HISTORY of EMPLOYERS'

ASSOCIATIONS in the

UNITED STATES

Clarence E. Bonnett, Ph.D.

VANTAGE PRESS • NEW YORK

PREFACE

THE FACT THAT there has been available no history of employers'
associations in the English language is enough justification for
the appearance of this book. The additional fact that all histories
of labor movements have disregarded completely or minimized
the significance of organized employers and so gave highly
erroneous conceptions as to the actual conditions in labor-
management relations through the years, only reinforces the need
for this history. The third fact that only recently in economic
discussions have relationships received the attention their importance merits, still further warrants the writing of a book in
this field that brings out those relationships, and the actions and
counteractions between the organized employers and organized
employees. So, while this book is primarily a history of employers'
associations, functionally it is a history of labor-management
relations as well as of associations primarily and of unions as a
necessity to a full understanding of the forces at work.

To most persons, employers' associations are "bad" organizations which keep the "underdog" workmen from getting better
wages, hours, and working conditions in order that "bloated" employers can "profiteer" off the misery of working men and women.
To what extent, if any, is this conception true? Just how have
these associations functioned and what have been the motives
that governed those functions? Have they been merely instruments
of obstruction to the labor movement and the progress of the
masses upward? Even in the minds of students of the labor movement, employers' associations are thought of in relation to blacklisting unionists and fostering "iron-clad" or "yellow-dog" contracts. Surely, there is much need for enlightenment on these organizations and their functions as they relate to the development
of our present economic system. How much of this system is due
to their activities? Is it probably better or worse because they functioned so extensively in making the system what it is?

This book makes no pretense of being a complete history of
employers' associations, or even of the details of the activities mentioned. It has intended to be illustrative, and the selection of the

events and of part of the details has been guided by an attempt to set forth the typical yet retain enough of the unusual to lend interest to the narrative. The problem was to select from all the voluminous material those things which would be most informative and interesting to the reader.

There are a number of ways by which the material in the book can be organized. First, there is the purely chronological where events are given strictly in accordance with their occurrences. Second, the history of each association might be given connectively. Third, the activities could be each traced historically. Fourth, a varying combination of all these can be used, depending upon the event, the association, and the activity. The problem here resolved itself into the answer to this question: Which of the four methods would best bring out the important relationships? The chronological method certainly relates events of the time, but there are also relationships of continuity of association and of activity which are thus destroyed. The history of each association would have unduly expanded the book and required much monotonous repetition of activities. This history of activities alone would have disregarded the *interrelation* of activities, the action and counteraction in diverse methods and manner, and slurred over the importance of industry, the association and union involved and the relationship of the activity to the time. Probably no two people will agree as to the best form of organization. In this book, we have endeavored to use the chronological method, modified by divisions into industries and the relative importance of the associations in the industry in regard to their activities at the time. Frequently, we have left it to the reader to draw his own conclusions as to relationships and interpretations. Perhaps, many relations that we may have thought were obvious were not, and we may have also pointed out too fully the obvious ones. On these points, few readers will agree, since each has a different background.

In a field so controversial as labor-management relations, we have undoubtedly recorded many errors or inaccurate accounts. The author was once in the center of a so-called strike riot and had an unusually excellent place to observe the activities. No two accounts given of the riot agreed, and several accounts stated as facts things which were not so. Since this book relies upon accounts that are often contradictory, it has either stated both, or attempted to set forth the one that seems best confirmed by the circumstances. There are, however, many facts over which there is no real dispute; each side has simply stated the case in its own language—to one who understands both languages there is no real contradiction. Moreover, this book presents a much condensed account, and any condensation gives an inaccurate impression through its omission of many details, so a degree of inaccuracy is found in the summarized characterizations of activities and events. For instance, an anarchistic strike needs to have only one riotous bloody period of a few hours out of a months-old strike, or it may have a series of such riots in a strike lasting only a few days. In both cases, the strikes are characteristically anarchistic.

The book covers the period from the first recorded association through the year 1900. It traces the development of ancient associations in the old world to furnish a background to the development of associations in the United States. By 1900, all the various types of associations had developed. The author's book on "Employer's Associations in the United States" continues that story of typical associations, and his Labor-Management Relations develops fully association activities from the point where the other book leaves off, especially under federal labor laws, and action and counteraction to these and unionism. Accordingly, there is apparently no great need to continue the narrative to 1956, although that may later be done in a second volume should the demand warrant it.

In making the research for "Employers' Associations in the United States," the author uncovered some of the material for this *History,* but that study served to show how further material could be found, and how the process of learning new facts became accumulative. A case in point will illustrate. The exploration of the case of Snow *vs.* Wheeler led him to investigate the possibility of filed "briefs" in that case with the Supreme Court of Massachusetts. In the "briefs" in that case, and others, much material was discovered that was not available elsewhere. A chance reference to the *Law and Order Leagues* in connection with the citizens' alliance movement of the early twentieth century led to the investigation and discovery of the highly important activities of the

Law and Order Leagues in the crushing of the Knights of Labor. Where a highly important event (or association) has been overlooked in various current treatises, more detailed information has been given than in those cases where the event has been fully reported. In a study based primarily on original sources, it seemed incongruous to rehash, or to repeat, the accounts already given. The reader of this book has probably already read such accounts, but in any event, can easily do so. This method has served to shorten this book.

References—placed at the close of the text—are to paragraphs, as this method avoids needless repetition when interrelated facts are drawn from two or more sources, for instance, union and association; thus action and counteraction may be traced in the references when consulted.

Acknowledgments are due to persons and institutions who aided in the preparation of this book. Moral encouragement was much needed over the many years required to conduct the research and organize the materials. Among persons who greatly encouraged the author in making the study are: John R. Commons, John M. Blair, Louis Brandeis, Leslie J. Buchan, Walter Drew, Robert W. French, Arthur Holder, Fred E. Inbau, Frederick Juchhoff, William J. Phillips, Jr., Noel Sargeant, James B. Trant, Elsie M. Watters, . . .

Among staffs of libraries who went beyond their "line of duty" in supplying materials are those of: Library of Congress, American Federation of Labor, Boston Athenaeum, Cleveland Public Library, John Crerar, Harvard University, Louisiana State University, Missouri Historical Society, National Foundry Association, New Orleans City Archives, New York Public Library, Supreme Court of Massachusetts, Supreme Court of the United States, Tulane University, University of California, University of Chicago, University of Colorado, U. S. Department of Labor, Wisconsin Historical Library, . . .

Articles based on materials herein were published in the *Annals* of the American Academy of Political and Social Sciences, *Commercial and Financial Chronicle, Encyclopedia of the Social Sciences,* University of Southern California *Law Review,* and the *Eduardo Lambert Memorial.*

Among persons who aided greatly in proof reading or careful typing and checking, are: C. E. Bonnett, Jr., Mrs. Elizabeth Arbo, Mrs. Mamie W. Bonnett, Mrs. Dorothy B. Moseley, Mrs. Emily Brett, Mrs. Mary Faulk, . . .

Current discussions of the great number of *mergers* suggest that clarity as to the field covered by this book requires a statement that mergers and the like are *not,* included, although "trusts" in the forms of price-fixing associations are, if they meet the tests of the standard definition: An employers' association is a *group* which is composed of, fostered by, or controlled by employers, and which seeks to promote the *employer's interests in labor matters.*

CONTENTS

CHAPTER 1

INTRODUCTION

THE LABOR-RELATIONS PROBLEM AN ORGANIZATION PROBLEM

THE LABOR-RELATIONS problem, when fairly and adequately considered, requires among other things a serious and extensive study of organizations of employers for dealing with this problem. This statement holds true, whether the problem is considered in its current aspects alone, or in all its evolutionary phases. In its current aspects, organization is the predominant factor, and the evolution of the problem shows clearly the growing importance of organization. Too often the labor-relations problem has been considered as simply a series of problems of individual laborers or organizations of laborers. The real problem, however, is too complicated and has too many ramifications to be approached with a finality from such a partial viewpoint as that of either the laborers or trade unionism. Employers' associations must be considered at every point of the discussion.

The Approaches to the Problem require consideration. A casual examination of the forces at work in any recent outstanding event in the world of labor, for instance, the coal strike of 1949, the Chrysler strike of 1950, or the political campaign of 1954, will show it is inadequate to approach the modern labor-relations problem either as simply one concerning the laborers, or even as a hodge-podge collection of problems of the laboring class. The issues in each of these events were clearly organization issues. Powerful organizations were distinctly involved. In the coal strike of 1949 the issue over which the deadlock occurred was the question of an employer-financed union-welfare plan, which could not be an issue between an individual employee and employer. Moreover, the United Mine Workers of America was not the only union concerned in that conflict; the Progressive Miners, the CIO,

the AFL, the Steelworkers, and the Autoworkers were interested
parties. Coal mine operators' associations were mainly appeasatory, only a few operators were belligerent. A number of other
national employers' associations interested themselves in the conflict and the attempts at settlement, through propaganda and ad-
vising the operators. The Federal Government was also deeply
involved: The Mediation Service and finally the President attempted to adjust the matter and the federal courts issued an injunction to enforce the calling off of the strike. The above enum-
eration by no means exhausts the list of organizations concerned.
Manifestly the problem has passed through the stage where either
the immediate laborer or even the laboring class, alone, is deeply
involved.

Careful consideration of the facts in the labor field will likewise reveal that the trade union point of view is also inadequate,
although is it more nearly correct than the "individual" or "hodge-
podge" points of view, since it does recognize in an incomplete
manner the great importance of organization in the problem. It
can be said as truly, although it would be just as inadequate, that
"The American labor problem is the problem of organized capital"
as to say it "is the problem of organized labor."

It is a problem in which organized labor and organized capital
are both involved, since trade unions and employers' associations
are always implicated in every important event in the labor field,
whether the issue is joined in a coal strike or in a national
political campaign. The modern labor-relations problem is essentially an organization problem—of employers' associations as well
as of trade unions.

The Partial Viewpoints are due to many reasons, of which
two main ones are: (1) Students of the labor-relations problem,
almost universally, have had a bias in favor of the laborer or the
trade union, and so saw the problem solely in the light of the
laboring class or of trade unionism. There is much in the textbooks in the labor field to confirm such an explanation. (2) It is,
however, just as possible that the once prevailing assumption of a
"strict parallelism" between trade unions and employers' associations, misled many students to believe that an understanding of
trade unions was all that was necessary to an understanding of

employers' associations, and accordingly, of the labor-relations problem. The assumption, however, is highly erroneous, as one of many challenging facts relating to the rival organizations will show, namely, there is no "strict parallelism" in number of members in the rival organizations. A union has relatively many more members than the corresponding association in fields equally well organized. The ratio for even local organizations is rarely less than 10 union members to one association member, while for international organizations the ratio is as high as 800 to 1. This fact means that the smaller group does not need the vast unwieldy machinery of the larger group. If the smaller body maintains itself against the larger, it must use different methods and means. With fundamental differences in form, function, means, and methods there can be no "strict parallelism" in fundamentals. Superficial resemblances are beside the point in an understanding of this problem.

Since trade unions do not typify, and are not the exact counterpart of employers' associations, an adequate comprehension of the problem demands that associations be studied as intensively as unions and not merely in an incidental way simply to furnish explanations of trade union activities. Only recently has even this been done. For this reason such conclusions as "Unions fail because they go into politics," needs to be reconsidered. Why did the Knights of Labor fail? Why did it go into politics? Have many unions failed without going into politics? Will unionism triumph or fail? Will "union recognition" become universal; and if so, when; if not, why not? What are the main trends in the industrial conflict?

A study of employers' asociations throws much light on such questions, but that is not its sole or even main purpose, since such questions present only a partial view of the problem.

The Labor-Relations Problem Defined.—The very conflicting ideas expressed in the numerous definitions of the labor-relations problem suggest one of the essential elements, namely, that of conflict. This problem presents the recurrent question of adjusting the conflict of interests between employers and employees as reflected through and generally magnified by their rival organizations and of adjusting it so that the necessary production of goods and the rendering of services may be carried on. In short, the problem involves the adjustment of the conflicting issues between unions and associations. The adjustment, as well as the conflict, vitally concerns other groups and individuals. Ultimately, the one reason for production is the consumer; it is to be expected that he will insist that his interests must not be unduly sacrificed while rival organizations of employers and of employees fight out their differences or combine against him to extort excessive prices. On the other hand, the consumer may be halted in his demand for commodities and services when the accompanying conditions and terms actually sacrifice either the employer or employee. Thus, we see that the problem involves an adjustment of the conflicting interests of the consumer, of the employee, of the employer, and of their various organizations, and includes even the government itself. These conflicting interests are not confined to individuals alone; the major conflicts are usually between rival organizations of some sort. Not often does a conflict between an individual and an organization come into prominence, and rare indeed are the momentous conflicts between isolated individual employer and employee. As a matter of fact, organizations, and especially leaders, often find it to their self interest to magnify issues in the conflict in some way, if not in many ways, to enlist on their side other individuals and groups, and so draw these into the conflict. Other individuals, groups, organizations, and institutions than those drawn into the conflict as partisans are also affected, in fact, may even be punished for taking a neutral stand. Nearly everyone is affected by the methods and means used in the warfare. The mobilization of mighty forces in the modern industrial conflict has thus become of vital concern to society itself. The labor-relations problem is one of our greatest social problems.

Issues in the Conflict often rise out of organization. Hitherto, discussions of the problem have generally placed the emphasis upon the *issues* ("evils" or "problems"), overlooking the fact that most of the issues are either primarily organization issues, or have been reflected through and magnified by organizations. Wherever there is a conflict of interests, issues can always be found or made or magnified by powerful rival organizations. Without organizations to foster and magnify them, most *issues* would never be heard of. Accordingly, issues and organizations require concurrent study, and not a treatment as separate entities.

Organization Complicates the Problem not only by a complexity of organization issues but also by inter-organization conflicts, such as "jurisdictional disputes," fights between associations, and fights among various types of unions. Jurisdictional disputes between trade unions arise because the workers are *organized* into two separate groups which do not readily conform to industrial changes. For instance, the carpenters' union for many years insisted that its members had always set the doors and placed the windows in all buildings erected by union men. The metal workers' union, however, insisted as strongly that the change in the material from wood to metal placed the work in the trade of its members. Was the process or the material to determine to which union the work belonged? The carpenters' union refused to accept the decisions of various boards, councils, etc., which awarded the work to the metal workers. As a result, the contention between these two unions caused building contractors much trouble whenever they employed workmen from the two unions on "unionized" buildings containing metal doors and windows until the manufacturer of metal frames, through the courts, forced an adjustment of the issue. He was aided by the League for Industrial Rights— an employers' association.

Organization Issues are legion, among which are: "union recognition," "the check-off," "seniority," "workshop control," "the boycott," "the streamlined blacklist," "the closed shop," "exemption of unions from the Sherman Anti-Trust Act," "abolition of injunctions in labor disputes," "limitation of apprentices," "standard workday," "standard rate of wages," "standard rate of work," "waiting time," "union representation on corporation boards of directors," "welfare fund," "guaranteed number of workdays," and the like. The list might be extended to cover practically all the so-called "evils," "problems," or issues; in fact, only such issues as hours of work, wages, method and time of wage payment, and working conditions that affect adversely the health or endanger the life of the worker may be issues apart from organization on either side. But even these issues are reflected

through and magnified into organization issues before they become
issues in the modern labor-relations problem. Again, even the
"remedies" of Adams and Sumner (solutions or approaches of
later authors)—with perhaps two exceptions when the remedy
is regarded in its narrowest application—are phases of organization. In this list of remedies, "strikes and lockouts" are clearly
manifestations of organizations. "Profit sharing" and "industrial
education" have been made organization issues, since they have
been advocated by employers' associations as a means of combating unionism. Profit sharing, and certain forms of industrial
training have been bitterly opposed by trade unions.

Growth of Conflict of Interests has developed with the expansion of the economic system. Under simple conditions, the
interests of employer and employee are mutual in carrying on the
production and in promoting the sale of the commodity or service,
but are in conflict in the division of the monetary return for the
"product" and in the determination of the conditions under which
production takes place. Usually both employer and employee are
conscious of their mutual interests. Each generally recognizes that
the regular process of production—subject to certain conditions
which promote the most advantageous sale of the product—is necessary to the relation of employer and employee; it provides the
fund out of which may be derived the wages of the employee and
the profit of the employer. Nevertheless, the conflict of interests on
occasions may become so sharp that both employer and employee
lose sight of their mutual interests, especially so when labor
troubles become chronic. In fact, the increasing complexity of
modern industrial, commercial, and financial conditions is tending
more and more to magnify the conflicting interests and to minimize
the mutual interests. These changing conditions thus have already
caused the labor-relations problem to assume a very serious if not
menacing aspect. No doubt much of the serious character of
the modern problem may be attributed to the fact that its evolution is now in the stage of the financial revolution—the financial
control of industry—and approaching the nuclear revolution.

The Financial Revolution.—While it has destroyed, in the
factories it dominates, the personal relationship between employer
and employee, it has by no means removed or lessened the cause

for personal animosity. The employees of today feel even more bitter toward the head executive of a corporation than the old-time workman felt toward an exacting employer-owner. For the modern employees often hear condemnations of the former who is held ultimately responsible for the policies of the corporation. The harsh things said are quite generally believed by the employees, largely because of the "inexorable rules" behind which foremen, department heads, superintendents, managers and others take refuge for their own short-comings. The employees cannot meet him personally or attach any redeeming qualities to him. Words in his praise spoken by supervisors or others generally fall on unheeding ears. On the other hand, writers who picture the old system of employer-owner and employee as ideal, have forgotten that oppression and bitter hatred then existed. There were, however, conditions then that helped to soften the harshness of the master; the master's wife or daughter or both, for example, might make extra efforts to be agreeable to offset the master's harshness. Again, the journeyman then might console himself with the thought that he would soon be a master and then could "show his authority," just as a freshman who has been severely hazed consoles himself with the thought that the next year he will be a sophomore and can take revenge on that year's freshman.

Devices to Lessen the Conflict under the financial revolution have been used to make the employees feel that their best interests are to be promoted by complete cooperation with the employing corporation. Among the various devices are those frequently classified as "employer welfare work" or "industrial betterment activities." "Work Councils," or employees-representation plans, are designed to serve the above-named end. Stock ownership by employees in the employing corporation is intended to tie up their interests more closely with the corporation by giving them the stockholders' point of view. The employees, however, do not gain control, and so are given a subordinate's viewpoint. While the conflict may thus be lessened, there still remain points on which interests may clash. The distribution of ownership among thousands of employees tends to facilitate the concentration of control in the hands of a few with lessened holdings of stock in the corporation under consideration. In fact, in the modern labor-relations problem, centralization of control, not concentration of wealth or ownership, is the significant thing. Distribution of ownership in great corporations is widespread and is growing, yet, at the same time the financial control of industry is centralizing. Instances of the rapid growth of wide distribution of ownership in corporations have been cited frequently. Cases are those of the American Telephone and Telegraph Company, the United States Steel Corporation, and Armour and Company.

Organization Complicates the Problem. All these devices, main organizations, super-organizations, and auxiliary organizations, with their numerous ramifications complicate the problem, not only in the highly organized field, but also in those trades, industries, shops, or factories that have not yet fully developed into the financial revolution stage. The problem would be complicated enough were the progress of industrial evolution uniform for all trades and industries. But, operating under unequal rates of evolution, organization has complicated and multiplied the number of methods which are employed in the conflict, whether for furthering or adjusting disputes. In fact, the wide range of conditions necessitates a multiplicity of types of organizations to deal with those conditions. So much have conditions favored main organizations, super-organizations, and auxiliary organizations, that it seems that each new organization begets both auxiliary and counter organizations. New types arise, and even marked specialization occurs.

The Evolution of Types.—While one might find among the associations today practically all the main historical types of associations, there would remain at least three considerations in favor of a historical survey: (1) The relative positions of the associations have changed, and the type that was formerly a dominant one may now be relatively of little significance in the current association movement. (2) The interdependence and interrelations of the associations themselves, as well as the trades and industries, have modified the modern type from its corresponding historical type. For example, the monopolistic medieval craft-gild with its dominating control over prices and labor in a community, and even over the government of the community, has no exact or unmodified counterpart in modern industry, although there are current associations of the modified gild type. (3) Many individuals find that the historical method enables them to view the development of the problem from its simple to complex stages, and thus to understand more clearly how the multiplicity of various types of associations with their involvements have complicated and intensified the problem by their different and often conflicting methods of dealing with that problem. It is especially under the third consideration that a study of the evolution of employers' associations, their structure, attitudes, and methods, will contribute to an understanding and better analysis of the problem. To make such a study is the purpose of this book.

The Evolution of Associations: Types and the Changes in Types.—Evolution has always been from the simple to the complex forms, from the general to the specific form. The development of employers' associations has been of this nature, as has the whole field of industry. The earliest forms of combinations of employers were simple, usually informal, temporary, and local, because trades and industries were generally local and the number of employers few in such local trades. A recognition of a common interest and an understanding—amounting almost to a code—among a few employers who could meet easily made an informal organization sufficient, when the employers were not already organized for another purpose, for instance, price fixing. When business is conducted on a large scale and thousands of men are employed by many different employers in widely separated localities, a formal association is necessary. In the early days, large-scale business existed only in trade and transportation; the isolation of workmen made it easy for a large employer to deal single-handed with any labor organization, since the controversy was usually limited to the immediate industrial, or rather commercial field. With the accumulation of capital, the extension of better means of transportation, the widening of the market, and the growth of large-scale production and all that these involve, has come a development of new types of associations. Industrial and financial changes have gradually forced a modification of the existing associations to types ranging from slightly fixed different ones to radically altered ones. The unequal rates of evolution in the various fields of industry have produced numerous types of associations. Unless all industry assumes a single united "trust" form, there will be increasing variety and complexity of associations.

Employers' Associations Are Not New, the types only are new. Employers' Associations are no new manifestation. They have always existed wherever and whenever the relation of employer has been well developed. The belief that associations did not exist in early times has arisen largely because they were generally small, informal, or secret—even all combined. The secret association reveals its existence through its powers to defeat the aims and aspirations or organized employees for "more"—more wages, more hours of rest or leisure, more control over working conditions, and more unionization concessions. The test whether an association exists is a functional one: is there concerted action among employers in promoting their interests in a particular labor controversy, or in labor matters in general? The general characteristics of the very early type of associations are probably about as follows: they were usually temporary, frequently informal, local and comparatively small, largely belligerent, occasionally and varyingly active, and confined to a "trade," but always as covert as possible.

Both associations and unions existed, largely as secret organizations, in ancient Greece. Unions were recognized by law under Solon, around 600 B.C., but were prosecuted later on account of their political activities. About two centuries later, subversive unionism was employed by Sparta to help defeat Athens in the war between the two cities: 20,000 men struck the mine owners of Laurian (near Athens) at the instigation of Spartan employers who promised the strikers better earnings and working conditions under a new regime. In 133 B.C., silver-mine operators were struck by more than a thousand miners, five miles from Sunion. The strikers killed the overseers, seized a castle at Sunion, also seized the town and the armories, armed themselves, and laid waste the countryside. They were finally defeated and most of them put to death. The members of a Crispinian union of shoemakers were thrown into a cauldron of melted lead near the close of the third century. The union, however, was vigorous down through the centuries until 1789 when it was suppressed. Romans tried to exterminate trade unions by persecution, murder, enslavement of their members, and innumerable other tortures, but only drove them underground to become even more secret organizations. Roman detectives, however, were able to unearth the unions.

A stone tablet unearthed in ancient Sardis shows that its building contractors were organized and appealed to the city authorities to take action against certain alleged abuses of unions in the building trades. As a result, these unions were required to issue a declaration under oath as to the terms by which they would abide; noteworthy of these is that the workers would not leave a job incomplete, as in a strike, if the employer paid promptly the wages mutually agreed upon. Apparently, compulsory collective bargaining is not new; and when it failed a form of compulsory arbitration was prescribed, at least, strikes in violation of the collective agreement were prohibited.

It is the change in types from the early times to the modern, that outlines the effects of industrial evolution on the association movement. The earliest formal employers' association of which we have definite knowledge is the craft-gild. The craft-gilds were organizations primarily of employers. In the early days an employer was called a "master," the youths who were learning the trade were called "apprentices," and the workmen who had learned the trade but who were employed by a master were called journeymen. The gild was controlled by the masters and it prescribed apprenticeship regulations, fixed wages and prices, and determined who should become masters. Gilds were often referred to as "corporations" because they were incorporated bodies. The craft-gilds of the Middle Ages were never reduced simultaneously to a single-type masters' organization, because of their different rates of evolution, and of the varied industrial conditions that confronted the gilds even at a given time. The general features of the craft-gild are such that a sketch of some phases of its development will perhaps suggest something of the characteristics of the more important types. That the craft-gild became an employers' association is evidenced by the growth of the master class and the servant class with the development of the employer's interest or attitude as it was antagonized by that of the workmen.

With this in view of obtaining a better understanding of the development of the labor-relations problem, let us make a review of the evolution of associations beginning with the early craft-gilds in Europe, and continuing with their development until associations arise in the United States, to which the study from then on will be confined. This review will indicate in a slight degree the strong relationship that exists between types and industrial conditions.

CHAPTER 2

THE SHOP SYSTEM—THE FIRST STAGE

THE DEVELOPMENT OF *Employers' Associations through the Craft-Gild Stage.*—In the history of the craft-gild, the early days are only occasionally illuminating on the struggles of employer with employees. The reason for this situation is that such struggles rarely receive much, if any, attention until they loom up in the life of a community. Not until industry progresses to the point where considerable numbers of workers are employed, or until a trade or branch of industry becomes monopolized, so that a strike shuts off the supply of goods or services or threatens the social order, do most of us, even today, give more than passing notice to labor troubles.

Thus, in the early days, only on such occasions at long intervals, did labor troubles or disputes manifest themselves in some form so that a record was made of them. A few illustrations taken from the record will demonstrate the existence then of employers' associations and their class interests and activities, although under the name of the craft-gild. Evidence exists today that as early as 1297, the craft-gild began to regulate apprenticeship. The ordinances of the Fullers of Lincoln—founded in 1297—prohibited the teaching of the craft before the apprentice had paid a fee to the gild.

Evidences of Class Interests and Organized Activity by Employers.—That labor troubles were occurring, and that employers were dealing with them by means of an organization can be concluded from the following provision in the ordinances, or by-laws, of the White Tawyers of London in 1346: "And if any serving-man shall conduct himself in any other manner than properly toward his master, and act rebelliously toward him, no one of said trade shall set him to work until he shall have made amends before the mayor and aldermen; and before them such misprision shall be redressed." Obviously, the existence of the employers' interest at this early time was clearly recognized by this gild, so much that it prepared to institute a blacklist against any rebellious workman.

Salzman says, "During the fourteenth century the strike was well known, and when a master would not agree with his workmen the other workmen of the craft would come out and cease work until the dispute was settled." Friction between masters and journeymen in this century was pronounced. "Strikes took place centuries ago, and with about as disastrous results as characterize the majority of the great labor struggles of the present day. At Breslau, in Germany, in the year 1329, brass workers inaugurated a strike which lasted for an entire year. In 1385 a strike of blacksmiths took place in Danzig, when the employers sought aid of the court, with the result that an order was issued by the municipal authorities that all workmen attempting to strike would have their ears cut off."

An Armed Conflict between Employers and Workmen.— The gild exacted of the apprentice an exorbitant entrance fee and of the new master a large feasting and drinking bill, as well as requiring from him the production of an elaborate and costly masterpiece or masterpieces which necessitated months of work and expensive materials, before he became a master. Under these conditions, says Unwin, "there grew up in every industrial center of Western Europe from the middle of the fourteenth century onward, a body of workmen in every craft who had no prospect before them but that of remaining journeymen all their lives, and who were therefore bound together by an increasing consciousness of a class interest which separated them from their employers. This development was especially characteristic of the various branches of the cloth manufacture. At Chester in 1358 [perhaps affected by the Black Death epidemic] the master weavers, shearmen, challoners, and walkers had reached such a pitch of exasperation with the conduct of their journeymen as to make a murderous attack upon them, with iron-pointed poles, baslards and pole-axes. . . . Instances of similar disputes in the latter half of the fourteenth century at Paris, Amiens, Chalons, and Rouen, concerning hours and wages and other conditions of labor are recorded in abundance; and they find a close parallel in the differences which arose during the same period between the masters and journeymen of the shearmen, the weavers, the cordwainers, the saddlers, and the tailors of London."

An Early Conspiracy Case.—In 1396, there was a dispute between the master saddlers and the journeymen saddlers of London. The associated employers brought the matter before the mayor and aldermen of the city. The masters contended that the journeymen had formed a fraternity and had entered into covenants for a great increase of wages; laws then prescribed maximum wages instead of minimum wages. The masters cited the great increases then demanded by journeymen, namely, from about $10.00 then paid, to varying amounts from $20.00 to as much as $50.00 yearly with board, as a link in the chain of evidence to prove the journeymen guilty of conspiracy. The masters and the journeymen were ordered to dissolve their fraternity and be subject to their masters.

So long as the journeymen's societies were supplementary to the masters' gild they were recognized by the gild and even established with its consent, otherwise they were suppressed, if possible, by the governmental authorities at the request of the masters. As early as 1362, ordinances of the Alien Weavers of London contained regulations designed to prevent workmen from combining to raise wages.

The beginning of fraternities of either journeymen or masters was apparently at a very early date. Unwin says that "society in the fourteenth and fifteenth centuries was literally honeycombed with fraternities in every direction." Among the various groups, each of which had its own fraternity, "bound together for the pursuit of their special class interest" were the wealthy merchants, the comfortable shopkeepers and the poor journeymen, but all "under similar social and religious forms and sanctions." These fraternities were essentially *secret* associations. Members were bound by oath to keep secret the proceedings, and this secrecy concealed practically all of the evidences of concerted action except under extraordinary conditions. The journeymen's fraternities at this time were "yeomen's" organizations, and Unwin has thus characterized the yeomen of this period: "The yeoman at the end of the fourteenth century was a journeyman on strike."

Masters Called Upon Governmental Authorities to Subdue Workmen's Organizations. In the year 1415, the mayor and aldermen of London, at the request of the gild, "made the wardens of the Tailors' Gild responsible for the existence of associations of journeymen tailors, which however were directed against the masters themselves." In 1420, in Coventry a group of journeymen tailors was ordered to disband, but it appeared again under a changed name, and was attacked again in 1425. The masters' gild of Coventry, however, in 1424, recognized the fraternity of journeymen weavers; likewise, the master shoemakers' gild of Bristol recognized the fraternity of journeymen of Coventry who had struck for higher wages and attempted to prevent anyone from working for the old scale of wages. The associated masters apparently were unable to handle the situation themselves and appealed to the town authorities—since the gilds were generally in control of both local and national government. The municipal officers intervened and virtually forced the journeymen to submit their case to arbitration.

Employers' Associations Were a Main Feature in German Industrial Life. "The conflict of organized bodies of masters and journeymen was one of the main features of German industrial life in the fifteenth century. The cities were drawn together in groups and opposing federations—representing the masters in a single trade on the one side, and the corresponding journeymen on the other—and they fought over the labor question in all its aspects with results that varied widely in the different trades and from one period to another."

The Craft-Gild Was an Employers' Association from Its Origin. It seems, then, from the above that the craft-gild from its origin was dominated by the employer's interest and dealt with labor matters. The craft-gild was an offshoot of the merchants' gild, for the interests of the two groups—craftsmen and merchants—grew apart with industrial developments, since the employer's interest differs from the trader's interest in certain respects, instances of which we find in modern associations. Unwin places the rise of the craft-gild at about 1328, and notes that craft-gilds become numerous and important, presumably for the first time in 1377. A list of gilds drawn up in 1328 consists largely of merchant gilds and wealthy manufacturing crafts, with about six out of the twenty-five belonging to the lesser crafts. The Black Death may have stimulated their formation to help meet the problems growing out of a labor shortage. By 1377 the number of crafts had increased to fifty-one, of which the lesser crafts were predominant, but by 1422, the number had increased to one hundred and eleven craft-gilds.

The craft-gild, therefore, might be either an organization of the wealthy or capitalistic class, or of the shopkeepers and small capitalists. The only element of a labor organization—trade union —to be found in these gilds was the journeymen's fraternity; but as this was forced by the masters to be supplemental to the gild which was controlled by the masters, and as only a portion of the workmen in the shop of the master craftsmen were journeymen, it can be seen that this element was almost negligible. The journeyman in the earlier period expected in due course of time to bcome a master and this expectation tended to keep him subservient to the master and the masters' gild. The masters' fraternity—sometimes called the "livery"—made even more secure their control of the gild which was of itself highly autocratic in form and function. Furthermore the craft-gild was a political power and so could direct against the rebellious workmen the force of the laws of the land, local and national; and it did later use this power to fix the legal rate of wages of the workmen and to prevent any increase it deemed unwarranted.

The masters' fraternity within the craft-gild fixed, if the gild itself did not, the prices of the products of the craft, and it is only fair to assume that it did not stop short of considering rates of wages. It is not denied that the gild, after the fourteenth century, regulated the relations between master and workman.

Gild Masters Had Wages Regulated by Law. It is definitely known that in the sixteenth century the craft-gilds were able to secure laws which prohibited increases in wages, stimulated no doubt by increased foreign trade, colonization, and importation of gold. Unwin states that in 1559 the wage question divided journeymen and masters and that during Elizabeth's reign (about

1563) the masters had wages fixed by law, which aimed at uniformity and strengthened the hands of the master and reduced the journeymen class to dependence.

Gild Regulation of Labor Troubles and Organizations is illustrated by their suppression of workmen's unions as shown in the ordinances of the English clothworkers, formulated in the sixteenth century or earlier. These ordinances stipulated that all "controversies between the livery and their apprentices were to be settled in the old way before the master at the Common Hall," and that "journeymen should make no unlawful assemblies, brotherhoods, congregations, and flockings together."

Craft-Gilds Became Highly Monopolistic. The desire for monopoly on part of the craft-gilds caused them, as industry developed, to take steps to restrict the right to engage in a craft to the families of the masters and the sons of the very wealthy. The entrance fee for apprentices was raised by degrees from about 60c to as high as $4,000.00 (the equivalent of the wages of the most highly skilled journeyman for about 100 years), while admission to the "freedom of the gild" (to become a master) rose to as high as $150.00, with a feasting and drinking bill, sometimes as high as $25.00 additional. Costly and elaborate masterpieces were required of the prospective master, after he had served first as an apprentice from four to seven years or more, and as a journeyman for three to five years. He had also to prove that he actually possessed sufficient capital to establish himself in business, usually at least the equivalent of two full years' wages, for borrowed capital was not generally allowed by the gild. These restrictions, however, applied generally only to persons not members of the family of the master craftsman. Eldest sons of masters were usually exempted from all restrictions. These restrictions necessarily aroused a class interest and antagonism among apprentices and journeymen but especially so among the poorer but ambitious workmen. "In the place of an oligarchy of landed proprietors, an oligarchy of capitalists stepped in." "In every single trade the gilds came into existence at the time when each trade was changing from small to great industry." The gilds, by making certain masters wealthy enough to become master manufacturers on a large scale, developed but ultimately broke down because of this great accumulation of capital invested in manufacturing, the increased use of machinery, improved transportation, and widened markets.

Workmen Resorted to the Courts. Complaining that the master clothiers had reduced wages, workmen in 1623, and again in 1630, had the temerity to petition the justices for an increase of wages, although apparently the masters generally controlled all the machinery of the local and national government.

Another Conspiracy Case.—During the years 1696 and 1699, there was a noteworthy contest between the master and the journeymen hatters over an increase of wages during a period of rising prices, and against any reduction of wages. The masters began a prosecution against the journeymen for conspiracy, and the journeymen retaliated by having an action brought against the masters for the illegal employment of boys. The suit against the masters was dropped, but the journeymen were greatly dissatisfied with the result of the issue, and the matter was fought over again in the latter part of the period, this time going to a higher court. The final outcome was a compromise as to wages.

Masters Secured More Legislation against Combinations of Workmen. In 1721, the master tailors in combination with other employers petitioned for and obtained an Act of Parliament prohibiting combinations of workmen, especially to raise wages. In 1799 another combination act was passed to deal with combinations of workmen which undertook to advance wages or reduce hours of labor. This act was supplanted in 1800 by a very elaborate combination act for dealing with such conspiracies. In spite of the combination law of 1721, a combination of journeymen struck. Riots ensued with resulting losses estimated from $75,000 to $100,000. The combination of masters was finally forced by the workmen to come to an agreement with them. The justices, then fixed the rate of wages for the year.

It was an Act of Parliament (Eighth of George III) which prompted Adam Smith to make this pointed remark on the situation then: "Whenever the legislature attempts to regulate the differences between masters and their workmen, its counsellors are always the masters." That act prohibited under heavy penalties all master tailors in London, and five miles around it, from giving, and their workmen from accepting more than about sixty-five cents a day except in the case of general mourning.

Masters Exempted from Combination Acts.—The combination acts, however, did not apply to the masters for two reasons; either of which alone was sufficient: In the first place, the masters dominated Parliament. In the second place, the masters' combinations were secret and conducted so covertly that to obtain direct evidence against them was extremely difficult. Their method of procedure is thus described by Adam Smith: "When masters combine together in order to reduce the wages of their workmen, they commonly enter into a private bond or agreement, not to give more than a certain wage under a certain penalty." Furthermore, he sets forth the advantages then enjoyed by the masters: "The masters, being fewer in number, can combine much more easily; and the law, besides, authorizes, or at least does not prohibit their combinations, while it prohibits those of the workmen. We have no acts of parliament against combining to lower the price of work; but many against combining to raise it. In all such disputes the masters can hold out much longer. A landlord, a farmer, a master manufacturer, or merchant, though they did not employ a single workman, could generally live a year or two upon the stocks which they have already acquired. Many workmen could not subsist a month, and scarce any a year without employment." And knowing these facts the masters had provided in the Combination Acts that no workman's organization should accumulate any funds whatever.

Combinations of Masters Had Apprenticeship Statute Repealed. The growth of large manufacturers reacted unfavorably on the small masters and they combined with the workmen in the enforcement of the Elizabethan Apprenticeship Statute. After several of the large employers had been condemned, the master manufacturers from many parts of England joined in petitioning Parliament for the repeal of the obnoxious statute. From 1803 to 1809, Parliament, in response to the petitions of the woolen manufacturers, had annually suspended the act for them, and finally in 1809, exempted them permanently from the application of the act. In 1814, however, the contest became general and bitter. While the great majority of the petitions received by Parliament favored the strict enforcement of the act and opposed its repeal, the master manufacturers desired its annulment and Parliament accorded them this favor. Its repeal was sought for two reasons: (1) because master manufacturers were being prosecuted for violating it; (2) because the strict enforcement of the statute would so limit the number of workmen that they could combine successfully against the master manufacturers and so regulate the trade. Naturally, the large employers made strenuous efforts to prevent such conditions and argued that "the persons most competent to form regulations with respect to trade were the master-manufacturers."

The Breakdown of the Craft-Gild; Its Decadence as an Employers' Association.—The craft-gild ceased to be an employers' association because there grew up within the group conflicting interests between the large wealthy masters and the small masters. The gild restrictions made possible the great accumulations of capital by the long established gild families. But the accumulation of wealth by these artisans led to the utilization of machinery and in turn required wider markets, and so the interests of the master manufacturer demanded the breakdown of the local restrictions of the craft-gild, while the interests of the small masters opposed that. The small masters, finding that their interests were now more nearly common with those of the workmen, united with the latter; at least, in brief, this was the process. The craft-gild was left by the master manufacturer to the small masters and the workmen. The gild thus came to assume a twofold character, and in this form has undoubtedly misled many present-day students in regard to its true character in its vigorous days. In its latter days it practically ceased to be an employers' association, and took on some of the characteristics of a trade union, but was not a true workmen's organization.

Associations of Master Manufacturers Were Secret and Informal. The manufacturers were relatively few and united informally. Accordingly, the dawn of the Industrial Revolution and the era of the breakdown of the gilds found employers' associations still existing, secret in nature, but now generally informal. They were thus characterized by Adam Smith: "Masters are always and everywhere in a sort of tacit but constant and uniform combination not to raise the wages of labor above their actual rate. To violate this combination is everywhere a most unpopular action and a sort of reproach to a master among his neighbors and equals. We seldom, indeed hear of this combination, because it is the usual, and one may say, the natural state of things, which nobody ever hears of. Masters, too, sometimes enter into particular combinations to sink the wages of labor even below this rate. These are always conducted with the utmost silence and secrecy till the moment of execution; and when the workmen yield, as they sometimes do without resistance, although severely felt by them, they are never heard of by other people."

We now pass from this brief review of employers' associations in Europe and go into an extended study of the development of American associations.

CHAPTER 3

THE EARLY EMPLOYERS' ASSOCIATIONS IN AMERICA

THE CRAFT-GILD *in America* differed from its European parentage. While America inherited the traditions of Europe in this matter as in others, her more backward industrial conditions—due in part to the restrictions in the policy of European master-manufacturers and merchants—checked the development here of any large number of employers' associations. It is possible that the gild of merchant shipowners, who were powerful in colonial days, hindered the early growth of strong gilds among the other master craftsmen. The craft-gild came to America and attempted its trade restrictions here, but met with the opposition of the royal ruling class whenever these restrictions were counter to the European master-manufacturer and merchant. The attempt of the gilds to control the trade within the city was made in New York as early as 1650, but was prevented by the royal authorities from interfering with the European trade.

The English precedent of wage fixing of skilled workers was tried out by the colonies, for example, Massachusetts Bay Colony as early as 1633; and by the towns in 1636, and as recent as 1777, when Newburyport established maximum wages ranging from six shillings per day for masons to three shillings with meals and bed; meals and bed were valued at one shilling.

In 1646, the Company of the Shoemakers of Boston petitioned for a charter to form a gild; this was granted. In 1647, the coopers also formed a gild. Gild privileges and regulations were common by 1670, but the hatters' gild was denied more privileges in 1671 by the General Court "until the hatters made hats as good and as cheap as imported hats."

These American gilds were not made up solely of self-employed workmen. This is shown by the records of apprentice indentures, as early as 1645 in Salem, Massachusetts. Complete records exist for New York City in the years 1695-1708 and 1718-1727; masters had taken in that time as high as five apprentices, while in Philadelphia in the years 1745-1746, one master took as many as three apprentices and a large number took as many as two. The term of apprentices in these days ranged up to as high as 19 years and the great majority were, in New York, for over seven years, and in Philadelphia, for over five years. In Philadelphia in the two-year period 1771-1773, one master carpenter took as high as six apprentices, while many other master carpenters each took from two to four apprentices, and the term of apprenticeship in this trade ranged up to 13 years. It may be noted that the master merchants (who were also shipowners), imposed unfavorable terms upon apprentices in their indentures; one master merchant, required the payment of a fee of $750, for a six-year apprenticeship, yet agreed to furnish no clothing to the apprentice, although it was customary for the master to do so. So favorable to the masters were the colonial laws relating to apprenticeship, it may be inferred that the masters were effectually united in obtaining such legislation. The exploitation of apprentices must have been reflected in the condition of the wage earners, but no clear case of the revolt of workmen has come to light—a riot in New York in the 17th century is recorded and it may have been in the nature of a strike. The masters, evidently secured favorable legislation in general. Boston in 1660 enacted a law that one must serve an "apprenticeship" (learner and servant) for seven years and must be 21 years of age before he was allowed to "open shop or occupy any manufacture."

Early Associations Were Local. The master carpenters of Philadelphia organized in 1724 under the gild title of "The Carpenters' Company." It had three sets of functions:

(1) It established a "book of prices" for carpenter work to provide for "fair" prices and "fair" wages.

(2) It provided assistance to aged, injured or otherwise incapacitated members and to their widows and dependent children left without adequate means of support.

(3) It furnished a hall for patriotic gatherings leading to the founding of the American Republic.

There is no record of a conflict of this association with the journeymen carpenters in that period. Its price and wage policies made it both a "trade association" and an employers' association as most craft gilds were. The evidence is fairly conclusive that a master bakers' association in New York City as early as 1741 prosecuted and obtained the conviction of a union of journeymen bakers for being in a conspiracy; this was used as precedent in the carpenters' case.* In 1791, the master carpenters of Philadelphia resisted a demand of the journeymen carpenters of Philadelphia for a shorter work day to commence at six o'clock in the morning and terminate at six in the evening with extra pay for overtime. How much earlier such associations dealt with labor matters, or how many of them did so, are questions that the available records of that day do not satisfactorily answer. That the craft-gild was not yet entirely supplanted by newer types of employers' associations is shown by the formation in 1785 of the General Society of Mechanics and Tradesmen, which in 1820, or earlier, began to aid in the support of a trade school.

Associations, moreover, resorted to politics: In the town of Newburyport in 1777 "pursuant to 'an Act of the General Court to Prevent Monopoly and Oppression,' it was voted by the Selectmen to establish . . . Maximum Wages" ranging downward from six shillings per day for masons to three shillings and found for day laborers [four shillings without found (meals and bed)].

Concert among Shipowners Defeated Striking Sailors. In a strike of sailors at Fell's Point, Baltimore, Maryland, on March 17, 1800, an informal employers' association—"a citizens' committee"—repulsed three separate attempts of a large mob of the striking sailors to board a vessel. The strikers had paraded to the wharf with fife and drum and flying colors, and tried to drive

---

* If we accept the view of Carroll D. Wright (Industrial Evolution in the U.S.) that there was a general strike of the journeymen bakers who were indicted by the master bakers for conspiracy, then we may conclude that the master bakers had an organization, either formal or informal. Should we, however, agree with David J. Saposs (Commons 1:53-54) that the master bakers combined to resist an ordinance regulating the price of bread, we need only to question if masters so well organized would overlook entirely the labor costs of making the bread and not consider or even attempt wage reductions before bringing themselves into conflict with the city government. It is not altogether improbable that both masters and journeymen may have combined to resist price regulation by the city.

off the ship a group of strikebreakers who had accepted $18 a
month, which was below the demands of the strikers. Both
strikers and citizens had a number seriously injured in this battle,
but no lives were lost.

Trouble was brewing in New York City about this time as
indicated by the publishing in the COMMERCIAL ADVERTISER, March
14, 1800, of an Act of the State of New York prohibiting any
alien sailor deserting a ship in violation of a contract he had
signed, or being absent without leave. The Act provided also for
the arrest and imprisonment of a violator until the ship was ready
to sail, when he was to be delivered to the shipmaster who paid
the costs. In October, 1802 (some writers say 1803), shipowners (generally merchants) of New York City refused to grant
their sailors an advance in wages from $10 to $14 a month. The
sailors struck and marched along the waterfront endeavoring
to induce or compel other seamen to join the strike. The owners
appealed to peace officers, and the drunken strikers were driven
off and their leader was jailed.

Association Combated Strikes and Resorted to the Courts. The
master shoemakers of Philadelphia were organized as early as 1789.
In 1796 and again in 1798 their organization unsuccessfuly resisted
an advance of wages demanded by the journeymen in each of
these years. In 1799, the masters attempted to reduce wages to
the level of the previous year. The masters entered into an agreement with each other not to employ any of the union men, presumably with the object of breaking up the union, "the Federal
Society of Journeymen Cordwainers." The masters finally compromised with the strikers on the amount of wage reduction. In
1804, when prices were rising, the union struck for higher wages
and obtained them, but on October 30, 1805, the Society of
Master Cordwainers of Philadelphia—as the association then
styled itself—held a meeting and resolved unanimously that no
higher wages would be paid. The resolution was signed by 46
master shoemakers. Although prices were then falling, the union
called a strike, and condemned newspaper accounts of the strike.
The masters defeated the strike and successfully prosecuted the
union leaders, in 1806, for being in a conspiracy to raise wages
illegally. Each of the eight defendants was found guilty and fined

eight dollars (which was about a week's earnings) and costs.*

In 1809, the Journeymen Cordwainers' Society of Baltimore ordered a strike on the master shoemakers, who caused twenty-nine of the union members to be indicted for conspiracy. Apparently only one unionist was tried, although there were at least two cases. He was found guilty. The outcome of the second case is doubtful. The concerted action by the masters at these times shows that they had some form of organization.

In New York, in the same year, (1809), twenty-two master shoemakers, following the examples of their fellow masters in the above cases, joined in the prosecution of a conspiracy case against the local shoemakers' union. The union offered to show, during the trial, that the masters had been for some time past in combination for the express purpose of lowering the wages of the workers, that the masters were in combination for the purpose of conducting the prosecution, and that the masters were making "an excessive profit on the labor of the workmen," but the court ruled that such evidence was irrelevant. The union members were found guilty of using unlawful means—epithets, social ostracism, and closed-shop coercion—but were fined only a nominal sum with costs. It appears that in a strike upon certain master shoemakers, the associated employers had the work done in shops not affected by the strike. The strike was thus broken, but these strikers discovered how they had been defeated, and the union of journeymen shoemakers ordered a general strike on all the masters, who then instituted the suit against the union for conspiracy.

In 1814, the associated shoemakers of Pittsburgh prosecuted the leaders of the local journeymen shoemakers' union for conspiring "with force and arms" to prevent employment of any non-unionist, as well as to raise wages. This suit, although compro-

---

* Saposs is in error when he contends (Commons 1:132-3) that the absence of a labor clause in the constitution of a masters' organization is proof that that body does not deal with labor matters. Quite a number of present-day employers' associations have no specific labor clause in their constitutions. The National Association of Stove Manufacturers during a period of over two years actually dealt with labor matters although its constitution specifically prohibited that. Moreover, associations, even today, frequently insist on "individual" bargaining.

mised, resulted unfavorably to the union. Under the terms of the compromise, the journeymen had to pay all the costs of the suit and go back to work at the old scale of wages over which the strike was called. In 1815, the journeymen struck again and were prosecuted a second time by the masters. They were found guilty of being in a conspiracy of using unlawful means to raise their wages, and were fined one dollar each and costs. An organization of employers, the Mechanics and Manufacturers of Pittsburgh, was deeply interested in the publication of the conspiracy trial.

The Character of the Early Associations was informal and secretive. This was clearly revealed by testimony of some of the employers who were witnesses at the trial of the Pittsburgh journeymen shoemakers in 1815. The employers testified that they met and talked over the affairs—wages and prices—but they never reached an agreement as to a uniform scale of wages. But they did agree unanimously to refuse to grant the journeymen's demands for higher wages, and likewise agreed to continue to pay the same wages they had been paying. It was constantly urged that the employers "should be all of one mind." There was never any written record of the discussions, nor did the employers enter into any formal resolution for carrying on the prosecution but each agreed to contribute something toward the fund. One employer thus stated the method of the masters' cooperation: "Employers met often in own defense when the journeymen turned out; often met afterwards to take a mug of beer."

Why the Labor Difficulties among the Shoemakers and Carpenters in 1809 and 1814? The labor troubles of 1809 and 1814 illustrate well the operation of economic forces on association activities. These troubles arose in the highest developed of the skilled trades and under economic conditions that characteristically exist when bitter labor disputes occur—namely at the beginning of or during the earlier part of an industrial depression. A study of the development of skilled trades in this period shows that the two highest developed ones were those of the shoemakers and the carpenters. These trades had led all the others in number of apprentices for some years. Naturally, organization would take place first in the most highly developed trades. When economic stress appears these organizations tend to become active. The period of 1808 and the early part of 1809 was one of the greatest depression, beginning in the shipping industry with the enforcement of the Embargo Act of 1808 and widening to other industries. Profits declined rapidly, although prices declined more slowly while sales almost ceased. The masters sought to reduce their costs of production by lowering wages to the old level, but the workmen resisted by means of strikes. The removal of the Embargo Act of 1809, relieved the situation by 1810, and the War of 1812-14 still further eased matters by widening the margin of profits through increased prices. Under these conditions, profits and prices outstripped wages in the upward climb, and the masters made the necessary concessions. The return of peace in 1814 brought with it extensive dumping of English manufactured goods. This put an end to the wide margin of profits of the manufacturers in America and forced a readjustment in the labor field. A general break in prices brings labor troubles, as it did in the years 1814-1815, and depressional unemployment follows.

The depression produced association activities and arguments for measures to meet it, primarily by checking or stopping the great importation of foreign goods. It was said that a day's wages in the United States in 1815 would support 17 persons one day with sufficient bread and meat, but in England, for the same time and manner, only five persons. However, wages were reported to be four times as high in the Western country as in New England, while corn was worth 50c in the former and 80c in the latter. In 1816 the Delaware Manufacturing Company—an organization of manufacturers—condemned reliance upon agriculture and urged that steps be taken to foster manufacturing—so to balance agriculture with industry—by stopping the enormous importations of foreign goods. One writer planned to meet foreign competition in manufacturing by using child labor to increase domestic production, and to pay child workers (as young as 7) $21,397,500 in wages. The Philadelphia Society for Promotion of American Manufacture in 1817 sent out a questionnaire of 20 questions on costs, conditions, quality of goods, workmen (habits, sex, manual, or machine), and similar matters. Wages and prices of commodities of 1789 were compared to those of

1819; for instance the ordinary day wage was 2d. Although great gains had resulted from the cotton gin, then regarded as the greatest labor-saving machine ever invented, factories had shut down and many thousands were unemployed. Operations were reduced from one-third to one-half; money stopped circulating; prices were demoralized by bankrupt selling; frauds of banks and their fear and jealousy of each other, "powerfully assisted too by the apparent determination of the United States Bank to eat up all the state banks immediately," helped to make the situation worse. Lengthy arguments were made that the vast unemployment was due to the great importation of foreign goods. In 1821, however, Albany printers compromised strike issues.

Masters Tried on a Conspiracy Charge.—In February, 1821, the master ladies' shoemakers of Philadelphia had agreed with each other not to employ any journeymen who would not consent to work for reduced wages, that is, at the old rate from which the union had forced an advance in a few months past. This time the union brought conspiracy charges against the masters. The judge bound the defendants over until the next session of the Mayor's Court, pointing out that the question whether there was an improper motive present in the conspiracy was one of fact for a jury to pass upon. He also intimated that the fact that the journeymen were also in combination might have a bearing upon the case. Whether this intimation of the court, or a rise of prices in the meanwhile, affected the case we do not know. Apparently, the case never came to jury trial.

Workmen Again Convicted of Conspiracy. The master hatters of the city of New York in November, 1822, when prices were falling, held a meeting and agreed to reduce the wages of the journeymen. To counteract this agreement among the employers, the journeymen had formed a society and had agreed not to work under a certain price. For making this agreement the leaders of the union were prosecuted and found guilty of conspiracy, although their counsel contended that the combination of masters had caused the combination of journeymen. The court ruled against such evidence and instructed the jury "that one conspiracy cannot justify another," presumably because the associated masters had not even threatened violence.

In 1824, the master tailors of Buffalo collectively refused to grant the demands of the journeymen tailors for higher wages. The journeymen struck, ostracized the "scabs" and took means to prevent their employment in any shop. The masters proceeded to prosecute the union leaders for conspiracy in doing "acts prejudicial to the community," and secured a conviction. The union leaders, however, were fined only two dollars each.

Other Conflicts between Associations and Unions around 1825. Strikes were numerous in this period, but the outstanding one seems to have been the strike in which the master builders were involved. In 1825, a committee of master carpenters of Boston issued resolutions adopted at a meeting of a considerable number of these employers. These resolutions condemned the demands of the union of journeymen house carpenters for a ten-hour workday. This action of the masters led to a strike by the union. The building union was defeated. New York shipbuilders, also, countered agitation by ship carpenters and caulkers for the ten-hour day. In 1825, 46 master builders of New York met and decided against an advance of wages (then $1.62½ daily) for the following year. In this period we find masters arguing that the better class of workmen of the present are the employers of the future, while unionists were contending that the poor were getting poorer and the rich richer.

In 1827, the master carpenters of Philadelphia, like the masters of Boston, refused to grant the demands of the house carpenters for a ten-hour day. One hundred and twenty-two master carpenters signed the resolution refusing to shorten the workday. The strike that followed was evidently a failure. In that year also in Philadelphia, the master tailors met a strike of the journeymen tailors by charging twenty-four of the union leaders with conspiracy. The trial before the Mayor's Court brought out the evidence that the masters were bonded together, at least informally, since the work of the struck shops was sent out to other shops to be done. Intimidation just short of physical assault by outside union pickets was practiced. The defendants were found guilty of conspiracy. In 1829 the master shoemakers of Franklin County, Pennsylvania, successfully prosecuted two leaders of the shoemakers' union for being in a conspiracy to drive from the town the workmen who had deserted the union; and to compel employers to deny employment to all nonunionists, to discontinue sending work out of town, and to grant a uniform and higher wage scale.

In 1830, as in 1825, the contests in shipbuilding were between the merchants and the journeymen primarily, although the master mechanics were the direct supervisors and employers. The merchants of New York City, after referring to the system of coercion of other workers by the union as to wages and hours, argued that the cutting of hours and advancing of wages would hurt the workers by driving the business to other ports where such restrictions were not imposed. The association also announced its intentions to blacklist all the unionists. Much has been said about employers combining to prosecute unionists for being in conspiracies to raise wages, but no reference was made to the unions' practice of intimidation—which was an illegal means.

CHAPTER 4

THE FACTORY SYSTEM

WITH THE ADVENT of the thirties, the factory system began to show its influence on the labor-relations problem in many ways although the shop system was still dominant. In general, the early types of associations in the United States were local, "trade" organizations which negotiated with the unions as to wages when business was very prosperous, but which became belligerent during business stress. In times of depression, there was practically no association activity, as need for such had not become great especially in the field of legislation and politics. Associations were found in highly skilled trades and only in the larger cities and their environs, where numbers of workers in the trade were congregated and business was conducted on an increasingly larger scale. Apparently no Southern or Western cities had yet developed any notable unions or associations, since the industrial conditions there were hardly yet ripe for such.

Yellow-dog contracts and welfare funds existed prior to 1832, according to Luther, who says that the contracts had no legal force. The provision of one reads:

"We also agree not to be engaged in any combination, whereby the work may be impeded, or the Company's interest in any work injured; if we do, we agree to forfeit to the use of the Company the amount of wages that may be due to us at the time."

Payment of wages was made monthly. Other provisions in this agreement (of the Cocheco Manufacturing Company, Dover, N. H.) dealt with wages, fines, and reprimands—to be determined by the Company—a "sick fund" of two cents a week, and an employee not to leave employment until after two weeks' notice or without permission of the agent of the Company, or to forfeit two weeks' pay. This was intended mainly to prevent the "quickie strike."

The large cotton mills were attacked for causing bad conditions, For instance, it was charged that "At Lowell, 72 persons (Irish) were found in one-half of a small house," and they worked 12 hours a day in the mills. Again, it was recorded that 1,000 women rose in rebellion in a large cotton mill when a fine of 12½ cents for late arrival was announced. The order was revoked.

Employers Resisted Movement for Shorter Workday. Master mechanics of Taunton, Massachusetts, refused to grant their machinist employees permission to quit work at sundown instead of 8.30 P.M. The machinists struck. In the early part of 1832, the master carpenters of Boston held a meeting and voted to call together the employing carpenters, masons, painters, and slaters to discuss the problem of a shorter workday. These employers met, considered the ten-hour day, and decided that it was inadvisable. But while the building contractors, it seems, really favored a shortening of the day's work, the merchants and shipowners of Boston were bitterly opposed to it and met and resolved "to discountenance and check the unlawful combination formed to control the freedom of individuals as to the hours of labor, and to thwart and embarrass those by whom they are employed and liberally paid." They contended that these labor combinations would drive trade from the city. They further resolved not to employ any journeyman who belonged to such combinations and not to utilize the services of any master mechanic who employed such journeymen—in unionists' terms, "to drive to starvation or submission" these unionists. These resolutions were signed by one hundred and six firms. Many journeymen struck to enforce the demand for the ten-hour day; shipwrights, caulkers, and carpenters struck quite generally, but the masons, painters, and slaters did not present a united front with other mechanics and laborers. New men readily took the strikers' places. The strike failed.

The merchants [shipowners] of Boston were troubled with a long list of grievances by the ship workers, one of which related to the need for early and late hours for ship repairing. The association argued that such hours were made necessary by the tides, and in this the union concurred. The merchants subscribed

$20,000 (a large sum then) to defeat the ten-hour movement. The Boston newspapers set forth the high wages of shipwrights— $2.50 a day from sunrise to sunset with two hours out for meals, for "tolerable" workers. While the strikers in Boston lost the ten-hour day—they won temporarily two hours for noon on account of the intense heat, so they could better resist cholera—the unions in New York and Philadelphia won the ten-hour day.

The strike of the ship carpenters in New York for the ten-hour day was won largely by a break in the ranks of the bosses up the river who granted it; the possible loss of business over-weighed their opposition to granting it. The strike lasted about ten days. But the union victory however, appears to have put an end to shipbuilding in New York City, and the men had to go elsewhere to obtain work.

The employers of Boston in 1833 again defeated a strike of the carpenters for the ten-hour day. In 1834 the shipowners of Bath, Maine, also joined in defeating the ten-hour movement in that place. Associated employers in New York and Pennsylvania were likewise successful in 1834 in defeating strikes of other craftsmen for the ten-hour day.

Certain events and issues of 1833 have interesting aspects. Noted men who were once workingmen were named and the fact commented upon. A Southern newspaper stated that Virginia, Georgia, and North and South Carolina were destined to become great manufacturing states, for that was the only way their planters could compete with those on the virgin soil of the West. The manufacturing would provide a market for provisions, better farming, increased population, and the like. A manufacturer, however, who shut down and threw men out of employment be-cause of falling prices and no profit was compared unfavorably to a slave-holding planter who cleared new fields with certainty of pecuniary loss. The record of a girl factory operative in a mill in Connecticut in June to August was given: in one week 1,575¾ yards and $9.45 for the week. Another rapid operative (dresser tender) earned $37.00 in a month, or $9.25 average a week. A citizens' committee in the vicinity of Williamsport medi-ated in a riot between two groups of Irish laborers employed on the Chesapeake and Ohio Canal and induced them to negotiate a treaty of peace and placed them on bonds to keep the peace.

Notice was given prominence to the holding of a convention by the workingmen of all New England. The Boston convention of New England workingmen in October appointed committees on: education, imprisonment for debt, condition of children in factories, condition of working women, and other subjects. It provided for speakers to spread its propaganda. A committee reported on the Thompsonville Manufacturing Company with the charge that it treated its weavers arbitrarily and oppressively; the report was published in the ARTISAN. The convention made plans to establish trades unions throughout New England. In November, unionists proposed a national convention, and resolved to vote for no public official who was not openly favorable—among other things—to a universal system of general education by means of manual labor schools supported at public expense and open to poor and rich alike; abolition of imprisonment for debt; effective lien law for laborers on buildings; and change or abolition of the state militia. The convention was called to meet December 9 at Philadelphia to promote the ten-hour day, general education, and regulate wages to make them adequate for the labor performed. Workingmen held a meeting in Baltimore to nominate candidates for President and Vice-President of the United States and selected a committee to state and carry out the objects of the meeting.

A society for promoting manual labor in literary institutions in New York was functioning in 1833, although others had failed. Its success was pointed out as a basis for other organizations elsewhere. A list of college presidents endorsing the movement was given. Reasons for such societies were set forth at length.

Employers Opposed Wage Advances, Some Attempted Reductions. The period of 1833-36 was one of great activity among the associations—in fact, association activities in this period reached a hitherto unprecedented height. The period was one of rising prices and increasing profits for the employer; the climax was reached in 1836 and a panic followed in 1837. Association activities, both as to character and extent were closely related to the price changes and the changing margin of profits. In the early part of the period, the employers were associated in checking rapid increases of wages, but in the later part, the associations vigorously resisted any wage advances. Prices did not begin to rise until in 1834, but the situation was not the same for all trades and industries. For instance, in 1833, prices were generally falling or were at a standstill, but in the early part of the year in the building trades the master carpenters of New York found it too unprofitable to continue for long their refusal to grant the demands of the local carpenters' union for advanced wages. As the strike was called at the beginning of the building season, the employers were at a strategic disadvantage and shortly made the necessary concessions. But prices in general were declining at this time and employers outside of the building industry undertook to reduce wages. The Master Hatters' Association of Baltimore in 1833 ordered a reduction in piece prices paid to the union workmen, on the grounds that competition from other towns where the piece prices had been reduced made it unprofitable for the master hatters of Baltimore to pay the old scale.

Efforts of the journeymen shoemakers' union of Geneva, N. Y., to prevent undercutting of the union scale of $1.00 a pair for making coarse boots led to a strike to force the discharge of a woman who undercut, and this in turn led to the indictment of the union for conspiracy in the noted case of People vs. Fisher. The case was appealed and in 1835 the upper court decided against the union's contentions. The master cordwainers were united in carrying the case through.

In 1834, prices began to advance but employers opposed immediate wage advances, because falling prices were feared shortly and they had just experienced great difficulty in reducing wages. Master bakers in New York City refused to grant the demands of the bakers' union for an increase in the piece rate with a minimum wage, limitations on number of apprentices, and a rest day on Sunday. The union struck and the masters advertised extensively for workmen who took the places vacated by the strikers. The shoe manufacturers of Lynn, Massachusetts, sent out the work to other towns and thus defeated the demands of the striking women shoebinders for increased wages. The shoe manufacturers of Lowell, apparently affected by the complete success of their fellow-manufacturers of Lynn, reduced the wages of the women factory operatives and were struck but the strike was of short duration. The manufacturers sent the work out to other towns, and thus broke up the strike. Mills at Lowell also were struck by girl operatives in large numbers. These paraded and in long lines attempted to break a bank friendly to the mills by demanding specie. They lost the strike. Railroad contractors were struck by 400 men for higher wages and daily allowance of grog. The contractors were attacked by strikers armed with clubs. One contractor was seriously injured. The militia was called out and 9 ringleaders were jailed. A wage increase, however, was won by the carpet-weavers' union which was also victorious in the Thompsonville Carpet Manufacturing Company conspiracy case.

Associations Resisted the Ten-Hour Movement in 1835. In May, 1835, the coal-yard owners of Philadelphia were struck by their workmen for a ten-hour day. Usually, this time of the year is not favorable to successful strikes by coal handlers. The employers offered to compromise on a day beginning at sunrise and ending at sunset, but with three hours deducted at the time workmen chose. The strike seems to have been a failure. It may have been this case which led McNeill to conclude that the employers in Philadelphia in 1835 were able to defeat the movement for a ten-hour day. However, in June, 1835, three different employers' associations in Philadelphia met separately and granted the ten-hour day, namely: the master builders granted this demand to their striking carpenters; the master bricklayers conceded the bricklayers the ten-hour day for the busy season, April 20 to September 20; and the employing sheet iron and tin plate workers also granted the ten-hour day. In general, the associations successfully fought the ten-hour day movement. On May 26, 1835, the Schuylkill merchants met and pledged themselves not to employ any laborers unless they agreed to work by the day from sunrise to sunset, with an allowance from that date to June 1st of one hour each for breakfast and dinner and, after June 1st, of one hour for breakfast and two hours for dinner. The merchants, furthermore pledged themselves not to pay "exceeding one dollar per day to laborers." In July, 1835, the building-trade employers of Boston defeated the second strike of their workmen for the ten-hour day. The master carpenters' and the carpenters' unions were prominent rival organizations in these strikes. Apparently, the defeat of these strikes didn't settle the matter, for McNeill reports that "In November, 1835, the master mechanics of Boston held meetings at the Exchange Coffee House to consider the question of altering the hours of labor. At the last one, fifty-two trades were represented and they resolved to fix the dinner hour at twelve o'clock instead of one." In New York, however, the master stone cutters were forced by a strike to grant the ten-hour day. After the strike was called they offered to make a concession of a two-hour noon, but the union refused to accept anything less than the ten-hour day and won. The master mechanics were likewise forced to grant the carpenters and other workmen a ten-hour day. The cotton mill owners of Paterson, N. J., were struck six weeks that year over the hours of labor, which prior to the strike were 69 a week, or 11½ a day. Many of the workers left town for other employment.

An Open-Shop Movement in the Thirties.—The ten-hour movement caused much bitterness among employers, since they desired long working days when prices were high and profits large. Although the tendency to belligerency was growing, concessions in the form of advanced wages were made in 1835 in some instances, with expressions of the justice of the workers' demands. The master bookbinders of Philadelphia met in June, 1835, and stated that the demands of their women bookbinders were just, and resolved that $3.00 a week was the minimum to pay. In contrast, the master cordwainers of Poughkeepsie, New York, refused to advance wages and were subjected to a strike.

Associations that Made Wage Concessions in 1835 Fought in 1836. The Ladies' Shoe Dealers and Manufacturers of the City and County of Philadelphia, in 1835, held a meeting and resolved to grant the demands of their striking workmen for an advance of wages made necessary by the increased cost of living and to advance the price of shoes to the customers in accordance with a list of prices fixed by the association. But in 1836 these employers resolved to resist any further increase of wages, and to combat any strike called. They were 82 in number, and they urged other employers to join with them.

The master tailors of New York City, in 1835, granted an

advance of wages to their workmen on strike. But in 1836, the association reorganized for defensive purposes when the union struck a second time for another advance in wages. The association proposed a scale of wages or piece prices but the union refused to accept it. Annual earnings of two union tailors were published: $1,945 for one, and $1,498 for the other. The masters issued a published declaration that they would not employ any member of the local trade union which demanded the closed shop. The association opposed the union standard rate of work and of pay as conducing to inefficiency and penalizing the most competent workmen. Twenty unionists were indicted for conspiracy; members were forced by the union to picket by a $5.00 fine, and workers who refused to strike were threatened with death. But so great was the terrorism, threatened workers feared to testify against the unionists. Sixty of the union leaders were found guilty and fined a total of $1150, and the judge condemned the combination as one of foreign origin and dangerous to this country. For that day, this trial resembled much the Danbury Hatters' Case of more recent times. The following quotation reflects some of the bitterness felt over the decision: "Employers never hesitated to exercise all the power they possessed. They combined and 'conspired' but escaped punishment; while their employees were made to feel the full weight of the law." In that year, however, a combination of employers failed to obtain the conviction of the plasterers' union of Philadelphia for conspiracy. In April, 1836, officials of the journeymen tailors' union were indicted for conspiracy and the employing tailors of Philadelphia organized to combat a strike by that union.

In the South, wages for skilled workers were higher than in the North as the South then had greater wealth than the North had, and the South had its labor conflicts. In August, 1835, an incipient riot was crushed in New Orleans by military force and the leaders of the movement were imprisoned. They were agitating against the employment of slaves as mechanics. At Natchez, Mississippi, in September, newspaper publishers resolved themselves into a society and discharged five members of the Mississippi Typographical Society for striking to force a publisher to discharge an apprentice.

The Open Shop Movement Became Widespread in 1836.
This year was full of bitterly fought strikes in which the unions
were generally defeated. For instance, in January, the master
carpenters of Boston won in the strike of the journeymen
house carpenters for the ten-hour day. In February building employers of New York began advertising for workers to meet a
threatened strike for $1.75 a day. In June, the shipowners refused
to grant a wage increase of two dollars a month (from $14 to
$16) and broke up the strike that followed. In September, sail-
makers struck. In 1836, longshoremen, riggers, and other dock
employees in New York struck for a wage increase and fewer
hours, but their places were quickly filled by nonunionists who
refused to leave and were threatened by the strikers. Apparently
the shipowners convinced the mayor that the militia was needed
to put down the strikers. Both here and in Philadelphia where the
scene was repeated and riot threatened, the armed forces broke the
strike. A riot by strikers on the Susquehanna Railroad was stopped
by the militia and three striking leaders held. In October the millowners of Lowell, Massachusetts, defeated the striking women
operatives.

During the year, employers, acting through their old organizations and through newly formed ones for this purpose, fought
wage advances as excessive, and resolved or agreed to refuse
to give work to any person who belonged to a trade union, in
order "that the workmen might not obtain the means of supporting one another," as unionism was threatening the creation of
capital and a shortage of articles requiring labor. Employers
formed such organizations in some instances in businesses which
were free from strikes, but generally a strike led to such action
on part of the employers. Union demands were fought so bitterly
by the Master Carpenters' Association of Philadelphia that it fostered a newly formed "Anti-Trades Union Association." A shoe,
cap, and hat manufacturer of New Brunswick, N. J., advertised
his freedom from union abuses, and his satisfaction with his nonunion workmen. The Employing Cordwainers of Newark, N. J.,
resisted a wage advance of 12 percent and especially opposed the
formation of a trade union among the journeymen who struck.
This association made an announcement that none of its members

would employ union men or pay the wages demanded by the union. The union, however, won the strike. The success of the union in Newark, N. J., was one of the causes that led the Employing Leather Dressers of the cities of New York and Brooklyn to make a similar announcement. The Manufacturers and Retailers' Association of the ladies' branch of the boot and shoe business of the city of New York was organized on April 8, 1836, to resist union demands and union regulations. This association urged other employers to organize into like associations and join with it in opposing "every injurious combination connected with the Trades Union." Newspapers—notably the New York COMMERCIAL ADVERTISER—were shocked by strikes, parades, and banners carried by unionists.

It should be noted that the strikes of 1836 were quite frequently over questions of wages, sometimes against wage reductions, and in many cases involved the question of union membership. While the issue over hours was not important, this year marks the peak of rising prices for most commodities, and the employers' associations (a number of which had formerly been appeasatory) now became belligerent and resolved to resist any further advances, or to reduce the recently advanced scales to a lower level. Since prices of raw materials and wages had advanced till profits were no longer large nor business especially good, the employers sought to retain a profit. They felt that wages were much too high. On the other hand, the workmen paid high prices for the articles they bought. The economic conditions necessarily resulted in conflicts and ill feeling. In 1836, merchant shipowners of New York City were struck by the longshoremen, riggers, and other shipping employees for advanced wages and a shorter workday. They threatened the strikebreakers; the mayor of the city called for the militia, and the strikers lost. Also, about this time, the shipbuilders of New York City—many of whom were merchant shipowners—were struck for the ten-hour day and conceded it. Later, they were for a wage advance of 25 cents a day; all but two yards granted it, but the other yards supplied strikebreakers.

In 1837, some employers of New York City attempted to induce a union of repair workers on ships to accept a wage reduction, but they countered with an offer to contract directly without the intervention of master mechanics, and at lower rates and utilizing the materials of the merchant-shipowners. Contractors of Rochester, New York, however, were struck by 150 men for higher wages—more than $4.50 a week, six shilling for 15 hours daily. Unemployment was increasing; an employer advertised for a mason and received 570 letters with postage due on each.

In 1840, ship-builders of Medford, Massachusetts, brought in workmen to break the strike of the workmen for the ten-hour day, but these were induced by the strikers not to work. The strikers sought work elsewhere, but business was dull until all contractors accepted the ten-hour day.

Masters Again Resorted to the Courts, in the noted case of Commonwealth *vs.* Hunt. The bootmakers of Boston had struck in 1835 for advanced wages and employers had conceded a satisfactory increase. The growth of nonunion shops in the following years threatened to break the union scale and nullify the union's gains. In 1839, the journeymen's union accordingly began an attempt to unionize all the shoemaking shops of Boston. Some of the masters resisted this attempt, and refused to discharge certain nonunion workmen on demand by the union. The shops of these employers were struck. One unionist, fined $1.00 for violating a union rule, was expelled when he did not pay the fine. He was advised by his employer to seek work elsewhere, because of a threatened strike. Seven of the union leaders were indicted for being in an unlawful combination: (1) with unlawful rules; (2) extorting money and conspiring not to work for anyone who employed a nonunionist; (3) compelling employer to discharge workmen; (4) conspiring to impoverish the plaintiff workman; (5) conspiring to impoverish other workmen. The union leaders in the case were not tried for being in a conspiracy to raise wages. The trial court found them guilty. On appeal to the Supreme Court of the State of Massachusetts, the decision of the lower court was reversed, largely on the lack of evidence to prove the counts of the indictments of illegal conspiracies to do unlawful acts. The plaintiff—proved by the union attorney to be an atheist —had not been allowed to testify. A number of employers had testified that their shops were not union ones; that they employed

both union and nonunion workmen; and that they had found
the union beneficial. One of the plaintiff's fellow workmen testified that the plaintiff was not a steady workman and was only a
passable one. The union attorney cited the similar rule of the bar
association and the medical association. Many persons have said
that the decision of the court legalized certain union practices,
but as subsequent cases show, it established in Massachusetts no
precedent favorable to such practices. It simply confirmed the
accepted principle that labor organizations, per se, were not
illegal.

*Economic Forces Were Adverse to Much Organized Activity
in the Forties.* The period of depression from 1838 to 1842 was
a factor in the disorganization of both unions and associations.
When workmen in large numbers are unemployed, the employer
holds the strategic position. During a depression an association
can defeat easily (even an individual employer usually can defeat)
any local organized group of workmen. It is by no means exceptional during these times for laborers to underbid their fellow
workmen, in order to get or retain employment. Under such
conditions, the employers are rarely called upon to put forth all
their united efforts. Now and then, there may be a flare-up but,
in general, inactivity of the rival forces was the rule. For instance in 1840, the Lowell millowners refused to grant a shorter
workday to their employees, and in 1842 the iron manufacturers
of Pittsburgh defeated a strike against the reduction of boiling to
$5.00 a ton. The strike lasted from February to July. So far as
the record at hand shows, this strike marks the beginning of a
momentous struggle between associated iron manufacturers and
the puddlers' union lasting over half of a century.

In the latter part of 1842, business began to revive, and with
it labor troubles returned. The workmen in their strikes showed
irritation and resentment that they had been feeling more in-
tensely as the depression wore out. Many employers had taken
advantage of the depression and consequent weakness of the
unions to subject the workmen to irritating conditions. In August,
1842, the manufacturing weavers of Moyamensing and Kensington, Philadelphia, were struck. Rioting occurred, looms were destroyed, and weavers who continued to work were assaulted by

the strikers. The manufacturing weavers were refused the use of a building that they had formerly used as a meeting place, because the strikers threatened to tear down the building if the manufacturers continued to use it. The rioting continued throughout the remainder of the year, and property of weavers who remained at work was destroyed, all to such an extent that in January, 1843, the militia was called out. But as soon as the militia was gone, the rioting broke out afresh. The manufacturers despairing of putting an end to the violence of the strikers, met with the weavers in conference in January, 1843, and temporarily settled the difficulty. In September of that year, the master weavers of Philadelphia met and agreed to give the wage advance demanded by the striking weavers. The weavers, however, went to work for those who first granted the advance demanded. This situation caused the employers' association to break up in a row, and then some of the masters granted a quarter of a cent a yard more than the weavers had demanded. In contrast, the employers' association blacklisted the women strikers of the Middlesex Mill at Lowell, Massachusetts, and they were forced to seek work in other localities in other fields. The workers struck against attending four looms instead of three. While this strike was in December, 1842, complaint was made about the blacklisting before a legislative committee in 1846, but the unionists failed to obtain any legislation to stop the blacklisting.

The period 1843 to 1847 was one of mild business revival, and concessions were not granted freely. In May, 1843, the brick manufacturers of Philadelphia were struck by the brickmakers for higher wages. The strikers rioted; in fact, they rode one brick manufacturer on a rail and forced him to sign the new scale. During the same month, the Chicopee mills increased the work without an increase in pay, and the women operatives struck but failed. However, business was prosperous enough in September, 1843, for the striking tailors of Boston to force some of the master tailors to grant higher wages. Here, again, the employers failed to hold together, for some still refused to grant the wage advance. In March, 1844, with business prosperous and the season at its best, the master tailors of Philadelphia felt compelled by a strike of a few days to grant the tailors' demand for a wage increase. During this year, most of the shipyards of Massachusetts, also of Bath, Maine, conceded the ten-hour day.

The iron manufacturers of Pittsburgh were forced by a strike —which lasted from May to the latter part of August, 1845—to grant the demands of the boilers (ironworkers) for an advance in wages of $1.00 a ton.

The attitude of employers in granting concessions during this pre-panic and panic period is reflected fairly in the following instances: In September and October, 1845, cotton millowners in Pennsylvania were struck by their operatives for the ten-hour day. The employers refused steadily to concede it, although they gave their consent to continued agitation to make the ten-hour day general in all cotton mills. In 1846, carpet manufacturers of New York City refused to meet in conference with the carpet workers' union over a reduction in wages announced by the association. Declining profits caused employers in 1846-7 to resist union demands, and many strikes occurred; immigrants were imported to break strikes and lessen union demands. In February, 1847, master weavers of Philadelphia (Moyamensing) defeated a riotous strike of the weavers for an advance of one-half cent a yard. The strike lasted a month. But in 1847, the master tailors of Philadelphia, by means of a strike lasting from June to October, were forced to grant the demands of the tailors' union for a wage advance. In 1847, the shipbuilders of Bath, Maine, bound themselves under heavy penalties to return to the system of working from sun to sun. A strike of several weeks resulted. One employer broke away from the association and hired the best workers on the ten-hour basis. A superintendent of a marine railway who had strongly supported the ten-hour movement was discharged on demand of shipbuilders, but was restored when a new superintendent learned the facts and refused the job. The panic of 1847 further tended to demoralize the union movement.

In 1848, a business depression set in, and wage reductions were again the rule. In February, 1848, textile manufacturers in Massachusetts reduced wages from 15% to 17% and their operatives struck only to fail in three weeks. The great proportion of the strikers in Fall River were foreigners. The cotton factories of Allegheny were struck by the operatives from July 4

to August 28, 1848, over the ten-hour day. The employers finally
granted the shorter day but made a corresponding reduction in
pay. In September, 1848, the coal operators of the Monongahela
River reduced the price for mining coal from 2c to 1¾c a
bushel, and the miners struck. In a few days the operators cut
the price to 1⅜c. The miners then offered to return to work for
1¾c, and the operators a few days later accepted the strikers'
offer. This strike apparently marks the beginning of an extended
series between the coal operators' association and the miners'
union.

In December, 1849, the iron manufacturers of Pittsburgh
agreed to reduce the price of puddling $1.00 a ton. On, or about
December 20, the men struck. According to one account the wage
reduction took place in January, 1850, affecting "puddlers, boilers,
refiners, scrappers, and heaters, and they struck." Strikebreakers
were imported from Europe. Rioting began and mobs of strikers
and their wives assaulted nonunion workers and destroyed mill
property. Six of the rioters were convicted, but were pardoned
by the governor of the state. The strike was broken and then
was called off in May, 1850. The reduction for puddling wages
was to $4.50 a ton. Although the manufacturers won the strike
much petty strife occurred during the succeeding years, especially aggravated by wage reductions corresponding to the declining price of iron, so that the puddlers had many grievances
real and imaginary. These situations in coal mining and iron
manufacturing are a part of the evolution of the labor-relations
problem, and are early stages in the development of a permanently organized conflict. This long-drawn-out struggle between
the unions and associations in the manufacture of iron and steel
illustrates, for instance, the growth and decline of one of the most
powerful trade unions in the United States as well as the develop-
men of an association into a powerful financial combination.

Foreign competition caused manufacturers to demand protective tariffs and to import the cheaper foreign labor, especially
to break wage strikes. John Aiken, a manufacturer, made a survey
of mills in England, Scotland, and Ireland in regard to wages,
and the like, and contrasted them with American wages and con-

ditions, publishing a series of articles in a Lowell, Massachusetts, newspaper and later in a pamphlet in 1849, "Labor and Wages at Home and Abroad." He set forth a wage theory of supply and demand—with profit as the motive for demand for labor. He condemned reformers and demagogues for trying to bring "class divisions" and foreign doctrines into America where conditions were so much better than abroad. He advocated tariffs to protect workers as well as manufacturers against products of cheap foreign labor.

Associations Held Strategic Position in the Fifties. They combined to blacklist union agitators. While the era of depression lasted, employers generally not only held the unions in check, but forced through wage reductions. When the depression passed, a great tide of immigrants made the supply of labor so plentiful that, with the exception of the building trades and perhaps the printing trades, the unions were quite generally demoralized. In November, 1850, the millowners of Fall River, Massachusetts, gave notice of a wage reduction and justified it on grounds of the depression, the improvements in machines, and the more favorable working conditions. The employers contended that the operatives by means of these could earn as much at the reduced rate as could be earned previously at the old rate without the improvements. The spinners struck. By June 1, 1851, the mills had secured enough nonunion workers to demoralize the strikers and break the strike. The reduced rates prevailed in all the mills. In September, 1851, the millowners of Three Rivers and Palmer, Massachusetts, defeated a strike of all the weavers over the question of wages.

The depression, however, favored reduction in hours. The unions in the building trades, then as now, held a strategic position and the master builders generally conceded the ten-hour day to the carpenters and masons around 1851, in some cases only after a strike, for instance, the contractors of Lowell, Massachusetts, were struck by carpenters and masons over this issue. Other employers in Massachusetts, who long had opposed the ten-hour day, in 1852, compromised by reducing the hours per week from 68 to 66. However, strikes at Amesbury and Salisbury were broken by strikebreakers imported mostly from Ireland. The strikers formed a double picket line and hissed all who went to work. They burned and cut the fire hose. They had boys throw stones and break windows of a boarding house for "scabs."

In 1852, a general rise in prices began and this made a wider margin of profit for the employer, but only workmen in strategic trades like the building trades, where the supply of laborers was not superabundant, could force wage advances. In May, the sewer laborers of New Bedford struck for advanced wages and compromised for a part of the advance demanded. In June, the hod carriers likewise struck and obtained a wage advance.

In 1853, strikes were generally of short duration and wage advances quickly made. In April, the manufacturing cabinet makers and the master carpenters of Philadelphia were forced by strikes of the cabinet makers and carpenters, respectively, to advance wages. The Master Plasterers' Association of Baltimore issued a notice of advance of wages of plasterers on April 1, 1853, to $2.00 per day, and of an advance in the price of plastering to 3½c a square yard. To meet the threat of building contractors to import plasterers, notice was given to master and and journeymen plasterers in other cities not to come to Baltimore, at least without reporting to association or union headquarters. Manifestly, this was a combination of association and union to raise both wages and prices, and to keep outsiders from competing. The Master Plasterers' Association and the Employing Bricklayers were notified by the hod carriers of a demand for $1.25 a day to meet the higher cost of living. The price-raising scheme did not work so well, and there were rumors that the association would dissolve. This was denied, and a meeting was called to harmonize matters. Employing house carpenters of Baltimore were notified of a demand by carpenters for an advance of 25c a day to meet rising costs of living. The journeymen carpenters had met and voted to take action to obtain a 25% increase in wages. The employing house carpenters refused to grant the advance, and the carpenters called a rally before striking. The employers broke ranks, a number gave the advance, and the strikers returned to those shops. The next day more employers agreed to give the advance. The master carpenters met April 14, 1853, to try to reorganize their ranks and work under the advance.

An Epidemic of Labor Troubles Hit Baltimore Employers in 1853. The mechanics struck and resorted to mass picketing. A group of the most prominent lawyers of the city, at the request of the president of the Employers' Association of Master Mechanics involved, gave an opinion that mass picketing accompanied by violence and the blocking of entrances to workplaces by crowds of strikers, so that workmen desiring to work were forced to quit, made a conspiracy. The lawyers cited three authorities and two were the conspiracy cases of the eighteen hundreds. The BALTIMORE SUN commented favorably on this opinion, and referred to the salutary typographical union in contrast to the turbulent one on strike. The union attorney cited Roscoe's Criminal Evidence that the common law gave workers the right to combine to raise wages—as well as employers to fix wages— but warned the strikers that they must refrain from intimidation.

The strike was directed mainly against the president of the association, and was for an increase of 15% in wages; however, seven employers were struck. The president denied that he had ever joined any combination to fix wages, as the union alleged.

The seven struck employers issued a joint statement that the strike caused them to associate; they paid as high wages as were paid for this work throughout the country, but were opposed to paying as high wages to the unskilled as to the skilled; individual merit to govern differences; moreover to grant the advance demanded would cause work to be sent elsewhere.

Strikers in considerable number returned to work in four of the seven struck shops. The strikers' committee stated that men had returned to two shops which had granted the 15% increase as claimed. Strikers at two other shops were asked to attend meetings of the union. One firm reported that outside pickets had blocked the entrance to its shop and forced its men to quit. A striker returning to work after three weeks contradicted the charge of the union committee that he was a faithless deserter; he had tried to prevent the disastrous strike; there was no prospect of settlement; most strikers had left the city for work elsewhere.

The unreasonableness of the strikers' demand for a 15 percent increase was set forth, and the pressure on the Baltimore and Ohio Railroad was condemned. A striker mechanic replied with epithets and condemned the above viewpoint.

The strike committee paid the fare of any striker to another city where he could obtain employment; the Philadelphia committe wrote that not only was there employment in that city for at least 100 men, but that a committee had collected funds from a number of cities. For instance, a committee had collected funds from about 300 mechanics at a meeting held in Trenton, New Jersey.

Union committees elsewhere continued to aid the Baltimore strikers; $300 was sent from each of four cities, and help came from even Atlanta, Georgia. Mechanics of Baltimore were called upon to perfect and extend the union and a mass meeting for March 29, 1853, was called for this purpose. The mass meeting met to perfect the organization of workers. However, 600 of the 800 strikers on Winans—the president of the association—returned, some at an advance. Of the 200 who did not return, some obtained better jobs and others an increase of 15 percent elsewhere.

The striking mechanics at a meeting on March 29, 1853, decided to publish a newspaper. Strikers met and selected delegates to a Grand Union which they were joining.

Engineers, firemen, and trainmen threatened to strike over new rules by the Baltimore & Ohio Railroad to work certain number of hours a day or have the wages reduced. The men won. About 1,000 boilermakers formed a union.

Master horseshoers of Baltimore refused to give $1.00 advance in weekly wages. One employer gave 50c. Workmen resolved to strike for $1.00, and to have those who accepted the 50c strike also. The employer who gave the 50c replied that he and his employees had agreed on this temporarily and that he would give as high wages as anyone. In contrast, the employing bricklayers met union demands for wage increases on grounds of higher prices.

In 1853, in Baltimore, shoe dealers of the ladies' branch met and organized to regulate prices of shoes and discuss other matters of mutual interest. They granted the justice of the workers' strike for higher wages, but felt that increased labor and material costs required higher prices for shoes. But higher prices met with strong sales resistance, so the issue was not easily solved. The association advertised widely for nonunion workers, but the shoemakers' union warned unionists and "scabs" to stay away from Baltimore during the strike: The coming of men "to work for the scab bosses" would subject the "scabs" to merited contempt and trouble." The union published a list of "fair" employers who paid the union scale with the advance of 20 percent. An added list was published a week later for the employers who had surrendered. The procedure was repeated elsewhere. Shoe manufacturers of Dayton, Ohio, however, were struck by a union of 100 members for wage increases. The attempt of the manufacturers to import scabs was met by the union issuing warnings to scabs to stay away from Dayton.

Hotel Owners Fought Union Demands frequently in 1853. In Boston, the owners refused to grant waiters an advance in wages and defeated the striking waiters by employing other waiters at once. Hotels of New York City were struck by waiters for $18 a month; some hotels granted the increase, others employed boys and girls. Some waiters remained at work or returned when demands were denied. Hotels of Philadelphia were struck by waiters for higher wages; one hotel employed women as strikebreakers. Hotels of Baltimore imported French waiters to break a strike of waiters for $18 a month.

Shipyards Were Struck in the East when they refused to grant increased wages but did not attempt to operate. Ship laborers of Baltimore demanded an increase of wages from $1.00 a day to $1.25 and work only from bell to bell, but apparently failed to get these. In 1853, the merchants of Boston defeated the shipjoiners on repair work in a strike for the eight-hour day, but granted it the following year. Joiners and shipbuilders of New York City—600—resolved to strike on April 1, 1853, for $2.25 a day. Master shipwrights and others were presented with a demand by the caulkers for a wage advance of 25c a day, to meet the increased cost of living. All steamship owners struck by firemen and coal passers granted the advance demanded.

Association Activities Were Varied and took place in many localities in 1853; some further illustrations follow: The master painters of Baltimore called a meeting for March 30, 1853, to consider the demands of the painters for $1.25 a day from April 1, and apparently granted them. The building contractors of Cleveland were tied up by strikes on a large scale. The master builders of Washington asked the carpenters to classify themselves before a wage advance of 15 percent would be granted, but the union refused to make the classification.

Newspapers of Boston and New York City showed a strong contrast. The morning newspapers of Boston were struck by all their printers for higher wages and all but two newspapers conceded the demand the same day as the strike. Newspapers of New York City fought a strike by the printers' union for higher pay and to enforce rules governing the conduct of employers. The strikers demanded $17 a week or 37c a thousand ems, an advance of $3 a week or 5c a thousand ems. Employers considered having the trade taught to girls for day work, as a means to break union control. Newspapers of Baltimore argued that a union making reasonable demands for wage advances had the employers' sympathy, but that arbitrary demands inevitably forced the employers to combine in opposition; in such a contest the association would win. Shortly thereafter the employing printers called meetings to organize. In the book and job printing offices, about half of the workers struck for higher wages on May 2, and most of the firms granted the increase demanded. THE BALTIMORE SUN referred to the season as one of strikes. It condemned the printers' union for its strike to force arbitrary rules on employers. An employer who offered to aid the struck employers was also struck. The strike spread and one employer opened up "quite a school" for teaching young persons printing. THE SUN denied that the employing printers had organized as a body acting in concert with avowed hostility to the printers' union; it was an independent. The issue was: Union rules and regulations were to be the bases of the contract with the employers, with the union reserving the right

to change its rules at any time. The union planned to publish its
own newspaper.

The Conflict Widened to Other Employers and Localities.
Employers of a different class of workers were beginning to experience organization troubles. The boss draymen of Louisville,
Kentucky, were struck for higher wages and the strikers paraded
their drays three miles long. Coal operators of Cumberland,
Maryland, were forced by a strike to grant higher wages and the
closed shop. Both a National Industrial Congress (8th) and
Southern Planters' Conference held meetings on the problems of
the day.

The first part of 1854 was still prosperous enough for wage
advances. In February, the shipyards of Philadelphia, after a
two-week strike by the journeymen shipbuilders and caulkers,
granted an increase that brought wages up to $2.50 a day. The
shoe manufacturers of this city also granted a ten percent advance to the boot and shoe workers after a few days' strike. In
April, the time was not so favorable for the coal shovelers of
Boston to strike for more pay. In August, wages were reduced
ten percent by the tack manufacturers of Taunton, Bridgewater,
Abington, and Boston. The first strike was at Taunton in opposition to the reduction and was lost. The movement spread to the
other cities named, but the strikers were defeated and the employers adopted a uniform scale of wages with the ten percent
reduction embodied therein.

In 1854, the New Orleans Typographical Union had forced
up the rates per thousand ems from 40 cents to 50 cents—a 25
percent increase and much above the New York rate. In 1855,
depression had set in and the Associated Press asked the printers
to return to the old rate. There were six newspapers in the Associated Press and one outside of it. The Associated Press was
formed to get telegraphic news at a lower cost per member and
to offset a virtual monopoly that the other newspaper—THE DAILY
PICAYUNE—had enjoyed through certain Eastern connections.
This fight led THE PICAYUNE to support the Typographical Union
against the Associated Press.

The association sent to New York City for 42 printers.
These arrived by steamship via Havana, but their arrival was

announced by THE PICAYUNE and the union called a general strike on all employing printers except THE PICAYUNE. The pressmen employed by the members of the Associated Press also threatened to strike. Threats of violence, persecution, and intimidation upon strikebreakers caused most of them to decide not to work. The strike gave THE PICAYUNE a great advantage over the members of the Associated Press. Time, expense, and uncertainty prevented the importation of more strikebreakers from New York City. THE PICAYUNE was charged with stealing telegraphic messages from the Associated Press through the local telegraph office, but THE PICAYUNE published a statement by its local manager denying such was the case. Under these circumstances, the association surrendered. Undoubtedly, the support given to the union by THE PICAYUNE was the real deciding factor. THE PICAYUNE upheld the union's demand for a "living wage," and said that the subscriber should be made to pay the extra cost.

Slack Business Lessened Strikes in 1855-56. In 1855, the cigar manufacturers of Suffield, Connecticut, were struck for an increase in wages. The strikers were supported financially by cigar workers of New York, Albany, Troy, Westfield, Springfield, and Fredenhills. Although a majority of the strikers had left for other localities in search of employment, the strike lasted between six and seven weeks and was finally settled by a compromise. But in 1856, the cigar makers of New York met with cigar manufacturers to equalize piece prices for making cigars throughout the state, undoubtedly with a view to reducing "cut-throat competition."

In 1855, the cotton millowners of Manchester, New Hampshire, defeated a strike of thousands of their operatives for a reduction of hours below twelve and one half a day. The owners, finding no profits in current prices, had no objection to the strike. Although the depression is usually recorded as beginning in 1857, there were manifestly factors at work to prevent the usual number of strikes during this period. The falling of immigration from the high point of 1854 also indicates an absence of much prosperity. Obviously the great number of immigrants who had come in the decade prior to 1855 had furnished so great a supply of labor that employers, during the slackening period of industrial activity, generally held the strategic positions, especially in all but the highly skilled occupations. The workers generally recognized this situation. An exception is to be found in the Irish laborers upon the wharves of Boston, for, in March, 1856, they struck unsuccessfully against the introduction of steam hoisting machines. The busy season in the building trades, however, was favorable to the carpenters in Philadelphia, for these skilled workmen struck and forced the master carpenters to advance wages 25c a day during the busy season. Also, from 1854 to 1858, the shipowners of New Orleans resisted strikes of the Screwmen's Union.

McNeill, like other unionists, apparently could not understand why employers quit giving concessions and started reducing those given when business slacked; this condition caused lost strikes, so that the breaking up of the unions was attributed to the panic and not to the excessive demands of the unions in declining business periods which contributed to the belligerency of the employers. Hence, McNeill concluded that the panic of 1857 tended to break up the unions.

The latter part of 1857 and most of 1858 were in a deep industrial depression. Wages were frequently reduced. Unionists argued then as now that employers can pay fair wages: "If the profits of their business are not sufficient to remunerate them for the trouble of doing business, *let the customer make up the balance.*" In 1857, the condition of workmen was so serious that a committee of an employers' association reported in 1892 that "manufacturers and merchants reduced the wages of the men in their employ to the point of bare subsistence, as the wages paid at that time conclusively show." In brief, the committee set forth that often men were paid in due bills—which the manufacturer bought from the stores for 75c to 80c on the dollar—and the merchant, to get his profit, overcharged the workmen, or gave short weight, or did both. This was done to such an extent that workmen were thus defrauded of about one-third of their wages. Laborers' wages were 65c to 75c a day, machinists and blacksmiths received $1.00 to $1.25, and molders earned from $1.00 to $1.38 a day. Molders, for instance, usually paid by the piece, received pay only for good "work" that was placed in the mounted stove ready for the market, and lost all good "work" that was broken in the process of cleaning, milling, or mounting, and sometimes even all the castings taken to fill orders for repairs. These practices gave rise to the Molders' Union in 1859. Thus reported committee No. 4 of the National Association of Stove Manufacturers in 1892, in relation to "Labor Organizations." The employers took the lead in establishing a national organization; local organizations of founders and molders had opposed each other in an important strike in Philadelphia in May, 1855. In 1858, iron founders met at Albany, New York, formed an association, and issued a circular advocating a national league of employers to import labor from Europe to take the place of strikers and workmen made discontented by union agitation. Three strikes were on in the molders' trade then. The practice of importing labor grew greatly thereafter. In 1859, iron founders of the Eastern and middle states formed a National Founders' League and sent abroad for molders to break strikes. In July, foundries of Albany, New York, had been struck for ten weeks because they had reduced wages and retained wages as a guaranty against striking.

Not even highly skilled workmen could obtain their demands during this period. 1858 was not a favorable year for unionism. That year, the glass factories of Glassboro, Williamstown, Port Elizabeth, and Millville, New Jersey, began to indenture apprentices extensively, to which the union objected very strongly on the ground that the apprentices would make factories nonunion and break up the union. In July, 1858, all the glass factories in New Jersey were struck by the glass blowers to enforce demands for a wage advance, restriction on number of apprentices, vacation in July and August (which probably was the real reason with many workers for the strike) and to fix the time for commencing and closing the blast. But the factories imported men and broke the strike. The union dissolved. In April, a few workmen formed the "United Sons of Vulcan," as a secret union, but its weakness caused its suspension until the more favorable time of the outbreak of the war in 1861. Union leaders had come to believe that unionism was retarded by slavery, and they had found that it was comparatively easy to form unions in the cities but difficult in the country.

Wage reductions continued in 1858. In April the millowners of Chicopee reduced wages 20%, and defeated the strike of the women weavers and of the other workers who later joined the strike. While the textile manufacturers of New England in general reduced wages during 1858, few were struck. But as business began to revive, the operatives struck for a return to the former level. The millowners of Salem, Newburyport, and West Springfield defeated the strikers, but the strikers won in one mill at Adams, and in the mills at Blackstone and Uxbridge. In 1858, manufacturers of Fall River granted an advance of ⅓ of that demanded by the spinners' union and by the outbreak of the war had granted the other ⅔. But the union went to pieces during the war. In general, the employers defeated the strikes of 1858 that were called when business began to improve to enforce a return to the wage rates paid before the panic.

In 1859, employers were not so successful, especially in the shoe industry. In February, the ladies' branch of the shoe manufacturers of Philadelphia were struck by the shoemakers who demanded a uniform price throughout the city, with an advance from 6 to 12% in the various shops. After a six weeks' strike the manufacturers generally conceded the demands. In March the men's branch of the shoe manufacturers of this city, after a week's strike, granted the 5% advance in wages demanded by the workers. Likewise, the shoe manufacturers of Natick, Massachusetts, were forced by a strike in August to advance wages. Apprentices struck in Boston. Hat manufacturers of Philadelphia, in July, reduced the scale of prices for hat finishers from 25 to 50%, but were forced by a three-week strike to restore the old scale. Coal dealers and operators at the Richmond wharves in Philadelphia reduced wages from 15c to 12c an hour, and apparently had no great difficulty in defeating the strike that resulted. The coal operators of the Monongahela Valley, and in the counties of Allegheny, Washington, and Westmoreland, however, had to deal with riots when the miners struck over the question of the capacity of the cars used in the mine. The strike was a failure. The shoe manufacturers of Lynn, Massachusetts, (138 factories) likewise had serious trouble, when their workers struck in 1860 to force a restoration of wages to the old scale.

The strike lasted seven weeks; scabs were assaulted and wagons taking work into the country were overturned and the cases of shoes and materials taken away. The manufacturers obtained special policemen, had Boston policemen come to Lynn, and had the state militia to stand by to stop the rioting. The strike spread through eastern Massachusetts. The manufacturers, however, imported men from Maine and New Hampshire, and the strikers soon began to seek their old places at the terms laid down by the manufacturers. These instances indicate that strikers are prone to use violence in periods immediately following depressions and in strikes about to be lost. It seems that the strikers then give vent to pent-up bitterness of months of endurance of what the workmen regard as oppression and meanness by the employer during the period of depression.

In 1861, the first American miners' union was formed; "foreigners . . . were the organizers and officers." It was destroyed by employer opposition in defeating strikes and by the resulting internal dissensions in 1867-68.

Business had not fully recovered from the panic of 1857 before the panic of 1861 came with the outbreak of the Civil War. Thus the years between 1857 and 1863 were generally depressed, and the strikes relatively infrequent, although sometimes attended with great bitterness. The workers were at a strategic disadvantage. The Civil War, with its great waste of economic resources and with its great drain on the labor supply for men under arms, changed this situation.

CHAPTER 5

ASSOCIATIONS IN THE CIVIL WAR AND POSTWAR PERIOD: ATTEMPTS TO FORM NATIONAL ORGANIZATIONS

THE CIVIL WAR—with its waste, inflation, large profits, and labor shortage—brought about renewed activity among the associations. Prior to this time, most of the associations were confined to the few industrial communities of the nation. The few national associations were not comparable to those of today; industry had not yet developed to the point where they were required. This period was one in which railroad transportation was widening the market and railroad managers were really the first national group of employers to come into conflict with the unions on anything like a nationwide basis. Furthermore this was a time when the iron industry was developing with great rapidity and associations in this field became prominent for the first time. Previous to this we have read of very few associations in any of the central states such as Ohio, Indiana, Illinois, Kentucky, and Michigan, but now with the extensions of railroads, the development of the iron industry, and under the stress of war, associations began to spring up in this region.

It may be recalled that the employers had been masters of the situation in the period beginning with the panic of 1857 and were inclined to resist the demands of the unions, although the latter now enjoyed the strategic position. Since the margin of profit was large, the resistance was largely verbal. Concessions are usually made to workmen when prospects for large profits are excellent, although protest may be frequently made by employers. Organization, however, took place so that only necessary concessions were made. The movement did not have much momentum until the war had been under way for over a year. In 1862, however, the association activities became more pronounced, and fighting, as well as conferences, took place.

In 1862, rising prices led to higher wage demands. The

shipyards of Camden, New Jersey, were forced by a strike of the ship carpenters to advance wages from $2 to $3 a day. The coal operators of Bevier, Missouri, although the winter season was near at hand, proposed a reduction in the price for mining coal, but the union demanded 9 cents—an advance of 1 cent a bushel—and based its demands on the high cost of living due to war prices. The strike was bitter and soldiers were brought in to maintain peace and order. After three months, however, the operators granted an advance to 10 cents and for a time paid 11 cents a bushel. About the same time the coal operators in the Belleville Trace, Illinois, were struck for an advance in wages. They imported Belgians as strikebreakers, but many of these left when their expenses were paid by the strikers. The association lost after a nine months' struggle; strikes had become quite general and rises in the prices of coal made wage increases easy to grant.

Strikes Increased in 1863. In New York City there were strikes of machinists, street railway employees, house painters (of Brooklyn), house carpenters, safe makers, lithograph printers, iron-clad ship workers, window-shade painters, horseshoers, sash and blind makers, cigar packers, glass cutters, coopers, stage drivers, confectioners (also of Brooklyn), and tin-plate and sheet-metal workers. Umbrella manufacturers defeated a strike of workers for higher wages and better conditions. Freight houses of Albany, New York, were struck by the laborers who engaged in a riot. Hat manufacturers of Orange, New Jersey, were struck. Boston had strikes of boilermakers, varnishers and polishers, wood sawyers, riggers, and plasterers.

Coal-mine owners in 1863-5 fostered strikes to boost or keep up the price of coal (a practice continued through the century), but they also attributed the high price to high wages paid to the miners. When the coal operators of Pittston, Pennsylvania, in 1863 granted their striking miners an advance of 10 cents a ton, several times that advance was added to the price of coal. However, the Coal Exchange of Pittsburgh met to resist "the unreasonable demands" of striking miners and to ask the cooperation of newspapers in ending the strike. Moreover, coal operators of the

Schuylkill region broke up the miners' union, charging the union officials with disloyalty and having them imprisoned.

Founders and Molders Fought Each Other. Foundrymen had refused to confer in 1862 with the molders' union over wages and the rising cost of living. In February, 1863, however, eight foundrymen agreed to a scale of wages, but demanded that the union abandon its limitation on apprentices. Moreover, employers generally insisted that each firm should deal with its own employees—this showed concert of action. Associated foundry owners tried to break up the Philadelphia local union (the backbone of the molders' union) and called upon foundrymen everywhere for cooperation, especially not to employ any Philadelphia molders. The strike lasted from February until October, and the union was defeated through instructors teaching green hands in the shops. Foundrymen of Cincinnati also broke with the molders' union over apprentices. During 1863, the Iron Founders and Machine Builders' Association of the Falls of the Ohio organized to resist the union scale of wages and union restriction on the number of apprentices. This association was composed of foundrymen, machine builders, and other employers of iron workers. The Louisville and Nashville Railroad was represented in the membership of the association. Limited to Louisville, Kentucky, New Albany and Jefferson, Indiana, it was a local association, but it tried immediately to induce employers in the principal cities of the United States to organize into local associations and cooperate with it in resisting the unions. It attempted to help carry out a nationwide blacklist of any workmen who had gone on strike against any of its members. It made appeals for immigrants and other workers to come to Louisville where "labor is scarce and wages advancing." It published a scale of wages and the like.

Strikes in foundries and machine shops making government war materials and in navy yards at Brooklyn, New York, and Charlestown, Massachusetts, during the war, led to arrests of strikers and to attempts by state legislatures (New York and Massachusetts) to prohibit any interference with workers who wanted to work. This was said to be part of a general campaign to crush unions. Strikes in St. Louis caused employers to combine to get a military order prohibiting picketing of any plant doing government work. A similar order was issued at Louisville, Kentucky. Anti-picketing laws were passed in Ohio, Minnesota, and Pennsylvania, and considered in Missouri. Some vagrancy bills had a similar purpose.

As a result of the activities of a group of employers in the vicinity of New Haven, Connecticut, in resisting the demands of the International Molders' Union, there was formed in 1864 in New York the American Iron Founders' Association. Representatives from New England, New York, New Jersey, and Pennsylvania were present at the organization meeting. It refused to recognize the molders' union. It considered reducing wages 10 percent, but a threatened strike prevented it.

Iron foundries of San Francisco were struck by the molders for a wage increase of 50 cents a day, time and half overtime, and a minimum wage of $4 a day. The foundrymen advertised in Eastern newspapers for replacements and imported sufficient strikebreakers to break the strike although the Journeymen's Iron Molders' Protective Union of California gave notice in FINCHERS' TRADE REVIEW, repeatedly warning any iron molders not to be "led to believe you can work in San Francisco without first joining our association—the members of said association being prepared for any and all emergencies."

The Iron Founders' Association of New York used an "honorable discharge" system for new employees (they had to furnish a written discharge from previous employer). One association member was charged with using the foundry in Sing Sing Prison (New York) "To train up scabs and strikebreakers." The association was likened to the Employers' Association of the Eastern States, although its members agreed not to employ union men but failed to live up to the agreement.

The Iron Industry was far from a unity in 1863. The Association of Engineers of New York issued a circular announcing its opposition to wage increases and to unions generally. It published statements showing high wages paid, and sent a committee to the President of the United States to counteract a union committee calling on him. The association provided for a blacklist of certain

machinists, and the union lost its "greatest strike on record."
Massachusetts employers of machinists were charged with combining to keep down wages by refusing to employ anyone who
could not show a recommendation from his most recent employer,
stating wages, class and kind of work done, his specialty, and his
character. Machine shops of St. Louis were struck again by the
machinists' union in 1864, which partially won the strike by
"divide and conquer" tactics; however, the employers refused to
sign the "written agreement" offered by the union. In some form
or other, the trouble was still on in 1865, although the union
claimed a double victory. Boiler manufacturers of St. Louis
combined in 1865 in using the "honorable discharge" system
and in reducing wages 20 percent, but were defeated by the machinists and boilermakers' union. Later in the year, the boiler
manufacturers and machine shops of Baltimore were struck over
wage reductions. Rochester employers of machinists and boilermakers failed in an attempt to reduce wages, as the unionists
sent away the "surplus imported labor." Master mechanics met
in Brooklyn to resist the "unreasonable demands of the union."
Employers of Philadelphia rejected a proposal of the machinists
and boilermakers' union for a joint union-association committee
to settle all disputes, on the grounds that it was "an outside
agency." The association was condemned by the union, as was
the New England Iron Manufacturers' Association for attempting
to break up the union. Similarly, iron manufacturers of Boston
and vicinity adopted anti-union resolutions in 1865. The iron
manufacturers of Pittsburgh, however, dealt with the unions and
appointed a conference committee to meet with a union committee of puddlers to fix wages from time to time as the price of
iron varied. In 1863, the joint conference committee met to fix
wage scales, but badly fluctuating prices of iron conduced to
a strike which the union won, and caused a sliding scale of wages
to be agreed upon in February, 1865.

Shipowners Combined.—The merchant-shipowners of New
York City in 1863 granted striking longshoremen an advance from
15 to 20 cents an hour. But the shipowners of Buffalo, New
York, used Negro strikebreakers, who were assaulted after a
white picket had been shot. A raid upon Negro quarters followed

and, in the resulting riot, three Negroes were killed and 12 severely beaten. The Ship Owners and Shipbuilders' Association of Buffalo in 1864 issued a circular on the "exorbitant demands" of the Ship Carpenters and Caulkers' Union, its "dictation, arbitrary rules, and regulations." The association added that "The day is not far distant when they will modestly ask an equal distribution of property if not arrested at this point." It resolved not to employ any member of the striking union; it offered wages of $2.50 a day, and filled its yards with "goon men" from abroad. It proposed to form a permanent association. The New York Central Railroad, the New York and Erie Railroad, and others were associated as member shipowners. The union won. Likewise, after a two weeks' strike, it won a wage advance from the shipyards of Baltimore. In 1865, these yards were struck again by the white caulkers to force employment of white foremen exclusively (instead of Negroes). Shipbuilders of Albany, New York, were threatened with a strike in 1865.

The High Cost of Living Led to Wage Demands. The continued waste of war, the consequent shortage of products, the transfer of much labor power from the farms and factories to the army, and the money inflation—all combined—led to higher and higher level of prices and to enormous profits to the employers whose products were in great demand. But they led also to repeated demands by the unions for higher and higher wages, partly because of the increasing cost of living, partly because of the desire to share in the enormous gains made by the employers. In some industries, however, the employers were suffering rather than profiting by the war, but their employees were facing the rising cost of living and so they demanded higher wages. The situation called for united action by employers in checking or resisting union demands. Thus, manufacturers of Worcester were organizing to reduce wages, due to a falling off of business. Wagon manufacturers of Philadelphia were struck for bringing in other woodworkers (wood choppers, log rollers, and laborers) at lower wages and to break up the wheelwright's union. Likewise the manufacturing potters refused to grant the flat pressers an advance in the piece price for making saucers. After several weeks the issue was compromised favorably to the union which, however, was financially exhausted and soon collapsed.

Employers Were Organizing extensively in 1864. An Employers' General Association of Michigan was proposed to be made up of affiliated associations to resist union demands. Brewers organized in Baltimore. Bakeries of Chicago jointly issued an unusual number of circulars when struck by the bakers' union. Associated employers of New Britain (near Lowell, Massachusetts) issued statements against employing union men. Employers in New Jersey combined in opposing an anti-store order law. Millowners of Cohoes, New York, refused a wage advance and were struck. Nail manufacturers of Fall River, Massachusetts, granted a 25 percent wage increase but were struck, as were other manufacturers in Massachusetts, when wages were reduced as prices fell.

Merchant tailors were struck in 1864 in St. Louis, Chicago, Buffalo, and Pittsburgh by the tailors' union for wage advances and, in New York City, to force union recognition. In St. Louis, the merchant tailors organized against union opposition to women seamstresses as well as "exorbitant wage demands." They refused to "recognize" the union, which would not call off the strike until the employers signed the agreement. Although the union won in New York City, it was months in beginning to recover from the strike. In 1866, the merchant tailors of Wilmington, Delaware, reduced wages and were struck by the tailors' union.

Morocco manufacturers of Philadelphia were struck by the morocco finishers' union over union recognition and a wage advance. They induced the Wilmington, Delaware, employers to discharge all union members as these were aiding the Philadelphia strikers. High prices were attributed to the union. By "divide and conquer" tactics, the union caused some employers to break away from the Morocco Exchange, but the strike was still on a year later.

Shoe manufacturers on government work in Philadelphia and in Newark, New Jersey, were struck in 1864 for wage advances. In 1865, boot and shoe manufacturers of Albany and Troy, New

York, were struck for a wage advance of 10 percent and because the shops posted a notice that union men would no longer be employed. One shop broke with the association and offered higher wages to nonunionists, but strikers refused to desert the union. The association advertised for strikebreakers. The strike at Albany was settled by a 5 percent advance and removal of the anti-union notices.

The employing curriers (leather) of Boston, Woburn, Salem, and South Danvers, Massachusetts, acted in concert in non-recognition of the curriers' union. They offered to pay the wages demanded but would not employ union members as these would not work with nonunionists and a large number of apprentices. Strikebreakers were imported from Canada. The Boston union won higher wages and established an apprenticeship system, but the unions of Salem and South Danvers expired, only to be re-organized later.

In 1865, employing curriers in Baltimore, in Newark, New Jersey, and in St. Louis were struck by the curriers. A wage reduction, over which the employers divided, was the cause of the Baltimore strike; the employment of men who had not served apprenticeships caused the St. Louis strike.

Railroad Managers Cooperated Nationally in 1865 in combating a union strike. The managers of the railroads centering in Chicago and of the railroads of the Eastern states assisted and cooperated with the officials of the Galena and Chicago Union Railroad in breaking a strike on that road. The railroad managers of Chicago promptly rejected the union proposals and, in the strike that ensued, were furnished engineers by the Eastern railroads to break the strike. The railroad managers of Chicago also reduced wages of certain workmen 15 percent. But the railroad managers of Buffalo had more trouble reducing wages from $2.50 a day to $2, then to $1.75 for 1,500 railroad workers, who struck (as they had done and won two years before). Conspiracy proceedings were begun against the officials of the picketing union and soldiers were used as strikebreakers. As the number of railroad managers is small, they can cooperate without a formal organization and they have done so through the years with the minimum of formality.

The Growing Belligerency of the Associations was evidenced in many ways. They tried to obtain state legislation penalizing unionists for using violence on persons and property, threats of intimidation, molesting, obstructing, and the like to force workmen to go on strike. Even the General Court of Massachusetts fostered the organization of an association of shipbuilders to make rules and regulations controlling the building of ships; in other words, to form a gild of masters—or both an employers' association and a trade association. Also, about 1864, the Braddock collieries installed independent-employee ["yellow-dog"] contracts and maintained these for many years. Employing printers of Rochester, also of Binghampton, New York, unanimously agreed "not to submit to the imperious demands made upon them" by the unions. The Western Associated Press adopted a resolution regarded by unionists as blacklisting of discharged printers. The Employing Printers' Association of New York City formed in 1862, discussed incompetent workmen and the apprenticeship system, which is interesting because of the boast of the printers' union that all its members are competent workmen. The Northwestern Publishers' Association was charged with planning to break up the typographical union, but 1864 was hardly the time for serious attempts to crush a union of highly skilled workmen.

Employing printers of Boston (1863-4), Chicago (1864), St. Louis (1864-5), New York City (1865), and Albany, New York (1865) were struck. The Chicago publishers, led by the CHICAGO TIMES, established a joint stock fund to finance a "Typographical Female Seminary" to instruct girls in type setting. It had 40 pupils. The typographical union was defeated. When the employing printers of St. Louis reduced wages and were struck, they sent to Chicago for strikebreakers, who were badly beaten up by "rat exterminators" on the Illinois side of the Mississippi River. Book and job printing shops of Boston were struck in 1863, and newspapers a year later. Weekly wages of compositors were published to show how high they were. The strikers established the BOSTON EVENING VOICE to present their side, to give strikers employment, and to compete with the struck newspapers (like the ST. LOUIS DAILY PRESS of the St. Louis strike, and somewhat similar to the

CHICAGO WORKMEN'S ADVOCATE). Newspapers of Albany, New York, were struck for refusing to discharge workmen who were "obnoxious" to the printers' union.

The belligerent employers, however, did not always win. In the summer of 1864, the glass factories of New Jersey refused to advance wages of the highly-skilled workmen in glass-bottle blowing. The glass bottle and vial blowers struck and within a week forced the employers to grant a 33 percent increase in wages.

Among the devices used to check unionism were: increasing number of apprentices, women workers (notably compositors), importation of workmen from Europe, Negro strikebreakers, requiring letters of recommendation from former employer (all of these had to be written by hand), machines, and anti-union shops. For instance, the Piano Manufacturers' Association barred all workmen who would not sign to leave the union and thus threw 1,200 men out of work.

Importation of foreign labor was fostered by organized employers in the United States and by unions abroad. It was not limited to strikebreakers, but functioned to increase the supply of skilled labor and thus keep wages of such workmen from rising rapidly. The American Emigrant Company and the Foreign Emigrant Society were either the same or closely allied. The "Company" was chartered by Congress, it seems. Its (or their) object was to import skilled labor especially and so caused unions to denounce this and the company or society frequently. Moreover, American unions contended that trades unions in England and Scotland arranged for the emigration of "surplus" skilled workers to America.

Building Trades seem to have been adversely affected by the war. In these trades, it was customary to advance wages in the spring and reduce them in the fall. But these spring advances were not always secured without a struggle, especially when the trades were somewhat depressed. Although wage reductions were the rule, not everywhere was depressed in 1863. Master builders of New York City were forced to grant striking carpenters $2.25 a day to meet the increased cost of living. Contractors on the treasury building in Washington, D. C., were struck twice by carpenters, masons, and laborers. In 1864, master builders of

St. Louis were struck for wage advances by the bricklayers,
carpenters, and painters. Some master builders granted the carpenters' demands for 50 cents extra a day and thus got the
best workmen—the divide and conquer tactics—and the union
carpenters won. Employers of Jersey City were struck by the carpenters and painters for a 25 percent wage increase. While the
master painters of Jersey City granted the painters' demands, those
of New York City were struck, but divided on the wage issue.
The Boss Plasterers' Protective Association of New York City
held a special meeting in 1864 and resolved not to grant the
plasterers' demands for higher pay. All master tinners of Evansville, Indiana, were struck by the tinners for refusing to grant a
35 percent wage advance. Proprietors of marble works of Boston
were forced by a strike of the marble cutters to grant an eight-
hour day. The Master Bricklayers' Association of Baltimore agreed
in 1864 to grant the union's demands for a wage scale, provided
the union would work exclusively for association members; that
is, the agreement was to be exclusive on both sides and not merely
a closed-shop one. This proposal was rejected by the union,
which feared that it would be blamed for the higher building
prices. The association then ordered a wage reduction of 50
cents a day, and the union struck. The master painters of Paterson, New Jersey, after a one day's strike, granted the painters'
union an advance from $3 to $3.50 a day while the master painters
of New York City lost a strike to reduce wages from $3.50 to $3
a day. The master masons of Jersey City were struck for a wage
increase. Some employers surrendered but others, refusing to
grant it, vowed to fight it out and get men from New York City.
In four days the strike ended by the union withdrawing the demand. The master plasterers of Brooklyn formed a league and
discussed reducing wages below $3.50 a day. In July, however,
they reduced wages but were struck, and restored them; the wages
were higher than in New York City and New Jersey cities, and
so set up competition which forced a reduction of 50 cents a day
to the level of the other cities. Master builders of Troy, New
York, combined to reduce carpenters' wages, and the bricklayers
of Brooklyn accepted a reduction of 50 cents a day (leaving $3).
But the master builders of Cincinnati, in October, gave the car-

penters an advance of 25 to 50 cents a day, while master plasterers of Boston were notified by the plasterers' union of a demanded advance to $3.50 a day beginning March 1, 1866. In December, 1865, the furniture manufacturers of Boston combined to reduce wages, were struck, and were boycotted by the cabinet makers' union, which started its own factory—all in accordance with the current widespread agitation for cooperative stores and shops.

Barrel manufacturers experienced strikes. Master coopers of New York City organized in 1863 to resist union demands, but when the coopers' union struck them (and Hudson River cities) in 1864, they divided in granting the wages demanded. Troy, New York, employers brought in outsiders to break their strike. Philadelphia master coopers issued a circular stating that the wage advances demanded (up from $9 to $15 a week) would make unprofitable existing contracts. Chicago employers gave their striking coopers a wage advance. Likewise the New York City and Brooklyn master coopers, after a two weeks' strike in 1865, lost to the union. But the master coopers of Chicago reduced wages from 24 cents down to 20 cents a barrel, and the coopers struck and formed a company to make barrels.

Iron industry employers continued their efforts to organize on a nation-wide basis, although the conditions for such an organization were not yet very favorable. In 1865, the foundries and machine shops of Detroit acted in concert against strikers and workers shifting jobs. They issued a circular dealing with a proposal to establish "protective" associations under three plans: local associations with affiliations, national associations likewise, and a congress or congresses of all.

Associations in the Postwar Period successfully opposed union demands in the industrial field, so union officials turned to "social legislation" such as laws prohibiting prison labor, regulating hours, apprentices, immigration, and even wages (on rare occasions). The leading union periodical then—FINCHERS' TRADE REVIEW—editorially said that Congress had the power under the "Welfare Clause" *"to do sundry things."* With the close of the war in April, 1865, came a slackening of industrial activity along with an increase in the supply of labor as the soldiers were mustered out. The strategic position held by the unions passed

generally to the associations. Wage reductions were made or proposed, and the strikes against these usually failed, although there
were exceptions among the highly skilled workmen, such as the
glass blowers. During the summer of 1865, the glass manufacturers of New Jersey and Pennsylvania attempted to reduce
wages 25 percent—to the rate of 1864—but the glass bottle and
vial blowers struck and won after a one month's strike, while the
window-glass blowers took three months to win. The druggist-
ware manufacturers' association of Philadelphia was charged with
pledging members not to employ workmen away from each other
and not to deal with "grievances." It was not until January, 1866,
that the glass manufacturers of Baltimore voluntarily restored the
wages of the glass blowers.

The Conflict in Mining Was Bitter. In 1865 when the price
of coal declined, the coal operators of Schuylkill County, Pennsylvania, cut wages for mining, largely to force a strike to cut the
production of coal. The union offered to take a reduction of 10
percent for miners and 15 percent for laborers. The strike was
bitter and federal troops were called out to maintain order.
The strike ended with a reduction of 35 percent for the miners
and 25 percent for the laborers, but within two months another
reduction was threatened by coal-mining railroads. The union
offered to take a 7 percent cut, but the operators declined. The
coal operators met in 1866 at Pottsville to condemn the outrages committed by striking miners in Schuylkill County, and to
denounce unionism. Unions from Hyde Park, Pittston, Plymouth,
Carbondale, and other mining communities met in Scranton and
decided to strike. Stores denied strikers credit, but some operators
acceded to miners' demands as winter neared. Coal operators of
Luzerne County, Pennsylvania, were struck in 1865 over wages,
but some of them were attacked by unionists as a "cabal" for
cheating miners in various ways, for their anti-unionism, and their
"yellow dog" contracts. In two Ohio cases, the associated coal operators (of Mineral Ridge and Massilon, respectively), reduced
wages and defeated the striking miners. At Mineral Ridge, the
miners were employed only as "free" men and the union was
abandoned. In 1865, coal operators were generally reducing wages
and miners were striking and losing, as the market was heavily

overstocked with coal. Nevertheless, coal operators were charged with combining and establishing the Emigrant Aid Association to bring in coal miners from Wales. Associated mine operators in Pennsylvania obtained a law to turn strikers out of company houses; and when the miners of Blossberg, Morris Run, and Fall Brook, in Tioga County struck, the operators acted together in the ejection of the strikers, as they had arranged for uniform leases and planned for joint action in stoppages of work. The ejection of the strikers was denounced by union officials and periodicals in bitter terms for a long time. A libel suit against the *Buffalo Sentinel* for its more vicious part in the union smear campaign led to its suspension. Repeal of the law was repeatedly demanded by unionists, and union members were given the names of legislators who had voted for the law and were urged to defeat the lawmakers, but did not.

Ore mine owners of the Lake Superior region, likewise, had strikes of miners and laborers, with riots.

Wage Reductions were numerous and varied in 1865 and against these, unions set forth their "wages purchasing power theory" with little or no effect upon employers with declining businesses. In some fields, however, business was picking up in September, but most trades were dull and labor plentiful, especially unskilled who usually accepted reductions or very low wages without protest. There was an exception. Contractors for cleaning streets of New York City, collectively, reduced wages of the street cleaners and were struck. Violence ensued. Strikers blamed it on agents provocateur of the contractors, who won the contest. Somewhat in contrast, Virginia planters met and agreed upon $5 a month as the wage for Negro workers. Strikes were not won quickly; even the skilled cigarmakers of New York City were still on strike. The nail manufacturers of Wareham, Massachusetts, defeated the skilled nail makers who struck for increased wages. The National File Manufacturers' Association had been formed in New York City in April with members from Rhode Island, New York, New Jersey, Connecticut, and Massachusetts. A wage scale was agreed upon.

Among the other employers' associations which attempted to

reduce wages and which were struck in 1865 were the boiler manufacturers of St. Louis (20 percent—were defeated), machine shops of Schuylkill County, Pennsylvania, and machine tool builders of Rochester, New York (who also reduced prices when tool builders of Fitchburg, Massachusetts, reduced prices of tools 20 to 25 percent). Metal manufacturers of Worcester, Massachusetts, met to consider wage reductions of machinists, but one maker of machinists' tools opposed the reduction and thus broke up the meeting. Reaper and mower shops of Auburn, New York, "all shut down to reduce wages." Master coopers of New York City reduced wages from $4 to $3 a day and strikers' places were filled with "boys" who were passed around from shop to shop as needed. Master plasterers of Brooklyn, however, lost in a fight over wage reductions. Longshoremen of Brooklyn and of Jersey City were on strikes over wages paid by the merchant-shipowners.

The situation was thus characterized by FINCHERS' TRADE RE-VIEW: Employers "are still forming combinations for the purpose of breaking up ours." Unions "must fight fire with fire." "Despots have combined to oppress the people, and the people have combined to resist them." "A fresh onslaught is about being made by capital on the wages of labor" because of: (1) fall in the price of gold, (2) return of a large number of soldiers, adding greatly to the number of unemployed, (3) increased foreign immigrant labor, (4) probable fall in prices (but not of cost of living), (5) decreased demand for manufactured products, especially by the Government. The formation of employers' associations is very disturbing, but the situation can be no worse than before the unions existed. We need international unions so as better to fight the attempts of associated employers to break up the local unions.

On the other side, the SPRINGFIELD UNION (Massachusetts) stated that the unions were driving business away from the large cities into the country, for instance, away from New York City to Bridgeport, Stamford, New Haven, etc., where people are independent. The AMERICAN ARTISAN added, "The true way to make wages high is to make capital abundant; the way to make wages low is to drive capital out of a trade or country. The best way to increase capital is for the workmen to save as much as possible and invest it in their shops."

Sliding Scales were an important development in the relations between iron manufacturers and puddlers. The puddlers were well organized in the United Sons of Vulcan and had a powerful local at Pittsburgh. The Pittsburgh iron manufacturers were informally organized. They and the union had had conferences and a joint committee for fixing wages since 1863. As the puddlers demanded wage advances when the price of iron rose and the manufacturers tried to reduce wage rates when the price of iron fell, frequent adjustments had to be made to meet the numerous fluctuations in that price. Moreover, the union, in time, realized that it could not maintain a high price for puddling regardless of the price of iron if Pittsburgh manufacturers were to compete successfully with the rest of the country. The sliding scale, based on a sort of "wages-fund theory," therefore, appealed to the puddlers' union when a Pittsburgh iron manufacturer proposed the idea at a meeting of manufacturers and puddlers. The fellow manufacturers ridiculed the idea, but the union accepted when he presented the arguments for it at a meeting of the union. It took a long series of conferences by the joint committee to work out a schedule acceptable to both sides. The scale finally agreed upon (on February 13, 1865) scheduled iron prices from 3½ to 8½ cents a pound with the corresponding prices for puddling from $4 to $9 a ton, with 25 cents change in the puddling rate for every ½ cent change in the price of iron. An added significance to this scale was that it became the *basis* for similar scales throughout the West; these were often higher than the Pittsburgh scale. To call the local Pittsburgh agreement "the first national trade agreement" as a labor historian does is an obvious misuse of the term national; it would be more proper to refer to it as an early instance of "pattern" bargaining, so characteristic of the steel industry today. Pittsburgh has long dominated the iron and steel market, often by devices that consumers have condemned, while the unions have often played a part in the game of sharing in the process and gains of high prices and profits.

The sliding scale, however, did not guarantee peace to the iron

industry. In July, 1865, the price of iron fell and made puddling
$5.75 a ton; there was also an extra dollar then for hot summer
months—a "hot fix" it was called. The puddlers thought that the
pay was too low and, accordingly, gave the 90 days' notice required for the termination of the scale. In the meanwhile, the
price of iron advanced so that puddling went up to $6 a ton.
The union then demanded $8 flat and the manufacturers agreed
to it. This rate was paid until near the end of 1866, when the
puddlers demanded an increase of $1, which the manufacturers
reluctantly granted. In a short while, all the iron manufacturers
in the adjacent country—practically all the important mills in
the United States—joined in giving notice of a general wage
reduction to $7. Unions refused to accept and the strike called
in December, 1866, lasted until May, 1867, when the old wage of
$9 was restored. During the strike, iron workers were imported
from Belgium but they proved to be incompetent. The strike had
produced a shortage of iron so that its price had advanced, but
Pittsburgh manufacturers had lost considerable trade and they
feared they would lose more. In July, the Pittsburgh manufacturers agreed to the restoration of the sliding scale, which "governed" for the next seven years through a period of bitter strikes,
according to McNeill. Wright says that the union struck only
after due notice or to help another union get better terms. However, employers usually welcomed short strikes which caused a
sharp rise in the price of iron. The period for the notice was
shortened to 30 days, and the range in the new scale was $6 a
ton when the price of iron was 3 cents, $8 when the price was
5 cents, with the graduations unchanged; later (1871) they were
10 cents for every 1/10 cent change in the price of iron.

In 1865, there were strikes on rail mills and other iron manufacturers in Cleveland and Buffalo over wage reductions or for
wage increases. The heaters of Cleveland and vicinity struck the
rail mills over a 30 percent reduction, which had been agreed
upon by all the iron masters in the West and so affected Buffalo
where the heaters also struck. They formed a national union to
meet the importation of foreign strikebreakers by associated employers. Helpers were also used as strikebreakers. Puddlers struck
the iron mills of Cleveland and Youngstown (as well as Pitts-

burgh which set the basic rate) for a wage advance and won
in a week. It should be noted that the Sons of Vulcan (the
puddlers' union) favored a protective tariff and opposed the importation of foreign puddlers by the manufacturers. On the other
side, the American Iron and Steel Association sought a high
tariff on iron and steel, and lower excise taxes. With the wage
scale tied to the price of iron, the union and association had
mutual interests in protective tariffs, and so divided the spoils.

Associated foundries were struck in 1864-5 in Cincinnati,
Chicago, Lowell, Massachusetts, and elsewhere. In Cincinnati,
they lost and gave a wage increase, planning later to reduce
wages. The Iron Founders' Association of Chicago and vicinity,
however, won by using laborers and apprentices trained by instructors in the struck shops; the association offered to assist
foundries elsewhere to resist unjust demands by unions. In Lowell,
the strike "continued," somewhat like in St. Louis where it had
gone on since 1860. Foundries in Detroit were struck over a
wage reduction and in Milwaukee over union recognition. The
year 1866 began with a strike on the foundries of Cambridge,
Massachusetts, over a wage reduction. Other foundries supplied
strikebreakers. In March, all stove founders of Albany, Troy,
and Buffalo, New York, met in Troy to arrange for a convention
to launch a national association. At this convention on March 14,
the American National Stove Manufacturers and Iron Founders'
Association was "permanently" organized. It prepared a notice
to be posted in members' shops stating its purposes among which
was the special one of "resisting any and all action of the Molders'
Union which shall in any manner interfere with our right to
control our own workshops and to manage our own business."
The posting of the notices in the shops of Albany and Troy caused
the molders' union to strike for their removal. The union started
a cooperative foundry. These notices precipitated strikes elsewhere in which the association was defeated in a majority of cases
including also Albany and Troy; foundrymen broke away to take
advantage of the loyal ones. The association was too young to
have developed its full strength for this preliminary test. In
1867, however, the contest was renewed and lasted about nine
months. As a result, the union was all but disrupted. Especially

in Pittsburgh this anti-union movement among the stove manufacturers was strong and successful. In January, these manufacturers had reduced wages 20 percent and the molders had struck. New men were employed but the union remained on strike for nine months and was completely broken up; none of its members could obtain work as stove molders until they had severed all connections with the union. The association extended over the territory in which there was any considerable number of foundries in the United States. The depression from 1867 onward till 1871 and a disrupted union made unnecessary any vigorous activity by the association, so it became dormant or dead only apparently to be revived later (1871) under another name, that of the National Association of Stove Manufacturers—at least, this new organization appeared in 1871.

The foundries and machine shops of New Orleans were struck in 1866 by the molders and machinists for the eight-hour day and increased wages. A cooperative foundry and a machine shop were started by each of the unions, and the union foundry advertised to do the work cheaper by 20 percent than any other foundry in the city.

Union Demands for Concessions Were Fought in 1866. It seems to be an age-long union theory that the best way to prevent wage reductions as a depression approaches is to demand wage increases (with a shorter workday) and other concessions, but such practices lead to an anti-union attitude by employers, who try to disrupt the unions. Newly formed associations, however, in their attempts to disrupt unions have sometimes been disrupted instead. A case in point is supplied by the shoe manufacturers of Marlborough, Massachusetts. They agreed to stand together to break up the union; they offered to pay the advance demanded, provided the workmen would abandon the union. The strike, however, helped to cause the price of shoes to advance and this led some manufacturers to break faith and compromise with the union. The association thus went to pieces. Each manufacturer as an individual began to make terms with the union. In the summer of 1866, the pottery manufacturers of New Jersey were struck by the potters' union (flat presser) and after a three weeks' strike were forced to concede the strikers' demands for a wage advance. But the street railway companies of New York City refused to grant drivers increased wages and were struck. Shipowners of Brooklyn were struck by longshoremen for higher wages, while shipyards of Detroit agreed to advance wages to $3.50 (from $3), but one yard tried to reduce wages 50 cents (to $2.50) and was struck. Marble shops of St. Louis were struck by the Marble Cutters' Society for recognition; the union called the marble manufacturers a "monopoly." Similarly, the plasterers and painters on strike in St. Louis said that "employers in that city combined to break up the trades unions there." The master painters of New York City were struck over the eight-hour day. Master painters of Washington, D. C., refused to grant 50 cents a day advance but when struck a few surrendered while the others met and resolved to fight. Master painters of Baltimore, however, when threatened with a strike, gave increased wages to the painters although a depression was on in Baltimore and elsewhere. Master builders of New York City were struck by the carpenters during the months of May and June.

In 1866, associations were quite often anti-union and attempted often to reduce wages; reductions were usually followed by strikes for restoration. Associated iron manufacturers met in Pittsburgh and decided to reduce wages for rolling mill hands, who struck from Pittsburgh to Cleveland and West. As noted above, puddlers struck also and won. Glass manufacturers of Pittsburgh were struck in February by "helpers" for a wage increase. The manufacturers met a week later and decided to reduce the wages of blowers 25 percent (which had been granted only three weeks before), but blowers won the strike. Machine shop employers of Baltimore were charged with combining to destroy the machinists and boilermakers' union, which was then on strike on railroad shops over wages and overtime rates. A strike of several weeks against the employing free stone cutters of Boston caused them to postpone their announced wage reductions. Employing stone cutters of Cincinnati bound each other with a bond of $1,000 not to employ any union stone cutter for a year. The stone cutters "struck." Daily newspapers of Richmond, Virginia, reduced wages, but the printers struck and started a newspaper themselves. When the printers of Keokuk, Iowa, struck the newspapers for increased wages, one newspaper surrendered at once and so got all the business. Cigar manufacturers of Suffield, Connecticut, when struck over wage reductions, brought in strikebreakers from other cities.

Associations Resisted Reduction of Hours. In October, 1866, mill owners of Fall River, Massachusetts, were struck by spinners to force a reduction of hours. After two weeks, the mill owners granted it to take place January 1, 1867. Later in 1867, the mill owners attempted to reduce wages, were struck again, and were forced to maintain the old rate. But in January, 1868, they reduced wages 18 percent, but offered to restore one-half on March 1. The workers declined but struck without success. After the ten-hour day had been in effect 21 months, the mill owners returned to the old workday but the workers did not strike since the times were depressed. Threatened with a strike in 1866, all the cotton mills of Blackstone, Massachusetts, and vicinity (including Southbridge), conceded the eleven-hour day; it had been 13. Cotton mills of Auburn, New York, however, blacklisted the striking spinners. Some cotton mills went on record favoring reduction of hours, if made generally. In fact, the wide-spread slacking of industry favored reduction of hours with no advance in hourly rates or piece prices; a strike at Bedford, Massachusetts, led to reduction in hours to 11 daily, but as daily wages were reduced proportionally, the strike failed. A few other textile mills elsewhere granted the ten-hour day in 1866, but most associations resisted, were struck, and defeated the strikers and blacklisted them. In 1867, the mills of Lawrence and Lowell, Massachusetts, were struck by the mule spinners to force a reduction of hours. The owners employed new workers and ignored the strikers. The defeats and blacklistings occurred again in 1868, and efforts to revive the crushed unions between 1868-70 failed. The woolen mills of Auburn and Utica, New York were struck over a ten-hour day by spinners. The mills were filled with replacements and strikers were arrested for "parading and intimidating" the "scabs," but were acquitted. The carpet manufacturers of Philadelphia reduced wages and defeated the resulting strike. Wool manufacturers were organized primarily for high tariffs in the National Association of Wool Manufacturers, with 201 members in 1865 from Ohio, Pennsylvania, New York,

New Jersey, Maryland, Delaware, and all six New England states. It was formally organized November 30, 1864. So national organization of unions was met by national associations of employers, as the occasion arose.

Hours were a problem for the shipowners in 1866. Master shipwrights and caulkers of New York City joined in issuing a statement against the eight-hour day. The workmen retaliated by offering to do the work for the shipowners direct as quickly and at less cost than through the master shipwrights. Most of the newspapers supported the master shipwrights and the strikers lost. Ships sent from New York City to Boston to be repaired during the strike caused the workmen at Boston to strike. Shipyards at New Orleans were struck over the eight-hour day, but one yard broke with the association and violated the agreement. The renegade was reprimanded by the owners of the other seven yards. This strike led to the passage of an eight-hour law for the navy yards in 1868.

Unions, faced with increasing unemployment, wage reductions, and mechanization, along with more strenuous opposition of associations in the industrial field, with low attendance at union meetings, and their periodicals suspending, turned to legislation and politics, and agitated for international unions, for the eight-hour day, eight-hour laws, anti-prison labor laws, child-labor laws, and laws checking immigration, and regulating apprenticeship. So the associations had to extend their activities likewise. Union agitation for laws favoring unions was very extensive through the union press, officials, mass meetings, and eight-hour leagues, especially for eight-hour laws—federal, state, and local—as well as reduced hours by collective bargaining and strikes. Hearings by legislative committees, and investigations by special commissions were conducted on eight-hours mainly, but even apprenticeship was included. Employer opposition was shown largely by arguments in the commercial press and magazines, which were condemned by the unions. Associated employers were divided in their opposition to anti-prison labor laws. Manufacturers defeated a child-labor law in Massachusetts. Employers, however, still sought anti-picketing laws.

On February 12, 1867, the master mechanics of Boston

held a mass meeting and appointed a committee to formulate resolutions in regard to union demands for increased wages and decreased hours, and "arrogant dictation," e.g., as to apprentices. Employers on March 7 resolved to take as many apprentices as they judged best and to control them, free from any dictation by journeymen. The association also resolved against the eight-hour day, to stand together as one against any strike to coerce an employer to grant unjust demands, to resort—if necessary—to a complete stoppage of work (lockout), and to appeal for co-operation to all capitalists. They stipulated also that in the future all contracts were to have a clause for non-liability in case of a strike. "The resolutions were made in a firm, conciliatory spirit"; "ten hours for a day's work was not a burdensome tax on men's energies"; "labor was the only true capital of this country, and . . . reduction of hours . . . would virtually subtract from our resources and increase the necessaries of life." A resolution was added to meet the threat of the plumbers' union to open a shop of their own and work ten hours a day to take customers away from association members—customers were called upon to continue to patronize association shops. The following trades were represented by the association: master masons, plumbers, plasterers, painters, slaters, freestone cutters, carpenters, granite cutters, machinists and boilermakers, founders, copper and tin roofers, and coppersmiths. An executive committee of representatives of each of these trades was appointed with full power to take any considered measure for the interests of the employers, to solicit other employers and have them sign the resolutions.

Associations in Chicago and other cities had the problem of a shorter workday in 1867. The employing coopers were struck for a shorter workday. The employing stone cutters offered the workmen $4.50 for a 10-hour day, $4.00 for a 9-hour day, and $3.50 for an 8-hour day. The workmen chose the third alternative. But the other building trades employers resolved to continue the 10-hour day and pay employees by the hour. The master bricklayers of Philadelphia resolved not to yield the 8-hour day, or to pay any higher rate of wages. The master masons of Newark, New Jersey, were struck by 200 masons for $4.00 per day. Five employers granted it at once, others offered it after April 1, but strikers demanded the increase at once. Many master painters of New York granted $4.00 a day and 4 o'clock quitting on Saturdays. The master plumbers of New York City notified the journeymen that the 10-hour day would be required. The master plumbers of Boston were struck when they voted to return to the 10-hour day; the 8-hour day had been granted in 1866.

Conflicting trends were in evidence elsewhere. According to McNeill, the glass manufacturers broke up the glass blowers' union in 1867, but not for long. While the employing bluestone cutters and flaggers forced a demand for $4.00 a day, the iron manufacturers of Buffalo were struck for nine weeks for reducing the pay for puddling $2.00 a ton. While the molders' union of Pittsburgh won a strike against a wage reduction of 20 percent in a strike lasting most of 1867, the East and West combination of founders broke up in the early part of the year after fighting the union in 1866. However, when the molders refused to accept wage reductions and equalize wages in the West (Cincinnati) with the East, the founders reorganized formally and adopted a wage scale. The head of the molders' union, informed by his secret agent or spy among the founders, urged the acceptance of the reduction. The association denounced union dictation; all efforts to negotiate failed, and a strike was called. The unions had trouble with piece work—which it conceded was advantageous to a few workmen, but enabled employers to destroy local unions. Employers were charged with conspiring to poison the minds of union members against their officials.

Associations of Coal Operators; their organization and the development of their activities in the coal-mining industry make up a series of significant events of the reconstruction period. Prices fell with currency contraction in 1866-67, coal operators attempted to reduce wages, and when the miners struck, imported Negroes, Bohemians, and Italians to break the strikes. These strikes, however, were only preliminary skirmishes in preparation for the battles of the seventies; they were rather indecisive. For instance, the coal operators of Bevier, Missouri, fought the union unsuccessfully in the spring of 1868. During the period 1863-68, there had been minor strikes in which the union gained increases in the fall only to lose them in the spring. This time the operators proposed a reduction to 5c while the miners demanded an increase from 6c to 7c a bushel for mining coal. The operators brought in nonunion men and, when the situation became serious, had the state militia called out. Before the summer was over, the coal operators decided that it was more profitable to grant the union demands than to continue to fight. Only minor strikes occurred here between 1868 and 1872.

In June, 1866, the coal operators of the Monongahela River reduced the price for mining coal from 4c to 3½c a bushel. At the higher rate miners could earn $9.00 a day. The miners struck and probably failed to win the old rate then, since the time of the year was unfavorable. But the scale was doubtless restored before the winter season was over. For, in September, 1867, the same association of coal operators again attempted to reduce the price from 4c to 3½c, but the strike that lasted until October forced them— or induced them through higher prices for coal—to restore the former scale. But in June, 1868, when the summer weather gave the coal operators the strategic position, the miners struck to force the coal operators to allow the eight-hour day as required by law, unless an agreement were signed to the contrary. The strike lasted until September, when the miners returned to work on the old terms. The coal operators of Schuylkill County were also finally struck.

In 1867, coal operators north of Broad Mountain in Pennsylvania organized as the "Mahanoy Valley and Locust Mountain Coal Association," embracing all the larger colleries in that region. This association is said to have used the blacklist. Influenced by the success of this association in handling labor disputes before they reached the striking stage, other associations were organized in 1868-69. Among these were the "Coal Association of the Southern Coal-field of Schuylkill County," the "Shamokin Coal Exchange," the "Mount Carmel Coal Association," and the "East End Coal Association," all formed in 1868. On November 19, 1869, the Anthracite Board of Trade of the Schuylkill Coal Region was organized by representatives from each of the above named associations, and controlled over 4 million tons. It was incorporated and acted as a unit in dealing with the mine workmen; neither organization included all possible members yet were practically monopolies. Union leaders noting the monopoly wanted a share of the gains.

In May, 1869, the coal operators in the anthracite region of Pennsylvania were struck for a period of five months by the miners who demanded regular work throughout the year by means of an eight-hour day, restricted production per man, and a sliding scale of wages. The coal operators threatened to import Chinese but did not. On June 4, the coal operators' association met and offered the miners a sliding scale, but included in their proposition clauses against union dictation. The miners accepted the proposed wage schedule. They declined to consider the clauses relating to union dictation, made a counter offer [which the operators accepted], and returned to work.

The coal operators of Luzerne and Lackawanna counties refused to grant the basis system—sliding scale—and the miners struck in July, 1869, but went back to work September 1 at the old prices.

On December 29, 1869, the Anthracite Board of Trade held a meeting and offered terms for 1870, a basis of wages with a sliding scale for meeting advances in the prices of coal above $2.00 per ton, for the year 1870. The unions declined to accept this basis as it meant a reduction of wages; estimated at from 25 to 40 percent less than the old scale. It also required the miners to pay all costs for materials and tools used in mining. The miners refused even to consider the proposal, and struck in 1870. Some of the members of the association disliked the proposal and finally removed restrictions, so that many miners resumed operation and men returned to work. On February 18, the association withdrew the old offer and made a new one, with 30 percent reduction in basis price, but the miners refused. This refusal united the coal operators and they agreed to stand by that offer, but the men persisted in their refusal. In July the men offered a compromise proposition which again divided the coal operators, and the Board formally accepted it under strong protest as to its justice. An agreement was signed on July 29, 1870.

A new agreement was drawn up in 1870 for the following year, but the union members rejected it. In 1871, it was charged that the different operators in the anthracite region had entered into a combination and instituted a blacklist, probably because of the numerous local strikes called in this region from 1865-69. The basis had been maintained until 1871, when a general strike ensued over the reduction in wages due to the fall in the price of coal. The Northern districts reduced wages and the miners of Schuylkill County were ordered out by the union. A general suspension followed. Strikebreakers were imported and riots ensued. The militia was called out, but the strikers seized the guns of the soldiers and forced the mines to suspend operation. The conditions became so serious that a Pennsylvania legislative committee made an investigation. Arbitrators were selected to settle the dispute, which involved the "right to hire and fire" union men and the wages to be paid. An umpire had to be called in because the other arbitrators could not reach an agreement. But even then the matter was not finally settled, due to the bitterness of the struggle. Apparently neither side was satisfied with the award. At the first sign of renewed trouble, the coal operators made an appeal to the miners individually, and the union countered with a proposal for arbitration of the question of wages. Temporarily a truce was patched up and a sliding scale and a plan of arbitration agreed upon. However, the price of coal fell. Workmen struck one of the coal companies and it agreed to pay above the scale price. This caused a demand in the other mines for the same terms. The association expelled the offending coal company but the rupture broke down the plan of arbitration.

In 1868, there were some wage advances. The glass factories of New Jersey were forced by a strike to grant the glass bottle and vial blowers an advance of 15 percent in wages. Likewise, the shipyards of Camden were forced by a strike of the ship carpenters to advance wages to $3.50 a day.

The railroad managers were threatened with a strike of all the locomotive engineers at St. Louis, Missouri, because the former had combined to help each other against the union, but its officials held to the plan of settling each dispute separately.

Associations used a variety of measures to defeat unions in 1869. Employers began extensive advertising abroad for labor. Local advertisements were used to reduce wages in outlying districts. The master shoemakers of Milford, Massachusetts, sued

Cronin—a union organizer—for damages for inducing workmen to leave the employ of Walker and other manufacturers. The court held Cronin liable for damages. A carriage manufacturer put into operation in his factory a company union with a profit-sharing plan, but the men broke it up and it was followed by a mutual benefit association for sickness and death—the company put in a dollar for every dollar that the employees put in. Welfare plans are not new. Employers then, also, had to argue against the Eight-Hour League's increased purchasing power theory for workers through wage increases and hours reductions. Reduction of hours by the Government was advocated by the unions and opposed by the employers on grounds that such reductions would set precedents for private industry—and the unions found the opposition very strong. In the spring of 1869, workmen in the navy yards had their pay reduced one-fifth for an eight-hour day, but were offered the usual rate for the ten-hour day, yet very few would accept. Although President Grant issued a proclamation that wages were not to be reduced, the law was not enforced. The President issued a second proclamation emphasizing that there would be no wage reductions on account of the reduction in hours, but the law was not observed. Congress then passed an eight-hour law in 1872 for all employees of the Government, and two months later a protest to the President about its nonobservance caused him to refer the matter to the Attorney-General of the United States whose decision, however, was adverse to the work-men. Another bit of evidence of the coming conflict was shown when the Massachusetts Bureau of Labor Statistics, established in 1869, made investigations which led a group of employers to attack it vigorously.

In 1869, growing belligerency by employers was shown as prices fell. The cigar manufacturers of Cincinnati reduced wages and defeated a 19-week strike against the reduction through the use of unskilled laborers and molds and machines for making cigars. The cigar manufacturers of New York City were struck also in 1869-70 for reducing wages. The union won only two out of seven strikes in 1870; the union was unable to meet its obligations and issued worthless checks to strikers for strike benefits. The union lost its fight against the introduction of molds as well as wage reductions and was practically disrupted before the panic of 1873. In the period 1871-75, the union lost 54 strikes out of 78, of which 64 were against reductions in wages.

However, when the pottery manufacturers of New Jersey reduced wages, the pottery workers in every branch struck in all the factories belonging to the manufacturers' association. After a five months' strike, prices improved and the manufacturers offered somewhat better terms which the workmen accepted. During the same year, the master printers of Trenton, New Jersey, were forced by a strike to advance the wages of printers 8 percent, but they defeated the demand for an increase of pay for overtime.

Associations Reduced Wages and made the year 1870 notable for proposed and actual wage reductions. On February 15, the coal operators' association of the Tuscarawas Valley, Ohio, gave notice that the price of mining coal would be reduced to 80c a ton on March 1. The coal miners struck. In September, the miners became demoralized and asked for work on the employers' terms. Likewise the glass factories of New Jersey made a reduction in the wages—amounting to 30 percent—and defeated the strike that resulted. In 1871, however, employers in Boston compromised with striking plasterers on a wage increase.

Textile Manufacturers Defeated Unions in 1870. On June 29, the textile manufacturers of Fall River, Massachusetts, posted notices in all their mills that a reduction of wages, averaging about 8 percent, would be made in about a week in all the mills. The millowners disregarded a petition by the spinners not to make the reduction. The employers likewise disregarded a memorial from the spinners who proposed that the matter be arbitrated or the reduction be only ⅔ of that announced. After waiting two weeks for definite action on part of the millowners, the spinners struck, and thus forced out of employment all the other operatives. The millowners brought in nonunion spinners, but not in sufficient number to operate the mills to normal activity. After the strike had been on for some time, a nonunion spinner was assaulted. Riots followed. Firemen, policemen and even the militia were called out to suppress the riots. Millowners called on the mayor and had him call together the Board of Aldermen who met and authorized the mayor to utilize a hundred or more special police-men, and to offer a reward of $100 for evidence to convict any person who assaulted a strikebreaker. The morale of the strikers was finally broken, and those whom the millowners would employ returned to work. The strike was a complete failure. Those who believe that an employers' association does not exist until it is formally organized may find the following current comment on the above strike illuminating: "The employers were a unit in taking such action as made a cessation of work possible and probable. They agreed together to cut down wages and decided beforehand upon all the minutiae connected with the change. It appears that the meetings of the manufacturers' combination were somewhat in-formal. The reasons given for the reduction were two: the example of other manufacturers, and the conclusion that as much money was not being made in the business as they contemplated."

In October, 1870, the manufacturers of knit goods at Need-ham, Massachusetts, signed an agreement to reduce wages 5 to 35%; the reduction was to be effective until May 1, 1871, when the old rates were to be restored. The proposed reduction caused the workmen to strike. A conciliation board between the asso-ciation and the union had been organized about four years before, but the association had withdrawn from it. When the board was established it agreed upon a wage reduction. Two years later —when business revived—it compromised on a wage increase. In October, 1869, the association had asked the union for a pro-posal as to what its members would accept for wages, but the union made no reply. The manufacturers in 1870 were undoubt-edly influenced in making their reduction by the success of the textile manufacturers of Fall River, as well as by business condi-tions. In Marlborough, however, the manufacturers were struck because of the employment of nonunion men and, with the ex-ception of one manufacturer, were forced to grant the union's demands.

Falling prices and declining profits lead to belligerency by em-ployers, but union officials act on the theory that every con-cession once obtained must be retained at all costs and more demanded. So pronounced were these conditions in this period that an "open-shop movement" seemed to be inevitable even in the late sixties.

CHAPTER 6

THE OPEN SHOP MOVEMENT OF THE SEVENTIES

THERE IS EVIDENCE that there was a distinct "open-shop movement" beginning as early as 1872. The movement in the boot and shoe industry broke up the Knights of St. Crispin. Its power was felt in the coal-mining industry and it developed great strength in a general drive against the eight-hour day.

Associations in the Boot and Shoe Industry. In 1870 most of the boot and shoe manufacturers of Lynn, Massachusetts, were organized into an association called "The Board of Trade." The boot and shoe manufacturers were planning to reduce wages, and the union—the Knights of St. Crispin—struck to force acceptance of a verbal agreement by the employers not to do so. The board issued a statement that the manufacturers found "it impossible to prosecute their business with any certainty of success under the vexatious and arrogant demands of the Crispin organization and, accordingly, they were determined to endeavor by concert of action to find some means through which they might free themselves." However, one of the prominent manufacturers of the city addressed a union meeting and pledged the union to have a committee of five manufacturers appointed to meet with five from the union to form a conference committee to reach an amicable agreement on the question of wage reduction. The association members branded the conciliatory manufacturer as a traitor. But his influence was great and his committee consisted of the most prominent manufacturers, so that the association manufacturers had to abide by the action of the conference. The meetings of the conference committee were stormy, and it required two full days for it to agree on a scale of piece prices. At the end of the year a new agreement was reached, but in 1872 the employers broke away from the conference committee. The boot and shoe industry, however, was not free from labor troubles even during the life of the agreement.

The boot manufacturers of Worcester, in January, 1870, issued a contract for the workmen to sign. The workmen objected strenuously and it was withdrawn. The manufacturers then issued a notice to the effect that they would give preference in future employment to the men who worked during the late strike. Finally, the manufacturers signed an agreement to withdraw all rules and schedules, to pay former prices before the difficulty, and to take back the strikers without discrimination as fast as needed; the union agreed to withdraw its rules. Manufacturers in Marlboro were struck because of the employment of nonunionists but, with the exception of one manufacturer, were forced to grant the union's demands within two weeks.

In 1871, the shoe stitchers of Lynn struck in two establishments because the boss stitchers attempted to reduce the wages of the highest paid and increase those of the lowest paid, that is, to make the wages more nearly uniform. The boss stitchers held a meeting and resolved to ask every girl to sign a statement to give two weeks' notice before she quit or forfeit $5.00. Any girl refusing to sign was not to be employed in any other establishment. The women stitchers held an indignation meeting and resolved not to be bound by such rules. The boss stitchers, fearing a general strike in all the establishments, withdrew the rule.

Association Broke Up the Union. In 1872, under the stress of competition in a falling market, the boot and shoe manufacturers of Lynn, Massachusetts, became belligerent. They withdrew their representatives from the joint conference committee. The union tried to arrange a meeting with the old committee of the association, but its members had disbanded and so no reply was made to the union communication. The manufacturers began to intimate that wage reductions would be made and refused to appoint a new committee to confer with the union committee. When the union appealed to the former members of the association committee, as individuals, they treated the union committee with contempt. The result was that the workmen struck. The manufacturers now began to organize on a permanent and formal basis, so as to mobilize their fighting strength. Funds were raised to form a war chest, and agents were sent to solicit other employers to join in the movement. The employers met and adopted a formal resolution not to employ any union member, and 50 manufacturers signed the resolution. More than 2,000 additional workmen went on strike. A union committee visited individual manufacturers but every one of these refused to consider any union proposition, no matter how many concessions by the workers it might contain, on the ground that such action would involve some recognition of the union. As the association had no regular fighting organization, the manufacturers acted together in obtaining nonunion workers and in sending their work to manufacturers in other cities to be done. Boot and shoe manufacturers throughout Massachusetts now united in the belief that the Knights of St. Crispin must be crushed. In a short time, the treasury of the union was exhausted, and the men broke ranks and sought jobs as individuals. The Knights of St. Crispin had made it a death struggle and it received its death blow. In 1873 the union surrendered its charter. The employers' association had attained a complete victory.

The association used a combination of devices to destroy the Knights of St. Crispin. Nonunionists, including Chinese workers, were imported. Chinese strikebreakers, especially in shoe making, were an innovation on a large scale in this period. Work was sent to other communities to be done. Some prison labor was utilized. Machines were installed to replace skilled workmen. But most subtle, was the tying up of union funds during the crisis in the struggle. These funds were kept from the union by two renegade former union officials refusing to turn the money over to newly elected trustees. The old trustees charged the union with being an illegal monopoly. The union sought an act from the legislature of Massachusetts to incorporate so it could handle its funds in its own name. The (state-wide) association's attorney lobbied against the bill but finally lost. The union appealed to an equity court for an order (mandamus or injunction) to compel the renegades to turn over the money. They were defended by the association's attorney even up to the Supreme Court of Massachusetts. The final decision was rendered only after the union had been destroyed. It is noteworthy that this apparently first injunction in a labor dispute between an association and a union was sought and obtained by a union. The association's attorney, knowing that precedent favorable to the union had been established in another injunction case where a union used this method to recover its funds, nevertheless, employed the delays of litigation to deprive the union of its funds in the hour of its greatest need. Had the union officials sensed that business was declining and a panic approaching they might have adopted a less arrogant attitude, and possibly accepted wage reductions as necessary. Shoe manufacturers elsewhere, for instance in Brockton, had joined enthusiastically in smashing the "arrogant" union. The victory of the association was so complete that the manufacturers felt the need for the association was practically gone, and the organization lost much of its vigor. The panic of 1873 and the fierce competition during the period, 1873-75, undoubtedly were contributing factors, since that competition lessened the manufacturers' feeling of mutual interests with one another.

That the Knights of St. Crispin had lost its prestige and power elsewhere is shown in the following case: The boot and shoe manufacturers of Stoneham had granted an increase of the piece price upon a certain kind of work on a special contract. When the next supply of work came in it was of the same kind, but the manufacturers notified the women workers that the old prices would govern the lower scale. The women struck. The manufacturers began rapidly to employ nonunion workers. When the strikers saw that their places were being filled, they deserted the union and sought their old jobs at the reduced prices. However, no striker who took any prominent part in the strike was re-employed. Under such conditions, the Knights of St. Crispin lost members in large numbers, and the entire organization rapidly went to pieces before the panic of 1873 occurred. Boot and shoe manufacturers no longer feared it. Aided by the machine, the employers now had the strategic position formerly held by the skilled handicraft workers.

The following quotation is illuminating as to the causes of the failure of trade unions, especially since the Knights of St. Crispin met its death blow before the panic of 1873; THE IRON AGE said editorially, August 14, 1873—the panic broke on September 18, 1873, over a month later:

"A year ago this order was the most formidable labor organization in the United States. It was very strong in numbers, and included within its ranks so large a proportion of those engaged in the various branches of the shoe manufacturing industry, that it exercised an almost absolute control over the trade. But the mistake made by the order was in arraying itself in open and declared hostility to capital, and inviting by overt acts the organized opposition of employers, and in the struggle which ensued capital triumphed. Indeed, it became a question at one time whether the union would ruin the trade or employers break up the union, but labor had no resources with which to maintain a struggle against the resources of capital, and the order was driven to the wall."

Belligerency Shown in the Building Trades was strong in the seventies. In 1869, the New York Master Builders' Association was a federation of only nine different trades in that city. In 1872, however, employers perfected an organization which successfully resisted the eight-hour strikes. The first strike involved 7,000 workers in the building trades but soon extended beyond these until it became a series. The strike began in March and grew until as many as 11,000 workmen were on strike at one time. In June, a conference was held by 400 employers to secure concerted action for the maintenance of the ten-hour system. The Employers' Central Executive Committee, formulated in conference over the strike, evidently contemplated the organization of a national federation. The test met by the new association was severe. According to a well-informed contemporary, "The most extensive strikes that have occurred in this conutry have had for their object the reduction of the hours of labor, the largest being that of the summer of 1872, in New York City, for eight-hours. In this 90,000 men were engaged. It was the best organized and best conducted of any within our knowledge." The movement had attained some success before the new association had begun to act. For instance, the master carpenters of New York were forced by a strike of the carpenters to grant the eight-hour day. The master carpenters were induced to renew the strike, which they did by announcing for a nine-hour day. They defeated the strike of the union and later increased the hours to ten.

The Employers' Central Executive Committee was a significant movement which warrants an outline of its origin, powers, activities, recommendations, and the reasons for its short life. It was formed on June 18, 1872, as a result of a meeting of a large number of employers. Its powers were: "To call meetings, to draft rules for the government of employers, to submit plans for their consideration, and to take such other action for the protection of manufacturers and other employers as may be best calculated to bring about concert of action." Under the last clause of its powers, the Committee carried on an extensive propaganda against the eight-hour strike according to a current report. "The Committee kept itself in communication with the newspapers, and by consultation with the reporters, succeeded in influencing the tone of the public press. It next appealed to the intelligence of the better class of workmen by putting in their hands a pamphlet printed in English and German. This pamphlet exerted a great influence over the more sensible mechanics."

This pamphlet was addressed "to the intelligent workmen" to convince them that a reduction in hours per day from 10 to 8 with no reduction in pay would be unwise for the New York workmen because a rise in prices would be necessary for the employers to meet the increased costs due to the curtailment of production, and competition by foreign and domestic country producers would take away the business from New York if the prices were increased; such a situation would mean the ruin of business in New York and the need for workmen to go elsewhere to seek employment as the ship carpenters had to do after they won their strike, and were the 8-hour day made general, prices would rise, and workmen would find their wages would buy less than before. The workers were informed that they were entirely capable of looking after their own interests without the unwise advice of trade unions and secret societies, or the unwholesome teachings of men with minds warped by disturbances in Europe, for the employers of yesterday were workers and the workers of today will fill the ranks of the employers of tomorrow.

In July, the Committee called employers into conference and sent out a questionnaire on the best means of preventing strikes, or resisting strikes, on legislation restricting right to strike, on employers' associations for trades in general, on possibility and desirability of replacing union men with nonunion men, and on organizing the workers who opposed union restrictions and aggressions.

This association concerned itself with "Industrial-betterment activities" or "welfare work." It is well to note here that an association entered into such activities as long ago as 1872. "The Committee devoted much time to a serious consideration of the duty of employers to look after the interests of their men by providing a room, for instance, where they could read or enjoy light amusements, and by establishing a more general intimacy with them." The Committee contended that if the employer kept himself aloof from his men, and simply studied how cheaply he could employ them, and how much work he could obtain from them, he should not complain about repeated strikes; for, argued the Committee, it could not be expected that an advance in wages would always satisfy discontented workmen.

The recommendations of the Committee show that it was distinctly an "open-shop" association which urged cooperation and wider organization among the employers. The recommendations were:

"First—That workmen be employed and paid by the hour, because it would open the door to the establishment of harmony between the duration of the laborer's day and the nature of the labor performed, which can never be done in a violent manner.

"Second—When strikes occur it would be wise for employers to meet in consultation, in order to determine the best course to pursue.

"Third—It would be well for employers to discourage trade unions by every fair means; by insisting on their right to employ workmen independent of any restriction imposed by a combination of men; by extending encouragement and protection to independent workmen who desire to improve their condition by working longer hours or by extra exertions; by the introduction of the piece-work system as far as possible; by an extensive employment of apprentices under master workmen.

"Fourth—It would be well to take a kindly interest in the welfare of their employees, by seeing that their individual efforts are appreciated.

"Finally—It would be wise for employers to encourage by their example everything that tends to perpetuate the dignity of labor by training up their children in such a manner that each may become the master of some trade."

The Committee found employers at fault in the management of their workmen; too infrequently no attempt was made to operate the shop with nonunion men; "If a demand is made by the men, they [the employers] either submit or shut up their places, and reduce the question to one of brute force."

The Committee held the employers themselves largely responsible for the lack of harmony among employers. It pointed out that employers frequently conducted their businesses in an independent exclusive manner so far as others in the same branch of industry were concerned, and that each employer usually regarded as rivals all other employers in his field of business, with the result that all pursued "a cutting and carving policy, on account of which few succeed." The Committee urged employers engaged in the same business to meet at intervals to discuss the principles and problems of their business, and *to act in concert.*

It seems pertinent at this point to recall that "concert of action" among employers in labor matters is the best test as to the existence of an employers' association, formal or informal. So universal is the "cutting and carving policy" among unorganized employers in any branch of business, that only when there is some form of organization is there even a semblance of harmonious relationship among competing employers. Emergency associations, accordingly, do not "socialize" the employer and moderate or destroy his individualism. Actually they maintain his individualism in face of the assaults of unions upon it.

It was the "cutting and carving policy" that caused the association to have a short life. The victory over the union took away, in the minds of the employers, the need for the association. "When there is danger of a concerted labor revolt employers are ready to combine together and hold meetings and put up money, but each considers his duty at an end when there is no longer danger of disturbances in his own shop." So reads a concurrent comment, which concludes pessimistically: "As to the cooperation of employers among each other, it is very probable that there never will be any effective union of the kind." The treasurer of the association later complained that while it issued much printed matter for which each member was assessed $20, $200 was still unpaid. However, $2,500 was collected to prosecute law-breaking strikers. It needs to be noted, however, that associations which grow up suddenly in an emergency and which are designed to meet that emergency usually pass away when the emergency is over. The permanent associations, in contrast, usually require a long period for agitation and organization and so are not created simply to meet an emergency, but rather to deal with an ever-present or frequently recurring problem or a series of problems. The labor-relations problem has become "chronic" whenever an incongruous mass of employers from all sorts of trades, businesses, and industries can be held together long. Certain writers who have not understood this fact, have concluded that all belligerent associations are by nature of an ephemeral character. Although some "emergency" associations may continue to exist in a semi-dormant state for some time, ready to spring into action, should a new emergency arise, they usually die off in a few months after the first emergency passes. Such was the fate of the Committee, which continued to exist for a few months after the noted strike —which lasted only three months—the Committee did not use its authority to call meetings, because no emergency arose. The association was not "killed" by the panic of 1873; at the most the panic may have prevented the calling back to life of a dead organization.

Other associations were involved in the fight against the eight-hour day. Andrews charges that one association bound its members, with a sum of $1,000 each, to break up the unions, and that "a combination of merchants of Boston pledged themselves to drive the shipwrights, caulkers, and gravers to submission or starvation, and pledged $20,000 for that purpose." In 1872, the furniture manufacturers of New York defeated an attempt of the cabinet-workers' union to enforce the eight-hour day by an eight-weeks strike, as the manufacturers elsewhere convinced their workmen that the move was unwise at that time. Without support from the other unions, the strike failed.

Associations in the Iron Industry were neither all belligerent, nor all conciliatory in 1872. The boiler manufacturers of Paterson, New Jersey, refused to grant a wage advance of 25% demanded by the boilermakers' union. When the boilermakers struck, the manufacturers discharged all union men and the strike was regarded as a failure at the end of three weeks. On the other hand, in April, 1872, a committee of the Iron Manufacturers of Pittsburgh met a committee of the guide-mill rollers' union and adopted a sliding scale which, with a few changes, remained in force until June 1, 1881. In May, 1872, the iron manufacturers agreed with the bar and nail plate rollers and heaters upon a scale that remained in force until October, 1879, and the scale then agreed upon remained in force until June 1, 1881. The early scales between the puddlers and iron manufacturers had no time limit —a 30- or a 90-day notice by either party terminated the scale— but the new scales, noted above, had a one-year limit, and were renewed frequently with no major change. The changes then, when made, were almost exclusively in advances in prices on the card; other changes such as those in processes were not yet significant.

While older associations were being struck, new ones were being organized in 1872-3. The master masons of Chicago were struck by the bricklayers and the master tailors by the journeymen tailors, while the National Association of Stove Manufacturers began its career of price-fixing and later dealt with labor matters.

Belligerent Tendency among Associations in 1873. As noted before, the period immediately preceding a panic is usually marked by an increased number of strikes of some duration and by belligerency among the associations. Every outstanding panic in the United States has been preceded by a pronounced "open-shop" movement. The great growth of unions in periods of prosperity inspires, on one hand, the workmen with a feeling of power, and on the other hand, the employer with resentment at the encroachment of the union upon his cherished "right to run his own business as he sees fit." In something like four cases out of five, the employer is never "friendly" to the union—he simply does not trouble himself with fighting a union that is too weak even to make demands. But when the union issues a challenge, he fights. The employer feels that the periodic demands of the union for repeated advances in wages will soon leave him no profit; private enterprise depends upon the profit motive—a fact union officials

seem to forget. Moreover, a theory has been expounded in association circles that "exactions and restrictive reactions of unions"
are the primary causes of panics. There is another theory quite
prevalent in textbooks on labor problems that unions are disrupted
by panics or politics, when most frequently such unions have already received their death blow before the panics, or before they
have immersed themselves in politics. If there were no panic and
depression, the union might sometimes recover from the blow dealt
by the association. If the union were not defeated in its attempts
to obtain its demand in the industrial field, most probably it
would not go into politics. The panic came on September 18, 1873,
but it was openly stated by those in touch with the situation that
even by July the trade unions in this country were rapidly losing
power over the workingmen. In May, it was clear that the temper
of the employers had changed, and an almost universal determination was evinced by them, as they stated it, "not to submit to
further aggressions." Employers throughout the years 1873 and
1874 were repeatedly and strongly urged to organize. The necessity for employers' associations was expounded at length. The formation of and activities of The National Federation of Employers
of Great Britain were set forth to enlighten American employers
as to their duties and possibilities. The attempts of the unions "to
control capital" were strongly condemned. At the beginning of
the year employers were told that,

"The success of the trades unions is due solely to the fact
that they have nowhere encountered organized and determined
resistance. Capital is notoriously cowardly and selfish. It is easily
frightened by a formidable demonstration which threatens a
diminution of current profits upon investments and, as the rule,
always ready to seize a present and momentary advantage, without
regard to future consequences of such a policy. Manufacturers engaged in a common trade are very ready to meet and discuss matters of mutual interest, but they rarely keep faith with each other
when they can make a profit by breaking their agreements."

The success of the boot and shoe manufacturers of Massachusetts in disrupting the Knights of St. Crispin inspired other manufacturers elsewhere to attempt the destruction of the union in their
locality. For instance, early in the year the five principal manufac-

turers of boots and shoes in Baltimore signed and published a card that they would not allow themselves to be ruled by any organization whatever, and that they would employ any workmen they saw fit to hire. The shoe manufacturers, however, were unsuccessful in their attempt. They refused to employ members of the Knights of St. Crispin, but after a ten-day strike, gave in to the union.

Associations Generally Defeated the Unions. Associations defeated strikes for reduction of hours in a number of trades in Philadelphia in June, 1873. In July, the lumber mill owners of Williamsport, Lycoming County, Pennsylvania, refused to reduce the number of hours from 12 and 13 to 10. The workmen struck. Rioting occurred, nonunion men were assaulted and troops were called out. The association won the strike by August 1. The glass factories of New Jersey reduced the wages of the window-glass workers 20 percent, and defeated the union in the strike that followed the announcement of the reduction. Employing coopers of Boston defeated a strike of 400 coopers and broke up the union. However, in 1872 and 1873, sugar refineries were struck by the coopers' union to force the refineries to use only local union-made barrels.

After the panic, workmen were strongly advised to accept wage reductions. Even appeasatory associations demanded such reductions of the unions. The rolling mill owners met at Cincinnati, Ohio, on November 12, 1873, and agreed to post notices calling upon the workmen to accept reductions in wages running from 10 to 25 per cent. The agreement was signed by 13 mill owners from Cincinnati, Louisville, Portsmouth, St. Louis, Covington, Indianapolis, Chattanooga, and other cities in Tennessee. The shipyard owners of Camden reduced wages, but compromised on the amount when the ship carpenters struck. The stove manufacturers of Cincinnati, through their association, made a formal demand upon the union of stove molders for a reduction in wages. The union appointed a committee and requested the association likewise to appoint a committee to confer on the matter. The two committees met jointly, and after debating the various propositions and counter-propositions offered by each side, finally reached and signed an agreement, fixing the wages for one year, which was said to have been one year of peace such as had not been known in the trade for many years. However, the agreement lasted only a year.

Strikes against Wage Reductions Usually Failed. In November, 1873, a number of newspaper publishers of Pittsburgh notified the printers that wages would be reduced from 45c to 40c a thousand ems. The printers refused to accept the reduction. Word that the newspapers were planning to employ nonunion men caused a strike to be called on all newspapers. The union lost the strike; the men had to accept the reduced rates, and the union virtually disbanded on November 27. Conspiracy charges were brought into court against a number of the strikers, but were later dismissed when it was seen that the union was broken up.

Railroad managers combined in November in reducing wages because of reduced business and earnings. The Brotherhood of Locomotive Engineers struck and won on one railroad, prevented the cut on others by the remonstrance, and lost on the others after losing the strike. The railroad managers continued to fight the union and gave assistance to any struck railroad; they refused to deal with union grievance committees to discuss and adjust through conference the grievances of the workers. Moreover, a law against sudden strikes was advocated to meet such a situation as that produced by the strike of the locomotive engineers.

There were other manifestations of belligerency. During the winter of 1873-74, mass meetings of the unemployed were broken up by police in a number of cities, presumably at the instigation of groups of frightened employers. Blacklisting of strikers was quite general in the period 1873-76. Great hostile combinations of employers and of workmen fought each other bitterly. Ten thousand cigarmakers struck the cigar factories of New York City and lost. A ten-hour law for all women and children in the textile industry was passed in Massachusetts. The reorganized spinners asked for an advance in wages but the manufacturers refused and the union postponed pressing its demands. The Lowell mills, however, were struck but defeated the strike. One union publication thus summed up the situation—and employers quoted it: A period of unemployment followed by greatly reduced wages made workers feel that the injustice was great. Their discontent was so strong that men quit work rather than accept the wages offered. In depressions, strikes are long drawn out; some employers welcome strikes. Short, sharp, and decisive strikes are the best type for success, and the most strategic time is at the beginning of a marked business expansion.

Coal Operators and Unions Clashed in the early seventies. The coal operators of Bevier, Missouri, however, were not successful in making their mines open shop. By 1872, the operators had reduced the price for mining coal from 7c to 5c a bushel. The miners then demanded an increase to 6c; the operators refused, and the union struck. After trying for five months to operate the mines with nonunionists, the operators granted the union's demands. During the strike, one of the operators became bankrupt.

Bitter disputes continued in the anthracite region during this period. Although in January, 1872, the committees of the association and of the union had met and agreed upon a new contract and the basis for the year, disputes arose in 1873. For a time, operators refused to recognize or negotiate with union officials but made their proposals directly to the miners. Some of the operators became dissatisfied with the action of their association and resumed work on the old basis, but a railroad [railroads owned mines] cooperated with the association and placed high rate charges on coal from this section so that no mine could operate until all could work under a common agreement. It was charged that the operators and the railroad managers had met in secret council in Philadelphia and agreed upon a very low scale of wages. During this time attempts had been made to arbitrate the dispute over "hiring and firing union men" and wages. Arbitrators had been selected but failed to agree, so an umpire had to be called in. He decided that nonunion men should be allowed to work and that the operators should not combine against members of the union. The wage question was also arbitrated and a compromise sliding scale was awarded by the umpire, but neither side was satisfied with the award, and the trouble continued. Both union and association attempted to make deals outside the other organization. Then a temporary truce was patched up.

In September, 1873, the panic broke and the price of coal fell.

The union struck one of the coal companies against the sliding-scale reduction in the price for mining coal. It immediately granted rates above the sliding scale, and this grant led to general demands for the higher rates accompanied by strikes in violation of the agreement. The operators conceded the increase and the arbitration award was abandoned. The association expelled the offending operator. In the conference between operators and the union, the miners refused to accept reductions in the contract for 1874. Although the five railroad corporations which controlled almost all the mining and transportation of anthracite coal reached an agreement with the union on a wage schedule, the combination was condemned as the worst sort of monopoly, and the depression finally broke the price of coal and forced a wage reduction. The miners struck but lost after a five-months strike and their union was practically crushed.

Operators in the Mahoning Valley (Ohio) imported Swedes and Italians to break the miners' strike there in 1873; in the meanwhile, iron manufacturers found out how to use cheaper coal than that of the Mahoning Valley.

One of the developments of this period was pronounced legislative activities. In 1873, the state of Illinois adopted a law relating to strikes by coal miners, especially to prevent intimidation of strikebreakers by strikers. Undoubtedly this law was the result of a concerted demand by the coal operators. The Pittsburgh Coal Exchange and the Railroad Coal Producers' Exchange met in joint conference in February, 1873, to adopt measures in opposition to the miners' screen bill under consideration by the legislature of Pennsylvania. A committee was selected to go to Harrisburg to lay before the legislature the objections of the operators to the bill. This committee, when it appeared before the committees of the legislature, found that the union had also sent delegates at the same time. Both the union and the association committees were heard upon the bill, and views and arguments were given at length. After quite a struggle, the legislature passed the bill in modified form and it was signed by the governor of the state, but the association committee had secured certain modifications by which it thought the law could be nullified. But rivalry between two associations prevented complete nullification.

The rival groups were in the railroad and the river mines in the vicinity of Pittsburgh.

In an effort to adjust their differences, the coal operators of Pittsburgh and vicinity met on March 1, 1873, to endeavor to make prices for mining uniform in the railroad and the river mines. Unanimous agreement apparently was not reached although the proposal for 4c a bushel was agreed to by a large majority. Nevertheless, the operators did not abide by the agreement. In July, 1873, the coal operators of Pittsburgh and vicinity notified the miners that all contracts to be acceptable must adhere to the old rates and methods of screening. In this manner the coal operators sought to nullify the "miners' screen law," which had been modified at its passage to exempt those who made an agreement for other methods than the one provided for in the law. The miners refused to make an agreement under the terms proposed by the operators. However the union proposed other terms which the Coal Exchange met and accepted. The railroad coal operators accepted, but the river coal operators refused to abide by the terms proposed by the union, and endeavored vainly to induce the railroad coal operators to discontinue the higher rates. The miners struck the river mines but after about six weeks offered to return at the old rates. The operators turned down the offer. Later the river miners returned to work, presumably as individuals, at the old rate of 4c a bushel.

In September, 1874, however, the coal operators along the railroads leading into Pittsburgh were struck when they proposed a reduction of wages. Italian immigrants were employed, and clashes between these and strikers occurred. The sheriff had to call out an armed posse to maintain peace. The Italians left in December, but the strike continued until March, 1875, when the men returned to work at reduced prices. Strikes in the coal mines of Pennsylvania were attended with violence and often with murder.

A similar mixed situation seems to have existed in the anthracite region. The operators of the Schuylkill region met with the miners in conference over wages for 1874, but the miners refused to take a reduction. However, in January, the operators reduced wages on the schedule with $2.25 as a basis and 9,000 miners struck during the month of January. But the railroads which controlled most of the mining and transporting of anthracite coal reached an agreement with the miners on a schedule of wages. This combination of miners and railroads was a typical collusion against the consumer. We have already seen that the Anthracite Board of Trade was belligerent during the year, so the situation was rather confused.

The coal operators of Arnot, Tioga County, Pennsylvania, issued a notice that all miners were required to answer a questionnaire in regard to their union affiliations and to pledge themselves to leave the union if members, or not to join it if they were not members. The miners ignored the notice but were forced by the managers to answer the questions or quit. A strike resulted on November 24, 1873. Those who quit or struck were ordered to vacate the company-owned houses they occupied. The coal operators employed nonunion men in considerable numbers. However, in March, 1874, the trouble was compromised and the notice and the pledge were withdrawn.

A Fierce Struggle between Strong Unions and Powerful Associations marked the years 1874-75. The unions in coal mining and in iron manufacturing were strong and usually dealt with powerful associations in the respective fields. Coal mine operators eliminated many of the union leaders by offering promotions to superintendencies. The business and industrial depression reacted upon even these powerful appeasatory associations to produce a belligerency very similar to that of "out-and-out" "open-shop" associations. It was a period of bad faith by both union members and employers, since a chance to make a gain by breaking faith and taking an unfair advantage was resorted to by someone whenever a favorable opportunity came.

The coal operators of Tuscarawas Valley, Ohio, in 1874, reduced the price for mining coal from 90c to 70c per ton. They had lost a strike over a 15 per cent reduction in 1873 and compromised. The union asked for a conference, and this was granted by the operators. The conference finally agreed to arbitrate the wage issue. The referee, upon whom final decision rested, decided that the wage reduction should be 19c instead of 20c, but that the operators should reduce the prices of power, oil, and rent of company houses to correspond to those in the Mahoning Valley. Both sides accepted, and a conference then agreed upon allowances for deficiency work, such as veins of coal under four feet, turning rooms, break-throughs, wet entries, wet rooms, and rotten and bad roofs. The miners for only one company demanded a check-weighman which the company refused and these men struck. Offered an increase of 9c by the company (to 80c a ton) to withdraw the demand, the miners accepted. This led all the other miners in the Valley to demand 80c a ton, over the opposition of the officers of the miners' union. The operators granted the demand and the union officers were berated for not obtaining better terms.

The coal operators of Hocking Valley, Ohio, gave notice in 1874 that, on and after April 1, miners would be paid by the ton of screened instead of mine-run coal as formerly. This action amounted to a reduction of wages and the miners struck. After three months, however, the strikers were forced to accept the operators' method of payment.

In October, 1874, the coal operators of St. Clair County, Illinois, were struck by the union to obtain a uniform price of 4c a bushel for mining coal and union recognition under which all nonunion men were to join the union. The operators organized a company of militia and the state of Illinois furnished this company with arms. By November 17, the strikers were defeated.

Association Activities Widened. During this period there was a marked tendency for associations to become more formal in a hard fight. Employers can easily break away from an informal organization, but formal associations frequently impose obligations or require deposits, bonds or other devices to bind the members to the organization; in the period, manufacturers bonded themselves $1,000 each to break up union dictation. During a strike, an employer may break away from an informal association and reap large profits, either through high prices when production is limited or by getting customers permanently away from the other employers, or by both means. In fact, sometimes the situation is even more pronounced, for there are cases where one manufacturer has incited or supported a strike on another manufacturer and has done so in order that the former might profit at the expense of the latter. Usually such cases occurred in the active competitive area of the rival manufacturers when it had not yet become generally nationwide. Accordingly, in this period the need for great powerful national associations had not yet fully developed. Local advantages of fuel, transportation, and market for products were generally so vastly different in the various sections of the United States that no association or combination for the maintenance of a given uniform scale of wages, prices, or contracts, had yet been practicable. "All such efforts previously made were total failures." However, agitation for certain national associations was going on. For instance, the United States Potters' Association was formally organized in 1875, as a result of previous agitation. There was also strong agitation for the formation of an employers' association in the iron industry to protect both labor and capital from the tyranny of the trade unions. It was freely suggested that the iron masters of the country form associations on the basis of an agreement not to employ any man in their works who could not show a discharge from his last employer. Employers began to use this "discharge system" and "open-shop" contracts. A description of their operation of the former system reads in part as follows:

"This system consists in the adoption of a rule to the effect that any men who shall actively engage in a conspiracy to deprive a manufacturer of the control of any detail of his business, or to compel him to advance wages upon the threat of a general strike, shall be promptly dismissed, without any papers, and that no man shall be promptly given employment who cannot show a clean discharge from his last place or give a satisfactory reason for having left it. . . . The rail mills generally have adopted this system. . . . Several of the largest bar mills are also working under it and others promise to adopt it."

"In some large establishments, favorably located for such an experiment, no man is now given employment who does not repudiate all affiliation with trade unions and agree not to join them so long as his name remains on the payroll. Where such a policy can be adopted, it is certainly the best and most effective way of guarding against conspiracies."

It was frankly stated then that "the result of either system would be to break up the unions, and protect both master and men against a further tyrannical exercise of their power for evil." Thus employers were continually urged to unite to emancipate industry from trade-union control, and were instructed as to plans used here and even in England, to insure employers against strikes. Among the devices "to combat the trade unions, and stop the war made upon capital by the unions," were auxiliary employers' associations. An organization for the emancipation of labor from the tyranny of the trade unions was fostered among workmen at this time, and was commented upon editorially in the leading periodical in the iron industry—THE IRON AGE.

In view of the general belief in textbooks on labor problems that the unions of this period were going to pieces because they had gone into politics, it should be noted that the associations were making bitter war upon the union in the industrial field, and gave relatively little attention to the political field. In making this fight, the associations then used methods which many regard as recent inventions of twentieth century associations, namely, the late welfare plan of the Lake Carriers Association, the late open-shop (yellow dog) contract of a number of associations, for example, the Cripple Creek Mine Owners' Association, and finally the late company union of Ex-President Post of the Citizens Industrial Association of America. An instance of industrial betterment activities of associations in a specific case is:

The manufacturers of St. Louis organized in 1874 under the name of the St. Louis Manufacturers' Association. Among the objects of this association were: To promote harmony and good feeling between employers and employees. To encourage working classes in securing cheaper and better dwellings, and encouraging frugality and thrift among them.

Wage reductions were the main causes of the strikes and the associations generally won, although there were exceptions; for instance, the morocco manufacturers defeated a strike of their workmen for a wage advance in 1874. The window-glass manufacturers of Pittsburgh reduced wages 15%. The workers struck, but were forced to return to a 25% reduction, and shortly thereafter to suffer another reduction of 15%. Likewise, merchant ship-owners of New York City reduced wages of longshoremen, who engaged in a general strike against the new wage scale. The calling of a general strike was condemned then on the ground that it would drive the masters of the ships into the combination of the proprietors of the steamers. The union, however, rescinded its general strike action, but prohibited its members from working for those who joined the merchants' combination to reduce wages. In contrast, the employing potters of New Jersey proposed a 10 to 20 per cent reduction in wages for their different classes of workers, but were persuaded not to do it by a threat of the potters' union that if wages were reduced it would petition Congress to reduce the tariff on crockery to a revenue basis. This action was probably the main cause for the formation of the United States Potters' Association in 1875, for, in later years, such threats did not stop wage reductions. Political activity was shown when the Philadelphia Board of Trade sought in 1874 to curtail the powers of the Bureau of Labor Statistics of Pennsylvania so that the Bureau could not inquire into labor conditions. Appeasatory activities gave way to belligerent in the case of the Stove Manufacturers' Association of Cincinnati, which proposed a wage reduction in 1874, and in a joint meeting with the union committee reached an agreement, only later to propose another reduction and refuse to meet the union committee. A strike resulted and "union recognition" was ended for several years.

The coal operators of the Lehigh, the Upper Lehigh, the Wyoming, and the adjacent anthracite coal fields met in Philadelphia, December, 1874, to fix the wage basis for mining for the coming year. Although coal operators conferred behind closed doors, it leaked out that wages were to be reduced and the miners began preparations for a general strike. While no positive formal action was taken in regard to a reduction, the general sentiment of the meeting favored it. It seems that the operators adopted policies which they should have known would bring about strikes by union officials without foresight, so as to allow the mines to remain idle for months during the deep depression, since anthracite was generally regarded as a luxury coal.

The anthracite coal strike of 1875 was bitterly fought. When the union miners walked out, the coal operators brought in non-unionists. When these were assaulted and the operation of trains interfered with, armed troops were brought in to help in the operation of both the trains and the mines. Neither side was willing to yield, so that the matter could be compromised or settled in any field or on any particular matter. Wages were reduced for engineers, firemen, and pumpmen, as well as for the actual coal miners, and these also struck to force a restoration. The miners on strike in the Wyoming Valley resolved not to go back to work by districts, but all at once, or all remain out. The operators continued to refuse to concede any demands of the unions. Mobs gathered and men carried concealed weapons, and riots or even pitched battles seemed imminent. There was violence, incendiarism, and pitched battles. The coal operators thought that the governor of Pennsylvania was too sympathetic towards the strikers to take vigorous action against violence by the strikers. President Frederick B. Gowen of the Philadelphia and Reading Railroad Company—one of the most important anthracite coal-mine-owning railroads—became a notable association leader during the strike. He went among the coal operators throughout the anthracite field to get accounts of the outrages committed by or in the name of the strikers. He submitted a list of over 200 outrages committed upon persons, usually the nonunion workmen or strikebreakers in the Schuylkill and Shamokin regions alone. This list was presented in the course of an argument he was making before a committee of the legislature of Pennsylvania. His argument was made to convince the legislature that it should officially rebuke the governor of the state. The result was that the governor later sent a message denouncing lawlessness in the strike and suggesting remedies to stop it.

In April, it became apparent that the strike was failing and, in May, the strikers accepted the employers' terms. Prosecution of leaders in the riots and disturbances by the association yielded disappointing results to the employers concerned, for Siney and Park were regarded as the most conspicuous, and they "suffered nominal damages" only, at least so the association felt. That the coal operators used Pinkerton detectives to break up the "Molly Maguires" is the most widely known feature of this strike, and needs no elaboration here. The associations have set forth at length the outrages charged against the "Molly Maguires," and the unions have denounced strongly the methods used to break up that organization.

The coal operators of the Clearfield coal district were struck in April, 1875, because they refused to grant a 10 percent wage advance. After two to three weeks' suspension, they employed new men and had these well provisioned. This was the time of the year when the union could hardly expect to succeed. But the strikers assaulted the strikebreakers and drove them out of the district. Others were attacked. The sheriff and special guards were able to restore order. The operators refused to deal with the union miners in any form or manner, and filled their mines with non-union men. Those who went to work were forced to leave the union and sign a pledge not to join it or to engage in a strike thereafter.

The coal operators of Tuscarawas Valley in August reduced the price of mining 10c a ton (from 80c) but after a short strike compromised on 75c a ton.

Only in depressed times is it usual for miners to accept wage reductions in the latter part of the year when the mining of coal for winter is on or about to begin. In contrast, wages are not usually advanced in, say, April or May; for this reason, it seems strange that the miners of the Clearfield district would strike at this time of the year during a depression with serious hopes of winning an advance in wages.

Wage reductions were general during the depression, and in the current literature that catered to the employing class, workers were frequently advised to accept wage reductions. With business slack and the labor supply plentiful, an employer could weed out union men from his shop. Employers were urged to require all workmen to sever all union connections and contract not to join any union. The "open-shop" campaign had not died with the passing of the "emergency" associations of 1872.

Wage Reductions and "Open-Shop" Victories were frequent in 1875. Among the instances are: The glass factories of New Jersey reduced the wages of the window-glass workers 17%, and defeated their strike of three months. The textile manufacturers of Fall River, in February, reduced wages 10%. Conferences were held between the association and the union but employers insisted on a reduction that the workers would not accept. The manufacturers later refused to grant a restoration of even one third of the reduction and a strike resulted. The manufacturers had become members of an association which provided that the struck corporations would be compensated for a part of the loss they sustained in the strike—a feature found in rather recent permanent associations. In an association of that day it was an indication of a perfecting of fighting forces for continuous or frequent recurring labor troubles. However, business revived somewhat and optimism caused the employers to believe that the depression was over. Accordingly, they agreed they would restore on April 1 the old wages before the reduction, provided the workers would return to work by March 13, which they did. The business revival proved to be temporary; in August the manufacturers again made a reduction in all the mills, and the strike was renewed. This time the millowners declared that the question had become a direct issue between the trade union and the employers who would no longer tolerate unwarrantable intereference of irresponsible committees. In October the operatives returned to work after signing a contract not to be governed by union rules. Manifestly, the open-shop contract is not a recent development in the industrial conflict. Similar strikes occurred in Newburyport, Roxbury, Wilbraham, and Lowell textile mills with the same results to the strikers.

Wage Reductions in the Iron Industry produced a series of strikes. The iron manufacturers of Pittsburgh in November, 1874, asked for a conference with the puddlers' union to discuss a proposed wage reduction through a modification of the sliding scale. The price of iron had fallen below that provided for in the scale —the price was 2½c, or lower, and the lowest provided for in the scale was 3c, which accordingly fixed $6.00 as the lowest price paid for puddling. The association gave the 30 days' notice for the termination of the scale (which had governed for seven years) and proposed to reduce the price for puddling $1.00 on a 3c scale or "card." The union countered with a 50c reduction on a 3c card with the 3c rate to be the minimum basis. No agreement was reached and the strike was called in December. Twenty-three concerns were involved. Negroes were imported to do the work,

and a riot was feared by the manufacturers. Troops were held in
readiness for instant service, but no riot occurred. The importation of Negro puddlers, however, caused the rollers and heaters
to strike, but the workmen returned to their jobs in March when
negotiations between the puddlers and the manufacturers were
resumed. In March, 1875, the manufacturers offered to arbitrate, but the puddlers refused. On April 15, the manufacturers
met and agreed to make individually an offer of $5.50 a ton, but
to the puddlers as individuals and not through the committees
as before. One of the reasons which caused the manufacturers to
offer this concession arose from the situation in which outside
manufacturers were giving at least moral, if not substantial financial aid to the striking puddlers. There were other points at issue,
for instance, the custom had been to pay during the summer
months what was known as "the hot dollar" which was an extra
dollar a ton on account of the hot weather at a hot job. "The
hot dollar" was not paid in the summer of 1875, so the reduction was actually bigger than the quoted price would indicate.
Finally, the manufacturers signed a scale which then ranged
from $8.50 a ton for puddling with iron at 5½c a pound to $5.50
with iron at 2½c, and in which a change of 10c in the price
of puddling was made with every change of 1/5c in the price of
iron. The price of iron continued low, and in October the iron
manufacturers demanded a reduction of $1.00 a ton. Only after
a long series of conferences between the committee of the association and the union committee was a compromise agreed upon
of a reduction of 50c, that is, the price was to be $5.00 without
the scale. This price was of short duration. About December 16,
1875, after many more conferences, an agreement was reached
that for 60 days the price would be $4.50, but no agreement
was reached after the 60 days. The old price held during the
long series of conferences from February to May when both committees decided an agreement could not be reached. The union
wanted a twelve-months scale, June 1 to May 31, but the association stood for the indefinite period with notices. The puddlers
offered a 50c reduction from $5.50 with 2½c iron as a minimum
on the scale, but this price was in excess of what the manufacturers would grant. During the summer the question of the hot
dollar arose since the manufacturers had not paid it during the

previous summer. The manufacturers offered a compromise of $4.62½c with the scale, but the puddlers insisted on $4.75 as a minimum with the scale. Finally, the manufacturers offered $5.00 until October, and $4.75 from October to June without the scale. The puddlers refused and struck for $5.00 on a 2½c scale. In two weeks the manufacturers broke apart and many then signed the scale as individuals. Later all signed as individuals. The union knew that the association always attempted to reduce wage scales in the winter, so the adoption of the expiration date as June 1, was a victory for the union. This scale was continued in effect for a year and was renewed annually until 1880.

As the Pittsburgh scales were the bases for scales throughout the West and affected those of the East, difficulties at Pittsburgh produced disturbances elsewhere. During the Pittsburgh strike, the most prominent periodical in the iron industry declared that the strike had become a contest between the employers and union and as such it possessed national interest. This periodical openly advocated that the power of the union should be broken and the working men emancipated from a pernicious and debasing servitude which it imposed. As may be expected naturally, the victory of the union caused profound regret. Among the strikes occasioned by the Pittsburgh strike, were those at Troy, Harrisburg, and Reading.

The iron millowners of Troy, New York, in October, 1874, proposed a reduction in the wages of the puddlers. The employers met with the workmen's representative in conference. The puddlers refused to accept the reduction and they and the other workers struck. The employers imported nonunion men, and had the Police Commissioner appoint some 80 policemen and to assign 12 of the regular force for duty at the mills. The iron masters paid the imported workmen a bonus of $3.00 a day, in addition to the $4.00 a ton for puddling. The iron manufacturers trained up green men to take the places left by the strikers. This step broke up the strike of all but the puddlers, and the defeated workmen deserted their unions and sought work on the employers' terms, about April 1, 1875. The puddlers remained on strike, but in May conferences were held and the strike ended, but the union was not recognized. The strike contributed to the consolidation of a number of the firms, which in turn facilitated the consolidation of the iron and steel industry, and that in time became the model of what the open-shop could accomplish. It is noteworthy that in the appeasatory iron industry and in the appeasatory anthracite coal and railroad field are the first marked tendencies to the combination-and-consolidation stage characteristic of the "Financial Revolution."

The iron masters of Harrisburg, in 1874, defeated the puddlers in a four-month strike against a reduction of wages from $6.00 to $5.00. The men were forced to return on the employers' terms and to sever all connections with the union. The iron masters at Reading and elsewhere met with the same resistance by puddlers' unions and generally enforced a reduction as the result.

Mediation by an Association occurred in 1874 when the Board of Trade of Ironton, Ohio, appointed a committee to inquire into the causes of the first difficulties between the employers and employees in the local iron mills. This committee found that the dispute and strike grew out of a wage reduction to the Pittsburgh level. The Board requested both sides to submit the dispute to a board of arbitration selected by the parties to the dispute.

The influence of the Pittsburgh strike was also felt in Cleveland, Ohio, where the iron mills were struck in 1875, because they reduced wages in accordance with Pittsburgh reductions. The nail mills of Wheeling, West Virginia, were struck in 1875 by the feeders and helpers. The Wheeling wage scales governed the nail mills of the West.

The amalgamation of various trades into one union in 1876 brought together a great diversity of interests and resulting dissension within the ranks of the union and was noted by the employers.

As we proceed with the discussion of the development of the associations, we need to keep in mind that the outstanding appeasatory associations of half a century ago were in the iron and coal industries. The reasons for this situation were that combinations to fix the price of coal and of iron products existed and the unions played a part in forcing members of the combination and even independents to maintain prices. The Schuylkill Coal Exchange met on November 8, 1875, and fixed the prices of coal and adopted rules and methods to deal with members who did not comply strictly with the price regulations. The old anthracite coal combination broke up in 1876, due partly to a new realignment of business concerns into another combination, for the combination of mine owners and railroads in the anthracite field called forth condemnation in THE IRON AGE: "In the combination of miners and carriers we have a monopoly of the worst kind." Similarly, the Western Iron Association met in Pittsburgh in April, 1876, and agreed upon the prices of iron.

Other association activities in 1875 included: The Western Hardware Manufacturers' Association was organized in 1875. The cigar manufacturers of Cincinnati reduced the price for making cigars $1.00 a thousand to offset a revenue tax of that amount. A combination of employers in San Francisco broke up the bricklayers' union after it had outlasted all the other unions but one in maintaining an eight-hour day; the other one was smashed in 1877 in a strike for higher wages. The Fall River manufacturers posted notices of a wage reduction on August 1 of 10 percent. The weavers, carders, and spinners struck, and the manufacturers refused to take on any employee until he signed an "iron-clad" contract not to quit in concert with other workers, and not to belong to any union. After nine weeks the workers returned under the employers' terms which included also the ten percent wage reduction. The militia was called out during the strike and prevented a threatened riot. Union leaders were blacklisted, and the weavers' and the carders' unions disrupted. Only the spinners' union survived, but its members signed the "iron-clads" with mental reservations. During 1876, the mills made another ten percent reduction; union officers tried to prevent the spinners from striking. Some spinners struck and lost, others deserted the union.

The National Association of Stove Manufacturers had been organized in 1871-72 for the purpose of regulating the price of stoves, and so fearful was this organization that any attempt to deal with the labor relations problem would produce discord in the association, it prohibited such by a formal pledge and a "rule" at the time of its formation, so as "not to permit of the discussion of any question relating to labor." However, the rule was repeatedly violated, until its repeal years later. The tariff on iron received the active support of the unions in the iron industry, thus aiding in keeping out foreign competition. Furthermore, these unions played off one manufacturer against another, until the manufacturers finally decided to hold together, if not by one means then another. The unions by their early victories helped to prepare their opponents to mobilize and consolidate forces a quarter century later so as to deal the unions a death blow in the "trades" in this industry where the best organized unions in the United States prevailed. When the manufacturers as individuals and as a group began to feel that it was not the most profitable thing to negotiate with the unions, the "open-shop" in iron manufacture became assured. The manufacturers showed an unmistakable belligerent trend when they began the process of training up green hands to take the places permanently of skilled workmen on strike. Employers were becoming concerned about the supply of skilled workmen especially since apprenticeship had been allowed to decline. At this time, 1875, Pennsylvania passed a law relating to apprentices. A revival of interest in apprenticeship is also shown by discussions of the subject and the question why employers did not take more apprentices. The iron manufacturers were reminded of union contract-breaking; were instructed by discussion of the "dead levelism" of unions and, among other things, its effect upon apprenticeship; and were told what the employers' associations of Great Britain were doing.

Employers were reminded also that they held the strategic position, for it was pointed out to them that depression and lower wages increased the efficiency of the laborer, who worked harder when he was at work, and who rarely took a lay-off as he so often did during prosperous periods, because the difficulty of finding a job made him appreciate highly his present job.

Wage Reductions Continued to be made in 1876. In the early part of the year the iron manufacturers of the Shenango Valley gave notice to their rollers that the rate of pay would be cut 20 percent. The rollers struck. In November, the stove manufacturers of Troy, New York, decided to reduce wages, because they said wages were higher in Troy than elsewhere, and that accordingly the increased cost of production of stoves produced in Troy made it so they could not meet outside competition. In March, the coal

operators of Tuscarawas Valley, Ohio, announced another reduction of 10c a ton for mining coal, thus bringing the price
down to 65c. The miners struck and would not compromise. The
operators brought in new men, but these were assaulted; in fact,
an actual battle took place. Armed guards, detectives and the
militia appeared on the scene. The operators cut the price to 60c
and imported more nonunion men. In May the strike collapsed,
the miners accepted 60c a ton, and sought work where they could
get it as individuals. In March, 1876, the coal operators of Co-
shocton, Ohio, reduced the price of mining coal 10c. In 1877, the
operators refused to restore the old rate asked by the miners and
these struck. Finally, the miners offered to compromise for 5c
advance with semi-monthly cash payment of wages. The operators
rejected this. After a 12-weeks strike the miners returned to work
with no advance, but the operators did arrange to pay wages in
cash every two weeks.

Troubles in Glass Industry in 1876. The glass manufacturers
in Pennsylvania and Ohio were struck because of a dispute growing out of the use of a crimping machine for glass chimney tops
to which the workers objected. Nonunion men were imported and
the strikers lost; increased output was demanded and wages were
reduced. In June, the glass manufacturers reduced the wages of
the glass chimney blowers 10 percent and the men struck, but in
September were forced to restore wages to the old rate to get the
men to return to work. In August, the Western Window Glass
Manufacturers' Association met in Chicago and decided to pay the
"tending boys" a sum equal to 55 percent of the wages received
by the blower instead of on a piece basis, but the "tending boys"
struck against this change. In Pittsburgh alone, 20 factories were
shut down because of the strike.

Wage Reductions in Shoe Industry.—In 1876, the union of
shoe workers in Massachusetts was revived and received back
its charter, and the Shoe Manufacturers' Association of Lynn,
which seemed to have lost much of its vigor during 1873-75, and
all of its belligerency, restored the board of conciliation, which
was composed of representatives from each of the associations
and the unions. This board settled a number of disputes during
the year. In 1877, the shoe manufacturers reduced wages of the

workers and were struck. The negotiatory attitude of the association seemed to have been of short duration, for the strike led the manufacturers to confer on means to "free their shops from union dictation." The association adopted a resolution not to employ any person subject to the union. Nonunion men were employed, but in February 1878, the association modified its nonunion declaration. The strikers then returned to work. Later wage reductions were made, but the union was so weakened that no strike was called.

The textile manufacturers of North Adams, Massachusetts, refused to pay overtime rates for extra time worked by the operatives, and these struck. The manufacturers threatened to close the mills and the strikers returned under the old conditions.

CHAPTER 7

THE OPEN SHOP MOVEMENT OF THE SEVENTIES
(Continued)

"THE STRIKE EPIDEMIC *of 1877*" was so called because of the widespread character and the bitter fighting, as well as the number of strikes. Among the outstanding strikes of the early part of the year were those of the molders at Troy, New York, of the coal miners in Western Pennsylvania, of the glass workers at Pittsburgh and Steubenville, Ohio, of the steel workers, of the coopers, and of others at Cleveland. All these were over-shadowed by the great railroad strike of the year. Most of these strikes were lost by the workers, and one of the factors in these defeats was the great number of unemployed men. The depression had not yet passed, large numbers of men were idle, and workers were still advised to accept wage reductions. Employers were urged to discharge surplus workmen rather than try to keep them, with only partial work, as a means to lessen labor troubles. Obviously, the discharge of these partial-time workers would undoubtedly increase the army of the unemployed, who, in many cases, would quickly serve as strikebreakers; it would put "fear in the heart of the worker" who was not discharged that he would lose his job too if he didn't increase his efficiency, "by digging into the work"; it would reduce the payroll, first, by the amount that was formerly paid the surplus workers for time when they were not really productively employed and, second, by lowering wages through increased competition among the unemployed for jobs. Employers were also told that labor troubles had been averted by an employer who gave workmen plots of ground to cultivate so as to raise food and employ idle time, which otherwise might have been spent in listening to strike agitators. It is perhaps true that strikers never fight more bitterly than in a period immediately following the recovery from a depression. This bitterness may be attributed to a number of things such as the long self-denial required, by the depression making workmen desperate in their strikes, and

by their resentment at what they believe has been too hard
bargain-driving by the employer that produces hatred and desire
for revenge.

It may be the same desperation is one of the primary causes
of unions engaging actively in politics. Their failures in the industrial field have undoubtedly contributed in the past to their willingness to attempt some other means to attain some degree of success,
if only a seeming success. "The Labor Party" was of special interest to the associations in 1877 and, so far as the sources consulted show, for the first time. Apparently, the entrance of unions
in politics heretofore was regarded as of little or no importance
or consequence to the associations. Now, the situation had
changed. Clearly, the ramifications of the labor-relations problem
were extending. Of course, resort to politics was a remedy for
the importation of alien strikebreakers, even from China; for
instance, the Chinese Six Companies in San Francisco (each
company represented a different part of China) up to 1877 had
imported 148,600 Chinese.

The Great Railroad Strike of 1877 was a distinct part of the
"open-shop drive of the seventies." The leader of that "drive"
was President Frederick B. Gowen of the Philadelphia and Reading Railroad—an anthracite-coal-mine-owning railroad. He had
extensive experience with collective bargaining. He antedates by a
quarter century, at least, some of our twentieth-century "fathers
of the open-shop movement," or "fathers of employers' associations." Nor was he the first "open-shop" leader in the United
States, but he was the first "open-shop" leader in the early dawn
of the great consolidation stage or "Financial Revolution," and
he brought to bear the great power then possible to the employers
against trade unions. He was aggressive and carried the fight to the
enemy, and he dealt the unions smashing blow after blow. With
these facts in mind, we can better understand the strikes on the
railroads, in the coal mines, and in the iron industry in these
epoch-making days of association history. The railroad managers
were expecting, if not actually looking for trouble. Early in the
year railroads asked for legislation in the various states prohibiting
the willful and malicious obstruction or impairing of the operation
of railroads by any act, or by *means of intimidation,* or *conspiring*

to do so. By March of the year this legislation was enacted in at least one state—Michigan.

In March, 1877, the Philadelphia and Reading Railroad required all of its locomotive engineers to withdraw their membership from the union. This was a move made by the railroad in anticipation of a strike, since detectives in the rank of the union reported to Mr. Gowen on the union's plans. The men generally agreed to leave their union, but on April 14, most of the men struck. President Gowen, knowing the union's plans, had nonunion men ready to fill the places of the strikers. The strikers tried, with little success, to get these men to quit strikebreaking.

The railroad managers were well organized for the strike, although generally their pooling agreements were quickly broken. On May 29, these managers met in Chicago and pooled their freight, fixed the rates, and agreed upon a general and uniform reduction of wages of 10%. They imported workers heavily from Hungary to break the strike. Hungary was "flooded with advertisements." Land-grant railroads advertised widely in Europe for immigrants to settle land, as well as to work on railroads and break strikes. Agents were employed to solicit immigrants. Jay Gould so testified in 1880. Other employers had the railroad agents procure strikebreakers abroad.

The notices for the wage reductions were evidently designed to bring on a strike—whatever the motives may have been for bringing this to pass—to smash the unions may have been the only motive, although the interest of England in the matter and the reaction there, suggested that financial motives or graft may have also been present, since the railroads were then in a grafting and stock-watering stage. For, the manner in which notices were given for the reductions were regarded in England as one of the causes for the "railroad rebellion," as it seems that nearly every railroad took some step or steps to irritate further the men into a bitter strike; for instance, the Baltimore and Ohio Railroad tried to pay 10% dividends at the time it reduced wages 10% and made public announcement of these actions.

Wage reductions alone did not produce a general strike. But when the railroads entering Pittsburgh added to the wage reduction an order to engineers and trainmen to run "double headers" without any extra help or pay, and at reduced pay, the strike came. In the railroad world, a double header means that two engines are attached to a train which, of course, hauls about twice the number of cars that a "single header" does. Accordingly, this meant more work for the trainmen and more danger to engineers, firemen, and trainmen, for the railroad equipment of that day was of a highly dangerous type.

In July, 1877, the greatest strike in the United States till then broke out on the Baltimore and Ohio Railroad in West Virginia, spread to other railroads—Pennsylvania, Erie, Lake Shore, etc. The strike covered from the Atlantic seaboard to the Mississippi River—12,000 miles of railroad, 60,000 strikers; the regular army and militia called out, 100,000; scenes like civil war. On Sunday, July 22, in Pittsburgh, militia brought in from Philadelphia fired on a crowd killing 20 men, women, and children, and wounding many others. The militia fortified itself in a roundhouse and picked off besiegers, but others set it on fire. The militia driven from the burning roundhouse was attacked by mob and lost 20 killed. The mob took possession of the city, smashed, looted and burned railroad cars and other railroad property—shops, buildings, and equipment. Pennsylvania Railroad's losses were $5,000,000, of which it recovered afterwards $2,000,000 from the county. Rioting took place at Reading, Scranton, Allegheny, Altoona, Harrisburg, and Philadelphia. Many of the railroads compromised; wages and conditions were bettered, and Vanderbilt gave his men $100,000 for not striking.

The strike of 1877 was called a "rebellion" because it extended half way across the continent and was accompanied with violence, arson, and bloodshed in actual battles. It became general, because the wage reduction of 10% was general, as was some form of irritation such as the rule increasing the length of trains with no additional brakemen, when all brakes then used were hand brakes. The railroads employed nonunion men and published extensive statements of the wages paid to the different trainmen on the various roads to show how well the strikers had been paid. The strike spread from Albany in the East to Kansas in the West. For instance, on July 2, 1877, conductors, engineers, firemen, and brakemen employed on the New Jersey

Central, the Morris and Essex, and the Lehigh Valley railroads joined in the strike. The railroads had sheriffs read the "riot act" to the strikers, and when this was inadequate had the state militia called out. Riots occurred quite generally: state militia and federal troops were called out to maintain law and order and to stop interference with the operation of trains. But clashes between the troops and strikers took place. Railroad property was destroyed. Rioting, pillaging, and burning of railroad property were extensive, especially in Pittsburgh. Other workers than on the railroads joined in the strike. The situation was undoubtedly further aggravated by the large number of idle men, some of whom were tramps who then were very numerous. Among these were men who seized upon the opportunity to pillage and burn property of the railroads, and even to shoot to kill when caught and shot at. The strikers themselves had, among their numbers, men who were in a temper to do almost anything to damage the railroads or wreak vengeance on those designated as strikebreakers, scabs, or even more odious names. As a result of riots, violence, and interruption to traffic, the railroads lost, it is estimated, over 50 millions of dollars, an enormous sum in that day. Vigilance committees were formed at Pittsburgh, at Zanesville, at Harrisburg, and doubtless at other places where the committees did not get into action as at the places named. With the organized power of the railroads, supplemented by the federal troops, the state militia, the local police, and the hidden force of vigilance committees against them, the strikers had no organization which could bring them success. The drive of the railroads was organized on a national scale; and the resistance of the strikers was localized, violent, and futile. Federal injunctions apparently played a part on some railroads, especially those in receiverships. Not only was the strike broken but the strikers were blacklisted by all the railroads.

Citizens' Committees during the strike period of 1877 functioned successfully when the usual police force and even the state militia had failed. In the Pittsburgh riots, the citizens' committee was highly effective. To this instance, another case may well be added here.

In Scranton, Pennsylvania, in 1877, a citizens' corps was

organized to meet the strike situation there. The mayor called upon the businessmen for organization to sustain the legal authorities in preserving peace and good order and guarantee protection to property. This corps became involved in an actual battle with strikers, and a number of the strikers were killed. Members of the corps were tried but were finally acquitted by the courts. The corps played a very important part in ending the strike.

Strikes in Coal Mining in 1877. A citizens' corps also functioned to end a strike in Steubenville, Ohio. The coal operators there had a dispute with the miners in regard to payment per car for mining coal because of the varying amount the car might hold. The operators also refused to grant an advance in wages demanded by the miners and a strike resulted. The operators attempted to put other men to work. The miners countered with a demonstration. The mayor called upon the citizens for a posse to suppress the disorder. The citizens' corps ordered the strikers to disperse, and when they refused the leaders were placed under arrest. Nonunion men then went to work and, after a five weeks strike, the union admitted its defeat. On October 16, the strikers sought work at the old wages. Coal operators in the Lackawanna region refused in 1877 to advance the price for mining coal. The strike lasted from August to October, riots occurred and troops were called in, but the strikers were forced to return to work at the old rates. The coal operators of Tuscarawas Valley, Ohio, likewise, refused in August, 1877, to advance the rate from 60c to 70c, and paid no attention to the request of the union for a conference on the matter. Later the association arranged for a conference when the union proposed "arbitration." The "arbitrators" (or conciliators) met, but since there was no referee or umpire, the arbitrators deadlocked, and nothing was done—which, of course, was a victory for the association, as the old rate remained in force. A coal strike on the coal operators at Des Moines, Iowa, beginning in August, was called off in November. Coal operators of LaSalle County, Illinois, however, were forced by a strike to pay the miners (300 in number) on gross weight of coal mined instead of for screened coal.

The Iron Industry had its usual share of labor trouble in

1877. The iron manufacturers of the Schuylkill, Lehigh, and Susquehanna Valleys announced wage reductions ranging up to as
high as 25 percent, and the workers struck. A riot at the Pen-
coyd Iron Works, Philadelphia, grew out of a strike—ended by
the sheriff swearing into service the special police sent there by
Mr. Gowen. In January, 1877, the iron and steel millowners of
Cleveland, Ohio, posted notices that wages would be reduced
13 to 15 percent, when the mills resumed work. The workmen
later demanded their old wages and struck in March. The strike
continued for several weeks. The iron manufacturers of Pittsburgh in 1877 signed an agreement with the puddlers' union for
a scale with $5.00 the minimum on a 2½c card. Most of the
iron manufacturers throughout the West had signed, during the
previous year, a scale the same as the Pittsburgh, but the Eastern
manufacturers paid lower wages, and for this reason, the Pittsburgh manufacturers contended in the conference that they should
have wage concessions to meet such competition. This agreement,
however, led the rollers and heaters to renew their demands. The
heaters had demanded in May a restoration of wages to those
before the reduction. The manufacturers refused the demands of
the heaters, and the furnaces were shut down during the strike.
The rollers also had their grievances, but apparently both groups
of workers returned to work on the old basis. Then when the
puddlers won out, the rollers and heaters asked for equally favorable treatment.

The Stove Manufacturers of Albany and Troy, New York,
were struck because they refused to grant the demands of the
molders' union in regard to piece prices, apprentices, the union
rule prohibiting the employment of nonunion men, and work
before 7:00 A.M. The issues finally were resolved into one over
helpers and apprentices, and the molders agreed to pay the helpers. Some of the manufacturers sought to get prison labor to break
the strike. The manufacturers began to employ nonunion men
rapidly and gave the strikers notices to that effect. The union at
first disregarded the notices, but soon the strikers learned that
nonunion men were going to be obtained in considerable numbers.
Large numbers of the strikers soon sought their old jobs as indi-

viduals. Later, the remainder of the strikers saw the futility of extending the struggle. However, the stove manufacturers lost considerable trade on account of the strike.

Other Associations in Labor Troubles in 1877. The manufacturing potters of New Jersey, in January, reduced wages 16 percent, and defeated the resulting 16-week strike of the potters in all branches. The glass manufacturers of Pittsburgh were struck by the chimney blowers over the introduction of a patent chimney crimper. The manufacturers, then resorted to a revolving mold which could be operated by unskilled workmen. The glass factories of New Jersey reduced wages 20 percent and defeated the strikers. The employing coopers of Pittsburgh refused to grant the demand of the coopers' union for 20c a barrel when the rate was 18c. The coopers struck and the employers granted the 20c. The union apparently thought it had not asked enough so it shortly demanded 23c. The employers refused and defeated the resultant strike. After weeks of idleness, the strikers got what work they could at 18c. In September, 1877, a combination of 32 cigar manufacturers of New York fought a strike of the cigar workers for an increase of wages. The strike lasted 107 days and over 1,000 families who made cigars in their tenements were dispossessed by the sheriff. A relief committee supplied the needy strikers with food and other necessities of life, and unions elsewhere grew rapidly as the result of the strike; the striking union, however, had only 131 left of its original 7,000 members when the strike was over.

In contrast, strikers forced concession from other groups of employers in the following cases. The silk manufacturers of New Jersey were forced by a 13-week strike of the silk ribbon weavers to maintain wages when the manufacturers sought a reduction. The cigar manufacturers of Cincinnati were defeated in a two-week strike by the cigar makers. The issue was the use of women and children to operate machines—a struggle of skilled handicraftsmen against the machine operated by unskilled laborers. The shipyards of Camden, New Jersey, were forced by a strike of the ship carpenters to advance wages. This contrast is all the more marked in that wages were advanced at this time when generally strikes against reductions were failures, and the advance was made in an industry which was relatively a declining one in the United States.

In 1878, the prices for cloth had fallen so low that the mills of Fall River, on March 12, gave notices of another 15 percent reduction in wages—a total of about 45 percent since 1870—the millowners rejected counter offers of the spinners' union for part-time operation, and two weeks after the reduction, prices of cloth fell still lower. Mills then operated on part time—alternate weeks for 18 weeks, but two-thirds of the mills were reported on the verge of ruin. Treasurers of three of the larger mills were later convicted of defaulting with large sums of money from their respective companies. Workers who had invested their life savings in these mills lost all.

There was no real recovery from the depression and in the years, 1877-78, strikes against associations were unsuccessful in general. The associations could well argue that strikes did not pay. Unions, then, as now frequently won the strikes called on the independent or nonassociation employer, but, as a rule, such strikes are not the outstanding ones in any period of time. Workmen and employers especially were told that the power of the unions was weakening.

The Growth of Political Power of Trade Unions was accurately appraised by the associations: "The labor party has become consolidated and united and of importance enough to be courted and their [leaders'] wishes consulted." The organization and affiliation of unions on a national scale—that is, covering the area where materials may be supplied in a strike—were discussed and the significance of these in future labor struggles was pointed out to employers. While the associations believed it impossible for a socialist uprising in the United States to be successful, measures provided for meeting such a threatened movement were outlined and the movement itself discussed. The associations clearly perceived two of the weaknesses of the labor party movement: (1) the many points of disagreement among reformers, especially as to methods: and (2) their lack of knowledge outside of a very limited field. Histories of trade unions quite generally attribute the failure of the labor party to disagreements and the period of prosperity, but it is more probable that the very limited knowledge of the leaders of the movement made it possible for the associations to foster the disagreements to the point where disharmony wrecked the party—the simplest and most effective means of all that the employers could have used.

The Influence of Labor Agitators was not underrated, as the following statement shows:

"They are not groping after an issue. They have one, distinct and well defined, and they also have one by which they mean to reach the object they are seeking. The aim is to control labor and its wages—the means, consolidation, or mobilization of all laborers. This is the dream of the labor agitators. To its realization these men are giving the most positive and intelligent efforts of their lives. The leaders in the movement are organizers of no common or inferior kind but know how to control men, to unite them, and to organize them. They are determined to succeed, because they believe that the only way to reach the ends they have been aiming at is by such united efforts as we have suggested. There is another phase of this impending struggle that is well to consider. These men propose not only to control themselves and their fellow laborers and prevent working under price by wage laborers, but they propose to prevent manufacturers from selling under price. It is no secret that during the past year certain manufacturers of iron needed only to drop a hint, and not a ton of iron could have been made in certain mills that did not sustain prices fixed by associations." Unions were condemned for attempts to fix wages, and apprenticeship was discussed with a view to its restoration as a means to increase the supply of skilled workmen. The failure of the school system of that day to train mechanics was discussed and the fact lamented. At that date, it was clearly perceived that the school system of that day was causing an overcrowding of clerical positions. Accordingly, industrial education was urged. The relation of the machine to the problem was well understood; and the employers' associations had demonstrated in the strikes then current that the machine and unskilled laborers could break a strike of skilled workmen.

Attacks Upon Unions were made on points familiar to readers of present-day discussions of unionism. No attack upon unions has been more persistent than that the unions level down the most efficient workman to that of the least efficient in the group. The losses sustained by workmen in even the "won" strikes, it was argued were greater than the gains, and so the strike policy of the unions was accounted bad. The problem as stated in current discussions of that day was, "How to increase productiveness and wages?" Perhaps the fact that the preceding years had been ones of marked depression and that the times were still too depressed for strikes to be successful, led to the statement, "In the often-quoted language of Adam Smith, it is a good time for labor when two masters are running after one workman and it is the reverse when two workmen are competing for one master." In August, 1878, trouble with enormous numbers of tramps continued to be great, so the army of the unemployed was still very large, and two workmen were competing for every job. Laws were enacted to deal with the problem of tramps but all that these laws were intended to do was to drive the tramps away. Under these conditions, it may readily be seen that trade unions which had to deal with belligerent associations were generally crushed. The associations had an abundant supply of labor and were using machines in breaking strikes so only those unions which could deal with an appeasatory association or with independent or nonassociation employers could have much strength in the industrial field. It seems clear then that, in this period, the unions went into politics as a second resort, if not in a final effort, to forestall defeat. In this effort, the unions instilled more fear into the ranks of the employers than they did by all their "strike rebellions." The association employers felt that so long as the old established government continued to function as it had in the past, that the suppression of riots in strikes was a matter of course. But when the unions were threatening to gain control over those governments, the employers saw that success by the unionists in gaining such control meant the wreck of the whole economic structure of that day. The associations saw the possibilities of the movement and began early to study its weaknesses and the result was the expected one.

Employers were informed of important developments and what other employers were doing to meet the labor-relations problem. Employers were told what the employers' associations of Great Britain were doing. Shop rules of certain manufacturers were given at length for the information of other manufacturers. Agitation of 1779 was pointed out, and a poster reproduced which was originally dated June 16, 1779, which called a mass meeting to "Rouse and catch the Philadelphia spirit; rid the community of those monopolizers and extortioners— . . ." To the employers of 1878, the words of the old poster sounded very familiar. Reformers of today like to quote the words of some employer or association leader in some period before the twentieth century and to compare it to some statement by a present-day employer, the above instance shows that the method was used long ago and by the other side.

Mr. Franklin B. Gowen, President of the Philadelphia and Reading Railroad, was active in propaganda for the open shop. For instance, on April 5, 1878, he delivered an address at Pottsville, Pennsylvania, on "Trades Unions and Labor Reform." The address was published to give it wide distribution. Mr. Gowen was an able association leader in that day. It was he, more than any other man, who was responsible for the breaking up of the Molly Maguires and the methods used in doing that. In association circles he was given great credit for putting out of existence the Molly Maguires organization. All later developments show he was badly tangled up in his financial dealings—but in this, as well as in other respects, he was a product of the times, for corruption, graft, and crooked high finance were characteristic of too many of the railroad magnates of that day. Accordingly, his attack on labor reform and his onslaught on trades unions and Molly Maguires suggest many interesting speculations, for which there is no space here.

In the Legislative Field there were two outstanding events in the year 1878. In the early part of the year, legislation providing for voluntary boards for arbitration was proposed in Pennsylvania. A congressional inquiry into conditions of labor was conducted by a special committee under the above title. Both events indicated a trend to seek the aid of the government in adjusting labor troubles. Both indicate a recognition of the growing intensity of the labor-relations problem and an extension of its ramifications.

Also union officials went in a committee to Washington to fight for a high protective tariff in 1878. A committee was appointed in each congressional district to call upon or communicate with the representative in Congress in favor of higher tariff on old rails.

In the Industrial Field the year 1878, like its predecessor, was marked by wage reduction. The proprietors of the iron and steel mills of Philadelphia met on August 15 and reduced the wages of the iron and steel workers. The reductions ranged from 10 to 40 percent. The wages of the puddlers, for instance, were reduced 65c, that is, from $4.25 to $3.60 a ton. All the various classes of workers affected went on strike. The proprietors imported non-union workmen and guarded them by means of special police. Finally, the strikers in October gave up the struggle and sought work at the reduced wages. The success of the employers was attributed to the fact that "the manufacturers have virtually united, pledging themselves to stand by each other, and thus they have gained their point."

In view of the fact that the Philadelphia scales largely governed those of the East, it was hardly a mere coincidence that, on August 15, the identical day on which the Philadelphia iron manufacturers met and agreed to reduce wages, the iron manufacturers of Kingston met to deal with the question of wage reductions. A new schedule of wages had been proposed to the workmen, but they had announced they would resist such a reduction. The reduction in puddlers' wages was identical with the reduction at Philadelphia, namely 65c a ton, (that is from $4.25 to $3.60 a ton). Those employed on time were cut 10%, while the reductions of the rollers were as high as 40c, so the range in Kingston was the same as at Philadelphia. When every detail in a scheme carried out by two groups of employers in different sections of the country corresponds so closely, some relationship exists between them to bring about such concert of action. Manifestly such concert of action is a highly efficient method of crushing unions.

In contrast, the Pittsburgh iron manufacturers renewed the old scale with the puddlers without changes. A current comment on the wages paid to puddlers, says: "If it is asked why these prices are paid it can be readily answered. In some cases the financial condition of mills is such that they cannot stop even for a day to fight it out. In other cases, as we have so often stated, there has not been the unity on the part of the manufacturers; and still again, some mills have contracts with their men that when there is a strike at other places they shall not join it, but let the others pull the chestnuts and they reap the benefits. One thing is certain—this thing will not get on the right basis until union is met by union, until manufacturers of iron in this country have a complete organization and one to which they will be just as faithful as the men are to their union."

The nail manufacturers of Wheeling, West Virginia, notified their employees that wages would be reduced at the end of 30 days, but the notice was withdrawn in the face of a threatened strike. Had the employees tamely submitted, the reduction, without doubt, would have been put in force, so it seems that the association either felt itself too weak for a fight, or that the cost of the fight would be greater than the gains from the wage reduction.

The National Association of Stove Manufacturers, although its members were prohibited by its constitution from discussing labor questions in the conventions, on January 16, 1878, spent a considerable portion of the annual meeting considering the question of prison labor. This problem had grown out of the Albany-Troy strike of iron molders. The President of the Association brought up the matter in his annual address and a special committee was appointed to consider the matter. Discussions on the floor of the convention indicated that stove manufacturers in general were opposed to the competition of firms using prison labor. The association resolved that the committee should use all honorable means to have all contract prison labor abolished; and, if this could not be obtained, to have all goods made by prison labor stamped as products of prison labor. Acting under this resolution, the committee aroused laborers in opposition to contract prison labor, and began organizing groups to oppose such labor. The committee urged political action—candidates were to be required to state their position on the question, and no vote was to be given for a man who would not pledge himself to work to abolish the system. The stove manufacturers using prison contract labor had organized to meet the agitation for the abolition of the system and even used page advertisements to counteract the propaganda of those who sought the abolition of the system. In the following convention (January, 1879) the National Association of Stove Manufacturers adopted a resolution that the various states should not allow over 10% of prison labor to be employed in any one line of business. Much opposition to prison labor was expressed, but the feeling was that this restriction was the best obtainable method of dealing with the problem. In other words, if it could not be abolished, to dilute it would be best.

Coal Operators' Associations in general reduced wages during 1878. In certain instances the combination of coal operators endeavored to advance the price of coal by curtailing production and thus throwing miners out of employment, in others, by reducing wages and thus causing strikes to be called. In the first instance, "the Western Coal Association, a combination that controls the price of anthracite coal west of the water routes, met in the Coal and Iron Exchange in New York City on Saturday the 30th ult. (August, 1878). Both coal companies and railroad lines were fully represented. An adjustment of transportation rates was agreed upon, making them uniform to competing points, and prices of coal were advanced 25 cents per ton." As a result of the allotments of the above coal combination, mining was suspended in the mines of the Lehigh Coal and Navigation Company and the Schuylkill region. The coal operators of the Monongahela Valley, in May, 1878, reduced the price for mining coal from 3c to 2½c a bushel, and defeated the resulting strike. At the beginning of the season for winter mining, another strike took place to force wage increases. Reductions had been made, until in some mines, a price as low as 1¾c a bushel was paid. The miners demanded 2½c in the first, second, and third pool mines and ordered all men there to quit. The coal operators of Plumb Creek, Sandy Creek, and Turtle mines, near Pittsburgh, finally forced the miners to agree to go to work for 2½c a bushel. The coal operators of Mansfield Valley, Pennsylvania, were struck by the miners when their demands (for 2½c a bushel for digging, a union check weighman, and 76 pounds to the bushel) were not granted. Likewise, coal operators along the Pan Handle Railroad were struck because of their refusal to grant wage demands and allow a union check-weighman. The demand for a union check-weighman grew out of the general belief among miners that the company weighman was guilty of the practice of crediting the miners with only part of the coal they had mined. The union demanded that the company allow a union-paid check-weighman to observe each individual weighing and keep a record of weights. The coal companies, for a number of reasons, opposed this demand. Like the railroad owners, the coal mine owners were not troubled with scruples, in fact businessmen then were none too scrupulous, either in their dealing with each other, or with their employees. The following is an instance of a rather general practice: In Jackson County, Ohio, the "furnacemen and ore diggers get $1.00 a day nominally for their labor, but as this is in script payable in goods at the companies' stores, the actual pay is but from 60 to 70c a day." Such practices prepared the grounds for union agitators or organizers and gave the nonunion shop or "open shop" a bad reputation.

In the "West" of that day, coal operators' associations were functioning in labor matters. Coal operators of Clay County, Indiana, refused to advance the price for mining coal 10% a ton and were struck at the beginning of the winter coal mining season. Coal operators at Zanesville, Ohio, refused to advance the price of mining coal ¼ cents a bushel and were struck. The coal operators of LaSalle, Illinois, were able to force the dissolution of the local miners' union; miners had struck in 1879 for extra pay for "extra work." The coal operators of Stanton, Illinois, however, had the militia called out to protect their mines from destruction threatened by striking miners. The coal operators of Bevier, Missouri, in September—the beginning of the winter mining season—agreed among themselves to reduce the price of mining coal from 5c to 4c a bushel. The miners struck. One of the operators attempted to operate his mine with coolie labor. Finally, an adjustment was made and the miners returned to work. The coal operators of Richmond, Missouri, refused in September to grant an advance of 1c a bushel for mining coal, and the miners struck. The operators met and agreed to offer ½c advance on a six-month contract—for the winter season—but the miners refused. Later, however, the miners went back to work for 4½c a bushel. The coal operators of Boulder Valley, Colorado, in September refused to grant $1.00 a ton for mining coal and were struck. In ore mining, the mine owners of Mt. Vernon, Pennsylvania, were struck by the ore miners who refused to accept a reduction of 10c a ton for mining.

Glass Manufacturing had its share of labor troubles in 1878. The glass factories of New Jersey were forced by a strike of the window-glass workers to advance wages 10%. In contrast, the glass manufacturers of Pittsburgh defeated strikes by various glass workers, and operated on a nonunion basis: In November, 1878, the glass manufacturers of Pittsburgh refused to confer with the glass workers over a "uniform list" prepared by the union, because it lowered output. The manufacturers met and agreed to issue a notice that work would be done by the hundred instead of "turn," that the manufacturers would make such articles, use such molds, and hire or discharge whom they pleased, and would "not submit to dictation in any form." The manufacturers were undoubtedly encouraged to take such a stand by the success they had obtained over the workmen in table-glass manufacturing. In September, these workmen had threatened to strike for about a 25% reduction in production, but the demand was withdrawn by the workmen as untimely. Twenty-four factories were involved.

The notice by the association caused the union to withdraw the "uniform list," but the manufacturers provoked a strike of the glass workers indirectly by reducing wages about 12½%, although they had formerly declared that the question was not one of wages but of methods and products. Eleven factories with 15 furnaces were affected. The factories started operating with nonunion men; in fact, six out of the eleven struck factories began operating with green hands, who were trained to do the work. The association refused to make any compromise, although the strikers offered many concessions. After the strike had been on for several months, strikers offered concessions which one firm accepted, but its action was immediately disapproved by the associated manufacturers. By June, 1879, another firm had compromised, but the other nine concerns had trained up an adequate force of nonunion workers. In August, 1879, the strike was called off by the union.

In Shoe Manufacturing, the associations dealt vigorously with striking unions in 1878. The shoe manufacturers of Marlborough, Massachusetts, reduced wages and shoe workers struck. New men were imported, the strike failed, and the union was completely broken up.

In the following account we have an interesting development of the "open-shop" movement in the boot and shoe industry. The ratio of 1500 Chinese laborers to 800 strikers is noteworthy, as well as the haggling over wages, but, more important, is the fact that the strikebreakers to be furnished were "contract laborers" and that defeats by such means as this led the unions into the legislative and political fields—in this case for a Chinese Exclusion Act. The account in question reads thus: "The boot and shoe manufacturers of Chicago are considering the proposition of the Chinese Six Companies of California to furnish them with 1,500 Chinamen, half-skilled and half-green workmen, at 75c a day for three years in place of 800 strikers. The plan was regarded favorably, but the general opinion was that from 40 to 60c a day would be adequate remuneration. No action was taken, but a further conference will be had with the agent of the Chinese Companies."

Although the above plan was considered at a time when unemployment was great in the United States, it could hardly be said that the unemployment situation had been relieved when the following occurred in April, 1879. The "exodus of the Negroes" is usually dated as beginning much later, and there are many who think that "the South has no labor problem." An abbreviation of the account is given as illuminating in a number of vays: "The planters of Madison Parish, Louisiana, have placed themselves in communication with the Six Companies at San Francisco, with a view of ascertaining whether a supply of that kind of labor is attainable, and, if so, on what terms. They likewise appointed a special agent to furnish the companies with a full description of the soil . . . climate . . . resources, etc., as well as the qualifications necessary to the kind of work which will be required of the Chinese in the event of their coming there." The Six Companies replied that they could not furnish any considerable number of field laborers for Louisiana. "The agent of the Southern planters . . . announces that the suggestion relative to sending to Hong Kong and chartering a ship will very shortly be acted upon, as the planters of Louisiana, Alabama, Mississippi, and Georgia, are becoming greatly alarmed at the rapid exodus of the Negroes."

The Chinese Six Companies, in connection with this case, said they did not bring their people to the United States, "nor make contracts to let out their labor to white men or corporations," but were "simply benevolent societies and nothing more." However, McNeill charges that the Six Chinese Companies were formed at the bidding of avaricious capitalists to import Chinese laborers into the United States. "The secret history of the Six Companies may never be written; but the accomplished fact stands out before the world that these companies brought over to California hordes of "coolie" laborers under contracts and conditions more baneful to our civilization than the importation of the African slave." In 1879, the sentiment in California was shown by the overwhelming vote against Chinese immigration 154,638 to 883 for it.

In other fields the situation was generally unfavorable to the unions. In November, 1878, cotton manufacturers of Philadelphia reduced the weavers' wages 1c a yard. The weavers struck. The manufacturers imported new hands and had them protected by the police. In January, 1879, the strikers sought work at the reduced wages. The granite cutters of Quincy, Massachusetts, however, forced the contractors by a strike to agree on a partial wage advance demanded by the cutters before the strike. One of the employers violated the agreement by employing nonunion men, and the cutters' union in 1879 struck all the other employers on the ground that the agreement of 1878 was being violated. Instead of complying with the union's demand to force the "open-shop" employer to adopt the union shop, the employers met and agreed not to employ any union men whatever. The strike was not called off as late as October, 1880, and so may be regarded as a complete "open-shop" victory. The employing stonecutter sent his ornamental work to New York City to concerns there to be done. The union branded his shop a "scab" one, struck it, and would not allow anyone to work in it until he paid a fine of $500. He paid it, but sued for recovery on grounds of extortion by an illegal conspiracy. The court decided in his favor.

In the far West, however, both railroad and silver-mine owners, notably of the Comstock Lode, Virginia City, Nevada, were forced to give the miners' union and the machinists' union, unqualified closed shops. The miners' union drove off all nonunion workmen.

Prosperity Changed the Labor Situation. In the early part of 1879, in all three of the great staple industries of that day—iron, coal, and glass—strikes were in progress. Although the resumption of specie payment took place on January 1, the depression continued for about five months longer. Under the continued depressed conditions, discussions set forth the "waning power of labor unions." It is interesting to note at this time that historical accounts of labor unions were given, for instance, the molders' union was cited as an organization which had been at one time one of the most powerful in the country, but also one which had its power broken a few years before 1879. A detailed account of the Knights of Labor was given mainly to show that it was essentially too weak ever to attain great power. Although union periodicals reported strikes still on at Scottdale and Cincinnati, both had been lost for some time—a procedure that led to remarks that unions make themselves ridiculous. Discussions of "technical education for apprentices" with advocacy of public industrial schools were becoming more frequent, as the result of the feeling of the need for highly skilled nonunion labor. In June, business activity was becoming great and a boom then was seen to be ahead. With the boom, the strategic position of labor unions was changed, and the shift in the situation was quickly realized: "Strikes and rumors of strikes abound in nearly every industry and it is noticeable that labor is successful;" "affairs wore a different aspect a year ago." In August, demands for wage increases and strikes were frequent, but usually the strikes were called on individual firms rather than groups of firms. But with the change in financial conditions and the shift in strategic positions in strikes came the use of the injunction restraining picketing. Prior to this time, the union pickets stationed themselves outside the struck shop or establishment and induced, or coerced by intimidation, the nonunion men to quit work; but only when there was a riot, would the police or military forces take charge. Now an appeal to the courts brought relief through an order from the judge restraining the activities of union pickets under penalty of being adjudged guilty of contempt of court and fined or imprisoned. The above discussion is the first that we have found relating to the issue of injunctions in labor disputes. That employers were promptly informed in regard to this remedy at equity, shows associations were active and the struggle was growing more intense. Contrary to Commons, the employers promptly made use of this new method, as the following pages will show. Moreover, the "blacklisting of scabs" by union men was likened to blacklisting of union agitators by the manufacturers, to set forth that the unions were guilty of practices very similar to those which they strongly condemned when done by the manufacturers.

Foresight was evident in the discussions in regard to labor contracts and the changed conditions; it was questioned strongly whether an employer should even attempt to hold workmen to contracts at low wages for a year in the face of general price advances.

The attitude of employers toward arbitration was also changed by the boom. When the employers held the strategic position, they often preferred to fight the matter out, but when surplus labor began to disappear, arbitration seemed to offer a means to prevent stoppages of work when production was highly profitable. Joseph K. Weeks (Secretary of the Western Iron Manufacturers' Association) delivered an address on arbitration before the Pittsburgh Chamber of Commerce, which was so impressed that it published in pamphlet form for circulation among manufacturers and laborers in that district 10,000 copies of the address. Mr. Weeks was otherwise quoted at length on "industrial arbitration and conciliation" (now generally known as "collective bargaining"). Illustrations of rules for the formation and government of boards of conciliation and arbitration were published for the information of employers who might desire to utilize such boards. As pointed out above, the early part of prosperous periods tends to be favorable to appeasement, while the closing days of prosperity and the depressed times following are usually unfavorable or belligerent.

Prosperous times also foster new organizations. Employers, when profits are good, no longer feel the need for economizing in association dues, and are interested in proposed plans for maintaining the profitable conditions, especially in the "get-together" plans. During prosperity, arguments in favor of combination are presented in convincing form, especially to the employer who finds demands for wage increases are keeping up with the price advance for his product. The Carriage Builders' National Association was one of the new organizations of this period; and the New England Manufacturers' Association began to function actively during the year.

The open-shop movement, however, did not die when business began to boom, although Mr. Gowen was ready to desert it in favor of a combination of association and union to control prices. Time had shown that the Molly Maguires had been wiped out through his efforts and under his leadership. Mr. Gowen, however, continued the fight on other organizations similar to the Molly Maguires. He complained of a secret order, known as the "McNulty Gang," which he charged was formed to burn breakers and commit depredations upon the property of strike-affected coal operators. It would seem that these secret orders had learned in the fate of the Molly Maguires, how to rid themselves of Pinkerton detectives, or, at least, to keep such "spies" out of the order, for Mr. Gowen apparently did not obtain evidence enough to proceed against the "McNulty Gang" as he did in the case of the Molly Maguires. Later on, however, the conditions under which Mr. Gowen was ready to abandon the open shop as a principle will be set forth.

In Coal Mining strikes were extensive in 1879. Wages were the dominating cause of the strikes; these were sometimes called against wage reductions, sometimes called to force advances. The coal operators in Osage County, Kansas, were struck in March, 1879, when they attempted to reduce the rate for mining coal one cent a bushel. The operators then offered to compromise on ½c reduction, which would leave the price paid at 3c a bushel. At Richmond, Missouri, the coal operators, who had made wage advances in the fall of 1879 for the winter season only, were struck at the beginning of summer and the strike extended into the winter season without the contestants reaching an agreement on wages. In Clay County, Indiana, the coal operators defeated the striking miners and blacklisted the leaders of the strike. Other strikers returned to work at the old terms. The coal operators in Kanawha Valley, West Virginia, were threatened with a general strike in December, 1879. The coal operators dealt with as many as 15 strikes in the period 1877-78 and were distinctly belligerent. They had trouble with miners striking in 1879; a long and bitter controversy followed. But the price for mining coal was 3¼c a bushel in January, 1880. The miners' union was said to have been connected with the Knights of Labor.

In the Ohio coal region, coal operators were struck rather extensively in October and November, 1879, and in most cases over refusals to grant wage increases. Coal operators in the Nelsonville, Ohio, Valley were forced by a threatened strike to advance the price for mining coal 10c a ton. In November, 1879, the coal operators in the Tuscarawas Valley were struck because they refused to advance the price for mining coal to 85c a ton. The miners offered to arbitrate and the operators accepted with the proviso that the price should be fixed upon the screen basis, but the miners rejected the proviso. Conferences, proposals, and attempts to arbitrate all proved futile and no compromise could be effected. Perhaps the fact that the union had once violated its pledge to accept an arbitration decision, caused the coal operators to place little faith in a second arbitration proceeding with the miners' union. It is as probable, however, that the majority of the coal operators too strongly favored the "open shop" to bind themselves to an arbitration decision on matters in general. The coal operators imported Negro miners, and when trouble arose between these and the strikers, the militia was called out to maintain law and order. In May, 1880, the strikers saw the futility of the strike and called it off. In the Hocking Valley, the coal operators were forced by the miners to advance the price for mining coal from 50c a ton to 60c, and five weeks later to 75c. Two weeks later the price was forced to $1.00, but it remained there only two weeks. The operators then reduced the price to 75c, but the miners struck. The miners had offered to accept 80c before they walked out. The operators agreed among themselves to bring in new men. Finally the men returned to work at the reduced rate. Conferences were held by the operators and miners, and on April 1, 1880, the operators proposed a sliding scale by months. The miners insisted on 80c a ton. In July, the coal operators reduced the price to 70c, the miners struck, but lost and returned to work at the reduction. On October 1, however, the operators advanced the price to 80c.

In the Anthracite Coal Fields, the year 1879 records an attempt of the miners' union and certain coal operators to form a combination to restrict the production of coal, and accordingly advance the market price of coal. The Schuylkill Coal Exchange issued circulars on wages to be paid during certain months, intending to standardize wages in that region. In March, delegates of the coal miners of the anthracite coal region met to take action to restrict the production of coal by a general strike. The coal operators did not send delegates with full authority to act for them, so the miners adjourned without any definite action. Previous meetings of the delegates of the coal operators and of the miners had been held to form a combination to suspend coal mining until prices were better. The coal combination, however, was unable to advance the price of coal because of the refusal of the Lehigh Valley Railroad Company to cooperate in the deal. Mr. Gowen, of "open-shop" fame, and President of the Philadelphia and Reading Railroad Company, was a leader in the movement for the combination of coal operators and miners to control the price of coal. The company addressed a letter to its employees stating that it could not, under the circumstances, make a proposed large increase in wages for coal mining. But Gowen did advance wages (about 4%), and this caused miners in the Wyoming and the Lackawanna coal fields to demand a 10% advance. In December, the coal operators of Tioga County conceded an advance of 10% in the rate for mining coal, but in January, 1880, refused a second advance. On March 1, the miners struck, and on May 1, the operators granted the advance demanded by the miners. In the Hazelton region, coal operators were struck by the miners who demanded a sliding scale with

15% advance in wages for every dollar advance in price of coal a ton. Coal operators in the Mahanoy district in July offered an advance of 5c a ton to their striking miners and many returned to work.

Appeasement in Western Pennsylvania.—In the early part of the year, belligerency, rather than negotiation, was the rule, but in the latter part the reverse was true. At the beginning of the year the Monongahela River coal operators were still refusing to grant the demands of striking miners for 3c a bushel for mining. In February, some of the operators broke away from the association and granted the miners' demands. Others held out and, in March, the strike seemed to have failed, for men were returning to work at 2½c a bushel. The coal operators at Elizabeth—which is in the Monongahela Valley—were struck also for an advance to 3c a bushel and in their attempts to operate their mines with nonunion men, had to have deputy sheriffs to protect their property. In March, there were 1,000 "striking" miners camped near Elizabeth to persuade the miners at work to quit. The striking miners in the Monongahela Valley are said to have joined, in March, the Knights of Labor. The strike then became general. The miners camped at West Elizabeth, were reduced to about 50. The men at work joined with the strikers. The coal operators lost the strike in April, and advanced the price to 3c a bushel for mining. The success of the strike in the Monongahela Valley caused other miners elsewhere to strike for 3c, for instance along the Pan Handle Railroad, and on the Chartiers Branch from Washington to Mansfield, but at some of the Pan Handle mines the men returned to work at the old scale. After an eight-weeks strike, all the miners resumed work but, as business had improved greatly, an advance was made. Coal operators along the Pennsylvania Railroad, east of and near Pittsburgh were confronted with demands for a 10% wage advance.

The coke manufacturers in the Connelsville Coke region defeated a strike of the miners for a wage advance. The owners declared that they would "blow out" and quit operating before they would pay an increased price for coke. By May 1, most of the strikers had returned to work at the old rate of wages. In November, the operators at first refused to grant the miners' demands for a wage advance, but when the miners' union issued an ultimatum that the rate of wages would be advanced or a strike would take place, a number of firms immediately complied by giving an advance in wages. Negotiations between the miners' union and the operators' association began. Various scales were proposed, two by the miners and one by the operators, but all were rejected. The operators showed their books to the union leaders to convince the latter as to the price received for coal. A compromise was finally reached of 3½c—which meant an advance of ½c a bushel. The operators requested the union to make the price of 3½c uniform, that is, it was to apply to nonassociation as well as association operators. This is frequently a task which an appeasatory association sets for a union with which it deals.

The coal operators of Western Pennsylvania, on September 25, 1879, appointed a conference committee to meet with a committee of the miners' union to draft a plan of conciliation and arbitration. The operators had refused at first to appoint such a committee, but the union leaders finally induced the association leaders to try to reach an agreement on a conciliation board. The joint committees met and selected a special committee of six to draft a plan of conciliation and arbitration. "Rules for the formation and government of a board of conciliation and arbitration for the coal mines of Western Pennsylvania" were drawn up and published for the general information of employers. In its original form, the object of the plan was to settle all questions of wages. However, during the year, the River Coal Exchange of Pittsburgh had refused to deal with the miners' union on the grounds that the exchange did not attempt to legislate for its members in labor matters. After some discussions among both the railroad and river coal operators, they appointed a committee to confer with the union officials. A call for a meeting of both the river and railroad coal operators was issued in September, and as a result a conference committee was chosen to meet a union committee. A board of arbitration was agreed upon, and rules were finally adopted to govern matters coming before the board. The board was composed of 18 members: 4 operators and 4 miners from each of the river and railroad mines, and a secretary each for the operators and miners. Among other matters agreed upon was a provision that "neither operators nor miners shall interefere with any man on account of his being a union or nonunion man." But some of the more prominent river operators refused to join the board. The old conflict between the railroad mine operators and the river mine operators prevented the original plan from being carried out, for the river mine operators would not endorse it, since the union members (on the board) insisted on a higher rate than the river mine operators would pay at the prevailing prices for coal—a fact that the operators convinced the union officials was the case. Accordingly, only the railroad coal operators and the miners formed the board; there were thus five members each from the operators' association and the miners' union.

The board met in Pittsburgh in November and fixed the price for mining coal at 3½ cents a bushel. The river mine operators did not pay as much. It seems that the railroad mine operators, in the business boom, had agreed in October to give the miners this advance of ½ cents a bushel over that paid before the winter season. However, in December, the coal operators along the Monongahela River granted the miners' demands for 3 cents a bushel, and the Railroad Coal Exchange was forced to withdraw its proposed reduction from 3½ to 3 cents because of a threatened strike. The lack of a unified organization among the coal operators to agree on rates for mining coal was clearly apparent at this time.

The issue between miners and operators had several phases. The miners' union demanded that the price for boiling iron be used as the basis, since the price of iron largely determined the price of coal; the operators argued that the price of coal should be the basis of wage rates. The operators yielded, but to prove their contentions as to the price of coal and profits and losses, the operators allowed the union officials to inspect the books of the companies. The union representatives had come to the conferences bound by instructions from the union, although this was contrary to the rules of the board, so the board deadlocked. It finally agreed to refer the matter to an umpire they had jointly selected, but he could not serve. The board would not agree upon another umpire, and the board broke up. The operators then set the price for mining coal, and the miners in the Pittsburgh district struck. These miners on strike in 1879 were ready to give up when a school teacher, reading law in Pittsburgh, overheard discussions of the Pittsburgh Coal Exchange and reported them to the union. Later the union made him its president with unlimited powers. In 1880, the union demanded the acceptance of its scales. The exchange refused to grant this. The union then drew up a sliding scale based on the price of iron, but the exchange again declined to accept the basis for a scale other than the price of coal. The miners then demanded 4c a bushel, and struck to enforce the demand, but lost the strike. Attempts to establish a board of conciliation and arbitration likewise failed in the Shenango Valley, where the coal operators asked the miners to submit their demands to a board. This board, however, could reach no agreement on the demands; the union representatives lacked the power to accept with finality the compromises of the conference, for these had to be approved by the miners in mass meeting. The board failed to select the umpire before the deadlock was reached, and then he could not be agreed upon. In November, 1879, the coal operators of the Mahoning Valley, Ohio, defeated a strike of the miners, and these resumed work at the old rate. Miners were also striking in Blair and Clearfield Counties, Pennsylvania.

In the Iron Industry the labor situation was a clear reflection of the change from depression to boom times. The iron manufacturers of Pittsburgh in the early part of the year, 1879, after trying for a long time to put up prices of their products and failing, decided to reduce wages on an average about 12 percent, although the range considered was 10 to 25 percent. It was contended that strikes and high wages were driving manufacturers from Pittsburgh. The pressure of other iron manufacturers upon the Pittsburgh iron manufacturers to lower wage rates is indicated in the following quotation from the leading periodical in the iron industry: "Millowners in other localities have uttered curses both loud and deep against the policy of the Pittsburgh Manufacturers in their dealings with the unions, which has kept wages in certain branches at a high figure. Pittsburgh manufacturers have been urged and pleaded with to change their policy, and make a strong and united attempt to break the power of the unions. They have hitherto virtually refused to take the course suggested, but the policy of the workmen is rapidly forcing them into a position where they will have to adopt prompt measures to defend themselves, and to secure rates of wages that are somewhat in keeping with the selling price of iron and the wages paid in other districts." According to McNeill, the Pennsylvania manufacturers attempted to destroy the Amalgamated in its third year by discharging its leaders; the fight was taken up in the following year by the Eastern manufacturers; and during these years, strikes were generally defeated.

In May, the iron manufacturers of Pittsburgh asked the puddlers' union for a modification of the scale—which had a minimum of $5.00 on a 2½c card. The puddlers refused and the mills closed down. At a conference with the union officials, the iron manufacturers proposed arbitration but the union members rejected this proposal, and discharged the union conference committee. The manufacturers had declared that they would not sign the old scale again, but in a few days thereafter, the boom times began. The manufacturers surrendered after the strike had lasted only one week. The heaters, rollers, and all other classes of skilled labor joined with the puddlers in the strike. The employers conceded everything the union had demanded. The manufacturers gave as their reasons for the quick surrender the general strike, and fear that competitors would get all the trade just when business was getting to be good. The strikers believed that they had won a great victory; they felt that it was significant because it was the first real test made of strength of the amalgamation previously formed of the unions of each of the puddlers, heaters, rollers, and other skilled iron workers. Perhaps we should note here that the employers maintained the fiction of independence and each signed as an individual the scale with his workmen— neither the union nor association "signed" the scale. THE IRON AGE'S comment on the strike, in view of the above facts, indicates that the lines of the future conflicts would be on a more extended scale and greater unity within the association: "There is one noteworthy feature of this strike, and that is the united front of the manufacturers both in advance and retreat. . . . Heretofore, there have been broken and struggling lines. This time every manufacturer refused to sign, every mill was closed, and remained closed, and when one signed, all were ready."

During the year, the rolling mill owners of Pittsburgh conferred with the rollers in regard to wage reductions, but apparently prosperity made such unnecessary. An agreement existed between the owners and the union on wages. A committee of the Pittsburgh iron manufacturers agreed on a sliding scale for rolling with the bar and nail mill rollers and heaters' union.

The Western Nail Association, in April, 1879, resolved to appeal to their skilled workmen to accept a reduction in wages to conform with the wages paid in Eastern mills for similar work. The Western nail manufacturers contended that they paid from 33⅓ to 50 percent more than Eastern nail manufacturers. The nail manufacturers of Wheeling, in May, notified the nailers that the scale of wages then in effect was not satisfactory and asked for a conference on May 31. We should recall here that the Wheeling scale governed other scales in nail manufacturing throughout the West. On June 1, the Wheeling nail manufacturers gave a 30 days' notice to terminate the agreement between them and the nailers' union in regard to the prices for cutting nails. The modern wire nail had not yet threatened to displace the old-time cut nail, which then required a more skilled and expensive process than the modern wire nail. The agreement between the nail manufacturers and the nailers' union was made in 1873, and provided for a sliding scale. The nailers' threatened to strike when the notice was served, and the manufacturers withdrew the notice. Again, the beginning of "good business days" had its effect upon the association's willingness to avoid a fight; and the nail manufacturers of Wheeling compromised with the nail plate rollers on 55c a ton. A few days later the manufacturers of Wheeling offered the muck rollers 68c a ton until a sliding scale could be decided upon—an advance of 8c a ton—and the rollers accepted.

In October, 1879, a conference committee of iron manufacturers and of nail mill rollers and heaters signed a sliding scale with prices ranging from 4c downward to 2½c, and wages from 97c down to 65c a ton for heating and rolling, with 1/10c change in prices and wage reductions 3c, 2c, and 1½c—3c for each 1/10c between 4c and 3½c, 2c between 3½ and 3-1/10c, and 1½c between 3c to 2½c. Nail plate rolling was 10c less per ton than bar rolling.

Wage reductions in the depression and wage advances in prosperity were general in the iron industry. A few instances are given. The stove manufacturers of Wheeling, West Virginia, Bridgeport, Ohio, and Martin's Ferry, Ohio, reduced wages 10 percent in February, 1879. But the stove manufacturers of Quincy, Illinois, were struck on October 3, 1879, when they refused to advance the wages of the molders 10 percent. The iron mills of Cincinnati were struck when they reduced wages for rolling in March. Likewise, tack manufacturers of Taunton, Massachusetts, reduced wages in May and their workmen struck. These manufacturers had combined to regulate prices as well as to deal with labor matters. In September, the blast furnace owners of the Mahoning Valley were struck for a wage advance of 15%. One furnace owner compromised with his men on a 10 percent advance. However, the stove manufacturers of Albany, New York, refused to grant a 20 percent advance in wages to the molders, and a strike resulted.

Prosperity Fostered Combinations of Associations and Unions. In May-June, 1879, mill owners and weavers in Pennsylvania met in a series of conferences to arrange a uniform scale of prices and to advance wages ½c a yard for weaving. All the large mills agreed to the new schedule, but some small operators declined. The union called strikes on these operators. The associated millowners and the weavers at work joined in supporting the strikers until the small operators surrendered. In September, the carpet manufacturers of Philadelphia combined with the carpet weavers' union in a joint organization "to protect the interests of both employers and employees, and establish a feeling of harmony and cooperation between them regarding the prices for labor, etc."

The open-shop movement, however, remained alive in other fields. The textile manufacturers of Fall River brought in new operatives to break a strike of the spinners. Although business revived in 1879, the employers refused to grant demands for ten percent restoration in wages. Negotiating committees of union and association failed to reach an agreement. The union then proposed arbitration, but the association rejected arbitration and issued a circular that the employers "did not propose to allow outsiders to run their business." After weeks of rebutting association arguments, the spinners struck. The association sent out agents to procure "knobstick" (or nonunion) spinners. Agents were paid expenses and from $3.00 to $12.00 for each strikebreaker obtained, and the strikebreakers were paid from 50 to 60 percent more than the wages received by workers before the strike. The nonunionists were protected against the violence of the strikers. Each strikebreaker was supplied with a revolver to defend himself against the strikers, and barracks were erected in the millyards to house, feed, and entertain the strikebreakers. Unions all over the nation sent in funds to aid the strikers, and meetings were held in a number of cities to create sympathy and build up support for the strikers. The association, however, took further steps to starve the strikers into submission; storekeepers were asked to deny credit to the strikers and landlords put strikers' families out of tenements; and large numbers of strikers were arrested and fined, so that the union treasury was drained more rapidly. Strike benefits were further reduced from the $1.50 a week in grocery orders to unmarried men, and 25c additional for wife and each dependent child. Unions put on a troupe which gave shows in several cities and raised considerable money for the strikers. The manufacturers consistently refused to arbitrate under any conditions. Propaganda by the association finally broke the ranks of the strikers, and a group that had been served freely with liquor returned to work. Others shortly followed, and the union called off the strike. Many of the strikers were "victimized" and could not obtain their old positions or new ones because of blacklists. Likewise, the associated steamship companies defeated a strike of longshoremen in New York City at a cost to the companies of $250,000. The strikers returned to work on the terms laid down by the companies. The broom manufacturers of Chicago defeated a strike of the broom makers for a wage increase. Cigar manufacturers of Chicago were also struck for the same reason with the same results to 1,200 strikers.

In the Glass Industry, prosperity changed the situation from belligerency to negotiation. The strike against the "patent crimper" beginning in 1878, continued into 1879 and lasted almost two years, when the strikers returned to work on the employers' terms. The Pittsburgh lamp-chimney manufacturers, in July, held a conference with the workers and reached an agreement which made some concessions to the workers. Under the terms of the agreement, the crimper was to be used, 300 chimneys were to be a "move," and wages were to be $1.83 a "move." The "opener," to which the union strongly objected was to be used, *if necessary,* to enable the Pittsburgh manufacturers to compete successfully with Eastern manufacturers. The glass manufacturers (11 factories) of Pittsburgh made several propositions to the striking glass pressers, and, as a result, the strike of nine months duration came to an end. The gatherers were to be paid by the hundred instead of the "turn," but the blowers were to be paid on the old basis. The window-glass manufacturers of Pittsburgh refused in September to grant the cutters an advance in wages; in a few days the cutters withdrew their demand. In January, 1880, however, these employers, after a short strike, granted a 10 percent advance in wages to the glass cutters, the layers-in, the layers-out, and the teasers. The glass factories of New Jersey in general were forced by a strike in 1879 to make a 10 percent advance in the wages of the glass workers. However, the hollow-glass manufacturers in Southern New Jersey refused to grant an 8 percent advance in wages, and bound themselves for 12 months and closed down on July 5.

On September 1, 1879, the window-glass manufacturers of Baltimore planned to start up, having offered the glass blowers a 10 percent advance in wages over those paid in 1878, but the blowers refused and demanded a 15 percent advance. The window-glass manufacturers were organized to restrict production and control prices. They formed an Eastern and a Western association, and a national association which included all the window-glass manufacturers of the United States. The National Glass Manufacturers' Association had adopted the practice of restricting production and had an understanding with the union for suspension of production for 60 days in July and August, 1879. The Baltimore glass manufacturers had been acting under that practice and understanding. Undoubtedly such "combinations," "under-standings," and "joint" organizations between the unions and the associations served in many instances to give the unions a reputation for "restricting output," "holding up" the independent employer, and "monopolizing" the trade, but these combinations also helped to strengthen and enrich the large manufacturers, who, in time, became too powerful for the union.

CHAPTER 8

THE FINANCIAL REVOLUTION IN ITS EARLY STAGES

THE LABOR SITUATION *in 1880* contained new developments especially in the field of politics and before the courts, while in the
industrial field strikes against wage reductions were rather general.
The policy of employers and their associations in boom times to
recognize, to appease, and to *combine* with the unions against independent employers and the customer, was a policy that conduced to the growth of unionism. The desire for immediate profits,
as we have seen above, led even a noted "open-shop" leader—
Mr. Gowen—to arrange to combine with the coal miners' union
to increase the price of coal by restricting its production. Mr.
Gowen, however, was still a hero in the eyes of many employers
for, in 1880, it was said that "Mr. Gowen, not merely directed the
campaign of law and order against crime, but he led it in
person . . . For years he has labored with zeal and intelligence
to break up the organized system of crime in the coal regions, and
has relentlessly pursued to the gallows enough of the Molly
Maguires" to break up completely that organization. This praise
of Mr. Gowen again at this time indicated the beginning of a
reaction against the policy of appeasement and in favor of the
more spectacular functioning of "open-shop" associations. In
fact, during the year, the National Labor League was formed in
Pittsburgh, [to quote] "of temperate, frugal, ambitious, and intelligent workingmen" "to put an end to strikes." Such organizations are usually of the fostered, temporary "emergency" type
in the early days of the so called "open-shop" movements; in
later days they were called "company unions." In the political
field, manufacturers in 1880, in a number of instances, intimidated
workmen politically through circulars issued and distributed
among the workmen. Undoubtedly, this activity among employers
is the main reason why the elections of 1880 showed such a
decline in the so-called "labor-vote." It was only a daring laborer
who risked his job by voting against the expressed wishes of

his employer and the employing class; the employers did not limit their activities in governmental matters to politics alone; they appealed frequently to the courts for aid in restraining certain union activities. For instance, an injunction against union picketing was issued in Zanesville, Ohio, in January, 1880, and employers were again informed of the efficacy of this remedy. Other instances of employers appealing to the courts in labor disputes, especially in conspiracy cases, were very frequent in 1880 and 1881. Employers were instructed as to "the law of conspiracy and trade unions"; also as to "the rights of strikers" and "the rights of strikers to entice workmen." It is, of course, fairly clear that the conspiracy cases were brought to court by an independent employer or indirectly by a belligerent employers' association. Among the new developments of 1880, was the establishment of "workmen's relief associations" on railroads, in mines, and in factories. It was frankly admitted that "sometimes the main object is to avoid any liability arising out of accidents."

The Current Discussions of the year still lamented the decline of apprenticeship; apprenticeship schemes were outlined with a view to its restoration. A full recognition of the importance of the foreman in labor disputes was given in an article on "The Model Foreman." Moreover, grounds for agitation were seen in the "store system," that is, paying the workmen in store orders and requiring him to purchase only from the company store at high prices, and accordingly it was condemned. Employers were also informed as to important events in union circles, especially the coal miners' convention at Pittsburgh.

Much written in those "ox-cart days" has been issued as new and original in recent years; a few illustrations follow:

Employment for all must be found by some means. Only through employment can there be wages, and through wages, the buying of food, clothing, and other necessities of life.

"The existence of a million tramps is a standing threat against the stability of our institutions. They are the unorganized militia of incipient rebellion; and the attempt to suppress them by violent measures will fail in the nineteenth century, as well as it did in the sixteenth century. . . . The crisis that we are rapidly approaching is not local."

"It is the policy of the government to protect her citizens from the influence of cheap labor and overwork. For cheap labor means a cheap people, and dear labor a dear people. The foundation of the Republic is equality. The cheap laborer is an irresponsible agent; the dear laborer, an independent citizen."

"Combinations of workingmen for the protection of their labor are recommended alike by reason and experience. There must be organization of workmen, and there must be organization of employers. Instead of being constantly in conflict, there should be—there must be—harmony between these two factors. Employers should combine to pay good wages. They will then have to fix the price of their products, if they are producers, or whatever their position in the social and industrial world may be, in proportion to the wages paid."

"Labor is thoroughly organized and marshalled on the one side, while capital is combined on the other; each powerful to destroy the other if they engage in conflict, but equally powerful to assist each other if they work in harmony. The contending forces are thus in a condition to treat. The great result achieved is that capital is ready to discuss. It is not to be disguised that until labor presented itself in such an attitude as to compel a hearing, capital was not willing to listen, but now it does listen. The results already attained are full of encouragement; the way to a condition of permanent peace appears to have been opened."

"The great curse of industry and the fruitful cause of difficulty is a foolish obstinacy and a false pride. Meeting as equals, and discussing subjects of common interest as sensible men seeking for the facts and inclined to moderation and concession if need be, have had a marvelous effect in removing this pride and obstinacy and bringing about that respect and courtesy that must be the basis of all friendly negotiations between capital and labor. These meetings have also given the men a knowledge of the conditions of trade and its necessities, which they could not get in any other way and, from this knowledge, they have been led to moderation in demand or willingness to concede reductions that otherwise they would not have possessed."

"The theory of the relation of employer and employed has been recast, and their attitude to each other, and of both to the state and society greatly altered. Even the individuals of the class maintain quite different relations to each other, and to the industry as a whole in which they are engaged. Legislative restriction of labor has been abandoned entirely or greatly modified, the laws of conspiracy altered, trades-unions legalized, and the body of labor legislation (beginning with the Statute of Laborers and covering a period of 650 years which has been 'the effort of a dominant body to keep down a lower class which had begun to show inconvenient aspirations') practically removed from the statute-book. The common-law doctrine of non-restraint of trade and the theory of non-interference with the liberty of the subject have been greatly qualified by legislative enactments, such as the factory, truck, and employers' liability acts; *laissez faire* has been degraded from an eternal and inflexible law to a simple rule of conduct that may change with circumstances; competition has been acknowledged to be imperfect; combinations are multiplying; the wage-fund theory has been exploded; and the economic man discharged from his onerous duties, and one with 'sympathies, apathies, and antipathies' employed in his stead."

Discussion of industrial conciliation [collective bargaining] and arbitration became very prominent, and legislatures in 1880 began to enact laws for voluntary arbitration. Iowa, Kansas, Massachusetts, New Jersey, and New York all passed laws on arbitration by 1886, and many labor bureaus were established by states and by the United States in this period. Of the three possible methods then considered, the emphasis then was on *voluntary* adjustment of labor disputes by the organized groups: (1) employers and employees each associated in antagonistic groups fighting it out, (2) cooperating associations of employers and of employees, and (3) government intervention and compulsion. Those in close contact with the disputes knew then that "There may be strikes and lockouts that do not involve an association of either employer or employed, but they are rare. A combination is usually a feature of these labor contests." Moreover, it was recognized that unionism had brought about the decline of cotton mills in New England in the 1880's.

In the Iron Industry, strikes were frequent in 1880, sometimes to force wage advances, sometimes against wage reductions. Under the sliding scale of wages, the decline in the price of iron in the early part of the year caused great reductions in wages of puddlers and other skilled workers but were accepted by the skilled workers without demur. The rolling mills of Pittsburgh were struck by unskilled laborers when the mills reduced the daily wage from $1.50 to $1.25. The strikers lost and returned to work at the reduced rate. In February the Western Iron Association agreed on a sliding scale for knobbing with wage rates varying both with change in prices and with scrap, refined, and pig iron. A more complicated sliding scale was adopted by the joint conference committee of union and iron manufacturers for rolling various gauges of sheet metal. In February, the Pittsburgh iron manufacturers, after a series of conferences with the rollers, practically granted the demands of the rollers' union; for instance, on a 4c basis, the demand was for $11.30 a ton for #24 sheet steel, and $11.00 was granted; for muck rolling, the demand was 92c, and 90⅝c was granted. This scale, however, did not last unchanged through the year. In July and August, the manufacturers held a series of conferences with the muck rollers to revise the scale of wages agreed upon in February. The cause of the demand for a revised scale was the change in the wage schedule for puddling. The revised scale was based upon the puddling scale, and was to be 12½ % of the wage for puddling. In addition, however, the manufacturers agreed to pay the wages of the blooming boys, who were formerly paid by the rollers. The puddling scale at Pittsburgh was revised in June after the usual amount of negotiation. The puddlers demanded an advance of 50c on a 2½c card. The manufacturers offered to sign the old scale with the upper price for iron to go to 5c. In February, the price of iron had gone to 4c, which brought the rate paid for puddling up to $7.25 a ton, so the possibility of 5c iron did not seem remote. However, in April the price fell so that puddling went down to $5.80. Under the prevailing conditions, the manufacturers' offer was quickly rejected by the union. The manufacturers refused to grant the 50c advance and the puddlers struck. A few mills in the district signed the scale with the advance. In a few days the association surrendered and by resolution authorized manufacturers to sign the scale as individuals—

which was the usual procedure. Through its conference committee, the Pittsburgh Iron Manufacturers' Association agreed during the year with the Amalgamated Association of Iron and Steel Workers—the union—on sliding scales for puddling, knobbing, heating, rolling, and muck rolling. Nevertheless, petty strikes, several in number, were called upon the Pittsburgh iron manufacturers after the agreements and scales were signed, and in violation of them. As a result some millowners refused to employ union men any longer. Later this situation developed into an open-shop movement in the manufacture of iron in Pittsburgh.

The blast furnace owners in general resisted demands for advanced wages in the early part of the year, and later tried to make reductions. The blast furnace owners of the Mahoning Valley were struck by the blast furnace workmen for higher wages. The owners in the Connellsville Coke region refused to grant increased wages to the cokers and miners. The owners declared they would close down before they would grant the demands of the workmen. These demands were: for cokers, $1.00 (80c was paid); for miners 40c a wagon (35c was paid). At Zanesville, Ohio, the blast furnace owners, on February 3, advanced wages, for instance, some from $1.50 to $1.75 a day. In May, however, notices of reductions were made by a number of blast furnace owners. Some workmen accepted the reduction, others refused, and the furnaces in those cases were "blown out" and closed down.

Iron manufacturers west of Pittsburgh quite generally made wage advances during the year. In March, representatives of rolling mills of Cincinnati, Ohio, Covington, and Newport, Kentucky. held a two-day conference with representatives of the iron workers and agreed upon a sliding scale based on the selling price of iron. The scale was a compromise and was to remain in effect until June, 1881. This scale was strongly influenced by the Pittsburgh scales, and in turn, governed the scales of other rolling mills in Ohio, Kentucky, Indiana, Illinois, and Missouri. On June 1, however, the associated rolling-mill owners of Cincinnati proposed a new scale, which was rejected by the employees. A strike resulted, but when the Pittsburgh strike ended and the scale was signed, the Cincinnati employers agreed to a scale that gave the employees an advance and all returned to work.

In Chattannoga, the iron manufacturers had attempted to crush the union, but had failed in the use of the "starving-out" method. Accordingly, the association made arrangements with the Pennsylvania Railroad to offer cheap rates to iron workers from points in Pennsylvania to Chattanooga so that such workers might be imported cheaply.

In Wheeling, the muck rollers struck and forced the manufacturers to grant the scale demanded by the union, but the nail mill owners won in a 13-week strike by the nailers' union against an allowance of 18% for self-feeding machines.

While the scales and policies of the Pittsburgh iron manufacturers dominated the Western mills, the scales and policies of Philadelphia dominated those of the East. In the Eastern mills, wage advances took place in the early part of the year, only to be succeeded by reductions before half the year had passed. In February, when business was good, the mills in Philadelphia, Conshohocken, and Norristown, Pennsylvania, advanced wages of boilers $1.00 a ton, which made the price $6.25. But in a few weeks the price of iron declined and a business reaction set in. In March, iron mill owners in the Schuylkill Valley were struck for a 10% advance in wages. Mills in Central Pennsylvania were also struck. The iron mill owners of Harrisburg, in March, refused to advance the wages of puddlers from $5.00 to $6.00 a ton, and the men struck. The proprietors had offered $5.50 as a compromise. Both puddlers and proprietors went into the conflict with a determination to win. Similar demands by the puddlers were made in most of the iron mills of Eastern Pennsylvania and the proprietors similarly offered $5.50 as a compromise. At one time 57 mills were idle and 20 others were scheduled to shut down. However, some puddlers, for instance at Pottstown, accepted the compromise. In a short time the puddlers at Norristown admitted their defeat and within two weeks the puddlers in Central Pennsylvania had returned to work at the $5.50 rate, and the strike was called off. Within a week, the rolling mills of Eastern Pennsylvania gave notices of wage reductions. The Eastern Iron Masters' Association members agreed to reduce, on May 1, the wages of all classes of skilled laborers 10 to 16%. The Association made a comparison showing wages of iron workers were much higher in the United States than in England. All the mills of South Harrisburg posted notices that wages of puddlers would be reduced 50c a ton on June 1. The rolling mills of Central Pennsylvania were likewise notified that their wages would be reduced to $4.50 a ton—a dollar reduction.

Unionism in the iron mills of the East was growing and was more extensive in 1880 than the iron manufacturers would concede. The number of union strikes also indicated the growth of unionism. The manufacturers, under these conditions and the state of business, apparently felt that the earlier a test of strength was made the better.

The iron mill owners of Philadelphia reduced the wages of the boilers from $5.25 to $4.25 a ton and the puddlers struck on May 25. The puddlers intimated they would accept a 75c reduction, then proposed a $4.50 minimum based on a 2½c card. But the owners met and proposed a scale which the puddlers rejected. The proposed scale of the owners had a minimum with iron at 1-9/10c a pound. All six of the mills signed a statement that they would employ no member of the union. The Kensington mills offered the striking puddlers a sliding scale to be accepted by July 23 on penalty of a refusal to employ any of the strikers in the future. After an eight-week strike, a compromise scale was adopted and this scale governed the Eastern mills.

The National Association of Stove Manufacturers was still opposing prison contract labor and was working for a limitation of such labor in any one industry, not to exceed 10%.

The foundries of Pittsburgh apparently experienced during the year more labor trouble than foundries elsewhere. About the first of February, the machinery molders struck for an advance in wages and the stove molders struck for a return to the old "card" rates. In about a week, 23 firms in the machinery manufacturing group granted a wage advance of 15% and signed the scale demanded by the union. The stove molders, however, were not so successful. In March, the foundrymen divided on the demand of the pattern-makers' union for a 15% wage increase, as 16 firms granted the demand while 8 refused and were struck. In April, the machinery manufacturers reduced wages of molders back to the old rate before the advance in February, and the molders struck. In May, the reduction was withdrawn and the molders returned.

The foundrymen of Louisville, Kentucky, and Jeffersonville, Indiana, were struck in August by the molders to force an advance of 25% in wages. At Jeffersonville, the molders were defeated so badly, that their union was broken up. But the union in Troy, New York—scene of most bitter strikes—prepared in August to take a wage reduction.

In contrast to the foundrymen, the master horseshoers of Cincinnati, after a strike of the journeymen horseshoers, granted a wage advance of from $2-$3 a week.

Associations in Coal Mining had more than their usual share of labor disputes in 1880. It is clear that the coal operators lacked at this time concerted action on a nation-wide scale; for in some places operators were advancing wages and granting other concessions while in other places operators were reducing wages. In January, the coal operators of Western Pennsylvania were struck for an advance in wages. The rapid advance in the price of iron had caused the miners to feel that they were not getting their share of the prosperity in the iron industry where the use of coal played so important a part. The miners' union had proposed a scale based on the price of puddling, but this scale involved an increase in wages regarded as excessive by coal operators and outsiders generally. The reaction to this scale caused the union to modify the scale downward although still based on the price of iron. The coal operators published lists of miners' wages to show how high these wages were even at the old rate, which was generally 3½c a bushel, although in some of the river mines only 3c was paid. It is noteworthy that during the strike it was pointed out that the strikers in the mines of Pennsylvania were mostly foreigners. Only a very few operators signed the union scale. The miners in the river mines soon returned to work at the old rate and without a scale. The miners in the railroad

mines, however, withdrew the demands for a scale when the
Railroad Coal Exchange rejected all those proposed. The union
finally demanded 4c a bushel, but the association refused to
grant that and the miners, after being on strike for over five
weeks, returned to work at the old rate.

Strikes in the Pittsburgh district were a part of the regular
procedure of collective bargaining in coal mining. In July, the
operators of the "fourth pool" withdrew a formal proposed reduction in wages because the miners threatened to resist it. The
operators who maintained wages brought pressure on the union
miners' officials to force two other operators to pay the same
rate. By calling strikes on the lower wage operators, the union
officials accomplished the result desired by the other operators.
Elsewhere in mining regions, in October and November, mines
were organized by the union officials who called strikes upon
operators paying below the scale, so as to protect the operators
who had granted wage increases.

In July, coal operators at Pittsburgh were struck and the
strikers called a mass meeting to stop "black-legging" or "scab-
bing."

In August, the miners of Western Pennsylvania broke up
the Board of Arbitration, but in September asked the coal operators for arbitration of issues.

In September, the Railroad Coal Exchange granted an increase
in the price for mining coal of one-half cent in anticipation of
the miners' demands. The Exchange also responded to the
unions' plea for cooperation by stating that it was willing to comply with existing laws relating to scales for weighing coal and
check weighmen, provided the person selected by the miners
was not personally objectionable to the mine owners. It also
fixed the price of coal at 7c—an increase to the miners of one-
half cent.

In October, the coal operators of Elizabeth, Pennsylvania, on
the contrary, proposed to reduce wages from 3½c to 3c, but
the miners resolved to hold out for 3½c. Competition, strikes,
and collective bargaining even then constituted an involved
process.

In July, coal operators of the Hocking Valley and Shawnee

region resolved to shut down and pay off all miners who refused to work for 60c a ton, to put in mining machines, and to distribute the production *pro rata* so that all operators could fulfill their contracts. They prepared to blacklist all strikers, but compromised in August with miners on 70c a ton. In contrast, coal operators of North Lawrence, Stark County, at the same time granted 75c a ton, and accepted union propositions. But coal operators at Coalton, Ohio, brought in new men to beat a strike in September. These were threatened with death by the strikers, and the militia was called out to prevent riots. A few days later, coal operators were struck at Corning, Ohio. Negroes were imported and supplied with arms and ammunition since trouble was expected. The militia was called out to suppress riots. Battles took place and the strikers were driven back. The strike spread through Hocking Valley and more troops were called out. In the meanwhile, coal operators in Salineville, Ohio, won a three-months strike by miners against wage reductions.

The withdrawal in October of all but one company of troops from the Corning region caused Negroes to leave. But the trouble continued; a mine operated by white nonunionists was invaded by strikers, and only the arrival of the sheriff and three companies of troops stopped the expulsion of the new men by the strikers.

Coal operators of Hocking Valley in October were forced by a strike to advance wages 10c a ton—from 70 cents to 80 cents. In December, coal operatives in the Hocking and Sunday Valleys were struck for semi-monthly to supplant monthly payment of wages. All operators in Nelsonville, Haydenville, New Straitsville, Gore, Shawnee, and Rendville were struck. Married men are often given preference in employment for various reasons, one of which is that they are not so quick to strike as unmarried men are. The coal operators of New Straitsville, Ohio, preferred married men mainly for another reason. These employers planned to discharge all unmarried miners because the money paid in wages did not return so rapidly and surely to the treasuries of the employers through the general stores and "check" system as it did when paid to miners with families to support.

The married men, however, struck and forced the operators to abandon the plan.

There was another development about this time in the Schuylkill coal region that was of considerable interest to the coal operators there, namely, the revival of the Workingmen's Benevolent Association which had been crushed in 1875 by the associations under the leadership of Mr. Gowen. The Schuylkill Coal Exchange was still issuing schedules of wages.

The coal operators of the Cumberland region in Maryland were struck in February because only a few operators granted the demand of the miners' union for 65c a ton. However, even at the time of the strike the prospects were that soon all would grant the demand. At this time the coal operators of Shenango Valley paid the miners 70c a ton, and the coal operators in the Mahoning Valley paid 65c. In the Shenango Valley, however, the miners struck, and in March the coal operators compromised on a 10c a ton advance and ended the strike. The coal operators of the Mahoning Valley were invited to meet on March 15 to consider a proposed sliding scale of the miners' union. This scale was based on the price of pig iron in the Pittsburgh market. The coal operators of Houtzdale Region, Pennsylvania, suffered from repeated strikes in the early part of the year—nine times in three months. The first strike was for a check weighman and this demand was no sooner granted than a second strike followed with the demand that the operators pay the wages of the check weighman selected by the union. In turn, the drivers demanded 25c a day advance in wages, the trappers an extra 10c a day, and the miners an additional 10c a day. But the granting of these demands was followed by other demands and other strikes. The drivers now demanded a ten-hour day, and this was granted. The miners then demanded a ten-hour day, which was granted. The miners demanded another increase of 10c a day and struck. But this time the operators began to ask where the end would be. The strike involved 3,000 men. About the same time, however, the coal operators in the Monongahela Valley were considering reducing the price of mining from 3½c to 3c. The coal operators of the Tuscarawas Valley, Ohio, were struck for 90c a ton, the price to be paid for the coal before it was screened.

In other regions, miners met with more resistance and various nonunion methods, although in a few instances the unions' reliance upon sliding scales prevented a breakdown in the collective bargaining. For instance, the miners and manufacturers in the Ironton, Ohio, district signed a sliding scale in which miners' wages were based on the price of nails per keg and of merchant iron. The nail association of Wheeling, West Virginia, showed the miners that a reduction in the price of nails necessitated a reduction in wages. The minutes of the association were shown to a union official at the request of the miners. However, the operators in the coke regions brought in outside laborers. The coke works in the Connellsville region in May reduced wages for mining coal and drawing ovens. Most of the men struck but finally returned to work on the terms offered by the operators. In December, the nail mill operators refused to make an agreement with the coal miners at Wheeling. The miners demanded a schedule with a 2½c minimum, and a 6¼c advance with every 25c advance in the price of a keg of nails. Only one mill conceded the demands, and 4,000 men and boys struck. Coal operators in June, in the Massillon, Ohio, district defeated a strike of miners by importing Negroes from Virginia, and the miners returned to work on the operators' terms. In March, coal operators at Belleville, Illinois were struck for a 4c rate. They granted the demand, but filled most of their contracts from other mines where the rate was 2½c. In May, the coal operators of St. Clair County (which includes Belleville) determined to break the control of the miners' union; the miners received 4c a bushel, worked 8 hours a day, and restricted the output per man to 50 bushels a day. The operators combined and agreed to close all their mines simultaneously and to keep them closed until the miners accepted the operators' terms. The threatened conflict caused the governor of the state to instruct the sheriff of the county to use every means in his power to protect property and preserve peace.

During the year, a strike in Leadville, Colorado, against a wage reduction was won by the mine owners. Some mines were closed; others imported strikebreakers whom the strikers tried to induce to leave. Armed guards at the mines fired upon the intruding strikers. "The Safety Committee of One Hundred" ordered certain union leaders to leave the community, but only three obeyed. The Governor of the State declared martial law.

In the Building Trades the business boom brought about increased activity in building, which incited unions in these trades to demand increased wages or a reduction in the hours of labor. In March, 1880, the contracting builders of Cleveland were forced by a strike of the bricklayers to advance wages 25c a day. In the same months the cut-stone contractors of that city, after a strike, reduced the hours of stone cutters to 53 a week, with no reduction in pay. In Paterson, New Jersey, the master painters, also in March, refused to advance the wages of the painters to $2.75 a day, but a strike lasting only two days caused the employers to make the advance demanded. As March in the Northern states is the beginning of the building season, March to May is the strategic time when business is good for the union to make demands and obtain concessions. In May, Chicago contractors, after a strike granted the bricklayers a 25 percent increase in wages. The contractors of Newark, New Jersey, in July, 1880, were struck by the bricklayers and masons for an increase in wages, but apparently it was too late in the season and in a slight business depression.

In Glass Manufacturing Wage Advances were generally granted by the employers in 1880. In May, the flint and lime glass manufacturers of the United States met in Philadelphia for the purpose of discussing the labor-relations problem, "in the hope that an understanding can be arrived at which will make strikes less formidable." In June, the flint manufacturers met and appointed a committee to bring about a general stoppage for one month out of July, August, and September. The green-bottle manufacturers shut down during the hot months, as their workmen refused to work then, even for extra wages. The window-glass manufacturers customarily shut down during the hot months. The Glass Manufacturers Association, east of the Alleghenies decided to close down directly during the hot months, if arrangements could be made with the workmen to that end. However, dissatisfaction of the workmen caused a general closing in May, and the glass blowers of New Jersey did not return to work until September 19. The factories of New Jersey, in general, had been forced by strikes to advance wages 10% in 1880, and to pay wages in cash instead of in "truck" or store orders. The glass manufacturers of Schetterville, Glasstown, and Millville, New Jersey, had been struck by the boys employed there for a 10% rise of wages, which was granted in January of the year. The glass manufacturers of New York granted their glass blowers a 15% advance of wages in April before the difficulty could be adjusted. In the glass factories of Williamstown, New Jersey, however, the employers took steps which caused the union men employed there, who had gone to Trenton to lobby for the passage of an "anti-truck law," to seek work elsewhere. As a result the local union collapsed.

The Western Window Glass Manufacturers' Association met in Pittsburgh in August and acceded to the demands of the window-glass blowers for an advance of 10% in wages. The Window Glass Manufacturers' Association of Pittsburgh, however, decided not to grant demands for increased wages until trade was better. The layers-in and the layers-out of Pittsburgh struck for a 10% advance but the association defeated the strike. The window-glass manufacturers had granted the packers a 10% advance in wages in February in accord with the previous advances to other glass workers.

Association Activities Increased in Range, rising from 1880 to the climax in 1886. For instance, master barbers of New York City combined with journeymen to put the 5c shop out of existence—such collusions against the public and the low-price competitor were a usual form of collective bargaining. On the other hand, the Axe Manufacturers' Association blacklisted the leader of a strike of the axe-makers' union in Cleveland. He was barred from working at his trade in 62 factories, and found work only as a common laborer until a nonassociation factory in Saginaw, Michigan, gave him a job. This factory, however, was "induced" to join the association and blacklist him. The union was broken up by the strike. In June, the master bakers of New York City were struck by the bakers' union and forced to come to a union meeting to sign collective agreements providing for a maximum 12-hour day except on Saturday when the maximum was 15, the right of the workmen to board where they

pleased, and the men to be employed through the union labor
bureau instead of through saloons. Master bakers in Chicago,
New Orleans, St. Louis, Newark, and other cities, as a result,
had to deal with bakers' unions, but they collapsed during the
year under indirect assault. Shoe factories in Chicago, with one
exception, defeated a strike of the shoemakers' union for a wage
advance, but other factories were struck to force the discharge
of green hands. In February, the employing tanners of Cincinnati
met and agreed not to grant demands of the tanners and curriers'
union for a wage advance. Although 200 workmen struck, in
three weeks they returned on the employers' terms. In August,
the horse-collar manufacturers of Cincinnati likewise defeated a
four-weeks strike of their workmen for a wage advance. But the
harness manufacturers of New Jersey were forced by a four
weeks' strike of their workmen to advance wages 10%. The
Carriage Builders' National Association through subscriptions
raised over $8,000 to found an industrial school in connection
with the Metropolitan Museum of Art of New York City. Lec-
tures were given and studies made relating to carriage building
two or three hours on three nights of the week. Tuition was
nominal.

In April, the Manufacturers' Board of Trade of Fall River,
Massachusetts, after a strike by spinners on 10 out of the 53
mills of the city granted an increase of 10% in wages. With the
exception of Lynn, Massachusetts, New England mills gave the
increase to unionists and nonunionists alike. Only a few manufacturers granted the union's demand for weekly payment of wages
at this time, but granted it in September when the price of cloth
fell heavily and wages were reduced 10%. Although committees
of the union and of the association did not reach an agreement,
the union after much discussion voted not to strike. The textile
manufacturers of Lynn, Massachusetts, failed early in the year
to convince the spinners that business conditions did not warrant
a wage increase and, refusing arbitration, were struck. Spinners
were brought in. The strikers attempted by peaceful persuasion,
then by intimidation and assault to keep the imported strikebreakers from working. Strikers were required to vacate company
houses. By October, the strikers admitted defeat and sought work

as individuals. Likewise, the mills of Cohoes, New York, broke a strike, disrupted the union, and blacklisted the active unionists.

In February, 18 cigar manufacturers of Cincinnati organized an association which required all their employees to renounce the union and sign a pledge not to join it. This was the reaction to a strike called on one manufacturer to force him to discharge some nonunion workmen. During the strike which followed, the association refused to deal with the union, even to receive its letters. After 6 weeks the association withdrew the obnoxious pledge and the manufacturers were permitted to employ anyone they pleased, union or nonunion. In Chicago, however, the cigar manufacturers granted 1,300 striking cigar makers part of the wage increase demanded.

In January, the barrel manufacturers of Cleveland won a 10-day strike by employees over a reduction of piece prices by about 15%. But, in August, the barrel manufacturers of Cincinnati were forced by a strike to advance the wages of coopers 15%. In July, the sawmills of Jacksonville, Florida, obtained special policemen to guard strikebreakers. In two battles beween these policemen and the strikers, two policemen and three strikers were wounded and a number of strikers were badly clubbed. Among other manufacturers struck were Chicago shoe manufacturers, Paterson, New Jersey ribbon mills, and New York City piano manufacturers.

The Year 1881 witnessed increased unionization, strikes, and resentment by employers against aggressive union tactics— all rising to the climax of 1886. The greatest activity was in coal mining and the iron industry.

Coal Mining Experienced Strikes, Conspiracy Trials, and Legislation. Basing wages on the retail price of coal caused trouble for the mine operators. Pittsburgh miners threatened to strike for 5c a bushel, because retail coal dealers had advanced the retail price of coal 57-1/7%, while the miners' wages advance was only 33⅓%—an advance from mining of 1c before October 14, 1880, to September 16, 1881, and of the retail price of 4c per bushel. They demanded that the retail price be reduced to 9c instead of 11c. The dealers cut the price to 10c.

D. K. Jones (General Secretary for the miners of Western

Pennsylvania) and Hugh Anderson (a pit boss of a mine in
Allegheny County) were convicted of conspiracy for inflammatory
utterances at a meeting of coal mine strikers to induce them to
remain out. They were tried under the conspiracy law of Pennsylvania. Each was fined $100.00 and costs and imprisonment
of 24 days in the county jail—a total of $400.00 in fines and
costs. Many coal operators were present in the courtroom, and
great interest was felt in the case. Appeal was made to the Supreme Court, but the lower court was sustained by the Supreme
Court.

Strikes were called for various reasons. Coal operators in the
Lower Monongahela coal region were struck because they refused to employ check weighmen. Coal operators in Westmoreland County, Pennsylvania, were struck by miners for an advance
in wages of 10c a ton. The coal and coke operators of Fayette
and Westmoreland Counties defeated the four weeks' strike of the
miners and coke drawers. But coal operators at Paint Creek, West
Virginia, were struck to force the discharge of three Negro
miners. The houses of the Negroes were shot into, the Negroes
returned the fire and drove away the strikers. Coal operators of
Belleville, Illinois, mining district were struck although some
operators had secured pledges from the miners to work for 3c
for a certain time; these men refused to strike. The strikers
threatened to drive away the men at work with drawn revolvers,
but the sheriff arrived in time to prevent a conflict. The miners
asked that a committee of businessmen of Belleville be appointed
to settle differences by arbitration. The coal operators on the
railroads in the neighborhood of Pittsburgh—the Railroad Coal
Exchange—gave notice to their men of a reduction from 3½c
per bushel for mining to 3c, effective May 2, 1881. The coal
operators defeated a strike in Hocking Valley in June; strikers
returned to work at 70c per ton, but Nelsonville miners remained
out for 80c. Later they gave in and the miners at New Straitsville
and Haydenville also returned at 70c. In September, however,
coal operators in Hocking Valley granted the miners' demands
for an advance from 70c to 80c a ton and a general strike was
avoided. Before the strike, Hocking Valley miners received 70c

a ton, Tuscarawas miners, 85c; Mahoning Valley miners 65c; and Pittsburgh miners 91c a ton. The coal operators of the Hocking Valley met and requested the miners to call a convention where the operators might meet them and discuss terms of a contract for a year. Such a conference was held and terms agreed upon, but the miners referred the matter back to the union, and delegates were chosen for a second conference. In making demands for further concessions, the miners cast some doubts upon the contract, although the union claimed the contract was made upon the terms previously agreed upon. Coal operators (railroad mines) of Western Pennsylvania conceded demands of miners for an advance in mining from 3c to 4c—there had been no general strike among coal miners in Western Pennsylvania for 2½ years. Coal operators of Tuscarawas Valley decided to grant an increase demanded by striking miners (from 85c to 90c) and the men returned at once. Operators and blast furnaces in Connellsville region were struck twice in the year because they would not concede wages of 1c a bushel to the miners, instead of 30c a wagon of 33½ bushels. Coke drawers were asking 80c instead of 70c per oven for drawing coke. The strikes failed.

The coal and coke employers in Western Pennsylvania fought the store-order law. Although the act went into effect on the 1st day of September, 1881, no change was made in the mode of paying the workmen; the employers awaited prosecution for violating the act. Then a test case was made; they claimed to have found a flaw in the act. The employers thus hoped to render it inoperative.

Wage strikes were widespread. Coal operators reduced wages of miners at Corning and Rendville, Ohio—the reduction was from 80c to 70c a ton. Over 300 white miners struck, but 300 Negroes remained at work. Coal operators of MacAllister, Indiana Territory, were struck by miners (300 to 400) for a wage advance, and attempted to get men from West Virginia. Coal operators of Starkville and Las Animas, Colorado, were struck by miners for an advance of 15c a ton.

Mine owners in Marquette region were struck for a Saturday half-holiday for day shift, and Saturday night holiday for night shift, with full pay for a ten-hour day. The strike lasted only a day or so and was defeated. The miners at Jackson City, Michigan, were out on strike for seven weeks.

In the Iron Industry, the Cincinnati strike was the most notable of the year. In June, 1881, the iron manufacturers of Cincinnati, Covington, and Newsport, refused to sign a new scale of wages demanded by the iron workers, and the employees struck. The advances demanded ranged from 10 to 36 percent. The manufacturers offered to pay the old wages, which were 5% above Pittsburgh rates. The manufacturers met a second time and determined not to concede the wage advance; they resolved upon a proposal for separate conferences between employers and employees. A general conference committee of the union met a committee of the manufacturers but reached no decision. A second conference was held, at which employees offered to accept 10% above the Pittsburgh scale, but the manufacturers rejected it. The union prepared a new scale of prices which the manufacturers considered and rejected. The employers imported nonunion men from the East, but the strikers induced these to quit. More nonunion men were advertised for with similar results. One small mill granted union demands and another mill operated with seceding unionists and imported nonunionists. On August 9, proprietors from cities in the Mississippi Valley met and resolved to pay no more than the Pittsburgh scale, and to employ only nonunionists. On October 23, another conference between manufacturers and unionists was held. Conferences were continued until finally an agreement was reached; both sides made concessions. The struggle had lasted five months. The employees agreed to return to work at the old scale of prices, but after June 1, 1882, Pittsburgh scale of prices were to prevail. Pittsburgh manufacturers were charged with having incited the strike to ruin Cincinnati mills. With Pittsburgh wage scales, Cincinnati competed more advantageously with Pittsburgh, but workmen were dissatisfied.

Other employers in the iron industry had labor troubles. Boiler manufacturers at Pittsburgh were struck by boilermakers for an advance of 25% in wages and overtime rates. Some manufacturers granted the demands. Iron manufacturers of Pittsburgh, through a conference committee, met a committee of workmen to discuss scales of wages. Individual arrangements had hitherto prevailed. After four conferences, agreement was reached and scales adopted with practically no change. Compared with the scales of 1865, the ranges were: with iron at 2½c a pound, price for boiling per ton was $4.00 in 1865; $5.50 in 1881; at 8½c in 1865, $9.00 per ton, against 5c in 1881 and $9.30 per ton. In September, the demands of the workers for a payday every two weeks was granted. Iron manufacturers at Portsmouth defeated a strike of puddlers for advance of 50c. Mills of southern Ohio, Indiana, Illinois, Northern Kentucky, and Missouri, were struck by puddlers for a $6.00 basis; $5.50 was the current rate. Iron manufacturers at Atlanta, Georgia; Knoxville, Tennessee; the one mill at Zanesville, Ohio; Scottdale, and McKeesport, Pennsylvania; and Wellsville, Ohio, were running independently of the union, although all were technically "struck." Iron mills struck in 1881 by iron workers included mills at Oxford, New Jersey; Catasauqua, Ferndale, Scottdale, and McKeesport, Pennsylvania; Wellsville, Zanesville, Portsmouth and Cincinnati, Ohio; Newport and Covington, Kentucky; Aurora, Indiana; Wyandotte, Michigan; St. Louis, Missouri; Knoxville, Tennessee; and Atlanta, Georgia —Mills at Ferndale, McKeesport, Wellsville, Zanesville, Knoxville, Atlanta, St. Louis, and one mill at Portsmouth continued to run in spite of the strike.

Although there were said to have been 46 different sliding scales in effect in 1881 with various branches of labor among the members of the iron workers' union, iron manufacturers reached agreements with the union with difficulty often after long strikes. For instance, conference committees after lengthy strikes agreed upon sliding scales at each: Wheeling, Cincinnati, and Philadelphia. Iron mills of Berks and Montgomery Counties had trouble with iron workers over an advance in wages. Iron manufacturers at Harrisburg, Pennsylvania, were notified by puddlers of a demand for advance. Iron manufacturers of Savannah, Georgia, imported about 150 men to break a strike there. The strikers met the train to drive the new men away. Chain manufacturers of St. Louis were struck to enforce the discharge of nonunion chainmakers. Increased use was being made of Negro workers in iron manufacturing and mining especially in strikebreaking. Nail manufacturers of Wheeling were struck by feeders for an advance in wages from 2/5 to 1/2 of what the nailers received. The manufacturers were putting in self feeders and were aided in it by the nailers. They were forced also to advance the price of mining in their mines to accord with the advance in price of nails per keg. Even tin manufacturers of Pittsburgh were struck over wage advances ranging from 12 to 50 percent and compromised. Employers of machinists and blacksmiths in Pittsburgh had demands made for 25 percent advance in wages. Some master tinners met in conference with tinners and others, and agreed to give the advance demanded, but a majority of employers were not represented.

Foundrymen were forced by strikers to advance wages. Stove manufacturers in St. Louis, Cincinnati, and Pittsburgh, in February and March, granted demands of stove molders for a wage advance; 10% in Pittsburgh, and 15% in the other cities. Stove molders in Troy, Wheeling, and New Albany, made similar demands; in New Albany for a 25% advance, but were offered only 15% advance. Machinery molders in Cincinnati struck for a 25% advance, while those in Pittsburgh demanded and obtained only 10% advance. In April, foundries in Erie, Pennsylvania, granted their striking molders an advance but foundrymen in Paterson, New Jersey, defeated a one-week strike for a 15% advance. Advances were demanded by striking machinery molders in Chicago (25%), Cleveland (15%), and elsewhere and were generally granted. In August, stove manufacturers in the Schuylkill Valley were struck by stove molders for 10% advance in wages (Reading, Royer's Ford, Spring City, and Middleton). One concern in Reading compromised by offering molders 5% increase then and remainder later; another gave the 5% advance without qualification. Foundry proprietors of Louisville, Kentucky, were struck by molders in October for 15% advance in wages. All owners refused to grant it, but during the strike four firms granted the demands, while three refused.

In the Building Industry, wage advances through strikes were frequent. In March the contractors of Newark were forced by a strike of the masons to advance wages, and in April by a second strike to $3.00 a day. Contractors in New York City were struck in September for an advance of 50c a day and granted it. In Philadelphia in October all large employing stone cutters were struck by 240 stone cutters and workers for a reduction of hours from 10 to 9. In May, the Master Bricklayers of Philadelphia met and resolved not to employ any bricklayer who had left his former employer for higher wages, and to discharge any employee when that fact was made known. The bricklayers' union conferred with the masters and induced them to withdraw the notice. In October, the Mason Builders' Association of New York City met and decided to reduce the wages of bricklayers from $4 to $3.50 a day, and 1,000 bricklayers struck. In December, building contractors of Wheeling, West Virginia, were struck by bricklayers and hodcarriers over the employment of nonunion men. In June, the master sheet-metal workers of Philadelphia were compelled by a one-day strike to increase wages of tin roofers from $1.75 and $2.00 a day to $2.50 a day. The granite manufacturers of Newark, New Jersey, were forced by a strike of the granite cutters to advance wages 50c a day. Again in March, 1882, the granite manufacturers were struck and compromised with the granite cutters for 25c advance in wages per day in lieu of 50c advance demanded.

In the Glass Industry, the struggle had an international aspect. The manufacturers had made concessions which seemed reasonable, but fought against disadvantageous terms. The glass-bottle manufacturers met in Chicago in January, 1881, and decided that the expense of grinding fruit jars, formerly borne by the men, should be paid by the manufacturer. Window-glass manufacturers met in Chicago in convention in January and resolved on a stoppage for 3 months (June 1 to August 31), although any manufacturer who reduced wages of skilled labor 20% might run until July 1, but no resumption of work was to be made until all whose wages had previously been advanced had been cut 20%. Pittsburgh manufacturers on May 24 endorsed this action but the union resisted. Factories were shut down on June 1.

Window-glass manufacturers and workmen of Pittsburgh conferred in August over a sliding scale for the ensuing year based on the selling price of glass. The scale signed gave an advance of ten percent. In September, glass factories of Pittsburgh were struck by bottle and chimney, or finishing, boys. The strike spread to the carrying-in and the mold boys in pressed glass factories who demanded 5c (on 35c) per turn. All returned at the manufacturers' prices. In October, both the bottle- and window-glass manufacturers of Pittsburgh were struck by their "fillers-in" and "teasers" for a 15 percent advance, but after a conference compromised on $1.00 a week advance. Glass manufacturers of Pittsburgh were at a disadvantage in competition with those of Bellaire and Wheeling where lower wages were paid to the workers. A largely attended meeting was held in Pittsburgh to consider an effort to make the wages of glass workers of Bellaire and Wheeling uniform. Nothing definite was done, but a later meeting was scheduled.

Glass manufacturers felt themselves compelled to deal with the glass blowers' union which had an almost complete monopoly of the skilled craftsmen, even organizing the workers in Europe (to prevent them from being brought to America as strikebreakers as they had been on occasions). The association was generally forced to accept the union's price lists of wages, although there were strikes over a number of issues. One nonassociationist was successful in cutting piece prices by importing German glass blowers.

In the Printing Industry, an anti-union trend was evident. In May, the newspaper proprietors of Pittsburgh granted, under protest, the demands of the printers for an increase of 5c a thousand ems. One of the newspapers imported men from Cincinnati and the workmen struck before the imported men arrived. One of the strikers assaulted a nonunion man and was killed. This caused the newspaper to discharge the Cincinnati men and reinstate the strikers. On May 30, 1882, the newspaper proprietors acceded to a new scale of wages submitted by the printers. The conflict between the employing job printers of Philadelphia and union compositors inaugurated in 1881 by the latter organizing a strike for increased wages grew in bitterness. A movement was started among the employers for forming an organization to oppose the demands of the journeymen. The employers pledged themselves to employ none but nonunion compositors in their respective establishments. None of the firms suspended worked on account of the strike. A conspiracy case grew out of the strike. The managers of THE PHILADELPHIA PRESS, anticipating a strike of the compositors, brought in new men from New York and discharged 40 compositors who denied they were going to strike. The employers had recently organized to eradicate unionism.

Strikes were mainly against individual employers, but instances were frequent of strikes against groups of employers. In May, the master horseshoers of Philadelphia were forced by a strike to grant a wage advance to their workmen. In July, the lumber mills of Eau Claire refused to reduce the hours of labor daily from 12 to 10, following an increase in wages, so the workmen struck. Nonunion men were imported. The strikers resorted to intimidation and violence. The militia was sent in and the union lost the strike.

Strategic moves by employers during the period included among others the following: Manufacturers appointed presidents of unions as foremen and managers to weaken union loyalty and to obtain leaders for supervisors. Trade schools were being established to supply skilled workmen as well as designers.

Associations usually defeated the unions in other fields, but made concessions in certain instances. In January, one hundred weavers of Suncook, New Hampshire, struck against a reduction of wages. The strike lasted two weeks and failed. The employers reduced the wages of men from $1.50 to $1.00 and women from $1.35 to 90c for eleven hours' work. In June, the carpet manufacturers of Philadelphia met with the weavers' union to negotiate a new agreement for the coming six months. The weavers asked for an advance of 1c a yard for weaving, but the manufacturers were unanimously against it, and won in the second conference. In Danbury, the hat manufacturers were in a conflict with the hatters' union over its restriction on the number of apprentices. The largest manufacturer obtained men from other places by the hundreds to learn the trade. The strikers gave up their union cards after about a four-week strike. Workmen earned from $3.00 to $10.00 a day when the trade was active. In Jan-

uary, the hat manufacturers of Orange, New Jersey, compromised
with the striking hatters on a demand for 10% increase in wages.

Cigar manufacturers of Paterson, in August, were struck by
cigar makers for a wage advance and were forced to grant it,
and in May, 1883, were again forced to advance wages ($1.00 per
thousand cigars) and to limit the number of apprentices. The
cigar manufacturers of Pittsburgh, however, divided when confronted in October, 1881, with demands for an increase in the
price for making cigars; some granted the increase, others were
threatened with strikes. The five leading cigar manufacturers of
Milwaukee combined against the cigar makers' union which had
demanded and secured an increase in wages from all cigar manufacturers. But the new association had prepared and posted in
the shops a new set of rules which abolished or abridged certain
custom-honored privileges of the workmen. A strike was called.
The association pledged each individual member not to yield
to the union's demands. One manufacturer, employing many
workmen, broke away from the association, but the others imported nonunion labor and defeated the union which called off
the strike as a failure.

Among the other group contests, these are worth noting:
The South Side tableware manufacturers of Pittsburgh voluntarily advanced the wages of their employees 10 percent. New
Jersey brewers were struck by the brewery workers for a reduc-
in hours of labor per day and double pay for Sunday work. The
strike failed. Livery stable proprietors of New York were threatened with a strike of 400 coachmen for an advance from $10.00
to $14.00 a week. About 19,000 cotton handlers struck in New
Orleans. A number of draymen worked under protection of
mounted police, but little headway was made by the imported
workers who did not understand their duties and returned home.
After a 13-day strike, the issue was compromised; the employers'
association agreed to make no discrimination against union men,
but the employer was to have the right to hire and fire whom he
pleased. The wages agreed upon were: draymen $3.00 a day;
longshoremen 40c an hour, 60c for night work, and 80c for
Sunday. A general strike at Galveston, Texas, on September 2,

involved longshoremen, car drivers, oil mill laborers, cotton pickers, and others, but only the longshoremen won their demands. The master bakers of Newark, New Jersey, were struck by the bakers for a reduction of working hours to 12 a day and were forced to concede it.

CHAPTER 9

COLLECTIVE BARGAINING INTENSIFIED THE CONFLICT

UNIONISTS DISREGARDED RECESSION *of 1882*. In 1882, the labor question was foremost in the minds of many employers, especially members of the National Association of Stove Manufacturers, because of the demands of the molders' union. The many labor troubles were an indication of lessening business activities to which union officials gave scant consideration in their demands. Weak unions crumbled under these conditions. Strikes were called by unionists against nonunionists in efforts to control the fewer jobs. For instance, union feeders struck against nonunion nailers in nail mills. A contemporary states that never before had there been so many or so important strikes, actual or threatened; not even in the great strike period of 1877 were the forces and issues so involved or great. The situation led to an investigation by the Committee of Education and Labor of the Senate of the United States.

Some strikes were caused by demands of unions for wage advances, some because employers tried to reduce wages to accord with falling prices and slackening industrial activity. Employers were becoming increasingly belligerent toward unions which would not accept reductions when prices were falling; manufacturers during booms often broke away from their associations when prices were rising, made liberal concessions to unionists, and grabbed at the possible increased profits. But rapidly diminishing prices or profits caused concerted resistance to any union demand. Union officials generally acted quickly on rising prices and increasing profits, and usually obtained wage advances for their followers, but their policy to fight wage reductions even under adverse business conditions often caused association belligerency.

This belligerency expressed itself also in legislation and propaganda. For instance, unions then sought anti-Chinese immigration laws to keep out cheap Chinese workmen and attacked the Chinese Six Companies for fostering immigration, but exporting merchants of New York City (especially those sending goods to China) united in opposing such legislation. The Chinese Six Companies were made up of merchants (Chinese); the merchants chose the officers and committees from among themeslves, but they levied dues of $10 to $15 not only on themselves but on every imported Chinese workman. The Companies were associations to promote the interests of the Chinese immigrants especially in obtaining employment. The immigration increased the trade between China and the United States to the profit of the merchants.

A conflict was conducted over anti-conspiracy laws, which the unions wanted abolished. The "Hearings" of the Senate Committee (see above) contain much testimony on the issue, with charges by unionists of the unfairness of such laws, and challenges by associations for instances and proof. Undoubtedly, the combination movement was growing rapidly, heading toward a high peak in organization. Conspiracy charges, accordingly, were varied: (1) unions were in a conspiracy against youth to keep young men from learning skilled trades through apprenticeship or trade schools; (2) manufacturers were conspiring criminally with each other and with the unions against consumers and independent employers, much like unions were conspiring against employers.

In the Iron Industry, collective bargaining with its concomitant strikes was still conducted. Pittsburgh iron manufacturers held a series of conferences during April and May with the union committee over new wage scales with advances demanded by the union; for instance, puddlers demanded $6.00 instead of $5.50 on a 2½c card. The firmness of the manufacturers not to grant advances finally caused the unions to withdraw practically all demands except those of the puddlers and scalpers, but these were not granted. Likewise, the Wheeling iron manufacturers faced a demand by the nail plate rollers for a rate uniform with Pittsburgh (from 63c to 70c). The nailers also asked for changes in the scale, for example, on lengths and weights. Conferences were held, but action was deferred until the Pittsburgh scale was settled. The blast furnaces of Wheeling also were

affected by a demand by the fillers for an advance from $1.75 to
$1.90 a day. The iron manufacturers of Wheeling and of Youngs-
town, following the refusal of the Pittsburgh manufacturers, refused to sign scales for wage advances or changes in the methods
of doing work.

Under these conditions, the manufacturers of iron in the
West organized formally and permanently. Previously, they had
united temporarily, but lacked "cohesion or plan, each member
afraid of the other." The organization was completed at Pittsburgh, June 7, 1882, to deal with the labor question only, and
not to conflict with the Western Iron Association in dealing with
prices. The association had district branches to meet their specific problems. It was believed then that with two strong organizations justice would be oftener done than with one weak one,
and the other side well organized, but all attempts to make a
national scale failed.

A widespread strike resulted in May—125 mills, 2,415 furnaces, and 45,752 men were involved. The strike spread over
the Pittsburgh district, the Shenango Valley, the Wheeling district, the Mahoning Valley, the Lake region, the interior of Ohio,
the Ohio River mills below Wheeling, the Cincinnati district, the
St. Louis district, the Chicago district, and the Detroit district.
Of these, 6 mills signed the scale, but 103 mills remained idle,
and 16 operated partly. Of the 16, some of these were in Cincinnati where striking puddlers were ordered by union officials
to go back to work, because they had a special contract to work
until the Pittsburgh scale was agreed upon, and to accept that.
Union officials approached manufacturers individually with in-
ducements; although two more mills signed the scale, the manufacturers of the West were united as never before. In July, they
held a very large meeting and reaffirmed unanimously their resolution not to make any advance in wages. In August, manufacturers individually began to offer to resume operations if the
workmen would accept the old scale, otherwise nonunionists
would be employed. By the end of the month, mills were opening on a nonunion basis. Nonunion contracts were used and
publicised among the employers. Undoubtedly, demands by
"oath-bound" unionists regarded as exorbitant by employers

generally, were responsible to a great degree for the development of the so-called iron-clad or "yellow-dog contract."

Union strikers were blacklisted by iron manufacturers not struck; these nonunion concerns did not desire the agitation which might result. Union officials were discharged by certain concerns, including Mr. Gowen's railroad, in order to help break down the union. Foreign strikebreakers were imported by some iron manufacturers. Circulars were issued on wages and the control of business, showing the unreasonableness of the unions demands. One article attacked trade unions as failures. The National Tube Works brought a conspiracy suit against union officials; and it remained nonunion after the strike.

It was believed then also that the strike would remove the main causes for the strike—falling prices for finished products and the high price for raw materials—and that the mills would gain from higher prices for their products and lower prices for their raw materials. The prospect for temporary profits was a temptation to some of the mills to break from the association and sign the union scale, and union officials pointed out the inducement. However, lack of demand for iron caused its price to remain low.

In September, the unions called off the strike and accepted the association terms, and attributed the failure of the strike to lack of funds. In Cincinnati, however, the union struck for four days against the Pittsburgh price, but at a conference with the local association drew up an agreement governing wages and shop rules.

The falling price of iron caused rejection of the scale in certain localities, and notices of wage reduction were issued quite generally in November and December. Bessemer steel rail manufacturers gave notice of a 20% reduction in wages, the union refused to accept but offered to take a 12½% reduction. A further fall in the price of rails led to the manufacturers changing the 20% to 33% which the union was forced to accept after losing a four-month strike.

More specifically, some of the activities of the associations, with union counter-activities, and interesting variations, were: In Cincinnati, a joint association and union committee visited

Pittsburgh to learn first hand what the wage scales and conditions were in the rolling mills there. Although a settlement was reached between the union and association, the helpers struck for Pittsburgh prices, but the puddlers who paid the helpers refused to grant those and the strike resulted; actually one union struck against another. In the Chicago district there were conflicting tendencies. In June, 1882, iron and steel manufacturers in the vicinity of Chicago were struck by some of their workmen for higher wages. Nonunion men were brought in and boarded within the mills which were fenced in to protect these and the nonunionists. The nonunionists, however, proved to be so incompetent that the manufacturers conceded the demands of the strikers. The Calumet Iron and Steel Company at Irondale, near Chicago, granted, in August, an advance of 10 percent demanded and agreed with the unions to accept the Pittsburgh scale when made. In Chicago, however, the association and union committees met but disagreed on the amount of wage reduction—the union proposed 12½%, the association 20%. At another conference held in October, 20% reduction was finally agreed upon, but the duration of the reduction—5 months or a year—was left undecided. Another conference was held in December.

Among the interesting variations in the strikes in the iron and steel industry in 1882 were the following series: The Homestead strike in March grew out of an anti-union move by one company, but it "resulted in bringing out the Amalgamated Iron Association [the union] on one side and the iron manufacturers on the other." It was finally settled by having union men work on one shift. Twelve representatives of the Western rolling mills —of St. Louis, East St. Louis, Belleville, and other cities in that vicinity—met in St. Louis, May 25, as a continuation of one held earlier to determine a schedule of wages for the coming year. The manufacturers resolved not to grant any advance in wages. Although union and association had agreed to be governed by the Cincinnati scale, the workers struck in June but resumed after six weeks under the Cincinnati scale. In December, the puddlers struck again for $6.00—50c above the Pittsburgh prices—and in violation of the Cincinnati agreement. In June, the

Cleveland rolling mills were struck, they hired nonunion men, and many strikers returned as individuals on the employers' terms. One mill failed during the strike. All the rolling mills of Youngstown, Ohio, were represented by their proprietors at a meeting held July 26, when they resolved unanimously to maintain firmly the stand they took at the beginning of the strike and not sign the proposed union scale. One of the largest mills offered the men to resume at the old scale, otherwise they would start with nonunion men, which they did. The proprietors of the blast furnaces in nearby New Castle, Pennsylvania, notified the men of a reduction of 25% in August if the furnaces were not to be shut down. The men accepted the reduction. There were strikes at Steubenville, Ohio, in June, and later in Wheeling, West Virginia. The latter strike was still on in September, but in October work was resumed at a scale with a few advances over the old scale arrived at after a number of conferences. In May, the steam boiler manufacturers of Cincinnati refused to grant a wage advance of 15% and declined to arbitrate the issue. The boilermakers struck. Finally, the manufacturers offered to compromise on 10% and the strikers accepted. In November, the iron and nail manufacturers of Greencastle and Terra Haute, Indiana, were struck by the puddlers who desired to maintain a 50c a ton differential above Pittsburgh prices. The manufacturers insisted on Pittsburgh prices, since they were working under an agreement similar to the Cincinnati one. It is clear from the above instances, that "pattern bargaining" is not new in the iron and steel industry, and that Pittsburgh then "dominated the scene."

In Eastern Pennsylvania, there were two conflicting trends. In May, the iron manufacturers of Philadelphia reduced the card rates for bar iron from 2.8 to 2.6, thus causing a reduction of wages of iron workers on the scale. The rolling mill manufacturers of Philadelphia met November 20, and reduced the price of iron to 2½c, a reduction of 2/10, which on the scale lowered wages somewhat. On November 22, the steel mills gave notice of a 10% reduction of wages on December 1, and no trouble was expected or later reported. In contrast, blacklisting of puddlers by iron manufacturers occurred at nearby Norristown and Pottstown. Puddlers who had struck the Phoenix Iron Company applied for work at mills in Norristown and Pottstown, but were refused employment, although men were needed at both places. The mills had issued orders that no one involved in the above strike should be employed. "A number of the leading officers of the Iron Workers' Union had been discharged, not only by the Iron Company, but by the Philadelphia and Reading Company, in order to break up the union. The strikers are being refused work at various other mills in the Schuylkill Valley." Foreigners were imported to break up the strike on the Phoenix Iron Company's seven large mills. The strike ended on March 7, 1882; all union men were discharged and refused employment.

Stove Manufacturers, faced with declining business in 1882, became more belligerent as business declined. In February, the stove manufacturers of Pittsburgh and Allegheny met and refused to grant a 10% advance in wages demanded by the stove molders. After a two weeks' strike, the manufacturers compromised with the molders for a 5% advance. In March, the stove manufacturers of Troy, New York, refused to grant the demand for an increase of wages scheduled by an equalizing committee of the molders' union. The manufacturers issued a lengthy statement on the dispute, in brief, that prior to 1877, the union had forced advances until they could not compete with Western concerns because of the higher wages. They then reduced wages to those paid elsewhere and did so until 1880. In the period up to 1882, they had made two advances of 15% each—much higher than elsewhere. The demand for equalization in 1882 was based on prices for the highest class of stoves and would not allow for inferior stoves to be produced. This statement caused the union members to repudiate the demand, but they asked for an adjustment of grievances at individual foundries, which was attempted in a confused manner. The manufacturers offered the old prices and all five concerns signed the statement. A conference adjusted the grievances and the molders returned to work. But, in December, the manufacturers reduced wages 15%, were struck by 2,000 workmen, and closed their foundries, as business was poor. Likewise, the foundries in Pittsburgh planned to reduce wages about January 1, 1883; one foundry had already cut wages from $2.75 to $2.00.

The National Association of Stove Manufacturers repealed in 1882 its constitutional restrictions on consideration of labor problems; they had violated the constitution for years by discussing such matters as prison contract labor and proposed laws against it. The LABOR TRIBUNE—a union journal—stated that the discussions of the Association were mainly on how to circumvent, encompass, and suppress labor organizations, especially by hiring journeymen teachers, filling the floor with boys, and making molders out of these in a few months. The Association had extended discussions of prison contract labor.

Coal Operators Who Had Bargained Collectively Fought Bitterly in 1882. The year began with the organized coal operators complaining to the union that the Waverly Coal Company of Pittsburgh was allowed to undersell them and do as it pleased while they were complying with the demands of the union. As the result of this pressure, a long contest between that company and the union finally resulted in a conspiracy and libel suit being brought against the union officials. Although combination among the coal operators and collusion with the union were more widespread, adverse business conditions conduced to belligerency especially toward a union which demanded wage increases and would not accept reductions with falling prices. In March, coal operators at George's Creek and at Cumberland, Maryland, reduced wages, and justified the reduction because of the lower wages in the Clearfield, Pennsylvania, region. A notice signed by the president of twelve coal companies that wages would be reduced 15c a ton caused the strike, although an increase in the hours was said to have been also a cause. The miners offered to arbitrate. The union in the Clearfield region—partly to meet the Cumberland argument—presented the coal operators there with a demand for a 15c increase—2,000 to 3,000 men were involved—but the operators gave no consideration to this or to a second and third circular making the demand for an increase and for "conciliation." Members of union committees calling upon various employers were discharged in a number of cases. The union struck "primarily to force conciliation;" the operators brought in nonunion men to operate the mines, had those guarded, and had the union officials arrested for "intimidation,

threats, unlawful assembly, and conspiracy." The Knights of
Labor addressed the presidents of the Maryland and of the
Clearfield Coal Exchanges proposing conciliation at least twice,
through its Grand Executive Board. The Clearfield coal operators
had broken up the local miners' union some years before by
utilizing the law of conspiracy, and were victorious again in
1882—the men returned to work on the old terms. The Cumberland coal operators insisted on hiring individually and refused to take the men back in a body; they obtained nonunion
miners from Baltimore, Richmond, and elsewhere, and the
strikers returned as individuals. Negro miners functioned as
strikebreakers, and foreign miners were brought in by install-
ments. The strikebreakers were accompanied by armed special
guards, and were placed in specially erected buildings guarded
by special officers. Some of the foreign strikebreakers had been
sent back by the strikers, but the operators, aided by the Baltimore
and Ohio Railroad, crushed the union, as they had done in 1875.
The active unionists were blacklisted locally and elsewhere.
Among the other interesting events, three are worth mentioning:
The coal operators notified the county that it would be held
responsible for any damage done by the strikers; they also appealed to the Governor of Maryland for protection of their property and that of the strikebreakers; and coal operators at Lonaconing, Maryland, refused to confer with the strikers because the
letter making the demand was not sent to the President of the
"companies' combination."

Some coal operators were struck for not advancing wages;
others were struck because they had made reductions. Operators
in Western Pennsylvania, including Pittsburgh, were struck because of wage reductions. The operators had reduced the sale
price of coal from 7½c to 6½c, which meant 3½c for mining
on the scale; the miners demanded 4c for mining—and 7½c as
the sale price. Some of the strikers at Pittsburgh were charged
with conspiracy. After four and a half months, the strike was
called off; by then the miners realized that they had struck
against the market. In March, coal operators of the Tuscarawas,
Mahoning, and Salineville districts reduced wages for mining coal
because the operators in the Hocking Valley had done so and

they competed with the Pennsylvania mines. The railroad operators were struck when they made the reduction. Negroes were imported in large numbers and some Hungarians were brought in. In August, the strikers gave up and the reduction became general. At about the same time, the coal operators of Shawnee, Straitsville, Monday Creek, and Hocking Valley, were struck by drivers who demanded an increase in wages from $1.75 to $2.00 a day. The operators offered the miners 70c for six months and 60c for the other six months of the year, but the miners rejected the offer at first. In April, the miners demanded an increase of 10c a ton, then struck, and again returned to work at the reduced rate. The miners' union had issued a general circular to the coal operators of Ohio not to make the wage reductions. In October and November, however, operators in these districts faced demands for a 10c increase. The operators of the Tuscarawas district granted the increase, but those of the Mahoning Valley denied it, were struck, and defeated the strike. In May, the coal operators of Mineral Ridge, Ohio, reduced the rate for mining coal; the miners struck, were out until August and September, but returned not only at the reduced rate but with larger screens—no miners were paid for the coal which went through the screens. But the coal operators of Sherman, Ohio, were struck when they refused to advance the rate, but after ten days granted the increase. The coal operators near Denver, however, steadfastly refused to increase rates, and those of Beaver Valley, Pennsylvania, posted notices of a 10% reduction on October 1.

The anthracite coal operators not only engaged in collusive bargaining with the miners' union but also had spies among the miners to report upon the out-spoken miners, presumably for discharge and blacklisting, but were warned of the possible reaction. The companies, however, met in New York and agreed upon restricting production so as to advance prices. Accordingly, the miners of Wyoming and Lackawanna Valleys were given work only about half-time for a period of four months when the price of coal advanced. The coal operators, learning of the dissatisfaction among the miners over the half-time and the present scale—undoubtedly through reports from the spies—granted an advance of 10% on July 1, before the men even demanded it.

In the Glass Industry, competition between the West and the East involved both associations and unions. The Western Window Glass Association held a meeting early in 1882 and discussed the labor question at length. "It was resolved not to work during July and August, and all manufacturers pledged themselves not to start their factories after that time unless wages in the East and West are equalized." The difference was said to be from 20 to 25 percent lower in the East for skilled labor, which allowed the Eastern firms to undersell the Western ones. The Western Association and the union met at Pitttsburgh and agreed upon a scale of wages; for the West the scale was practically the same as the old one, but for the East it was provided for an advance of 10%. The scale was signed by the two organizations without consulting the Eastern manufacturers, and the question whether they would accept was presumably left to the union. The union made the demand for the 10% increase, the Eastern manufacturers refused, and were struck for over five months. The glass manufacturers of New Jersey imported about 1,000 glass-blowers from Belgium, Germany, and the north of France. The strike was carried over in 1883, was settled, and broke out again later in the year. The union thus helped the Western manufacturers by putting the Eastern ones largely out of competition for nearly a year. The bottle and vial manufacturers of New Jersey, however, requested the union of bottle and vial blowers to appoint a committee to sit with an association committee in conference to deal with wage schedules and other disputes.

In the Building Trades, Cincinnati added another instance to its strike-ridden activities. Early in 1882, the master carpenters met to consider the demands of the carpenters' union, and determined to make a strenuous resistance to the advance demanded. The masters' association refused even to confer with the union, so it appealed to a newly created board of arbitration of the Board of Trade and Transportation which was "composed principally of merchants and manufacturers of Cincinnati, whose members had not forgotten the disastrous labor strikes that occurred in the city the previous year." At a meeting on March 21, the board of arbitration was created and its members selected at a subsequent meeting. The Builders' Exchange also had a committee elected to take part in the proceedings. The Boss Builders' Association (the master carpenters) not only refused to recognize the carpenters' union but also declined to arbitrate. It did, however, appoint a committee to meet the arbitration board to present its reasons for its actions. It presented statements from other cities to show that carpenters' wages were not so high there as the union claimed they were. The one outstanding instance of wage advances was that of the building contractors of Allegheny granting, in March, a minimum of $15.00 a week, to those then receiving that or more, a 10% advance. The Board of Trade Arbitration Committee, however, decided unanimously that the master carpenters of Cincinnati should grant part of the union's demands, namely, $3.00 a day for first class, $2.75 for second class, and $2.50 for third class carpenters. The master carpenters continued to refuse to arbitrate or confer and, after a month's strike, the strikers returned to work as individuals on the employers' terms.

The master cornice-makers and tin-roofers of Cincinnati were struck on April 28 to force unionization of all the shops in the city, especially four large nonunion concerns. Nine independent firms had granted the union's demands for "a standard wage and shop rules," but the union made the strike a general one, so the nine firms revoked their agreement with the union. Both union and nonunion shops then organized, and 39 of the 43 shops decided not to recognize the union in the future. The association refused to confer with the union but did offer preference in employment to the old hands who returned by May 15. After lasting three weeks, the strike was a failure.

The employing plasterers of Cincinnati, however, were not so successful. They refused to grant the plasterers' union a wage increase of 50c, and the union struck. For seven weeks neither side made any overtures, but in the latter part of May, the employers met and offered two alternate compromise propositions, both of which were rejected by the union. On May 29, the association met again and conceded the union's demands.

The contractors of Newark, New Jersey, were struck in May by the bricklayers and masons to aid a strike of building laborers, but the strike failed; the bricklayers and masons had failed in July, 1880, in a strike for wage advances but had succeeded in March, 1881.

In the boot and shoe industry of Cincinnati, a Board of Arbitration and Conciliation was formed in 1882. It was made up of five members, selected by the Shoe Manufacturers' Association, and five members selected by the unions—one each by the lasters, cutters, bottomers, finishers, and stock fitters. In 1882, it settled minor disputes and agreed upon a bill of wages for the entire trade. A "lockout" was settled in 1883, but the Board broke up in 1884 when the association refused to amend one of its rules which the unions held was adverse to their organizations.

The Textile Industry, in 1882, took definite steps to resist unionism. The Textile Manufacturers' Association met in Philadelphia on January 3, 1882. While it had decided, in 1882, to raise a fund for establishing a textile school for artisans, it still lacked nearly one-fifth of the $25,000 required. A report relating to the matter was printed, since it contained arguments for the school, for instance, to train workmen so as better to meet foreign competition. The association resolved to call a public meeting in behalf of the school, which was established later. The Fall River Manufacturers' Board of Trade was charged with attempting in 1882 to break up the spinners' union by discharging and blacklisting all business agents and members of the union's committee. The Board was said to have had a spy in the union ranks to report on union officials, but had sent him away as soon as the union found out about him. The Board also employed a spotter to visit all the mills to detect any of the blacklisted men who were working under assumed names. The union supported the blacklisted men until they could find employment in other localities. The Fall River strike was called against wage reductions by the companies who had large earnings the year before and was broken by the importation of strikebreakers from other parts of the country and from Great Britain. The textile manufacturers of Lawrence, Massachusetts, were struck by the mill operatives, on account of a wage reduction. The textile manufacturers of Lowell, however, declared that they could not grant the demands of the mule spinners for an advance in pay in January, but that in the Spring if and when trade improved they would be able to make some advance. In April, the textile workers offered to arbitrate the issue, as they then knew that trade was dull.

Iron-Clad Contracts Indicated Growing Belligerency, when used by associations. "Understandings" between a nonassociation employer and his nonunion workmen that none shall join an "obnoxious" organization have probably always existed and will continue to exist so long as there is the employer-employee relationship, and may conduce to industrial peace. However, these contracts assume a different aspect when utilized by associated employers. In June, 1882, the associated manufacturing potters (7) of East Liverpool, Ohio, met and prepared a notice to their employees that the firms would no longer employ or retain in their employment any member of the Knights of Labor. As the men would not sign, the factories were closed on June 16, in what is called a "lockout." After eleven weeks, the manufacturers prepared another pledge for the workmen to sign but it did not require the men to leave the union. The workmen accepted it, but the manufacturers, recognizing the loophole in the previous pledge, offered a new "iron-clad" agreement. The manufacturers operated with nonunion men and with former union men who had signed the new pledge. Unionists who would not sign the pledge were "locked out" months later. Likewise, the Manufacturing Potters' Association of Trenton, New Jersey, was struck and refused to hire any members of the Knights of Labor. However, some years later, the matter was referred to the Executive Board of the Knights of Labor by the association. The meat packers of Chicago concertedly demanded that their employees promise not to belong to any union. The employees struck, but the militia was held ready to help the sheriff maintain law and order. It is doubtless true that the pledge or "oath" of the Knights of Labor caused associations to attempt to counteract that by a pledge or "oath" not to join or belong to that union; however, some of our largest unions in 1956 still have that "oath," although the yellow-dog contract has been outlawed by the Federal Government and several states.

Belligerency toward unionism was shown in a number of ways. In May, tanneries in Chicago that refused to grant an increase of wages of $1.00 a week, or that posted a notice stating only nonunion men would be employed were struck. Conferences failed and the men were defeated after striking for 72 days. The quarry owners of Lemont, Illinois, were nearly as belligerent; they refused to grant a wage increase in April, the men struck, but Italians and other nonunion men were imported. The men had been organized by the Knights of Labor, which, however, gave the strikers no financial support, so they lost the strike. In May, 500 brickmakers in Cook County, Illinois, struck against a reduction of 25c a day in wages, although the brickyard workers were demanding wage increases. The Brick Manufacturers' Association of the South and West Divisions of Chicago then tried to bring in nonunion men, but the strikers induced these to leave. A conference was called, but only two employers attended; its failure was attributed to the members of the Association bonding each other in the sum of $500 to make a compact resistance to the union demands. The Association appealed to the mayor of Chicago for protection to the nonunion men it was bringing in, but the mayor refused to send the police before the threatened trouble broke out. The Association then conferred with the union leaders but granted only half of the union's demands. The Brick Manufacturers' Association of the North Side also made the same concession to its striking workmen. Chicago employers had other labor troubles: the master horseshoers were struck by 350 journeymen for machine-made shoes and 25c a day advance. Moreover, a Team Owners' Benevolent Association was beginning to function. The master bakers refused to grant increased wages and a shorter workday and were struck in April. Conferences were held and the strikers urged to return at a dollar a week increase. However, men very active in the union could not obtain employment in the city, so a cooperative bakery was established for a number of obvious reasons.

The conflict manifested itself in various ways and localities; of which the following are illustrative: On June 18, 1882, freight handlers in New York and Jersey City employed on the Pennsylvania, the Erie, and the Delaware and Lackawanna railroads struck for an increase in wages from 17c to 20c an hour. The companies employed nonunion men, and the union sought an injunction. After a two months' strike, the men gave up and sought their old jobs, but the companies required the returning strikers to abandon the union. The upholstery factories of Milwaukee, however, were forced by a strike to increase the wages of the upholsterers about 20%. An event in Rochester was somewhat unusual: 168 industrial establishments threatened a general lockout "because of a labor combination against one of them." This was averted by an appeal of business men for arbitration and a referral of the matter to committees. However, during the year, 400 carriage makers struck. Around this time, cigar manufacturers locked out two rival unions of cigar makers to force an end to jurisdictional disputes. After long negotiations, the matter seemed to be settled, but the old dispute soon returned. Also to be noted here is the fact that the Carriage Builders' National Association of the United States issued a circular advocating trade education in the public schools, but school officials paid little attention to it. The Association then established a school for its own trade.

The Year 1883 was marked by the great number of strikes in the coal fields throughout the nation. Nevertheless, Pittsburgh still dominated the labor-management relations in the United States. Pittsburgh was the heart of the iron and steel industry. Iron and steel were essential in the economic development of the United States, and coal was necessary in the making of iron and steel. Wood was still important in the newer regions, but it had ceased to be a real competitor to coal in making iron and steel. The collusion between the unions and associations in the iron and coal industries conduced to the growth of unionism although unions and associations regularly fought over their respective shares of the spoils. That collusion set a "pattern" in other industries and localities, in which union officials tried hard to restrict "cut-throat competition" between employers and prevent "ruinous" prices. The sliding scales were intended to give the unions a generous share in rising prices, but the unions objected strenuously to taking the reductions when prices fell. If these facts are kept in mind, it is not difficult to understand the militancy in periods of falling prices. The "bad" or "unfair-employer" explanation fails to explain why the one and same employer is "fair" at one time and "unfair" at another.

Collective Bargaining in the Iron Industry in 1883 encountered the problem of wage reductions with falling prices. The Association of Western Iron Manufacturers met in Pittsburgh in April to consider a new scale of wages to be proposed to the workers, with reductions corresponding to those prevailing in the East. The conference committee of the manufacturers met with the union committee but reached no agreement in April. The Association met in May and endorsed the decision of their conference committee not to grant the union's demand for the old scale. But the drift toward a strike caused the manufacturers to sign the old scale with few modifications after a conference with the union. Dissension among the manufacturers was evident; it was the West against Pittsburgh. However, the averting of the strike was well received. IRON AGE thus commented editorially on the situation: "The formation of the association of manufacturers has had the effect that we anticipated for it and that we believed it would have, when years ago we urged the manufacturers to meet organization by organization, believing that this, instead of being conducive to strikes, would prevent them by making each side more reasonable."

Other developments among the associations elsewhere in the iron industry in 1883 were: The workers in the Bessemer steel works of the West, who had refused to take a 20% reduction in wages were finally forced to take 33⅓ off. The Iron Manufacturers' Association of Philadelphia, who paid workmen on a sliding-scale basis, met monthly to fix the price of iron, which of course determined the wages for the same time. The Bethlehem Iron Company of Philadelphia defeated the iron workers' strike by using nonunion men. The Cleveland rolling mills reduced wages 25%. The Vulcan Steel Works of St. Louis reduced wages of tonnage men 33⅓% and of mechanics 10 to 15 percent, and were struck. Edgar Thomson Steel Works at Braddocks, Pennsylvania, reduced wages around 12½ to 15 percent—none in some cases, and as high as 20% in others. Puddling at Elmira, New York, was cut to $4.35; at Phoenix-ville, Pennsylvania, to $4.00, and almost generally through Pennsylvania to $4.00. Blast furnaces throughout the Schuylkill Valley reduced wages 10%. A Chattanooga mill gave notice of reduction from 10 to 25 percent. Wages of iron workers at Reading were reduced, and the E. G. Brooke Iron Company was struck because its reductions were from 11 to 12½ percent—the workers were willing to take a 10% cut. The Pencoyd Iron Works of Montgomery County did likewise with the identical results. But reductions at Pottstown and by the Roane Iron Works were accepted by the workers. The Allentown rolling mills reduced puddlers' wages from $4.00 to $3.75, and other wages in proportion. But the Coatsville Iron Works was struck because it cut the puddlers' wages from $4.00 to $3.50. Reading Iron Works refused employees an advance and a strike took place at the pipe mill. Nonunion men at work for the Springfield (Illinois) Iron Company were fired upon and one killed. Investigation showed that the nonunion men led the attack and the man killed was the leader of the attacking party. The Centralia (Illinois) Iron and Nail Works was struck because it changed from the Cincinnati scale to the St. Louis one. The boilers wanted $6.00, and were offered $5.75—an advance from $5.50. The workmen at the nail works struck again, repudiating the agreement made after the previous strike and lost. But the striking nailers at Fall River, Massachusetts, gave up their strike against a wage reduction by the manufacturers and returned to work in large numbers. Likewise, the striking iron workers of Somerset, Massachusetts, called off their strike and sought their old jobs—the manufacturers had reduced wages 10% "because poverty and distress stared them in the face." The nail manufacturers of the West, especially at Wheeling, were restless under the rules of the nailers' union and awaited a favorable opportunity to throw off the burden.

Strikes in the Coal Fields in 1883 occurred through January to May, and from August to December, and were mainly against wage reductions. Arbitration was tried out. Attempts to control "cut-throat competition" were also present. In January, the coal operators of the river mines at Pittsburgh reduced wages from 4c to 3½c. Miners of Western Pennsylvania proposed arbitration to the coal operators for the settlement of their disputes.

The coal miners in the Belleville mining district, St. Clair County, Illinois, met and resolved to dissolve their union. In February, the coal operators of Mineral Ridge, Ohio, reduced the price for mining coal 10c a ton, the miners struck, but after a week decided to accept. But it took the miners of Salineville, Ohio, five weeks to decide to accept the same reduction. In March, the coal operators of Nelsonville defeated a three weeks' general strike over working conditions. Tuscarawas coal operators, who had been planning for some time to reduce wages because of the competition of Hocking Valley coal, decided in April that the price of mining was too high by 10 to 15c a ton and appointed a committee to confer with the miners. In April, the coal operators of Coalton, Jackson County, Ohio, "upon consultation, unitedly refused to concede that advance" demanded by the entrymen whose wages had been reduced a few days before. A wage reduction of 25c a day had caused 800 miners in 25 mines to strike. During a three weeks' strike, conferences were held between association and union until an agreement was reached providing for sliding scales of wages based on the Hocking Valley scale but 5c above it. The coal operators of Bellaire, Belmont County, Ohio, reduced the price of mining coal ½c a bushel, and the miners struck. After a protracted struggle between the association and union of 42 months, a settlement was made in which the operators withdrew the reduction and the men returned to work. The "associated operators" of Braidwood, Illinois, and vicinity, announced a reduction in April of 5c per ton for mining coal with the expectation of a strike. The coal operators of Del Ray, Carroll County, Ohio, reduced the price for mining coal 10c a ton and the miners struck. After a month of conferences between the union and association a compromise was reached making the reduction 8c instead of 10c. In September, however, the miners demanded an increase of 10c (winter prices) but the operators refused to grant it and the men again struck. In a week's time the operators made the concession. Coal operators of the Hocking Valley were struck over a reduction of 30c a day in wages; all miners at New Straitsville went out on strike but shortly accepted the reduction.

Arbitration was resorted to successfully on occasions. On

May 1, the railroad coal operatives (Pittsburgh region) reduced wages for mining coal to 3c a bushel and the miners struck. Conferences were held but failed. "A second attempt at arbitration" in the railroad pits near Pittsburgh failed in May, 1883, as the first attempt had failed in 1879. "Committees representing both sides were appointed but, on meeting, found that the miners' representatives were not endowed with full power to act and the operators refused to proceed until they were." The board could not agree on either scale or a price for mining and so adjourned *sine die*. Pennsylvania had passed a law providing for industrial arbitration in 1883, and the coal miners of Western Pennsylvania petitioned for a tribunal for the coal industry. Finally the miners' proposal to settle the dispute under the Voluntary Trade Tribunal Act was accepted by the operators and the tribunal selected. It ordered the men to return to work pending the hearing. The tribunal tried to settle the dispute without an umpire but was finally compelled to select one. His award was accepted by both sides—it gave the miners 3¼c a bushel. In September, the umpire was called in again to settle the question of a fall advance; he awarded 3½c a bushel, which award both sides accepted. Arbitration in Western Pennsylvania and in Iowa favored the miners' union.

In May, 1883, the coal operators of Churchill, Ohio, reduced the rate for mining coal; the men struck, and within a few days the operators restored the old rate and the men returned.

In August, 1883, the coal operators' association in the fields of Iowa and the mine workers' union held a conference which agreed upon a plan for arbitration. A number of coal operators, however, among them some railroads, refused to be bound by the action of the association or to submit to the arbitration plan. The miners had agreed to protect the association operators against the competition of outside operators, but failed to do so, yet demanded higher wages so that the association members were at a disadvantage competitively. The increased wages were granted in October, but in the spring of 1884, the operators reduced the rate per ton. In September, 1884, the miners again demanded an increase and the association agreed to it if the outside operators would grant it. The union struck both association and outside operators. A compromise of half the amount demanded was offered but refused. The coal operators imported nonunion men but these men were prevented from working by persuasion, threats, and by deportation by the union. An injunction was issued to restrain these union activities. The state militia was called out to maintain order. Finally the miners accepted the compromise. A sliding scale was put in effect in some of the mines. It is worth noting that railroads, depending then almost entirely on coal for their locomotives, disliked strikes which cut off their supply of coal; so they were not always friendly to the miners' union. In fact, they were charged with combining with coal operators to prevent even the operation of a union cooperative mine—there was no Interstate Commerce Commission to prevent highly discriminatory rates against such a mine.

In September, coal operators, often after a strike lasting usually less than two weeks, granted an advance of 10c a ton. This was true for the associated coal operators of Wadsworth, of New Philadelphia, and of Mineral Point [Tuscarawas Valley], Ohio. At McLuneys, they granted an advance of 20c. But in October, coal operators of the Mahoning Valley, of Meigs County, Ohio, and of East Palestine, Ohio, refused advances; the miners struck, but after strikes lasting from two weeks to two months, returned at the old rates.

In November, 1883, the coal operators of the "Fourth Pool Coal District" of the Monongahela River met the miners in a conference over a wage advance demanded by the union. They agreed to submit the issue to an arbitration board later known as "The Trade Coal Tribunal of the Monongahela River." This board could not agree and so called in an umpire who decided in favor of the union, but only four firms paid the back wages due the miners under the award. The miners struck, established a camp, and endeavored to keep nonunion men from working. Some of the nonunionists were annoyed by the strikers and had them arrested and fined for conspiracy. That broke up the camp. In 1884, the coal operators proposed a wage reduction, but refused to arbitrate, and the men struck. The miners finally returned to work at the reduced wages. Arbitration in the Monongahela River section had been used in 1883 and probably prior to decide disputes as to differences in rates paid in the Second and the Fourth Pools. The operators of the Fourth Pool wanted a difference of one cent a bushel; the miners, one-half cent. The difference had been one-half cent for 10 years, and the umpire decided that the 10-year rate should be maintained. Operators of the Fourth Pool talked of not abiding by the decision, although they had previously agreed to abide by the award.

In the Glass Industry, the contest between the East and West continued through 1883. The Eastern window-glass manufacturers refused the demands of the workers for increased rates to 10% less than Western rates. The workers struck, but the manufacturers imported workers from Belgium and when the strikers interfered with these, obtained injunctions and started suits for conspiracy against the unionists. Since the union failed to equalize the wages, the window-glass manufacturers of Western Pennsylvania and of New York attempted to reduce the wages. The workers struck. Instead of importing foreign workers, the manufacturers combined in purchasing Belgian glass to supply their trade during the long stoppage of work. They imported 50,000 boxes. The strike ended after seven months, a sliding scale was adopted, and the men returned to work at the old wages but with the price of glass higher—largely because of the strike. However, when the price of glass came down, the workmen received lower wages; moreover, the union agreed to put no limit on the individual's production. In September, the window-glass manufacturers of New Jersey were struck again over a 10% increase in wages and a uniform method of paying for piece work, quality considered. The manufacturers again attempted to bring in and use foreign workmen but found them unsatisfactory after a five months' trial, and conceded the strikers' demands. The window-glass manufacturers of Ohio had practically an identical experience with the union that the Western Pennsylvania manufacturers had, even to the strike lasting into 1884.

The Boot and Shoe Industry had a belligerent tendency in 1883. The boot and shoe manufacturers of Cincinnati had trouble with the Knights of Labor over its demand that a shoe manufacturer discharge a nonunion workman. The association supported him. The union appealed to "the board of arbitration and conciliation in the boot and shoe factories of Cincinnati," but the manufacturers did not appear at the meeting of the board to present their case. They offered to open their factories to those who would come as individuals and make the proper arrangements. They continued to refuse to submit the issue to arbitration. Finally, on May 24, the manufacturers agreed to appoint a conference committee to adjust the dispute at the factory where the trouble originated. This was done and the strike ended. In June, the board of arbitration changed a number of its rules to make it more useful. In September, the shoe manufacturers of Burlington, New Jersey, attempted to compel their workmen to leave the union. After a three-months stoppage, the men acknowledged their defeat, and most of them abandoned the union. In Marblehead, Massachusetts, 12 shops were struck by the lasters.

In the Stove Industry, wage reductions were the issue in 1883. The stove manufacturers of Cleveland, in January, reduced the wages of the stove molders 15%, and closed their foundries to enforce it. After three weeks, they opened their foundries at the old price. A committee of stove manufacturers of Albany and Troy, New York, was appointed to confer with a union committee on a wage reduction. These manufacturers had a committee visit Western foundries to ascertain wages there and found these to be 16 to 17 percent lower than the wages in Albany and Troy. The stove manufacturers of Pittsburgh and Allegheny reduced the wages of molders 5% and expected 400 molders to strike.

Telegraph Companies were struck in 1883 by the linemen and the commercial operators for increased wages, equal pay for women for equal work throughout the country, abolition of Sunday work without pay, and adjustment of a number of minor grievances. Two of the companies granted the demands but the others remained firm. The strikers were demoralized and gave up the strike in about six weeks, largely because the railroad operators would not strike or refuse to send commercial messages. The weakness of the Knights of Labor was revealed by its failure to aid the strikers financially or morally. The strikers were ordered back to work and most of them obtained their old positions. The companies abolished Sunday work without pay, but as the payment for Sundays added increased costs, the companies displaced as rapidly as possible the higher salaried men for the cheaper grade.

Railroads centering in St. Louis were charged with black-listing striking switchmen.

Employers in various fields listed below were forced to advance wages or make concessions to the unions in 1883. In the Spring of 1883, the cigar manufacturers of Cincinnati refused to grant an advance of $1.00 a thousand for making cigars, but after a week's strike conceded it. In like manner, the cigar packers, after a two-weeks strike, received an advance of 20% as a compromise of their original demand for 25% advance. In May, 1,300 cigar makers of Chicago struck and forced the manufacturers to give them a bill of prices, and in December again defeated the employers. In April, 3,000 bricklayers and stone masons of Chicago struck for eight weeks to force the contractors to grant increased wages of 50c a day. Association members had pledged themselves not to employ any union men after a certain date. In October, 1883, (also in 1884) the plumbers of Chicago struck *against* an eight-hour day during winter months, and obtained, by compromise, a longer working day. In March, 1883, (and other years), the master painters of Paterson, New Jersey, granted advanced wages over the cut rate of the Fall—$2.75 a day after a two days' strike. In March, the harness manufacturers of Cincinnati granted the harness workers an increase of wages, without a strike. Although building contractors of New York City readily granted higher wages, they were struck in 1883 to force the discharge of nonunion workmen, but won largely because the strikers gave up. An upholstery firm of Milwaukee ran overtime in 1883 but paid only 1¼ time, which was contrary to the union's constitution. From December, 1883, to April, 1884, wages were reduced 10 percent in all shops; the workmen accepted the reduction without a strike. Wages were restored in April 1884, but trouble sprang up over the overtime rate paid by the above firm, which finally discharged its union men. Then the employers reduced wages 10 percent and prohibited union agitation in their shops. The union broke up.

In the Political Field, probably the investigation and hearings by the Senate Committee on Education and Labor supplied the outstanding activity for both sides. The hearings functioned as a sounding board for the theories of radical unionists and conservative employers. Proposed laws were advocated and certain current ones denounced or upheld in accord with the partisanship of the speaker. Many of the arguments and theories expounded then are current in the 1950's. For instance, in 1883, there was much complaint about overproduction—too much iron, too much woolen goods, too much cotton goods, an overstock of many things; more produced than the markets will consume. Again— an abstract of an argument states that:

Unions are very favorably regarded by manufacturers and mining operators, who feel that it is easier to obtain their required labor through union officials than by dealing directly with the workmen. Such employers appreciate fully the conservative influence of unionism. It has done much to establish harmony. It prevents strikes, curbs unruly spirits, and fixes wages with equity. When the organization is perfected, labor will be so completely under control that no refractory or unruly *individual* can create a strike or labor disturbance. With the employer it will be a mere business matter. Clothed with the legal authority to forbid the employment of nonunion men, the union would feel the full necessity to keep mines and mills in operation to get wages for the men and would moderate the demands for advance in wages and compel submission by the men.

Among the proposed laws advocated by unions were: legislation against iron-clads, or independent-employee contracts; against blacklisting of unionists; abolishing the law of conspiracy as applied to unions; against foreign contract labor; against prison-contract labor; against the "truck system"; requiring check-weighmen; and the like. Employers were advocating public trade schools to make up for the deficiency caused by the decline of the apprenticeship system, and a government which maintained law and order especially in strikes. Unionists were very bitter about the law of conspiracy, and employers complained strongly about the "professional agitator."

Company unions and profit sharing were tried out in this period; for instance, Brewster & Company formed an "industrial association" of its workmen with a profit-sharing plan (10% of the firm's profits). But the plan broke down because of a strike for the eight-hour day.

CHAPTER 10

THE BOOM IN ORGANIZING UNIONS AND ASSOCIATIONS: THE LAW AND ORDER LEAGUES CRUSH THE KNIGHTS OF LABOR

WHILE THE YEAR 1884 was relatively quiet in organizational activities, it was laying the bases and furnishing the arguments for these activities in the following years. The years 1885-86 marked the height of the boom in both unions and associations; in fact, the unions began their decline in the early part of 1886 and remained relatively weak until their growth was greatly stimulated by the Boer War and the Spanish-American War.

Association Attitudes Varied in 1884. That some unions in 1884 were similar to the Molly Maguires was readily inferred by the recurrent references to the destruction of those gangsters. Undoubtedly, as a part of the reaction and counteraction, workmen who petitioned for changes or against abuses were summarily discharged by many manufacturers, as actual or potential agitators. Unionists then argued against arbitration in any form; they favored only "industrial conciliation"—later called "collective bargaining." While some associations agreed not to employ any members of specified unions—notably, of the Knights of Labor—the Board of Trade of Cincinnati appointed a committee to try to persuade employers and workmen to confer over differences in order to avert strikes. Strictly speaking, it was a mediatory organization, as a "conciliatory" organization is made up of the parties to the dispute, and an "arbitration" board is made up of "outsiders," usually with an umpire to settle the dispute between the contending parties. The Master Builders' Association of New York was formed to resist a strike. Manufacturers in California organized a state association.

The association movement was beginning to become extensive throughout the year—to meet the expansion in union activities. Local associations were very active, especially in taking stands which caused unionists to strike, like reducing wages.

The period was likewise one of abnormal advocacy of collective bargaining (then called "industrial conciliation [and arbitration]") as the method of solving all labor disputes. Unionists were propounding the recently revived "purchasing power" theory that too low wages were the cause of depressions. There were also both indirect cooperation and conflict: A United States Bureau of Labor Statistics was advocated as a means of furnishing statistics to support the labor argument of protectionists; but trade schools were fostered to increase the supply of skilled workmen.

Association support of trade schools is illustrated by the Carriage Builders' National Association, in convention, discussing technical education, hearing reports on apprenticeship, and subscribing $700 to aid the New York Technical School. A group of textile manufacturers subscribed $36,000 for a technical or industrial school, but at the time merely established a department of chemistry in the Pennsylvania School of Art. The Master Plumbers' Association of Philadelphia founded a plumbers' trade school which was open two evenings a week, but only apprentices working at the trade could attend. The Chicago Manual Training School was established in February through efforts of the Commercial Club of Chicago.

Because of the depressed conditions during and at the close of 1884, reductions in payrolls were general. These were accomplished in two ways: cutting wage rates and laying off workmen. Instead of cutting the wage rate, railroads laid off men as a method of avoiding strikes. Employers in iron, coal, textile, and pottery industries reduced working forces and, in many instances, cut wage rates.

In the Iron Industry, employers threatened to resist union demands for the old scale with extensions to other trades and slight modifications. Wage reductions were proposed, but after a series of conferences, the associated iron manufacturers conceded practically the union demands. The Western Iron Manufacturers' association held a meeting in Pittsburgh, May 1, and endorsed the action of the committee on conference in demanding a 10 percent reduction and not granting the union demands. For a time, both sides seemed determined not to yield. The manufacturers then petitioned the courts for an arbitration tribunal as provided by law. But in the next conference held, the association conceded the old scale with modifications, as demanded by the union. In Cincinnati, the workmen demanded the Albany scale—which was about 10 percent higher than the Pittsburgh scale—but the iron manufacturers refused to grant it. Finally, after heated discussions, on June 18, manufacturers and workmen agreed to sign the old scale. However, wages were reduced in the Eastern rolling mills; Philadelphia led, then the others followed because, they said, of competition in prices by those who had reduced wages, and because the range of wages paid was considerable among the different places.

Agitation for reduction of wages in the iron and steel industry was being conducted not only in the United States but also in England. The lower English wages were used as an argument against advances here. Iron manufacturers told ironworkers repeatedly that the puddlers' insistence upon very high wages would cause steel to be used in the place of iron, as was done by the nail manufacturers of Wheeling. The nail mill owners of Wheeling used steel in making nails and threw the puddlers out of jobs; and these incited the nailers to demand 20 percent advance for making steel nails over iron (or cut) nails. The union tried to boycott steel nails and to get consumers to do likewise. The nailers, however, refused in September to demand the 20 percent extra for making steel nails. The Western Nail Association endorsed the action of the iron manufacturers in demanding a wage reduction. The nail manufacturers of the West, especially at Wheeling, were restless under rules of the nailers' union and awaited a favorable opportunity to throw off the burden. Moreover, the nail manufacturers of Massachusetts gave simultaneously notices of a reduction of wages of nailers of 15 percent. The nailers struck; a compromise was thought probable. After 12½ weeks the strike ended. The reduction was found to be necessary to enable New England manufacturers to make nails in competition with Pennsylvania manufacturers. In fact, New England nail manufacturers still paid wages above those paid by Western manufacturers, and supplied customers by buying nails in the West and selling them at a profit greater than making them.

The foundry owners of Cincinnati defeated a nine months' strike by using nonunion labor and apprentices to do it, although the foundries had to be conducted as though in a siege for weeks. Every offer of settlement or compromise by the union was promptly rejected. "The local manufacturers have a strong and united organization and propose to stand by one another in defending their interests," a contemporary said editorially, in part, "If they will do this they can forever remain independent of union control, to their own advantage and that of their labor." Likewise, the stove manufacturers of Troy, after a three months' strike, defeated 2,000 molders and forced them to accept 20 percent reduction from the wages of the past year. Strikes by the molders' union, however, were ruinous to the Troy foundrymen.

In the Coal Fields, labor troubles were notable in the Hocking Valley; in fact, they led the Ohio General Assembly to appoint a Hocking Valley Investigating Committee to investigate and hold hearings on them, during which many issues were aired including company stores and drunken miners. The Columbus and Hocking Coal and Iron Company was called the Hocking Valley Syndicate and, although not consolidated with the Ohio Coal Exchange, worked in harmony with it in regard to the reduction in the rate for mining coal. It was made up of formerly independent operators. The Ohio Coal Exchange was an organization of 12 different operators and was incorporated. In January, the associated coal operators proposed at first a reduction of 10 percent in wages, but after a conference with the union, held it up until late in March, when a 20 percent reduction was offered. Miners were asked to accept the reduction because of competition by operators elsewhere who had reduced wage rates. This time the conference failed and a strike resulted. The operators met and agreed to pay off the miners and bring in new men. These were brought in from July 1 on; some Negroes were imported. A mine was set on fire. The operators were put to extraordinary expenses for guards to protect their property and the nonunion men who were working in the mines. It also cost the operators heavily for transportation of the nonunionists to the mines who did not work long enough to pay back the cost of transportation. Negroes were obtained by agents of the operators from Virginia and elsewhere. "Iron-clad contracts" were not used until after the strike began. McNeill states that the coal companies lost millions of dollars by the strike, yet failed to break up the union. The Hocking Valley Railroad proposed to reduce the freight rate on coal 20 percent provided the miners would accept the 10 percent reduction in the rate for mining coal—to equalize the competitive situation. While the union lost the strike, it was able to demand an increase from 50c to 60c in October, and through a board of conciliation, was able to get it. The board, with five members from each side, deadlocked on the points at issue, but when a referee was chosen, and he had heard long arguments by each side, he decided in favor of the wage advance.

The operators and miners in the railroad coal mines near Pittsburgh were able to reach an agreement through their "arbitration" tribunal without calling in an umpire. A sliding scale was agreed upon as a compromise. The tribunal also laid down certain rules, such as enforcement of the law relating to checkweighman, enforcing uniform rates, and the use of the correct size of screens.

The river coal operators near Pittsburgh, however, refused to increase the rate from 3c to 3½c, as demanded by the miners, who struck. The river coal operators refused to arbitrate; it was their usual attitude to refuse arbitration; and the miners repeatedly struck until they were in a deplorable condition as the result of the long-continued strikes. The operators imported Hungarian laborers for the Fourth Pool, and a serious situation resulted.

In March, 1884, the coke manufacturers, as a result of agitation begun in 1883 in the Connellsville coke region, formed a "Coke Pool." Thus one more organization was added to the growing list of combinations to deal with wages, competition, and the like.

A strike in the Southern coal fields of Colorado in 1884, led the mine operators to bring in nonunion men, including Negroes from the South. Armed detectives were employed to protect the nonunion men at work. Out of this strike grew another one, namely on the Denver and Rio Grande Railway, which was closely connected with the coal mine operators. Many outrages were committed, especially in the destruction of property by dynamite and otherwise. Vigilance committees of citizens and counter vigilance committees were formed, the latter to watch members of the former. Many detectives were *employers*—a development that became very important later on, but of which the union officials apparently never learned. The strikers lost.

In the Glass Industry, there was still the conflict between the Eastern and Western manufacturers as well as between them and the union. The glass manufacturers of New Jersey and Eastern Pennsylvania met in conference with the glass workers, July 29, 1884, and effected a compromise for a 5 percent advance in the scale over the past year; the workers had demanded a 10 percent advance. Under the new arrangement, these workers, it was said, received 10 percent less than the Pittsburgh workers. Shortly before this, the Window Glass Manufacturers' Association and the Window Glass Workers' Union had abolished their sliding scale—for the West—because they could not agree upon the basis for a new one. Instead they returned to the fixed rate with 10 percent reduction from the old prices of 1881, but with a few modifications. In December, however, the glass manufacturers of Pittsburgh reduced wages from 10 to 20 percent, and the workers struck. The strike lasted from December 1, 1884, to January 1, 1886, and ended in a compromise. During the strike, some of the manufacturers were able to operate only about half-time, a number of them trying German blowers but finding them inefficient. The fact that Belgian workers contributed to the support of American workers on strike may explain why American glass manufacturers imported glass instead of workmen. The attempt of the glass workers of America and Belgium to form an international union shows that there was a recognition of the growing international character of the problem of labor relations at this early date. Only about a third of the strikers could obtain work in nonassociation glass factories at the old rates. Nevertheless, the union was not broken up, although it met with great resistance in Ohio. In December, 1884, to September, 1885, the glass manufacturers of the Ohio Valley caused the workers to strike by seeking to change from "turn work" (time basis) to "piece work." The strikers offered to compromise, but the manufacturers refused to recognize the union. Finally, however, the manufacturers were forced to grant the demands of the strikers.

Other interesting association activities in 1884 were: On July 7, an organization of brick manufacturers attempted to reduce wages but lost the strike, but a second group of brick manufacturers succeeded when it did so on July 21. Carpenters and joiners of Chicago struck for increased wages, but the contractors secured nonunion men and the strikers were worse off than before the strike. Jay Gould defeated the telegraph brotherhood, and thus enhanced his reputation as an enemy of unionism, later to become an outstanding one in the history of the United States labor relations. Unusual for the year 1884, was the granting by New York employing framers to the framers' union of a demand for a wage advance ($3.25 from $3.00) for a ten-hour day, after an eight-day strike. Later in the year hours were reduced to 9 and wages to $3.00 (8 hours on Saturday) by mutual agreement. In contrast, the upholstery factories of Milwaukee, Wisconsin, reduced wages 10 percent during the period from December, 1883, to April, 1884, and the workmen accepted the reduction in all shops without a strike. When the wages were restored in April, however, trouble sprang up over the overtime rate paid by one firm which finally discharged its union men. Then the employers reduced wages 10 percent and prohibited union talk in the shops. The union broke up.

Other association activities for 1884 carried over into 1885, and need to be related as a continuing event. Among such activities are those of the associated streetcar companies of New York City, of the Mason Builders' Association there, of the hat manufacturers, and of the textile manufacturers. In New York City, in 1884, a spy in the union furnished employers with the names of the union officials and the most active members of the horse-railroad (streetcar) men. Company inspectors and superintendents spied on the men after the day's work. The blacklisting of unionists by the companies kept the union from growing. In January, 1885, 40 unionists were discharged for union activity, but by January, 1886, the union had obtained nearly all the horse-car drivers and, in a few weeks, organized the conductors completely. The companies refused to adjust the grievances of the workmen, and were struck around the first of the year in serial order. One company after the other signed the agreements after short strikes, even the hardest company was brought into line, and some which tried to break agreements were forced to abide by their contracts. Meanwhile, the companies tried to weed out all the unionists; one of them had its men take an oath that they would not belong to any labor organization; about 100 men were discharged and blacklisted, and many of these changed their names so as to obtain work. Strikers used violence in their strikes.

The Mason Builders' Association was formed in 1884, and in Januray, 1885, appointed a conference committee to confer with unions to settle all disputes. In April, 1885, an agreement was reached with the bricklayers' unions—with wages 42c an hour for nine hours a day, but eight hours on Saturday at eight-hours pay. Disputes between association and union were settled by a joint "arbitration" committee of five from each side—with an umpire provided but not used in the next eight years.

Many well-known events often have been the culmination of events years before. The collusion of the hatters' union and the hat manufacturers in the eighties finally resulted in the noted Danbury Hatters' case. McNeill—a noted unionist of that day—declared that the Hat Manufacturers' Association was well pleased with the unionization of the hat shops in 1884, as the union guarded well the interests of the association members against the "foul" shops. In brief, these events took place: On November 17, 1884, the leading hat manufacturers of South Norwalk, Connecticut, attempted to put in effect a reduced scale of wages. The workers struck. The firms imported nonunion workers and there were brawls between these and the strikers. One dynamite explosion occurred. The manufacturers refused to arbitrate. The goods of the struck firms were boycotted and cooperative factories were organized. After the strike had been on for three months, the firms still refused to arbitrate, but in April, 1885, the em-

ployers conceded a large part of the workers' demands. The
workers took the issue into politics and won the first battle. The
employing hatters attempted to form a national organization—a
pool—in which there would be a monopoly of labor and capital
combined, but it was not fully accomplished. The competition of
the Danbury hat manufacturers was given as the cause for the
wage reduction. Prior to 1885, the fur hat manufacturers of
Danbury, Connecticut, were more frequently victorious than their
workers in their recurrent contests. The aid of the Knights of
Labor changed the situation so that, in 1885, when the hatters'
union proposed that the fur hat manufacturers form a national
organization, the manufacturers accepted the proposal and a
convention was called in New York on October 28, at which an
estimated 95 percent or more of the capital invested in the
United States in this business was represented. The opposition
of the hat manufacturers of New Jersey prevented the formation
of a truly national association. A local association was formed
in Danbury—The Fur Hat Manufacturers' Association of Danbury—and in December entered into collective agreements with
the fur hat makers' union and the finishers' union. Conferences
were held in the following years and new clauses added to the
agreements. The trimmers' union, however, refused to enter into
any agreements, although urged to do so by the association. The
association forced the issue by a posted notice containing a pledge
that each worker would endeavor to have such an agreement
made, and followed that up with a lockout which caused the
trimmers' union to sign an agreement. The coners and clippers'
union at a later date signed an agreement. By these agreements,
wages were increased and the prices of hats advanced. It seems
that collective bargaining in these years was usually of the collusive type, and especially so in the hat industry.

In the textile industry, profits became so low in 1884 that
the Fall River Massachusetts Board of Trade announced a wage
reduction to follow those made in mills in other cities. Workers
in 10 mills struck, but the millowners broke the strike by importing "knobsticks"—or nonunion—workmen. One of the mills was
burned, but no evidence could be obtained to prove that the
strikers were guilty. A statement made in 1884 about the de-

pression seems to be from a rather recent day: "There were millions of men and women in want of bread, notwithstanding 'the abundant harvests' . . . and the cry . . . went up from millions of farmers of 'Too much wheat' . . ." Depression caused the manufacturers to work only part time, and in 1885, wage reductions elsewhere led the Fall River mills again to reduce wages.

Frequent notices of manufacturers closing down due to lack of demand were evidences of the depression. Discussions of labor-reducing machinery and of the policy of reducing work force or wages, indicated the current thinking. Unemployment was not improved for "free laborers" by the State of New York making shoes and clothing by using prison labor.

The Year 1885 Was Notable for the Growth of Unions and Associations. They fought each other and combined against the consumer. Competition was blamed for all the industrial evils of the day: depression, falling prices, and reduced wages. The evidence seems to indicate that union officials took the lead in urging employers to combine to raise prices, so that wage reductions would not be necessary. Actually, there was so much discrimination—for instance, in railroad rates—that the combinations encountered much difficulty in maintaining "uniform prices." Union officials attempted to "police" the industries, as they do today in the clothing industry. In any event, union officials fostered organizations of employers for the purpose of having these bargain with the union. It was not a "class conflict," which was then expounded by radical union officials; it was more like incipient fascism. Many of these union-association combinations carried in themselves the elements of their own destruction; for the combination led to a merger or a "trust" which became so powerful of itself it no longer had need for the union to help it to control prices and so it became nonunion. In other cases, the power, arrogance, and doctrines of the union officials so frightened employers that they set about the destruction of the union. To many employers the great growth of the Knights of Labor was alarming; its increase of 75 percent in members from June 30, 1884, to June 30, 1885, was noted with apprehension.

In the Iron Industry, the low price of iron caused a number of reactions during the year 1885, among which was the demand of iron manufacturers for further wage reductions. The Western Iron Manufacturers' Labor Organization announced in January that the June, 1885, scale should have a reduction for puddling from $5.50 to $4.00 (reduction of more than 27 percent) with corresponding reductions in other wages, which were based on the puddling price. Iron was selling much below the 2½c card price, but $5.50 had been set as the minimum in the old sliding scale. The reductions were said to be necessary because other iron manufacturers had reduced wages much below this. Other reactions to the low price of iron can be understood better by noting certain factors. The Amalgamated (the merger of the unions of iron workers) had not only helped the iron manufacturers get a high protective tariff, it even advocated the prohibition of foreign goods competing with those produced by *union* workers, just as it opposed the importation of foreign workers under contract. But the resistance by the unions to wage reductions and to lessened labor costs of production, with the falling prices, caused employers to seek new devices, machines, and methods to reduce those costs, for instance, the substitution of steel for iron and the high wages for puddlers. At this point, the union's own statistics on strikes are pertinent: "From 1876 to 1885, inclusive, the total number of legalized strikes was 93 . . . [of which there were] 61 over wages, 17 over the right to organize, 3 over signing the scale, and 12 for miscellaneous reasons . . . 28 were successful, 61 unsuccessful, and 4 compromised." With two-thirds of its strikes unsuccessful, it would seem clear that the union was over-aggressive in its demands.

The Western Iron Manufacturers asked for a conference with the union. This was held and the manufacturers conceded the union's demands in relation to the method of calculating prices on the 2c card, but no agreement was reached in regard to old rails or to the 10 percent extra allowed, or in regard to the sheet scale. The differences were referred to committees composed of the sheet rollers and of manufacturers, and of users of old rails and representatives of their workmen. The other part of the scales was signed: 2½c price, $5.00 for puddling; 5c price, $8.00 for puddling—a 50c reduction with $5.00 the minimum, no matter how low the price of iron went. The reason for the association giving up the struggle was that the manufacturers of sheets and the users of old rails—the points in difference—had signed the scale individually and had started running, so the other manufacturers thought it was not worth the while to fight under these conditions.

The iron manufacturers of Mahoning and Shenango valleys, in Cincinnati, Youngstown, Wheeling, and other outside districts, protested against the action of the Pittsburgh manufacturers in surrendering to the union after the short, but practically complete, general strike. These Western manufacturers withdrew from the Western Iron Association and proposed organizing another association of their own. Actually, only 9 mills in all the West signed the scale, and 7 of the 9 were in Pittsburgh; and 15 of the mills turned nonunion. In the Youngstown district—the Valley and Cleveland had resolved to close down the rolling mills commencing February 15, and remain closed until after June 1, when they expected a low scale to be adopted. Many iron manufacturers were failing during this period. In September, however, the striking iron workers at Cleveland decided to return to work. But the Western nail mills were generally strikebound throughout the year.

The Western Nail Association met during July, 1885, and decided to persist in its demands for: a reduction of about 19 percent in wage rates with no distinction between steel and iron nails, nailers to pay for machines broken by negligence, and feeders on automatic machines to receive 25 percent less. The manufacturers gave notice that the striking nailers must return by a certain time or remove their tools; they failed to return by that time. The manufacturers attempted to operate with feeders and with such nailers as instructors as could be secured from other sections. The association pledged its members to retain the feeders in employment when the strike ended, and sent a circular to the feeders informing them about the pledge. While not up to full capacity, the mills did fairly well with the feeders taking the nailers' places. The association refused conferences with the union on the grounds that new nailers had been employed and could not be displaced, since the employers had obligated themselves to the new workmen. By February, 1886, when another conference with the union was refused by the association, about 1,000 machines were being operated by nonunionists—the trained feeders; some manufacturers had granted the Mingo scale of 19c on $2.25 card with 10 percent reduction for self-feeding machines. The price of nails later fell to as low as $1.90 a keg, and some manufacturers offered a compromise of 17c on a $2.20 base.

New England nail manufacturers were presented in 1885 by the nailers with a demand for 10 percent increase in wages; the nailers struck but later returned on the old basis.

In the Coal Fields, strikes were more widespread than had been for years. With one notable exception, groups of coal operators around Pittsburgh had their regular allotment of strikes as the concomitant of their collective bargaining. The notable exception was that of the railroad coal operators of Western Pennsylvania whose sliding scale—range, price of coal $4.00, for mining $2.00; $7.75, $4.60—enabled the operators and miners to adjust their differences without even calling in the umpire.

The coal operators in the Pittsburgh railroad mines, however, who had conceded 3c were asked to pay 4c, and operators who paid only 2½c were called upon by the miners' union to pay 3c. Miners asked for a conference, but after about two weeks' strike, they returned to work at the old rates, defeated. In April, likewise, coal operators in the Monongahela Valley were struck over a demand for 3c, which the miners then won, but the operators reduced the rate to 2½c and even 2c in the late summer; after three months' striking, some of the miners returned to work at 2½c. Some of the strikers shot down nonunionists in Allegheny County. The year 1885 closed with the strike still on. River coal operators near Pittsburgh won a seven-weeks strike ending in October when the men returned to work on the operators' terms.

Coal operators and miners met in a convention in Pittsburgh in December, 1885, to discuss means to avoid the numerous coal strikes, by adjusting differences over wages. A scale was formulated for the bituminous coal districts and referred to the miners and operators of the various districts for approval. In February, 1886, the scale was approved—from 56½c to 95c a ton depending upon markets and conditions in the mines—and a board of conciliation for each state with a national board for final adjudication was agreed upon.

Other strikes in the coal fields included that of 1,100 coal miners against the operators of LaSalle County, Illinois, in April against wage reductions. The strike failed. A strike in Macoupin County, in March, was against wage reductions and for wage advances. The strike prevented wage reductions, but the operators refused to arbitrate the question of wage advances. The coal operators' association of Centerville, Iowa, notified the miners that wages would be reduced on April 1, and 325 miners struck but lost the strike. Coal operators of the Birmingham, Alabama, district were called to meet in September and devoted a large measure of their attention to labor questions. The Warrior Coal and Coke Company was struck over the importation of Italian labor, but the matter was compromised. Coal operators in Perry County, Illinois, were struck in October by 300 miners and forced to increase wages, reduce prices for miners' supplies, and agree to arbitration of future disputes.

The widespread coal-mine strikes caused a conference of miners and operators to be held in Chicago, on October 15. A joint committee of three miners and three operators was appointed to invite the cooperation of all engaged in coal mining in America and to call a meeting of operators and miners in a joint convention at Pittsburgh. Conferences were held between the operators and miners at which the operators proposed a compromise of 7½c reduction. The miners countered with the proposition that this would be accepted until October 1, 1888, when an advance of 2½c must be made. The operators refused and the conference broke up. The Coal Association refused to arbitrate because of the dissension within its own ranks as to the amount of reduction; some of the operators had demanded as much as a 20c reduction. It was the dissension between the Eastern and the Western operators that caused the national annual conference to break up in 1888.

Coal operators of the Hocking Valley, Ohio Central Region, and Ohio Coal Exchange met in November, 1885, and decided not to grant the miners' demand for a 10 percent wage increase.

The matter was submitted to arbitration in the Hocking Valley, where the operators were using machines as the result of the strike. These operators became noted for their use of the "iron-clad" or anti-union contract, yet engaged in collective bargaining quite regularly when their workers were not on strike. The following sworn statement by a coal operator before the Hocking Valley Investigating Committee revealed the situation which led to efforts to control competitive conditions: "There are organized operators in all the various coal fields, so far as my information extends. There is an organization in Central Ohio of coal operators for the purpose of regulating prices, and for the purpose of settling matters that may be of common interest." Actually, the attempts of rival coal operators' associations to control competition through the agency of the union led to many of the strikes that were noted as "coal-mine wars" of a bloody character.

In the Shoe Industry, there were both appeasatory and belligerent associations functioning in 1885. In October, the shoe manufacturers of Lynn, Massachusetts, formed an association to deal with labor disputes in a conciliatory manner by means of a tribunal with an impartial arbiter. Unions have been charged with having driven shoe manufacturing, in part, away from Lynn to other cities; in any event, some of the other cities preferred fighting the unions, specifically those connected with the Knights of Labor. An elaborate scheme for "arbitration in the shoe industry" had been worked out with rules to govern the shoe manufacturers and the Knights of Labor, yet the scheme could not operate successfully because of all sorts of dissension.

In the autumn of 1885, 42 shoe manufacturers of Brockton, Massachusetts, associated to maintain the right of the worker and employer to make individual contracts. The association issued a notice on November 12 setting forth the wages for lasting and stating that it was the right of the employer to hire or discharge any worker, and that it was the right, likewise, of the worker to work whenever and wherever it was to his best interest to do so. The lasters' union struck, and the finishers' union then followed. A committee from all the shoemaking unions in the city called upon the president of the association to arrange for arbitration, but he refused, as he also did later to a committee from the

Knights of Labor. The strike of the 5,755 operatives tied up the 42 factories, but 40 other factories ran at full capacity. This caused the smaller manufacturers in the association to become restless because their machinery was idle, interest was accumulating on borrowed capital, and their competitors were taking away the markets. The association voted to leave the matter to its executive committee; it met with the union committee and accepted a modification of the "Philadelphia Rules." These rules provided, among other things, that no employee should be discharged for union membership or activity. The ten-hour day was adopted, and a conciliation committee of six each from the association and the union was created to settle all difficulties. But the new committee could not agree upon wages for the lasters, and three arbitrators were chosen. They proposed a compromise, which was accepted by both sides until the following year when the contest broke out again.

In the Glass Industry, negotiations between the flint-glass manufacturers of the Ohio Valley were broken off in August, and the settlement of the long-drawn-out dispute seemed then to be as far off as it was when the strike began. The Western window-glass manufacturers and workmen had joint conference committees in September to agree upon a scale of wages for the next year, but referred the matter to sub-committees with power to decide. The glass manufacturers of Pittsburgh who had been struck by the prescription glass workers over a 20 percent reduction in wages, after a strike lasting over a year compromised in December on a 10 percent reduction.

Other association activities in the East included wage reductions; for instance, in the Spring of 1885, the manufacturing potters of New Jersey proposed reductions from 10 to 25 percent, but a conference between the Manufacturers' Association and the union resulted in a compromise under which wages were reduced only 5 percent. About the same time, a combination of granite manufacturers of Rhode Island and Connecticut attempted to get all New England manufacturers of granite to join them in reducing wages 15 percent. When the workmen threatened to strike, some of the members of the association withdrew the reduction; the other members were later forced by the strike to restore the wage rates, and one of them became a "union job." The manufacturers of Barre combined to crush the union in Vermont. At South Ryegate, Vermont, a concern notified its men that it would not employ unionists. The unionists struck, and published a notice in a Boston newspaper warning workers that the firm was being struck and branded as "scabbed." The strikers refused to retract and were charged with conspiracy. These instances constitute a record of the first widespread attempt of the granite manufacturers to deal with unionism.

In February, the oyster packers of Annapolis, Maryland, reduced the price to shuckers from 20c to 15c per gallon and they struck. The packers, however, secured other help. In April, the tin-canmakers struck the factories for an advance, asking for 30c per hundred for two-pound cans and 35c for three-pound cans. On May 1, a compromise of 25c and 30c respectively was reached, but in two weeks, the factories cut the rate to 25c for both sizes. In July, the strike ended with the prices 30c and 35c, but by October the prices had been forced up to 60c and 65c. In August, the shipbuilding yards cut wages of ship carpenters and caulkers from $3.00 to $2.50 a day and the men struck, but in May, 1886, the strikers, after repudiating a settlement made by a committee of the Knights of Labor, later accepted it and the wage reduction, along with an agreement of the shipbuilders to employ only union members.

Association activities in the West were fast growing more extensive, affecting even lumbering in Michigan. From July to September, the salt and lumber millowners of Bay City and the Saginaw Valley were struck for a ten-hour day. At first, 150 Pinkerton detectives were brought in, then 10 companies of state militia were called in. The millowners refused to meet the committee of "outside organizers." The employers gained from the strike through the rise in the price of salt. But when the shingle-mill owners of Muskegon refused to grant the ten-hour day with no reduction in wages, the shingle-mill workers struck and won. The strikes in Michigan over the ten-hour law of that state spread to a mill in Wisconsin, and that mill was boycotted. As a result, the millowners of Marinette and Menomine met and declared a general lockout. This caused a number of sawmill employees to petition and promise the millowners not to be subject to any union and to work for the former wages, provided the mills would start up. The associated millowners replied that they would start up as soon as sufficient workmen signed the petition. Outside logging and jobbing contractors, however, came in and employed the strikers in such numbers that the mills could not resume full operation that year. In contrast, in August, master tailors of Leavenworth locked out the tailors, refused arbitration, and defeated the union's demand for a new bill of prices.

Associations of boat owners were also active during 1885. The tugboat owners successfully resisted the demands of the linemen and firemen on the tugboats at Milwaukee and defeated the strike partly by working themselves. In April, employers at Cheboygan, Michigan, refused to grant increased wages to "rivermen" or "drivers" who struck unsuccessfully since other men were easily employed. In May, the Vessel Owners and Captains' National Association was formed in Boston. At Galveston, a joint committee of businessmen and of the Knights of Labor settled a strike over Negroes employed by the Mallory Steamship Company—the strikers lost. In the Far West, however, the sailors were organized and started hitting at shipowners one by one—the unions have long practiced the strategy of "Divide and conquer."

The master bakers of Milwaukee organized to resist the demands of the bakers' union for a ten-hour day and abolition of the "boarding" system. The union boycotted two bakeries it had struck, but the men returned to work as individuals and the strike failed. This instance, however, seems to have been exceptional. The master bakers established a weekly trade paper to counteract the weekly union paper published by the bakers' union, as the latter had attained an astonishingly large circulation almost at once, and it revived the bakers' union everywhere it had members. Concessions were forced from the master bakers in practically every large city primarily by boycotts on nonunion bread.

In the Building Trades, one of the most notable incidents of 1885 involved the Master Plumbers' Association of Milwaukee.

Its members agreed not to employ a plumber unless he could show a certificate from his previous employer. Numerous conferences were held between the association and the union with the issue sharp: The union insisted on working only with union men while the association asserted the right of the employer to employ and discharge whomever he saw fit. Finally the association resolved not to employ union men under penalty of the forfeiture of $1,000 each. The union submitted a new proposal at the final conference, but this was refused by the association. Both association and union issued lengthy statements to the public. The strikers organized a cooperative shop—another illustration of the establishment of a cooperative to give employment to strikers and hurt the business of employers fighting the union, not to give lower prices to the consumer as its primary object. The association imported men, but the union induced many of these to leave the city. The master carpenters of New York, however, were forced by a strike to grant the nine-hour day and $3.50 daily wages, and the Master Builders' Association of New York City and the bricklayers' union entered into a joint arbitration agreement in April, 1885. The employing lathers of Chicago were struck also and forced to grant the lathers increased wages in April. Again, in October, the master plumbers of Chicago were forced by a strike to abandon the eight-hour day for a longer working day in winter.

Among other associations struck over wages were the brick manufacturers of Cook County, Illinois (Chicago), and of the outskirts of Detroit, the employing coopers of Cook County, the master horseshoers, and the metal manufacturers, both of Chicago. In May, 650 brickmakers of Cook County struck against a 50c reduction of wages and won, but the brick manufacturers of Detroit defeated a strike of the brickmakers for higher wages and denied that they were in "combination." In July, 750 brickmakers struck against a 50c reduction and refused the manufacturers' offer of 25c reduction and won. But, in June, 800 coopers obtained an increase in wages, and again in October, 700 won a strike for increased wages, while 100 striking coopers compromised. While the master horseshoers of Chicago failed to force wage reductions, the metal manufacturers were forced by a strike of 1,300 metal workers to grant wage increases and changes in working rules.

Although some thought that boycotting had largely failed, there were others who thought that it should be legally suppressed. "Manufacturers and others who are being 'boycotted' in New York are quietly arranging to have a bill presented and pressed for passage at the next session of New York Legislature, making boycotting a misdemeanor, punishable with heavy penalties."

Association activities extended to other fields such as technical education, legislation, and detecting agitators, of which the following are cited: The Carriage Builders' National Association continued its support of a technical school in New York. The Philadelphia Textile Association cooperated in establishing and maintaining a school of weaving and textile design in Philadelphia. The glass manufacturers of New Jersey met with the union committee on apprentice limitation and refused to grant the union's request. It was pointed out then that "Employers are beginning to see that the supply of trained workmen will not remain inexhaustible if nothing is done to replenish it." One trade association issued a circular to public schools urging training of mechanics in public schools.

Associations opposed both the law against contract immigration labor and the Chinese Exclusion Act. They opposed the unions' attempts to have the Pennsylvania conspiracy law changed. Conspiracies were condemned in England between unions and associations, for example, in the nut and bolt trade, by which employers were forced to join an association by having the union call a strike on them if they remained outside. Associations usually fought union legislative proposals in labor relations and rarely sought legislative acts. Secondary boycotting was thought to be illegal as a conspiracy.

In regard to associations using detectives to war on agitators, it is a matter of record that there were at least two classes of detectives other than the Pinkerton type, namely, workmen loyal to their employers, and other employers. Moreover, the "great exposure" by Joseph R. Buchanan, printed on November 25, 1885, and recorded in Commons' *History of Labour in the United*

States (Vol. 2, p. 146) was really a fraud, for the so-called "confidential circular to employers" had been published at least seven weeks before the "exposure." IRON AGE published it in full on October 8, 1885 (p. 18), and thus commented on it: "Pinkerton's Detective Agency has issued a circular to all employers of labor, volunteering their services in settling labor disputes. The method will be to obtain information by supplying applicants with 'a detective suitable to associate with their employees.' " The book you are now reading supplies abundant evidence that very few association activities are really kept secret, although some union officials and political investigators attempt to make it appear that associations are "very secret" organizations.

The contest between the Knights of Labor and Jay Gould's railroads—which assumed great significance later—had this interesting turn in 1885: The strike on the Wabash system of railroads was settled by the following agreement: "That no official should discriminate against the Knights of Labor, or question the right of the employee to belong to our Order. That all employees locked out June 16, 1885, or who came out in their support since that date, should be reinstated as fast as possible. That no new person shall be put to work by the officials of the company until all the old employees locked out, or came out since the lockout, who desire employment, are reinstated."

While associations were beginning to organize in 1885, they were still largely local or sectional, like the Merchants and Manufacturers' Association of Cincinnati, organized in the latter part of the year. On the other side, the Knights of Labor was a national organization and its growth called for a reaction on the part of the employers. Among the many statements in regard to the conditions—which were alarming to employers—this one by McNeill is pertinent:

"In the winter of 1885, and the spring of 1886, the Order grew with unprecedented rapidity. Never in the history of the world were the workingmen everywhere, of all trades and callings, so aroused to the needs of organization. Local assemblies were multiplied by hundreds, and thousands of men were enrolling daily. With this influx of new members, undisciplined and ignorant of the failures of the past, strikes multiplied as though a contagion spread from one end of the country to the other. This wonderful and unnatural growth led the Executive Board to place a check upon further organization, and in District 30 (Massachusetts) led even to the suspension of the initiation of new members."

When strikes multiplied like a contagion, employers felt compelled to meet organization with organization. This did not mean that the employers attempted to "parallel" the unions in order to get the most effective counter-organizations. The unions had apparently no organizations "parallel" to the highly effective "law and order leagues" formed in 1886 to fight the Knights of Labor.

Around 1886, New Associations Began to Form, among which were the United Typothetae of America, and the Stove Founders' National Defense Association; both under totally different names are in existence today. The former, during its early years, was concerned with the question of the shorter workday, but the latter was wrestling with the union over piece prices and related problems. In 1886, the General Managers' Association of railroads centering or terminating in Chicago was formed with 24 members. This Association crushed the American Railway Union in the noted railroad strike of 1894.

The year was then a new peak in strikes. A general strike for the eight-hour day was called May 1, and the Haymarket Riot in Chicago occurred on May 4. Many strikes were conducted in New York and Massachusetts, as well as in the West where the crucial struggle was mainly centered. During the year the Knights of Labor reached its height and began its decline during a campaign against it by both local and national employers' associations.

The most noted strikes of the Knights of Labor occurred in 1886, and those which attracted most attention—like the great Southwestern Railroad Strike—proved failures. Its greatest gains were secured by "the use of the boycott, as in the Dueber Watch-case Company, or by conciliation, as in the case of the horse-railroad employees of Boston."

The effect of strikes in 1886 was marked. The demand for merchandise in some instances was paralyzed as the purchasing power of a great number of people was diminished; the money market was disturbed, and in many instances manufacturers closed their establishments, or at least reduced their working force, to avoid accumulating stock at a higher cost of production.

Collective Bargaining—then called "voluntary conciliation" —was vigorously advocated, even throughout the period 1886-1900, and was tried extensively in the latter part of that period, namely 1892-1901. A current statement, widely circulated, sets forth an interesting viewpoint, and is as follows:

"The labor question is the great topic of the hour. Everybody is discussing it, but nobody knows how to settle it. In several places committees of employers have met committees of workmen, and after repeated conferences have agreed upon a basis of settlement, but something always occurs to make one side or the other feel aggrieved, and a pretext is soon found for a reopening of the question. Manufacturers affirm that they would have no serious trouble if they had only their own employees to treat with. It is the outside committees who undertake to arrange matters with which they are not fully acquainted that in most cases make all the trouble. Men who have spent money and time for years in building up a business do not like to explain their affairs to strangers. It is on this point that the disagreement in Beverly between the shoe manufacturers and their workmen is likely to turn. There are circumstances peculiar to every shop or factory and every town, and the best way would be to let each plant settle its own grievance."

It is noteworthy that "outsiders" then were the main complaint by employers.

Men who testified to the success of voluntary arbitration and conciliation were listed: Rt. Hon. A. J. Mundella, Sir Rupert Kettle, Thomas Hughes, Lord Derby, David Dale, and unionists Thomas Burt, Wm. Crawford, John Kane, Edward Trow, Geo. Broadhurst, and Geo. Howell. But the collective bargaining advocated was often a conspiracy against the consumer. For instance, the argument was offered (abstracted):

Combinations of manufacturers, like unions which fix and maintain minimum wages in the face of an over-supply, have maintained advanced prices and so avoided the necessity of wage reductions. The transactions between an individual worker and an employer in the privacy of a counting-room, with hunger and want forcing the laborer to accept what is offered does not constitute in any practical sense, an open labor market, where the law of supply and demand has free action. It is neither self-evident nor is it capable of proof that it is in accordance with public policy for goods to be sold at rates which mean great loss or ruin to the manufacturer, or for wages which mean distress to the workmen to be paid, when by their joint combination, fair profits and good wages can be obtained. Employers or employees associated together have the right to pursue a course which their judgment dictates, the same as individuals, acting as individuals, have the right to pursue. Reasoning *a priori,* the judgment of the many—of the organization—is more to be trusted in labor matters than that of the individual. When the organization is made up of members of but one class, with the same purpose, grievances, and passions, the judgment may be a biased one, but not necessarily more so than that of each individual, and a biased judgment is not always an unjust one. But when the combination is made up of both classes and from both parties to these differences, then the judgment of such a body, with its opportunities for ascertaining both sides of the question and for securing information that both do not possess, increases the probabilities that "the determinations of such a body are more nearly right than those of individuals actuated only by their individual sense of their own interests." "At the hands of a committee representing many manufacturers, injustice and oppression would be impossible."

The failure of combinations through the "individual's trickery" was discussed elsewhere.

"Shop arbitration" also was advocated and the scheme of "The Shop Council" was set forth in 1886 by James C. Bayles in a book bearing that name. It advocated the formation of shop committees of "representatives named or chosen by the parties in interest," by the men working in the shop and by the employer, and each given an equal voice, so as to avert trouble by conferences and clearing up misunderstandings.

Both federal and state governments considered arbitration boards. The House of Representatives in April passed a bill providing for arbitration on the railroads by a board made up of three members: one selected by the corporation, one by unions, and one by the other two members. Cleveland's message to Congress advocating a National Board of Arbitration was condemned as unwise. New Jersey passed an "arbitration law" providing for a board of 5 persons; one representing the union, one the employer, two the department of labor, and one chosen by the other four. A Board of Arbitration was also formed in Massachusetts.

Attacks on the Knights of Labor were condemned; its destruction was held to be impossible, and attempts to do so inadvisable:

"If any hot-headed and unreasonable men in the League shall by work or act create the impression that the movement is antagonistic to organized labor and seeks to oppose it with hostile influences, the resulting conflict is likely to be disastrous to both sides, and no good will come of it."

"Those who imagine attacks from without can destroy it are greatly mistaken. At the present juncture nothing could be so useful to the order of the Knights of Labor as a little persecution." In 1886, the Knights of Labor added to its membership "by the tens of thousands weekly." "So great was the increased membership that even the largest cities were unable to provide hall capacity for the meetings."

Nevertheless there were strong indictments of labor organizations, and repeated prophecies of their impending collapse, especially if they became mere boycotting and strike-making machines. But advocates of collective bargaining asserted emphatically that:

"Unionism is here and will not depart. It is growing yearly in power, in wisdom, and in organization. It cannot be crushed out; it will not permit itself always to be ignored nor despised." "An organized crowd is usually neither as wise, nor as conservative in its actions as one that has put itself under the restraint of laws, precedents, and officers." "A weak union which represents but a part of a section or trade is timid and cowardly yet tyrannical, and seeks to make up in bluster and flagrant injustice what it lacks in power. But a strong union can be just and generous without fear of being charged with cowardice, and when there is beside it a strong employers' association, strikes and lockouts will be of rare occurrence, peace will be assured, and production go forward under the most promising conditions."

"With its growing power and intelligence, with its larger liberty and freedom of action and combination, with the removal of the legislative burdens under which it has staggered and the imposing for its benefit of other burdens not on labor itself directly but on industry—and with the abandonment of certain economic theories that rested upon it like a horrible nightmare—illusory, but as dire and distressing as though real—labor has come into possession of a new and larger life."

"Wise men are not antagonizing organized labor. They are going with it, and seeking to lead it by safe paths to practicable and desirable ends, to counteract the michievous teachings of half-educated demagogues, and to help the honest and industrious workingman to attain everything which is to his good."

In July, 1886, a reaction had set in and was clearly apparent. The anti-union movement in 1886, in one instance, was met by the unions by a resort to legal action. A contractor attempted to use convict labor in constructing a capitol at Austin, Texas, and his job was branded as a "scab job." He then attempted to get granite cutters from Scotland, and his agent brought in 78 granite cutters and 8 tool sharpeners. The union tried by legal action to block these at New York, but succeeded only in getting some of the imported men to remain in New York. From these, the union obtained the contracts made by the agent in Aberdeen, Scotland. These contracts were sent to Texas, and suit began against both the contractor and the syndicate which imported the men.

In the Legislative Field. In 1886, unionists contended that the Chinamen controlled the boot and shoe trade; "He is the servile unit in one of the Six Companies." Legislation against immigration of contract labor was demanded by organized labor. Union domination in legislative halls was definitely recognized. It not only prevented legislation it regarded as inimical, but it forced the passage of laws which in theory and principle were a complete reversal of the policy of our Government from its origin. Notable instances of these are the anti-Chinese and the anti-contract labor laws. On the other hand, "committees of

manufacturers sought in vain to be heard before the Ways and
Means Committee" and obtained a hearing only when union
officials in no uncertain tones demanded that hearing. Unionists
also appeared before the Ways and Means Committee in March,
1886, in opposition to tariff reductions, and apparently were very
effective.

The eight-hour agitation aroused opposition; one of the most
effective arguments against it was:

"Over 200 St. Louis employers and manufacturers have recorded the opinion that the adoption of the eight-hour system
will not affect their business, but that it will surely end in a reduction of wages and a consequent injury to the laboring classes.
They also state that the movement, if put into force, will be
met with the piece system and the method of payment by the
hour."

Twelve demands were made by the Knights of Labor on Congress in 1886. One was a child-labor law and the others were
in an omnibus bill—"bills approved by the Congressional Labor
Committee."

In 1886, complaints were made that gas and electricity were
displacing coal, that coal-producing machinery was being used,
that the mines were overcrowded with men, and that there were
"too many mines and too many miners."

"Will Employers Organize?"—was a question that, under
these conditions, grew in importance:

"A movement is on foot and letters are being sent out
quietly to arrange for a national meeting of business men and
manufacturers to be held some time next month, to take action
toward devising means of defense against the power of organized
labor. There is nothing definite yet arranged, but the opinion of
business men is being asked in confidential circulars which speak
of demands and how to put employers in a position to withstand them."

The argument for widespread organization of employers was,
in abstract form, as follows:

Capital is timid and selfish, individualistic and not cooperative. It is therefore highly vulnerable to the attacks of organized
labor which has grown powerful and aggressive. The individual

employer lacks the resources in both capital and skill to compete with organized labor on a national scale. He is unable to meet either a strike or boycott when these are conducted by a national labor union. No employer can resist a ramified secondary boycott. A local issue may be magnified by a national union into a national one, or one which involves an entire industry. The only recourse of the individual employer is to close his plant and leave it closed, in the hope that his employees will finally recover their common sense and return to work.

Organized labor makes more and more unreasonable demands as its machinery is perfected for enforcing them. Every victory over an employer makes the conquest of the next employer easier, so long as employers do not unite. The power of organized labor is beyond the law—too great for any irresponsible group to exercise. As its power grows, it becomes more and more uncontrollable. Organized labor is as selfish as capital and less intelligent, and cannot be expected to use its uncontrolled power wisely. An opposing force is needed strong enough to produce a balance of power. This requires a powerful national federation of employers backed by strong local associations.

"Law and Order Missions" in all the large cities of the country to teach the masses of the people a set of 10 principles relating to government and labor were advocated in a booklet by C. C. Bonney: "The Present Conflict of Labor and Capital" (1886). The author appealed to the "money makers" for financial support in this undertaking. The booklet was prompted by the Haymarket Riot of May 4, 1886.

In New England, the cotton manufacturers were organizing for "mutual protection" and the knowledge of this fact stopped one important strike before it gained headway. The manufacturers of brass and iron steam and water fittings also effected a settlement of certain labor difficulties by means of a very complete organization and were in a position to defend any of their number from "oppression or injury by organized labor."

Even then doubts were expressed: "To what extent the organizations forming among employers in many branches of manufacturing will aid in restoring the men to reason remains to be seen."

Law and Order Leagues.—The spearhead in the attack upon the policies of the Knights of Labor and upon that body was the organization of law and order leagues, fostered by Jay Gould. The Knights of Labor conducted a strike upon the Gould railroads in the noted Southwestern strike, which began on March 6, 1886, and lasted two months. It was called to force the Texas Pacific Railroad to reinstate an employee at Marshall, Texas, who was discharged for infraction of rules. Martin Irons, the union leader, was opposed by Gould who was indicted by unionists as the "bitter enemy" of the Knights, which he "had determined to crush, in order to screw down wages." "Both sides fought with desperation." All trains were blocked, all traffic stopped. "In the beginning there was rioting against which the state authorities were powerless." Strikers "seized the cities of St. Louis, Sedalia, Atchison, Kansas City, Parsons, Fort Worth, Little Rock, and Texarkana, besides lesser places." Sedalia was controlled by a Knights of Labor mob under Martin Irons and a reign of terror instituted. The business of the city was paralyzed. A law and order league—highly secretive with recognition signs, grips, and pass words—was formed, and afforded protection to the replacement employees and railroad property. The league was not only very effective locally, it had a profound influence on business men in other cities. Sabotage was practiced especially upon engines of the Southwestern system. The law and order leagues were formed at once at St. Louis, DeSota, and Wyandotte and operated secretly to break up that violence with the same telling effect as at Sedalia. Through an intelligence corps operating among the strikers, plots to commit violence were learned in advance, and pressure was brought upon peace officers and public officials, including state governors, to take steps to prevent it as well as to prosecute violators. Thus the strike was broken. Membership in the leagues was secret, but their existence and purposes were recorded at length in publications circulating among employers. Yet Powderly knew nothing of their existence; in fact, the only reference we have found to them in union literature was in the *Railway Clerk* for December, 1939, nearly 54 years after the leagues were formed. Unions then had no research departments to do intelligently the reading to acquaint their officials with such significant facts.

The law and order leagues grew rapidly. The first one, as noted above, was organized in Sedalia, Missouri, and they soon spread to other cities on the Gould railroads and elsewhere— cities like Scranton, Pennsylvania, Bloomington, Illinois, Joplin, Springfield, and Kansas City, Missouri, Evansville, Shelbyville, and Columbus, Indiana, and Pittsburgh, Kansas—and had a "magical effect in crystallizing public opinion." "With the design of preventing labor disturbances," the leagues soon had a membership of 17,000, many of whom were in St. Louis, Missouri. With the leagues functioning efficiently, the railroad officials—Gould included—refused Powderly's request for arbitration of the strike on the grounds that the courts were dealing with the situation satisfactorily. The Southwestern strike paralyzed the Knights of Labor.

With one victory to their credit, the law and order leagues grew and extended their influence directly and indirectly. Directly, they added to their membership and exerted powerful political pressure upon public officials. Their propaganda affected both employers and public opinion. The following statement of principles of the parent League is illuminating:

The Central Board of the Law and Order League (St. Louis, Missouri) issued a circular to its chapters, especially in regard to political conditions.

"The Law and Order League stands organized upon the principle announced in its constitution. It insists upon the enforcement of law. It insists upon the preservation of peace, order and quiet in the community. It insists upon non-interference by any man, or any set or association of men, with the lawful rights of any other man, or set or association of men. It insists upon the right of every citizen to work or not work as he pleases, and to make and carry into effect such lawful contracts as may be agreeable to himself and other contracting parties. It insists that their fellow-citizens in their various walks of business, whether as employees or proprietors, must and shall be protected in all rights guaranteed to them by the Constitution and laws of the

State, and that men, or associations of men, who violently interfere with these rights are law-breakers and rioters who must and shall be crushed out. It presents an uncompromising and united antagonism to riotous or anarchical demonstrations, to all forms of boycotting, and to the use of all unlawful and violent means to rectify supposed personal wrongs.

"It insists that all political parties shall nominate for offices of public trust men of character, capacity and integrity, and to such only will we give our suffrages. It insists that bad men, whether rioters, anarchists, public plunderers, political ringsters, sympathizers with turbulency and turbulent elements, men who pander to vicious or venal voters, bad and incompetent men generally, shall be defeated at the primaries and at the polls, irrespective of their party connections or proffered connections.

"It insists that every citizen is in duty bound to faithfully discharge the duties devolvent upon him as such, especially in his participation in the work of primary meetings, nominating conventions and elections. It insists that no man can neglect these duties or shift them upon his fellows without doing violence to his honor and patriotism. It insists that all judges, prosecuting attorneys, grand and petit jurors, shall do their whole duty without fear or favor and that in so doing they will have the unwavering support of this League. It insists that all public offices shall be administered solely for the public good, and that they shall not be used for political advancement or private gain. It insists that all law-abiding and patriotic citizens of the community should associate themselves together and aid in carrying into practical effect the enunciations of this League. These are the organic principles of the Law and Order League. To them every member stands pledged with his time, energy and means, and around them all good citizens of all shades of political or religious creed can rally as around the flag of our common country.

"No honest man, under the obligations of this League, can countenance any political candidate who is in sympathy with any associations or practices which are hostile to the foregoing declarations. The League reposes in the judgment of its members as to how they should act in individual cases. The influences of the League are intended to be, and are, in fact, in harmony with its declarations. But to assume a position as a political party, or to dictate to the individual judgment of its members as to what is right or wrong or to in any wise limit the personal freedom in the exercise of the elective franchise is, in the opinion of the Central Board, neither wise nor in harmony with our declared principles. Counting among its members men of all shades of opinion on party matters, the Law and Order League is concrete and a unit by virtue of its principles, which are above all parties and interfere with the proper functions of none, so long as they operate within the limitations of law. If the future should bring about a marshaling together of anarchical or law-breaking or boycotting elements for the purpose of measuring political strength with the patriotic people of the community or country, a united political action by the League as such might in such an issue be advisable. Sufficient unto the day is the evil thereof.

"No work ever undertaken in this community is more important as bearing upon its peace and prosperity than the work of the Law and Order League. Give to the world the assurance that here labor and capital, which are mutually dependent upon each other and essentially the same, are fully protected; that public trusts are administered for the public good; that taxation is at a minimum; that all rights of life, liberty and property are safe not only by reason of law, but by reason of a living active public sympathy that will not brook their infraction; that enterprises of all kinds can be safely entered on, because every opportunity for success will be offered, and immediately the stream of immigration that is spreading over the great West will flow to St. Louis as surely as the magnet turns to its pole. These are the things that are needed more than your great river, or your iron mountain, or your mines of mineral and ore. Capital and brains and muscle made out of sea marshes a great commercial Holland, and they will always gravitate to the place where they can operate with safety. What, then, are the immediate duties of the members of the League? Register, vote, and see to it that not only you who are Leaguers, but that your neighbors also do both. The league can safely trust the individual conscience of its members to do that which is right, and as becometh a good and patriotic citizen."

The Conservators' League—a law and order league under another name—was organized April 24, 1886, and held an open meeting July 28, 1886, to discuss aims and objects. It was chartered by the State of Illinois. Proceedings of "councils"—supreme and local—were secret. It dealt with labor matters, mainly political.

On July 28, 1886, Chicago Council No. 1 of the Conservators' League of America held an open meeting for a discussion of the aims and objects of the organization: The Conservators' League of America was organized "to counteract these injurious results (paralysis of business from labor troubles) and to protect these all-important business interests, and thus promote the highest good of the country." The League was incorporated under laws of Illinois. It was organized:

"To unite in one organization all men who believe in the supremacy of the law and are willing to join in putting in motion a great moral force to uphold the law and conserve alike the rights of the employer and the employee, to protect business from disorders and from all unlawful interference, and to promote a better understanding of the true relation of the employer and employee, maintaining the rights of each and adjusting their differences," "to watch and guard against legislation—to stand between and antagonize the utopian schemes of a class who seek to overthrow the present order of things, and say to the members of such organizations: Thus far shall thou go, and no farther."

It indicted unions, but the most serious charge was union dictation to business men who had no organization to meet the extortions and plots of unions. "To supply this deficiency and furnish a means to combat the new and dangerous enemy of the business world," the Conservators' League had been formed. Its Councils had already reached into four Western States, and many believed that it was destined to be the largest and strongest of all exclusively secular organizations in the world: "Business men present expressed themselves in favor of the league." The league was organized April 24, 1886, by the formation of a Supreme Council. Subsidiary councils were formed under the control and advice of the Supreme Council; the Chicago Council No. 1 soon had several hundred members. The proceedings of the councils were secret. This caused some to fear that it would fail quickly and completely:

"The kind of men who are needed in the membership to give it character and dignity, and to command for it the support of public opinion, will not join a movement which plots in secret even for the conservation of institutions held precious by the American people. Proceedings which need to be surrounded with secrecy will everywhere be regarded with distrust and suspicion. The value of such an organization as the league is said to be will depend chiefly, if not wholly, upon its educating influence."

Effects of the Leagues' Victory. Indirectly, the law and order leagues by proving the vulnerability of the Knights of Labor, as well as by propaganda, conduced to the organization of other associations. The conditions, however, were the main factors. Accounts of the functioning of two other associations will illustrate these points. The organizations of employers was thus heralded (abstracted):

The sudden and unexpected collapse of a threatened serious strike at the Whittenton Mills, Taunton, was caused by the discovery that the mill belonged to a huge organization of textile industries of New England, which has been formed so quietly that it received no notice. It extended over Rhode Island and Connecticut, and included 49 large woolen mills, with such cotton mills as the Lonsdale and Hope Mills. It was organized for mutual protection. It did not recognize the authority or dictation of the Knights of Labor in any way, but used arbitration in the settlement of strikes. It grew rapidly in numbers, it gave each strike due consideration and assisted only those manufacturers who were unfairly treated by their help. Another association, embracing all cotton mills of any importance in Maine, New Hampshire and Massachusetts, was also quietly organized. This Massachusetts association was a league of cotton mills to which woolen mills were admitted, while the Rhode Island Association was formed by woolen mills and subsequently admitted cotton manufacturers. During March the cotton mills of Massachusetts quietly organized for mutual insurance against labor disturbances. The cotton-manufacturing industry was better adapted to the formation of such an organization than many others, because it was composed of a number of large mills rather than a large number of small ones. The quiet organization was conducted with much expedition and it was ready to meet the attempt of the mill hands to secure the discharge of workmen who were not members of the union. The entire woolen, as well as the entire cotton, interests of the three states were included. The association took the form of a mutual insurance company organized on the basis of the respective payrolls of its members, but it was not a corporation and had no stock. The yearly payrolls of the Massachusetts mills which joined amounted to $15,000,000. Plain cottons, colored cottons, prints and ginghams were all represented in the list of members, and every leading cotton mill in the state joined. Its aims were not in any sense "aggressive," and their purpose was not to attack the Knights of Labor, but simply to protect their members against unjust persecution. Its methods of self-defense were not made public.

Chicago foundrymen joined the Association of Manufacturers in Metal, and its formation "had a salutary effect upon dissatisfied employees." Under its constitution and by-laws, the workman had the alternative of working 10 hours for 10 hours' pay, or not working at all. Very few of the foundries, however, were in full operation. Some of them had not attempted to work, while others were working only a small portion of their capacity. It determined to prosecute all cases of intimidation of workmen by strikers, and had warrants issued for five men who were charged with intimidating laborers at the Calumet Iron and Steel Works which then had a serious strike.

In 1886, the brass manufacturers of New York refused to grant a reduction of hours to 9 a day, but the Brass Manufacturers' Association met at Pittsburgh and resolved to recommend that each member grant the men 5 hours out each week (Saturday half-holiday) which the union accepted in lieu of the 9-hour day. In October the manufacturers desired to return to the 59-hour week. The men struck but failed.

The Manufacturers' Association of Brass, Steam, Gas and Waterworks Supplies, a protective league among the brass-goods manufacturers of the United States was formed in March, and included the manufacturers of brass and iron steam and water fittings; it represented 98 percent of all the capital invested in this business. Forty-four firms were then enrolled in the membership, employing about 10,000 men. Mr. A. F. Foster, of the United Brass Company, was president. The organization was effected for the ostensible object of establishing uniform prices, but later adopted as its primary purpose "to protect the trade against the unreasonable demands of organized labor." Its attitude was "defensive, not aggressive." It tried not to antagonize the Knights of Labor, or to refuse "any reasonable and proper demand of labor"; but resisted vigorously "any attempt to dictate to manufacturers who shall be employed or how their business shall be conducted." "In our organization," says Mr. Foster, "we have a mutual insurance plan. In case of a strike the manufacturer will receive a benefit to an amount graded by his payroll; all our workmen are Knights of Labor, but we make no objection to that. We want fair play, and they will find out who is who. We favor arbitration and desire to avoid all trouble." A contemporary accounts states that (abstracted):

The effectiveness of this organization was shown in a most striking manner. The workmen of Peck Bros. & Company, of New Haven, had demanded an advance in wages, the reemployment of one of their number who had been discharged for disobeying orders, and certain changes in the method of conducting the work. The company tried to adjust the difficulty itself by offering concessions to the workmen. All its endeavors, however, proved fruitless, and there appeared to be every prospect of a long and bitter struggle. Peck Bros. & Company then turned the whole affair over to the hands of the association, and no sooner did the men discover the strength of the organization with which they were dealing than they withdrew all their demands and returned to work.

This association met in Pittsburgh on May 11, 1886, and adopted a 10-hour day resolution. It also favored national and state legislation establishing boards of arbitration for settlement of industrial disputes.

In summary, the collapse of the Southwestern strike about the first of May corresponded to the rise of widespread militancy of employers' associations toward the Knights of Labor. This was also reflected in the reaction of unionists; a notable illustration is the Haymarket Riot on May 4. There are warnings and lessons from the conflict of the Law and Order Leagues and Knights of Labor applicable to the current situation, but those are not those usually pointed out by union partisans.

CHAPTER 11

THE BOOM IN ORGANIZING ASSOCIATIONS AND UNIONS (Continued)

THE LAW AND Order Leagues not only stimulated employers to organize to resist unionism in the industrial field, they also influenced associations profoundly to attempt to utilize governmental agencies to check the abuses of unionism. The shock of the widespread resistance to unionism and the new zeal with which public officials upheld law and order in strikes, undoubtedly functioned to make the highly zealous union leaders resort to further violence as in the May Day Haymarket Riot; in fact, cases of unions using dynamite were listed, among which were striking-dry-goods clerks in New York City, striking miners in Hocking Valley, strikers at Beverly, Missouri, and car strikers at St. Louis, Missouri. Prior to the victories of the Law and Order Leagues, the eight-hour day was being conceded in an amazing number of instances. Almost over night, the process reversed itself, and many concessions were as suddenly revoked.

In the Political and Legislative Fields, associations showed a variety of reactions to union activities as well as undertaking their own political ventures. The eight-hour riot in Chicago, in which firearms and dynamite bombs were used and six rioters and five policemen killed, not only stimulated the associations to urge public officials to do their duty in punishing the persons responsible for the riot, it alerted associations to union violence and caused them to take steps in preparation for stopping future violence. But many of the associations' activities preceded the May Day riot. For instance, this statement was made about April 1: "The manufacturers of Rhode Island, anticipating unfriendly legislation and labor agitation injurious to their interests, formed about two months ago an organization known as The Slater Club, which includes about all the manufacturers of any account in the State. . . . They have agreed to stand by each other's interests in any contest, financially and otherwise. The most important feature is a 'blacklist'—that is, a list of persons who may quit the employment of any mill in the State for causes which may be offensive to the employer. This list is to be transmitted to other Rhode Island mills in the combination, and the persons so listed are to be excluded from employment in the mills, and thus compelled to leave the State or seek some other line of work." Likewise, the New York Chamber of Commerce met on April 27, to consider means to enforce "existing laws for the protection of all classes of our citizens in the peaceful pursuit of their business." The Chamber recommended arbitration of differences between employers and employees.

In June, "Newark manufacturers, embarrassed by numerous boycotts since the conspiracy laws were repealed in 1882, . . . (planned to) petition the Legislature through the Board of Trade, that the laws be reenacted." Boycotting cases were frequently dealt with as criminal conspiracies in 1886 and prior, but in Baltimore in July, the injunction began to be used and thereafter was often employed. In October, Pennsylvania's law against store orders— enacted June 29, 1881—was declared unconstitutional and void by the Supreme Court of the State, as a violation of the freedom of contract. The Court ruled that, "The act is an infringement alike of the rights of employer and employee, and is an insulting attempt to put the laborer under legislative tutelage which is not only degrading to his manhood, but subversive of his rights as a citizen of the United States." In December, it was stated that, "To prevent excesses of possible labor organizations among the Negroes, ostensibly to protect the farmers, the Senate of North Carolina has passed a bill by a large majority declaring that "it shall be deemed a conspiracy and shall be a misdemeanor for any persons united, organized, associated or banded together to interfere by threats, force or in any other way with any contract between any employer or employee."

Industrial education was promoted by associations as a means to lessen the monopoly power of unionism. In July, 1886, the Master Plumbers' Association, in convention in Philadelphia, discussed the apprenticeship system and considered the possible benefits to be derived from establishing trade schools. It endorsed a five-year term of apprenticeship and agreed to lend its influence to establish trade schools. It considered congressional aid in fostering trade training and the addition of technical departments to public schools with skilled artisans as instructors. It also considered the grading of workmen and the issuing of cards of proficiency. In August, the Apprentices' Library of the General Society of Mechanics and Tradesmen of New York City—established in 1820 and containing 70,000 volumes—was made open to the public for the first time. In September, the green-glass manufacturers planned to open four schools for apprentices in Southern New Jersey to accommodate from 100 to 150 apprentices. In October, the Carriage Builders' National Association met in New York and its committee on technical education reported favorably on the work done in the classes supported by the association at Broadway and Twenty-seventh Street. In November, the Industrial Association of New Jersey met in Hoboken for the "object of presenting to the people of the State the subject of industrial education in the common schools."

In the Iron Industry, employers threatened to resist, in 1886, union demands for the old scale with extensive modifications. Wage reductions were proposed, but after a series of conferences with union officials, the associated manufacturers conceded practically the union demands. The Pittsburgh iron and steel manufacturers met on May 28, and appointed a committee to negotiate with the union committee. The joint conference committee met a number of times, although the differences were unimportant. Some differences were postponed, and the scale signed was practically the old one renewed. As the Pittsburgh scale governed the West, there were no major difficulties there. In the East, however, the Philadelphia Rolling Mill Association met on June 21, to consider the ultimatum of the 1,500 iron workers employed in the rolling mills for the establishment of the 2c basis. The association's refusal caused a four weeks' strike and then the demands were conceded. The scale ranged from $3.85 on a 2c card to $8.30 on a 5c card.

The associated nail manufacturers were not so appeasatory. The year 1886 opened with the nailers' strike on, and it lasted six to nine months more. The Western nail manufacturers continued to train up feeders to take the place of nailers. In previous strikes, the association had done this spasmodically, now the "under hands" were used systematically and persistently by practically all the manufacturers. Not only did the manufacturers pledge themselves to the feeders to retain them as nailers when the strike was finally called off, the manufacturers kept faith with the feeders. The feeders and nailers at work formed a protective "union" to meet the union of the striking nailers. The Western Nail Association met in Pittsburgh in February and resolved not to accede to the demands of the nailers, but to pay only 17c for cutting 10d nails on a $2.25 card; to fulfill their pledge to the feeder-nailers, the association could enter no conference with the striking union that would interfere with that pledge. As these were the points of difference, no conference could reach an agreement should one be held. One of the association members compromised with the strikers for 19c and for 10 percent reduction instead of 25c when self-feeders were used; he was expelled by the association. The strikers had been hoping that the spring trade would cause concessions to be made, but the one-member-compromise complicated matters. The striking feeders charged the compromising nailers with broken faith; and the conflict became a three cornered "union" fight. The association met again in February, March, and April, each time resolving to fight it out and renewing its pledge to the feeder-nailers. From January to the middle of February the number of nonunion machines rose from 780 to 1,000 in operation. In April, the nailers withdrew from the Amalgamated Association (union) of Iron and Steel Workers, and formed an organization of their own in order to resist the 10 percent reduction which the nail manufacturers demanded and which the Amalgamated was willing to concede. After nearly 13 months' striking, the nailers accepted a scale with 17c on a $2.00 card, up to 25c on a $3.75 card, with 10 percent reduction for self-feeders. The scale proposed by the association at the time of the strike ranged from 15c to 20c on $2.00 to $3.00 cards, while the strikers demanded ranges of 21c to 24c on $2.25 to $3.00 cards. The question as to the feeders was not settled. The striking nailers at Wheeling did not return to work until in August at the reduced Pittsburgh scale, which was one cent less than the Amalgamated's. The Pittsburgh nailers returned in September. The rise in the price of nails helped to end the strike.

In Cook County (Chicago), Illinois, iron workers struck in May for an eight-hour day with no reduction in pay: 400 failed and the attempt at arbitration was unsuccessful; 200 compromised on eight hours with nine-hours pay; 500 struck later against reduction in wages, but failed; and 25 striking machinists in May failed to get an eight-hour day.

Among the Foundries in 1886, the most significant event was the organization of the Stove Founders' National Defense Association—later known as the Manufacturers' Protective and Development Association—with 62 charter members. It was organized by the National Association of Stove Manufacturers at a meeting in June, with the object of enabling "manufacturers to deal with organized labor on a plane of equality." It was intended to provide the organized stove manufacturers the means for settling labor disputes through an executive committee considering and acting upon any demand by the unions and resulting dispute which could not be settled in the foundry where the issue arose. The complaint or dispute went first to one of four district committees, chosen by a nominating committee. The manufacturer could appeal an unfavorable decision of the district committee. If the district committee was sustained, and he refused to abide by the decision, he was left to his own resources in further dealings with the union. If he was sustained, his patterns were distributed among other members to make his stoves for him during the strike. In other words, the new association was set up as a belligerent organization in order to fight the molders' union; not until 5 years later did it hold conference agreements with the unions. Stove founders were then having much trouble with the molders' union in regard to apprentices and helpers, and had been subjected to the "divide and conquer" strategy of that union through the serial strike. They organized "so that by hanging together they might not be taken in detail and in that way they would by joint action be able to make headway against the simultaneous action of workmen when dissatisfied." Undoubtedly, they were greatly influenced by the very recent victories and propaganda of the Law and Order Leagues.

A strike at the Bridge & Beach foundry at St. Louis over an advance in wages was taken up by the SFNDA in 1887 and the patterns distributed, some of them going to Troy and Albany, New York, and causing suspensions of work by the unionists there. However, the struck foundry asked for the return of the patterns in May, as it had defeated the strike by means of apprentices and helpers.

Although the jobbing and machinery foundries had no national organization and business was reviving, local associations usually defeated the unions in whole or in part. In May, foundries in Chicago were struck by the molders for both an eight-hour day and wage advances, but the strikers returned at ten hours and no wage advance. In Millville, New Jersey, in August, a citizens' committee effected an adjustment of the labor troubles at the works of R. D. Woods & Company's pipe foundry. It advised the men to return to work and, after hearing the employer's propositions, they decided to do so. In August, the foundry proprietors of Paterson, New Jersey, were struck by the molders' union to enforce a new schedule of wages. One foundry tried to get another to do its work, but the molders there struck and were discharged. In September, a general strike was called on all the foundries except a small one which had granted the demands of the union. Then foundries at Ramapo, Newburg, Newark, New York, Brooklyn, and other places offered the Paterson manufacturers castings at prices lower than it cost to make them at Paterson. The molders' union tried to induce the molders at the outside places not to make castings for Paterson foundries, but failed. Some of the strikers returned to work without getting the $2.50 a day demanded. However, by January 15, 1887, all the firms conceded the wage increase and signed an agreement with the union. The molders' union usually used violence then to make the strike costly to employers; cheaper castings were not enough. Actually, more molders applied for work than could be used, and molding machines were introduced, so far as the record shows, for the first time in breaking a strike. Of course, the improvement in business justified a wage increase.

In the Coal Fields, operators were very reluctant to make concessions in 1886, partly because the business revival was slow in reaching them, partly because of the hostile trend toward unionism engendered by the law and order leagues. In January, the Monongahela Valley (river mines near Pittsburgh) strike ended with the men returning to work at the reduction to 2½c. The coal operators of Mineral Ridge (near Youngstown), Ohio, in January, were led to submit their differences with the union to a board of arbitration. A referee was chosen and he gave a decision favoring the advance of wages demanded by the miners —11 percent. Such boards, it seems, were a factor in the later formation of the Central Coal Fields. Coal operators in Logan County, Illinois, in February, were struck by miners for certain demands. Companies conferred with 260 miners and compromised on the demand to sell the miners their supplies cheaper; but 280 striking miners failed to get their demands. The Interstate Convention of Coal Miners and Operators met at Columbus, Ohio, in March, admitted West Virginia to the deliberations of the body, with an equal vote with the other four states—Ohio, Indiana, Illinois, and Pennsylvania. It adopted the Pittsburgh scale of wages for mining for the year May 1, 1886, to May 1, 1887. The scale ranged from 60c to 95c in various districts. A board of arbitration consisting of two operators and two miners from each of the five states was created for national questions, and similar state boards were recommended for state and local questions. Des Moines, Iowa was included in the scale at 90c. This was the beginning of the later so-called "Central Competitive Coal Fields." Nevertheless, coal operators, in April, reduced the wages of the coal miners in LaSalle County, Illinois, and defeated a strike of 1,100 miners. Likewise, the coal operators in the Mahoning Valley refused to grant the miners' demands in December for 10 percent in mining rates, and the miners struck.

The coal operators of George's Creek coal region were struck in March because they refused to increase the rate for mining coal from 40c to 50c—5,000 men were involved. The operators notified the men to remove their tools and paid them off. The union conducted the campaign weakly and in a conference with the operators, practically withdrew the demands. On May 19, the men returned to work at the old rate, but in March, 1887, the operators voluntarily granted the 50c rate.

The Philadelphia and Reading Railroad, on December 27, 1886, gave notice to the "topmen" employed on its piers that their wages would be reduced from 22½c to 20c an hour on January 1, 1887. This caused a strike which soon involved all the different coal companies along the New Jersey coast, in fact, the strike spread over three states. There was some violence and a few lost their lives in the strike disturbances. Pinkerton detectives were employed. The company finally withdrew the reduction but the strike lasted about three months.

Coke operators were struck in January, 1886. The strike was extensive, but one firm made concessions and operated. There were riots and bloodshed. The strike spread and with it increasing personal violence and bloodshed. Other businesses were seriously affected, some shutting down. A recently passed law prohibiting women from working in coke ovens cut down earnings of families and was one cause of the strike; company stores were also a cause. The strikers won because the strike caused a rise in the price of coke so that wages were advanced: mining from 27c to 30c a wagon of 30 bushels, drawing ovens from 55c to 60c, and leveling ovens from 8c to 10c. The Pittsburgh Coke Syndicate met on April 19, advanced the price of coke and agreed to grant an advance of wages on May 1. Coke operators, on October 19, were presented with demands by workmen for wage advances, for scales on tipples, reduced price for tool sharpening, uniform price for coal delivered to workers for domestic purposes, and semi-monthly paydays. The Syndicate called a meeting for November 19, and invited the Coke Producers' Association and the independent operators to meet at the same time and place. In the conference with the miners' committee at this meeting, the operators refused to grant any of the demands. Miners offered to submit the issues to a board of arbitration but the operators declined. The miners' union joined the Knights of Labor preliminary to a strike. However, the unions gave the operators a month to consider the demands; these were compromised and the men received concessions.

In the Wood-Working Industries, the main issue was the eight-hour day, although wages were also an issue. In January, 1886, the barrel and keg manufacturers of Cook County, Illinois, reduced wages, were struck, and defeated the strike of 800 coopers. But, in May, after the law and order victories, there was marked resistance to the eight-hour day. Then, the organized wagon manufacturers of New York defeated a strike of the wagon makers for reduction in hours of labor. The Employing Carriage and Wagon Manufacturers' Association of New York met and resolved not to grant the eight-hour day but to continue with the ten-hour day. Members of the Association who had already conceded the eight-hour day escaped expulsion by agreeing to return to the ten-hour day. The strike continued for some time but the association defeated it. On some issues, associations were divided; for instance, the National Wagon Manufacturers' Association met in Chicago in December. Although it took no official action, the sentiment of the association was against the employment of convict labor: 31 manufacturers present represented 70 percent of the wagon product of the United States; while 25 percent of the wagons were made by convict labor.

Associations of furniture manufacturers led in the fight on radicalism. In May, however, the furniture manufacturers of Chicago arbitrated a strike by 300 furniture workers which ended in a compromise. The Furniture Manufacturers' Association of New York pronounced the eight-hour day impracticable and agreed to protect employers against interference or intimidation. The Furniture Manufacturers' Association (national) met in Chicago, May 9, and adopted resolutions declaring a day's labor to be ten hours, and "That no members of this association will knowingly employ in his factory any communist, anarchist, nihilist or socialist, or any person denying the right to private property or recommending destruction or bloodshed as remedies for existing evils." The furniture workers attempted to continue the eight-hour struggle in Baltimore, but were resisted by a newly formed association of employers who bound themselves by rules and fines to keep their factories closed except for ten hours work per day. The union disintegrated and the men sought work as individuals.

Other May strikes were defeated. The mill and lumber vessel owners were struck by 8,000 lumbermen in Chicago for two weeks. The lumber companies of Chicago defeated also a strike of 1,300 lumber laborers for an eight-hour day and a wage increase. The railroad car manufacturers of Detroit defeated a strike over hours and wages. The piano manufacturers of New York defeated a strike and the movement among the piano makers for an eight-hour day.

Two other strikes on wood-working associations were somewhat unusual. In June, the picture frame workers struck because the employers violated their agreement. In December, cooper shops of Cincinnati were forced by a five-weeks strike to grant increased wages. In contrast, in January, 1887, the master coopers of Elliott City, Maryland, were struck for an increase in the price of making barrels, but informed the strikers that the increase would be given them if they could get the flour mills to pay more for the barrels. The strike was called off. In May, 1886, most of the broom manufacturers of Chicago defeated a strike of the broommakers for a shorter workday.

The Building Industry was hard hit by strikes for the shorter workday in 1886. The building contractors of New York felt very uncertain as early as January over the eight-hour law and had clauses placed in all collective agreements providing for reconsideration of their terms if the law was enforced. In February, the contracting masons of Providence, Rhode Island, held a meeting to consider the demands of the bricklayers and masons' union for a reduction in the hours of labor from 10 to 9, and granted the demands for the nine-hour day with daily wages of $3.00. On May 8, they met again to consider the situation, as they found themselves badly handicapped by the nine-hour day. They voted to return to the ten-hour day and decided that union men should not refuse to work with nonunion men. This action caused a strike. Nonunionists were brought in who did the work, and the union remained on strike throughout 1887. After they had decided to return to the ten-hour day, the employers refused at all times to arbitrate. In the spring of 1886, the Masons and Street Contractors' Association of Rochester, New York, in conference with the journeymen bricklayers, plasterers and masons' union granted the nine-hour day for trial during that season. At the close of the season, the association reported that because of the great increase in the cost of building due to the reduction of hours, the ten-hour day would be restored April 1, 1887. The association offered 50c an hour for the extra hour, but the union declined and struck. Finally, the union won the nine-hour day with the proviso that when necessary union men should work an extra hour at 50c. An agreement including also shop rules was signed.

The Master Builders' Association of Boston, however, was more belligerent. It authorized, in May, 1886, a statement saying it stood irrevocably upon the ground it took in April that it would have no conferences or agreements with unions which thrust themselves between the workmen and the employer; when the workmen got ready to come to work and presented themselves at the shops or at the buildings under construction, they would be put to work on the ten-hour standard if their places had not been previously filled. In October, the association was obtaining signatures of all contractors in the building trades—whether located in Boston or any other Eastern city—to an agreement for mutual support and protection. It proposed that wage rates be paid by the hour instead of by the day, so that cutting the hours would not add unduly to costs. This belligerent organization campaign among the master builders on a widespread scale undoubtedly helped to check the movement for the eight-hour day.

Around May 1, the issue of the shorter workday reached its height in the building industry. The Builders' Association of Detroit and affiliated associations signed an agreement with the carpenters and joiners to establish the nine-hour day from May 1, 1886 to May 1, 1887, with 5 percent advance in wages on August 1, 1887. The agreement required that six months' notice be given to the other side by the side desiring to change the agreement. An eight-hour strike affected all manufacturers of architectural iron work in St. Louis, Missouri, in May, 1886. It spread to other cities, affecting from 2,000 to 3,000 workmen in St. Louis, 1,500 to 1,800 in Milwaukee, Wisconsin, 1,800 in Pittsburgh, Pennsylvania, and 4,000 in Boston. But 50 firms, employing nearly all the men in the tin and sheet-iron trade of New York City granted the nine-hour day without a strike to force it. The Master Decorators and Painters' Association of New York granted a reduction of hours to nine, and wages of $3.50 a day, at a conference between the association and union. The union called strikes only against individual employers during the year. The Master Painters' Association of Brooklyn granted the nine-hour day with wages of $3.00, but the agreement was verbal and a dispute arose over the time to begin and end the day's work. The resulting strike failed and wages were reduced to $2.70. Later some firms attempted to return to the ten-hour day, but a strike defeated this movement. While the building contractors of East St. Louis, Illinois, were forced by a strike to grant the eight-hour day and an increase of wages to 30c an hour, the employers of Chicago, Illinois refused to arbitrate with the carpenters and joiners and defeated the strike for an eight-hour day. In early May, among others in Chicago, 500 stone laborers and mechanics, 200 lathers, and 90 steamfitters struck building contractors for an eight-hour day with ten-hour wages. The laborers and mechanics won through arbitration, and the lathers through negotiation. In Chicago, in the latter part of May, the sash, door and blind manufacturers determined to return on January 1, 1887 to the ten-hour day against the strong opposition of the workmen. The employer who submitted the resolution was struck at once but defeated the strike by employing other men. Among the other associations in Chicago which returned in June to the ten-hour day, were the plumbers', the foundries', the galvanized-iron firms', and the steamheating plants'. The strike on the Chicago Master Masons' Association was a long one and was finally arbitrated. In fact, strikes in the building trades of Chicago in May were quite extensive over the shorter workday. The contractors of Newark, New Jersey, held a meeting and decided to ask the carpenters' union to postpone to June 1, the demand made in March for a nine-hour day with wages at $2.75. The union refused and struck on May 3. Some employers granted the demands but most did not. After about a week, an agreement for the nine-hour day with a minimum wage of $2.50 a day, was reached. On May 3, the master plumbers of Newark, New Jersey, refused to grant the plumbers a reduction from the ten-hour day to nine hours for five days a week and eight on Saturday. The plumbers struck. The employers offered a nine-hour day, and the strikers countered with an eight and one-half hours on Saturday. Finally, the issue was referred to arbitration and the decision favored the employers—a 54-hour week.

In Baltimore, the Master Builders' Association was confronted with demands for the union "card system" and for the eight-hour day. A number of the building trades unions—the bricklayers, the slate roofers, and the plasterers—asked for the nine-hour day originally, while the tin and sheet metal workers and the stone masons changed their demands from the eight-hour day to a nine-hour day. Thus, with the exception of the carpenters, all the unions in the building trades asked for the nine-hour day, which was granted. But the carpenters insisted on the eight-hour day; some of the contractors granted it, while others did not and were struck.

Wages were also an issue in 1886. In April, the contractors of Cincinnati, Ohio, were forced by a three-weeks strike of 400 hod-carriers to grant a wage increase. The master painters of Newark, New Jersey, in April, granted the painters' demands for $3.00 a day but later, when times became dull, discharged a number of men and refused to pay $3.00 a day as a minimum but wanted to pay the men according to ability. The painters struck but the strike was a failure. In Buffalo, the plumbers demanded $3.00 a day from the master plumbers.

Organization issues were sharp in 1886. The associated contracting bricklayers of Cincinnati locked out all union men because of a hod-carriers' strike. The Master Plumbers' Association of New York City in August had a sharp dispute with the plumbers' union over the employment of apprentices. The association locked out 82 journeymen over apprenticeship rules and 350 journeymen struck to enforce the union rules on apprentices. The master plumbers refused to submit the dispute to arbitration in October, although the secretary of the board advised it. Collusion was practiced; the Association of Blue Stone Dealers of the City of New York had the Blue Stone Cutters and Flaggers' Union declare a strike and boycott, in March, against nonassociation employers although these employed union men and paid the union scale of wages. In September, the Central Labor Union of New York City ordered a general strike on all employers of the brown-stone cutters.

Employers were organizing superorganizations to check the abuses of unionism. The Builders' Exchange of Pittsburgh—composed of building-trades employers—adopted a constitution stating that its objects were "the promotion of industrial and mechanical interests among the various trades and to adjust controversies and misunderstandings as far as practicable without recourse to the courts."

A conference of the leaders of building-trades and master plumbers' associations of the Eastern District of the United States was held in New York City in August and discussed plans and recommendations to lay before the Executive Committee of the National Association regarding the then recent labor troubles in New York—they were planning a central organization to take concerted action when occasion arose in opposition to strikes. The master plumbers had made a strong effort to enlist all the building-trades employers in the struggle, and the various association leaders favored the superorganization. The president of the master plumbers' association, in an address, stated that the time had come to combine against the walking delegates and in defense of the apprenticeship system, so that young men would not be obstructed in learning the trade. Boston and other cities— which had the superorganizations—were cited as cities in which strikes were much less frequent. Representatives were present of master plumbers, masons, painters, ironworkers, marbleworkers, builders, and manufacturing steamfitters; and they planned an incorporated "Amalgamated Building Trades Exchange." A committee was selected to ascertain the workings of the Boston and Baltimore associations and to report on them. The problem was then made more acute by the journeymen strikers opening up "cooperative shops" to compete with their former employers.

In the Glass Industry, there were two unusually important developments during 1886; the attempt of the union to abolish apprentices in certain factories, and the formation of national associations. American manufacturers of window glass were much disturbed over an attempt by Belgian manufacturers to reduce the wages of their workmen to meet the 10 percent reduction recently made by the American manufacturers and accepted by their workmen—which had been done, it was claimed, to meet foreign (Belgian and other) competition. The window-glass workers' union proposed a combination of American manufacturers and workmen to aid Belgian workers resist the reduction. This was undoubtedly one of the competitive factors which led to the formation of national associations here; one was formed in 1886 by 54 of the 57 glass manufacturers in the United States.

The Western green-glass vial and bottle manufacturers met in May, in Pittsburgh, to consider the wage scale for the next year, and considered a reduction of from 10 to 20 percent. The question of apprentices, however, soon overshadowed the wage question. In July, the Glass Manufacturers' Association of New Jersey refused to grant the glass blowers' union's demand for abolishing apprentices for the years 1886 and 1887. A strike resulted. A conference was held and a compromise reached, which, however, was rejected by the union members. Local compromises were then effected by local conference committees. Then the state-wide union offered to compromise, but the association declined. Although the executive committee of the state-wide union authorized all locals to make compromises, this action was declared illegal by the state-wide union itself. Disgusted with the great dissension among the union officials, workmen quit that union and organized another and went to work in July at reduced wages of 5 percent and with two apprentices to a factory. The green-glass manufacturers of New York, New Jersey, and Pennsylvania took a very strong stand against the demand for the glass blowers to abolish apprentices, and the Glass Manufacturers' Association declared such demand arbitrary and detrimental to the interests of all concerned. It not only considered establishing training schools for glass blowers, but later aided in establishing four of these in New Jersey. In September, the glass manufacturers of New Jersey and elsewhere were struck by the window-glass workers for an increase in wages. A conference was held but the strikers' demands were not granted. Shortly thereafter, the demand for an advance in wages made upon Western window-glass manufacturers was withdrawn and the glass workers at Pittsburgh signed the past year's scale. In September, the bottle factories of Maryland were struck by the glass blowers against an increase in the number of apprentices and the old ratio was continued. In December, however, the green-glass blowers struck over a wide section to force the abolishment of apprenticeship. Glass manufacturers of Baltimore signed an agreement with each other to shut down if employees did not take a 15 percent wage reduction and allow two apprentices to each blast. The employees refused.

In Transportation, the most noted strike of 1886 was on the Southwestern System, and has been discussed above in connection with the Law and Order Leagues, but other railroads were struck. On April 20, 1886, the General Managers' Association was organized in Chicago to deal with an eight-hour strike on the railroads there. The railroads in Chicago resumed business May 10; the Baltimore and Ohio Railroad alone conceded the shorter workday. In August, the labor injunction was used by the Lake Shore Railroad against the striking switchmen.

The Vessel Owners and Captains' National Association met in Boston in October with 100 members present representing about 1,000 vessels. It was being organized "to establish a uniformity in coasting freight rates and for the benefit of that branch of the merchant service." It met in New York in November, "adopted a constitution and appointed a committee of 15, representing every State from Maine to Virginia, for the purpose of securing Congressional action in favor of the abolition of compulsory pilotage"—the law requires a vessel entering a harbor to take on a union pilot at a high fee although the captain of the vessel may know the harbor as well as the pilot does. Apparently, this is the first time this issue has been dealt with by an organization covering several States.

Detroit shipbuilders were handicapped by concessions made to strikers and 400 fewer men were employed by these concerns after the strike; the work had gone to competitors at other ports. Shipbuilders of Detroit and Trenton (18 miles from Detroit) had repudiated the Knights of Labor and its wage scale.

The Pacific Coast Ship Owners' Association was organized on June 7, 1886, with 73 members representing sailing vessels only, but of about 90,000 tonnage. The cause for the organization was that the seamen wanted to "run the owners' business," to dictate terms, to commit unlawful acts, such as cutting the rigging and assaulting the captains and others, over a period of eight weeks. The seamen had organized in 1885 and started hitting at the shipowners one by one. The seamen struck against the shipowners' organizing, adopted arbitrary rules and resorted to violence. The association defeated the three months' strike and established a schedule of reduced wages that lasted about two years.

In the Textile and Related Industries, association activities became increasingly belligerent as the year 1886 passed. Textile mills were struck by operatives for advanced wages and shorter workdays. In March, the cotton mills of Manchester, New Hampshire, were struck by 300 weavers and forced, after a three-months strike, to grant an increase in wages. Cotton weavers also struck in Massachusetts and Rhode Island in March, to around 2,250 strikers; and 2,000 carpet weavers struck in Philadelphia the same month. In August, cotton mills of Rollinsford, New Hampshire, were struck by weavers for a uniform scale of prices and against deductions for imperfect work. The strike failed. Likewise, two spool and bobbin factories of Dover, New Hampshire, were struck for a reduction of hours. The employers hired nonunionists and the strike lasted only one day and was a failure. About 150 textile manufacturing firms in Philadelphia organized in May for "mutual protection" as "The Manufacturers' Association of Philadelphia." Representing $150,000,000 in capital, the association was formed "for the establishment of fair and uniform wages, the prevention of strikes, the setttlement of differences between employers and operatives, and the protection of the members from worthless and incompetent operatives." In October, it decided to make a test case with the Knights of Labor which had ordered a strike against an "objectionable" foreman. At first, 15 cotton mills threatened to close, shutting down 2,000 looms and throwing 4,000 hands out of work. In November, the threat of closing down extended to the entire association and included 100 firms employing 26,637 workers and having a weekly payroll of $208,000. The issue, however, was settled at a conference between the aid committee of the association and the General Executive Board of the Knights of Labor. But the Fall River, Massachusetts, manufacturers refused in November to grant spinners higher wages on the grounds that an advance of 10 percent had been made a few months ago, and that higher wages were not warranted when very low dividends had been paid.

The silk manufacturers of Paterson, New Jersey, in May, refused to grant the demands of 900 dyers for a new schedule of wages, hours, and working rules. These rules governed output, number of apprentices, minimum wages, shop committees, no Sunday work, early quitting on Saturdays, and time and one-half for overtime. The dyers struck but at the end of three days all the firms but one had conceded the demands. However, in July, a large silk mill of Paterson prepared to move to Harrisburg because of recurring labor troubles in the former place which manufacturers were anxious to escape. The silk manufacturers were particularly interested in the establishment by the Paterson Board of Trade of a "permanent board of arbitration for the settlement of questions between workers and employers in that city."

The Knit-Goods Manufacturers Organized and fought in 1886. The National Association of Knit Goods Manufacturers was organized in March, and local associations affiliated with it or were organized about this time. Among these locals was the Employers' Association of Cohoes, New York. In March, the Cohoes knitting mills were struck for three weeks by over 6,000 workers for restoration of the 1884 schedule of wages (10 to 15 percent above the rate at the time of the strike), semi-monthly pay, no discrimination against any member of a labor organization, and no reduction in pay if the ten-hour law were passed; these were granted. In June, 47 manufacturers of Philadelphia, employing over 12,000 workers, organized the Associated Manufacturers of Hosiery and Knit Goods for "mutual protection." It was the result largely of union demands for wage increases ranging as high as 55 percent in factories making the finer grades of goods and as high as 200 percent in the cheaper factories. In October, the associated knit-goods manufacturers of Cohoes decided to sustain one of its members who had been struck for a wage advance and primarily for promoting an apprentice. The local association invited the strikers to return to work and when they did not, because of the advice of union officials, the national association declared a lockout affecting also mills elsewhere. The association then declared that any members of the Knights of Labor desiring to return to work must first withdraw from the union. The association refused to deal with the union officials on the ground that the strike was in violation of an agreement between the national association and the national executive committee of the Knights of Labor. The strikers lost. Amsterdam, New York, knit-goods manufacturers had a similar experience: one of its members was struck because he promoted an apprentice to a new machine. The national association tried to conciliate the issue, but the union leader refused, and the national association now declared a general lockout, for reasons given above. While the strike was on, the strikers drew up a new wage schedule and presented it to the association, which rejected it in a joint conference with the union. Meanwhile, the police arrested 100 pickets on order of the mayor, who was also a manufacturer. Twelve pickets were sent to jail when they refused to put up $250 each as security for their good behavior. The strike was called off after six months, in May, 1887, a failure.

Associated Clothing Manufacturers and boss tailors had laboi troubles in 1886. The clothing contractors of New York were struck by the tailors over wages and hours by the button-hole operators and the cloak makers over wage increases. The tailors and button-hole operators obtained concessions, but the strike of the cloak makers was a failure. The Clothing Manufacturers' Association of New York signed an agreement with the United Clothing Cutters of New York, providing for a nine-and-one-half hour day with Saturdays half-holidays during the Summer months, and that no strike or lockout should be called without notice being given and a conference held. Nevertheless, that association was struck by the cutters because of the employment of nonunion men by two firms which had been struck, and upheld by the association. The strikers were ordered back to work by the Arbitration Committee of the Knights of Labor on the ground that the strikers had violated their contract. The settlement left the employers free to employ whomsoever they pleased. On May 15, the boss tailors of New York locked out the tailors because the union refused to call out the workmen of independent boss tailors and because the union would not combine with the association "in raising the trade generally." The difficulty was finally settled by conciliation. Manifestly, collusion in the clothing industry is an old practice.

The Clothing Manufacturers' Association of Newark, New Jersey, made an agreement with the tailors providing for: the abolition of the discharge system, exclusive employment of union men, a week's notice to be given before leaving or discharge, reinstatement of employees who had been ill, and conciliation of disputes. The association, however, later in the year inaugurated the "honorable discharge card" system, but the union after several conferences secured its abolition. In contrast, the wholesale clothiers of Milwaukee, Wisconsin, defeated a strike of the shop tailors and one of the clothing cutters. The shop tailors wanted wages restored. The employers refused to deal with any union committee, but offered to deal with their own employees. After six weeks, the shop tailors' strike was called off, and they received about 10 percent increase in wages. But the clothing cutters lost their strike in about three weeks and their demands for an eight-hour day with no reduction in pay. They did, however, obtain a Saturday half-holiday without reduction in pay. On the contrary, the master tailors of Eau Claire, Wisconsin, were forced by a strike of the tailors to advance wages 25 percent. Clothing manufacturers of Cook County (Chicago), Illinois, in April, granted the clothing makers the eight-hour day at ten-hour wages without a strike but the tailors' strike caused the pay to be for a nine-hour day. In May 863 tailors and 421 cloak makers struck—the cloak makers demanding also 20 percent increase in wages—as well as reduction in hours. Compromises resulted. In April, the clothing manufacturers of Springfield, Illinois, were struck and compromised with the striking tailors for a wage increase.

Hat manufacturers had some trouble with the union label and wage reductions in 1886. In January, the hat manufacturers of Orange, New Jersey, refused to use the union label and were struck. After several weeks, the manufacturers agreed to use the label and the men returned to work. In February, the Hat Manufacturers' Association and the national union met in New

York and reached an agreement on the use of the union label. This caused factories in Essex County, New Jersey (including Orange), to use the union label. On May 10, the Association of Hat Manufacturers of Newark, New Jersey, which had organized shortly before, "locked out" about 600 sizers by reducing the rate for sizing hats. Some manufacturers broke away from the association. On the third day of the strike, the secretary of the association sent for the union conference committee and asked it for a proposal, which was refused until the "lockout" was declared off. The association met, declared the "lockout" off, and in a conference with the union conceded the strikers' demands and also an arbitration procedure for future disputes.

Laundrymen, collar, cuff, shirt, glove, and fur manufacturers experienced difficulties with unions in 1886. As far back as 1879, the manufacturers and laundrymen of Troy, New York, had considered the organization of a permanent and formal association but nothing important had been done prior to 1886. Then the Trade Association of Employers of Troy—shirt and collar factories—was involved in a strike on one of its members, and locked out the union employees in all the firms. The association had refused to negotiate over a partial restoration of wages to the 1885 rates. The strike was declared off by a union official who called it unjust, and the strikers went back at the manufacturers' rates after six weeks of striking. On the other hand, collar manufacturers of New York were struck by the collar and cuff makers for an increase of wages. The strike ended by conciliation after one month and five days. The associated shirt manufacturers of Jamesburg, New Jersey, locked out 2,000 employees when it became known that they had joined the Knights of Labor. Glove manufacturers of Gloversville, New York, were struck for higher wages by 6,000 workmen. The glove manufacturers of Gloversville organized a Fulton County Glove Manufacturers' Association and put out a price list which reduced wages 15 percent from the 1885 levels, while the union demanded a 10 percent increase. Conferences between the association and union committees finally settled the difficulty by restoring the 1885 wages or better. An agreement as to shop rules was also signed. In April, the Manufacturing Furriers' Association of New York was struck by the furriers' union for the eight-hour day. The association issued a statement to show that the furriers received high wages, and refused to deal with union officials or answer their demands and communications. In reply to a union circular, the association, however, issued a circular to its workmen arguing against the eight-hour day and the strike. The association resolved not to recognize the union or treat with it on any basis whatever, and promised protection to any workmen who would return to work under the terms and conditions existing prior to the strike with wages to be adjusted by the individual employers. The strike failed.

In the Shoe Industry, there were no unusual developments in 1886. In February, all the shoe manufacturers of Milwaukee refused to sign a union price list for piece work on machines, and the employees struck. After many conferences and much wrangling, the manufacturers gave in one by one. In June, the Shoe and Leather Association of Lynn, Massachusetts, appointed subcommittees to prepare new lists of wages in each department, covering all prices in making shoes. The association took the lead without regard to the union's desires. In July, the shoe manufacturers of Newark, New Jersey, after closing for stock taking, gave notice that before they resumed, they had to be assured that no advance in wages would be demanded, but that certain reductions would be accepted. The union submitted a new schedule with advances. The factories were closed for six weeks. In the second week in August, however, an agreement between the association and the union was reached granting increases ranging from 5 to 20 percent. Likewise, in September, the labor troubles at Brockton, Massachusetts, which had kept the 39 associated shoe factories idle for four weeks were settled by the factories yielding on nearly every point. Although collective bargaining had been carried on in the shoe industry for many years, McNeill complained that in 1886 the shoemakers and the Knights of Labor had to invoke their entire strength to exercise the right to organize against the tenacity of employers to hold to assumed perogatives, even in Massachusetts. These unions had successfully conducted boycotts and ruined businesses in certain cases, for instance, Brennan and White, formerly prosperous shoe manufacturers were boycotted out of existence in 1886.

The activities of the leather manufacturers were quite diverse. In April, 1886, the leather manufacturers of Newark, New Jersey, held a conference with the leather japaners' union and agreed to do away with the sub-boss system. They asked the union committee to submit wage schedules, but this was rejected by the manufacturers because of the large advance (about 50 percent) in wages. The manufacturers then held a meeting and revoked their agreement to abolish the sub-boss system and agreed not to pay any wage advances. After a five weeks' strike, the manufacturers agreed to advance wages 25 percent and abolish the sub-boss system. In June, however, the leather manufacturers' association in Essex County, New Jersey, supported one of its members in a dispute over the wage schedule and the maximum output as agreed upon by the association and union. The association, in August, resolved not to treat with union representatives, and the union struck. Nonunion men were employed in large numbers and in 30 days the strike had failed. In September, the National Morocco Manufacturers' Association met and appointed a committee to promote "all lawful efforts to maintain their position in controlling their business."

The harness manufacturers of Newark, in May, refused to grant a new schedule of wages demanded by the harness makers' union, but offered an advance of 10 percent, which the union refused. The manufacturers then offered to grant 25 percent to the stitchers and 10 percent to all other workers, but again the union declined. After a five weeks' strike, however, the strikers wearied and accepted a 15 percent advance and returned to work. Other harness manufacturers in New York defeated a strike for equalization of wages. The strike lasted 3 months and 17 days. The firms were boycotted but that also was a failure.

In the Meat-Packing Industry, the issue in 1886 was the ten-hour day. In April, the butchers of Chicago were "locked out" by the packers for joining the union. The meat packers of Chicago formed an alliance and resolved to return to the ten-hour day by August 1. The workmen resisted the return to the longer day and 16,000 workmen struck in October. On November 6, a general strike was ordered on all packers by the Executive Committee of the Knights of Labor. The packers declared war on the unions. Thousands of workers were brought in from elsewhere and the militia was called out to protect them, and the hopelessness of the strike was soon apparent. In one week, Powderly called off the strike, and the strikers got their jobs back only when these were not filled by newcomers. Moreover, a pertinent comment then made, pointed out that "a peaceful condition, however, can hardly be expected so long as union and non-union men are working together, and the end can hardly be foreseen." In September, the butchers in Maryland struck but failed to force their employers to reduce the day to ten hours. An attempt to arbitrate the issue failed, the strike broke up, the union dissolved, and later the employers shortened the day voluntarily. There was also a general strike of the sheep butchers in New York, that was settled by conciliation.

Among the Brewers, the normal appeasatory attitude had a belligerent turn around May 1, 1886. The St. Louis Brewers' Association began a fight upon a newly organized local union in 1886—a new union is often over-aggressive. On May 1, the union retaliated by placing certain beers on the boycott list, especially that made by the president of the association. The association then declared that on September 4, any brewery worker who had not severed his connection with the union would be discharged. The brewers refused to recognize the union and a general strike was called on September 2. The union was soon defeated. In October, the union boycotted all the breweries except one, and on January 6, 1887, the association signed an agreement with the union to be effective until May 1, 1888. The secretary of the association later declared that after that date the association would no longer recognize the union. One brewery which discharged union men was boycotted. On June 1, 1889, 17 St. Louis breweries formed the St. Louis Brewing Association —an English syndicate—and was boycotted by the union. Two other firms disparaged the union and were boycotted. In April, 1891, members of the St. Louis Brewers' Association discharged 33 union workmen because they belonged to a union boycotting the association, and this caused the union to lift that boycott. The boycott was thus narrowed to two firms on which the boycott was made nationwide. One of the three outside firms —Anhauser-Busch—had entered into negotiations with the union in June, but it was not until September 25, 1891, that a satisfactory agreement was reached.

The master brewers usually made concessions to the unions, mainly to avoid union boycotts on beer. The master brewers of Chicago settled all difficulties with the brewery workers' union by conciliation and arbitration. On June 10, 1886, the New York and New Jersey Brewers' Association signed an agreement with the union providing for exclusive employment of union workmen, high-wage schedules, and arbitration.

Cigar Factories clashed with the cigar makers in 1886. In January, 14 member firms of the United Cigar Manufacturers' Association of New York City, to help two of their fellow members who had been struck, ordered a lockout in all the factories which together employed 7,000 workmen. The manufacturers hoped also that the lockout would compel the cigar makers to accept a new schedule of prices issued on January 1, which involved a wage reduction from $1.00 to $2.50 per 1,000 cigars. The contest in New York City was complicated by bitter rivalry beween competing unions. In June, the cigar factories of Baltimore refused to grant the demands of union cigar makers for a new "equalization" scale of wages and 930 men were involved. The union obtained an injunction restraining the manufacturers from using the blue label of the union on nonunion cigars. The factories gave up one by one and conceded the union's demands. The tobacco (not cigar) manufacturers of Milwaukee granted the eight-hour day without reduction in pay.

The Bakeries were also more belligerent in 1886. The bakeries of Newark, New Jersey, became involved in trouble with the bakery-workers' union over the partial use of the union label, reduction in hours, and increased wages. The majority of the bakeries had granted the union's demands but failed to use the union label. The bakeries organized and tried to increase the price of bread one cent to cover the increased cost of labor, but the association failed to obtain the most important bakeries as members. In contrast, the Master Bakers' Association of Buffalo, on June 1, adopted two rules, namely: "That one week's wages of the bakers should be retained so that men would not strike suddenly; (and) that employers should blacklist undesirable workmen." A strike was called but failed.

Some other associations granted union demands in 1886. In April, the brick manufacturers of Baltimore granted increased wages to the brickmakers. In May, the Chicago brick manufacturers were struck by the brickmakers for a shorter workday with no reduction in daily pay and lost through arbitration. The merchants of LaSalle County, Illinois, gave their clerks a shorter workday without a strike. Steel file manufacturers of New York failed to carry out their promise to restore wages when business revived, so the file makers struck. After three weeks the issue was compromised. But the metal manufacturers of Chicago, in February, defeated a strike of the metal workers over restoration of wage rates to a higher level. Moreover, the cotton manufacturers of Georgia and South Carolina organized in July to resist strikes.

This tidal wave of formation of employers' associations to check the abuses of unionism, even to crush it, continued well into 1887.

CHAPTER 12

ASSOCIATIONS CONTINUE DRIVE ON THE KNIGHTS OF LABOR

WHILE THE ASSOCIATIONS in 1887 continued their drive on the Knights of Labor, they also came to grips with other unions. Associations won most of the larger strikes of 1887. For instance, the strike of the 90,000 New York and New Jersey coal handlers and sympathizers, of the 8,000 New England shoe factory employees, of the 26,600 Chicago building trades employees, of the 25,000 Lehigh, Pennsylvania coal miners, and of the 25,000 Connellsville coke burners, all failed. The situation in 1887 was then thus characterized:

"Miners are idle in Pennsylvania; sawmills and their operatives are idle in Michigan and Wisconsin; thousands of men are thrown out of work in stone quarries adjacent to the city; the pressed brick trade is affected all over the United States; thousands of dollars have been lost to the railroad companies; every branch of manufacture identified in any way with the building trades—and their number is legion—is a direct sufferer from this and every other strike of similar nature."

In June, internal dissension in the Knights of Labor was reported great and growing, and the fights between assemblies were causing numerous strikes on employers without issues. In July, the Order was said to be fast disintegrating; according to a current analysis:

"The causes which have led to this deplorable state of affairs are not far to seek. First, the K. of L. have exhausted themselves and impoverished their treasuries through their innumerable strikes and labor dissensions. They have suffered defeat in almost every recent fight which they have waged against their employers, and consequently they have come to place but little confidence in the advantages and capabilities of their organization. Besides this . . . a deep seated conviction has entered the minds of the thinking members of the order that the management of affairs is not all . . . it should be."

The victories of the Law and Order Leagues over the Knights showed employers what united action could accomplish when well directed:

"Realizing at last the magnitude of their common danger, employers have been taught to make a common cause of resistance. Organizations have been formed in different lines of business, and at the present time two strikes are in progress in which the good faith of the members of employers' associations is to be put to the test. Manufacturers have only too often looked on complacently, if not gleefully, when the operations of rivals were being interfered with by contest with their men." (The lockout of the silversmiths and the strike of the stove molders are the two strikes referred to above.)

The matter of "good faith" of the employer was discussed in a number of connections, of which three instances will serve to illustrate some of the pertinent points made: (1) It was held that an employer had a responsibility to his nonunion workmen when he shut down indefinitely and set adrift those workmen to get jobs when all other concerns were unionized. (2) The Newark, New Jersey, Manufacturers' Association placed members "under heavy bond to conduct their business hereafter independently of the Knights of Labor, . . . if the shops close, only men who abandon that organization will be employed." (3) "Good faith" by the employer requires that he treat workmen so that their attitude will change:

"The man regards his employer as his natural enemy. They are, in his opinion, as bound to quarrel as cat and dog. To have a feeling of gratitude toward an employer is a weakness of which he is ashamed, to say the least."

"Capital cannot say to labor, 'I will take all of you into partnership and for the benefit of the concern I expect you to labor 300 hours extra; in return for this I will pay you out of the profits, if any there be, $6.00 for your extra work.' Such games as that have been tried repeatedly in this and other cities and failed. The insurance scheme of the Pennsylvania Railroad was of this kind. It had only the good of the company at heart, and was perfectly regardless of the men. Much was expected, and much gratitude was asked, but nothing was given in return. A failure was deserved and should have been most signal."

It was recorded that the year's events had caused a general feeling among the employers that employers' associations were valuable institutions, particularly in regulating wages and restraining injurious competition. It was noted also that unions were causing the removal of manufacturers from industrial centers.

In the Government Fields, there were court decisions, legislation, and political activities. The boycott was declared illegal in Connecticut in April, while the futility of the boycott in Chicago when combated by vigorous employers' associations was pointed out. Attempts of workmen to prevent employment of other men, or deter them from working, by calling them "scabs" was held to be an unlawful conspiracy by the Supreme Court of Vermont in May. The conspiracy case of shoe manufacturers against a "strike agitator" was also cited. The legality of strikes and boycotts was discussed and early cases reviewed; and the right to stop strikes—by compulsory arbitration and other legal action—was also considered. The injunction issued by Judge Welker in the New York, Pennsylvania and Ohio Railroad strike was noted. Discussions of the "difficulties in assisting labor," sympathetic strikes, the costs of strikes, and N. O. Nelson's profit-sharing plan were published in the IRON AGE. That profit-sharing plan was then thought to be a great success along with another case cited. There were expositions of other issues such as the policy of company houses and stores, the apprenticeship question, and the great boom of manual training in the public schools. It was noted that in the Cleveland Manual Training School a machine shop and a carpenter shop were established in 1887.

Associations were also concerned with legislation and politics. In March, alone, the Connecticut legislature considered a law for the incorporation of unions; Congress passed legislation prohibiting the importation of alien contract labor and providing for arbitration, but the President refused to sign the bills into law; and the Missouri legislature defeated a bill for the support of the state militia, but enacted a law making intimidation a felony "for anyone, by threats of violence, to induce an employee to quit work," with the penalty two to five years in the penitentiary; and "to prevent one from accepting employment, by threats or violence," with penalty of a fine of $100 to $1,000, and county jail. Legislation dealing with prison labor was proposed in Illinois. In January, 1888, courts of conciliation were proposed by legislation in Iowa. Moreover, the union candidate for mayor of Chicago was defeated in April, 1887.

A countertendency, however, was shown by the Paterson Board of Trade and the local assembly of the Knights of Labor agreeing upon an arbitration plan in May, 1887. But the Manufacturers' Association of Newark, New Jersey, placed its members under heavy bonds not to employ members of the Knights of Labor. Moreover, it was pointed out that most unions were composed largely of foreign-born members.

The Iron Industry was relatively quiet in 1887. In March, the iron manufacturers of the Mahoning and Shenango Valleys, Ohio, began to form an association, since most of them did not belong to the Western Iron Association. In June, the furnace owners of New Castle, Pennsylvania, were struck for a 10c a day advance in wages and submitted the question to arbitration. The arbitrators decided in favor of the furnace owners. About two weeks later, the Amalgamated Association (union) of Iron and Steel Workers went on record as "unalterably opposed to the system now applied" for arbitration of labor disputes. Accordingly, they held conference after conference with the iron manufacturers at Pittsburgh in June in a demand for 10 percent advance in wages and "extras." While 70 manufacturers met and decided against both the advance and "extras," after many conferences, they granted the advance and some "extras." In July, it was found that the Amalgamated had apparently outwitted the Western Iron Association by the omission of one clause which provided for 10 percent reduction on heavy work. In December, the Pittsburgh manufacturers were presented with a new scale and, while conferences were held, some manufacturers had already signed the scale.

The National Association of Sheet Iron and Steel Manufacturers was organized in June—sheet iron was already beginning to displace iron castings as superior in a number of fields. This, of course, had an adverse effect upon both foundries and molders.

Competition often manifested itself through substitution of better products. For instance, the nail manufacturers and nailers held informal conferences on means to reduce the cost of producing small nails to meet the competition of the tack manufacturers, but no decision was reached in regard to possible wage reductions, although the conferences were carried over into the year 1888. In January, 1888, the Wheeling nail manufacturers refused to deal with the Amalgamated in regard to a revision in the wage scale upward, because of competitive conditions which apparently the union officials did not understand or chose to ignore.

In Stove Manufacturing, the belligerent Stove Founders' National Defense Association made history in the noted Bridge and Beach strike. On March 8, 1887, a member of the SFNDA— the Bridge and Beach Stove Manufacturing Company of St. Louis, Missouri—was struck by the molders' union to force a wage advance of 15 percent, later reduced to 10 percent. The firm offered to compromise by promising to grant 10 percent advance on June 1, and then offered 5 percent advance at once with an additional 5 percent in June, providing prices of stoves could be advanced. The local association had decided that the price of stoves could not be increased under market conditions, so the offer of the 10 percent was withdrawn. The SFNDA sent its executive committee to St. Louis to hear both sides, but the union failed to convince the committee. The SFNDA then opened negotiations with the President of the International Molders' Union, and renewed the offer of the split 10 percent increase. The molders struck and the SFNDA distributed the patterns of the struck firm among the members of the association in that district, but the molders there struck against working with the "hot" patterns. When the 20 firms employing 1,125 molders in the fourth district—in St. Louis, Chicago, Belleville, Leavenworth, Quincy, Keokuk, and Milwaukee—were struck, the patterns were sent to the third district, and finally into the second district as the molders struck when the patterns appeared.

The sending of the patterns from shop to shop with the resulting strikes caused much comment:

"Many of the manufacturers who assumed the obligations

of the Defense Association did so for the 'moral effect,' and with no idea of being called upon at any time to take patterns from other foundries and make goods for them." It "should at once abandon the plan." "All the foundries now running could not make work enough from the patterns of those closed by strikes to amount to anything." "No manufacturer really wants castings made in any other foundry than his own, or would send his valuable patterns outside to be entrusted to the tender mercies of hostile union molders." "The patterns . . . have passed around from hand to hand, followed by strikes in the majority of cases." "Molders sometimes worked on the patterns because they thought that the distribution was a subterfuge to close foundries, not to get castings." Two reasons for closing foundries apparently were to cut heavily the sources of union funds to support the strike, and to sell off a great surplus of stoves at high prices induced by the strikes.

In other words, the sending of the patterns around functioned as a sort of a lockout to starve out the strikers and deplete the union treasury while the association members prospered from the sale of stoves on hand. However, it had its anti-union aspects that indications were growing more numerous that employers throughout the country were beginning to change from a defensive to an offensive attitude to meet the aggressions of the labor organizations. The conferences between the union and associations during the strike came to naught. The conduct of association members was puzzling to the uninitiated observer, for instance, a conference of the principal members of the association in Detroit led to a lockout of 2,800 men for 4 weeks there although the shops were not unionized, while in Philadelphia, the foundries which had closed, opened up and used the struck patterns. The stove manufacturers of New York met in April and decided to stand firmly against the strikers. In Leavenworth, Kansas, the Great Western Stove Manufactory was struck when the struck patterns appeared, but when these patterns were recalled later, the men had to return on the open-shop basis. The great secrecy with which the association conducted its affairs during the strike tended to confirm the belief that the association was a combination to advance the price of stoves by creating an artificial scarcity through stimulated strikes. In any event the IMU was defeated, the Bridge and Beach shop was operated by nonunion helpers, apprentices, and others, the patterns recalled, and after 6 months, the IMU discontinued its support of the St. Louis strikers. The strike made the SFNDA powerful, but produced a number of reactions in the molders' union, such as lessening their aggressiveness toward employers but increasing it toward the Knights of Labor, for instance, the Knights of Labor lost their strike at the Delamater Iron Works because members of the molders' union acted as strikebreakers. On the other point, in January, 1888, in Albany—noted for its molders' strikes—a member of the SFNDA, Rathborn Sard & Co., was enabled to reach an agreement with the molders to make no reductions or advances in wages for a year, to retain 10 percent of their wages as a forfeit in case they struck, and to grant that amount in case of a lockout; a shop committee was to settle all grievances.

In the Coal Fields in 1887, the main issue was wage advances, but there was also marked dissension between the great rival unions, as well as division among the coal operators. In January, the Board of Arbitration in the Mahoning Valley dispute awarded a 10c advance (from 55c to 65c) a ton for mining coal, but left other wages unchanged. In February, river coal operators near Pittsburgh were struck for about two weeks. In April, the Pittsburgh railroad coal operators finally formed an association with 31 members representing a capital of $12,000,-000. Each member paid an initiation fee of $25. In May, the coal operators of Pennsylvania were served with a demand by the miners for a 10 percent advance. On May 18, the bituminous coal operators of Ohio, Indiana, Illinois, and Western Pennsylvania, met with the miners' representatives from these states in an organization known as the Interstate Joint Board of Arbitration and Conciliation and formed to fix rates a year in advance. It granted an advance of 5c a ton for May—as agreed upon previously at a meeting in Columbus for a year—but the opposition of Northern Illinois operators made the grant conditional. These operators contended that Central and Southern Illinois operators had not lived up to it and that it should not be given unless all districts united on it. It was resolved that the 5c advance would be for May, but if operators did not give it universally by June 21, all were freed from the obligation. Northern Illinois operators refused to pay the 5c advance and thus broke up the arrangement. But the Joint Board, on June 22, ordered an advance of 5c on the scale fixed at Columbus from May 1 to November 1, 1887, but no further advance was to be made from then to May 1, 1888, if the coal operators of Illinois did not pay the Columbus scale. The Illinois situation was due largely to a fight on the Knights of Labor by the Miners' Amalgamated —the bitterness between these organizations was so great that representatives of the Amalgamated refused to meet coal operators in conference if representatives of the Knights were present. By November, the Illinois operators had been induced to conform; so another 5c advance was made.

The Anthracite Coal Strike of 1887-88 was important enough to lead to an investigation by a Select Committee of the House of Representatives of the United States. It began in September, 1887, in the Lehigh region. The coal operators refused to recognize or communicate with the union representatives on such grievances as excessive dockage, "pluck-me stores," and exorbitant profits on powder and equipment, as well as over a wage advance. The coal operators contended that under the sliding scale in operation, wages could not be advanced without an increase in the price of coal which the public would not stand. More than 23,000 workers struck in the Lehigh, Columbia, Shamokin, and Dauphin regions. The strike affected the Schuylkill, the Philadelphia and Reading Railroad, and the Wilkes-Barre collieries. The strike on the Reading and Schuylkill collieries came to an end in February on the employers' terms. Lehigh miners started to return to work in March, and the strike was declared off officially in the latter part of March, a failure. In the Wilkes-Barre region, attempts to evict strikers from company houses failed in a court test in November, 1887.

Dissension among the coke operators marked the great coke strike of 1887. The Producers' Association and the Coke Syndicate were united in March in their determination not to grant the demands of the workers for a 20 percent advance in wages based on the rise in the price of coke from $1.50 to $2.00 a ton. The operators had offered a 5 percent advance. Finally, the issue was arbitrated, but the umpire decided that there should be no advance in wages until coke rose further in price. The union then sent an ultimatum for a 12½c percent advance or a strike in May. The coke operators replied that the cost to produce coke in the Connellsville region was greater than elsewhere in the United States. The strike was called and 15,000 men were out of employment. No effort was made by the operators to fill the strikers' places and no workmen were evicted; so there was no occasion for disturbances until an attempt was made in one instance, to save the coke in an abandoned oven by a group of laborers. A mob of 400—mostly Negroes and Hungarians— assaulted the laborers in a deadly manner. In conferences between strikers and operators, the operators insisted on the arbitration award. The strikers declared they would not accept it, but would return to work if the price of coke was reduced to $1.50, which the operators refused to do. Pinkerton detectives were imported in large numbers to protect the men who returned to work. But when the notice was given when the works would resume operation and when men did return to work in large groups, no trouble occurred. The strike was declared off unconditionally in the latter part of July. However, one large concern—the Frick Coke Company, a Carnegie company—broke with the associated operators and granted the strikers' demands. The coke operators met in September and decided emphatically not to pay the advance in wages granted by the Frick Coke Company; they adopted a sliding scale, equalizing wages throughout the region but with no general advances. The operators held conferences with the representatives of the Knights of Labor, but the competition of the Allegheny Mountain and the Clearfield Snow Shoe districts with lower wages (about 15 percent) and lower freight rates (about 15 to 20c a ton), caused the coke operators to be uneasy. The three months' strike cost both sides heavily; it was a defeat for the strikers; but it did not improve the competitive position of the coke operators.

Among the brass manufacturers, there were continued organization and a strike. The National Association of Brass and Iron Steam, Gas, and Water Works Manufacturers successfully formed

a number of local associations during 1887. The Brass Manufacturers' Association of New York City and Brooklyn resolved
to abolish the Saturday half-holiday on the grounds that competition made the sixty-hour week necessary. The brass workers
protested and on Saturday at noon struck to the number of 3,000
to 4,000 but returned to work on Monday. This was repeated
the following week but on the next Monday they were locked
out. The dispute was referred to the State Board of Arbitration,
and the association conceded the fifty-nine-hour week.

The Chandelier Manufacturers' Association of New York had
a somewhat similar dispute. Its strike of 1886 was settled in
1887 on the basis of the fifty-five-hour week—ten hours daily
with Saturday a half-holiday. But at the close of 1887 season,
the Association gave notice that the Saturday half-holiday would
be discontinued except during eight weeks of summer, and refused to grant the union a conference on the matter. The New
York Association tried to get associations in other cities to declare against the Saturday half-holiday but failed. Attempts to
have the dispute arbitrated were unsuccessful and the union
eventually lost the strike.

In the Glass Industry, labor-management relations were
rather unsettled in 1887. The glass manufacturers of Pittsburgh
were struck by the mixers and teasers, but the strikers, for the
third time, declared the strike off and returned to work. The
window-glass manufacturers of Pittsburgh and the West averted
a strike in October by the workers accepting a five percent advance instead of the ten percent demanded. All the ground-glass
factories in New York and the Eastern states were represented
at a meeting held in New York in November in private proceedings at which they decided, on account of the strike in the West,
to conduct a general lockout at the end of the month affecting
7,000 members of the Flint Glass Workers' Union of America.
In 1887-88, the glass manufacturers of the Ohio Valley locked
out the glass workers rather generally. The chimney and prescription departments of the unions had held joint conferences with
the manufacturers and agreed upon a scale of prices, but the other
departments had not and, in many cases, could not get the manufacturers to confer. A number of firms were strongly opposed to

meeting the union officials. The manufacturers, however, assembled to consider what action to take and the majority finally decided in August to meet the representatives of the workers. Conferences were held and all questions settled but one —that of docking the gatherers for defective work they had done. This caused a deadlock and a strike was called for November 25. Meanwhile, another conference was held and the strike order revoked, but the matter was not clearly decided. The manufacturers later withdrew from the understanding and on December 2, issued new lists and shop rules which were objectionable to the union. On January 1, 1888, 28 factories employing over 28,000 workmen locked out their workmen. The glass chimney manufacturers proposed a compromise which was rejected by both sides. Conferences were held in February between union and association committees but no agreement was reached. After several weeks' discussion, the conference agreed upon a scale of prices and an agreement was signed.

The Building Industry was one of organization and turmoil in 1887. The Master Builders' Exchange of Philadelphia was formally organized in January. In February the master builders of New York City met to form a protective association to resist the encroachments of the unions. A Committee from the master roofers, plumbers, carpenters, steamfitters, stone cutters, and material dealers, among others, was appointed to report the plan for organization. On March 14, about 500 employers in the various building trades met and formed the "Building Employers' Protective Association" with the object "fairly to consider the rights of the employee as well as the employer." The master plumbers, who had much to do with the formation of the larger organization, had trouble with the plumbers' union during the year. They were struck over apprenticeship rules but defeated the union in a long-drawn-out strike. They had about 100 boys in the plumbing class of the New York Trade School. That was one of the results of the union's opposition to the employment of apprentices. The Master Plumbers' Association had a trade school committee which prepared the examination questions for the boys, diplomas were given to those who passed, and their term of apprenticeship was reduced one year. The master plumbers also

had difficulty with the union over a building concern which refused to break its contract with a master plumber and was boycotted by the Central Labor Union. Although bargaining collectively with the plumbers' unions, this association not only helped
form the aggressive National Association of Builders, but sent
delegates to its June convention.

The National Association of Builders of the United States of
America was formed in Chicago in March, 1887, to cooperate with
169 local associations in the building industry. It was the result
of a convention called by a group in Boston in January which met
for the purpose of discussing the feasibility of a national association. The idea originated with the Master Builders' Association
of Boston in 1886; it called the preliminary meeting at which the
object of the new association was stated to be "the establishment
of uniformity and harmony of action in all matters that directly
affect the interests of contractors, manual workmen, and all concerned in the erection of buildings in the United States." The
March convention adopted a "Declaration of Principles" (abstracted):

"This Association affirms that absolute personal independ-
ence of the individual to work or not to work, to employ or not
to employ, is a fundamental principle which should never be questioned or assailed, and is not a subject for arbitration, although
there are still many points upon which conferences and arbitration
are perfectly right and proper, and on these points associations
should confer together to the end that strikes, lockouts, and other
disturbances may be prevented. A uniform system of apprenticeship should be adopted by the various mechanical trades. Manual
training schools should be established as a part of the public
school system, and trade night schools should be organized by
the various local trade organizations for the benefit and improvement of apprentices. Payment by the hour—not day—for all
labor performed other than piece work or salary work should be
made. Architects and builders should be required to adopt more
effectual safeguards in building in the process of construction,
so as to lessen the danger of injury to workmen and others.
There should be adopted a system of insurance against injuries
by accident to workmen in the employ of builders, wherein the

employer may participate in the payment of premiums to the benefit of his employees; also in securing the payment of annuities to workmen who may become permanently disabled through injuries received by accidents or infirmities of old age."

These "Principles" are noteworthy in that, while asserting the rights of the *individual,* they anticipated workmen's compensation by nearly a quarter of a century, and old-age pensions by nearly a half-century. Although employers' associations have been the main institutions in the maintenance of the *rights of individuals* and the *system of private enterprise;* collectively, employers may be in advance of unorganized employers, standard unionism, and union officials. It should be noted again that associations led in the fight for industrial education. This is shown again in the Objects of the Association:

"The fundamental objects of this association shall be to foster and protect the interests of contractors and all others interested in the erection and construction of buildings; to promote mechanical and industrial interests; to acquire, preserve, and disseminate valuable information connected with building trades; to devise and suggest plans for the preservation of mechanical skill through a more complete and practical apprenticeship system, and to establish uniformity and harmony of action among builders throughout the country."

In this connection, the National Association of Master Painters at their convention in New York in July adopted a resolution favoring the system of apprenticeship with the *length of the term to be determined by the local associations.*

Local builders' associations throughout the United States fought not only against the shorter workday and higher wages, but also against "union encroachment upon the employers' business." But of all the cities, Chicago had its full share of labor disputes in 1887.

In Chicago after the carpenters in April led off with a strike, and were followed in May by the hodcarriers on the masons and builders, strikes spread to all the building trades. There were issues over wages, hours, payday, rival unionism, the closed shop, and walking delegates, among the complex of the causes for the strike and lockout. The bricklayers and stonemasons struck to change the payday from Monday to Saturday—so they could have their week-end spree, it was said. After the carpenters had struck with the others, a general lockout was declared by the builders. The Chicago builders were then the latest acquisition to the growing list of employers "organized to resist the encroachments of organized workingmen." Operating through the Builders and Traders' Exchange, they effected a compact organization of the building interests of Chicago in view of the diverse character of the trades involved. The movement included not only those engaged in the actual work of erecting and finishing houses but also those dealing in materials. Among the businesses represented in the Exchange were: architectural iron work, Portland cement paving, brickmaking, builders' hardware, electric work, fire brick and clay, fire proofing, galvanizing iron work and cornices, glass, granite, lumber, elevators, lime and hair, mantels, grates, brass goods, paints and oils, plumbing and gas fixtures, sash, door and blind making, molding, sand and gravel, sewer pipe, steam heaters, terra cotta, and wire and iron work. All pledged themselves to stand by their fellow members in case of trouble with employees. After the lockout was declared, not even material could be purchased; the Material Men's Association of Chicago supported the lockout. The Illinois Association of Architects, and the recently formed National Association of Builders took part in defeating the unions. Builders considered making declarations on: no recognition of the union, return to the ten-hour day, freedom of employment to workmen from outside Chicago, and pay according to ability. Over 20,000 workmen were idle and these said the movement was aimed at destroying the unions. In reaction, the bricklayers added to their demands of the Saturday payday, the closed shop with recognition of the walking delegate, the eight-hour day, and limit of two apprentices to an employer. The associated builders then adopted a nonunion declaration of principles (part of those of the National Association of Builders). Among the principles (or employers' terms) were; individual contract required of workmen, right of employer to employ whom he pleased and so on, and right of the workmen to work when, where and how he pleased, apprenticeship without arbitrary restrictions, nine-hour day, Monday payday every two weeks, and minimum wages for bricklayers and stone masons to be 45c an hour. The National Association of Builders investigated the dispute and issued a long statement to the public. The Chicago Master Masons' Association led in the conduct of the strike-lockout. It fought the old union but offered to recognize and deal with a new union "not founded on brute force." It issued an appeal to certain strikers; those who had laid by a little money, those who had joined the union under compulsion, those not in accord with the ruling clique, those who believed in arbitration, and those who looked forward to becoming employers. The appeal to them was for them to form a new union based on the principles laid down by the Builders and Traders' Exchange. An attempt was made to operate with nonunionists, local and imported. The employers had a conference committee which constituted a plan and organization of a "central Council of Builders" to have control of the strike. The Council was made up of delegates from the "Metal Workers' Associations" (masters, cut-stone contractors, contracting steamfitters, plasterers, gravel roofers, masons, painters, carpenters, and galvanized cornice manufacturers, North side brick manufacturers, fireproof manufactuers, nonunion stone yards, and the Builders and Traders' Exchange. The material men began to break away from the Council because of their maturing obligations. The bricklayers' union became willing to arbitrate but the master masons declined until the bricklayers withdrew the demand for the Saturday payday. The Master Masons' Association then agreed to arbitrate all other differences and issued an address to the public containing the offer. The bricklayers declared the nine-weeks strike off on June 23, but the lockout remained because of the questions of the closed shop and walking delegates. The bricklayers rejected the master masons' plan for arbitration and proposed a plan which the master masons accepted—five chosen by each side and the eleventh elected by the ten. Master masons qualified the questions for arbitration by excepting their "stated principles." Pressure was brought by the other contractors to have the entire matter settled. An agreement was finally reached and the joint board functioned for a number of years.

Builders and other contractors were struck in New York

State. The contracting cornice makers of New York were struck in May for an advance and uniform wages. But the employing carpenters of Brooklyn conceded in April the nine-hour day with eight hours on Saturday and with no reduction in pay. Likewise, the employing carpenters of Troy signed an agreement granting the eight-hour day and 30c an hour, but withdrew the shorter day in about a year. The master builders of Rochester were struck by the masons' helpers and laborers for $1.75 a day and caused a temporary derangement of the building trades of the entire city.

The building industries of Omaha, and Lincoln, Nebraska, had strikes over wages and the shorter workday, and organization issues. In April, the Master Painters' Association of Omaha was struck by the painters for a nine-hour day with an advance in wages from $2.50 to $3.00 for a ten-hour day. The strike lasted until May 21. The Association agreed to the nine-hour day, to pay the painters $2.75 and the paperhangers from $2.75 to $3.75 a day, and to give union men preference in employment. The Association kept the agreement until June 18; by this time, sufficient nonunion men had been found to work at a lower wage. When these were imported, the union men struck a second time. The Association issued a statement contending that the union had broken the agreement by the second strike and that thereafter no dealings would be had with the union. As the Association obtained plenty of nonunion men, the strike was abandoned on July 18. In April, the master plumbers of Omaha met and organized, and considered the demands made upon them by the plumbers' union. They entered into an agreement to pay $3.50 and $4.00 a day for nine hours, and to observe certain union rules as then demanded by the union. Later they granted another union demand that all nonunion men be discharged. In May, the sewer contractors of Lincoln were struck because they would not grant increased wages to the sewer laborers, but defeated the strike. In May, the brick manufacturers of Omaha held a meeting, signed an agreement among themselves, and published it stating that they would not make any concessions to the brickmolders who had struck for 25c a day advance—from $2.50 for ten hours with a required output of 6,000 bricks. The strikers, after being out until May 18, won the strike. In June, the employing bricklayers and plasterers of Omaha were struck for six days for a wage increase of 25c, and granted a part of the demands of the unions.

Other cities throughout the United States had disputes in the building industry in 1887, usually for the shorter workday. In January, the architectural iron contractors of Cincinnati defeated the demands and strike of the architectural iron workers for a reduction in hours. After a six weeks' strike, they returned at the old terms. In May, however, the "outside" contractors of Cincinnati granted at once the demands of 1,000 striking carpenters for a reduction of hours from ten to nine, but the mill owners refused and, after a six weeks' strike, all the strikers returned to work—the outside carpenters at reduced hours, the inside ones at ten hours a day. In March, the master plumbers of Cleveland refused to grant the demands of the plumbers' union for an eight-hour day, equal wages of $3.50 a day for all journeymen, and any helper or apprentice who handled the tools of the trade to be paid not less than $3.00 a day. The master plumbers paid off the men when they struck, sought other men, and thus defeated the strike. On June 1, the contractors of St. Paul were struck by the carpenters' union for a nine-hour day with ten hours' pay. The contractors employed nonunion carpenters, only to be struck by the other trade unions when the nonunion men appeared on a job. The strikers tried to organize cooperative organizations to build without contractors. Many conferences were held and finally, after a 60-day strike, an agreement was reached that the nine-hour day would be granted on January 1, 1888, but only about one-fourth of the contractors carried out the agreement. In May, 1887, the New Haven builders were struck by the plumbers, carpenters and painters for the nine-hour day. The master tin roofers of Philadelphia, however, granted the demands of the journeymen for a nine-hour day in March.

Wages and walking delegates were issues in other cities. In March, in St. Louis, "the mechanics and building bosses" agreed upon wages for the year—the bricklayers got a 5c an hour increase but all the others were unchanged. In August, however, the boss stone masons of St. Louis declared a war on walking delegates and declared that they "would take no commandments from any union in regard to apprentices, journeymen, or payday."

In July, the contractors of Detroit refused hod-hoisting engineers an advance in wages, and defeated their strike. The Brickmakers' Exchange of Baltimore was struck by the brick carters for an advance in wages from $2.50 to $3.00 a day and was finally forced to grant it.

The box and barrel manufacturers and millers had trouble with unions in 1887. In April, the millers of Minneapolis "at a secret meeting resolved 'to fight the scheme to the end' " of the coopers for a union committee to run the business on a cooperative basis as a means to win their strike against the millers. In July, the employing coopers of New York City were presented by the coopers' union with an extended list of demands to be complied with by August 15. Among the demands were the ten-hour day with nine on Saturday, the closed shop, no man to be discharged except for negligence or drunkenness and then the reasons to be stated, wages $3.00 a day, Saturday paydays, abolition of piece work, and apprentices to be limited to one to every ten journeymen. The coopers had also struck in sympathy with the longshoremen. The employing coopers used carpenters as strikebreakers for a while. But as the strike of the longshoremen failed, the strike of the coopers also was a failure. The barrel manufacturers of Buffalo, however, were struck by the flour barrel men and, one by one, conceded the union's demands of one cent increase in the piece price of making a barrel. The box manufacturers of Baltimore, in August, granted the box makers a guaranteed one-year price for boxes and agreed to a large number of details. One firm was struck to force it to sign. The box manufacturers of Cohoes, New York, joined in "an open revolt against the assumed powers" of a union official who demanded that discharged employees should be reinstated and that boxes should not be supplied to certain firms objectionable to the union, on pain of a boycott. The box manufacturers won.

Employer-Fostered Unions or Auxiliary Employers' Associations came into prominence in 1887. Mayor Hewitt of New York City suggested that "the workmen who believe in liberty of action organize for their own protection. The idea was well received by business men and a hearty support, moral and financial, was pledged to the movement." In June in the Chicago building trades dispute (discussed elsewhere), a very favorable report was given out on the progress of the new independent union of bricklayers and stone masons, to the effect that it was assuming definite proportions and promised to become an important factor in the labor world. A second meeting was held at the Builders and Traders' Exchange for the purpose of effecting the organization. It was said that "the men present were an unusually well-appearing crowd of workingmen, and the proceedings were unmarred by any of the riotous demonstrations so often occurring in the other union. The platform and code of principles adopted by the master masons were ratified. It was decided to call the new society the Chicago Bricklayers and Stonemasons' Union." It was designed that "this shall be the first of a number of unions extending all over the United States and Canada, and that these unions shall form a national organization." A similar movement was already under way in several cities at that time. In August, another of these organizations was being strenuously promoted, and the following statement is given in abstracted form to show the character of the new union:

"With a view of avoiding all strikes and securing as harmonious relations as possible between employers and workmen, a new organization was recently started at Deering, a manufacturing suburb of Chicago. Its objects and principles are so different from those of most unions that it is worthy of special notice, inasmuch as it proposes to adjust all grievances in a spirit of friendliness toward capital. Well-called the Progressive Order of America, its constitution declared that its objects were the promotion and maintenance of harmony and good will between employer and employee, and the protection of their common interests from injury by strikes or other riotous union demonstrations not in harmony with the civil government of the United States. Only citizens of the United States were admitted. There were to be no strikes; only arbitration and moral suasion were to be used. Employees not taken care of by these means were to be supported by the Order until they got other employment, but other men were not obligated to leave their jobs to force employers to terms. There were to be no boycotts. Leaders of the Order were encouraged to make it national."

Another illustration was supplied by the textile workers in Kensington, Philadelphia district, forming an anti-strike federation of 15,000 members to be governed by arbitration between employers and employees.

In the Shoe Industry in 1887, associations showed marked belligerency. "An extraordinary movement in favor of free shops" was initiated in January by the shoe manufacturers of Worcester, Spencer, North Brookfield, and Brookfield, Massachusetts. New terms of employment were drawn up under which workmen were required to ignore the Knights of Labor and not to be influenced by any union whatever. The men had to agree to work ten hours a day under the appointed foreman or overseers of the firms hiring them. The manufacturer reserved the right to hire and discharge men as he deemed it best for his own interests. The worker obligated himself to work one year except in the case of giving a reasonable notice of the desire to discontinue the contract and the employing firm consenting. The workmen further agreed "to have nothing to do with any strike or interference with the prosecution of labor by other men." Only on these conditions could men go to work. The shoe manufacturers thus associated produced $15,000,000 goods in the previous year. Apparently, they were trying to complete the rout of the Knights of Labor. During the shoemakers' strike in Brockton, Massachusetts, in March, shoe manufacturers successfully introduced shoe-lasting machines into the shops. Thus another highly skilled trade was ended, and the strategic position of trade unionism weakened. In May, the four months' strike on 19 prominent shoe manufacturers of Worcester, Massachusetts, collapsed and the "independent contract established." This meant a defeat for practically all the unions in the shoe industry in New England. The Knights of Labor lost its test case.

The Shoe Manufacturers' Association of New York intervened in the case of a strike on one of its members over the demand by the union for the discharge of a foreman, and upheld the union. But, in a strike called on another member to force the discharge of a nonunion workman whom the union had refused to take in, the Association took up the matter and resolved to make resistance to unreasonable demands and to make their shops nonunion. The strike failed at once. A strike on the shoe manufacturers of Rochester developed the fact that, while they had a strong organization, they had wholly omitted wage rates from the scheme of their action, each firm arranging its own schedule—a characteristic of permanently belligerent associations which had not yet developed in the United States. The strike was called over wages, Saturday half-holiday, and limitation on apprentices. The manufacturers met and promised to guarantee to any individual who accepted employment in their factories that no arrangement would be made with any union which would affect his employment. They further declared that if the strike extended beyond December 12, they would pledge each other to employ no men except as individuals. The strike failed, new men were secured, and many of the strikers returned as non-unionists.

Nearly all the leading leather manufacturers of Newark, New Jersey, formed an association with the object of excluding all workmen who belonged to the Knights of Labor from their shops. The lockout was placed in full operation. The Association offered to guarantee no wage reduction for a year and to give two weeks' notice to a man to be discharged.

The glove manufacturers of San Francisco met the union's demand for a uniform schedule of piece prices by posting notices of a schedule with reductions ranging from 20 to 50 percent of the former piece prices. In the strike that followed, the union was defeated.

The silk manufacturers of Paterson, New Jersey, were presented by the unions in February with a revised set of rules requiring strictly union shops, reduction of hours to 55 a week, and an advance in wages. After much negotiation, three of the smaller firms conceded the demands; the others refused. Arbitration was resorted to without success. A strike was called. The Association refused to compromise, since it was determined to break up the union, and in this it practically succeeded, as the strikers returned only on the terms set forth by the Association. Even the dyers' union had an identical experience with ten of the silk manufacturers. However, the dyers' union had insisted on examining the accounts of the various manufacturers. The strike caused 60 mills, employing 18,000 workers, to close for lack of dyed material. The 1,600 dyers returned on the manufacturers' terms of wages, no concessions, and no recognition of the Knights of Labor.

Belligerency was shown by other associations in related industries. The Cohoes, New York, manufacturers of knit goods refused to use the union label. Three of the largest clothing manufacturers of Grand Rapids, Michigan, in April, defeated the striking tailors in their demand for the restoration of the previous year's wages.

Even master brewers were belligerent in 1887. The Master Brewers' Association of Baltimore was struck in May because it refused to grant the wage increase demanded by the brewery workers. The union had nonunion beer boycotted. After a number of conferences were held, the Association signed an agreement ending the strike. The agreement contained practically no concessions—only a very slight increase in wages to one class of employees—but did reduce to writing many of the rules and working conditions generally accepted in the industry. This is called "face-saving" for the union officials. However, the Master Brewers' Association of New York refused to agree to employ union men exclusively and to deal with the union representative officially. The Association had an agreement by which all members were pledged to protect each other in strikes and lockouts and, accordingly, the association supported one of its members who was struck over the employment of nonunion men.

The year 1887 ended with the cigar makers of New York City striking President Hirsch of the Cigar Manufacturers' Association, who not only reduced wages but also discontinued the use of the union label on the grounds that it was offensive to his customers.

In Transportation, both water and rail, there were strikes in 1887 involving organization issues. In January, longshoremen struck the coal companies in New York and Brooklyn. The strike had spread from the New Jersey coast and was over a wage increase. The real issues were the sympathy strike and war on the Knights of Labor. The coal companies acted in concert. Foreigners were hired as strikebreakers, nonunion boatmen were protected, Pinkertons were employed, former longshoremen were blacklisted, an injunction was issued against the union boycott, and union officials were sued for being in a conspiracy to prevent longshoremen from working. However, a dynamite explosion took place on one boat. Meanwhile, the coal companies controlled prices through their exchanges, such as the Schuylkill and Lehigh exchanges. The strike was lost by the longshoremen because of the great army of unemployed who took the risks involved in taking strikers' places with the hope of getting permanent employment. With employers and nonunion workers given protection against union violence, it was otherwise relatively easy for the employers to break a strike by workmen who had no great amount of skill. In December, the Shipowners' Association of the Pacific Coast was charged with causing sailors to be discharged who were working on the wharves and in the lumber yards of San Pedro, with the avowed purpose of forcing these sailors to go to sea in order to relieve a scarcity among sailors and lessen the high wage. The sailors both on land and on vessels at San Pedro struck. The Association sent in strikebreakers, but the strikers got them drunk and they refused to work, although the Association retained their luggage. All efforts at arbitration failed. Longshoreman who had struck also were replaced generally with new men; later, many of the strikers were given employment on the Association's terms. In March, the Philadelphia Vessel Owners' Association at its annual meeting advocated the establishment of a schoolship at that port. The Lake Carriers' Association, organized a few years before "in the interest of the carrying trade on the Great Lakes . . . (and) instrumental in bringing together the most prominent and influential men in this business for concert of action in freight rates and all matter pertaining to the advancement of steam navigation," held its annual meeting in Buffalo in March. The strike of the dock workers at Cleveland, Ohio, affected the unloading of ore by vessels, but the railroads granted the 25c a day advance demanded—bringing the wages up to $2.00 a day—and the strike was over.

Injunctions were issued restraining strikers on both the New York, Pennsylvania and Ohio Railroad, and the New York, Lake Erie and Western Railroad by a Federal Court. Judge Stone in giving his decision in the case of the second-named railroad stated that it was the first instance *in Ohio* that a labor injunction had been issued by a Federal Court. The Baltimore and Ohio Railroad had maintained a training school for two years and had brought up the number of apprentices to 150 in March in shops employing 4,000 workmen. The Pennsylvania Railroad had established a "relief system" that was condemned even by employers as unfair to the workers, yet it caused the employees on that railroad to dissolve their Mutual Benefit Association, which had at one time 7,000 members, within a year after the "relief system" was installed. Railroads quite generally established these "relief systems" in the late eighties to deal with cases of injured workmen. The Knights of Labor refused to support a strike of engineers and firemen on the Brooklyn Elevated Railroad and the strikers lost in July. In December, the Philadelphia Railroad strike was to prevent deunionization. Thus, the railroads reflected the prevailing spirit of belligerency toward unionism, especially the Knights of Labor. A strike on the San Francisco Cable Railway was followed by two explosions with more threatened if the strikers' demands were not met.

In the Printing Industry, the contest between the master job printers and the printers' union became national in 1887. The United Typothetae of America was organized to resist the demand of the International Typographical Union for the nine-hour day. It was made up of master job or contract printers as distinguished from newspaper publishers who owned their own print shops. It began agitating for trade schools as early as 1888. There were, however, local contests in the printing industry. The New York Typothetae refused to sign an agreement with the printers' or compositors' union for a new scale of wages because it also required exclusive employment of union men, or the closed shop, which was still a bitter issue in the 1950's. The master printers offered to arbitrate the issue, but the union declined and lost the strike in October and withdrew the union "card rule" as a requirement under the schedule. In October, the job and newspaper offices acted in concert under the name of the Employing Printers of Rochester, New York. The association refused to grant a new schedule of wages to the typographical union. The printers struck.

Conferences between the association and union brought no results. The association refused to arbitrate, the strike was declared off, and the printers returned at the old rate. The master job printers in Chicago were struck by the printers to change from the ten-hour to the nine-hour day. The union conducted its picketing very effectively, but the association invoked the Illinois conspiracy law, enacted at the past session of the Illinois legislature. The case failed because the prosecution did not produce "convincing" evidence—often a difficult matter to do in strike cases.

Organizations in agriculture and related industries were forming or functioning in 1887. In March, an "Anti-Convict" Contract Association was formed. Among the members were manufacturers of agricultural implements, wagons, and the like, who opposed the contract system for prison labor, but they failed to offer acceptable substitutes for it or at least to get them adopted. The Western or Northwestern Plow Association was formed in August, 1887, to control prices and advanced them in less than two months. It was composed of plow manufacturers in Illinois, Wisconsin, Minnesota, Iowa, and Missouri. In October, the Carriage Builders' National Association adopted its almost annual resolution urging an increase of mechanical schools in connection with public schools. In Brooklyn, the master horseshoers were presented with a new wage schedule by the horseshoers calling for a wage increase and the eight-hour day. In a meeting between the bosses and the workmen, the bosses refused as one man the demands of the union. Then the union struck and some of the bosses had a conference with the union officials and made terms. All the bosses then met and the bosses who had made terms with the union revoked the agreements. The bosses invited the union to a conference but the union refused to meet all of them together. A lockout was declared and the union lost. In the packers' strike and after, Armour and Company was especially attacked because it had led the packers in breaking away from the eight-hour day, so it was actively boycotted by the Knights of Labor. In Akron, Ohio, where the boycott was very strong, Armour and Company notified its agents to start six retail shops in March and to sell direct to the consumer at "any price and charge the loss." Moreover, planters in Louisiana were struck in November by plantation hands in one section of the sugar district. Such strikes usually failed because of the surplus of labor in November.

An interesting contrast of associations—one belligerent and the other appeasatory—is shown in the following instances of their labor troubles. The associated manufacturers of silver goods in New York, Brooklyn, and Providence locked out 1,200 employees because they joined the union. In June, however, many of them returned to work individually. On the other hand, the Ball-Room and Park Proprietors' Association of New York had a provision in its by-laws requiring the exclusive employment of union men, and generally employed members of the Knights of Labor. There were two other rival organizations among the waiters. One of these rival unions—the United Waiters—struck members of the Association but failed and then boycotted these members. The Association issued a lengthly public statement of its position, its rules, and its wage schedules. The growing rivalry between the Knights and AFL unions caused employers much trouble in the next few years.

The years 1888 and 1889 were relatively quiet in association activities because the Knights of Labor was in the rapid process of disintegrating, and the American Federation of Labor had not attained much strength. Some of its affiliated unions were powerful, but the AFL itself created no fear among the associations. Most of the association activities during these years were in the building and brewing industries.

In the Building Industries, there were notable association activities in Omaha and Lincoln, Nebraska, in 1888. In March, the Brick Contractors' Association of Omaha, was struck by the bricklayers because it would not grant an eight-hour day with $4.50 daily wages. A conference was held by the association and union at which the association offered $5.00 for a nine-hour day, but which the union refused to accept. The association issued a lengthy statement setting forth its viewpoint and the reasons why it would not grant the demands of the union. The association made public a proposed agreement to employ men without regard to union affiliations, to protect them, and to pay $5.00 for a nine-hour day. Nonunion bricklayers were imported. Although a conference was held in May between the association and union, nothing was accomplished and the bricklayers lost the strike. In March, the cut-stone contractors of Omaha were called upon by a union committee with the demand for an eight-hour day on April 1. Another conference was held on March 25, at which time the union's demands were granted with the modification that the eight-hour day was not to take effect until June 1. The union refused but offered to compromise on May 15. On March 29, however, the contractors posted in their shops a set of resolutions adopted March 28 at the convention of the Missouri Valley Association of Cut-Stone Contractors. These resolutions declared that men would be employed without regard to union affiliations at wages not to exceed 45c an hour, no extra pay for overtime, no dictation by union leaders, and no limit on the number of apprentices. The contractors had entered into an agreement with the quarry owners that stone should be furnished only on recommendation of the contractors. The union struck but the contractors imported nonunion men and broke the strike. Likewise, the Master Plumbers' Association of Omaha was belligerent. It had planned to lockout its workmen on May 15, 1889, but was anticipated by the plumbers' union which struck on May 13. The issue was "union recognition." The association asked for a committee of five from each side to arbitrate the issue, but the union replied that it had nothing to arbitrate. The association endeavored to have dealers of supply material to boycott one of its members who had surrendered to the union, but he obtained a restraining order enjoining such a boycott. Finally, the master plumbers went to work as workmen, and other master plumbers from Lincoln offered their services. These broke the strike.

The issues were not so sharp in Lincoln, Nebraska, in 1888. In May, the cut-stone contractors were struck over their refusal to grant the stone cutters $3.50 and $4.00 a day, classification of workmen, and fewer apprentices. The union's demands were practically all granted. The contractors of Lincoln, however, were fearful that the powerful Missouri Valley Association would cause the quarry owners to refuse to sell stone to any contractors not conforming to the MVA rules, as the Lincoln contractors' agreement with the union had not done. The union agreed to make no objections to these contractors joining the MVA. On June 1, the brick contractors of Lincoln formulated rules governing the hours of work and the scaling of wages according to the ability of the workman. Most of the firms, however, violated the rules, preferring to pay the fine rather than have a strike. A few firms were struck because they tried to put the rules into effect, but only 16 bricklayers were affected.

Associations in New York State were active in resistance to the shorter workday and increased wages in 1888. After a series of conferences, the master painters of Rochester, in March, granted the painters a nine-hour day with no reduction in wages, to take effect in new contracts. The boss plasterers of Buffalo after a two-days strike conceded the demands of the plasterers for a nine-hour day and $3.00 daily wages. The master steam-fitters of New York were struck because they refused to grant the eight-hour day with increased wages and to abolish the system of requiring a recommendation from the previous employer. Some of the employers weakened and granted the demands. The union opened up a cooperative shop which employed a number of union men. In a month the strike was over. In contrast, the Builders' Exchange of Troy took vigorous steps to stop interference by strikers with nonunion men who were imported to work as carpenters in Troy. The trouble arose over the demands of the carpenters' union for the eight-hour day with an advance in wages. The contractors refused to give more than the old wages for the nine-hour day. Neither side would conciliate or arbitrate. The carpenters lost the strike because the contractors employed all non-union men. In May, however, the Master Plumbers, Gas and Steam Fitters' Association of Troy signed an agreement with the plumbers' union, after the union had struck to enforce its demands for an eight-hour day and limitation of apprentices. The Master Painters' Association of Troy was struck by the painters' union for the shorter workday and increased wages. Apparently, the union temporarily won most of its demands, only to lose them when times became slack. During the strike the association denounced one master painter for granting the demands and expelled those of its members who compromised with the union. Undoubtedly, other associations disliked the effect produced on other unions by the master painters' concessions; in any event, the union alleged that "By a combination of bosses, consisting of boss masons, boss carpenters, and boss plumbers and painters, there was an agreement to break the eight-hour system."

Varying somewhat from the usual are these instances: Association strategy contributed heavily toward making the painters' strike in Chicago in April a "fiasco." Unusual pressure by outsiders affected the outcome of a strike in Duluth, Minnesota. On August 2, contractors on public works there were struck by laborers and carpenters for $2.00 and $2.25 a day, respectively. After much agitation by citizens and other parties, both sides to the dispute finally chose representatives who conferred and agreed upon $1.75 for laborers and $2.00 for carpenters. The San Francisco Board of Trade issued a widespread appeal to laborers, skilled and unskilled to come to the Pacific Coast.

Associations in the building industry carried on an extensive propaganda for trade education in 1888. In February, it was reported that the manual training schools under the Industrial Education Association of New York City were full to overflowing. The Master Builders' Exchange of Philadelphia had a scheme for training mechanics in trade schools with one year less at the trade for proficiency in that school. The Exchange accepted a gift by Colonel Richard T. Auchmutty—the founder of the New York trade schools—of $3,000 annually toward the support of a trade school in Philadelphia. The school opened in 1889 with seven departments; bricklayers, painters, plasterers, plumbers, carpenters, blacksmiths, and stonecutters. It was an evening school with nine-months terms, three evenings a week with practice at the trade outside. The school was established because of the unions' restrictions on apprentices. The masters and journeymen bricklayers of Philadelphia finally agreed upon rules defining the relations between them and their apprentices through the operation of a joint committee. Colonel Auchmutty offered also a large sum of money to the Builders' Exchange of Boston to help establish a trade school there. The Builders' Exchange of Pittsburgh planned a building for the Exchange which contained, among other things, a basement for a trade school for the various building trades. The Builders and Dealers' Exchange of Cleveland started a trade school with work in three branches—plumbing, carpentry, and masonry—with evening classes for a five-months term. Preparations were made for a new building for further expansion. The Wilmington Board of Trade in 1888-89 began agitation among national associations for congressional legislation establishing "national mechanical trade schools on the apprenticeship principle."

The National Association of Builders discussed extensively arbitration proposals and adopted one in 1888. In 1889 it made great efforts to have a largely attended convention, at which there was strong advocacy for the establishment of trade schools. It compiled a list of associations in the building industry in 1889, namely; local builders' associations and exchanges 62; local master carpenters' associations 26; local master masons' associations 30, and one state association; 41 local, 8 state, and one national master painters' associations; 56 local, 4 state, and one national master plumbers' associations; 7 local master plasterers' association; 3 local, and one national master roofers' associations; 3 local, and one district employing ironworkers' associations; 2 local and one national master sheet metalworkers' associations; 10 local, one state, one district, and one national cut-stone contractors' associations—all told, with the NAB, 262 associations. The NAB, also took note of a case in which a jury awarded in 1889 a contractor $3,700 damages against a union for a boycott circular. The court also gave both a preliminary and a permanent injunction against the bricklayers' union.

While there were relative few strikes in 1889, these associations in the building industry functioned thus: The master housesmiths of New York signed an agreement with the housesmiths' union fixing hours, wages, and working rules. The Marble Industry Association signed an agreement with the marble polishers, bed rubbers, and sawyers, thus ending a strike for a wage advance. The employing plasterers, threatened with a general strike of the plasterers, conceded the increased wages demanded by the union. In April, the employing painters resolved to return on May 1 to the nine-hour day, but after a 16-day strike conceded the eight-hour day. The Master House Painters' Association of Buffalo was forced by a strike to grant the painters' demands for a shorter workday. During the negotiations, the association attempted to deal with the men individually and not recognize the union, but the union forced recognition. The Master Painters' Association of Buffalo offered to grant the nine-hour day from March 15 to October 15 with no change in wages, but the painters wanted also a wage increase and got it with the eight-hour day. The Builders' Exchange of Buffalo, during a series of conferences with the building trades employees, was unwilling to grant the nine-hour day with no reduction in pay. The carpenters and painters decided to strike. The Exchange offered to concede the nine-hour day after several months when the current contracts were completed, and the unions rejected this plan. The unions offered to set the day at May 1, instead of April 1, but the Exchange rejected this offer. The unions, however, won their demands from the builders as individuals generally. The associated master painters of Syracuse refused to grant increased wages to the painters who struck and forced the employers individually to grant the demands in whole or in part. The Master Plumbers' Association of Oswego granted a wage increase and an eight-hour day to the plumbers after a short strike. The master carpenters of Staten Island formed an association and, on June 9, locked out members of the carpenters' union who demanded an eight-hour day on Saturday—with nine-hour days the rest of the week. The matter was compromised, on June 16, on a Saturday half-holiday with five hours' pay. Over a year before this, it was reported that "the Saturday half-holiday was an experiment which has proved to be a failure. . . . The commercial exchanges one and all have pronounced against it as detrimental to business interests." The workers largely spent the morning planning what they would do in the afternoon and anxiously wanted to get to do it. The result was an inefficient half-day. In August, the master cornice and skylight makers of Yonkers, New York, were struck by their workmen. After the strike had lasted five weeks, nearly 50 percent of the trade still refused to grant the union's demands. Finally arbitration was offered, accepted, and an agreement made.

In the Brewing Industry, there was distinct belligerency in 1888, although the brewers are characteristically appeasatory

toward unionism. Moreover, while the brewery workers' union
has received concession after concession from the brewers, it is
nevertheless one of the most socialistic of long established unions.
The whole philosophic justification of collective bargaining is
challenged by the way it has functioned in the brewing industry.
In April, the United States Brewers' Association revolted against
"union dictation," and a statement issued by its President Miles
says in part:

"At a meeting of representatives from all over the United
States, at which the situation of the labor question throughout
the country was thoroughly discussed, the testimony was uniform
that where the most arrogant demands of trades unions had been
unwisely complied with, the employers had suffered the most
trouble and annoyance from the labor unions, and the opinion
was equally unanimous that the time had come when the trade
must refuse any longer to make contracts with labor organizations, and insist on their right to deal individually and directly
with their men. The circular now published is the culmination
of that discussion, and the entire trade is unanimous upon it. This
is not a local affair, but is national in the fullest sense of the
word, and it is not confined to one branch of the brewing trade,
but includes the ale and porter as well as the lager beer brewers
in every State of the Union. We do not expect any trouble, but
if the men go out on strike hereafter at the dictation of any trade
union or organization they will stay out."

Nevertheless, within two weeks, 5,000 brewery workers were
"locked out" in New York and vicinity, and more brewers were
planning on employing nonunion men. The brewers found "it
difficult to lift themselves out of the old rut." Abstracted and
summarized, their old policy and the causes for the change have
thus been stated:

The leading master brewers are consolidated in the United
States Brewers' Association, under the rules of which they compete with each other in the extension of trade or in the advancement of individual interests. But they are banded together in
all matters affecting the general weal, and in particular they
present a solid front against strikes or other aggressive actions of
labor organizations against members of the association.

During the period of brisk business, the association encouraged unions, so that it could deal with them more easily than with individual workmen. Later the association changed its views, and opposed labor organizations that antagonized the employers' interests. Contracts between union and association had been made in April, 1886, and 1887. But in 1888, trouble arose in Milwaukee. Certain master brewers were boycotted, and the Milwaukee association appealed to the USBA, which championed the cause of the Milwaukee breweries, and resolved not to renew the agreement with the union.

The U. S. Brewers' Association announced that the breweries had pledged themselves not to take advantage of any boycotted brewery. The union boycott of the Milwaukee breweries was thus made ineffective, but the union enlarged the boycott to include all breweries in the "pool." The association met this move by a lockout of all union men in the "pool breweries" on which the boycott was declared. Nonunion men and union men *as individuals* were employed. The master brewers refused to arbitrate. The union lost because the boycotts were not highly effective. The association, however, demanded the removal of the boycott by a certain date under penalty of refusing to hire any union man tied up with the unions doing the boycotting. The unions refused.

The U. S. Brewers' Association had 516 members in 1884 and 698 in 1888, when it produced about 80 percent of the total product of the industry in the United States. When it broke with the union, the association voted against any reduction in wages or increase in hours, and its President Miles urged its members to study the labor problem. The boycott extended even to San Francisco, where the Brewers' Protective Association dealt with boycotts by various unions from 1888 to 1892, and locked out workmen during one of the boycotts.

In the Iron and Steel Industry in 1888, collective bargaining was carried on through strikes and conferences as previously, but the dissolution of the outstanding association was the most significant development of the year in the industry. The iron and steel manufacturers at Pittsburgh met May 9 to consider and formulate a scale of wages for the coming year. Circulars had been sent out to members notifying them of the appointment of a scale committee and asking for suggestions and opinions. The manufacturers said that they had to have a reduction and proposed one, while the union demanded practically the old scale. They were deadlocked in June. Meanwhile the Western Iron Association held a number of conferences and discussed the proposition of shutting down the mills for three months as a solution to overproduction, but reached no agreement in June. On June 29, the conference committees of the Association of Manufacturers of Iron, Steel and Nails, and of the Amalgamated (the union) met but could come to no agreement since each side insisted on the adoption of its scale unmodified. Finally, the manufacturers suggested compromising, but the union struck. Then the manufacturers started one by one to sign the Amalgamated's scale. It was then proposed that the association require each member to put up $20,000 as a forfeit for breaking the compact among them by signing an unauthorized scale. This must be distinguished from the practice of the association adopting a scale and each manufacturer signing it individually. This had been the practice since 1874, although in 1882, and again in 1888, an attempt was made to reach a national agreement.

Dissolution of the Association of Manufacturers of Iron, Steel, and Nails took place in 1888. The *Amalgamated Journal* has stated that this association in 1882 was formed to forestall, by defeating the union, a demand for $6 per ton for boiling, but its dissolution led to a system of divisional conferences in 1893. This association was separate and distinct from the Western Iron Association which dealt with prices and had a more limited part of the industry. The following is an abstracted account of the association:

Its principal object was to unite the iron and steel processors of Pittsburgh and further Western cities in support of a common policy on the labor question—to meet the issues presented by their workmen through the Amalgamated Association (union) of Iron and Steel Workers. Committees of conference of association and union met annually to discuss rates of wages and adopt a scale that was binding on both organizations for a period of 12 months from July 1. In 1888, they deadlocked because basically of the low price of iron and steel products. In July the rolling mills shut down generally, but manufacturers singly began to sign the Amalgamated's scale, and at the end of three weeks, those who had not signed stated that they would not continue to keep their mills closed with their trade going to their competitors. As a result, the association released the members from all pledges and practically issued an order for dissolution.

The association actually went to pieces and was not reorganized the following year.

The blast furnace operators of the Mahoning Valley notified their men that wages would be reduced 10 percent on March 25, 1888. The men asserted correctly that their wages were already 10 percent less than in the Shenango district, only 30 miles away. However, the men, after a short strike, accepted the reduction and returned to work. The furnace operators, however, granted an increase in November, 1888, but posted a notice of reduction on March 1, 1889, which would wipe out that advance. A related industry, the limestone quarry operators of the Mahoning Valley were struck in February, 1889, because they refused to grant their workmen a wage increase. The proprietors met at Youngstown and resolved not to be dictated to by the Knights of Labor, and to pay the old wages. Attempts were made to operate with nonunionists.

In the Glass Industry, the issues in 1888-89 were wages and apprentices. In April, 1888, the flint glass manufacturers were struck, and the main issue was union limitation of apprentices. The manufacturers desired to be unrestricted in the number of apprentices. In the fall of 1888, the American Flint Glass Manufacturers, after holding a number of conferences with union committees, had a meeting and drew up a new wage schedule which reduced wages 15 percent, and asked the unions to approve it by the first of the year 1889. The association closed its factories in New York, New Jersey, Pennsylvania, and Maryland, until the union answered, disliking very much to employ union men exclusively or to have union approval for the discharge of any man, and to have the number of apprentices greatly limited. In April, one of the firms broke from the association and signed the union scale. This marked the start to the ending of the lock-

out, since other establishments soon did likewise. On account
of the scarcity of glassblowers in this country, manufacturers
attempted to supply themselves from abroad without previous
contract, and thus obtained a number of workmen. In December,
1889, the Glass Manufacturers' Association of Pennsylvania
clashed again with the Knights of Labor over the number of apprentices who might be employed.

The glass manufacturers were not alone in avoiding the contract labor law. It was said then that "the contract labor law is
practically a nullity; so far as it has any efficacy skilled labor is
excluded, while the padrone and his counterpart of various na-
tionalities meet with little impediment."

In Coal Mining and related industries, there was little activity in 1888, but more in 1889. In September, 1888, the coal operators of Bevier, Missouri, were presented by the union with a
schedule of wages and prices for mining coal that meant an
advance over those then prevailing. The operators refused and a
strike was called. The operators then offered 60c a ton—a 10
percent advance—and the miners refused; their demand was for
95c for riddled (screened) and 78c for unriddled coal. Negotiations were broken off. One operator offered 74c and the miners
accepted. Other operators attempted to import nonunion workmen. One of the coal operators was killed after he had shot at a
mob that jeered him, and some of the strikebreakers were shot
at and wounded. In 1889, there were a number of strikes on
coal operators in Missouri, but most of them were unsuccessful.
In some strikes, as many as 26 mines were involved. Railroad
coal operators in Pennsylvania advanced the mining rate 5c a
ton on November 1, 1888—74c up to 79c—and the mining rate
agreed upon in conference between operators and miners was to
be 74c from May 1 to November 1, and then 79c to May.
Northern Illinois coal operators, organized into a "Coal Association," agreed to reduce the price of pick mining 10c a ton—
also placed at 15c—on May 1, 1889, and were struck. The
operators claimed that the decline in the price of coal made such
a reduction necessary since the competition of other mines, especially in Southern Illinois, made it impossible to pay the old
wages. By August 1, many of the 10,500 miners involved and

their families were starving and were being aided by the public through contributions; they claimed that wages at the operators' rates would not cover the barest necessities. A compromise was made as to wages; it should have been made three months before, for striking against an adverse market showed poor union leadership.

The coke operators in the Connellsville region in January, 1889, refused requests of workers for conferences over a new scale proposed by the union that called for advances in wages of miners and drivers of 5 percent and of all other employees of 4 percent for each 10 percent advance in the market price of coke. Some men struck. In July, 1889, the coke operators were presented by the coke workers with a demand for a wage reduction. The coke workers asked the operators for a conference and named a day, but no operators met the union delegates, so a strike was ordered. The operators contended that with the prevailing prices of coke, no wage advance could be made. But the operators were defeated and granted a 12 percent increase. Operators signed a scale good for six months, with no change in wages with changes in the price of coke. The coke workers' organization was highly efficient and took the coke operators by surprise. A number of the smaller coke operators in the Connellsville region decided to organize as the Connellsville Coke Exchange, and by a directory protect the Exchange and its members from losses on contracts by reasons of strikes or unavoidable accidents—a sort of strike insurance at this early date.

In the strike movement of 1888-89 in the bakers' trade, the master bakers in New York and Brooklyn made common cause. They issued and posted in their bakeries a set of "shop rules" against which the bakers' union protested as a means to destroy their union. These "rules" stated that no changes in hours or wages would be made, that the employer should hire and fire as he pleased, that there should be no outside interference, that workmen were to be dealt with as individuals, and that each man must subscribe to the "rules." The union struck but the employers soon obtained other men and the strike failed. In February, 1889, the Boss Bakers' Exchange of Syracuse made a considerable reduction in wages. The bakers struck and boycotted the bakeries that would not pay the former wage. The boycott caused the Retail Merchants' Association to recommend that the bakers be taken back at the old wages, and on May 1, the difficulty was settled by the bakeries conceding the union's demands.

Shoe manufacturers functioned in other fields than merely breaking strikes in 1888. They left in increasing numbers the industrial centers to go to quieter retreats because of labor troubles. They applied for an injunction to stop placards or banner-carrying by men walking back and forth in front of a struck shop, and they obtained a favorable decision from the Supreme Court of Massachusetts around August 1, 1888. On the other hand, the conspiracy case against shoe manufacturers of Weymouth, Massachusetts, was dismissed by the court around July 1. A workman who had struck was blacklisted and sued his former employer "for conspiracy to prevent his earning a living." It was admitted by defendant's counsel that the plaintiff was discharged in pursuance and in consequence of an agreement among the manufacturers.

The Fall River textile mills were struck by 6,000 weavers about April 1, 1889, for an advance in wages. The employers refused to yield on the ground that they could not afford to raise wages. The workmen returned only after exhausting their surplus funds. While the strike closed practically all the mills, it lasted only about two weeks.

In 1889, the Employing Knee Pants Makers of New York signed an agreement with the knee pants makers' union, restoring prices and doing away with charges for machines and the like. The contractors had attempted but failed to have a lockout declared on all the union workers.

Somewhat unusual was the strike called in 1889 on the Silk Manufacturers' Association of New York. The union thought that the manufacturers were seeking to import workers and it also demanded a universal price list. An advance of wages was granted as a compromise. But the American Silk Manufacturers' Association thought that more workers should be trained in that industry, so it proposed to establish an evening school and appointed a committee to plan the matter.

In transportation, there were a series of strikes by the engineers in 1888 on the Burlington, the Wabash, the Northern Pacific, and the Santa Fe Railroads. All were lost, although Swinton says that the firemen's union scabbed and the engineers on the Burlington finally won. There was also a street car strike in New York City in 1889.

Shipbuilders on the Great Lakes were presented in 1888 with demands by ship carpenters and caulkers for the nine-hour day with wages at $2.75 a day. The employers met at Cleveland on February 25, and decided to resist all demands and to adhere to the current regulations.

Quite a number of associations were new in the handling of strikes and other labor matters and varying results followed: In 1888, the master hack carriage drivers of New York granted, individually, the demands of the livery-stable employees for a wage advance. But, in October, the feather manufacturers of New York were struck because they reduced wages. On December 1, the manufacturers formed an association of 8 firms. In January, 1889, the union submitted a schedule of prices but it was rejected. The employers acted together, gave preference to non-union workers whenever shops resumed work, and gave them the union scale. In March, the strikers admitted their defeat and gave up. But the contractors for convict labor at the state prison in Trenton, New Jersey, unanimously refused, in 1889, to renew their contracts with the state unless the law of 1887—requiring the label of "Prison Made"—was repealed. In July, 1889, in New York City, the HERALD, the WORLD, the SUN, the TIMES, and the MAIL and EXPRESS organized and cut down the pay of the compositors and adopted a set of rules. The union called on the managers who refused to compromise. A strike resulted and one of the proprietors withdrew from the association, and this practically broke it up. A compromise was soon reached.

Two topics were prominent in the discussions of labor matters in 1888-89; the law of conspiracy, and do strikes pay? Actually, it was contended that the independent worker got as high wages as the union man, without the losses due to strikes and the cost of maintaining unions.

CHAPTER 13

ASSOCIATIONS CONTINUE TO ORGANIZE

ASSOCIATIONS CONTINUED TO organize in the nineties, but association activities in 1890 were greater in the building industry—where the shorter workday was still a fighting issue—than in any other industry. It was estimated that 25,000 workers obtained the eight-hour day by strikes in May. However, these were normal collective-bargaining manifestations involving AFL unions. Likewise in the foundries the AFL molders' union was involved in conflicts, but the degree of belligerency was greater. In any event, the "honeymoon" between associations and AFL unions was fast losing its "sweetness," as the fear of the Knights of Labor was converted largely into contempt. As a contemporary stated it, there was an uprising against "the tyranny of trades unions":

"Combinations of manufacturers and corporations to resist the alleged extortions and tyranny of labor organizations are becoming more frequent. . . . A number of the richest corporations in the country have formed an alliance against strikes. Among the corporations which are members of the combination are the Westinghouse system, both in . . . (Pittsburgh) and elsewhere, the Yale Lock Company, the Colts Arms Company and four or five other big factories in Connecticut, and presumably the Pullman interests. The compact agreed to is that in case a strike occurs to enforce unreasonable demands—whether the strike be against one or all of the associated factories—all work is to cease. The strikers are to be allowed to remain idle until they see fit to return to work, and no factory is to employ any worker who may have left another factory on a strike; neither is any associated factory to seek workers during a strike from any other federated works. The institutions named employ between 50,000 and 60,000 workers, and directly support some 250,000 to 300,000 people, exclusive of other interests depending upon earnings of these people. It is claimed by these manufacturers that the action of their workers has caused the alliance."

Of the alliance, the Yale Lock Company and Westinghouse in Pittsburgh were struck. When the brass molders struck the Yale Lock Company, it employed nonunion men who were so badly persecuted that it shut down, then opened up and had employees sign individual contracts which asserted the employer's right to hire and discharge.

It was realized that, while the Knights of Labor had been crushed, AFL unions differed very little in their militancy toward employers, some of whom were ready to crush the AFL type of union: "Employers have learned how to make combinations among themselves, and by so doing to oppose an effective barrier to combinations of labor. By this means, through their greater command of material resources, the aid of combinations of manufacturers has sometimes been invoked for the purpose of crushing labor unions." Undoubtedly, the demands of the unions for "back pay" to penalize "faulty" employers and to reimburse strikers for time lost in a strike caused by the alleged fault of the employer, seemed to be a process of getting pay for striking and an exercise of tyranny by those unions. It is also noteworthy that the New York law against runaway apprentices was invoked in August, 1890, because the shortage of skilled workmen enabled these apprentices to get journeymen's wages. Moreover, the fight over apprentices still continued in the glass industry. Also, serious consideration was being given to employee stock ownership as a strike preventive. With strikes threatened, the labor situation seemed to be very serious, especially strikes for the eight-hour day.

In the Building and Closely Related Industries, the National Association of Builders by resolution in February left the matter of the eight-hour day to the local associations. This clearly indicated that the builders were divided on the issue with a great number of them favoring it—in other words, the unions could win it easily against such division. However, that was then more nearly the real eight-hour day and not the current "basic" one with overtime pay.

During May, 1890, many associations granted the eight-hour day after being struck. Among these was the master builders' group of New York City who were struck by the carpenters; it signed an agreement with that union granting also 40 cents an hour wages and giving the walking delegate the right to inspect all work. A strike forced the boss carpenters of Yonkers to grant the union carpenters' demands for the eight-hour day and to set beginning and quitting times. Chicago builders, after a short strike, yielded the carpenters the eight-hour day without a wage cut. Carpenters' strikes on the master builders of Philadelphia for the eight-hour day caused them individually to grant it shortly. In contrast, the planing mills of Erie, Pennsylvania, were struck by their employees for eight months over recognition of the union and the shorter workday. Similarly, the planing mills owners of Buffalo refused "as one man" to make any change in the hours as demanded by the union and the men struck. The owners declined to arbitrate, the strike died out, and the men went back to work. However, the employing lathers of New York City were forced to grant the eight-hour day by a strike, and later on in May were forced by another strike to conform to the union wage schedule, while on July 8 they were compelled to give every union man the wages called for in the schedule. The Employing Plasterers' Association of New York City, after a strike, reached an agreement with the plasterers' union for an eight-hour day. The master roofers (slate and metal) of New York granted the eight-hour day at $3.50 without a strike. The master roofers (metal) of Brooklyn met to consider the demands of the union for the eight-hour day but could not reach a unanimous decision to oppose it, so it was granted by many employers, and the others were struck. Nonunion men were employed and the association refused to have these discharged. Finally, a conference was held and the matter settled by a contract practically granting the union's demands.

In some places, there was still a contest over the nine-hour day. The boss carpenters of Staten Island granted the union carpenters' demands for the nine-hour day without a strike or other trouble. But the Master Builders' Association of Boston defeated the attempts of the carpenters' union to secure a shorter workday either by strike or voluntary arbitration; the association, however, adopted an apprenticeship agreement. The Builders' Exchange of Boston resisted the demands of the carpenters' union for reduction of hours from ten to nine, while the mill owners refused to arbitrate and defeated the union strike. In June, the master carpenters of Cincinnati were forced by a six-weeks strike of the carpenters' union to "recognize" the union and reduce the hours to nine.

It should be noted that by August, striking carpenters had generally won the shorter workday very largely from builders as individuals and not through agreements with builders' associations—the old strategy of "divide and conquer." This condition led to the formation of a strong Builders' Exchange of Pittsburgh in November, because "the contractors in the various lines of trade were practically at the mercy of labor unions, and that as a means of protection they should continue in an organization, and thus be able more successfully to deal with the demands made by labor unions."

Organization issues, as well as wages and hours, were fought over in 1890. The carpenters' union notified all the boss builders, carpenters, and contractors of St. Louis that wages would be advanced 5 cents an hour. Seventy-odd bosses refused to grant that demand and stated that they never would acknowledge a union which claimed the right to fix wages. May 1, 1891, was the date set for a general strike and four weeks prior to that date, the union again repeated its demands. In the meanwhile, 52 bosses met and organized the Boss Builders and Carpenters' Association, and determined to resist to the last. The strike took place and many of the bosses, having profitable contracts on hand, broke away from the association and granted the union's demands, until practically all bosses had given in when the strike was called off on May 20. In April, 1890, the Master Plumbers' Association of Chicago was struck by about 1,000 plumbers for uniform wages. The Master Plumbers' Association of Brooklyn, which had been organized for several years, had a strike called on an independent plumber to force him to join the association—the plumbers' union had agreed previously not to work for a nonassociation master plumber. The strike lasted only six days and succeeded. The master painters of Binghampton, New York, after some trouble, were induced to sign an agreement to employ only union men and to pay wages for certain hours at the union scale.

Voluntary arbitration was being given a trial. The association of manufacturers of cabinet work and furniture of New York endeavored by voluntary arbitration to end a strike of union workers but failed. The National Association of Builders had a committee on arbitration which had drawn up a form of agreement providing for arbitration boards and a plan for settling differences between unions and associations in the building trades. The Mason and Builders' Association of Boston adopted this plan.

The trade school was said to be the answer of the National Association of Builders to the apprenticeship problem, and the Builders and Traders' Exchange of Chicago subscribed funds for a trade school. The Builders' Trade School of Philadelphia was very extensively advertised. Thus trade schools were being fostered in 1890.

It is of more than passing interest that the Builders' Exchange of Wheeling, West Virginia, was greatly weakened by strikes in the period 1888-90.

In related industries, two associations fought; both stuck together and won; one defeated a strike, the other a boycott. In May, the sash, door, and blind factories of New York were struck because they refused to grant the nine-hour day, and they defeated the strike. The Brick Manufacturers' Association of New York met in August to take action against a boycott by the Board of Walking Delegates of the Building Trades of New York City against the bricks made at Verplank's Point. The manufacturers had sent a committee of three to visit all the brick manufacturers along the Hudson River and in New Jersey, and the committee reported that it had secured the signatures of 97 percent of the manufacturers visited to an agreement not to send bricks to the New York market so long as the boycott was kept up. The manufacturers decided that they would continue to send bricks to New York for a few days so as to give the walking delegates one week to make up their minds. As the boycott was not lifted, the association put its boycott into action three weeks later.

The Granite Manufacturers' Association of Maine was formed in March, 1890, and was affiliated with the New England Granite Manufacturers' Association, also then newly organized. The Maine association resolved that the state of trade did not warrant any increase in wages or reduction in hours without a reduction in pay. On the other hand, the freestone contractors' association of New England voted to lockout all the union men in the employ of its members unless the union modified "certain evil practices." The union answered the proposal for modification by a strike and ultimately was defeated. Out West, the quarry owners of St. Louis refused to grant the quarrymen an eight-hour day with no reduction in pay. The strikers charged that the struck employers had all other employers refuse to hire any of the strikers, but the quarry owners denied the charge. Finally the strike was declared off by the union. Thus, the stone producers were drawn into the struggle over the shorter workday.

The Furniture Manufacturers' Association of New York locked out the furniture workers because the union demanded the discharge of a foreman in the shop of one of the association's members. In conference, however, with the union, the association agreed to employ union men exclusively, to reinstate all union men, to discharge all "scabs," to reduce the working hours to 53 a week, to discharge the union-condemned foreman, and to submit all differences to a joint conference. Such complete surrenders by associations made employers distrustful of conferences with expert union officials.

In the Iron and Steel Industries, the year 1890 was a quiet one for the iron manufacturers. A wage scale for both Eastern and Western manufacturers was proposed in June, but nothing came of it at this time. In June, the Eastern manufacturers were presented with a new scale but the issue was postponed a year. The iron manufacturers at Pittsburgh in July appointed a conference committee to meet with the union committee and, with a few modifications, signed the scale as presented by the union. The resulting scale was submitted to the mills of the South and West and adopted.

Foundries were struck in 1890 by the molders, especially in San Francisco, where 1,100 molders walked out in March. Although 42 nonunionists were imported at one time from the East, 36 proved worthless by deserting to the ranks of the strikers. The foundrymen, however, took the position that to grant the demands of the strikers would be fatal to the interests of the foundries, and that surrender by the workmen was the only acceptable measure. The issues were: apprentice ratio (union ratio one to eight journeymen), the eight-hour day, and union restriction of output. About half of the imported strikebreakers were "induced" by threats or actual violence to desert if other means failed. So further importation of nonunionists from the East was supplemented in August by sending patterns to Chicago where one of the foundries was struck because of the "hot" patterns. In May, Chicago foundries generally had been struck by the molders for an eight-hour day and more overtime pay. The strikers conducted the strike in a half-hearted way and only two foundries were affected a week later.

In contrast with the above and with the foundries in Cincinnati, five New York foundries signed an agreement with the Iron Molders' Union to employ only union men, to grant a ten percent increase in wages, to conform to the union's apprenticeship rule, to work only ten hours a day, and not to interfere with the union's shop committee. The foundry proprietors of Cincinnati, however, disastrously defeated the molders' strike for a wage advance. "Loafing on the job" by union molders (restricting output greatly) was the complaint of stove manufacturers who publicized this in September, 1890.

The Boiler Manufacturers' Association of Pittsburgh and Allegheny in June and July, 1890, suffered from the "divide-and-conquer" tactics of the union. The association met and decided not to grant the boilermakers' demands for a reduction in hours from ten to nine with no reduction in daily wage. After a two-weeks strike, however, several of the largest firms broke away from the association and signed an agreement granting the union's demands. In November, President James Lappan of the American Boiler Manufacturers' Association felt the need for more united action by employers and appealed to the boiler manufacturers of the United States and Canada to effect a more complete organization to stop price cutting and to combat "unreasonable" unionism.

In Coal Mining, the year 1890 was largely a typical collective-bargaining year in this industry. The coke operators of the Connellsville region were presented, on January 8, 1890, by the miners' union with a proposed scale of wages for mining and engaged in collective bargaining characteristic of the practice in this field. The coke operators replied that they could not pay such wages. No agreement was reached in conference but a compromise committee of three was appointed from each side to formulate a new scale from scales proposed by each side. Coal operators of Pennsylvania, Ohio, Indiana, and Illinois were threatened in February with a strike if a wage advance of 17c a ton was not made by May 1, 1890. In March, the miners' union proposed to the coal operators that they should organize to control prices and thus prevent "foolish competition in the selling price of coal." In June, the coal operators met with the miners in Pittsburgh and compromised on a scale of wages. In December, however, coal operators in the Birmingham, Alabama, region refused to grant the demand of miners for a wage advance in violation of an annual contract with still seven months before its expiration. The trouble was caused partly by agitators and partly by "boomers" who gave exaggerated reports of how cheap coal could be mined and iron be produced, and in general how profitable it was to invest in mining and manufacturing enterprises in the Alabama iron and coal districts. In this connection, it may well be noted that in 1891, the Mahoning and Shenango Valleys furnace owners stated that "the Valleys must get on to a much lower plane of cost to sell their products against Southern competition."

In Transportation, in 1890, the railroads entering Cincinnati defeated a strike of 800 freight handlers who demanded a 15c increase in their daily wage. Nonunionists were imported by the railroads. Somewhat in contrast, the railroads entering

Cleveland were struck by the switchmen for higher wages and a shorter workday. Compromises were effected in most cases; in others the strikers were defeated.

The Vessel Owners' Association of Cleveland, Ohio, decided in August to discharge all union men and to fill their places with nonunionists imported from the East, although the action threatened to cause a strike of all classes of employees connected with lake transportation. Transportation by sea, in November, was involved in the advocacy by the Marine Association of New York of a National Board of Commerce, similar to the British Board of Trade. The Marine Association was composed of 1,400 business men, embracing ship and steamship owners, merchants, importers, exporters, and others interested in commerce. It may be recalled that this association fought a longshoreman's strike.

In the Clothing Industry in 1890 the main issue was union recognition. The employing tailors of Syracuse defeated a general strike called to enforce union recognition. But the master tailors of Utica were compelled by a general strike to recognize the union. In April the Merchant Tailors' Exchange of Columbus, Ohio, refused to grant an advance of wages to the women who worked upon pants and vests in custom-made clothing shops, and the tailors struck. The Exchange offered three propositions upon which they would take the tailors back to work: (1) nonrecognition of the women as union members by the union; (2) no scale to be signed by the Exchange for making pants and vests; (3) tailors who continued at work to be reinstated in the union —all of which the tailors rejected. The employing knee pants makers of New York, however, were forced by a general strike to advance wages through a general strike called on April 19.

The clothing trade of New York City in 1890 had organizations of cloak manufacturers, cloak contractors, and the cloak cutters, whose interests were often in conflict. Accordingly, a strike of the cloak makers affected both the contractors and the manufacturers. These associations have opposing interests in certain respects, since the contractor wants to get the best price, while the manufacturer desires the lowest. Statements were made that the "outside" contractors had signed a compact to break up the union. Strikes were called but seem to have failed. Finally, a consolidated board of contractors, cutters, and operators was formed, and it held conferences with the manufacturers' association. But the association refused to grant the union's demands for recognition, the reinstatement of discharged union employees, and the discharge of "scabs." On July 12, the associated manufacturers, in accord with a circular it had issued, discharged all its union workers and opened up its shops to nonunion workers, but this effort failed. The association then submitted a proposed agreement, which the union rejected. Some of the manufacturers broke away from the association, the union declined the services of the Board of Mediation, while the association accepted. Finally, the manufacturers saw that the season was going by and other manufacturers were getting all the business, so the lockout was called off. An agreement was drawn up by the manufacturers and submitted to the union, and accepted by the leaders, but radicals in the union prevented its immediate acceptance. The cutters, however, accepted it. It provided for the employment of union members, the union was to accept to membership the nonunionists then employed who were not to be compelled to join, and the outside contractor system was to be abolished.

The Fur Hat Manufacturers' Association, in November, 1890, locked out the members of the trimmers' union because it insisted upon modifications of their agreement. The Association refused on the grounds that such modifications would make it differ from the other agreements with the other unions. Conferences were held prior to the lockout in an attempt to maintain the agreement, but the trimmers' union was obstinate and at a special meeting voted to give up the agreement. After the lockout was called, the Association asked the trimmers to confer with the other unions. The union refused but asked for an informal conference with the manufacturers. A formal conference was held, but it proved to be fruitless. The manufacturers then organized a new trimmers' union to work under the old agreement. Numerous conferences were held in an attempt to amalgamate the rival unions. Finally, a conference of the manufacturers, of the makers' union, of the finishers' union, and of the other unions chose a committee which adjusted the dispute by having the new trimmers' union taken over by the old union and the old agreement restored and the lockout ended.

In the Shoe and Leather Industry in 1890, association activities were mainly belligerent. The Shoe Manufacturers' Association of Rochester, New York—and a like one in San Francisco—locked out the shoemakers because they had declared a strike against one of its members who had introduced machinery into his factory. The Rochester association, on December 31st, withdrew all propositions that it had previously submitted to the union as bases for a settlement, and opened its shops to all who would agree to a set of association rules not favorable to unions. The workmen accepted the rules and returned to work. The Morocco Manufacturers' Association of Lynn, Massachusetts, was contending in October for the principle of free shops and had locked out about 900 men. Some of the factories were like small garrisons, provided with cots, cooking apparatus, and the like to withstand a siege. The Association resolved to employ no more Knights of Labor.

In 1890, in contrast, the master bakers of Buffalo were forced by the bakers' union to grant a new set of rules. Although most of the bakers conceded the demands a few "pulled themselves together and resisted the union." After a day or two of negotiations with the objectors, the workmen struck. The objectors, however, were mostly small concerns.

In October, the piano manufacturers of New York and Brooklyn were struck for the eight-hour day by the varnishers, but defeated the strike, which was called off in January, 1891.

Cigar manufacturers were somewhat appeasatory in 1890. The Cigar Manufacturers' Association of New York aided a struck tenement-house cigar contractor. The association was charged with having induced two men who refused to strike and whose names were published as "scabs" to bring action for criminal libel against the newspaper which published the names, an action, however, that failed. The association held a conference with the union committee, but refused to have the "scabs" discharged and wages increased 12½ and 15 percent, respectively, on certain jobs. The association proposed that the matter be arbitrated by the State Board or by a joint committee with an impartial umpire, or that the union take the "scabs" in as members after having punished them. The union rejected all proposals and later won its demands. The cigar manufacturers of Utica asked for a reduction of wages from one to two dollars a thousand for making cigars. A conference was held and the matter was "compromised." In a strike for a wage increase by nonunion cigar-makers (mostly girls) against the cigar manufacturers of Binghampton, New York, the cigarmakers' union intervened, picketed the struck factories, and were restrained by an injunction. Both sides engaged in an intensive legal battle, but finally the injunction was overruled by the highest court of New York.

Activities among other associations varied during 1890. The clerks of New Haven complained that they were blacklisted through an understanding which existed among the merchants of the city not to employ help away from each other. The harness manufacturers of St. Louis were struck by the harness makers to force a 15 percent increase in wages. A conference committee of three employers and three union men met and settled the difficulty and the strike was declared off. The hotel and restaurant owners of St. Louis were more belligerent. They refused to grant the demands of the waiters for a ten-hour day with pay of $10 a week of seven days. The waiters struck; new men were employed, and some of the restaurants were boycotted. The strike lasted 35 working days, and wages were lower after the strike than before it.

The Organization of Associations Continued into 1891. The Board of Manufacturers and Employers in California was organized in August. It was also called the Manufacturers and Employers' Association. It was formed as a defensive organization against union aggression, mainly the boycott. It did not deal with the question of wages, hence was not a collective-bargaining type of association, as most of the others were. It was a federation of associations, but a suborganization handled questions of trade unionism. It issued a "Manifesto on the Boycott." The National Board of Trade—a newly formed organization—met in January, 1892, and discussed, among other labor questions, the regulation of immigration. It was being recognized by employers that there was "too much indiscriminate immigration," and that selection was needed. It was then observed that "The rage for trade associations is of comparatively recent development. It has continued, however, until there is now scarcely a line of business in the country which does not maintain some form of an organization." While it was recognized that "Organizations of employers need improvement almost if not quite as well as organizations of workmen," there were pointed attacks made on these:

"[Workingmen's] most trusted counsellor [is] . . . some hired labor agitator whose advice is from the purely selfish standpoint of justifying his position by doing something [which is] . . . a sure means of magnifying his own importance, no matter at what cost. [Consider] . . . the small percentage of successful strikes, the amount of loss of wages, and the moneys paid by labor for carrying on strikes"; one must conclude that strikes generally have failed to better the condition of the working class but have led to improvidence and demoralization of the workingman.

In the Field of Government, associations were awakened to the need for association legislative activities by the unions proposing legislation to repeal the laws against conspiracy and boycotting. A bill of this sort passed the General Assembly of New York in 1891. It was noted, however, that the political and legislative influence of the Knights of Labor was nil, since the New York legislators ignored or ridiculed its demands while catering to AFL unions. There was combined opposition to the enforcement of the weekly payday law in Illinois in July, 1891. Compulsory arbitration was also proposed there. The National Association of Builders adopted a resolution against convict labor unless current prices were paid for the product or service. Coal operators of Pittsburgh strongly opposed a welfare fund bill providing for a special tax of one cent on each ton of coal mined to create a fund for the support of miners who might be injured in coal pits. The operators made "every effort to prevent the bill from becoming a law."

The courts were also involved. Associations were favored by a decision of the Supreme Court of Pennsylvania adverse to the exclusive ownership and use of union labels as a means to injure nonunion concerns. Injunctions were invoked in Massachusetts against boycotters, in Chicago against a furniture workers' union for violent picketing, and in Ohio against rioting railroad strikers. Association members were told that:

"Workmen may combine in unions for their own advancement, for the purpose of raising wages or fixing the hours they will work. Whenever they seek to secure these objects by threats, by violence or intimidation, or where . . . they seek to destroy and impoverish an individual, or when they seek to enforce their rules upon others, or to extort money, they commit criminal offenses for which they are subject to indictment."

Consideration of the question of the treatment of workers was given in some quarters—personnel administration had not yet developed. The employer's method of discipline of "jack-'em up," or "fire them," was a perfect set-up for the agitator. Foremen were often bullies, and so were many of the so-called "labor leaders"—neither possessed real leadership.

Employers were slow in recognizing that in fighting union demands they were generally successful if they stood together, and that unions usually won their demands when employers divided or acted as individuals. But as they continued to organize and resist union demands, they learned that the "divide-and-conquer" tactics of the union officials required full coordination of the employers if they were not to be defeated.

In the Building and Related Industries, association activities continued extensive in 1891. A survey of building trades' associations in the United States in 1891 showed that there were 616, with builders' exchanges leading with 92, lumber manufacturers following with 84, and plumbers with 82. Master carpenters and journeymen of Chicago were preparing for a strike on April 1, as the old agreement was very unsatisfactory. In New York City, the employing (or contracting) bricklayers, marble workers, plasterers, plumbers, and steamfitters united into associations roughly corresponding to the trade, and thus were a form of "trade" associations. In these trades a joint annual conference of representatives of the association and the union attempted to settle disputes by fixing wages and choosing an arbitration committee to settle intervening disputes but left the nonassociated employer subjected to strikes without these instrumentalities presumed to prevent those. Nevertheless, the building trades associations in New York City were not free from strikes as the account below shows. Pittsburgh associations, however, had their full quota of strikes, and mason contractors in various cities had a comparable record.

In Pittsburgh in 1891, building trades associations were struck May 10, for 60 days for a shorter workday and increased wages. The associations involved included the employers of 1,600 stone masons, 500 plumbers, 275 tin roofers, 30 tile layers, 600 stone cutters, 375 plasterers, bricklayers, house painters, hod carriers, carpenters, and electricians. The associations defeated the strikes, and all the men—excepting the bricklayers who remained on strike—returned to work July 9 at the old hours and wages.

The mason contractors were among the most active of the building trades in 1891. In March, the mason contractors of Grand Rapids, Michigan, at a conference with the masons and bricklayers' union, instead of accepting the old scale of wages, presented a new proposition that the union should work exclusively for members of the builders' exchange since the employers had employed union men exclusively, and that the wages of the stone masons should be cut 5c an hour. The union refused and struck. The contractors could not obtain sufficient nonunion workmen and as union strikers took contracts, the employers surrendered after six weeks. They granted the nine-hour day and gave the stone masons an advance of 5c an hour. In March, the Mason Builders' Association of New York was forced by a strike of the bricklayers to grant the eight-hour day with no reduction in pay. The demand was granted at once and a joint agreement was signed which, while granting the union's demands, required the union to submit its grievances to the joint arbitration board before striking. Likewise, in May the mason builders of Brooklyn granted at once the eight-hour day with no reduction in pay to the striking bricklayers. In April, the mason builders of Kingston were forced by a strike to grant the bricklayers a reduction in hours to nine and wages of $3.00 a day. The strike ended the same day it was declared. In May, the mason builders of Utica, New York, immediately granted striking bricklayers and masons the nine-hour day (reduced from ten) and wages of $3.00. In May the contractors of Yonkers were compelled by a strike of bricklayers and plasterers to increase wages from $3.50 to $4.00 a day for a nine-hour day. The mason builders of New York granted striking hod carriers an increase of 3c an hour in wages. The mason builders of Brooklyn (54 firms) averted a strike by giving the hod carriers an eight-hour day with no reduction in wages; the bricklayers had won this only by striking. A number of firms refused to grant the demands and were struck; 16 of these granted and 13 still refused. When the strike failed, the other firms reduced the rates. The mason builders of Kingston, after a two days' strike granted the demands of the hod carriers for a nine-hour day with wages at $1.75 a day. The hod carriers in some instances forced the contractors of Milwaukee through strikes to advance wages from 21c to 27c an hour. But the mason builders of Corning, New York, were struck unsuccessfully by the hod carriers to aid other unions. The Mason and Builders' Association of Milwaukee was also confronted with demands for exclusive employment of union men, an increase of wages, and (in some instances) for a shorter workday. The unions in the building trades had organized a Building League and agreed not to work with nonunion men. In April, the League submitted a new scale of wages to the contractors, and when the demand was not granted, the bricklayers and stonecutters struck. The issue between the stonecutters and the contractors was finally compromised (after a five-weeks strike) by a fifty-cents advance in daily wage, while the bricklayers received an advance of 2½c an hour.

Contracting carpenters likewise had clashes with the unions of carpenters in 1891. The Milwaukee contracting carpenters association issued a set of "shop rules" in April, stating among other things that the employer reserved the right to employ or discharge whomever he saw fit without regard to a union.

On December 30, 1890, the carpenters' union notified all the boss builders, carpenters, and contractors in St. Louis, Missouri, that wages would be advanced 5c an hour. Seventy-odd bosses refused to grant the demand and stated that they would never acknowledge a union which claimed the right to fix wages. The other bosses did not reply. May 1, 1891, was the date set for a general strike, and four weeks prior to that date, the union again repeated its demands. In the meanwhile, 52 bosses met and organized the Boss Builders and Carpenters' Association, which determined to resist to the last. The strike took place and many of the bosses, having profitable contracts on hand, broke away from the Association and granted the union demands until practically all bosses had given in by May 20, when the strike was called off. In Sea Cliff, Utica, and Tarrytown, New York, the master carpenters of each were compelled by strikes of the carpenters' unions to grant a nine-hour day (reduced from ten). In December, 1891, a committee of the Master Carpenters' Association of Middleton, New York, met a union committee and agreed to grant the nine-hour day on May 2, 1892, with no reduction in pay, but the master carpenters, with one exception, failed to fulfill their promises.

To train young men in the trade, the newly organized Builders' Exchange of Pittsburgh planned a trade school similar to those in New York, Philadelphia, and Chicago; but in Boston, the unions and associations representing the building trades agreed that in the trade schools of that city no one but indentured apprentices should be allowed to enter. "The Boss Masons' Association of New Jersey resolved to employ pupils of the New York Trade School to fill the places of striking bricklayers. Their services could be had, it was stated, at $1.50 a day. Non-union journeymen were offered $1.05 a day, the wages paid heretofore." The National Association of Builders advocated trade schools and a more perfect apprenticeship system under which sufficient young men would be apprenticed. A new manual training school opened up in Philadelphia in February.

Arbitration was extensively debated at the annual convention of the National Association of Builders which drew up an elaborate plan of arbitration, but which, however, voted down a resolution favoring the fostering of "proper unions."

Other woodworking employers had to deal with strikes in 1891. The planing mills of Erie, Pennsylvania, were struck by their employees for eight months over recognition of the union and the shorter workday. On May 1, the master stair builders of St. Louis were struck by the carpenters to force an advance in wages of 5c an hour and a reduction in hours from nine to eight. The union won. While outside the building trades, the four months' strike of the ship carpenters was defeated by the ship owners at the lake ports for an eight-hour day, and the strikers returned to their old places at the old terms. The Boss Framers' Association of New York was organized to resist the demands of the framers' union for an increase of 5c an hour and seven hours on Saturday. The association offered terms which differed from the union's demands in certain respects, such as classifying the workmen, examining contracts of employers, and weekly payment of wages. As all attempts at settlement failed, the framers struck on May 1. On June 15, the issue was compromised and the union gained all its points except the weekly payment of wages. Although the association signed the contract, the union struck on June 23 to force the employers individually to sign the agreement, which they did the same day.

Employing lathers made concessions in 1891. In New York City they were forced by a series of strikes to grant a wage increase to the lathers. In Brooklyn, they were forced by strikes to grant the eight-hour day and increase the daily wage of the lathers. In Milwaukee, the contractors granted, after many conferences during which many proposals, counter proposals, and compromises were discussed, the striking union's demands for an eight-hour day and 32c an hour wages. The employing plasterers of Milwaukee refused to grant the plasterers' demands for a 5 cents per hour increase in wages and were struck on March 15. The union, however, comprised only a part of the plasterers in the city, and the nonunion men remained at work.

The Furniture Manufacturers' Association of New York in response to an appeal for protection from one of its members who was struck by the cabinet makers without submitting the dispute to arbitration as required by the agreement between the association and union, demanded that the union order its men back to work pending negotiations. The union refused on the ground that the firm had not asked to have the matter handled by the association. The association appealed to the Board of Walking Delegates which requested the union to order its men back to work and it did so.

The Lumber Trade Association of New York City in May refused to reply to the demands of the lumber handlers and truck drivers for a new scale of wages and union shop rules. On May 4, all the men struck one of the members of the association. The struck firm employed nonunion men and continued operations; then the union boycotted it. It appealed to the association, which ordered its members to close their yards until the boycott was ended. The association was supported by lumber dealers elsewhere. The chairman of the executive committee of the association and the president of the union board of delegates held a conference and reached an agreement, which was rejected by the association. The association announced that it would hold no more conferences with the board of delegates, but its repudiation of the agreement created considerable dissension among members of the association. About this time, however, the Brooklyn dealers closed their yards to help out the association. The association offered on June 1 to reinstate the workmen if the boycott would be declared off, but the union demanded also arbitration of wages and hours. On June 6, the association announced that on June 8 it would open the yards as open shops with nonunion men employed as individuals. This ended the strike.

The Brick Manufacturers' Exchange of Denver accepted a scale of wages and output, but the brickmakers struck on April 20 against it. The employers had great difficulty in obtaining and keeping new men under conditions of union tactics and violence. A riot occurred in which two men were killed and the union leader crippled for life. The employers were tried and acquitted, and the strike was called off by the union as a failure.

Master painters had varying degrees of success and failure in dealing with unions in 1891. In April in New York City, they granted the eight-hour day to striking painters. In Grand Rapids, Michigan, they were struck because their association refused to grant the nine-hour day. The union struck only after considerable correspondence had passed between the association and the union. Then a conference was held at which the union received the nine-hour day and full "recognition" so that only union men were employed thereafter. On May 1, however, the master painters of St. Louis defeated disastrously a strike called by the AFL painters' union. The employers were enabled to do this because a local painters' union, older and stronger than the AFL union, was very unfriendly toward its younger rival. In November, master painters of Mt. Vernon, New York, defeated a strike of the painters for a nine-hour day with wages at $2.75. But the master painters of Utica, New York, granted the union demands for nine hours on the first five days of the week. The master painters of Milwaukee defeated a strike of the painters' union for an eight-hour day; they had offered a wage increase.

The master plumbers and steamfitters were not very active in strikes in 1891. In May, master plumbers of Sioux City, Iowa, were struck by the plumbers, gas and steam fitters, and helpers for a reduction in hours from 10 to 9 with no reduction in wages. The union won. Likewise, the master plumbers of Dubuque, Iowa, refused to grant a new scale of wages and reduction of hours demanded by the union of plumbers and steamfitters, who struck and won the wage demands. In August, the Master Steam and Hot Water Fitters' Association of New York City granted the demands of the striking steamfitters for rules and an agreement. But the Master Plumbers' Association of Yonkers defeated a strike for reduction of hours from nine to eight with no reduction in pay. Likewise, the contractors of Milwaukee refused to grant the demands of the steamfitters for an eight-hour day and an advance of 5c an hour in wages, and defeated a strike which lasted over a month.

In two instances, the master sheet metal workers were belligerent. The master sheet metal workers and manufacturers of St. Louis in May were struck by the sheet metal workers to enforce demands for an eight-hour day—from ten hours—with no reduction in pay, and the adoption of certain union shop rules. "The employers acted in strict concert. They had lists of all strikers; the names of the objectionable men . . . were marked . . . About fifty copies of those lists had been divided among the employers." The strike died out by October 1, a failure. The contractors of Milwaukee defeated the tin and cornice workers in a four-weeks strike over a wage of 25c an hour and the eight-hour day.

In April, the Iron League of New York City offered the housesmiths' union an eight-hour day with corresponding daily wage reduction, and contended that their contracts were based on the old hourly rate. The housesmiths' union, 3,500 in number, struck for the same daily wage on May 1, but after six weeks declared the strike off and went back to work at the old terms. Almost identical events took place in Brooklyn, but some of the employers who had granted the union's demands went back to the nine-hour day. Moreover, the Iron League of New York City and Brooklyn defeated a six-weeks strike of the architectural iron workers' union for the eight-hour day and the signing of a new agreement. The foundries making architectural castings were struck in New York and Brooklyn in sympathy with the house-smiths. Likewise, the architectural iron foundries of St. Louis were struck on May 1 for increased wages and the eight-hour day instead of the ten-hour day. The foundries ignored the architectural iron workers' union's demands. "The proprietors acted in concert, and after six weeks' struggle their determination was not weakened the least." They even refused compromise offers. The strike was declared off on June 13, a complete failure.

On May 1, contractors of St. Louis, Missouri, felt themselves compelled to grant the demands of the team owners for $4.00 a day (instead of about $2.50) because the latter threatened to have a city ordinance enforced which regulated the size of the wagon bed, and accordingly of the load.

In May, the quarry owners of St. Louis were struck by the quarrymen for an eight-hour day with wages they had received for a ten-hour day. On May 11, a conference between the owners and the union resulted in a compromise on the nine-hour day with no reduction in pay. Likewise, the marble companies of St. Louis were forced by a strike of the marble setters—and profitable contracts—to grant the union's demands for $3.00 for an eight-hour day instead of $2.50. Somewhat different was the strike on the paving contractors by the pavers and rammermen of New York against the handling of nonunion blocks of a granite company which had employed nonunion stevedores. The "contractors brought their united influence to bear to have the particularly objectionable stevedores removed, and they were successful."

In the Iron and Related Industries there were strikes on the Eastern iron mills, on the blast furnaces, and on the foundries of San Francisco, in 1891. In June, the wage committee of the Association of Manufacturers of Iron, Steel and Nails met with the committee of the Amalgamated Association of Iron and Steel Workers and agreed upon a new scale for West of the Allegheny Mountains. It was signed by most manufacturers. There were, however, some Pittsburgh manufacturers who were nonunion or open shop. In July, rolling mills elsewhere brought strong pressure to bear upon the sheet and iron workers' union of St. Louis by stating that they would annihilate the international union if it did not make the local union enforce the union rules against a St. Louis rolling mill which was underselling the other mills by 10 to 20 percent because it did not conform to the union rules. The local union demanded that the firm conform to the rules and refusal brought on a strike. Nonunion men were obtained with some difficulty but the proprietor operated as a nonunion mill. The Eastern manufacturers, when presented with a new scale, generally refused to sign and a strike was called, but failed. The rolling mill owners of Lebanon, Pennsylvania, defeated a strike of 500 workmen beginning July 1 and ending October 15. The strikers were allowed to return only as individuals. The striking ore handlers at Cleveland resumed work in June pending arbitration; a compromise was agreed upon, the men receiving 9½c— ½c per ton less than they demanded of their employers. The furnace operators of the Mahoning and Shenango Valleys reduced wages of workmen on June 8, an average of 10 percent—"to meet Southern competition." In October, however, the blast furnace owners of the Shenango Valley were forced by a strike to restore wages paid before the shut-down on account of the coke strike. The advance amounted to 10c to 15c daily. The blast furnace owners of the Mahoning Valley, however, met on October 8 and decided to grant a general advance of 10 percent to all blast furnace employees.

The strike of the molders on the foundries of San Francisco spread to the building trades because of the boycott of nonunion iron by the building trades workmen. The building trades employers appointed a committee to take action to meet the boycott, and while they had not proposed to antagonize their workmen on questions of wages, they insisted on their right to employ whomever they pleased and to use the nonunion iron. The protracted strikes finally caused the employers of the city to organize a federation of an aggressive character. It was then said of the new organization that:

"Ere long there will be few employers of labor in San Francisco who will not be found in its ranks. It was bound to come. . . . and having come, it is bound to stay as long as there shall be employers and employed. It will not be confined to San Francisco, but before the year is out will have embraced the whole State, and finally the Union . . . One cardinal maxim laid down by its founders is that employers shall not be dictated to as to whom they shall employ. The proceedings were enveloped in secrecy."

"Manufacturers and others interested in industrial pursuits in this city have grown tired of the numerous strikes and boycotts, which have become alarmingly frequent of late. The manufacturers are organizing, and we are promised here a grand federation of manufacturers to offset the Federation of Labor. This would never have occurred were the trade unions of this city only reasonably prudent. But they have sown the wind and they are likely to reap the whirlwind. The iron men began the resistance somewhat over a year ago, and now it looks as if the struggle would become well-nigh universal."

In November, the molders' strike completely collapsed.

The Philadelphia Foundrymen's Association organized in November with 40 firms, and its object was the "advancement of foundry interests. . . . It has nothing to do with the fixing of prices or the regulation of trade matters . . . It is organized on the plan of the Builders' Exchange." In contrast, the National Association of Stove Manufacturers had a "uniform cost system" in 1891 for the "automatic regulation" of prices. Foundrymen were complaining of the scarcity of molders and laid that scarcity partly to union restrictions on apprentices.

In the Coal and Coke Industries in 1891, the strike of the coke workers was notable. The coke operators of the Connellsville region held a conference on January 3 with their workmen to consider a wage scale proposed by the union. The operatives' conference committee characterized the demands as "unreasonable and unfair": an increase of from 15 to 20 percent was demanded, while the operators were contending that there should be a reduction because of the business depression. At a conference held on February 2, the operators proposed a 10 percent reduction, but both sides were unyielding. The coke operators were "strongly entrenched." On February 9, the coke workers struck for a wage advance and reduction of hours. The strikers assaulted men who remained at work. Conferences between the employers and strike leaders were held up to March 3, on which date all the leaders were arrested for conspiracy, riot, and assault. Federal injunctions were obtained. But the strikers continued their assaults and destruction of property. A large number of deputy sheriffs were sworn in and special guards and Pinkerton detectives were employed. Pitched battles occurred. The state militia was called out. Attempts of the operators to start with new men were only partially successful under the warlike conditions. Imported workmen deserted to the strikers. It was openly stated that some iron manufacturers were aiding the strikers: "At least one iron manufacturer . . . stated that he had furnished the men with sinews of war." Seven strikers were killed and others wounded. Finally enough new men and deserting strikers were obtained on the coke operators' terms to operate fully and the strike collapsed. But the coal operators of the Ohio Valley were struck and forced to grant a wage advance.

The year 1891 started off with a demand and threatened strike on the coal operators of Central Pennsylvania who shipped their product to tidewater for 50c a ton net instead of 50c gross. The coal operators of Ohio, Indiana, Illinois, and Western Pennsylvania were apathetic over a threatened coal strike in April. The miners demanded the eight-hour day, which operators refused to grant. The strike was deferred by the miners because of the defection of miners in some sections and the great expense of the coke strike mentioned above. Coal operators of Iowa, however, were struck for six weeks beginning in June, and announced that mines were being rapidly exhausted and that many of them would soon be mined out. In October, the railroad coal operators of Pittsburgh district refused to grant 10c a ton advance in wages and were struck by about 12,000 men. After five weeks the strikers were defeated and returned at the old wages. The Indiana State Association of Bituminous Operators were struck by 8,000 miners over higher wages. This strike helped to cause a coal famine. The defeat of the Pittsburgh miners conduced to the defeat of the Indiana strikers. In December, the miners admitted their failure to obtain the eight-hour day.

In Clothing and Related Industries, manufacturers and contractors were distinctly belligerent in 1891. In February, the strike on 47 contracting cloak makers of New York by 700 employees had reached its 72nd day and was apparently lost. In May, the leader—Barondess—of the cloak makers' union in New York was convicted of extortion of money from the manufacturers to settle the strike. He tried to escape to Europe, but was caught and returned to New York. On March 7, the Clothiers' Exchange of Rochester was struck by the cutters in a dispute over the work, wages, and number of apprentices to a shop. The Exchange announced that all men returning to work would be required to sign an individual agreement and renounce the union. The Exchange was reputed to have raised a pool of $166,000 to which its members had paid in from $2,000 to $22,000—two percent of their sales. No man was hired unless he had a letter of recommendation from his previous employer. The Exchange opened its shops on March 13, fullhanded. In May, one of the union leaders—Hughes—was caught at extortion and convicted, but 21 of the clothing manufacturers were indicted for conspiracy.

Illustrative activities of other soft-goods manufacturers are: The cap manufacturers of New York refused to grant the demands of the blockers for a wage increase, and the strike became general. The manufacturers declined arbitration and the association announced that no man would be reemployed if he did not leave the union. Union officials were arrested for conspiracy and the association was charged with thus trying to break up the union. After the strike had lasted three months, the association asked for a conference with the union officials but the conference failed when held. Union men deserted the union and thus broke up the strike. The Hat and Cap Manufacturers' Association of New York was organized during the strike. The Suspender Manufacturers' Association of New York was struck by the suspender makers over the employment of a nonunion man by one of its members. Finally, the Association induced some of the strike leaders to repudiate the union and return to work; the strikers then stampeded back to their old jobs. This is one of the few cases where the association used the "divide and conquer" tactics on the union.

Some of the diverse activities of other associations are: The New York shirt manufacturers, especially of Troy, protested against the employment of convict labor in making shirts. The morocco manufacturers of the Eastern states proposed the establishment of a technical school in connection with the University of Pennsylvania, in which attention would be directed exclusively to the chemistry of tanning. The Manufacturing Furriers' Association of New York was forced by a strike to grant their workers the eight-hour day.

In the Brewing Industry in 1891, the outstanding instance of belligerency was in St. Louis; the other associations tended to be appeasatory. The brewers of Syracuse granted the 60-hour week, and the strike ended the same day it began. The brewers of Troy, New York, granted a reduction of hours on Sunday from two to one, a wage increase, and union shop rules. The brewers of New York, threatened with a general strike of the firemen, signed an agreement with the union fixing hours, wages, and shop rules. In contrast, the St. Louis brewers were belligerent—for brewers. The St. Louis Brewers' Association—comprising all the St. Louis breweries but two small ones—began a fight upon a newly organized local union in 1886 (as recounted above). The union boycotted the brewers and the brewers banned the union and defeated it. In January, 1887, however, the brewers signed an agreement with the union effective until May, 1888, after which the Association announced it would not recognize the union. The brewers were boycotted for about the third time or more. In April, 1891, the association caused 33 union men to be discharged because they belonged to a union boycotting it. Then the boycott was withdrawn. One of the three large breweries— Anheuser Busch—entered into negotiations with the union in June, but it was not until September 25 that a satisfactory agreement was reached. The Brewers' Protective Association of San

Francisco also dealt with boycotts by various unions from 1888 to 1892, and locked out the workmen in at least one of the boycotts.

In September, 1891, the Window Glass Manufacturers' Association and the union committee conferred on gatherers' wages but reached no agreement and 10,000 men were thrown out of employment. About two weeks later, they met again in Pittsburgh and decided that the work would be resumed at the prices and rules of the previous year. The Window Glass Manufacturers' Association of Indiana was formed in August and adopted a resolution declaring "that no glass shall be made until wages, rules, and usages are settled to the satisfaction of the Manufacturers' Wage Committee, and until said Wage Committeee shall have notified each manufacturer through the secretary of the date of starting."

Other industries were relatively quiet. A few instances from some of these will illustrate activities in varied fields. The Boot and Shoe Manufacturers' Association of San Francisco had nine members in 1891. Because a manufacturer introduced a lasting machine, the workers struck and the association declared a lockout. In January, the Tanners and Leather Manufacturers' Assosiation of Milwaukee, after refusing to grant a list of prices demanded by the tanners' union, submitted a price list in which the wage rates were cut five percent. The union rejected the list and ordered a strike. All union men were discharged by the association members. The association brought in nonunion workmen from the East and bound its members by a bond of $1,000 each not to employ any of the strikers at wages higher than in the scale submitted by the association. In June, one member withdrew from the association and employed all his old employees at the old scale. However, this desertion did not break the ranks of the association, as so often formerly happened almost immediately.

The textile mills of Newark, New Jersey, defeated a strike of the textile workers. In April the strike was declared off and many sought their old jobs. Textile manufacturers defeated in April in the Massachusetts legislature a bill reducing hours of women and children in their factories to 58 a week, on the grounds of Southern competition.

Among others, the butchers, the bakers, the canners and axe-makers contributed to association activities during the year. The Boss Butchers' Association of New York refused to grant the union's demands for reduction of hours and limitation of apprentices. The union dropped these demands and signed an agreement with the association—a rather unusual proceeding. But the master Bohemian butchers of New York granted the demands of their striking workmen for wage increases and reduction of hours. Likewise, the Hebrew master bakers in New York City granted the demands of their striking bakers for a wage increase and better working conditions. Other master bakers in New York City were struck for a reduction in hours from 14 to 10 and granted it. Although the salmon canners of the Northwest proposed to cut wages one cent per fish, they were forced by a strike to restore former prices. In September, war was also conducted between the American Axe and Tool Company with 12 factories and the unions backed by the AFL. In October, the job printing shops of Pittsburgh refused to grant the job printers and pressmen increased wages, so the workers struck in a strike that extended into 1892. In contrast to the above, the New York Chamber of Commerce, in order to educate seamen more effectively, took entire charge of the schoolship St. Mary.

CHAPTER 14

COLLECTIVE BARGAINING AGAIN INTENSIFIED
THE CONFLICT

NOTED DEVELOPMENTS OF 1892 include a large number of sympathetic strikes especially in the building industry of New York City. They also include many double exclusive agreements between association and union—only union men were to be employed and they were to work exclusively for association members. In contrast, there was the great growth of nonunion concerns. In other words, the issues were growing sharper, and the strikes were more bitterly contested, often bloody, like at Homestead. These events—and others detailed below—foreshadow a panic or marked business recession. In fact, unemployment in certain industries was increasing and making the combating of strikes easier because of the surplus men anxious to take the jobs claimed by the strikers. Another outstanding development was that of high union officials (former or resigning) taking jobs as association or corporation officials. In union circles, such shifting has been usually regarded as the highest order of treason. Whatever motives caused the shifting, loyal unionists regularly denounced these officials for "selling out to the enemy." But it is conceivable that their shifting, at least in part, reflected a general reaction toward unionism.

In February, it was noted that cheap prices penetrated every section and were going lower, and that there were too many immigrants. It was recognized that it was "a day of small margins" because of competition and low prices. On one hand it was pointed out that wages were leveling off, they had not fallen correspondingly to prices. On the other hand, associations were combining with unions—giving the unions their "spoils" in "stabilized" or higher wages—to "stabilize" the industry restricting production and preventing price cutting. Undoubtedly, these were the main factors in the Stove Founders' National Defense Association's becoming negotiatory with the Iron Molders' Union and signing the "Conference Agreements" in 1892. Because prices were falling, strikes for wage advances or against reductions in the early part of the year were usually defeated.

As early as March, it was freely predicted that a crisis was impending, that wages had to be reduced, and that an alarming labor contest was coming. The "anarchy of overproduction" was discussed as a contributing factor to that crisis and contest. Employers were charged with forcing strikes, among other things, to curtail production. Manufacturers and operators cut prices in spite of agreements among themselves and with the unions, and cut them well below market quotations. When union officials insisted that certain wages should be paid in accord with certain prices as given in market quotations, employers offered to show their books to prove that much lower prices were received. Union officials retorted that if employers did not keep faith among themselves, how could the unions trust them?

Unions, however, gained higher wages and other concessions by their strikes on the World's Fair at Chicago but as a result received much unfavorable publicity.

Various phases of unionism were under attack. Among these were condemnations of the walking delegate and his practices, especially his "arbitrary" and "dictatorial" orders and attitude. Discussions of the trade union—in contrast with the "labor union" like the Knight of Labor type—while pointing out its accomplishments also called attention to its defects, inconsistencies, and failures. Union boycotting and sympathetic strikes—a form of boycotting—produced a hostile reaction among employers; for instance, in a strike and boycott upon Wheeler and Company of Bay City, Michigan, the company appealed to the merchants to help it break the strike and boycott, which they did by positively refusing to aid the strikers in any way—that is, one boycott offset the other. A more detailed illustration of the reaction toward unionism was supplied by the Board of Directors of the Manufacturers and Employers' Association of San Francisco, whose members employed 40,000 workmen, in its declaration of May 6, 1892, that (abstracted):

"The time has come to put an end to boycotts and the pernicious interference of trade unions with the internal affairs of business. Eastern competition has proven to be serious under union interference. Several factories have gone East and more are expected to follow. The manufacturers do not complain of the wages. If permitted to do business in peace the manufacturers could pay these wages and prosper. The union leaders seek to control the men and the manufacturer cannot manage his business to the best advantage then. Walking delegates have been bribed to boycott competitors, and walking delegates have exacted bribes for immunity from the boycott. Agitation is the life of unionism. This activity is good for the paid walking delegate, but it is ruinous to business and calamitous to industrious working men. Watch your employees and discharge boycotters. Patronize boycotted firms."

The growth of nonunionism was remarkable. Lists of nonunion concerns were published, the lists grew longer with each publication, and thus stimulated other firms to join the lists until the growth became great. The Homestead strike was a startling demonstration of the growth of nonunionism. While great strike losses to employers contributed to anti-unionism by themselves, the losses to the workers tended to raise doubts in the minds of workers as to possible gains from unionism. These were further increased by showing workers how much they had gained from modern improvements, made against the strong opposition of union leaders.

In the Field of Government, the compulsory pilotage bill was defeated—a bill sought by pilots' unions to force vessels to use a pilot whether they needed him or not to enter harbors in the United States. Associations were advocating federal incorporation and legal responsibility of unions and the regulation of immigration. On the other side, the Chinese Six Companies of San Francisco employed counsel to test the validity of the Chinese Exclusion Act. Far more significant but almost unheralded was the first application of the Sherman Anti-Trust Act to unions and the issuance of a federal injunction by Chief Justice Fuller under that Act to restrain a strike in New Orleans. As a violation of the freedom of contract, the Illinois Anti-Truck Law was held invalid; the law was directed mainly at company stores and the payment of wages in "store orders."

While the pardoning by the Governor of the State of New York, on petition of 60,000 persons, of Joseph Barondess was undoubtedly a great political victory of the unionists over those who had him prosecuted, the resulting publicity hurt unionism. It was proclaimed that he was a grafting union leader who terrorized the cloak manufacturers of New York by sudden strikes, violence, and extortion. The demand by the thousands of unionists for his pardon seemed clearly to be an endorsement by them of his unethical and illegal practices, and created in the minds of many that such practices were common under unionism. Moreover, the idea that unionism and lawlessness were inseparable was confirmed by the history of labor troubles in Western Pensylvania and elsewhere, and justified a contempt for local government—to quote:

"Until the root of the evil is reached by a radical reform, employers of labor will be forced to rely upon the Pinkerton service, which they pay out of their own pockets, or be provided with protection by militia at the first sign of trouble, at a great cost to the community and, in the long run, unbearable inconvenience and suffering to the citizen soldiery . . . [or] the employment of a State police, which could be quickly concentrated at any one locality."

In later years, the State police was established and then fought bitterly by the unions for many years. In this field many years have been spent in advocacy, followed by many years to obtain repeal, of a highly controversial measure.

In the Iron and Steel Industry in 1892, associations were organized for more effective collective bargaining at about the same time of a rapid growth of anti-unionism, demonstrated spectacularly in the Homestead strike. The Association of Iron and Steel Sheet Manufacturers met at Pittsburgh February 23 and adopted a constitution and by-laws. Reports were read by each of the four scale committees appointed at a previous meeting. These committees represented sheet-bar mills, tin-plate mills, sheet mills, and fire-bed mills. An Executive Committee of three was appointed to draw up a scale for each of the four kinds of mills based on the reports of the four committees. These scales were then sent to each mill and submitted by each individual concern to the

sub-lodges of the "Amalgamated" union of iron workers for consideration by these lodges, which reported on the scales to the
union convention. The manufacturers made no attempt to reduce wages generally, but endeavored to correct discrepancies
which had crept into the wages paid by sheet mills. A Committee
was appointed to call upon the American Tinned-Plate Manufacturers' Association of the United States to get it to consolidate
with the Association of Iron and Steel Sheet Manufacturers.

The Tinned-Plate Manufacturers' Association of the United
States, with 35 members, met February 24. After considerable
discussion of wages to be paid by association mills, a committee
was appointed to formulate a wage schedule, and did so. The
proposal of the Association of Iron and Steel Sheet Manufacturers
for uniting the two bodies in some manner was referred to the
board of managers for final action. Likewise, the choice of
method of raising funds was referred to this board with the suggestion that an assessment be levied on the product of each firm.
The initiation fee was $50.

Pittsburgh iron manufacturers met on June 15 with the
Amalgamated (union) and each side presented its scale. The
manufacturers contended that bar iron had been selling for a
long time at 1½c a pound or less, while the scale minimum was
2c; and that many improvements had been made but that the
workers had absorbed all the benefits. To these contentions,
union officials replied that they were "unable to see how a reduction of wages would be of any benefit to the manufacturers as
such reductions would undoubtedly be shared almost entirely
by consumers." The manufacturers' scale proposed heavy reductions, for example, to cut from $5.50 to $4.50 on a 2c card
for boiling. Conference after conference was held without an
agreement, and a shutdown resulted. Finally, when all but two
clauses were agreed upon, the manufacturers proposed arbitration, but the union refused to arbitrate. After 17 meetings, the
manufacturers conceded $5.50 on a 2c card—which was the old
rate, but some rates, for instance, in the finishing department
were cut as much as 10 per cent or more. A few individuals had
signed the union scale before agreement was reached in August
after two months of conferences.

Meanwhile, the wage committee of the Iron and Steel Sheet Manufacturers' Association met in conferences with the union committee from June 17 until in July. The first conference lasted ten hours. The manufacturers' scale proposed a number of changes in rules and conditions, but with reductions only in shearmen's wages and that because of improvements increasing their earning power. Final agreement on all but three points was reached at a conference lasting from 2:15 p.m. to 4 a.m.— nearly 14 hours. But the next conference stalled on the three points. In July, final agreement was reached.

In contrast, the proposed scale of the Association of Manufacturers of Iron, Steel, and Nails, submitted to the Amalgamated, contained heavy reductions, like in the proposed Pittsburgh scale. Likewise, the bar iron manufacturers of the Mahoning and Shenango Valleys and "other points west of Pittsburgh" submitted to the Amalgamated a scale with heavy reductions. But the wire rod manufacturers, in conference in June with the Amalgamated, found that their differences were not great and scheduled another conference to complete the agreement. Likewise, the jobbing mills met and arranged for a conference with the Amalgamated and agreed upon a jobbing mill scale in August. But the wire nail manufacturers, in conference in August with the Amalgamated, convinced the union that wages should be reduced 8 to 10 per cent in the scale.

The manufacturers of the Mahoning and Shenango Valleys conferred with the Amalgamated but reached no agreement. They conferred again at Youngstown after the Pittsburgh conferences were over and adopted the Pittsburgh scale, with minor changes, at the August conference. The rolling mill manufacturers of these valleys had discussed scales extensively and had decided to break away from the Pittsburgh scale, but, of course, the Amalgamated would take no less, and practically got it. The association members had been dissatisfied with the situation for several months. That dissatisfaction expressed itself when the Mahoning and Shenango Valleys Iron Manufacturers' Association met in March, with 17 of the 20 member firms personally represented and discussed the proposal to disband the association. The discussion, however, caused the members to vote unanimously against the proposal and to take steps "looking to the material strengthening and the extending of its (association) influence and benefits."

The pig iron manufacturers of the Mahoning and Shenango Valleys, in March, reduced wages 10 per cent for all blast furnace labor on the grounds of the low prices for crude material. Clearly, there was unrest by manufacturers because of falling prices, and by unionists because of actual and threatened wage reductions. In March, likewise, a general movement was started by the furnace operators in the Birmingham, Alabama district to reduce the wages of the furnace and coke laborers 10 per cent.

The unrest in the iron and steel industry manifested itself in many ways. One was by a rapidly growing list of concerns that became nonunion. Another was by former officers of the Amalgamated becoming association officers and corporation officials. The third manifestation was the Homestead strike.

The nonunion movement in the iron and steel industry apparently showed greatest headway in Pittsburgh in August and September when a considerable number of firms became nonunion. As the number grew in September, imposing lists were published, and the number of workmen employed by these firms rose in September to 100,000. Unions were usually defeated where unionism was the issue.

Instances of former officers of the Amalgamated changing their allegiance were: Ex-President John Jarrett of the Amalgamated was made secretary of the Iron and Steel Sheet Manufacturers' Association—a secretary was then the real executive officer of an association. Likewise, Ex-Vice-President James H. Nutt of the Amalgamated was appointed by the Mahoning and Shenango Valleys Iron Manufacturers' Association to have full charge of their labor matters. Even President William Weihe of the Amalgamated severed his connection with the union to take an executive position with the Oliver Iron and Steel Company of Pittsburgh. The Amalgamated union was then one of the foremost unions in the United States.

The Homestead Strike was unmistakably an anti-union manifestation, in which violence reached new heights. Several battles were fought. In the first battle, 300 Pinkertons had been brought in, and in a fight between them and the strikers a number of men were killed. Fifty deputy sheriffs were brought in and 100 nonunionists were deputized. In a second battle, 7 men were killed and one wounded. For the third battle with the Pinkertons, the strikers built forts and had two cannon. They fired on a boatload of nonunionists and Pinkertons and drove them back. The Pinkertons were forced to surrender and leave, after receiving severe beatings while captives; and about 25 were killed. The militia was called out, and order restored for the time being. Congress appointed a committee to investigate the strike.

While the issues were given as the reduction of the wages of highly paid workmen and the nonunion shop, there was a socialistic element, possibly even an anarchistic one in the strike. Attempts were made to assassinate Chairman Frick of the corporation. Nonunion men were employed and brought in in increasing numbers and were assured of continuous employment. In retaliation, the union called more strikes on Carnegie mills. As strikers began to realize that the strike was failing, the violence toward the strikebreakers increased and there were more outbreaks and battles between the troops and the strikers. Breaks in the ranks of the strikers occurred among the older employees, especially at certain mills. The riotous disturbances led to strong demands for a state police. Although all departments were in full operation by September 1, the union officials still tried to keep the strike going. Prosecution of the strikers for killing Pinkertons and an official of the firm was begun early in the strike. At least 167 rioters were indicted by the grand jury and Berkman, a union leader, was sentenced to the penitentiary for 22 years. Although the strike had definitely failed in September, rioting and assaults continued. The advisory committee of the strikers was charged with treason to the state of Pennsylvania. Finally, the troops were removed, and the strike called off in November.

Organization among the foundry proprietors was aggressive in character in 1892. The Foundrymen's Association of Philadelphia grew to 80 members by July and to 100 by October. Agitation became strong to make it national with chapters. Among other things, it sought information as to wages paid to molders not only here but abroad. Thus, it was equipping itself to fight union demands. The machinery foundry employers of Cleveland were practically unanimous in opposing the demands of the molders' union for a minimum wage of $2.75 a day and for a set of union shop rules. Wages paid then ranged from $2 to $3 a day.

In the Building and Related Industries in 1892, the overshadowing development of collective bargaining in the industry was not one of industrial peace but of war in the form of a great number of sympathetic strikes. Instead of lessening the conflict, collective bargaining both widened and intensified it. Another development was the monopolistic practice of unions and associations signing double exclusive agreements by which they usually controlled the trade or locality in which they were strong to the detriment usually of outsiders and the consumers as well as of the nonunionists. The Iron League of New York furnished an excellent illustration of the intensification of the conflict:

"The iron manufacturers and builders have been organizing a league, which is said to represent about 90 per cent of the companies in New York and Brooklyn and Jersey City. The organization has been incorporated under the name of the Iron League. The manufacturers say that their fundamental idea is the same as that adopted by the employees. So that if the men employed on one building or in the shops of one company strike, the League will back the concern in its fight. None of the companies will employ a man who has struck while in the employ of any other company."

Because of sympathetic strikes called in New York City directed against the employment of nonunion men and variously affecting its members, the League gave notice on June 13 that by a certain date unless the strikes brought about by the Housesmiths' Union were discontinued, every member of that union in the employ of members of the Iron League would be discharged. "This course was approved by the United Building Trades, with which the Association of Building Material Dealers were affiliated." Everyone of the employees of the League's members denied that he belonged to the Housesmiths' Union and this nearly broke up that union, but it prevented the discharge of those workmen. The resolution of the League was to force the calling off of strikes against a firm in New York City which had been sympathetically struck because of a strike on a firm in Brooklyn. This action of the League helped to defeat the strike there.

In July, at a meeting of the Association of Building Material Dealers of New York City, the association resolved to support the Iron League and ordered a notice to be posted in the yards of its members against union dictation of its members' employees. The dealers were struck but hired some nonunion drivers and the strike collapsed.

By August, however, the conflict had grown and the League locked out all its union employees and employed nonunion men as a result of a contest over the discharge of a hoisting engineer. The Cartmen's Union declared a boycott on the members of the League, and the other contractors suspended work, so that 15,000 workmen were involved in the complex sympathetic strikes, boycotts, and lockouts. The builders and contractors thus joined hands with the League and the Building Material Dealers' Association to employ only such men as were "not subject to the orders of the walking delegates." In turn, the Board of Delegates of the Building Trades issued a public statement attacking the Iron League and the Building Trades Club of New York, and denounced the League for trying to crush the unions and create a monopoly.

Sympathetic strikes on employers in the building industry of New York City in 1892 became a "house-that-Jack-built" affair. Among the 18 sympathetic strikes called by the derrickmen in 1892, was a general strike of 36 days called in the Spring in sympathy with the hod-hoisting engineers. In July, however, the hod-hoisting engineers struck their employers sympathetically to assist the building material drivers in their strike, which was a result indirectly of sympathetic strikes relating to the Iron League. In July, the building contractors of New York City were sympathetically struck repeatedly because of the employment of nonunion men in other trades. The employing framers in New York were struck by the framers sympathetically to help the building material drivers in their contest with the Association of Building Material Dealers. Likewise, building contractors were struck sympathetically by the hod carriers for the same cause. Among the 13 sympathetic strikes called by the marble cutters in 1892 was one called in July to help the building material drivers. Among its 7 sympathetic strikes by the skylight and cornice makers was one called to help the same drivers. Out of 25 sympathetic strikes called in 1892 by each of the steamfitters' union and the steamfitters' helpers' union were those called to help those drivers and the housesmiths. The employing plasterers were struck sympathetically by the plastering laborers to aid the drivers. As the strike of the drivers grew out of other sympathetic actions going back to the Iron League and beyond, it is not necessary here to trace and record them all. Needless to say, there were other sympathetic strikes in New York City not related, as well as related to the above complex.

Among the other sympathetic strikes were: The blue-stone cutters struck sympathetically four times. The Association of Manufacturers of Cabinet Work and Furniture caused all union men to be locked out in three establishments in which ornamental plasterers were at work because the plasterers had struck in sympathy with the cabinet makers. New York builders were struck in sympathy generally in November to aid electric wiremen on strike. In view of this incomplete record of sympathetic strikes in 1892 among the collective-bargaining associations in the building industry of the New York City it seems fair to say that this experience proved that collective bargaining was not conducive to industrial peace, but actually provided the means and methods for conducting extended industrial warfare.

Unregulated collective bargaining also produced conspiracies against the public, the consumer, the outside employer, and the nonunion workman. These conspiracies were in the form of double exclusive agreements. Among the associations and unions signing such agreements was the Master Plumbers' Association of New York which signed a double exclusive agreement with the Journeymen Plumbers, Gas and Steamfitters and Steamfitters Helpers' Association (union) of America. A gas fitters' union was thus excluded because its members refused to join the contracting union, and they were locked out by the contracting association until they did join. The master plumbers generally have long been reputed to have sought monopoly conditions.

Another instance of the double exclusive agreement was supplied by the Tile, Grate, and Mantel Association of New York. In May, the association agreed to grant the union the eight-hour day at the old hourly rate, but was forced by a strike of the tile layers' union to give the eight-hour day with no reduction in daily pay. Moreover, an exclusive agreement on both sides was signed, which included wage rates, hours of work, and apprenticeship rules.

The Master Builders' Association of Baltimore in January conceded the eight-hour day to the bricklayers, marble and freestone cutters and granite cutters *with corresponding reduction* in *pay*. The carpenters asked for the eight-hour day with an increase in pay. The association submitted a proposed plan of arbitration which the carpenters rejected. The carpenters then stated that on July 5, the eight-hour day would be established and the wage would be 35c an hour. The association replied that the nine-hour day and $2.50 daily wage would prevail. The carpenters then offered to work eight hours for $2.50, but the association declined and a strike was called by the carpenters which lasted 10 weeks. The employment of nonunion carpenters caused the unions in the other trades to strike in sympathy. But the strike was called off and the carpenters lost; however, they accepted the association's offer of the nine-hour day at $2.50. The union card system—the closed shop—was abandoned and union and nonunion men worked together on the buildings. The strike of the mill workers was called at the same time as that of the carpenters, some factories conceded the eight-hour day, but others organized and fought the union. The new association imported nonunion men to some extent and sent some its work out of the city. The union failed because it was weak. The strikers returned to work at the end of three weeks at nine hours' work for nine hours' pay.

Strikes of master builders in 1892 were too extensive to be given in detail here. The master builders of Chicago faced strikes on May 1. In Pittsburgh strikes were called in 1892 on the master masons, plumbers, tinners, stone cutters, plasterers, house painters, and carpenters. Hours were the issue in many cities. In Ithaca, New York, in May the master carpenters, after a five-day strike by the carpenters conceded the nine-hour day and a slight increase in wages. But the master carpenters of Newburg defeated a three-day strike for the eight-hour day, while the master carpenters of White Plains, New York, conceded the nine-hour day after a three-day strike. In Grand Rapids, Michigan, the Master Carpenters' Association failed to reply to repeated requests of the Carpenters' Union for a nine-hour day with wages at 25c an hour, but apparently conceded both after a strike. In November, the Builders' Exchange of Pittsburgh announced that it adhered to "the rule which makes nine hours a legal day's work," and invited all builders' exchanges to a convention to be held in Pittsburgh on January 17, 1893, to deal with the issue. The Builders' Exchange of Pittsburgh endeavored to prevent an independent contractor from getting supplies to fulfill a contract to build a large building for a clothing house, which, to cater to and secure the trade of the working class, gave the contract to an "independent" who had not resisted the strike of the workers in the previous year. The independent appealed to the court for an injunction against the 64 members of the Exchange to restrain the conspiracy.

The Master Builders' Exchange of Philadelphia had other than direct strike activities in 1892. It obtained from the National Association of Great Britain a statement that showed that wages in Philadelphia were twice as high as in London. It had sheet metal work added to the trades taught in its trade school. In June the school bestowed 41 certificates of graduation upon young men for completing one each of the various trades taught. Thus, the exchange endeavored to increase the number of skilled men and to supply members with information to combat union agitation.

In connection with trade schools, J. Pierpont Morgan gave $500,000 to the New York Trade Schools and Phillip D. Armour endowed Armour Institute, as a manual training school, with more than $1,500,000.

The Association of Manufacturers of Cabinet Work and

Furniture of New York, in April, refused to grant the eight-hour day in place of the nine-hour day and defeated a 64-day strike of the machine woodworkers. The association, likewise, refused to grant in April the cabinet makers the eight-hour day with daily wages of $3.50. The association issued a manifesto arguing that even the nine-hour day handicapped the New York manufacturer in competition with manufacturers in other cities. The union struck. On May 10, the association gave notice to the strikers that unless they returned to work by May 16 they must remove their tools from the shops, and their places would be given to new men. The strikers did not return on that date, but on July 11, they abandoned the strike. In July, the association resolved to restore the nine-hour day from the eight-hour day in the case of the wood carvers because they had struck sympathetically to aid the cabinet makers. After a six weeks' strike, the association refused certain compromises but finally proposed that any manufacturer could work nine hours a day and give Saturday as a holiday, and the workmen accepted. However, 16 firms did not grant the Saturday holiday but gave an eight-hour day on Saturday. Their workers were out 25 weeks before they gave up. The association also ordered lockout of union members because unions had sympathetically struck, in one case, one of its members. After 72 days, the lockout ended in the defeat of the union. In another case, three of its members had been struck sympathetically. The contracting cabinet makers of St. Louis were struck in March by the cabinet makers to enforce their demand for the nine-hour day with no reduction in pay. The strikers won after a four-day strike. The planing mills, however, defeated the same demand by employing new men; after two months the strike was called off as a complete failure. Building contractors of Staten Island were forced by a strike to grant the hod carriers a wage advance of 25 cents.

The employing framers of New York City were forced by a two days' strike to renew an agreement with the framers' union. The employing framers of Brooklyn did likewise on threat of a strike. They also suffered from sympathetic strikes.

In related industries, in September, the lumbermill owners of Marinette and Menominee, Michigan, were struck for a wage advance. Conferences were held but accomplished nothing, since neither side would yield. The mill owners imported nonunion men and most of the strikers returned to work before the strike ended.

The fight for wage increases and the eight-hour day extended to employing elevator constructors and electricians. In April, the elevator constructing contractors of New York granted the eight-hour day to the elevator constructors' union. But, in April, the electrical equipment firms in New York refused to grant a wage increase of 25c to 50c a day to the wiremen. They struck one-half of the shops, and after 15 days were granted the demands by the struck shops soon to be followed by the others. In October these contractors were struck again because they had employed nonunion men, and for this, New York builders were struck sympathetically.

The Granite Manufacturers' Association of New England had an adjunct in the Paving Contractors' Association of New England. They cooperated in April in the lockout of the granite cutters. The employing pavers asked the pavers' union to make known in October its demands for the following January and year. The union declined and was locked out in New York since this was the principal market for paving blocks, and the pavers and rammermen there boycotted the products of the nonunion producers of New England by striking against using those products. Attempts at arbitration failed and the employers refused to compromise. They employed nonunion labor on the streets of New York. In July, the union gave up the contest and the employers took the union men back as such at the former wages and hours. The Granite Manufacturers' Association of New England brought pressure to bear upon the local manufacturers' association of Brooklyn to lockout the granite stone cutters there on July 13. The local union gave up after about two weeks and handled the "boycotted" granite. Likewise the local organization at Middle Village of the Granite Manufacturers' Association of New England locked out the granite cutters because they would not handle the "boycotted" stone and in three weeks forced the workmen to agree to handle it. In May, the Granite Manufacturers' Association of New England demanded that the expiration date of collective agreements with it be changed from May to January. The granite and paving cutters would not agree and were locked out by the association. The trouble spread to New York City, and manifested itself there in boycotts and strikes. Many conferences between the association and the national union decided nothing. The association employed nonunion men and resolved to employ union men only as individuals. In three months the strike was practically over, although it was not called off even after 17 weeks. Some granite was imported from abroad. All of the quarries signed "iron-clad" agreements (a new use for the term) among themselves not to recognize the union. The granite companies of Concord, New Hampshire, locked out the stone cutters in May because of disagreement over wages, but the granite manufacturers of Westerly, Maine, entered into an agreement with the granite cutters providing for "conciliation and arbitration" of their differences.

Union officials often break up these compacts by hitting at one employer individually so others gain at his expense, which he sees, and then breaks with the association. Or they convince an individual employer (in a rather general strike in the trade or locality) that he can make great gains by operating so he breaks with the association to reap great immediate profits and take customers away from his strike-bound competitors. Union officials know these weaknesses and play upon them regularly in "divide-and-conquer" tactics.

Processors of stone in the West also had labor troubles. In April, the marble companies of St. Louis were struck by the marble cutters for a nine-hour day with no reduction in pay. After ten days, the setters were called out in sympathy. While the marble concerns in the building industry conceded the demands, the ones in the monument business did not. In May, the quarry owners were struck by the quarrymen for a nine-hour day at the same weekly wages. But high water and other strikes made quarrying almost impossible as well as undesirable, so no concessions were made and strikers sought and obtained work elsewhere.

The employing stone cutters of New York City, in April, granted the eight-hour day to the blue-stone cutters who, however, struck sympathetically four times during the year. Likewise, the machine stone workers and hand rubbers struck sympathetically, and participated in the complex series of those strikes to aid the building material drivers. The Master Masons' Association of New York, on May 2, refused to grant the derrickmen's union demand for 25c a day wage increase but, after a ten-day strike, compromised on the issue and signed an agreement with the union, and then was struck sympathetically 18 times during the year; it gave the building laborers 30 cents an hour and the eight-hour day. Similarly, the employing cement masons of New York were forced by an eight-day strike to give a wage increase of 25c a day to the Cement Masons' Union. In August, however, the employers returned to the old rate and defeated the eleven-day strike which followed. In May, the contractors of Saginaw, Michigan, were struck by the bricklayers for $1.00 a day wage increase. In September, the Master Masons' Association of Boston and the bricklayers had a joint committee to which all questions were referred for adjustment; the scheme was indorsed by Secretary Sayward of the National Association of Builders: "It has been one of perfect harmony and illustrates the sort of arbitration that this association advocates." The Boston association granted the bricklayers, the stone masons, and the laborers a nine-hour day with eight hours on Saturday, time and one-half for overtime with double time on Sunday, Christmas, July 4, and Labor Day, and 25 cents an hour for the laborers and 42 cents an hour for the others. It also adopted an apprenticeship agreement. Thus, the master masons dealt with labor disputes during the year 1892.

The master plumbers met with a number of issues ranging from hours and wages to ownership of tools and double exclusive agreements. In April, the Master Plumbers' Association of Grand Rapids, Michigan, refused to grant the demands of the plumbers' union. Among these demands were exclusive employment of union men and a nine-hour day with ten hours pay. The association offered to grant the nine-hour day with nine hours pay, but it refused to deal with the union or any representative of the strikers on the ground that it would not recognize the union. However, it left the conferences to its individual members and in these conferences with the union the nine-hour day was granted. In April, the master plumbers of Dubuque, Iowa, were struck for the eight-hour day on Saturday and won. The Master Plumbers' Association of Rochester formulated a set of shop rules, all of which were acceptable to the union but one— that required the plumber (worker) to own certain tools to work on the job. The association, after a 10-day strike compromised on a requirement that the worker own only a portion of the tools. This issue is highly contradictory to the theory that workers want to own the tools. The most important case of double exclusive agreements was in New York City, discussed above. In a related trade, the master steamfitters of Philadelphia in October had to have police protection in order to carry on their work because of labor troubles.

The master painters in 1892, in two instances, defeated the unions. In April, the master painters of Syracuse divided in granting and refusing the demands of the painters and decorators for a reduction of hours from ten to nine. The majority of the masters defeated the union's demands. The strike was abandoned in two weeks. In May, the master painters and decorators of Grand Rapids were struck because the masters would not agree to employ union men exclusively. The masters issued a declaration that they would employ any competent workman, union or nonunion, as they saw fit. The striking painters planned to take painting contracts, but the strike was later declared off as a failure.

Other associations in the building industry reacted variously in labor disputes during the year. In January, the employing lathers of New York were struck for a restoration of a wage schedule from $2.00 to $4.00 rates. After a two weeks' strike, the demand was granted, but a few days later the rates were reduced back to the lower ones. In June, however, the employers were forced by a week-long strike to restore the higher rates for the season. In August, the employing plasterers of New York City divided in granting and refusing the demands of the plasterers' laborers; some granting the demands when the strike was threatened, others after a few days of the strike, and some not at all. These employers also suffered from sympathetic strikes during the year. The Employing Plasterers' Association of New York had an agreement with the union—Operative Plasterers' Society—to put in place all ornaments. This union struck to force the association members not to employ any members of the Ornamental Plasterers' Union and succeeded. But, in November, the employers of the marble mosaic helpers of New York granted them a wage advance of 25c a day without a strike. In contrast, the employing metal roofers of Philadelphia were struck by 158 workers for eleven days because they refused to agree to union rules, while the employing millers and millwrights of New York City and Brooklyn were forced by strikes to grant the eight-hour day. In May, contracting paper hangers of St. Louis were struck by the paper hangers to force a change from weekly wages to payment by the piece. Master plasterers of Philadelphia were struck over a wage increase.

In Coal Mining in 1892 there was, with one exception, minor activity among the associations. In May, the railroad coal operators of the Pittsburgh district met the miners in conference and agreed upon the old rate for mining. In Pennsylvania, strikes were called on coal operators in Jefferson Township, Hilldale, Monongahela City, Scott Haven, and Allegheny County—none of them large outside of Allegheny County (Monongahela River), and the largest strike was a "market-boosting" one. In August, however, coal operators of Tennessee went through all the turbulence characteristic of a major coal strike. The coal operators were "struck" over the issue of a convict lease system in the operation of the coal mines. The unionists attacked the stockades where the convicts were housed, destroyed property, and attacked persons working in and about the mines. Deputies and the state militia were sent in, and even 500 to 600 armed volunteers came from Chattanooga, Knoxville, and Memphis. Many of the volunteers were leading citizens of the State, and obtained their arms from hardware stores throughout the State that turned over their stocks of arms and ammunition to the volunteers to repel the armed unionist "invaders." Pitched battles occurred, three soldiers and six unionists were killed, and a number injured. The convicts, however, were withdrawn from the mines as a dangerous element under the conditions. The State made great efforts to bring the rioters to justice; 400 of them were arrested, and one of their leaders "was captured by a party of citizens and threatened with lynching, but was finally let off with the solemn promise that he would assist the officials in apprehending the rioters, and many who would otherwise have escaped have been captured by his assistance." The trouble was of a year's duration and had been "brewing" for some time. The unionists lost, since the convicts were returned after order was restored and the stockades rebuilt. The opposition of unions to Southern lynching has been of long standing, and the above illustration furnishes a partial explanation for that opposition.

Although at the beginning of the winter season when the demand for coal usually increased, the executive committee of the Monongahela River Coal Operators' Association met in September and decided that the price for mining coal should be reduced one-half cent a bushel, which would bring the price down to 3c. The proposed reduction affected about 8,000 men who were expected to refuse it and strike. Perhaps it should be remarked again that coal operators often welcome a strike as a stimulus to a weak market and to dispose of otherwise unsaleable coal. Nominally, the river coal operators lost.

In contrast—and there seem always to be exceptions among associations, their activities, and prosperity—the winter of 1892-3 was the most remunerative season enjoyed by the Iowa coal mines and mine workers for many years; in 1893, however, many persons were out of employment. The depression simply set in later there.

In the Clothing and Related Industries in 1892, association activities were limited largely to New York City and were relatively peaceful. In March, the clothing contractors of New York City were forced by a two-day strike to reduce hours of labor 14 to 11 in a day and to sign an "exclusive" or closed-shop agreement. In August they were struck for a week by the knee-pants makers and forced to furnish machines free of rent to the workers. The contracting cloak makers of New York City increased the wages of cloak makers when threatened with a strike. The Clothing Manufacturers' Association of New York City appointed two of their members to sit on an arbitration

board with two officials of the garment workers' union and a
member of the State Board of Mediation and Arbitration to settle
a dispute between a member of the association and his union employees. As a result of the decision of the board, an agreement
was signed by both parties. In April, the Merchant Tailors' Association of Menominee, Michigan, refused to grant increased
wages and the tailors struck; as the merchant tailors were then
overrun with orders the association committee had to make concessions. In September the Merchant Tailors' Exchange of Denver rejected a new wage schedule of the journeymen tailors' union,
which in turn rejected the one offered by the Exchange. The
union refused arbitration and a strike resulted. In November, the
hat manufacturers of Danbury, Connecticut, were struck because
they refused to "recognize the union." Similarly, seventeen suspender manufacturers of New York City defeated the union in
its demands for the exclusive employment of union men and a
wage increase in a strike lasting four weeks, but seven of the
24 manufacturers after a two-weeks strike granted the demands.

The clothing contractors of Baltimore were struck in July
by the Garment Workers' Union to enforce demands for a ten-
hour day, weekly payment of wages, and abolition of the "task
system." Previously, negotiations had been pending between the
Knights of Labor and the contractors, but a large number of the
members of the Knights of Labor seceded and joined the Garment
Workers' Union. The contractors at the end of two weeks agreed
to concede the demands of the strikers. The agreement, however,
bound the contractors to employ only members of the Garment
Workers' Union, and this brought on a conflict with the Knights
of Labor which aided the contractors who refused to sign the
agreement or who repudiated it; the Knights gave a charter to the
contractors. The struggle was bitter. The wholesale clothing dealers attempted to have the issue arbitrated but neither side would
agree to terms of adjustment. The Garment Workers' Union
lost and the workers returned on the contractors' terms.

The Manufacturing Furriers' Exchange of New York locked
out the fur workers in order to return to the nine-hour day from
the eight-hour day. It also gave notice that it would not discriminate between union and nonunion men. The Exchange had

been recently organized and the employers had granted the eight-hour day in September, 1891. After being out from March 15 to May 13, the workmen were forced to return to the nine-hour day. The Exchange had given notice that only those employees who had returned to work by May 23, would receive pay for a Saturday half holiday during three summer months. The Exchange adopted a "letter of recommendation for employees who left one establishment to seek employment at another"—unions called it a blacklisting system.

In Transportation in 1892, relatively few associations were involved in any notable activities. There were belligerent ones on railroads and drayage concerns in New Orleans. In contrast, the Lake Carriers' Association in October raised the wages of ordinary seamen about 50c a day and other classes of men in proportion. On the railroads, 10 railroad companies in western New York were struck by their switchmen because the railroads cut wages proportionally when the hours of labor were reduced by law from 12 to 10. Much rioting occurred and railroad property was burned. The militia was called out, and the strike was lost. The switchmen's strike in Buffalo was bloody, and the Reading Railroad system—to be specific in regard to belligerent attitudes—required new men taken on to replace "the trouble makers" to show that they were not members of any labor organization, and to agree not to join such—the so-called "iron-clad" contracts.

In New Orleans on October 22, a strike among the teamsters, warehousemen, and handlers spread to many classes of workmen, even street railway employees, and electric light men threatened to strike to further tie up the city in the general strike. "Merchants, finding that their business was affected, and that the regularly organized militia would probably be insufficient to cope with the mob, contemplated raising a force of several thousand men to act as auxiliaries, at the same time calling for the interposition of the Governor." Repeated conferences were held, attempts at arbitration were made, but the matter seemed stalled until a federal injunction—issued by Chief Justice Fuller of the Supreme Court, acting for the Circuit Court, as the first one under the Sherman Anti-Trust Act applied to unions for the first time—ended the strike over night. The strikers meekly accepted the concessions offered, and seemed paralyzed by the new instrument. The case became a precedent for the noted Danbury Hatters' and other less noted labor cases. The reasons given for the strike were demands for shorter workday and higher wages, but as the strike was a general one affecting nearly every workman in the city and was one of the first of that character in the United States, those reasons are inadequate: it was actually a broad test of the power of the unions of New Orleans, probably backed up by many of their nationals, against the poorly organized employers of New Orleans.

Steamboat owners also had labor troubles. In May, the longshoremen at St. Louis struck because the steamboat owners refused to grant a wage increase from 17½ to 25 cents an hour. After three days, the demand was granted, but later when the wages were reduced to 20 cents, the men did not strike. However, when the engineers struck, the longshoremen were asked to strike in sympathy and did so. The engineers struck the steamboat owners on the Mississippi River in June because the latter demanded that the former discontinue its affiliation with the American Federation of Labor. Some of the engineers withdrew and returned to work, the others were replaced with new men.

The year 1892 was one of many contradictions. While the steel industry—which was said to be the leader among industries —was suffering from falling prices and seeking wage reductions but, when stalled, turning strongly anti-union, there were indications that the textile industry was not following closely the steps of the reputed leader. The Fall River cotton manufacturers in July made an unsolicited advance of wages to their employees, and in November made another increase of 7 per cent, which restored wages to the old standard of 1884. Similarly, the master printers of Elmira, New York, signed an agreement increasing the wages of the compositors. In November, theatrical managers of New York were compelled by stage hands to pay increased wages—50 cents a night. Again, while the master brewers of San Francisco were still fighting the union boycott and using the lockout in 1892, the master brewers in New York, Brooklyn, Troy, and Grand Rapids, were making concessions to the unions.

In New York, Brooklyn, and vicinity, the breweries threatened by a strike against wage reductions conceded the old rates. In Brooklyn, the master brewers immediately signed an agreement containing a new clause about workers alternating weeks in the dull season, and also providing for the exclusive employment of union men. In Troy, New York, the Brewers' Association signed an agreement with the brewery workers' union providing for the exclusive employment of members of that union and containing many union shop rules. The first provision later caused a strike because the brewery drivers would not join that union which, however, lost the strike. Although the breweries of Grand Rapids, Michigan, were struck for a new scale of wages, a conference was held and the demands granted. While the master bakers in Detroit, Michigan, refused to grant the bakers' union the ten-hour day, higher wages, and day work, and were struck, the master pretzel bakers of New York City were forced by a strike to abrogate a shop rule requiring bakers to work seven nights a week instead of six, and to sign an agreement providing for wage rates and the exclusive employment of union bakers. Finally, a strike that was typical under the conditions of 1892 and reflects short-sighted union leadership was that of the boiler manufacturers of Chicago. After four months, they defeated the boiler makers' strike. It was called off August 31, and the strikers sought work on the old terms. The manufacturers, however, were not able to run their shops with full force, as much of their trade had gone to other cities, and they had insisted from the beginning that they could not make the concessions. Union leaders and workmen were warned that under the conditions striking was unwise: "It is not the employer who breaks down a strike, but the competing laborer out of work and anxious to fix himself in a place for the winter. Against this rival, present in large numbers, it it worse than useless for the striker to contend." Similarly, the Boston boiler manufacturers conferred with boiler-makers' committees and reached an agreement on a nine-hour day with a $2.00 minimum, but otherwise with a loss of one hour's pay (10 hours to 9). The workmen rejected the agreement and struck, but the 21 employers affected remained firm. Thus, the year 1892 was one of intense belligerency with bloody strikes, like in Homestead which was unusual but also in the Idaho mines which was not so unusual.

The year 1893 continued the depression which finally broke into a panic, and was, accordingly, one of increasing association belligerency toward unionism. It was among the collective-bargaining associations in iron and steel, and in coal mining, that belligerency showed up during the year. The bloody strikes led to much comment, even on strikes centuries ago. Moreover, unionists were warned that it was "no time to advance wages," and that workers elsewhere should not be misled by the high wages forced by strikers on the World's Fair. The methods of a professional "strike defeater" of England were set forth for the information of American employers if not also as a warning to unionists. The Homestead strike was recalled and the decline of the Amalgamated was pointed out in September. Its victories in conferences were producing an increasing number of nonunion shops, and thus were causes of its defeats. The great amount of unemployed labor was discussed as a source of surplus labor to defeat strikes and as a problem of methods of alleviating the distress. Wage reductions in November-December, 1893, were as much as 10 percent which was not unusual, and wage cutting continued into 1894. Some wage cuts were reported as high as 65 percent. Union officials had shown themselves to be experts in attack and holding ground, but apparently did not know how to retreat when necessary. It should be noted that the panic did not crack the Amalgamated; that was actually done in the events—so-called conference victories—that led up to the Homestead strike, and union violence could not save the Amalgamated as that had so often done for the miners' union.

Contrasts and contradictions were evident, especially on wages, most associations favoring reductions but some granting increases. In another field, most associations thought that immigration was excessive, but the Chinese Six Companies of San Francisco raised $60,000 from their countrymen by collecting one dollar per head, to fight the Geary registration law which went into effect May 1. While the "rights of labor (unions)" were set forth, anti-union contracts were required in increasing number against unions which demanded wage increases clearly against the trend.

In the Building Industry associations were active with the main issues the shorter workday and wages. Boston led all the cities in activities in 1893. In January, the Master Builders' Association of Boston discussed the demands of the unions for the eight-hour day. In March, the association conferred with the building laborers' union, arranged a schedule of hours and wages, and granted the eight-hour day with eight hours' pay. In July, the association refused to grant the demands of the hoisting engineers for advanced wages. In February, the Mason Builders' Association held a conference on the eight-hour day with the bricklayers' union. At a second conference the shorter workday was granted and a permanent board of arbitrators was chosen. In March, this association conferred with the stonemasons' union and agreed upon a schedule of hours and wages for the year 1893. While the eight-hour day was granted, one hour's pay was deducted. The conciliation committee agreed to meet monthly. In October, the Master Carpenters' Association of Boston was condemned by the carpenters' union for refusing to live up to an agreement granting the eight-hour day. In March, the Master Plasterers' Association of Boston met and drew up a compromise proposal in answer to the demands of the plasterers' tenders' union. On April 6, an agreement was reached and signed. In September, the Master Steamfitters' Association signed an agreement with the steamfitters' union that was exclusive on both sides.

Associations in the building industry elsewhere were generally appeasatory in 1893. The Master Builders' Exchange of Philadelphia resolved to recommend to the national organization a method of arbitration which would be universally applicable and recognize fully the rights of both employers and workmen. In January also, the Builders' Exchange of Grand Rapids, Michigan, however, refused to grant the demands of the bricklayers and stonemasons' union for the eight-hour day with nine hours' pay. On April 1, the workmen struck, but the contractors imported men from Chicago. Negotiations were continued with the strikers, and indicated that the Exchange was not wholly belligerent. In March, the Pittsburgh Builders' Exchange considered the establishment of a trade school at Morganza but the bricklayers' union opposed the school.

The building trades employers of Pittsburgh, in May, signed up all scales for the year, with the exception of an agreement with the stonecutters who had an old agreement which did not expire until June 1. A walking delegate sued by a member of the Pittsburgh Building Exchange for calling workmen out on strike two years previously was assessed 6¼c for damages to the firm. In June, the roofing companies of St. Louis, Missouri, were struck by the composition roofers for a wage schedule with increased wages, and negotiated a compromise. In September, the sewer contractors of St. Louis, Missouri, notified the sewer workers that wages would be reduced 20 percent October 1, and the men struck. Conferences were held and a compromise reached for a a 10 percent reduction. In September also, members of the St. Louis Woodwork Manufacturing Association issued a circular to their employees setting forth the schedule of wages, hours, and shop rules adopted by the association. The cabinet makers, machine hands, hardwood finishers, and carvers protested and were locked out. At first, the association refused to deal with the union committee, but later met with the committee and agreed upon a 10 percent reduction, although most of the strikers' places had been filled. About the same time the Iron League of New York was struck for the nine-hour day. Although against the trend, 1,560 plasterers of Philadelphia struck for about a month to force their employers to increase wages 5 cents an hour, which they obtained after rescinding an "obnoxious rule." However, the old rate of 40 cents an hour was restored within six months by mutual agreement.

Other associations in the building trades engaged in a wide variety of activities in 1893, of which the following are illustrations: The Society of Master Bricklayers of Philadelphia had a joint committee with the bricklayers' union to adjust differences and grievances. However, strikes took place on other associations. The employing plasterers of Wilmington defeated a strike of the plasterers for $3.50 a day—a 50 cents increase. In a three-weeks strike in Worcester, Massachusetts, the tinsmiths' union lost its nine-hour day campaign against united employers. Discussions of hard times was also extensive among builders.

In the Iron and Steel Industry in 1893, there was belligerency due to depressed conditions and the momentum of the previous year. A system of divisional conferences was instituted—one each for boiling; for bar, guide, and plate; and for sheet, tin, and black plate. The Iron and Steel Sheet Manufacturers' Association met in March and again in June and discussed the wage scale for the year commencing July 1. The association wanted the elimination of "extras." After a series of conferences with the Amalgamated, agreement was reached on June 29, and the old scale with a few changes was adopted. But the association asked for a reduction in September, the Amalgamated voted against giving its conference committee authority to accept a 10 percent reduction, and the manufacturers, with conditions becoming worse, demanded a 20 percent reduction. The association was in danger of disruption because the wage scale was competitively too high. One member withdrew and went nonunion. Another firm cut the scale 10 percent and its action severely affected all the other association members. The association met but postponed action, hoping the Amalgamated would vote for a conference, but it voted adversely on the grounds that the agreement was for an entire year. In November, however, the Amalgamated offered to confer on a 7½ percent reduction on the sheet scale. Finally, after a week of conferences, the union accepted a 10 percent reduction. The Pittsburgh rolling mills, especially the nonunion ones, were underbidding the Eastern mills by selling below the cost of production in the latter—the price for puddling in the nonunion mills of Pittsburgh was less than $4.00 a ton.

The Mahoning and Shenango Valleys Manufacturers' Association was requested in May by the Finishers' Union to confer on a wage scale for the coming year. The manufacturers talked of general reductions for all workmen ranging from 15 to 50 percent. The finishers asked for a continuance of the old scale, but in the conference the manufacturers refused to grant it. Likewise, manufacturers in conference with the Amalgamated reached no agreement. Other conferences were held but no agreements were made by July 1 for rolling-mill scales for puddling and finishing, so the mills shut down awaiting an agreement which depended upon the action at Pittsburgh by the Amalgamated and the Association of Iron and Sheet Steel Manufacturers— who were also stalled in conferences. In late September, the Pittsburgh manufacturers and the Amalgamated agreed upon a scale in the finishing departments with reductions of 10 percent, but no agreement on puddling was reached at that time. Finally, the rates in the Valleys were reduced and the dissatisfaction among the union members was great, as they did not understand the depression. In October, the rolling mills which had signed the $5.00 scale for puddling asked their workmen to help their employers meet the competition of nonunion mills where puddling was only $4.00, but no concession was made.

The blast furnace operators of the Mahoning and Shenango Valleys met on August 3, and decided to reduce wages 15 to 20 percent—the scale agreed upon was the same as that of 1886. Notices were posted that the scale would become effective on August 15. Reduction went into effect with only eight furnaces running in both Valleys. In October, the leaders on both sides admitted publicly that the prospect of agreement was very remote.

In November, a number of Mahoning Valley millowners met with a committee of the Finishers' Union and agreed upon a wage scale for the finishing departments. The scale was based on a 1½c card (instead of the old minimum of 2c) and had a number of other material wage reductions. The scale was perpetual—with three months' notice necessary to change or terminate an agreement.

The Amalgamated conferred with millowners (who were very much alarmed at developments) and promised as favorable a scale by its members. The union compromised in conference for a puddling (or boiling) scale of $4.75. The base was changed to 1½c, and the scale was to last until April, 1894. The finishing scale as signed by finishers and manufacturers was adopted as promised. In December, however, the iron manufacturers of the Mahoning Valley planned to notify the Amalgamated on January 1, 1894—with three months' notice—that a reduction of boiling from $4.75 to $3.75 would have to be made on the grounds that nonunion mills of Pittsburgh were paying less than $4.00. When January came, the notice was for $3.50, and the Amalgamated replied with a demand for $5.00. The manufacturers issued a circular letter in March, 1894, setting forth the arguments of the need for the reduction to $3.50.

There were contrasts among associations in regard to wages, even early in the year 1893. It was reported that in February, seven mills of the associated wire manufacturers were planning to reduce wages. In contrast, the Tinned Plate Manufacturers' Association met in June and decided that the current scale of wages was satisfactory, but that any advance would be resisted. The association chose a conference committee to uphold these decisions.

Among the foundries, there was strong resistance to any wage advances even by the newly appeasatory stove manufacturers. The Stove Founders' National Defense Association held several conferences with the molders' union in efforts to convince the union officials that times were adverse to wage advances. The union demanded a 15 percent increase, but intimated that a 10 percent increase would be satisfactory. The union officials, when informed that an advance in wages could be granted only if the prices of stoves could be increased, asserted that this would be "an easy matter if all the manufacturers stood together." But the stove manufacturers stood firm against the wage increase, convinced that a double conspiracy against the consumer to raise the price of stoves would not work under the depressed conditions.

The Foundrymen's Association of Philadelphia, in April, discussed the subject of paydays and the sentiment favored once a month only. The association, in May, was still agitating the formation of a national association with branches. On May 25, 1893, the Western Foundrymen's Association was organized with a constitution modeled after the Philadelphia association. The WFA voiced the opinion that wages should be left to local associations, but the relations and field of the FAP and WFA were live questions. The FAP congratulated the WFA on its formation. In July, the FAP obtained and tabulated wages of molders in foreign countries. In October, it discussed the advisability of wage reductions if passed down to the consumer in entirety.

The machine shops and foundries of Pittsburgh reduced wages 10 percent. This affected 8,000 workmen and the molders' union struck.

The boiler manufacturers of the United States were resisting the nine-hour day in 1893. In April, the boiler manufacturers and iron shipbuilders of Boston were presented with demands for the nine-hour day, exclusive employment of union men, and certain union shop rules. The manufacturers had been struck in May, 1892, for 13 weeks over the nine-hour day with ten hours' pay, and had compromised on the 58-hour week. In 1893, the association met and refused to concede the nine-hour day. In June, the American Boiler Manufacturers' Association of the United States met in Chicago and listened to a plea of a committee of the Brotherhood of Boilermakers and Iron Shipbuilders for a universal nine-hour day, but decided that it was undesirable. The Association also published a tabulation of wages in boiler shops in the United States for the information of employers in dealing with wage demands. The union, however, was successful in Chicago and Boston in getting the nine-hour day with no pay reduction, and had struck in New Orleans to get it as a part of the union's general campaign throughout North America. "After presenting a solid front for several days," the boiler manufacturers of New Orleans acceded unanimously to the union's demands. This action was precipitated by the granting of the demands by one of the leading manufacturers of the city." In July, however, the boiler manufacturers of St. Louis, Missouri, were struck by the union for nine-hours with no reduction in pay, and conferred with the strikers without reaching an agreement. The strikers lost; although one firm granted the demands, the other firms employed nonunion men and reduced the wages from 22 to 33⅓ percent for a ten-hour day. The union's "divide-and-conquer" tactics failed largely because of the depression. In August, the demand for the shorter workday was made on the boiler manufacturers of Bay City, Michigan, who refused. The shops were closed.

A contrast of association activities was afforded by the wagon makers and the master horseshoers in 1893. The Carriage and Wagon Manufacturers' Association of Boston met March 24 and resolved not to grant the demands of the carriage and wagon makers' union for the nine-hour day. Some manufacturers had already granted it, and a few withdrew from the association and granted it. In June, the Master Horseshoers' Association of Boston signed an agreement with the union granting the nine-hour day but requiring the workmen not to work for any employer who cut below the bill of prices—another double conspiracy.

In Coal Mining in 1893, marked belligerency developed among associations toward the miners' union. In May, however, Ohio coal operators and miners met in conference and agreed upon a wage scale. The agreement also provided for a joint state and local investigating committee to inquire into costs of production of mines and earnings of miners in various localities, to be compiled into a report and published. On April 1, the miners of Bevier, Macon County, Missouri, demanded that the winter rate for mining coal continue throughout the summer, but agreed in conference with the coal operators to accept the summer rate, provided the operators would allow check-weighmen. When most companies refused to put this in effect, the miners struck. As the state law required check-weighmen when the miners demanded and paid for those, the companies were forced to grant the demand. In the latter part of September, the coal operators at Bevier, Ardmore, and Huntsville, Missouri, gave notice to the miners that the summer rate for mining would continue and that the higher winter rate would not be paid. In figures, 50c instead of 60c would be paid because of the business depression. The miners of Bevier and Ardmore struck at once, and those at Huntsville joined them later but went back to work within two weeks. One of the companies was in the hands of a receiver and he applied to the Federal Court for an injunction restraining any intereference with the nonunion men the company had brought in. A number of leaders among the strikers were arrested and brought before the Federal Court. The result was that the miners called off the strike in fear that "Federal troops would be brought in." It should be noted here that union officials often place the blame on something else, as a "face-saving" tactic, when they know that the strike has been lost; in this case, the injunction applied only to one company and in no wise interfered with the conduct of the strike on all the other companies. In November, coal operators in Western Pennsylvania, likewise, reduced wages and the miners struck. The strikers destroyed property and assaulted employees who remained at work. They attacked one mine where armed guards were stationed with Winchester rifles and were fired upon and a number injured. Armed guards finally restored peace and the strike was defeated. It is of interest that the miners' strikes caused coal in some districts of New England to retail at $15 a ton in November.

In 1893, an agreement between miners and mine owners and managers of Leadville, Colorado, was reached fixing wages on a sliding scale based on the price of an ounce of silver.

Among associations in other fields there were new organizations acting for the first time for the record, as well as appeasement and belligerency by older ones. In January, the boss stevedores of New York organized, and a combination of shipowners on the Pacific Coast, militant to the Seamen's Union, threatened to cause general strikes. Likewise, the Clothing Manufacturers' Association of New York was militant in April. The association —composed of 30 of the largest firms in the city—applied for and obtained a temporary injunction from the New York Supreme Court restraining the locked-out unionists or the Federation from boycotting the goods of the firms. Later the injunction was dissolved. Then one of the firms made a test case in the Supreme Court for an injunction. It is rare for an association to apply for an injunction although it is the prime mover, because such action can raise questions of conspiracy and "clean hands" which would not be so evident if a seriously injured employer made the complaint. In October, the Clothing Manufacturers' Association of Boston had a controversy with the garment workers' union. Danbury hat factories were struck against wage cuts. As the strikers controlled the town politically, they voted $50,000 for their own benefit. Some factories gave in to the strikers; others improved matters, but the strike lasted from November, 1893, to January, 1894. But when the glass manufacturers of Cumberland and Gloucester Counties, New Jersey (Bridgeton, Clayton, Glassboro, Fairton, Medford, Elmer, and Mintola) reduced wages, the workmen accepted the reduction without striking because of the depressed conditions. In contrast, the Master Brewers' Association of Boston signed an agreement with the brewery workers' union providing for hours, wages, and working rules. Likewise, the textile manufacturers of New Bedford, Massachusetts, conferred with the mule spinners and compromised on a wage reduction of 10 percent. In June, however, restaurant owners in Kansas City, Missouri, were struck by waiters to force unionization. The union succeeded in most instances by "divide-and-conquer" tactics on the owners. In September, the manufacturing watch-case firms of St. Louis, Missouri, reduced the hours of work from 60 to 50 a week, because of lack of orders, but with no change in the hourly rate—which reduced the weekly earnings. The workers struck and failed. The Lake Carriers' Association, however, raised the wages of ordinary seamen about 50 cents a day and of other classes of men in proportion. Engineers and firemen struck the Toledo, Ann Arbor, and Northern Michigan Railroad in a boycott on cars of a nonunion railroad. A federal injunction ordered the strike called off, but another federal injunction issued in the West was not effective. A strike on the Lehigh Valley Railroad over unionism was lost in two weeks.

CHAPTER 15

ASSOCIATIONS COMBAT "ANARCHISTIC" STRIKES

THE YEAR 1894 was noted for its strikes. Union officials showed poor judgment in striking for wage advances when prices were falling and unemployment increasing. The strikes were usually conducted with much violence to prevent the use of strikebreakers which the depression and unemployment made plentiful. It was pointed out clearly, however, that the union officials were responsible for the violence which was organized and was conducted by persons fully equipped for war and destruction. The patterns of the violence indicated that it was carefully planned by top union officials. Had association officials done as careful planning, much of the violence could not have taken place, but these officials were usually of the appeasatory type and often believed that conferences (collective bargaining) would peacefully resolve the issues. However, when the violence occurred, they appealed to governors and other high officials (who often feared the political power of the unions and were condemned if law and order was not restored at once). Workers and union officials were warned that it was not a favorable time for striking —depression, unemployment, and labor displacing machines were among the unfavorable factors mentioned—and especially strikes for wage advances were regarded as very unwise. It will be recalled that this was the year of Coxey's army of unemployed marching on Washington, D. C. The ARU strike called forth much comment—from the "folly of unions in boycotting Pullman and the railroads" to the following characterization of the "Report of the United States Railway Strike Commission":

"The Report is incomprehensibly inaccurate and strongly biased. The issue of veracity has been raised by a cloud of witnesses, and if the report shall be received and made a part of the archives of the Government [and it was] there seems to be a necessity for a companion document making the necessary correction for the guidance of the historians of the future [which was not done]."

A characterization of the "anarchistic strikes" is properly a part of the record of 1894:

"Insurrections of more or less magnitude have broken out in 12 states." The militia was called out frequently and "bloody engagements have taken place, lives are sacrificed, property is destroyed, and the 'horrid front' of war has become a vivid reality in too many places."

Havemeyer, Rockefeller, Huntington, Jay Gould, Armour, and Vanderbilt were attacked by union leaders as the villains on the scene responsible for all the troubles of the day. On the other hand, 150 business men of Denver, including smelter managers, bankers, and wholesale merchants "met recently and issued an address to the business men of Colorado. The address urged them to join in a movement to regain the confidence of Eastern financial circles by securing the defeat of Governor Waite [who sympathized with "rioting strikers"] and the Populist Party in the coming election."

Moreover, the drive was on to organize the manufacturers of the United States on a national scale—an organization that spearheaded the propaganda directed against the abuses of unionism in both industry and government. This drive was begun by "the combined manufacturers of Cincinnati and its neighborhood" and was successful.

Likewise, the record shows that 1894 was the year in which the Civic Federation of Chicago held its "Congress on Arbitration and Conciliation," which was the forerunner of the noted mediatory National Civic Federation.

To show how sentiment had changed in a year of "anarchistic strikes," it is only necessary to cite the condemnation of an independent employee ("iron-clad," "yellow-dog," and anti-union) contract by the same source in 1893 with its plea in 1894 for discrimination by employers in hiring workmen and its justification of their contracts in keeping undesirable agitators out of work places. Likewise, it is interesting to note that union officials argued that "corporations stand together," "they supply each other with men, money, and equipment," "yet they attack the sympathetic strike."

With this background, the strikes of 1894 stand out as notable events in the history of labor-management relations.

The most noted strike of 1894 was the "sympathetic" or secondary-boycotting" strike of the American Railway Union. In May, 2,000 to 3,000 workmen struck the Pullman Car Company primarily for a restoration of wages to the level of 1893. There were other grievances: a statement of these is found in the classic one about the workman working in a Pullman factory, living in a Pullman house, walking on Pullman streets, buying from a Pullman store, sending his children to a Pullman school . . . going to a Pullman church to listen to a Pullman preacher, and fearing when he died he would go to a Pullman hell. In contrast, in 1884, the chiefs and commissioners of the various bureaus of statistics of labor in the United States [said then to be largely pro-union], in convention, determined "to make a full and extensive investigation of the economic experiment conducted by the Pullman Palace Car Company." Their report was generally highly favorable to the plan, which was held to be "worthy of emulation." The Pullman Company then operated its cars over practically all the railroads of the United States—mainly sleeping cars. The members of ARU refused to haul these cars, and struck when ordered to do so. The railroads centering in Chicago were members of the General Managers' Association, and these were the railroads first affected by the boycott and sympathetic strike. Attempts by the railroads to operate were met with violence both to the nonunionists (or strikebreakers) and to railroad property. The militia was ineffective against violence extending over miles of railroads. President Cleveland proclaimed that the United States mail must move. Federal injunctions were issued against the boycott, Federal marshals were sworn in and armed with riot guns, a regiment of the regular United States Army was sent in, and union officials were arrested for conspiracy and for being in contempt of court. The jailing of these leaders broke the morale of the strikers, and the stopping of most of the violence permitted traffic soon to be restored somewhere near normal. The widespread unemployment made it easy to obtain plenty of strikebreakers. The association refused to compromise on the issue. Railroad attorneys had been sworn in as special United States attorneys so that they could make the applications for the injunctions and conduct the proceedings before the Federal Courts. The strikers, especially the leaders and rioters, were blacklisted and could not get jobs on railroads. It has been said that this strike gave rise to the statement that "a strike without violence is a farce (joke, or dud), while one with violence is anarchistic and must be suppressed with all the power of government." The failure of the strike finished the ARU.

In the Iron and Steel Industry was to be found the confusion characteristic of the ending of an era of collective bargaining in which a highly prosperous industry divided part of the "spoils" with unionists who had helped to maintain a high protective tariff on steel. With falling prices and tariff reductions ahead of them, manufacturers often wanted freedom from union exactions, yet harbored an idea that unionists somehow might help to better the situation, and cause prices to rise, for instance, by preventing manufacturers from cutting prices. Unionists urged the manufacturers to combine and stand together resolutely on prices, but their combining solidly caused them to do so also against the unions. That was one of the ironies of collective bargaining.

The Association of Iron and Steel Sheet Manufacturers and the Amalgamated began their conferences on May 14 but did not reach an agreement on the wage scale until in July, and it was conditional. While there was no material change in the scale, the union agreed to reopen the matter if tariff duties were lowered. The competition of the nonunion and lower-wage manufacturers caused the association to put pressure upon the union to make strenuous efforts to unionize the price cutters. Union officials thus could argue that wage reductions by association mills would make it highly difficult for the union to appeal to the nonunion workmen. All this made for confusion.

In the Mahoning Valley, some manufacturers planned in March to operate nonunion if the puddlers would not accept a reduction to a $4 rate. In April, however, the puddlers agreed to that rate. On September 8, the Iron Manufacturers' Association of the Mahoning and Shenango Valleys met and refused to grant the blast furnace employees a ten percent advance in wages on the ground of low prices of steel. In November an association committee met with a committee of the Finishers' Union and readily agreed upon changes in the wages to conform to changes in the Amalgamated's scale.

The Tinned Plate Manufacturers' Association of the United States had its executive committee meet in June with the wage committee of the Amalgamated. But no agreement was reached because the association refused to sign the scale for the term of a year in view of a probable reduction of tariff and because the union demanded an advance of 30c for the shearmen (from $1 up to $1.30 a turn). In July, the old scale was agreed to, the demand for the advance was withdrawn, and a new scale was to be adopted in conference if the tariff duties were lowered. On September 5, the association met to discuss the wage reductions made necessary by the lowered tariff. At the conference with the union, the association proposed an average reduction of 25 percent, but the matter was referred by the union to its lodges. There, the members voted against the 25 percent reduction, but offered to take a 10 percent reduction. No agreement was reached. The manufacturers had threatened to operate nonunion if the union refused to take the 25 percent reduction, and they began to do so with wage reductions from 25 to 35 percent. The association was in danger of breaking up. Its constitution provided that all labor difficulties must be settled in conference (collective bargaining) and that wage scales signed by its secretary were binding upon all members. On October 1, when the mills shut down, six or seven concerns refused to be bound by the action of the association and continued to operate at the old scale with the understanding with the workmen that they would be allowed any concessions made later. Concerns started resigning and operating nonunion. Conferences were held by the Amalgamated with manufacturers independent of the union and compromises on reductions ranging from 12½ to 15 percent were reached. The Amalgamated had obtained an injunction against tin plate mills breaking contracts with the union, and so the mills sought new contracts, since the old ones were valid until a year had expired or new ones made. However, the mills thought that further reductions were necessary, and the confusion continued.

An instance of the confusion and disorder is supplied by attempts at mediation in the National Tube Works case. A citizens' committee—a Board of Trade committee—acted with a strikers' committee in conferring with officials of the National Tube Works Company at McKeesport, Pennsylvania, in regard to a wage reduction. An agreement was practically reached that the time was inopportune for wage advances. However, before the committee could report back to a meeting of all the strikers, a local newspaper got out an extra stating that a 10 percent advance would be given. As a result, the strikers voted down the recommendations of the joint committee. In the strike which resulted, rioting occurred, the company's property was stormed and all nonunion workers driven out.

The Foundrymen's Association of Philadelphia, in February, discussed the use of molding machines and the difficulty of getting a union man to operate them, either efficiently or at all. Later, these machines proved to be highly effective in breaking strikes of union molders. The association, in June, by resolution condemned the coal strike as unwarranted, and demanded that coal operators be protected by state authorities in the operation of the mines.

Strikes extended even to the iron mines. The iron mine owners of Ironwood, Michigan, started up in the Spring at reduced wages, but in June, a large number of men struck for the eight-hour day and more wages, which the owners had refused to grant. Union violence caused the militia to be called out. The chief union leader was finally jailed and the strike collapsed.

Gold mines were affected in 1894 by a violent strike. On January 20, five of the leading gold mine owners of Cripple Creek, Colorado, posted notices that, on February 1, nine hours would constitute a day's work. The eight-hour day had been the prevailing workday in a large majority of the mines, although nine mines still worked under a nine-hour agreement. The miners' union opposed the increase in hours and the mine owners declined to confer with the union on the issue. No men went to work on the nine-hour schedule. Attempts were made to have the issue arbitrated. The mine owners offered the eight-hour day with wages reduced from $3.00 to $2.75 a day. The union rejected this offer. Violence occurred. The militia was finally called out, and the sheriff of El Paso County (in which Cripple Creek is located) recruited an army of deputies who clashed with the strikers. These continued to destroy property. The representative of the mine owners met in conference with the Governor of the State, who had been chosen as arbitrator for the strikers. This conference failed to reach any solution. A later conference resulted in the mine operators granting the eight-hour day with a $3.00 wage.

In Coal Mining, the year 1894 was noted for its great coal strike, along with preliminary and supplementary ones. In February, the Hocking Valley coal operators met the miners' union in conference and proposed a reduced wage scale which the union rejected. Pick mining was 50c a ton. Coal operators in the Massillon district in Ohio failed likewise in February to reach an agreement with the union, and 3,000 miners were idle. In March, the presidents of the coal companies in the George's Creek region of Maryland posted notices calling for a conference with delegates of the miners. The miners met, selected delegates, but gave them no authority to bind the miners. At the conference (which was the first one held between the miners and operators since 1886), the presidents explained fully that the depression necessitated a reduction in the price of coal and, accordingly, of wages. The miners' delegates were convinced of the necessity, and accepted the reduction from 50c to 40c a ton. In the meanwhile, however, strikes were being called in other fields to prevent reductions. The United Mine Workers' organizers came into the Maryland fields and, after what for a long time seemed futile, finally organized the Maryland miners sufficiently to call a strike. Then they struck without presenting any demands or grievances; although the main cause of the dissatisfaction was the wage reduction, there were other grievances such as the "pluck-me" company stores. The attempts of the organizers and strikers to keep men from working at the mines both by peaceful and often violent means caused first an injunction to be issued and later the militia to be called out. Strikers were arrested for contempt of court and unlawful assembly with sentences suspended, and for assault and fined. The strike lasted 27 working days, involved over 3,500 men, and was lost. In April, the coal operators of the Pittsburgh district had taken no action to meet the miners' demand for increased wages—the demand seemed so incongruous—to 70c a ton basis. This demand applied to the mines in Pennsylvania, Ohio, Indiana and Illinois. The strike spread almost simultaneously from these states to Missouri, Iowa, Maryland, Tennessee, Kentucky, Alabama, West Virginia, Minnesota, and Indian Territory, but was rather ineffective in April and May because of the depression with its closing of factories. It was said that the strike was forced by the coal operators in Ohio who had great quantities of coal in storage as a result of the depression. They cut the price for mining so low that the miners struck, and miners everywhere struck in "sympathy." This striking, of course, enabled coal mines to sell the coal on hand for high prices but the strikers gained nothing. As characteristic of coal strikes, much violence took place in attempts to make the strike effective. The militia was called out and sheriffs and police were forced into action. Rioting took place, nevertheless, and 100 strikers were killed. Negro strikebreakers from the South were brought into Pennsylvania rather extensively, and this action caused more rioting. Much property was destroyed. Strikers turned into tramps and many starved. The coal shortage further deepened the depression by causing many other factories to close. Under other conditions, the strikers might have won:

"Even coal operators themselves conceded the justice of the miners' claims and professed willingness to advance wages in quite a number of localities *if competing operators would do the same.* Enough of them at one time were ready to settle the dispute to have given the miners a great victory, which could then probably have been extended over the entire coal country. But the obstinacy of the leaders in refusing partial settlements and in demanding a national adjustment changed the whole aspect of affairs."

The main strike lasted about two months; in some places advances were granted, in others none. There were a series of sup-

plementary strikes: (1) On June 18—about the close of the
main strike—coal operators in Jefferson County, Pennsylvania,
were struck. The strikers destroyed property and created a reign
of terror. They improvised cannons and commanded the hills.
The militia was called out and the strikers fled. (2) Coal operators in Alabama attempted to reduce wages because of Northern
competition. A cut of 10 percent was proposed, but the miners
rejected it on the grounds that the contract held until July 1.
The operators, then, offered a cut of 20 to 25 percent coupled with
a threat to use Negro and convict labor if the miners refused the
cut, as they did. The coal operators quickly began to hire Negro
and convict labor, and the strikers resorted to violence. Bridges
dynamited to isolate the mines were instances among the strikers'
violent activities. Deputies were employed at all mines, and convict stockades were heavily guarded. Troops were encamped at a
central location ready for instant calls. (3) In October, the coal
operators of Massillon, Ohio, and their striking miners agreed to
submit their differences to arbitration; the miners accepted the
award under protest. (4) In December, the Railroad Coal Operators' Association met in Pittsburgh to decide upon a new mining
rate to take the place of the old 69c rate, and decided upon 55c.
The association and union met in joint conference without reaching a settlement, but the question was referred to a committee
composed of three operators, three miners, and three disinterested
citizens of Pittsburgh. In the meanwhile the district rate for Pittsburgh was to remain at 55c. The association also adopted a resolution designed to bring about a uniform price in the district and,
until such was established, to pay wages competing mines paid.
This question was carried over into the year 1895.

The coke operators suffered from a violent strike in 1894.
On March 31, the agreement between the coke operators and the
workmen in the Connellsville coke region expired and no new
one had been agreed upon. The operators refused to grant a
wage increase and uniform wages which the union wanted, and
it struck. The strikers began to intimidate men who remained
at work and assaulted and beat up men at one of the coke concerns. The operators employed a large number of guards, obtained
deputy sheriffs, and armed them with Winchester rifles. Pitched

battles were fought. After a chief engineer had been murdered by the strikers in one of their battles, the citizens of Connellsville joined with the armed guards and attacked the strikers, killed five of them and wounded many more. That ended the strike.

One event in these strikes is of high significance although often recurring hereafter. During the great strike of the miners in 1894, the West Virginia coal operators, who were not struck since they were nonunion, obtained new markets for their coal and its excellence enabled them to retain much of that trade after the strike was over. This event profoundly affected union tactics in all the years since 1894.

In the Building Industry, associations in 1894 were unusually appeasatory considering the business depression. In March, the Master Plumbers' Association of Manchester, New Hampshire, faced the demands of the plumbers for a nine-hour day, five days a week, and eight-hours on Saturday with no reduction in pay. In April, the association met and refused to grant the demands; later it met and voted to employ by the hour. The plumbers struck. The first conference between the union and the association failed, but at a conference two weeks later the association granted the demands. In contrast, on October 31, the terms of the Master Plumbers' Association of Boston were accepted by the plumbers' union. In April, the builders, contractors, and material men of Chicago formed an organization styled the Central Building League, and planned a cessation of all building operations throughout the city beginning April 11, and continuing until an agreement was reached that would prevent the vexatious interference of walking delegates with the work. Some employers resumed work after about two weeks on unfinished buildings. Finally, concessions were made by both sides, but the plumbers rejected the terms of the master plumbers who attempted to resume work with imported men. Other associations made little resistance to union demands. In April, the Master Builders' Association of Lowell conferred with the bricklayers' union on wage standards. The Mason Builders' Association of Boston failed to agree with the bricklayers' union on wages, the matter was submitted to arbitration, the umpire reported, and his decision was accepted on July 9. By October, 50 contractors in Massachusetts had signed eight-hour agreements with the carpenters' union. Even the contractors' association and the cornice workers' union of Chicago reached an agreement in October, thus ending their long strike. The old schedule of wages—35c an hour for an eight-hour day—was restored, and the contractors agreed to hire only union men, who were to work exclusively for members of the association.

An excellent illustration of the types of associations in the building industry in 1894, resulting in part from the joint action of unions, is found in the United Building Trades of New York City, which was a "sort of congress" composed of delegates from associations of:

> Bluestone dealers
> Cabinet work manufacturers
> Employing plasterers
> Marble industry employers
> Master architectural workers
> Master freestone cutters
> Master plumbers
> Master stair builders
> Tile, grate, and mantel contractors
> Building material dealers
> Electrical contractors
> Granite manufacturers
> Mason builders
> Master carpenters
> Master painters and decorators
> Master slate and metal roofers
> Master steam and hot water
>   fitters and the Iron League

Two great problems of the building trades in 1894 were held to be "the decadence of the apprenticeship system and the unrestricted immigration of foreign labor." Trade schools for the former problem were advocated, and laws restricting immigration were urged for the latter.

Association activities in textile and clothing manufacturing were small in 1894 and related mainly to strikes over wage reductions. In April, the Cotton Manufacturers' Association of Fall River held its third conference with the mule spinners without reaching an agreement over wage reductions. The manufacturers were struck by the workmen, but the strikes generally failed. On August 16, the cotton manufacturers of Suncook, New Hampshire, announced that wages would be reduced on August 20. They were reduced 10 percent. After a few days the employees struck, and the mills were closed until September 10. Then they were opened to those who would accept the reduced wages. The strikers remained out for a week or so longer and returned. The strike was a failure. The silk ribbon factories of Paterson and four other cities in New Jersey were struck to force a restoration of wages to those before the reduction of 1893. Nonunionists were obtained and the strike failed. On Labor Day, an extensive strike against clothing contractors (and manufacturers) in New York City was inaugurated against the "sweating" system.

In order to show unionists why they should favor high tariffs, the manufacturers of pottery and the makers of collars and cuffs proposed a scheme "to pay foreign schedules of wages in the same trades plus American duties."

In January, the pottery manufacturers of Trenton, New Jersey, were struck (over a reduction of wages) by 4,000 of their employees. After six months of negotiating, the conference committees of the manufacturers and the potters had practically agreed to compromise on a reduction of 15 percent in wages from the old list when the potters' union suddenly withdrew the authority of the union committee to settle the strike, thus reaffirming the claim of the union to the old rate of wages. However, later a compromise was reached.

In July, 1894, the meat packers of South Omaha were struck by the butchers for an increase of 5c an hour in pay (also partly in sympathy with striking Chicago butchers). The packers obtained plenty of nonunion men, and when the strikers assaulted the strikebreakers, deputies were sworn in, and when these proved unequal to the task the state militia was called out. The strike was soon ended in failure.

A contrast was supplied by the salmon canners and the brewers. The salmon canners in the northwest proposed to cut wages one cent per fish but were forced by a strike of the fishermen to restore wages. The brewery owners of St. Louis, Missouri, held conferences with the beer drivers and stablemen during the year 1894, but no settlement was reached.

The year 1895 was a calm between the storms. Most union leaders had finally learned that there was a depression too deep for major wage advances, and that they, in combination with associations, could not boost prices at will. As a tactic to prevent possible wage reductions, union officials demanded wage increases, fully expecting only to retain the current scale as a "compromise." Employers began to note that one wage advance led to another and solved none of their problems.

Although the depression continued, employers felt the need to protect themselves by strengthening the old associations and creating more powerful new ones. In 1895, the National Association of Manufacturers was definitely forming to begin a career—slowly and weakly at first—as a permanent propaganda association opposed to the "abuses of unionism." The Pittsburgh Chamber of Commerce began an agitation for a local branch of the newly formed NAM. Associations were just beginning to learn how to combat strikes scientifically as a function of permanently belligerent associations. Moreover, factories more and more were seeking areas free from unionism, such as rural districts where workers were largely highly individualistic.

Particularistic solutions for the problem of labor-management relations began to appear, like, "this factory has never had a strike." "Profit Sharing" was also discussed as a solution to the problem, and ordinarily that is advocated only where profits are attractive. Other articles told "how to obtain the best results from the labor of employees"—a sort of beginning of personnel management. These discussions and the organization of associations are usually manifestations of an upturning business cycle; something in the political field—as distinguished from the industrial, unless it was unionism—probably caused the depression to continue.

The surplus of unemployed workers took the pressure off for

the establishment of trade schools. In November, the following events occurred: In Boston, efforts of the Builders' Exchange to found a trade school were fruitless. The Philadelphia Mechanical Trade School, however, got an appropriation of $7,000 for two years from the State of Pennsylvania.

In the Iron and Steel and Related Industries in 1895, there were conferences as usual, but no major strikes. The Iron and Steel Sheet Manufacturers' Association met May 21 and discussed the wage question extensively with the expectation of a demand for a 10 percent advance. They decided to refuse to grant it. Some of the members of ISSMA were also members of the Tinned Plate Manufacturers' Association, and they held an informal conference on May 23 on the wage question. In May, the TPMA met to consider wages and probable demands which it decided to refuse. The association met again in June on the matter, but when it conferred with the union the scale was signed in July and nothing said about advances. In August, iron manufacturers voluntarily advanced the wages of puddlers from $4.00 to $4.25 without regard to the terms of the scales, but without prejudice to the scales.

In October, the Merchant Bar Iron Association and the Eastern Bar Iron Association, through a joint committee, drew up an agreement for their consolidation into a National Association of Bar Iron Manufacturers. A convention was called to effect the new organization, which was formed December 3, 1895. In November, the Merchant Bar Iron Association, however, conferred with the amalgamated to settle the wage rate on the basis of the past two months' prices. The union thought the rate would be increased to $4.50 on the scale, but the price did not average 1-3/10, so the price for boiling remained at $4.25.

The Mahoning and Shenango Valleys Manufacturers' Association met in May and agreed to continue the association as the agreement was for a year only. A special meeting was called to consider wages at the blast furnaces. It was decided to restore wages to those prevailing in 1893 before the reduction. The Amalgamated demanded a $4.50 scale, and the association refused. The scale adopted in June had 1-1/10c as a minimum, but with the rate at $4.00, which was the old rate at 1½c as the

minimum. Above 1-1/10c, the rate was to be advanced 25c
with every 1/10c advance in the price, and to be $5.00 when
the price was 1½ c. Moreover, the Valley mills were promised
by the Amalgamated that it would use every effort to compel
the nonunion mills in Pittsburgh to pay the scale wages for
boiling and finishing and to recognize the Amalgamated; so the
Pittsburgh mills had this situation to face. Mahoning Valley mills
making cotton ties complained that Pittsburgh mills were paying
lower wages, and conferred with the president of the Amalgamated for an "adjustment." The association met the finishers'
committee in June, but reached no agreement then on a scale.
In September, the association, in conferences with the Amalgamated, advanced the wages of finishers 2 percent on the scale
on the basis of prices of bar iron—with every 1/10c advance in
price, wages were to be advanced 2 percent. In December the
association refused bluntly the demands of the blast furnace
hands for extra pay of 1½ time for Sundays and holidays other
than Christmas and July 4, and double time for these two days.
The demands were withdrawn.

In August the Mahoning and Shenango Valleys Manufacturers'
Association joined the National Association of Manufacturers.

Strikes by the Molders' Union in 1895 for wage advances
were conducing to organization of the foundries. In August, the
Foundrymen's Association of Philadelphia discussed arrangements for a National Association of Foundrymen. In October,
foundries in Lawrence, Massachusetts, granted the demands of
the Molders' Union. Foundries in Boston, New York City, and
Elizabeth, New Jersey, were struck in November by the molders
for advanced wages. In November, the Northwestern Machine and
Foundrymen's Association was formed at Minneapolis with O. P.
Briggs as Vice President. He was later branded as a "foe of
unionism." In December, the Foundrymen's Association of Philadelphia discussed strikes extensively. The executive committee
held that "it was an open question whether the association could
take any action in the matter, but the subject was ripe for discussion." After the discussion—which indicated that the association should prepare a "declaration of principles" of the right of
every man to run his own business and that the association should

support a struck member—the matter was referred to the executive committee for action. But the committee again did nothing. Then agitation began for action or for a new association for such action.

The Associated Manufacturers of Toledo, Ohio, was formed in October, 1895, with the object of protecting the best interests of the manufacturers of that city in reference particularly to *labor,* material, shipping, and the like. It was made up of bicycle manufacturers mainly but included other manufacturers. The bicycle manufacturers were struck within a few days by the tool makers for 10 per cent advance in wages. The manufacturers conceded 5 per cent advance to all employees instead of granting the 10 percent to the tool makers alone.

In July, the wire mills of Cleveland were struck for higher wages by about 3,000 men. On August 1, and again on November 1, wages were advanced 5 per cent—"one wage advance led to a demand for another."

The managers of the iron mines of the Marquette Iron Range in Michigan, in the Spring of 1895, refused to advance wages and were struck. The managers sent a joint letter to the union refusing to grant the demands but offering to make some advance to be agreed upon in conference with the men who worked in the mines and at their own particular mine. Finally, in September, the strikers called at the individual mines as required by the mine managers. Violence had caused troops to be called in. As a unionizing measure the strike was a failure, but it caused some wage advances.

In Coal Mining in 1895, the main issue was over "company stores," although wages were made an issue in nearly every case. In May, Pennsylvania coal operators were struck because of wage reductions below 1894 rates. In June, miners at Pittsburgh proposed to one company to work for 55c a ton in cash provided the company would close its store. They were asking 69c otherwise, but the company offered only 55c. In August, the Railroad Coal Operators' Association in the Pittsburgh district granted the union's demands for an increase, on October 1, of 4c for cash mines and 9c for mines with stores. The association agreed also to have check-weighmen, to give honest weights, to have uniform scales, and to provide all other means for uniformity. The agreement expired on January 1, 1896. In December, in a three-day conference, an agreement was reached for the year 1896. The mining rate was to be 64c from January 1 to March 1, and 70c for the rest of the year. Company stores were to be abolished or 20c extra per ton was to be paid for mining. Check-weighmen were recognized, paydays were to be semi-monthly, and a conciliation committee of five operators and five miners was established. In February, 1896, machine rates were fixed by that board for various mining machines. In May, the Indiana Bituminous Coal Operators' Association and the miners met and agreed on 60c a ton for mining coal until July 15. In July, no agreement could be reached, so the miners struck. The operators agreed in August to pay 60c so long as they could with profit. In July, coal operators in the Birmingham, Alabama, district organized, and Ohio County, West Virginia, coal operators were struck by 3,000 miners for an increase from 50c to 60c a ton for mining coal. Ohio coal operators were presented with demands by the miners for increased wages with a higher differential for mines with company stores, if the stores were not closed. In December, the operators declined to grant 60c per ton for mining where company stores were operated. In September, the coke operators granted a wage increase effective October 1, on demands by the union.

In the Building Industry in 1895, there was relatively little activity among the associations. The following events illustrate that activity: In January, 64 contractors and builders of Lynn conceded the eight-hour day. On February 28, the Granite Manufacturers' Association of Quincy, Massachusetts, and the granite cutters' union settled questions on wages which had been under consideration for three months. On May 2, the master plumbers of Lynn, Massachusetts, signed an agreement granting plumbers $3.50 a day. On July 1, 9 master plumbers of Brockton, Massachusetts, met to consider the journeymen's demand for a 50c advance in daily wages but reached no decision. On September 25, the Master Steamfitters' Association of Boston granted the eight-hour day with nine hours' pay. In October, the National Associa-

tion of Master Plumbers, its executive committee, and local associations condemned all prison-made goods. In November, the
Iron League of New York City was struck by the Housesmiths
and Bridgemen's Union over nonrecognition of the union, increased pay, and the eight-hour day. A strike was threatened by
the Central Labor Union unless the dispute was settled by
November 18. The National Builders' Association had a committee on trade schools (with Anthony Ittner on it who was
noted later for his belligerency toward unions), which reported in
November at length but found little progress in the movement
during the past year. In December, employers of steamfitters and
helpers in New York City reached a private agreement which
ended a strike lasting over a month and stopped a number of
contemplated sympathetic strikes. Terms of the agreement were
not made public. The Mason Builders' Association of New York
City signed an agreement with the building laborers' union and
had done so for three years past. The agreement fixed hours and
wages and prohibited strikes and lockouts without joint conferences first.

In the textile industry in 1895, activity was limited largely
to the Cotton Manufacturers' Association of Fall River, Massachusetts. It met on April 16 and voted to restore wages to the
schedule existing prior to August 20, 1894. It resumed operations
shortly thereafter and gave employment to 24,000 workmen at
the advanced wages, but the New Bedford mills started work
with 10,000 employees at the scale prevailing before the strike
in the Winter. On June 19, however, the Fall River association
decided not to grant the slashers' demands for an advance in
wages. On July 16, the association voted to pay a certain schedule
of wages to the slashers, along with reduced hours of labor. In
September, however, the association refused to grant the advance
in wages demanded by the weavers.

In the Clothing Industry in 1895, there were a number of
strikes involving conditions of work as well as wages and hours,
for instance in April:

"Five hundred garment workers employed in various sweat
shops in St. Louis, Missouri, inaugurated an entirely justifiable

strike last week. They do not ask for higher wages, but demand that their employers proved for them clean shops in which to work, fresh air, and proper sanitary conveniences."

Likewise, in April, the clothing contractors of Baltimore, Maryland, were struck by the coatmakers to force the employers to grant higher piece prices, the ten-hour day, exclusive employment of union coatmakers, free access to the shops at all times to the union representative for purpose of inspection, and to abolish the task system. After several conferences, the contractors granted all these demands and gave real-estate security for the faithful performance of their part of the contract as the union required. The strike ended in about 8 days, although the workers did not return to work generally until nearly a week later in which time the contractor bargained with the wholesalers for better prices.

The contracting pants makers, as an organization, passed a resolution in August not to employ members of the Pants-Makers' Union, on the ground that piece prices had to be reduced to leave the contractors a profit. The pants makers met and decided not to work until the contractors signed an agreement drawn up by the union. This agreement provided for the exclusive employment of union pants makers, the ten-hour day, weekly paydays, contractors to furnish all supplies and equipment, limit on discharging workmen, and free access to the shops by a union representative. The ranks of the contractors were broken in a few days and the agreement was signed one by one by many of the contractors.

In July, 15,000 members of the United Brotherhood of Tailors in New York struck their employers to force adjustment of future terms of employment, and further strikes were inaugurated later in August. About the same time, however, the clothing contractors of Boston signed an agreement with the garment workers providing a scale of wages and hours.

In the shoe industry in 1895, the Shoe Manufacturers' Association of Haverhill, Massachusetts, in April, accepted the list fixed by the joint conference board on cutters' wages, and in June, adopted the list of the State Board of Conciliation for machine lasting on the consolidated machine. In December, the shoe manufacturers of Marlborough agreed to submit the question of wages to the State Board of Arbitration.

Other associations were generally inactive in 1895. In March, however, the Bohemian master bakers of Northeast Baltimore were unanimous in refusing to grant the demands of their employees for higher wages and shorter hours. The union struck, and one of the master bakers broke away from the employers' ranks and granted the demands on the second day of the strike. In the course of about 10 days, other master bakers surrendered, but a few of the small master bakers held out and did their own work. In November, the cigar manufacturers of Detroit were struck to force through exclusively union shops. Although the striking cigar makers opened up a cooperative shop to manufacture cigars, the strike failed to unionize the cigar shops of Detroit.

The year 1896 was one of depression although there were periods with indications of business revival. Association activities were marked in the foundry industry and in the Rocky Mountain mines. Industrial peace elsewhere, especially in the iron industry and coal mining in the Central Competitive Field, was largely the results of exhaustion from the strenuous strikes of the immediately preceding years. It was also partly a result of the depression.

The new National Association of Manufacturers was said to have had a "tumultous start," and "a brief period of chaotic conditions," yet was known "as a powerful organization." Similarly, the new associations in the foundry industry attracted much attention. However, neither the newly organized associations nor the old ones seemed to be influenced in their price-fixing activities by the Sherman Anti-Trust Act of 1890. Probably the period of falling prices may have indicated to the enforcement officers that competition was working very effectively in spite of price-fixing associations and cooperating unions.

Illustrative discussions of 1896 were: apprenticeship, profit sharing, conservative influences in labor organizations, correct relations between labor and capital, improving labor relations, what becomes of seasonal laborers, and strikers act foolishly by striking in depressions. A discussion of "The Wage Scale and Labor-Saving Machinery" implied that the Amalgamated was making war on improved machinery. "A remarkable strike in Milwaukee" was noted in which the people boycotted the street cars, but the boycott was broken.

Politically, "free silver" was the overshadowing issue. While individual manufacturers held meetings on their own time to "educate" the workers during working hours on the issue, there is no record of any employers' association advocating that this be done. Such associations have difficulties enough with labor issues not to want further dissension on other issues. In December, Congress was considering a law providing for industrial arbitration, as about the only noted issue in the labor field.

In the Iron and Steel and Related Industries in 1896, the greatest association activity was among foundrymen. In January, the Association of Iron and Steel Sheet Manufacturers met with the Amalgamated in conference and found that the price of sheets had been at the base price and accordingly a reduction of 2 per cent in wage rates was made for January and February. The Amalgamated proposed a scale for puddling with a base of $4.50 on a 1-1/10c price and an advance of 12½c for every 1/10c rise in price up to 1½c and $5.00 for puddling. The association met with the Amalgamated, but reached no agreement. At a later conference at the end of June, the old scale with few changes was adopted. Similarly, the Tinned Plate Manufacturers' Association met on June 3 and discussed wage rates. On June 26, it conferred with the Amalgamated and asked for a 15 percent reduction for rolling and doubling, and a slight decrease for heating. The Amalgamated demanded a 10 percent increase. The old scale was practically agreed upon, but was left to individual manufacturers to sign. It was stated that the reduction was "asked" for political purposes; however, such tactics on both sides are characteristic of genuine collective bargaining.

In the Mahoning and Shenango Valleys, there were mixed trends during 1896. In May, the bar iron manufacturers of the Mahoning Valley met with the Amalgamated and found the price too low for any advance above $4.00 for puddling, or for any advance in the finishing departments. In June, the iron manufacturers of the Mahoning and Shenango Valleys conferred with the Amalgamated over a new wage scale but reached no conclusions, as the manufacturers then refused to grant 50c advance in the price of boiling on the basic scale. In July, however, the 50c advance was given and the scale prices were to be for 60 days. In September, the association and Amalgamated met in their bi-monthly conference and found no price change to alter the $4.50 rate. On July 30, however, the blast furnaces of the Shenango Valley (except New Castle) notified their workmen that wages would be reduced about 20 percent on August 1.

The Merchant Bar Iron Association conferred in March with the Amalgamated and found that the rate for boiling would be $4.00 and that a 4 percent reduction would be made in finishing rates, since the price of iron was less than 1-2/10c. On March 26, the association was reported dead—that it had disintegrated because it had attempted and failed to maintain prices in the face of falling markets. In April, efforts brought the association to life again.

Some associations, however, granted wage increases in 1896-7: Boiler manufacturers of Cleveland, Ohio, were struck by the boiler makers for 10 percent advance but agreed to return for an advance of 12½ cents a day. The coke operators of Connellsville had agreed to advance wages effective January 1, 1896. The can manufacturers of Baltimore were struck in May by the can makers who were granted an increase in the piece price from 15c to 20c a hundred cans. During the busy season several weeks later, the can makers struck again for an advance to 25c and got it. But, in the fall, the manufacturers reduced the price to 15c, only to be struck again in February, 1897, for 20c, which was granted.

In the Foundry Industry in 1896, there were at least five active associations. In January, the executive committee (of the Foundrymen's Association of Philadelphia) on protecting members in labor troubles reported "progress." The association sought expert advice, even from abroad, and had a paper read in February on the "Labor Question," that had been prepared by an English manufacturer and association leader of Sheffield, England. In April, the FAP jointly with the Western Foundrymen's Association, called a national convention of foundrymen to discuss, among other things, the question of apprenticeship. In

January, the WFA met and discussed labor questions, such as requiring molders to remain until quitting time if molds have been poured off, and the matter of overtime work and pay. The apprenticeship question was so important that its discussion was postponed to a later meeting so as to give it the fullest consideration. On March 18, that question was discussed and a communication from President Martin Fox of the Iron Molders' Union was read. Fox said that the apprenticeship issue ranked next to the wage question as one of the greatest causes of friction between employers and employees. The WFA had samples of its apprenticeship indentures published for the information of foundrymen and others. Strikes and a lockout at Cleveland made it "impracticable to hold the September meeting there" of the WFA, so a Chicago meeting was arranged. On October 21, the report of its committee of apprentices was presented and discussed. A scheme with indenture, bonus, and the like was outlined in the report—all designed to make apprenticeship attractive to both employer and apprentice.

The American Foundrymen's Association was formed at the convention which met May 12 and 13. A constitution and bylaws were adopted and papers read on apprenticeship and similar questions. Its membership was over 200. Its board of directors considered "the adoption of a uniform apprenticeship system," and "plans for protecting the members from the unfair exactions of labor organizations and against attempts of one employer to take advantage of his competitors by reducing wages lower than the rest. The success of the Stove Founders' National Defense Association has served as an incentive." The New England Foundrymen's Association had presented to it "a brief outline of the way the cost of stoves is kept as adopted by the [Stove Founders'] National Defense Association." So accounting as a method of price fixing is not new. A member of the SFNDA— the Detroit Stove Works—was struck by the stove mounters from May 26 to September 22, over the control of apprentices. The aggressiveness of unions in the foundries also caused the Pittsburgh Foundrymen's Association to be organized in September. Moreover, Southern competition in making castings and stoves caused the IMU to start a campaign to organize Negro foundry workers whose lower wages made it easier for the Southern stove manufacturer to undersell members of the SFNDA. Foundrymen were thus faced with this dilemma: They could not fight against "union exactions" and use the unions as instruments to prevent "price cutting." It was not long before a choice had to be made.

In Coal Mining in 1896, the coal operators' associations were still relying on the unions to restrict the "cutthroat competition" in coal, and one of the means was "uniform wages." Coal operators in the Pittsburgh district met in February and drew up an agreement among themselves to bind the operators to pay uniform wages and the miners to abide by the uniform rate. A fund of almost $12,000 was raised by assessment upon the capital stock of the companies to pay inspectors to see that the agreement was not violated. The Ohio and Pittsburgh combinations had difficulty in regard to their respective percentage of the business. In December, the coal operators and miners of Pittsburgh met in joint convention for three days but failed to agree on wages for 1897. The operators offered 60c from January 1 to March 31, and 65c from April 1 to December 31, but the miners insisted on rates of 70c and 79c for the two periods respectively. The dispute was carried over into 1897. Trouble had been threatened in the bituminous coal mines throughout the United States because the miners of Pittsburgh in October had voluntarily reduced the wage rate from 70c to 54c. The differential agreement for the various districts was said to have been violated by the Pittsburgh operators. The operators of competing states were in conflict with the miners' union because of the reduction. The Ohio coal operators then demanded a reduction, and the miners were advised by the president of the union to accept a reduction to 45c—which made the differential required between Pennsylvania and Ohio. But when the Hocking Valley operators reduced wages to 45c, the miners struck. Later they returned at the reduction.

The Railroad Coal Operators' Association met with the miners' union in February and March, 1896, and, on the basis of the uniform agreements, advanced the mining rate to 70c. This caused the Ohio rate to be advanced from 52c up to 61c—

according to the 9c differential. The river coal operators of the Pittsburgh district, in December, in conference with the miners offered an advance from 25c to 37c per hundred bushels effective July 1, 1897. Clearly, the mining rate was fluctuating greatly in spite of attempts to make it "uniform" and "stabilize" it.

In March, 1896, the Indiana coal operators refused the demands of the miners for increased wages, and the mines—with two or three exceptions—were closed. In March also, the bituminous coal operators of the Clearfield, Pennsylvania, region formed a district organization to "regulate local trade." In January, the Connellsville coke operators granted increased wages and the new scale went into effect on the first. Thus the coal operators struggled during 1896 with wages and prices against a badly fluctuating but falling market. This was partly because of the highly competitive nonunion coal from West Virginia, and that problem increased during the years until NRA in 1933 brought about a change.

The coal operators of Northern Colorado suffered from a strike because some of them substituted an eight-inch screen for a one-and-a-quarter-inch screen. This reduced greatly the pay of the miners as they were not paid for the screenings, or they had to take more time and effort to produce mostly large lumps of coal. A conference was held between the miners and some of the coal operators, and they agreed upon the restoration of the smaller screens. Coal operators not present at the conference refused to abide by the agreement, and they employed nonunion men. This action caused all the miners to strike again. Another conference was held and the points at issue compromised, so that where the larger screen was used, the pay was increased accordingly. A few of the operators continued to operate with nonunion men but they abided by the agreement as to screens and pay. Future disputes were to be submitted to a joint board of conciliation.

"Anarchistic" strikes took place in the metal mines in 1896. In July, the mine operators of Cripple Creek, Colorado, however, were "peacefully" struck for $3.00 for an eight-hour day and exclusive employment of union men. In June, the Leadville, Colorado, strike began because the demands of the Western

Federation of Miners for $3.00 a day were not granted. The mine owners and operators met and decided to oppose vigorously these demands. Attempts to operate the mines with nonunionists brought about riots in which property was destroyed and some men killed. The state militia was called out. In September, the operators tried to get men from the Lake Superior iron-ore region where men were idle, but very few came although high wages were offered; at least 1,500 men were needed to operate the mines. There was rioting and bloodshed, dynamiting of shaft-houses, and pitched battles between strikers and nonunion men. It cost the State of Colorado about $2,000 daily to keep the militia at the mines, and for the entire strike about a quarter of million dollars. Meanwhile, each side carried on its propaganda and war. When the managers offered to arbitrate the issue, the miners refused the proposition offered. A conference was then arranged between the two groups but no agreement was reached. The managers published certain propositions followed by another set in reply to the counter-proposals of the strikers. Then the management decided that no agreement could be reached and prepared to operate the mines on a nonunion basis. Again violence broke out. The strikers set about to keep replacement men from coming in by force when persuasion failed. Nonunion men were assaulted by strikers at every opportunity. Strikers armed themselves to control certain districts. One mine was dynamited and its workmen fired upon. Equipment about the mines was set on fire. Strikers and mine guards fired upon each other. An attack was made upon a second mine but the strikers were repulsed. From June, 1896, to January, 1897, there were periods of recurring violence. An agreement was reached in May, 1897. This was one of the strikes which helped to give the Western Federation of Miners a reputation for conducting "anarchistic" strikes, and led to warnings about other potential strikes.

In November, 1896, IRON AGE said editorially in regard to an announcement which it believed indicated "that the mining companies of the Butte, Montana district contemplated reducing wages 50c a day:

"The Butte district has become the seat of one of the most formidable labor unions in the country—an organization which has reached its present strength and temper because some of the leading mine owners have subordinated their business interests to the gratification of political ambition. . . . It is a notorious fact that the Butte men have been the ones responsible for the excesses committed in the Coeur d'Alene region, and it is a perfectly understood fact that any effort to reform the status of affairs in Montana will lead to a shotgun campaign unparalleled in the history of our labor disputes. So long as the managers who fostered the growth of the union for their own personal ends are in charge there will be no change."

Perhaps some day the history of the labor movement will reveal how often the workman has been ruthlessly exploited by union officials working hand-in-glove with power-seeking employers—a fact not at all in accord with the socialist theory of class conflict, as these anarchistic strikes superficially seem to indicate.

In the Building Industry in 1896, the associations were generally appeasatory and usually granted union demands, with the notable exception of those of structural iron workers. Although the master builders of Lynn, Massachusetts, refused in April to grant the carpenters' demands for a 25c increase in daily wages, the master carpenters of Detroit, Michigan, were forced by a strike of 1,500 carpenters in June to grant them an eight-hour day at 25c an hour. The Master Builders' Association (or Exchange) of Pittsburgh and the building trades unions agreed "to establish a permanent board of arbitration and conciliation for the settling and prevention of all labor disputes." The master painters of Boston were appeasatory by degrees; on May 1 they granted the eight-hour day, and on May 11, a daily wage of $2.50 to the painters' union which demanded these. But the Master Painters' Association of San Francisco was not quite so appeasatory. While the painters' union demanded and obtained increased wages, it failed to secure the general adoption of its "card system"—a sort of exclusive employment of unionists— under which apprentices had to serve three years and all painters had to prove their competency before being given a "card" and obtaining employment. The association was organized in 1892 with 25 members; it had 40 members when the strike was called, but grew to 80 members during the strike.

The Iron League of New York City was charged in May by the Housesmiths and Bridgemen's Union with paying the lowest wages for its class of labor of any place in the United States. In June, the union demanded an increase in wages up to 31¼c an hour for an eight-hour day. Firms outside the League granted the demands. The union renewed its demands in November for May 1, 1897, on the master builders and structural-iron contractors. In Chicago, in March, 1896, the contractors formed an association "to defend their interests when the Bridge and Iron Workers' Union demanded an increase from 37½c up to 45c an hour on the grounds of the hazardous nature of the occupation." The contractors asserted that iron workers could be obtained outside of Chicago for 25c an hour. The union suggested arbitration.

In the Clothing Industry in 1896, the employers were struck in Baltimore, New York City, and Massachusetts. In February, the Clothiers' Board of Trade of Baltimore was struck because of an alleged blacklist of union workmen through an agreement among the manufacturers not to employ a former workman of another member without that member's recommendation. After the strike was called, a wage increase was demanded by the strikers. The Board resolved not to accede to the union's demands, but to employ workers as individuals. The union presented an agreement but the manufacturers refused to sign or confer with the union representatives. A boycott was declared by the union but the strike was lost. The Board declared that the trouble was largely a fight by a union affiliated with the AFL to force out all members of the Knights of Labor; and that this was brought out in conference between the Clothiers' Association of Baltimore and the secretary of the cutter's union who demanded that only members of the AFL union be employed. The clothing contractors of New York City were charged by the Brotherhood of Tailors of planning to return to the sweating system, and 10,000 of the tailors struck in July to force a renewal of the contract to the 59-hour week. On October 1, 3,500 garment workers in Massachusetts struck to enforce a nine-hour day on their employers.

While the master brewers of Boston, on September 17,

adopted the agreement drawn up by the brewery union with wage scales, the master printers of Detroit, Michigan, refused to sign the scale prepared after several conferences with the book-binders' union, in which mutual concessions had been made. The union struck and won.

The New York Trade School [Auchmutty's] "also adopted the plan of having district committees appointed by several employers' associations, who make frequent visits to the schools, watching the progress of the pupils in the classes in their particular trades, and offering suggestions as to the instruction pursued."

CHAPTER 16

THE ERA OF UNION-ASSOCIATION COLLABORATION AND BEGINNING OF PERMANENTLY BELLIGERENT ASSOCIATIONS

THE YEARS 1897-99 form an era of sharp conflicts. Of these conflicts, there were extensive combinations of unions and associations against the consumer on one hand, and the development of permanently belligerent associations on the other hand. Collective bargaining became collusive bargaining in both the building and the coal industries, while other associations became disgusted with collective bargaining, turned to the open shop as the better way to industrial peace.

The year 1897 was largely a depression year in which manufacturers and other employers welcomed *general* strikes as a means of restricting production in a trade or industry. In other words, a strike on an individual employer was often disliked, while one on an industry-wide association was usually highly desirable. However, there were exceptions, and in those industries, the associations became tired of the endless bickering of collective bargaining with all sorts of strikes from the wildcat and the polecat, to the housecat (friendly, collusive) strike. Collective bargaining seemed to conduce to all three types, not to prevent them.

A picture of the strikes in 1897 is shown by the summary of 16 in Indiana in that year:

(1) 29 manufacturers of cigars and tobacco over nonunion goods.

(1) 10 manufacturers of electrical appliances over rule on imperfect work.

(1) 13 manufacturers of furnaces, stoves and ranges over nonrecognition of the union.

(12) 63 manufacturers of glass over higher wages.

(1) 6 manufacturers of leather over reduction in wages and union dictation.

All were strikes on associations or groups of employers.

Among the topics discussed during the year were convict labor, manual training schools, are the poor growing poorer? and the new eight-hour movement as a means to spread employment.

In the Iron and Steel Industry in 1897, there were threats of general strikes but none took place. It was a year of conferences. It was pointed out specifically that a strike was "an impotent threat," as a strike was "welcome to iron manufacturers if general." On May 11, the Association of Iron and Steel Sheet Manufacturers met and discussed the wage scale, and decided to ask that all "extras" be stricken out. In a conference with the Amalgamated on June 23, no agreement was reached. On July 17, practically the old scale was agreed upon. In April, the American Tinned Plate Manufacturers' Association was formed to take the place of the old defunct tinned plate association. The new association met May 21 and 22 and voted unanimously to deny the demand of the Amalgamated for increased wages and a new scale. In July, the conference agreed upon advances ranging from 8 per cent for rolling to 10 and 15 per cent for heating and shearing. Changes were also made in the "foot notes" to the scale. A conference by manufacturers was held on the bar-iron scale in Youngstown, Ohio, on June 30. The manufacturers, especially those outside the Youngstown district, insisted that radical deductions in the scale must be made. The latter stated that they would not abide by the agreement on the scale otherwise. In July, these (Mahoning and Shenango Valley) manufacturers met in conference with the Amalgamated on the scales for boiling and finishing, but the manufacturers refused to pay the $1.00 demanded by the union on the Pittsburgh rate. The scale agreed upon was a 1c card with $4.00, with 25c advance with each 1/10c, for instance, 1-1/10, $4.25—1-5/10c $5.25, for boiling. There were some other changes and slight reductions, but the scale or percentage reduction for finishers was not given. In November, the blast furnace owners of the Shenango Valley were considering favorably the union's demand for a 10 percent increase, since those in the Mahoning Valley had granted it. It is worthy of note that by August, 1897, practically all the Pittsburgh iron mills had become nonunion while the Valley mills were still union. Thus, the union scales given above are misleading as to the actual rates paid by the most of the Pittsburgh mills.

While not an association-wide strike, nevertheless, it involved an association member and is of considerable interest, so the following event is given: "On account of a strike of boys for an increase in pay of six cents a day, the Lake Erie Iron Works, at Cleveland, Ohio, have closed down in all their departments, thus throwing out of employment about 500 men." We should remember, however, that in depressions, employers often welcome strikes.

In the Foundry Industry in 1897, there was much association activity, much of it highly illustrative and informative as to the formation and functioning of associations. Most of it related to the agitation for and the formation of the National Founders' [now Foundry] Association as a negotiatory association, modeled after the Stove Founders' National Defense Association [now the Manufacturers' Industrial Relations Association]. An official of the SFNDA, Henry Cribben, and President Martin Fox of the International Molders' Union both strongly urged the formation of the NFA. It required much advocacy and agitation by W. H. Pfahler—a member of both the SFNDA and the American Foundrymen's Association, to launch the organization, and he was aided by a committeee of six other members of the AFA.

The NFA "had its inception at a meeting of the American Foundrymen's Association in Detroit in 1897 and took definite shape—in Cincinnati (as an organization) for the express purpose of handling labor questions in connection with foundry work —The progress made far surpassed that of the stove founders' organization both as to members and the magnitude of the establishments represented. The first few months constitute the most trying period in any organization, when a policy must be mapped, when decisions must be quickly made upon all kinds of questions and when conditions must be faced which could not be foreseen nor provided for." It standardized wages since it could not make them uniform because of the varying conditions through the country. Power of the association was brought to bear when employees' demands were unjust. Instances were given where the association upheld the workmen and convinced an employer he was wrong. Its success caused agitation for a similar association among proprietors of machine shops—the National Metal Trades Association.

The procedure and argument for the organization of NFA has thus been stated (abstracted):

The committee of the AFA—consisting of W. H. Pfahler of the Abram Co. Stove Company, Philadelphia, Pa., Wm. Yagle, of Wm. Yagle and Co., Pittsburgh, Pa., E. H. Putnam of the Chattanooga Plow Company, Chattanooga, Tenn.—appointed to consider the advisability of organizing a defense association within the lines, or in connection with, the American Foundrymen's Association, met in Detroit Monday and Tuesday, April 5, and 6, and after discussing the matter at length, prepared a report to be submitted to the convention together with some recommendations as to the best plan to be adopted. The report dealt with the matter in detail in all its phases. Mr. Pfahler had a great many years' experience in matters of this kind as a member of the Stove Founders' Defense Association, and his explanation of the workings of that society and the good accomplished had much to do with the committee's decision. An expanded committee of seven was appointed to serve as the Committee on Defense and was made up of Pfahler, Yagle, Putnam, H. M. Leland, Geo. H. Gibby, Alex Jarrecki, and Ed Maher.

At the Oct. 6, 1897, meeting of the Foundrymen's Assn. of Philadelphia, Mr. Pfahler, chairman of the Committee on Defense of the American Foundrymen's Assn. by invitation "addressed the gathering in regard to the progress made by his commitee."—He said: "Acting under the instructions of the convention the committee appointed to canvass the matter has been in correspondence with a large number of manufacturers, nearly all of whom evinced a desire to take up the subject and work out the problem of defense. There seemed to be no doubt in the minds of those corresponded with as to the advisability and practicability of the formation of a defense association. I called a meeting of the committee here about two months ago, and after a two days' session decided on a plan acceptable to the foundrymen. We corresponded with about 200 of the leading foundrymen of this country, selected at random, asking them if they were sufficiently interested in the matter to attend a meeting for a discussion of the subject. Although that invitation has been out only about ten days, we have already over 100 acceptances. I have therefore called a meeting to be held in Cincinnati at the time of the Western Foundrymen's Association, which will get those founders located west of Ohio to attend, and in November we expect to have a meeting in the East. Through those two meetings, we intend to make our plan acceptable. After those two meetings, the committee will meet to draft by-laws and put the association into working shape. In New England especially, where there was formerly a great aversion to anything of the kind, there are the strongest advocates in favor of an organization which will work with the unions, and the idea that the new organization they will have must be antagonistic is dying, because today the warmest advocates in its favor are to be found among the workmen themselves. They realize that in the new organization they will have a strength against agitation and the agitators, who are in the minority in the ranks of unionists. There is not 20 per cent of the members of the Molders' Union in favor of a strike, and yet that small percentage could bring about a strike. With the manufacturers organized they will have a support which is always maintained."

Pfahler addressed an informal meeting of the Western Foundrymen's Association and stated—that interests of labor and capital are not essentially antagonistic, that employers are not assiduously endeavoring to depress labor by crowding wages to the lowest point. He argued for the organization of employers in the foundry trade not to fight unions but to cooperate with them. "Uniform wages for the same character of work is the foundation stone; the rate of wages is a secondary consideration —High wages can easily be paid by foundrymen *if all his competitors pay the same rate*. High wages work no hardship on an employer if his labor cost is no greater than the labor cost in other foundries."

Foundrymen met in New York December 1, 1897, and heard a report and address by Pfahler eloquently advocating NFA. Resolutions were drawn up and sent to prominent foundrymen for their signatures—a committee on constitution and by-laws was appointed, and a general meeting of all the foundrymen in the country was called to organize formally on January 26, 1898. Committee met and drew up constitution and by-laws, and addressed calls to foundrymen to meet in New York, January 26, 1898. The date chosen was because the NAM met there January 25-27. Constitution and by-laws were adopted. The annual dues were $100. A reserve fund was created by assessments of 10c a molder a month. The methods provided for strike combating.

American Foundrymen's Association met and Martin Fox, President of the molders' union, addressed the association. Mr. Pfahler spoke in favor of the eight-hour day. President Francis Schumann of the American Foundrymen's Association in 1897 advocated shorter hours: "Lessening the hours of labor seems to me the most vital question available for immediate application toward the welfare of all, whether employer or employee. Instead of laboring night and day for short periods to meet spasmodic demands, is it not wiser to adjust the labor so as to bring about the equal distribution of work among the many? Is not the lessening of the hours of labor one of the most vital elements to correct the disturbances between demand and supply?" A report of a committee on apprenticeship was presented and discussed and a form of indenture recommended.

Western Foundrymen's Association discussed apprenticeship, classification of molders, and read a letter from Martin Fox. WFA had a supplementary report of the committee on apprentices with an indenture for manual training school graduates.

In Coal Mining in 1897, there was another widespread strike undoubtedly provoked by coal operators as a stimulant to a weak market. As a preliminary, in January, the coal operators of the Massillon, Ohio, district notified the miners of a reduction from 61c to 51c a ton, and 2,000 men quit work at once. In July, however, the Western coal miners' strike paralyzed an already depressed business. Many coal operators refused to go into any scheme of arbitration, claiming there was nothing to arbitrate. While falling prices for coal and the consequent wage reductions were the real issue, the miners had many other grievances: "The miner has been defrauded of a large percentage of his earnings by 'pluck-me-stores,' by false weights and screens, and in other ways until his condition has become deplorable." In prosperous times, coal operators had expanded their business, but in the depression following the panic, they competed strongly and underbid each other and cut wages. The strike was, accordingly, largely a result of the competition of West Virginia coal. During the previous 10 years, many inventions had been introduced in coal mining and elsewhere for the purpose of minimizing the cost of production. Vast capital, attracted by the larger returns of former years, was invested in mining, increasing the productive capacity very much in excess of the current market demands under an attempted "price maintenance" scheme. The condition was further aggravated by the policy of certain railroads, notably those operating in West Virginia, that brought the mine owners of West Virginia into competition with the mines in Illinois, Indiana, Ohio, and Pennsylvania, into the markets they long had had. Their combinations to maintain prices broke down under the West Virginia competition. Coal operators outside West Virginia continually urged the officials of the United Mine Workers to unionize the nonunion West Virginia mines and stop the "cutthroat" competition. But the West Virginia miners, knowing that they prospered most when their coals sold extensively in out-of-State markets, were very difficult to unionize. Hence, the violence used on them by union organizers and their gangsters until the nation had the "Bloody Mine Wars of West Virginia."

As pointed out above, coal from West Virginia was a large factor in breaking the 1894 coal strike. In order that West Virginia coal would not thus break the 1897 strike, the officials of UMWA sent their best organizers into West Virginia and the violence began. The coal operators of West Virginia obtained injunctions to restrain the organizers' activities. The "strikers" in West Virginia increased, many of them coming from idle mines outside the State. Agitation and the pressure on the local miners became great. Tent colonies and relief stores were set up in as many places as possible. "Strikers" marched along the roads to and near the mines, and violated the injunctions by intimidation if not by outright violence upon nonunionists and mining equipment and other property. A number of the "strikers" were arrested, tried for contempt of court, and found guilty, but their fines were paid, and if imprisoned others took their places. Only professionals could have organized the "bands" to function as they did to intimidate and terrorize the nonunionists into not working in the mines. These activities cut down greatly upon the amount of coal mined in West Virginia during the strike.

The violence on nonunion miners was not limited to West Virginia. For instance, on September 10, at Lattimer, Pennsylvania, a clash between the "striking" miners and deputy sheriffs resulted in the killing of a great number of the invading "strikers" who were attempting to force nonunion men to quit work.

In 1894, the union endeavored to get a "nation-wide settlement, and thus threw away chances to get desirable district settlements," but in 1897, it did not repeat this error. In the Chicago agreement in September, the committees of coal operators and miners agreed upon a scale which provided that 39c should be paid a ton for mine-run coal, 54c for coal passed over a ¾ inch screen, and 65c for coal passed over a 1½ inch screen, with allowances for clay, narrow veins, and the like. In November, Northern Illinois coal operators and striking miners, in conference, reached an agreement after each side made concessions, and ended the strike. But the coal operators and miners of the Pittsburgh district, after conferring on wages, postponed action until the interstate convention had met and acted on uniform wages, in 1898. It was noted in November, 1897, that the Anthracite Coal Operators' Association was dealing with prices.

In the iron ore mines, the companies in the Lake Superior region in February, 1897, reduced wages about 10 per cent, but the owners of the Ishpenning, Michigan, region in December decided to increase miners' wages 10 per cent.

In the Building Industry in 1897, associations generally made concessions to the unions. In February, the Builders' Exchange of Worcester, Massachusetts, conceded the nine-hour day, and the Master Painters' Association of South Boston granted the eight-hour day. On April 1, 41 master painters of Lynn, Massachusetts, granted the painters' union the eight-hour day with no reduction of pay, and on April 8, the Master Painters' Association conceded the union the eight-hour day and an hourly wage of 30c but only after a few firms had been struck. In May, the manufacturers of iron building material met and organized the Architectural Iron League of Chicago to deal with labor questions (and not to regulate prices). After a six weeks' struggle with the union, the League met the union in conference in August and agreed to pay 35c an hour and to drop helpers and allow only one apprentice to two journeymen. The agreement was to last a year and not terminate on 30 days notice as the old one did. In April, 41 master builders of Salem, Massachusetts, held a conference and decided not to grant the carpenters' and plumbers the eight-hour day without a wage reduction. In March, the master masons of Milwaukee, Wisconsin, were struck by 1,500 bricklayers and stone masons for 40c an hour and the eight-hour day. About the same time, the master bricklayers of Baltimore were struck by the hod carriers although it was during a depression in which they knew that many men were paying for jobs. In June, the Employing Plasterers' Association of New York "decided to resist the demands of union workmen to select their own foremen"—and locked out 3,000 plasterers.

Wide variations in association activities in 1897 are illustrated by the following events: Tannery owners of Chicago were struck in February by 1,500 workers but agreed to arbitrate differences before the State Board of Arbitration; the men returned to work at the old wages and hours pending hearing and decision. In April, 13 clothing manufacturers of St. Louis reduced the wages of the garment workers 35 per cent and they struck; the manufacturers were compelled to agree to restore the wage scale and recognize union rules. In May, the four-year strike of the American Flint Glass Workers' Union was declared off, after having cost the union over one million dollars. In December, 63 window-glass manufacturers in Indiana, after a prolonged strike, advanced wages from 13 to 17 per cent, and 15,000 men returned to work. In June, the Board of Trade of Brockton, Massachusetts, heard a report by its committee on statistics in regard to piece prices paid in their shoe factories, and on the advisability of the readjustment of these to conform more closely to those of other cities. In October, the propositions of the shoe manufacturers of Brockton were rejected and the strike continued by the sole fasteners' union. On August 7, master brewers of Boston signed an agreement with the engineers limiting work to 10 hours a day and fixing the rate of wages. On December 15, a committee of the Cotton Manufacturers' Association of Fall River, Massachusetts, proposed salary reductions of administrative officers as well as wage reductions of workmen. On December 19, the Western Massachusetts Typothetae met and voted to grant the 9½ hour day for a trial period of six months. The broom manufacturers of Chicago were struck by the broom-makers for a wage increase, but the strike failed, and cloakmaking firms of San Francisco locked out members of the cloakmakers' union. Master bakers of Boston were condemned by the bakers' union for opposing a bill for sanitary inspection of bake shops. Granite manufacturers of Quincy met the union and reached an agreement that the employers eliminate a non-discrimination clause from their bill of prices.

In 1898, there was relatively little association activity outside the foundry industry. In this industry, the unions were apparently trying out the new association—the NFA. In the iron and steel industry practically the old scales were continued. In coal mining the new interstate agreements designed to restrict competition went into effect. There were a few strikes in the building industry, as usual, and some in cotton manufacturing and the like. On the whole, it was a very peaceful year industrially.

Associations, however, continued to organize, mainly because of legislative threats, since unions defeated or stalled in the industrial field turn to the political field. In April, the Illinois Manufacturers' Association held its first annual banquet. The manufacturers came together to "map out a plan for their mutual interests, to talk over a campaign against class legislation . . . speeches were made . . . (by) Vice President Nathaniel French of the Sylvan Steel Company, Moline, on labor and wages (and by) President L. W. Noyes of the Aeromotor Company, Chicago, on benefits to be derived from the association." Likewise the Manufacturers' Association of Kansas City was a new organization in June.

Discussions of that year were varied, of course, but these

are illustrative topics. The Convention of the National Association of Manufacturers discussed technical education, and President McKinley attended its banquet. "Carpenter versus machinist" foretold jurisdictional disputes arising from using iron and steel in place of wood. The injunction issue was becoming bitter, but many believed that "the courts protect free labor." "The treatment of boycotts" was a discussion provoked by an unfavorable court decision. The new United States Industrial Commission was commented upon frequently. It was also noted in September that strikes were starting up again.

In June, the Iron and Steel Sheet Manufacturers' Association's wage committee met with one from the Amalgamated and asked that the 10 per cent differential for rolling steel over iron be stricken from the scale, but the union insisted on it. Other changes in the scale were unimportant. Manufacturers all over the West, in July, signed the Amalgamated's scale. In February, the Valleys Iron Manufacturers' Association and the Amalgamated held their bimonthly meeting in February and found that prices brought no change in the scale rates. They conferred in June on the next year's scale. In June, the "representatives of the leading iron and steel manufacturers of the United States appeared before the Senate Committee on Education and Labor on June 18 to protest against the passage of the pending bill"—acted upon favorably by the House—providing for eight hours on government work. In March, the war scare made possible a quick ending to a long effort to combine the furnace owners of the Mahoning and Shenango Valleys with those of Cleveland. In June, the furnace owners of the Shenango Valley were asked by workers for increases of 10c to 15c daily. In June, the conference committees of the tin plate manufacturers and Amalgamated met and adopted practically the past year's scale of wages. And in a related field, the boiler manufacturers of Erie, Pennsylvania, were struck by 500 boilermakers for a new scale of wages.

The National Founders' Association met in New York City on January 26, 1898, to perfect the organization. About 23 firms were represented among the 33 individuals, present, and only two-thirds of these firms joined although the others expressed sympathy with the movement. However, 75 firms had pledged themselves by letters. W. H. Pfahler was elected president and four district committees were chosen. Apparently much solicitation was still needed to make the association a success. The Foundrymen's Association of Philadelphia met on March 2 on call to hear President Pfahler of the NFA explain the advantages of the new association, but the address was postponed until the NFA was better organized. But on March 9, Stephen Holman, chairman of the First District Committee of the NFA addressed the New England Foundrymen's Associations on the merits of the NFA. This rather inauspicious beginning encouraged the unions to go ahead with their plans for higher wages and the like. The foundries of Pittsburgh faced in March a general demand of 200 molders for an advance of wages to $2.75, the rate before the depression. The foundries of Cleveland were struck in May by the coremakers for an increase in wages from $2.25 to $2.50. The strike caused most of the foundries to shut down; the foundries sent the large cores out of the city, and new coremakers were employed where possible. The NFA met again in June just before the meeting of the American Foundrymen's Association. W. H. Pfahler retired as president and H. W. Gates was elected. Secretary John A. Penton of the AFA was elected secretary also of the NFA. The constitution was ratified and committees chosen. President Gates of the NFA spoke before the AFA on the "Molder of the future and the need of an adequate apprenticeship system." The great activity in the foundry trade was attributed partly to the associations. In any event, the FAP on November 2 reported trouble in getting good molders on account of the good times.

Stove manufacturers in New York City were struck in March by the molders for increased wages and a shorter workday. The conference committee of the SFNDA met with the committee of the molders' union, discussed the labor situation, but made no change in the wage schedule.

In Coal Mining in 1898, the outstanding event was the adoption by the interstate joint convention of the coal operators' associations and the United Mine Workers of America of an interstate agreement, after a ten-day session. This agreement applied to the unionized mines of Western Pennsylvania, Ohio, and Indiana. The agreement provided for a uniform eight-hour day, an advance of 10 per cent in wages on April 1, and a joint scale committee of union and association officials to tabulate and perfect a scale to be effective for 12 months. The union members of this committee were the national executive board of the UMWA and the district presidents and secretaries, while the association members were two operators from each state. It was said that the operators adopted the eight-hour day to increase the costs of mining in the competing nonunion mines of Northern Illinois. In February, the coal operators and miners of Illinois in conference agreed upon a mining scale for the year April 1, 1898, to March 31, 1899. In January, the New York and Cleveland Gas Coal Company had its miners sign an agreement with it to work from January 16, 1898, to November 30, 1898, at a price of 10c a ton less than that paid for pick-mined coal in the same seam of the Pittsburgh district, provided the agreement for uniformity did not become operative. The price was, accordingly, to be 55c for coal over a 1½ inch screen. The coal operators of Pomeroy, Ohio, were struck by the miners in March, but the strike was broken and the local union disrupted. This period was one of combination, rate discrimination, and the like, often of one combination pitted against another. This was especially true in coal mining.

In the building industry in 1898, there were collective bargaining and strikes on a rather quiet basis. In March, proposed reductions by the employing bricklayers of St. Louis resulted in a strike in every branch of the building trades, since the local unions supported the bricklayers in their strike. In April, however, the master builders of Boston, in the annual agreement with the stonemasons' union, granted a wage increase of 3c an hour. In contrast, the contractors of Buffalo were struck May 1 by 400 structural ironworkers for a wage increase from 25c to 30c an hour—a demand made in January—and several large contracts were held up. In June, the master roofers of Boston conferred with the roofers' union before the State Board of Arbitration over the eight-hour day but no decision was reached. The Iron League of New York City began an agitation in July for forming a national organization into which it was proposed to take all

the large architectural iron firms in the principal cities of the
United States. The National Iron League was formed with head-
quarters in Chicago and met in September to perfect the organization.

In the textile industry in 1898, the State Board of Arbitration in February endeavored to bring about a conference between
the New England cotton mills and their employees to end the
six-weeks strike. In April, the strike on the New Bedford, Massachusetts, cotton mills was declared a failure by the weavers' union.
In the South, efforts were made to train up workers through
what was later called "vestibule schools,"—to quote:

"The Southern Cotton Spinners' Association has decided to
utilize the cotton mills under their control as textile schools for
the training of young men in that industry. The pupils are to receive careful instruction from superintendents and overseers, and
at the end of two years it is expected they will have obtained a
fair mastery of the practical details of the business, in order that
they may be independent of the judgment of subordinates. Moreover, it is calculated that during their period of instruction the
pupils will be brought into personal contact with the employers,
by which means better relations will be established between the
two."

The United Typothetae of America, in 1898, signed an agreement with the International Typographical Union granting the
nine-hour day in November, 1899. In 1898, a member of the
UTA—Henry W. Cherouny—addressed a communication to UTA
members in which he stated that the UTA and the trade unions
"united in one body are a legitimate power to fix rules of conduct
in business as well as prices for labor and printed matter, binding
all printers." He thought he was harking back to the gilds, but
he anticipated NRA 35 years.

Two other events in association activities may be mentioned
here to give variety to the record. In April, 1898, the Master
Barbers' Association of Boston, Massachusetts, agreed to close
shops at 6 o'clock Monday evenings except when that evening
preceded a holiday. In Indiana, three manufacturers of sewing
machines and materials were struck.

The year 1899 was one of business prosperity and extensive

association activity, notably in the foundry and building industries. It was a year of combination in disregard of antitrust acts by both associations and unions against the customer and other outsiders. In fact, President Theodore J. Schaffer of the Amalgamated Association (Union) of Iron, Steel, and Tin Workers of America in his testimony before the United States Industrial Commission favored combinations of capital in any industry, opposed compulsory arbitration, condemned woman labor in steel mills as injurious, noted machine displacement of workers, and denounced immigration for lowering working conditions in the steel industry—he believed that combinations had caused higher wages and were easier to bargain with collectively. It was recognized in informed quarters that industrial consolidations were producing revolutionary financial changes. Combinations had led to consolidations. For instance, the American Bridge Company was in the process of being formed of 24 companies—nearly all the leading companies in the field—and this company shortly became noted for its belligerency toward standard unionism. In contrast to the Amalgamated's attitude, the window-glass workers union got an injunction restraining the window-glass manufacturers of Indiana from transferring their plants to the window-glass consolidation.

On the other hand, increasing government intervention in labor management was being condemned in 1899 and 1900. It was charged that the law-making power was being used systematically to create a monopoly, for instance, penalizing employers for discharging men for belonging to a union, Chinese Exclusion Act, prohibition of aliens on public works, no contracting with foreign workmen abroad, laws against use of convict labor, and the like. Attacks on labor organizations as "trusts" were becoming more and more common, and unions were blamed with causing industrial unrest.

The relations of government, directly and indirectly, were discussed extensively, as illustrated by the following topics and events: Congressional hearings were held on an eight-hour bill for government work which bill was very much amended in the process. The eight-hour law of Colorado was challenged as to its constitutionality, and its passing upon by the court was said to be a cause for delay in ending the strike of the smelter workers in that State. In connection with this and other bloody strikes, State governors were warned in regard to their failure to protect fully the imported nonunion men in a strike, with the resulting bloodshed and death. The "rights of nonunion men" were commented upon in relation to a court decision involving those rights. It was pointed out that the city government of Chicago had to pay for the riot damages of the Railroad Strike of 1894.

England's industrial relations were set forth for the information of all concerned; illustrations were in relation to "industrial conciliation in England," and the "association movement in England." Finally, the investigation and hearings of the United States Industrial Commission—which did not limit itself to "industrial relations," but explored "industrial combinations," and varied industrial matters—provided a sort of sounding board for the views of experts and others in these fields, especially in matters in which these persons disagreed as to the extent, if any, governments should intervene. Undoubtedly, the great industrial activity resulting from the Spanish-American, and the English-South African wars stimulated much thought in regard to the industrial future.

The relation of high wages to poor work was discussed. It was noted also that output per worker fell off in prosperity, and that better results for arduous labor was shown when wages were low and employment hard to get; and that when jobs were plentiful (and workmen scarce), workers were less regular, changed jobs more frequently, were more independent, and struck more quickly and often. It was recorded that workmen—both skilled and unskilled in the Central West—were scarce, due partly to railroad work in new constructions and betterments, which were the results largely of enormous railroad earnings. Hence, there was much questioning in regard to employers working overtime when labor was scarce and paying the premium rate of time and one half, because of the greatly decreased output per man-hour—did it pay? Rising wages and decreasing output per man-hour, along with the growing certainty of labor disputes, were regarded as strongly adverse factors to any contract for future delivery. Moreover, the argument, heard so much in the past score of years, that "low wages mean restricted consumption" was rather new, but it was then partly answered with "most employers pay as good wages as their earnings permit." Neither then nor now was the relation of credit inflation made clear as a factor in higher money wages, and of the accumulation of capital as a necessity to higher real wages.

The revived prosperity caused comparisons to be drawn in regard to the period of the "nineties" with the "seventies." It was said that competition among manufacturers was the highest between 1870 and 1880 of any post-war period, and that the period was one of marked "cutthroat competition," due partly to the stimulus of the protective tariff causing many new industries to be established. In the "seventies," older men were displaced, and surplus workers with farm experience went on the "free land."

In the Iron, Steel, and Related Industries in 1899, strikes were rare in the basic industries, but occurred in the foundry and metal-manufacturing industries. Conferences were frequent, and collective bargaining *along with competition for workers,* was operating to give concessions in wages to unionists. In March, the iron and steel mills at McKee's Rocks advanced wages, and the Manufacturers' Association of the Mahoning and Shenango Valleys met and increased the wages of common laborers from $1.15 to $1.25 a day. At about the same time, the blast furnace owners of the Mahoning Valley restored wages to the basis of 1896— advances averaged about 10 percent. However, one wage advance led to demands for another, and these employers were presented with demands for another 10 per cent advance, which was granted on May 1, as a general one. It took a short strike at New Castle to force the employers there to grant an advance. In June, the blast furnace owners of the Mahoning Valley were asked for increased wages equal to those obtained in the Shenango Valley and through the strike in the New Castle district. Nevertheless, the conference of the Amalgamated with the Association of Iron and Steel Sheet Manufacturers found in May that the average price of black sheets for March and April was not enough under the scale for a wage advance. In June, the Amalgamated and the Association conferred on a new scale. The

Amalgamated demanded a 15 per cent increase and the Association granted an increase of about 11 per cent. The scale otherwise was practically unchanged. In September, also in November, the bi-monthly conference of the Amalgamated and the Association found that the average prices were not high enough to give any wage advance under the new scale.

The Manufacturers' Association of Youngstown conferred with the Amalgamated in May and found that the average price of bar iron had advanced so that puddlers were entitled to 25c more and finishers 2 per cent advance under the scale. In June, the association was confronted with a demand for a 25 per cent increase for puddling in new scale rates with all other wages based on the puddling rate. The compromise gave around 11 per cent. In September, the union-association conference found no wage advance was justified under the new scale rates based on the average price of bar iron. In November, the conference found that the advance in prices entitled puddlers to 50c extra and finishers to a 4 per cent advance.

The American Tinned Plate Association, in June, refused to grant a 25 per cent advance in wages, but the American Tin Plate Company in one mill about a week later granted about a 25 per cent advance to the Tin Workers' Union (not the Amalgamated) and for certain workers in that one mill as much as 100 per cent increase. These set new marks for the Amalgamated and caused it to change its demands. The Amalgamated dealt with each mill separately on a scale, but in July, the tin plate mills consolidated and advertised the large profits being made and this caused it to be struck for higher wages. Then the puddlers theatened to withdraw from the Amalgamated on the grounds that the tin plate workers dominated it. There was a strike on an Indiana mill by the local union over the discharge of its president for violation of a mill rule. The Amalgamated—on pressure by the Consolidation—ordered the strike off and suspended the president for 30 days.

In related industries, a strike on the boiler manufacturers of Chicago for higher wages and a shorter workday caused IRON AGE to note that such demands were driving business away from the cities to country plants.

In the foundry industry, the proprietors of the jobbing foundries were experimenting with the stove manufacturers' process of utilizing the molders' and other unions to help get better prices for the castings. The Foundrymen's Association of Philadelphia met February 1, 1899. "The secretary read several letters at a distance from Philadelphia all expressing themselves ready to support any movement tending to raise the price of castings." Prices were discussed at the March meeting of the Western Foundrymen's Association as to "the best means to secure higher prices for castings in view of the advance in the price of pig iron and other materials." The Philadelphia association was concerned over the scarcity of good molders, coremakers, and pattern makers.

The National Founders' Association's convention in March took action on the request of President Martin Fox of the IMU for a conference. The committee on labor troubles reported that it had conferred with the IMU committee in February and entered into agreements in New York City that were "eminently satisfactory" then. In March, the iron founders and molders of Cincinnati, Ohio, "amicably adjusted" their dispute and agreed upon a wage advance of 10 per cent effective May 1. The agreement was to last until March 31, 1900, unless terminated by a 30 days' notice. Several thousand men were affected by the increase. In April, the Iron Molders' Conference Board, which was composed of all unions in New York and New Jersey, called a conference to meet with the foundry proprietors "with the object of reaching an agreement by which strikes and lockouts can be adjusted"—a movement which culminated later in the noted *"New York Agreement"* between the NFA and the IMU. In the meanwhile, however, the foundries of Massachusetts and Rhode Island were struck by the molders in May for an advance in daily wages to $3.00, abolition of piece work, and recognition of the union card. The foundries refused to concede the demands, attempted to operate in part with nonunionists, and sent work to other foundries. Chicago foundries also were struck in May by the molders for a 10 per cent advance in wages with $2.75 a day minimum. Some foundries conceded the demands.

In May, the foundrymen of St. Louis, Missouri, met at a meeting of the St. Louis Manufacturers' Association and formed the

St. Louis Founders' Association. Mr. John Penton in 1898-99 was secretary of each of the National Founders' Association, of the American Foundrymen's Association, of the National Association of Manufacturers, and of Malleable Castings, but in May, 1899, tried to resign as secretary of the AFA. The AFA, by meeting in Pittsburgh, got 40 new members. In June, the foundrymen of Milwaukee, Wisconsin, met and formed the Milwaukee Foundrymen's Association. Likewise, the foundrymen of Buffalo, New York, met, formed an association, and adopted a constitution and by-laws modeled after the Foundrymen's Association of Philadelphia and the Western Foundrymen's Association. Thus, the organization of foundrymen spread, stimulated largely by demands of the molders' union, but also by what other organized foundrymen were doing to meet problems of labor and prices. By November, there were local foundrymen's associations in Boston, Buffalo, Chicago, Dallas, Milwaukee, Philadelphia, Pittsburgh, St. Louis, and St. Paul, among others.

The foundrymen began to experiment extensively with molding machines, which later became excellent means in preventing, as well as in breaking strikes called by the molders' union. President Martin Fox of the IMU "advised members to accept work on molding machines and bring out their highest possibilities." It was thought, however, in foundry circles, that the purpose of this strategy was to give the union control of the machines and minimize their competition with the molders, and such proved to be the case, especially in stove manufacturing.

In September, the Foundrymen's Association of Pittsburgh, among others, for example, of Milwaukee, adopted "card" prices. The molders of Pittsburgh, in October, appointed a committee to confer with the foundrymen with a view of getting a 10 per cent increase in wages. They struck, and Secretary Fenton of the NFA tried to effect a settlement. The matter was then referred to a local joint committee of molders and foundrymen. This committee likewise failed and, under the New York Agreement, the dispute went to a joint committee of the national organizations—the NFA and the IMU. The foundries, in individual settlements with the striking molders (and coremakers) showed that they had already given an average increase of 10 per cent, and were willing to give 5 per cent more. But the strikers insisted on $3.00 a day minimum for molders, and $2.75 for coremakers. No agreement was reached by the joint national committee, so the matter of the minimum rates was referred back to the local joint committee.

Foundrymen elsewhere were struck. At St. Paul, they ended a strike in November by giving molders a minimum of $2.50 and coremakers $2.00 a day. At Moline, Illinois, the foundries combated the molders' strike by having castings made elsewhere. In the Cleveland strike, the foundries obtained enough nonunionists who proved to be at least 50 per cent more efficient than the unionists were before the strike, so that 240 of the nonunionists, getting $2.00 a day extra as a bonus from the NFA, performed nearly as much work as the 496 striking molders did before the strike. The NFA, however, paid the struck foundries $1.00 a day for each idle place up to 70 per cent of the employees formerly working—that is, for about 107 unfilled places. Outside foundries also supplied castings, and two foundries preferred not to try to operate and risk union violence. In November, the iron foundries of Racine, Wisconsin, were struck by the molders for a minimum wage of $2.75 for bench molders and $2.50 a day for floor molders, with 10 per cent advance on piece work. The NFA settled the strike by granting the strikers' demands. In November, much satisfaction was expressed with regard to the work of the NFA, but the IMU was preparing to test it further, for in December the union voted on the questions of the eight-hour day and the abolition of piece work.

The success of the NFA and the great organizing activity among metal trades workers in 1899, led to agitation among proprietors of machine shops for a similar association, for instance:

"The menace even now overhangs the trade of a concerted movement to force the adoption of the eight-hour day in the machine shops. It would have been attempted last May but for the war with Spain, which caused the labor leaders to change their plans. They have not abandoned the scheme, but merely postponed it for a more favorable opportunity." The eight-hour day is a menace to our competing in international markets. "Our people should use every means in their power to avoid the forcing of such an issue. The best way in which this can be done is by the formation of an employers' association to handle labor questions, and such questions must not be handled imperiously, but judicially."

In the stove industry, the two sister organizations—the National Association of Stove Manufacturers and the Stove Founders' National Defense Association—were active in their respective fields. The NASM had under serious consideration the consolidation of all its member firms into one corporation to control the prices of stoves. The SFNDA members were far from agreement on the use of molding machines in stove foundries.

Agitation for a national association of hardware manufacturers was actively carried on in 1899, so that the organization, among other things, might consider the "question in regard to wages and the manufacturer's relation to labor."

Shipyards were struck in 1899. On June 1, all the shipyards of Baltimore were struck because they refused to grant the nine-hour day to the iron shipbuilders and the boilermakers, about 600 in all. Some of the shipyards conceded the demand at once, others granted it in a few days. By July 11, the strike was practically over and the nine-hour day in operation. However, when the ship caulkers, late in June, asked for 25c a day increase in wages, they were convinced at a conference with a committee of their employers that is was useless to press the demand. In July, the shipyards of New York City and Elizabethport, New Jersey, were struck by the iron shipbuilders and boilermakers for reduction of hours. The strike failed.

In iron ore and other metal mines there were strikes in 1899. In March, the iron ore mine operators of Ishpenning, Michigan, advanced the wages of 3,000 of their workmen. In April, however, all the mines at Ishpenning were closed down on account of the demands of the UMWA for higher pay—for more than the old schedule of over $2.25 a day. About 3,000 men struck, but the operators stood firm and accepted applications from nonunionists. Many strikers left for the copper region and other iron ore districts. Within a week the strike at the Marquette Range for the "recognition of the union" and exclusive employment of union men, was broken by the "resort of the operators to injunction proceedings and other prompt measures." The men returned to work.

Five months later, the operators announced a voluntary increase in wages of 10c a day taking effect September 1. In October, it was announced that the Iron Ore Operators' Association fixed prices. The ore dock managers of Cleveland, Ohio, met and decided unanimously in April to advance the wages of their men one cent a ton for handlers on the docks and 2c for unloaders in vessels. The matter was taken up later by the Lake Carriers' Association. This association in August advanced the wages of all the men employed on its lake vessels to the extent of 10 per cent. On September 30, the zinc mine owners of the Joplin, Missouri, district were struck by 90 per cent of all their miners in obedience to the order of the Missouri and Kansas Miners' Association (union).

In Coal Mining in 1899, the main strikes were in Kansas, but there were negotiations in other fields. The coke companies in the Connellsville, Pennsylvania, region granted about a 10 per cent advance in wages effective May 1. On May 13, a strike was called in Crawford and Cherokee Counties, Kansas, on the "Big Four" coal mining companies which refused to "recognize" or deal with the miners' union and discharged "active union men" or "agitators." The other (16) coal operators conferred with the union before the strike and reached an agreement (with which the "Big Four" refused to be bound), that provided for the eight-hour day, the check-off of union dues, and arbitration. The strike involved 2,150 men. The "Big Four" brought in Negroes from the South and, when the union "induced" these not to work, obtained injunctions, erected stockades, and policed these with armed guards. The union obtained a temporary restraining order to keep out the Negro strikebreakers, but this was later dissolved. The strike continued through 1899 and up to May 31, 1900. Negro importations were made and a few white miners came from West Virginia and the East, many of which the union caused to leave. One of the strike leaders was jailed for contempt of court. Finally the "Big Four" made some concessions—not including full union recognition nor exclusive union employment—and the strike was called off, largely a failure. Coal operators in the Pittsburg, Kansas, district in conference with the UMWA granted increased wages in a new agreement. In June, the coal operators of Leavenworth, Kansas, refused to confer with a union committee or grant increased wages. But, after a strike lasting from August 17 to October 14, the operators conferred with the unionists and reached an agreement.

In the East in 1899, the coal operators in the Birmingham, Alabama, district, in July, granted an advance of 55½c a ton for mining coal, and the coal operators of George's Creek, Maryland, in August, stalled for time on a demand for wage increases. The miners asked for 10c extra on the ton. The operators posted a notice stating that the competition of the Virginia mines made the increase a risky proposition for both operators and miners. Dissatisfied with the operators' attitude, the miners made more demands in December. The operators replied that as soon as a rise in coal prices justified an increase—which they believed would be soon—they would grant it, but they declined to confer with the union representatives. The union sent the operators a lengthy statement in regard to a conference and union recognition. On February 22, 1900, the operators issued a notice granting the 10 per cent increase, but refused in March to confer. The miners' union demanded a 15 per cent increase to correspond to that given in the competitive field of Pensylvania, and asked again for a conference. Some miners who attended union meetings were discharged, and the companies refused to reinstate them, even on the request of a committee of businessmen of Frostburg. On April 9, the union struck one of the mines. In contrast, coal mine operators of Midland, Cardiff, New Castle, and Spring Gulch, Colorado, were forced in December, 1899, by a strike to grant increased wages.

In the Building Industry in 1899, there was much association activity covering a wide area of the country. In the East, building contractors of New Jersey had more than their share of strikes, mostly for the eight-hour day. In April, the building contractors of Hudson County (Jersey City) were struck by the carpenters, bricklayers, and plumbers for an eight-hour day (with increased hourly rates), and granted it after a few days' strike—the contractors of Hoboken granted it in two days to some unions and in six days to another. It took 54 days, however, for the master masons of Madison, New Jersey, to be forced by a strike of the bricklayers and masons to grant the eight-hour day. In contrast, the contractors of Perth Amboy in April defeated a strike of 1,400 fireproofers for a wage increase—and within eight days. In May, lathing contractors of Paterson compromised with striking lathers on a wage increase. Master builders of New York City had demands made on them by the carpenters, mechanics, and other building trades unions for an advance of 50 cents a day—due to the increased cost of living and of rents—and for Saturday half-holiday.

The master painters of Cambridge, Massachusetts, in June granted the demands of the painters for the eight-hour day. On June 20, 1899, the system of arbitration between the Master Builders' Association of Boston and the bricklayers' union had been in effect eight years and had been instituted after a strike. In July, the Master Plumbers' Association of Hartford, Connecticut, did not reply to the demands of the plumbers' union for a conference over its demands for an eight-hour day, $3.00 a day minimum wage, and only one apprentice to a shop. The union struck. Conference committees were chosen, but the association would not grant the wage scale although conceding the other demands, so that an agreement was reached. The master painters of Bridgeport, Connecticut, defeated a strike called to force the discharge of nonunion men, by employing nonunionists to fill the places of the strikers. Contractors of Buffalo, New York, were struck by the structural iron workers in October for the eight-hour day and 33⅓c an hour—the old wages were 25c to 30c an hour for a nine-hour day. Agitation among the building trades of Portland, Maine, led to the formation of the Builders' Exchange among the building contractors, which decided that on and after April 1, 1900, its members would pay by the hour. The plasterers' union protested against this to the boss plasterers (who were members of the Exchange). The union struck, but nonunionists were employed, and it lost the strike. In December, 1899, the building contractors of Pittsburgh and Allegheny, Pennsylvania, were presented with a demand for the eight-hour day by 15 local unions, effective April 1, 1900.

On February 28, 1899, the granite manufacturers of Quincy, Massachusetts, were struck because they refused to grant 30c an hour minimum wages, but offered 25c. In March, they compromised. In December, the Granite Manufacturers' Association of New England refused to grant the demands of the granite workers and the granite cutters' union for the eight-hour day with a minimum wage of $3.00 a day.

The above events illustrate association activities in the building and related industries in the East, but there were similar activities in both Central States and in the West.

In Chicago, building trades disputes broke out not only in April—which is the normal time—but also in November—which was very abnormal. Among the associations in disputes in April were the cut-stone, the sheet-metal, and the ornamental-iron contractors, and the master plumbers' associations. The master plumbers, for instance, were struck for about a week before they conceded a wage advance of 25c a day. In November, however, the Master Plumbers' Association of Chicago published the rules of the plumbers' union to show how greatly these restricted output. The Builders' Association (Exchange) of Chicago also set forth the rules of the carpenters' union to exhibit their "exactions." It was said then that the "employing interests in the Chicago building trades are contemplating aggressive measures against the arbitrary rules of the building trades unions." In November, the Chicago Building Contractors' Council adopted an ultimatum—which they submitted to the unions—containing a long list of indictments and resolving against:

1. Any limitation as to the amount of work a man shall perform during his working day;
2. Any restrictions on the use of machinery;
3. The right of any person to interfere with workmen during working hours;
4. The sympathetic strike;
5. Restrictions on the use of any manufactured material except prison made;
6. The right of the unions to prohibit the employment of apprentices.

The associations represented in the Council were the Mason Builders' Association, the Carpenter Builders' Association, the Master Carpenters' Association, the Master Plumbers' Association, the Master Steamfitters' Association, the Master Plasterers' Association, the Sheet Metal Contractors' Association, the Architectural Iron Contractors' Association, the Constructural Iron Contractors' Association, the Marble Contractors' Association, the Fireproofing Contractors' Association, the Building Elevator Contractors' Association, and the House Draining Contractors' Association.

The union rejected the ultimatum. Then combinations of building-material dealers with sub-contractors and union officials were exposed. The combinations forced the use of their materials upon the building public, for example, the brick and tile manufacturers were cited as guilty. The unions appointed a committee to meet a contractors' committee to adjust the "differences." These were settled by the joint conference in which employers made many concessions and agreed to employ union men exclusively. The Chicago chandelier factories were forced in November to grant the metal polishers a reduction of hours from ten to nine. Fourteen shops belonging to the Sheet Metal Manufacturers' Association of Chicago, in November, locked out their employees, 400 in number, because a strike had been called against a member of the association. It was said that in the 20 year period, 1881-1900, associations in Illinois had ordered only 14 of the 95 so-called lockouts, and of the 14, the brickmakers had ordered 3 and the building trades 4. In other words, genuine lockouts are rare; and even employer-provoked strikes—often called "lockouts"—were relatively few.

In St. Louis, Missouri, in June, 1899, the architectural iron contractors were unsuccessfully struck for two months by the architectural iron workers' union to secure a reduction of hours and an increase in wages with a minimum of 30c an hour. In Kansas City, Missouri, electrical contractors were forced by a four-months strike to "recognize" the electrical workers' union. But only about half of the employing woodworkers of Kansas City, Missouri, granted the striking woodworkers their demands for the nine-hour day and 25c an hour.

In the West, in July, 1899, the master plumbers of Denver, Colorado, were notified by the plumbers' union that the wage schedule would be $4.50 on January 1, 1900. In March, the master painters and decorators of Denver were forced by a strike of the painters' union to grant an increase of wages from $2.50 to $2.80 a day—the union had demanded $3.00. In April, the brick manufacturers of Denver refused to grant a demand by the brickmakers' union for increased wages, and were struck. After numerous conferences failed, a compromise was finally reached which gave the strikers an advance of 25c a day. Likewise, the contractors of Denver compromised with the carpenters' union on a wage increase. In October, the contractors of Victor, Colorado, were forced by a strike to grant increased wages to the hod carriers and brick tenders in connection with the rebuilding of the burned district.

In the textile industry in 1899, the Cotton Manufacturers' Association of Fall River, Massachusetts, refused in January to confer with the Textile Council on wages or to grant the increases demanded. On February 2, the association discussed the union's demands and appointed a committee to settle the matter. On February 27, in a conference with the union committee, the association committee agreed to restore wages to the schedule prior to January 1, 1898, and to consider the adoption of a sliding scale. The union accepted the manufacturers' proposition on March 5. On March 3, the association conferred with the slashers' tenders' union, but refused to grant a more favorable basis than the above. On July 12, the association met and refused to grant demands of the firemen, who struck unsuccessfully on July 15. On November 3, the association met and voted not to grant the demands of the operatives for 10 per cent advance in wages. On November 20, a committee from the association conferred with a committee from the union and offered 5 percent advance provided a sliding scale was adopted. On December 1, the association granted a 10 per cent advance—which advance was made general by the New England cotton mills, and followed by the Southern mills on January 1, 1900.

In 1899, certain clothing contractors of St. Louis, Missouri, were unsuccessfully struck for two months by the garment workers' union for an increase in piece prices.

In the printing industry in 1899, the printing offices of Minneapolis, Minnesota, in September, averted a pressmen's strike by arbitration. In November, however, it took a three-day strike before the dispute was settled by "arbitration" between the association and union committee. In November also the association was struck by the bookbinders' union for a nine-hour day with ten hours' pay, which was conceded by the association and a five-year contract signed. On December 14, in Boston, Massachusetts, 14 printing firms granted the demands of the junior pressmen, piece feeders, and helpers for a wage increase of $2.00 a week.

The glass manufacturers of Cumberland and Gloucester Counties, New Jersey (Bridgeton, Clayton, Glassboro, Fairton, Medford, Elmer, and Mintola) had reduced wages in 1893 on account of the depression and the workmen had accepted the reduction without striking. But with the recovery in 1899, the nonunion manufacturers were asked in March by the union for a conference, which was granted. Nothing was decided at the first conference. At the second conference, the manufacturers refused to grant the union's demands at that time. These demands were: union scale of wages, cash payment of wages, and the "right to organize," or "union recognition." The union then dealt with the manufacturers as individuals. The union "had been forced" to organize the nonunion factories because their competition and cut prices had threatened to make unionized concerns become nonunion. The union obtained concessions from five manufacturers as individuals, but two of the larger firms refused to grant interviews to the union officials. The union then called a strike on these factories and tried to induce all workers to quit. The strike "spread" to all the nonunion factories. Nonunion men were imported, and special policemen and detectives employed to protect the nonstriking workmen and company property. Strikes were called on window-glass factories in sympathy and to unionize them. An injunction was sought against the strike leaders but not granted. After five months, the manufacturers began to break away from the association and sign as individuals an agreement with the union granting its demands. In this case, the union "cracked" the association instead of the association "cracking" the union, and did it by "divide-and-conquer" tactics.

In the food and brewing industries in 1899, there were varied association activities. The master bakers of Newark, New Jersey, were struck in May and June over a reduction in hours from 12 to 8, but did grant a somewhat shortened workweek. All non-union restaurants of Kansas City were struck by the waiters' union to force "union recognition" and it thus succeeded in unionizing 90 per cent of them. Such strikes are usually "polecat" strikes and succeed because of the effectiveness of union picket-ing and boycotting in keeping customers away; this type of strike was greatly on the increase, and may have been noted in the case of the glass factories above. In November, the hotel and restau-rant keepers of Denver, Colorado, were forced by a strike of the cooks' and waiters' unions to grant their demands. In August, the master brewers of Baltimore were struck by the brewery workers' union to enforce a demand for the nine-hour day, which the masters had refused at a conference in July. Then a confer-ence was held at the Brewers' Exchange and an agreement reached by which part of the strikers' demands were granted, and the strike was called off. The bottlers, however, had different de-mands, which the Bottlers' Exchange would not grant, and these were finally dropped.

Two other groups of employers were struck in 1899, and new variations appeared. In April, a committee of the Master Horse-shoers' Association of Boston, Massachusetts, met with a com-mittee of union horseshoers before the State Board of Arbitra-tion, which suggested that each side appoint a committee, these to meet, and settle their differences without a strike. This failed, many master horseshoers were struck on May 1, but on May 2, a large number granted the demands. In May, the Lake Carriers' Association was struck at Buffalo, New York, by grain shovelers, freight handlers, and other laborers on the docks. The dispute arose between the workmen and the contractors of the Lake Carriers' Association. Attempts were made by the State Board of Arbitration and the Roman Catholic Bishop of Buffalo to mediate the matter. It should be noted the increasing intervention of the governments into labor disputes through boards of arbitra-tion created by these governments.

CHAPTER 17

FORCES LEADING TO THE GREAT OPEN-SHOP
MOVEMENT OF 1902-16

THE YEARS 1900, 1901, and 1902 revealed more clearly the failure of collective bargaining not only to bring a degree of industrial peace, but also how employers turned more and more to national belligerent associations, most of them permanently so to deal with labor matters on a nonunion basis. Moreover, these associations were becoming more than mere strike-breaking organizations, they were beginning to concern themselves with industrial betterment activities—comfortable workplaces and the like.

The year 1900 in general was a prosperous year, but with depressed businesses, places, and periods. The stimulus to business from the wars—Spanish-American, and British-South African—was wearing off, yet unions were attempting to get "more and more" concessions "now," often in disregard of the consequences to the employer or even themselves.

Some of the unions faced industrial consolidations caused in part by union practices, notably so in the steel industry. A union in certain cases found that it now had to bargain with one company instead of with an association on which the "divide-and-conquer" tactics had so often been successful, for instance with the American Sheet Steel Company instead of all the sheet mills, with the American Tin Plate Company which absorbed most of the tin mills, and with the American Bridge Company instead of with 24 separate manufacturers and erectors of structural steel. While "industrial combination" was still advocated before association meetings, industrial consolidations had proved to be disappointing in results. Some formed in 1898-9 had already dissolved and others were preparing to do so. Although seven advantages claimed for them were listed, reasons were also suggested as to their limitations.

The "divide-and-conquer" tactic of the unions received a great and growing stimulus from its success in pitting one coal

operators' association against another so that the eight-hour day
had been almost thrust upon the mine workers by the associations in the Central Competitive Field in 1898. That grant intensified the demand elsewhere for the shorter workday, notably
in the building industry where increased mechanization had not
yet economically justified its introduction—which, accordingly,
increased building costs, so that great pressure was brought on
the building trade unions to eliminate their system of restricting
production. This fight was spectacularly illustrated in Chicago in
1899-1900, but especially in 1900.

Mechanization elsewhere, however, had functioned to arouse
fears of overproduction—to some people, including one noted
economist, the machine process was capable of practically unlimited production. The machine process was recognized as a
menace to trade unionism in a number of ways, hence union
hostility to the introduction of new machines. Unionists argued
that the shorter workday and other union methods of restricting
production were directed toward preventing overproduction and
widespread unemployment. With a view of forcing the shorter
workday upon private industry and spreading employment, union
officials continued to seek a Federal law for an eight-hour day
upon government work, but stronger opposition developed at
the congressional hearings on the matter so that it was not until
1912 when this sort of a law was enacted.

These and other union practices caused an adverse attitude
to unionism in many circles. Discussion often turned on the
"epidemic" of or "excessive number" of strikes, sometimes on
"public sympathy" in strikes, and occasionally on the "issues"
in strikes. Strike insurance was considered along with conciliation and arbitration as a method of meeting the growing problem.
Not only were the Chicago labor conditions viewed with anxiety,
the "labor policy of Great Britain was discussed with prophetic
vision—half a century ago—as a vital factor in England's declining industrial supremacy (abstracted):

The English manufacturer is bound hand and foot by unions.
Progress is impossible and retrogression seems inevitable. Unions
have come to stay, but they stand today largely for wrong ideas,
for example to benefit the incompetent worker. Strikes do not

settle anything; they usually fail, and are nearly always accompanied by violence and disorder. The organization of manufacturers who do not combine with the unions, as in England, is necessary to check the abuses of unionism, and bring about proper industrial relations.

This prophetic warning was given, of course, because there was a strong tendency for many people, even in association circles (like SFNDA, the Central Competitive Coal Operators' Association, and the like) to advocate following England's example of union-association combination against the customer. Union officials boasted of their lack of foresight and denounced it as "pie in the sky"; corporation officials frequently showed a lack of it; but association officials might be expected to have it. But the "uneconomic practices" of unions were not regarded as their only abuses; there was complaint about the "check-off system" of forcing an employer to collect union dues from unwilling unionists and at no cost to the union. The right of the employer to discharge "active union members" ("labor agitators" and "trouble makers") was vigorously asserted, and was upheld by courts around this time. It was pointed out that it was a duty of "town boomers" and cities seeking new industries to go to the legal limit in maintaining order in labor disputes and minimize if not eliminate lawlessness. It was pointed out that a lawless strike caused General Electric to close its Cicero (near Chicago) plant and move the machinery to Fort Wayne, Indiana, and Schenectady, New York.

Mediation was also a growing policy. For instance, a committee of Pawtucket, Rhode Island, businessmen called on the treasurer of a local struck manufacturing concern "with large interests" to get him to confer or "arbitrate" with the strikers. Somehow it was believed that conferences and arbitration could settle any dispute, although practically all the major disputes of the past decade had gone through a maze of conferences, as pointed out above. The National Civic Federation held a national conference, addressed by prominent men, on methods of promoting industrial peace.

Although interest had declined somewhat in trade schools, the Manufacturers' Association of New York "appropriated annually $500 for four years to defray the expenses of giving a young man an industrial education."

In the Iron, Steel and Related Industries in 1900, association activity in the basic industries was relatively small but was pronounced in the metal trades and foundries. In January the bimonthly conference gave the puddlers 25c advance, mill rollers 4 percent advance, and finishing mill hands 4½ percent advance according to the sliding scale. In regard to a new sliding scale for the year July, 1900 to July, 1901, the Amalgamated and the manufacturers were unable to reach an agreement by July 1, and the mills closed down. The bar iron manufacturers and the Amalgamated's conference committees adjourned pending a report from a subcommittee. While the sheet mill wages were agreed upon, no agreement as to the nonunion mills of the American Steel Company (the consolidation mentioned above) was reached. The company signed only for its unionized mills. The scale with the American Tin Plate Company (another consolidation) was not agreed upon. Conference after conference failed to agree upon a scale for bar iron; the manufacturers refused to give a wage advance, and the union committee did not have power to bind the union, since the matter had to be voted upon by the lodges. In September, the bar mill scale was settled by a compromise—$4.75 a ton on a 1c card, $5.00 on a 1-2/5c card and so on. Both sides made slight concessions to settle the tin-plate scale (in extensive footnotes to the scale). This scale, however, was not accepted by the American Tin Plate Company until modified late in September. Low prices (steel bars at less than 1c a pound) were the grounds on which manufacturers based their contentions that they could not maintain the high wage scales demanded by the Amalgamated. To stop its loss of members and give it restored financial strength the Amalgamated asked the manufacturers to give it the compulsory "check-off" of union dues. The Amalgamated might have obtained this when the union-association combination was at its peak, but the opportune time had passed with the growing list of nonunion steel mills in the late nineties, among these were Carnegie, Jones and Laughlin, and American Steel and Wire. A continuous wage scale was much discussed.

The National Metal Trades Association organized in 1899, perfected its organization as an appeasatory body in 1900, but as it developed more and more its resistance to the "divide-and-conquer" tactics of unionism it became increasingly belligerent. At this point, it may be noted that unions prefer to deal with appeasatory associations which combine solidly for higher prices and so pass on all increased labor costs (and others) to the customer; no such an association is wanted which stands united firmly against "progressive" union demands—"of more and more, now"—but unionism welcomes an association whose members "can be picked off one by one" until it surrenders. The following account of the formation of the NMTA is pertinent (abstracted):

On December 4, 1899, the second meeting of the NMTA was held in New York. Plans for the permanent organization of the association were perfected, and a number of nonassociation manufacturers were present to learn of the plans of the organization. The association consisted of manufacturers who employed machinists and was modeled after the SFNDA and NFA in objects and methods. Wm. H. Pfahler of the SFNDA addressed the meeting on the benefits derived by members of such associations. It was argued that "the universal agitation now going on in labor circles would indicate that united action on the part of employers is extremely desirable"—the machinists' union was agitating for the nine-hour day and minimum wages of $2.50 to $2.80 a day.

At the December meeting of the association, 50 concerns signed the constitution and bylaws. Two strikes instigated by the machinists' union were defeated by the association during its infancy. A "Circular Letter" issued by the NMTA contains the following explanations:

Labor is organized and is being strengthened daily, and each month and year is growing more powerful. Organized labor proposes to run and regulate your business. No one is immune from demands by unions. Assistance is afforded members of the association by: (1) arbitration [appeasement]; (2) furnishing men in a strike, or remuneration; (3) a natural feeling of respect by the labor element for the power of combination of interests activated by a common desire to maintain fair play and to protect its con-

stitutional rights; (4) competent advice; and (5) a restraining
influence upon employees from a knowledge that their employer
is a member of an organization which endeavors to protect his
interests. Why not accept the truth of the adage, "In time of
peace prepare for war"?

Chicago in 1900 became a battleground in the machine
shops as well as in the building trades. The machinists' union
demanded union recognition, a minimum wage of 28c an hour
for tool-room men and 32½c for die sinkers, a nine-hour day
with time and one half for overtime and double time for holidays,
free access to the shops by the walking delegate, discharge of
foundrymen after 60 days, restriction of apprentices, exclusion of
Negroes, new men must await prior employment of laid-off men,
and the closed shop. The employers "decided not to undertake to
settle the difficulty single-handed," since the character of the
questions and the interests involved were so important that they
"formed an organization under the name of the Chicago Association of Machinery Men." Its executive committee held several
conferences with a union committee without reaching an agreement. The association voted not to grant the demands and the
union struck practically every machine shop in Chicago. The
association employed counsel, and made "all arrangements to
resist the demands of the union to the bitter end." Association
officials consulted with the NMTA, with the Columbus, Ohio,
Metal Manufacturers' Association (which was struck by the machinists' union at about the same time), and with "other prominent
manufacturers in Milwaukee and other cities for the purpose of operating in harmony with them." Correspondence was also carried
on "with associations of manufacturers throughout the country."
More conferences were held by association and union committees, but no agreement was reached. The NMTA cooperated with
the local association and an attempt was made to conciliate the
differences on a national scale and this failed. Each side submitted a proposed agreement which the other rejected. The
president of the machinists' union threatened to call a national
strike extending even into Canada. The threat stimulated machine shop proprietors to begin to organize locally. "In view of
the advisability of concerted action among employers of ma-

chinists, local organizations, comprised of manufacturers in the various districts . . . [were] formed in all industrial centers." Among these was the New York and New Jersey Machinery Manufacturers' Association. Another was the Detroit Machinery and Metal Manufacturers' Association, also formed in March "to resist the demands of the machinists."

The union resorted to its "divide-and-conquer" tactics on the Chicago association by spreading the rumor that some machinery manufacturers had signed the union agreement. But the association immediately published a "card" signed by 68 manufacturers denying that any of them had signed the union agreement. Finally, in a conference between the NMTA and the IAM, an international agreement was signed at Chicago, with the issue to be decided by a board of arbitrators under an assurance of a nine-hour day in the near future and a slight increase in wages. Work was resumed at Chicago, Philadelphia, and Paterson, New Jersey, pending arbitration. A settlement had already been reached at Columbus, Ohio, but Cleveland strikers refused to work pending arbitration.

The NMTA conferred with the union—the International Association of Machinists—to arbitrate national issues. In May it passed resolutions on technical and commercial education. On May 7, it met in secret session principally to consider the Chicago Agreement. Its officers conferred with an IAM committee. Its convention discussed means of averting strikes, and a paper was read on "A History of the English Engineering Strike." It was the voice of the convention that proper steps should be taken to prevent any such calamity in this country. About a week later an arbitration committee was chosen to deal with the IAM under the Chicago Agreement. The early history of the NMTA gravitates around that agreement.

In Cleveland, the metal trades manufacturers met and organized the Cleveland Metal Trades Association, and resolved to refuse to grant the demands of the machinists' union for the nine-hour day with ten hours' pay, and union recognition. There were 58 concerns in the local association, and it had its offices jointly with the NMTA. When conferences failed, the machinists struck. The local association imported nonunion machinists and boarded them inside the struck plants. The president of the IAM threatened to call a nation-wide strike if the NMTA furnished any strikebreakers. He claimed such action by the NMTA would breach the Chicago Agreement. Some of the striking machinists broke away from the union and returned to work.

In November, the NMTA, in conference with the IAM, adopted an arbitration agreement providing for arbitration after negotiation failed. The NMTA had grown to 129 firms, and Gompers asked it to make agreements with other metal trades unions besides the IAM. These unions had met in conference and discussed the formation of a national metal trades department to make national agreements with the NMTA. The NMTA had conceded the nine-hour day effective May 1, 1901.

On April 12, the employing pattern makers of Cincinnati, Ohio, met and discussed the formation of a local defense association and the advisability of joining the NMTA.

The National Founders' Association held its annual meeting in February and discussed, among other things, apprenticeship, contracts with workmen, and the NMTA. The NMTA was represented at this meeting and carried on an agitation for members. The NFA's functioning was discussed editorially by IRON AGE as a "manufacturers' defense association." Comment on its methods and prestige is illustrated by the following:

In handling labor troubles, "one of the most interesting issues arose in Cleveland, and in that case, the association adopted the very successful policy of compensating from its own treasury those molders who remained faithful to their employers. Payment was made to each individual in envelopes bearing the printed name of the association, so that the molders were plainly informed of the source from which came the premium for their faithfulness."

"In order to show the respect which the National Founders' Association has commanded, we desire to illustrate by an instance which occurred in Brooklyn. The molders in a certain shop, feeling that they had a just cause for a demand, made same upon their employers; the demand, however, was refused. The representative of the union called and ordered the men to strike; they put on their coats, and were about to leave the shops when, in the course of the conversation, one of the employers stated that the question of settlement would be left to the National Founders' Association, they being members. The union representative said that put a different aspect on the case, and ordered the men back to their places, and the matter was referred to the chairman of that district."

In June, the national conference between the NFA and the IMU decided against the demands of the striking molders of Cincinnati, Chicago, and Cleveland, for 25c advance a day. Times were becoming less prosperous. No agreement was reached on a series of resolutions. About a week later, the NFA and the IMU, in a national conference at Detroit, withdrew even the temporary advance of 10 percent, and the Cleveland molders struck. The Cleveland Foundrymen's Association decided to leave the settlement of the strike to the NFA. The administrative council of the NFA personally viewed the strike. A bonus was paid to the men who continued to work during the strike, patterns were sent to outside foundries to make castings, and nonunion men were imported and paid $2.75 a day plus a bonus of $2.00 a day. The foundries had a large stock of castings on hand, accumulated during the machinists' strike. There was bitterness between the molders and machinists because the molders would not strike with the machinists, so the machinists worked on nonunion castings. The great falling off of orders made the time inopportune for the molders to strike.

The NFA continued to import nonunion men into Cleveland and appropriated $100,000 for this purpose, but the union pickets "induced" two out of every three of them to leave. About 175 imported men, however, were working in the foundries in September, and only about 50 more were said to be needed because of the depressed conditions. Patterns were sent to other shops. Contributions to aid the strikers were heavy from the outside. A clash between the strikers and nonunionists returning to their boarding houses resulted in a striker, a bystander, and a police officer being killed. Nonunion men were arrested but were bailed out by the local association. After nine months the strike ended by negotiation; the union returned to the shops but the nonunionists were discharged. The IMU claimed a great victory, but it was one of

the factors which contributed to the NFA ceasing to be a negotiatory association.

There were other strikes on foundries; for instance, those of
Youngstown were struck in May by the molders' union in the
general drive for the nine-hour day—and in this case for $3.00
a day. In November, the NFA was dealing with strikes at St.
Louis, Missouri, and at Springfield, Ohio, where nonunionists were
supplied.

The NFA with 364 members, in convention, began to consider measures for more effective strikebreaking. Its bonus system
was thought then to be novel; at least, no association had hitherto
made evident to all that it was paying extra wages to strikebreakers. Newspapers condemned it as an attempt to crush the
molders' union. Moreover, one of these strikebreakers took the
system into court by suing for $48.00 after having worked only
48 days out of the 60 he had contracted to work before he
received a $60.00 bonus. The lower court decided in his favor
but the NFA appealed. The NFA, in convention, appointed an
"educational committee" mainly for spreading propaganda—and
began the use of "certificates for loyal workmen . . . during
strikes" to whom members were obligated to give preference in
employment and to release them on leaves of absence for strikebreaking. This system reached its perfection under the NMTA in
the creation of a large body of highly skilled and efficient strikebreakers. The use of the molding machine and a corps of very
competent instructors in molding was better adapted to the foundry
and less expensive than that of certificate men. The molding machine was then hailed as "the solution of the foundrymen's difficulties and eventually his main safeguard." Manufacturers were
shown by lantern slides at the AFA convention how to use the
molding machines. The problem and uses of the molding machine
were discussed at length; the best results were obtained from
laborers, the poorest from skilled molders, although (and perhaps because) the IMU sought to control the molding machines.

Although appeasatory associations were beginning to show
a spirit of belligerency toward over-aggressive unions, the National Civic Federation was formed to promote industrial peace
through national conferences of very prominent men among union

officials, capitalists, and the "public." Moreover, the SFNDA was then regarded as a model organization, and was heralded for having the enviable record of years "without a strike." In fact, in 1947, it was very erroneously given credit for having "56 years without a strike."

In Coal Mining in 1900, there were new elements in the field, but the most significant matters grew out of the conferences between the UMWA and the various coal operators' associations in the Interstate or "Central Competitive Field," where they compromised on wage scales for the year. The 1900 conference was held at Indianapolis, Indiana, January 23 to February 3, and coal operators of Illinois, Indiana, Ohio, and Pennsylvania conferred with officials of the UMWA. It seems highly appropriate at this point to quote and paraphrase extensively, not only from the 1900 conference proceedings, but also from the 1910 and 1912 proceedings to show specifically the character of collective bargaining between the two great groups and the continuity of issues over half of a century. Collective bargaining in the coal industry has not only failed to bring industrial peace, but has also failed to solve the fundamental problems. Moreover, it has added to the problems as well as complicating the old ones. The quotations and abstracts from the conferences are given as they occurred in the proceedings—under their respective topics—both by years and pages; they are arranged under topic headings so as to set forth more clearly the issues:

1. *Competition of West Virginia must be stopped:*

(*1900*) "The operators of Indiana, Ohio, Pennsylvania and Illinois have been clamoring with the Miners' Organization ever since the interstate movement commenced to bring the State of West Virginia in; but up to this time the Miners have been powerless to control the price of labor in West Virginia, which is the greatest competitor today of all the other states in the competitive field."

To which John Mitchell, President of UMWA replied: "Have you not insisted in every convention held that a clause be inserted that the Miners' Organization would give you all possible protection against outside competition?"

And T. L. Lewis of the UMWA added: "The purpose of this

movement was to wipe out competition. First, we wipe out competition from a local standpoint as it exists in the various States, and, second, to wipe out competition as between the various districts . . . We have only a contract to wipe out competition which has two parties signing it in good faith, but when it comes to enforcing the terms of that contract, the miners are always expected to enforce it [against 'rebellious operators']."

By M. C. Lackey of UMWA: "This movement has been a factor in controlling the markets of the coal industry . . . it is also necessary that this convention . . . should *legislate for all the coal that is produced in the United States*." [italics added.]

By Chapman, operator: "When the Chicago Agreement was made and the eight-hour day granted and the 10 cents advance given you, . . . it was an unwritten part of the agreement that West Virginia was to be brought up or the other States would be relieved. It was not done." This was repeated at Pittsburgh a year ago. Now further opportunity and time is being given "to bring the West Virginia people into line, that the Miners of that State may enjoy the privileges that you do, and that the operators of West Virginia may not have the advantages over their competitors in Ohio, Pennsylvania and other parts that they have enjoyed and do now."

Mitchell urged operators to increase prices and share gains with the miners.

Morton, operator, said: "We cannot secure any extortionate profit from the manufacturing industries; we cannot secure any extraordinary profits from the railroad companies who use fuel." Only small amounts of coal at certain times sell at high prices.

Penna, Indiana Commissioner, coal operators, said that Indiana operators expect "to be put on an equality with her competitors, especially the great state of Illinois. . . . She will take nothing less."

Dolan, Pennsylvania operator, wanted large defense fund so miners could organize West Virginia and stop its competition.

(*1910*) Maurer, operator, complained of the competition of West Virginia and Kentucky's unorganized fields, and demanded protection against them; he said that the operators granted the eight-hour day and other concessions "with the distinct under-

standing and explicit promise of the miners to give to the operators of the four contracting states adequate protection against
competition of the unorganized fields." The promise was given
again in 1898 when the movement was renewed.

Fenan of UMWA: "If there is a proper understanding between them [nonunion coal operators of West Virginia] they can
add whatever advance will be granted here . . . to the cost of
production and *put it on the consumer."* [italics added].

Schieuderberg, Pennsylvania operator, said that the fierce
competitive conditions in Western Pennsylvania were due to
natural gas. "Natural gas is what caused the trouble and misery
in the Pittsburgh district."

Maurer, Ohio operator: "The great tonnage from the unorganized fields of West Virginia and Kentucky . . . is taking
away from us our markets and taking away the employment
which belongs to you."

Green, UMWA: "The operators at home [have] to stop the
kind of guerilla warfare they have among themselves" [in cutting
prices to get part of the declining markets].

Penna: "The coal operators of the competitive district are
not permitted to enter into any agreement to sell their product
as you are permitted to enter into an agreement to sell your
labor." *Hence, the coal operators have to rely on the union to
restrict competition.* "Everything they buy from a nail to a locomotive they buy at trust prices, and the smallest of these trusts is
not the United Mine Workers by any means. . . . With more
mines than are necessary to meet the consumption and with more
miners than are necessary to supply the demands . . . the result
is this competition—unbridled, unlimited, ruinous."

Chapman, Ohio operator: "If you were in the employ of the
operators of the nonunion fields of this country you could not
be working for their interest more effectually than you are doing
now in trying to increase the cost of Ohio coal compared with
their costs. Are you proposing to give your friends justice, uniformity, and equality after they have been acting with you for the
last twelve years? . . . You made promises in 1898 that you
have not kept. . . . You are weaker now in the nonunion fields
than you ever were."

Savage, UMWA: Operators who own mines in Ohio and West Virginia are willing to have their Ohio mines unionized but strenuously oppose unionization of their West Virginia mines. West Virginia operators would reduce wages if operators reduced wages in central competitive fields, and competition would not be lessened. "If you want any assistance from the miners to raise the price of coal, we are at your command any time."

Maurer, Ohio operator: "The Government of the United States and the Government of the State of Ohio say that we must compete." It is unfair for the President of the UMWA to urge operators to do illegal things, but the UMWA can raise wages of the nonunionists and stop the "unfair competition." Ohio operators are being crushed between high wages and nonunion competition. Operators want the union to do the restraining.

Chapman, Ohio operator: "Years ago we asked you, pleaded with you to bring the nonunion fields up to a scale of wages that would enable us to pay you the scale you asked for from time to time; and you promised to do it, but you have not done it; you have not kept the faith. We would be willing to pay the scale today and make the advance if you would put those people on a level with us in the cost of production. You know you cannot do it. You have made efforts to do it, but you are farther away from the goal now than you were in 1898, and you are getting farther away every day. You know you cannot enforce the scale of wages. In every district that you have attemped it you have practically lost out, and you are losing every day."

Lewis, UMWA: The Chicago Agreement provided "That the United Mine Workers' Organization, a party to this contract do hereby further agree to afford all possible protection to the trade and to the other parties hereto against any unfair competition resulting from a failure to maintain scale rates."

(1912) Field, Pennsylvania operator: Union leaders know all about "the enormous increase of West Virginia coal . . . and the conditions just as well as we do . . . also . . . that every time we have increased wages in our district you better satisfied the West Virginia miner, because he had his wages increased in proportion. . . . There is only one way to meet this condition. Decrease your wages, have the wages of the West Virginia miners decreased correspondingly, and when they are dissatisfied you will have a better opportunity to organize them. . . . We lost business last year because we could not meet competitive conditions. I don't see any way we are ever to meet competitive conditions unless we have a decrease [in wages]."

Hayes, UMWA: "If we reduce wages it will not be much of an inspiration to organize."

Maurer, Ohio operator: By wage advances and other concessions increasing the cost of production, the trade has been given more and more to West Virginia and Kentucky.

Penna, Indiana operator: The West Virginia operators oppose unionization "because they see and know from public and private sources how the employers are treated in localities where the union is strong. . . . It is cheaper to adopt those methods and pay the bill than it is to submit to the unionizing of their properties." They read reports of our meetings where it is urged "to unionize West Virginia for only one purpose, namely, to exclude them from the markets in order that we may replace their product with ours. . . . They read of the continued strikes and turmoil and violations of contracts in districts that are unionized and conclude that it is cheaper to remain nonunion.

"There is no law in this country preventing the miners from organizing unorganized territories, but there is a law . . . that would put the operators in jail if they were to meet and agree to maintain any schedule of prices. . . . The coal operators . . . have tried it. . . . There is no law that will put you in the penitentiary for trying to organize miners." Therefore, *you* (the union) *must do the job for us.* [italics added.]

Maurer: While the Sherman Anti-Trust Act and the Valentine Law in Ohio are in force, "we cannot carry out these theories [in regard to stopping competition among ourselves and from West Virginia], but if the union, with the cooperation of the operators, tries to get these acts repealed, the thing can be done. We tried to combine but the Attorney General of Ohio called us into his office and warned us to quit, and we did."

Chapman: "When we met in Chicago in 1898 and reestablished the Interstate movement the competition from nonunion fields was the element . . . that entered into negotiations in the

adoption of the scale made there . . . It was understood in that
convention . . . that the miners of the competitive field of the
four states were to bring the nonunion fields up to the price paid
for mining in those states, and unless they secured the adoption
of an eight-hour day at the next convention the competitive field
was to be relieved of these burdens. . . . The State [West Vir-
ginia] from which the keenest competition comes has increased
its production 350 percent, or 25 percent annually for fourteen
years. . . . Not only that but Eastern Kentucky and Tennessee
are doing the same thing and have the same relative increase in
their percent.

2. *THE UMWA a giant monopoly seeking super power:*

(*1900*) By John P. Reese, UMWA: "If we are going to the
expense year after year of building up this gigantic organization
and protecting the operator against unfair competition in the
market; if we are to protect him as we have done in the past,
and as they have a right to expect in the future, we have got to
be recompensed for our services."

Chapman complained of the "great defense fund as a menace
to the operators, also about the attempt to get a nation-wide
agreement as "the most colossal and combined trust in the shape
of labor that ever existed in the history of that country. All other
trusts would be but pigmies compared with that, and its effects
would be calamitous to the interests of this country. You would
place in the hands of your National Organization the power to
stop every line of railroad in this country, every line of steam-
ships that enter our ports, the power to stop every manufacturing
industry of this country, the power to close every public property
that produces light, pumps water or anything of that kind in the
cities of this country, the power even in the home, at the fire-
side, to put out the fire that cooks the food and warms the people
of this country."

McKay said that the purpose of the defense fund was to bring
that whole force on the operator who attempted "to cut the market
conditions."

Penna favored a strong union, defense fund, and wide organization. "If, however, that strength [of the UMWA] shall ever be-

come a menace to the public weal then the organization will forfeit its right to live and will die."

(*1910*) Lewis, UMWA: There was an argument for a clause "that there shall be no limit to the amount of deductions for the organization [UMWA]." Money was to be spent to organize West Virginia.

Chapman told the UMWA that it was a combination in restraint of trade and its check-off, although agreed to locally, was in violation of the law.

Zerbe, Ohio operator: "There are many operators" who feel that if they are to be "sand-bagged" every two years, "the time has come to go back to the old way."

Green, UMWA: "Our movement has for its purpose that the labor cost of a ton of coal shall be about equal in the different districts."

Penna: "The local officers assume to decide upon the competency and the efficiency, and the management is denied the right to decide that question. And invariably when there is an attempt made to move or discharge men because of their incompetency or inefficiency, or because of common, ordinary laziness, we are accused of being prompted by ulterior motives, and it means a fight in the mine, a long drawn-out squabble, investigations, meetings of committees, argument—in fact, it is easier and cheaper for a coal operator at times to keep a good-for-nothing cuss in his employ than it is for him to tread the devious course he is required to do to get rid of him."

"The demands contain certain things that will never be conceded, things that the rank and file of the Mine Workers of America do not want. . . . But every time we have been invited to come and reason together the miners have assumed to say what is fair, what is conservative, what is reasonable—no elasticity in it, no give, no move, it is absolute and fixed! The reasoning together we are invited to do is 'Come over here, get down, kiss our feet, let us trample on your head, take your medicine and say you like it.' "

There is an additional cost of production over the higher wages paid in unionized fields that is due to "the existence of the

union and the union's meddlesomeness and unwarranted interference with the operation of the property. That is not a small
item. . . . Here we meet you as men who profess to be fair and
who try to be fair; but when we go home and undertake to operate
the mines with union labor we meet with the criminally inclined,
with the men who have no respect for law nor order nor the rights
of others, who have no respect for anything but their own desires, with or without reason. . . . We have men who are provi-
dent and good, men who are ambitious to do more than make
a mere living. They work whenever the opportunity presents itself. They want to earn what they can. Then we have men of another class who do not want to work steadily and who will not
do so. As long as they get enough in one day to exist on they
will not work two days."

Lewis, UMWA, admitted that were extra costs of producing
a ton of coal added unnecessarily because of certain union activities, such as stoppages of work.

Zerbe, Ohio operator: The fault lies with the leaders not
with the miners; the UMWA has too much politics in its make-up.
"You are not here in good faith; you are not here asking it because you need the advance in pay; you are asking it because
someone committed himself by saying the miners would get it."

Penna: Unions have sniped off the operators regularly and so
long that the limit has been reached. Unionists have become dic-
tators and have told the operators to swallow it or choke.

(1912) The UMWA does not stand for efficiency. "It pro-
tects the inefficient equally with the efficient, and the greater
percent of the Mine Workers' labors are in protecting the inefficient, indifferent and careless men.

"Were I an operator and had it in my power I could resort
to any method to keep any trades union out of my mines, rather
than to submit to the galling meddlesomeness" recently displayed
by Illinois miners.

Maurer, Ohio operator: "I am not against organized labor
and . . . I have never been against organized labor. . . . But
when organized labor takes a position that is absolutely and un-
conditionally unfair; when it will not listen to reason; when it
will not consider facts that it knows are facts, then as far as West

Virginia is concerned, there is no incentive for me to continue being in favor of organized labor."

Penna: "Where the union exists and gets into the hands of certain individuals, coal companies do not control their properties. All they do is to become paymasters."

"In order to be mutually helpful to each other the operators agreed to what is now known as the checkoff for the miners' union, as a source of strength and for that purpose built it up."

"When the trades unions become stronger and more dominant and arrogant, and ignore the rights of the people entirely then legislation will have to deal with the trade union proposition and limit those powers."

3. *The issue of screened versus mine-run coal and union destruction of discipline:*

(*1900*) There was a long scrap over screened versus mine-run coal—the miners wanted to be paid on the mine-run basis; operators opposed it because miners were careless in shooting and handling mine-run coal.

Penna: In Indiana, the mine-run basis is required by law. The mine-run basis makes for poor mining practices—lower quality of coal—too much slack. We must employ only union men and cannot discharge them for too much slack. The mine-run system "increases the cost of production. It requires more men to keep a mine open and running. It lessens the percent of lump coal per acre of the company's investment without being of any benefit to the practical coal miner."

(*1910*) Every district which has gone from lump coal to mine-run coal as a basis for wages has been demoralized. The mine-run system has not merely increased costs to the operators and destroyed the value of his property, it has increased accidents— the killing, the maiming, and crippling of men, due to the extravagent use of powder, which is the easiest way to mine mine-run coal. When men mine coal on a mine-run basis they use more powder, they produce fewer tons of coal per keg of powder, and they do less mining. . . . it means more slate falling." This costs more to remove. "It results in a bigger percentage of screenings and a smaller percentage of lump coal. It means reckless shooting that results in accidents." Windy shots causing the destruction of the lives of all men in the mine did not occur until the mine-run system was introduced and now occur right along only where the mine-run system exists.

Thomas, Pennsylvania operator: "Under the mine-run system there is no incentive for a miner to produce lump coal. . . . The run-of-mine basis encourages carelessness."

Penna: "With the interference of the United Mine Workers' organization . . . discipline is not easy." Excess use of powder under the mine-run system sometimes kills shot firers, tears up the curbing of the shaft bottom and the shafts themselves, blows away the fans from the top, and the like—a "natural result of the mine-run system . . . a loss of life and property."

Zerbe: The union is unfair in demanding the mine-run system at prices for screened coal.

Feehan, UMWA: "I attribute 90 percent of the total number of strikes and suspensions of work that have taken place during the past four years to the fact that we have not had the mine-run basis."

Lewis, UMWA: Unions will not permit employer to impose on them the costs of legislation beneficial to them.

Schieuderberg, Pennsylvania operator: Laws, both objectionable and expensive, have been imposed on the operators and have added greatly to costs of production.

(1912) Penna: The mine-run system is the main cause of "loss of life and limb in coal mines. . . . It destroys every bit of skill there ever was exercised in the mining of coal. It destroys the efficiency of labor. . . . The burning of the excessive amounts of powder renders conditions in the working places more dangerous and a great majority of our fatal accidents and non fatal accidents come from the falling of coal and slate."

Taylor, Illinois operator: Operators use machines in Illinois in order to undercut coal and have less dust due to the careless mining under the mine-run system.

Lewis, UMWA: "Each side accepted in the final wind-up conditions they were not satisfied with, but agreed to them rather than go into a possible conflict, after having been on strike the previous year, 1897." The time is coming when the government will control the amount of powder used in a shot "because of the awful catastrophies that are occurring in the coal mines (and when) . . . the government discovers that windy shots are the cause of explosions that wipe out in an instant a number of lives."

Reese, Illinois operator: "Legislate the (union mine or pit) committees out of existence and you will legislate a thousand times more trouble away from the four states than you will be getting on the mine-run system."

4. *Increased wages and the cost of living:*

(*1910*) Maurer, Ohio operator: In 1908, miners of Ohio lost 95¾ hours per man on account of strikes and suspensions, while those of unorganized West Virginia lost 1¼ hours per man from the same causes.

Lewis, President UMWA demanded higher wages because the cost of living of miners had increased 60 percent since 1898.

Green, UMWA: Cost-of-living argument made the basis for wage advances when it is rising, and when workers cannot live properly, they are not going to produce, and there will be no profit for the employer.

Penna: Unions have increased costs of living to the consumer —coal, hats, shoes, etc. Then they demand increased wages to meet the increased costs of living, and so on in a vicious spiral.

Chapman, Ohio operator, showed how much greater the cost of mining coal was in Ohio than in West Virginia, but how miners in West Virginia made more annually at lower rates because they had more days' work.

Penna: "A trade union's . . . very existence is for the purpose of increasing the cost of living. It is organized and maintained for no other purpose than to increase the cost of living. Every time there is an advance in wages secured, every time there is a reduction in the number of hours of labor, it means additional cost to the consumer, and the component parts of any trades union, to the extent that they are consumers, must participate in and pay that advance. Every reduction in the hours of labor and every advance in the amount of wages paid is but a further inducement to secure still other advances and still further reductions in the hours of labor. And when the circle is completed it comes back again.

Lackey, UMWA: Miners must have advance in wages because cost of living has increased and they must maintain their "social standing"—"at least maintain themselves in their present status."

Penna: "Men working in the mines earn money in other ways; they do not all work exclusively in the mines. Of the men working in the mines are the lame, the lazy, the unwilling and the weak." Ability of the men to earn a living should not be based on a weakling nor on a giant. A wage advance, when miners are idle and markets for coal cannot be found, "would further reduce the opportunity to toil, and instead of bettering their condition would make them worse."

Chapman: Miners can make a living at present prices "if they have an opportunity to work. . . . Men who are producing the same commodity you are, cause your lack of opportunity to work. . . . We are not able to give you enough work for the reasons (that our high wage rates prevent us from keeping our markets against West Virginia competition)." Unionists do not want more work (employment) but more money for less work.

(1912) Lord, UMWA: "The contracts for all bituminous mines in North America are based on what is done in this conference."

Maurer: "And you will unionize West Virginia when you put them down to the point where they will have to become union men. You will never unionize them as long as you increase your wages and as long as you are willing to work one hundred days a year and let them work three hundred days a year. . . . They are making more money than you are . . . at the end of the year they have earned many more dollars than the miners of Ohio and Pennsylvania." Union wages and conditions are so costly that "they can work their mines every day while our mines are idle." They "can produce their coal from thirty to forty and fifty cents a ton cheaper than we" although they "pay the men pretty close to the wages we are paying you."

Walker, UMWA: "To undercut the nonunion men until we would starve them out . . . we would be in a mighty bad fix, and it would be hard for us to turn around and try to bring ourselves up again. . . . There is a certain amount of coal produced in mines where men in our organization work that will have to be

filled by them. The nonunion operators cannot fill all the demand.
. . . You have too much war going on in your own ranks, (so)
. . . I don't expect to get a single penny unless we are able to
convince you *it will cost you more not to give it than it will to
give it.*" [italics added].

Lewis, UMWA: "If the operators conceded everything we
asked we would go away from the city of Cleveland with regrets
that we did not ask more."

Maurer: "An increased price in mining will decrease your
earnings for a year. The four millions of coal that West Virginia
took from Ohio last year means a loss of $3,000,000 to the
miners (of Ohio). . . . You gained nothing by your last increase.
You may have gained in the amount you made per day, but you
lost in your tonnage and will continue to lose." During the suspension in Illinois and Pennsylvania, "the nonunion miners were
busily taking your markets and getting the benefit of your suspension." "Your action today is saying to organized capital, 'Invest your money in nonunion states'."

Chapman: "It isn't more work you want, but more money for
the work you do and less hours of labor. . . . (To concede) your
demands (will reduce) . . . the amount of work we will be able
to give you."

5. *Labor a commodity sold by the union:*

(1910) Lewis, President UMWA: "You men were here to
buy labor at the cheapest possible price you could convince us
we ought to sell it to you, and . . . we were here to secure the
very highest rate of wages for our labor that we could convince
our employers they ought to pay."

6. *Portal-to-portal issue:*

(1910) Lewis, UMWA: The question is where does a man's
working time begin—at the pit mouth, or where the change of
cars is made by the drivers, or at the working face?

7. *Operators wanting a strike:*

(1910) Lewis, UMWA: Some operators are gambling on a
strike and have stocked up coal expecting to make large profits
in case of a strike. Other operators are endeavoring to tie up
the entire industry until everyone signs.

(1912) McDonald, UMWA: "Some of the operators are not

very anxious to continue work after the first of April. The mere fact that they have stocked all the coal they could for the last two months in many parts of the country looked to us as if they were trying to prepare for a general suspension on the first of April."

8. *Machine differential an issue:*

(1900) Lackey, UMWA: "We ask that the man who operates the pick mine shall have an open field to compete with the man who operates a machine mine, and if it makes more money for the miner it makes more money for the operator also."

(1910) Penna: "Every step reaching that conclusion (7 cents differential in machine mining) is painted with dishonor and absolute dishonesty on part of the United Mine Workers."

(1912) White, President UMWA: "Nearly fifty percent of the total product is now produced by machine."

9. *Why the war on the "captive" mines:*

(1900) Dolan, Pennsylvania operator: "The small consumers pay nearly the same price for coal all the time. . . . the railroads, the Carnegie and the Illinois Steel Companies and such large concerns . . . are always asking for cheap coal . . . (but) are best able to pay for it."

(1910) Green, UMWA: Railroads extended their lines, labor-saving machines were introduced, new coal fields were opened up, new producers entered the market, and keen competition resulted. The price fell. The less efficient operators reduced wages and resorted to dishonest practices upon their employees, through company stores which charge excessive prices, through dishonest screens, through false weights, and through exorbitant rents for cheap houses, and the like. At least two miners were in every district for one man's work.

Railroads get operators to sell coal around cost of production to get that business, then steam trade, which is in close touch with the railroad officials, buys coal almost as cheap, so that the price must be raised on the domestic consumer, who complains and gets an anti-trust law. Coal operators get ICC to reduce railroad rates on coal, but the railroads fight the matter through the courts for years, and legal costs are high for both sides.

Railroads probably have an indirect interest in coal mines in West Virginia and will adjust rates for West Virginia.

(1912) Walker, UMWA: Railroads are acquiring coal mines in order to get cheap fuel. The steel industry is getting coal cheap; it is crowding operators out of the business by establishing "the market price at practically the cost of production." And both are a serious threat to destroy the unions.

The big coal consumers are backing up the enforcement of the Sherman Anti-Trust Act on the coal operators; "most of the big concerns . . . doing business on a nonunion basis are controlled by interests. . . . Some of them will make money out of their nonunion mines, if the nonunion mines work. . . . Railroad concerns dominate the mines in West Virginia. . . . men near Grafton have holdings of five, ten, fifteen and twenty thousand acres of coal land that is valueless while the railroads have the control they have. It does not matter whether you compel them to maintain different organizations and pay uniform freight rates, they will be paying themselves. . . . In Danville, Illinois, the advantage of the Steel Trust being able to use their own equipment and load and haul coal from Danville to Chicago gives them an advantage of 32 and a fraction cents over every other operator in that district."

Feehan, UMWA: "The operators of Western Pennsylvania, . . . Ohio and other states represented here have interests in West Virginia. They are not desirous of having the union there. They are just as strenuously opposing the organization as the operators who were in the business when they opened up. The same is true in the nonunion fields of Pennsylvania. Pennsylvania corporations have gone further than West Virginia corporations have in the way of securing protection. . . . The corporations in Pennsylvania secured the enactment of a law which gave them the protection of a military force, known as the State Constabulary, to eliminate the cost they were formerly put to of maintaining a force of coal and iron police. They make the citizens of our state pay for the maintenance of this military force. And when they are put in actual operation the thugs of West Virginia cannot begin to compare with them. . . . The nonunion coal corporations of Pennsylvania are not even put to the expense of hiring their thugs and . . . union destroyers; the citizens of the Commonwealth are taxed to bear that burden."

10. *Amending the Sherman Anti-Trust Act:*

(1912) Penna: "Now the miners have taken no hand in this affair (amending the Sherman Anti-Trust Act) and it affects them just as much as it does the coal operators. I believe a committtee from this body would have influence with that Senate Committee (on Interstate Commerce) if they appeared before it and said we would like to have the Sherman Anti-Trust Law amended so as to permit coal operators to enter into agreements on selling prices of coal to alleviate the situation; and to remove any fear of the coal operators we are willing that a commission be appointed, as is done now in the railroad interests, to say to the operators of this country that when they do agree on schedules of selling prices those schedules shall not be exorbitant, that they shall not be unreasonable or unfair."

Lewis, UMWA offered the following resolution:

"Whereas, It is recognized that there is a useless waste of our fuel resources in the development of the mining industry, and an unnecessary loss of life, and

"Whereas, The useless waste of fuel and the reckless loss of life is due to the competition in the industry that prevents any form of an agreement in establishing the selling price of fuel,

"Resolved, That it is the sense of this Joint Conference that a Committee of Operators' and Miners' representatives, of an equal number from the states here represented, together with the International officers of the United Mine Workers should be created for the purpose of using their influence to amend or have repealed such sections of the Sherman Anti-Trust Law and the anti-trust or conspiracy laws of the different states as prohibit mine owners from arranging a fair selling price of fuel, or that would prohibit miners and operators from arranging wage contracts."

11. *The secret committee proceedings:*

(1900) Sub-committee was appointed, and services of the stenographer were dispensed with.

(1910) Lewis, UMWA: Reference was made to the small

sub-committee which holds executive meetings and discussions are informal. After meetings were held on three successive days the sub-committee failed to agree and reported back to the full committee.

12. *Job selling:*

(1912) Walker, UMWA: accused mine managers of selling jobs, from $25 to $50 for a room or an entry.

In March, 1900, agreement was reached in the Pittsburgh district on a scale of coal mine wages for one year with advances, for instance, of diggers of 20c a ton.

Among the important coal strikes of 1900 was that in the George's Creek mines of Maryland, where many efforts were made to prevent it by the businessmen against strenuous ones by union agitators to call and continue it. A conference was granted by the president of the struck mine, but before it took place the miners issued a general strike order and, on April 11, the men went out. Some of the miners later returned to work for the 10 percent increase which was granted. The companies prepared for a long strike and began to close up their mines to protect them. The businessmen of Frostburg and Lonaconing endeavored to have conferences between the coal mine presidents and the representatives of the miners, but failed. The Cumberland Board of Trade and businessmen of Frostburg made an effort on May 1 to get large numbers of miners to return to work, but they were kept out by speeches of union organizers and the massing of union men at the mouth of the mines. An injunction was sought and obtained to restrain interference with miners who desired to go back to work. Many miners left the region for employment in other coal fields. Miners held a meeting and wanted to ask the leaders to call the strike off. "Mother" Jones appeared and gave the strike new life. In June, the Business Men's Committee of Frostburg arranged for a conference between the leader of the coal operators and a committee of miners, but nothing was decided. Miners and other workmen were assaulted and riots occurred. Many men were tried but only a few were found guilty. On July 10, the Business Men's Committee requested the miners to elect delegates to confer with the operators. At the conferences, the operators refused to grant the 15 percent demanded. On August 1, many men returned to work in spite of the efforts of organizers, marching men, and speeches. The sheriff had 100 men deputized to maintain order and, on August 3, the strike was declared off.

On August 28, 1900, the coal operators of Leavenworth, Kansas, were struck again. Conferences had been held but no agreement was reached because of the increased wages demanded. The strike was arbitrated finally, the workers reduced part of their demands for an increase, and a new agreement was drawn up governing wages and working conditions and signed.

Among the other strikes in coal mines—in the Davy, West Virginia, coal fields, the operators granted the miners an advance of 10 percent in wages, and the anthracite coal operators lost their strike. They said too much at the beginning of the strike. The strikers forced the operators to concede "every point they originally refused and declared impossible of consideration." They learned the lesson that "a union cannot be defeated by talking it down."

The squeeze play on the Illinois operators by the UMWA and the coal operators of the central competitive fields helped to induce the Illinois operators to form an organization which attracted considerable public attention as a promising solution to the difficult problem of obtaining industrial peace:

"An important organization has been formed in Illinois, named the Illinois Coal Operators' Association, of which Herman Justi is commissioner. . . . A prospectus just issued by Mr. Justi states that 'The Illinois Coal Operators' Association is possibly the first voluntary organization in this country of men engaged in industrial pursuits on a large scale to attempt, as it is attempting now, to prevent friction and to settle disputes with its employees by submitting its differences to a commission of its own choice, whose business it will be to take them up with . . . the officials of the Mine Workers' Union and settle them upon their merits solely." Arbitration was to be resorted to only when conciliation failed.

In metal mining, the mining companies of the Ishpenning, Michigan, district advanced wages of miners 15c a day—5,000 employees were affected—the wages were the highest ever paid in this district; and the Missouri and Kansas Zinc Mine Operators' Association (organized in December, 1898) attempted to follow the lead of coal operators' associations in regulating prices. Mining iron ore companies in July in Morris County, New Jersey, reduced wages and miners struck in a number of mines, but within a week strikers at some mines returned to work. The sheriff sent in deputies to maintain order.

In the Building Industry in 1900, the "Chicago Building Trades' War" was outstanding among association activities in this field. In January, an agreement was reached by the association and unions, although the carpenters and electricians were demanding wage advances for April 1—the carpenters from 42½c to 50c an hour, and the electricians for 25c a day more. The Chicago building trades agreement was ignored by several separate unions which were assumed to confirm it. This caused the association to consider a lockout. In March, most of the dissenting unions struck. The association felt "compelled to take the position that no proposal for arbitration will be considered and (that it) will accept nothing short of a complete surrender by the workmen." The real issue was not over wages—as we have seen above—but over "freedom of the contractor from the tyranny of the business agent and restrictions on output in the eight-hour day." Mechanization had not become great enough in the building industry to increase the output per man-hour so that a worker could produce in eight hours what he had formerly produced in ten hours; so the pressure was put on the workers to discontinue all sorts of practices which reduced output. In August, the struggle had been on for eight months; a few had weakened on each side but the main forces remained in stubborn opposition. Late in October, the Iron League and the structural iron workers' union reached an agreement and the union withdrew from the Building Trades Council. The same procedure was followed by the Master Plumbers' Association and the plumbers' union. Unions were thus settling differences with the separate trade associations.

The master builders (or master carpenters) elsewhere were active in resisting the demands of the carpenters' union in 1900. On January 15, the master carpenters of Plainfield, New Jersey, refused to grant the eight-hour day with nine hours' pay. One master carpenter discharged all union men in his employ because they would not quit the union. In January, the master builders of Winchendon, Massachusetts, granted the nine-hour day with no reduction in daily wages. On January 29, the Contractors' Association of Newark, New Jersey, reduced the wages of carpenters and helpers 50c a day and a strike was threatened. In February, the contractors of Great Barrington, Massachusetts, agreed to give the mechanics a nine-hour day to begin April 1, 1900. On March 9, the Master Carpenters' Association of Passaic, New Jersey, met and fixed the wages of carpenters at 31c an hour. In March, the contractors of Attleborough, Massachusetts, agreed to grant the carpenters a nine-hour day effective May 1, 1900. The building contractors of Greenwich, Connecticut, however, were struck on April 2 by the carpenters, masons, painters, and plumbers over the nine-hour day. The master plumbers granted an eight-hour day and the building contractors conceded the other strikers' demands. On April 4, the contractors of Westerly, Rhode Island, were forced by a strike of the carpenters' union to "recognize" the union and grant a nine-hour day. On May 1, the building contractors of Saginaw, Michigan, were struck because they refused the demands of the carpenters for an eight-hour day. On May 20, "the Master Carpenters' Association of Plainfield, New Jersey, held a meeting to take action on the communication of the Business Men's Association offering their good offices with a view to arbitrating the carpenters' strike." In May, the master carpenters of Boston, Massachusetts, were struck by the carpenters for the eight-hour day and a minimum wage of $2.50. In June, contractors of Fall River, Massachusetts, and elsewhere were hit by a general strike by the carpenters and tinsmiths for an eight-hour day with nine hours' pay. Master plumbers of Youngstown, Ohio, gave a wage advance. Contractors of Denver, Colorado, were forced to grant increased wages to the carpenters, bricklayers, lathers, painters and decorators, and the sheet metal workers. The carpenters also got a further concession of a Saturday half holiday. However, the contractors of Arapahoe County (Denver), during the carpenters' strike caused a clause requiring union labor in a contract for a public building to be declared illegal and void. The contractors of Colorado Springs, Colorado, were induced to enter into "an agreement with the trades' council by which the council was to furnish them with unskilled labor and they were to employ only union labor."

In May, the employing woodworkers of Minneapolis, Minnesota, were struck by 800 woodworkers who demanded unionized shops, ten-hour day, use of union label, and new wage scale. Out of 22 shops, 18 granted the demands while 4 refused. The Mill Owners' Association and the Lumber Dealers' Association of Denver, Colorado, were involved in a strike growing out of the refusal of a planing and lumber mill to employ union woodworkers exclusively. The strike was finally settled by granting the union's demands for complete unionization. On May 3, four box manufacturers of Bay City, Michigan, were struck for an advance in wages of 25c a day and, on May 17, settled the matter so the strikers returned to work. The mill owners in San Francisco and Alameda County, California, refused to grant an eight-hour day and on this account resisted a protracted strike around 1900.

Master plumbers' associations had disputes with the plumbers' union in 1900. In January, the Master Plumbers' Association of Denver, Colorado, was confronted by a strike because it refused to grant the plumbers an increase in wages. Negotiations caused the demand to be postponed until June 1, but on that date, business was so poor that the demands were dropped. On May 1, the master plumbers of Duluth, Minnesota, were struck to force them to sign a scale granting 50c a day advance in wages and a Saturday half holiday. A few days later the demands were granted. In May, the master plumbers of Pittsfield, Massachusetts, granted the plumbers the eight-hour day on Saturdays, while the master plumbers of Fall River were struck for the eight-hour day with nine hours' pay. In June, the master plumbers of Malden, Massachusetts, signed an agreement for the eight-hour day. But the Master Plumbers' Association of Hartford, Connecticut, refused to grant the plumbers' union an eight-hour day with a minimum wage of $3.00 a day, and the men struck. Dissatisfaction broke out among the strikers, the association refused to accept invitations to arbitrate, and the strike was called off. The Master Plumbers' Association of Greenwich, Connecticut, had trouble with their workmen over the date the eight-hour day was to be effective, and were forced by a strike to make it effective at once.

In 1900, the Master Plasterers' Association of Colorado Springs, Colorado, issued an order that journeymen who worked for nonassociation employers should be blacklisted, and the plasterers, hod carriers, and lathers struck. The order was rescinded. The master plasterers of Denver fought a strike called to compel them to carry a union card.

Contractors had issues with the bricklayers' union in 1900. In February, the Mason Builders' Association of Boston, Massachusetts, ageed with the unions of stonemasons and bricklayers on wages and hours of labor. In March, the contractors' agreement to grant the eight-hour day went into effect for the bricklayers. The master builders granted the building laborers' union the eight-hour day with a 28 cents a day increase. In March, the contractors of Holyoke, Massachusetts, were struck by the masons and bricklayers for 5c more an hour. The struck contractors brought in workers from outside the city, but after a month compromised with the unions for half the advance demanded. On March 31, contracting builders of Baltimore, Maryland, were struck by 700 to 800 Negro hod carriers for an increase in wages from $2.00 to $2.50, and in a week granted the demand. In May, contractors and bricklayers of Fitchburg, Massachusetts, agreed upon a nine-hour day until January 1, 1901 when the eight-hour day would prevail. The contractors of Colorado Springs, Colorado, were compelled in 1900 to give the bricklayers a uniform wage of $5.00 a day.

Master painters had disputes with the painters' union over wages and hours during the year 1900. In February, the contractors and master painters of Providence, Rhode Island, were notified that on May 1, the painters' and decorators' unions would require the eight-hour day with no daily wage reduction. On February 28, the unions voted to demand the eight-hour day and $2.50 daily wages. On March 2, the unions met and planned a campaign for their demands. On May 1, several shops conceded the eight-hour day, others remained idle; four of the largest firms refused to grant the demands and 400 to 600 painters were out of work. On November 10—when the painting season is usually over—the union claimed that the strike was not lost, as most of the shops—in number—had granted the union's terms and that the strike was still on the others. In February, the master painters of Easthampton, Holyoke, and Northampton, Massachusetts, met and voted to pay $2.25 a day wages. In April, the master painters of Boston were struck by the painters' union to enforce a minimum wage of $2.75 for an eight-hour day. The strike succeeded. The Master Painters and Decorators' Association, however, published a statement after the strike disclaiming responsibility in the matter. The master painters of Duluth, Minnesota, were struck by the painters and decorators to force the employers to sign a wage scale. In August, the employing painters of Bridgeport, Connecticut, were forced by a strike of the painters' union to discharge some nonunion men.

Granite manufacturers were struck extensively in March, 1900, by the granite cutters' union to enforce a new wage schedule with a minimum wage of $3.00 a day for an eight-hour day (instead of $2.65 for a nine-hour day). The strike extended throughout New England, affecting New Hampshire, Massachusetts, Connecticut, and Rhode Island associations as well as the New England Granite Manufacturers' Association. In New Hampshire, after about six weeks, the manufacturers and the union compromised on $2.80 for an eight-hour day; then the polishers struck for a nine-hour day and 25c a day advance in wages. In Massachusetts, the granite manufacturers of Quincy offered a compromise, but the union declined. The manufacturers submitted another proposition and this drew a counter-proposition from the union. After several propositions and counter-propositions had been offered, an agreement was finally reached and, on May 7, the men returned to work. In May, the granite cutters and marble workers of Fall River struck their employers for the eight-hour day and $3.00 daily wage, while the manufacturers and granite cutters of Chester signed an agreement for the eight-hour day and $2.80 daily wage. In Connecticut, some of the members of the Connecticut Granite Manufacturers' Association withdrew on account of the strike, but the New England Granite Manufacturers' Association supported the contention of the Connecticut association that it was impossible to grant the demands. Some of the firms compromised with the union, which called off the strike on the others as well. In Rhode Island, granite cutters' wages were $2.70 for the ten hour day, but they struck for the eight-hour day with $3.00 wages. A committee of manufacturers submitted a proposition to the Westerly and Niantic local unions of granite cutters, based on eight hours a day for six days a week, with a minimum wage. On April 6, both sides submitted propositions. The granite manufacturers voted on May 7 to adhere to their offer of 33c an hour, and no settlement was reached then. On May 22, the granite manufacturers of the state and the union agreed on 35c an hour, and the men returned to work.

Hat and clothing manufacturers, however, had relatively few strikes in 1900. Hat factories of Orange Valley, New Jersey, were doing work for the struck firm of Berge and Company and were struck in January. On August 7, the strike on Berge and Company was ended when it granted the closed shop. Clothing manufacturers in San Francisco, in a dispute with the cloak-makers' union, locked out the union members.

Vessel owners and shipbuilders had labor difficulties in 1900. In March, the vessel owners and ore shippers at Cleveland, Ohio, held conferences with the officials of the ore handlers in regard to an advance in wages. The conferences extended over two weeks and resulted in an agreement for a twelve-hour day, 20c a ton for unloading vessels and 25c an hour for overtime; other rates were agreed upon, holidays were named with picnics and excursions eliminated. In March, the new schedule of wages adopted by the Lake Carriers' Association was accepted by the new union of sailors without complaint. On May 6, the shipbuilding companies of Bath, Maine, which would not grant the ship joiners a nine-hour day with increased pay, were struck and forced to grant the demands of the union. On May 10, the shipbuilders of Calais, Maine, were struck by the caulkers for a wage advance from $2.50 to $3.00 a day, but, after a few hours of deliberation following the strike, granted the demand.

Increased wages, shorter workdays, or both were issues put before associations in various industries in 1900. The newspapers of Denver, Colorado, as a result of an arbitration decision, gave the press helpers an increase in wages. The master bakers of Trenton, New Jersey, were presented in May with a demand by the bakers' union for a radical shortening of hours, but the master bakers of Denver, Colorado, were forced to advance the bakers' wages. In June, the cigar manufacturers of Boston made a three-year agreement with the cigarmakers' union as to piece prices. In July, the green-bottle manufacturers of South New Jersey, in conference with the union, agreed to pay wages in cash as well as an increase. In December, the master barbers of Greenfield, Massachusetts, signed an agreement with the union for 11 PM Saturday closing time instead of midnight.

Master brewers' association in 1900 continued to make concessions to the brewery workers' union. In May, the Master Brewers' Association of Fall River, Massachusetts, signed an agreement with the brewery workers (engineers excluded) for $1.00 a week advance in wages. In May, the Master Brewers' Association of Boston was struck by the engineers for a new schedule of wages and hours; and in July, it conferred with the bottlers and drivers and signed an agreement granting them an advance of $3.00 a week. On August 4, the master brewers of Baltimore, Maryland, were struck by the brewery workers to enforce the signing of a new agreement for a uniform nine-hour day and an increase in wages of $1.00 a week. The master brewers granted the demands.

CHAPTER 18

SUMMARY AND CONCLUSIONS

DEVELOPMENTS AND EVENTS in labor-management relations have been so great since 1900 that only a sketchy summary of these can be presented here. As these developments have a very pertinent bearing upon conclusions drawn from the survey of the evolution of associations in the United States, they are outlined first so as to be before the reader as he reviews the conclusions.

Belligerent Trends.—While the Homestead strike indicated the end of appeasatory relations in part of the steel industry, the evolution of employers' associations into another stage—that of permanently belligerent associations—belongs largely to the twentieth century. That belligerency finally resulted in laws designed to outlaw, or at least, minimize the functioning of these organizations. The most outstanding belligerent associations have been dealt with specifically and in detail in my Employers' Associations in the United States—A Study of Typical Associations. Nearly a third of the century passed, however, before the intelligentsia of unionism largely recognized that these organizations were permanently belligerent and only then did they foster a series of pro-union laws (e.g. "Wagner Acts") to crush these associations. In 1902, Hilbert stated the theory of this school that such organizations were ephemeral in character while the appeasatory associations conducted relations with the unions on a stable business basis, so that all associations "tend sooner or later to form agreement with the corresponding unions."

Thus, while associations on occasions fought unionism, the type of association usually considered in weighty discussions of the labor-management relations problem before the turn of the century was the appeasatory type characterized by the Stove Founders' National Defense Association—later the Manufacturers' Protective and Development Association, and now the Manufacturers' Industrial Relations Association. That association has been recurrently but erroneously referred to as conducting industrial relations with the molders' union since 1892 without a strike!

Belligerent trends manifested themselves early in the twentieth century. In 1901, the United States Steel Corporation became belligerent and remained so until "organized" by the CIO under the Wagner Act. The National Metal Trades Association, although formed to deal with the machinists' union, broke with it in 1902, nearly smashed it in 1922, and was a special target of the LaFollette Committee in conducting a campaign to sustain the Wagner Act and promote other pro-union bills. The American Anti-Boycott Association—later the League for Industrial Rights —was formed in 1902 to utilize the courts to check extensive union boycotting, notably of D. E. Loewe & Company. The league was practically de-activated by the Wagner Act. The National Association of Manufacturers declared for the open shop in 1903, fostered the Citizens' Industrial Association of America in that year, and in 1906 sponsored the National Council for Industrial Defense—later the National Industrial Council. That council took over the legislative work of the CIAA when it went out of existence in 1907. The opposition of the NAM to legislation desired by the American Federation of Labor led to the exposure of the NAM's political and legislative activities by congressional committees of both the 63rd and 76th congresses. The National Founders' Association—later the National Foundry Association—became convinced in 1904 that it could no longer deal with the molders' union and has not done so since, although that union has been sustained by NRA and the Wagner Act. NFA almost put the molders' union out of business. In 1906, the National Erectors' Association ceased to be appeasatory toward the structural iron workers' union and fought that union through a long "dynamite war" which culminated in the conviction of union officials for various dynamiting crimes. In 1916, the National Industrial Conference Board was formed mainly to do research work in industrial relations for employers and associations, and in 1919, at the First Industrial Conference, defeated a resolution endorsing collective bargaining.

Among the varied types of belligerent trends are the following: the open-shop movements of 1903-16, of the twenties, and of the forties; the welfare plan of the Lake Carriers' Association; strong local belligerent associations in Los Angeles, Indianapolis, Cleveland, and other cities; litigation adverse to unionism as in the Danbury Hatters', Gompers, Duplex, and Bedford cases (boycotting), the Hitchman case (yellow-dog contract), the McNamara case (union dynamiting), the Coronado Coal Co. cases (union liability for damages due to violence), the Steel Seizure case, and finally in public thinking as expressed in recent elections and legislative developments.

A specific instance of belligerency (out of legion) is found in the attitude toward "peaceful picketing" as set forth in court decisions, notably in Atkinson T. & S. F. Ry. Co. v, Gee (139 F 282, 284): "There is and can be no such thing as peaceful picketing, any more than there can be chaste vulgarity, or peaceful mobbing, or lawful lynching. When men want to converse, or persuade, they do not organize a picket line." Later Supreme Court decisions have legalized peaceful picketing.

Appeasatory Associations not Always Appeasatory.—Among appeasatory and mediatory associations there were flashes of belligerency. Although the National Civic Federation fostered collective bargaining, notably in the anthracite coal strike of 1902, and intermittently down to the Wagner Act, it was strongly condemned in its last days as "fascistic." Associations in the building trades have been troubled recurrently by jurisdictional strikes and regularly by graft (exposed on occasions), and so at times have had belligerent traits. The Stove Founders' National Defense Association (MPDA & MIRA) was almost disrupted by "stoppages of work" (unauthorized strikes) and by resignations of members who then adopted the open shop; and only through NRA was it put back on the way to recovery. Collective bargaining broke down in bituminous coal mining and was reestablished mainly through NRA and the Wagner Act. While NRA fostered collective bargaining, this was often accomplished through company unions which had a phenomenal growth while NRA lasted. NRA itself was the result of a compromise under which associations conceded collective bargaining in return for the dubious legal right to fix prices—a government sanctioned collusion against the consumer. NRA was thus a form of fascism lacking only the "confederation" of associations and unions to enforce the "codes" of "fair practices, prices, etc." upon all parties. Then the Wagner Act was enacted and the government actively fostered unionism, although employer opposition was great until the U. S. Supreme Court, in 1936, held that the act was constitutional. The continued employer opposition resulted in the Taft-Hartley Act, which is still attacked by union officials as a "slave-labor act."

The belligerent trend in public thinking expressed through politics is shown by the overwhelming victory of Robert A. Taft for U. S. Senator against the combined opposition of all types of union officials and proponents of "fairdealism," and by the election of Dwight Eisenhower against the same combined opposition. It is likewise shown by the passage of open-shop legislation by at least 18 state legislatures (1955), notably in Texas, where all union "monopolies" have been outlawed.

Are Employers' Associations Anti-Social?—The preceding pages have indicated the answers to the questions in the Preface: Are employers' associations "bad" organizations which keep the "underdog" workman from getting better wages, hours, and working conditions? In the first place, "underdog" workmen in general are not and have not been members of unions and are rarely sought by union officials as members. A union with a million-dollar monthly income is not composed of "underdogs." By and large, union membership has been confined mainly to skilled workmen and not to the "underdogs." Unions of unskilled workmen unless supported by other unions of skilled workmen (e.g., building-industry laborers by carpenters and others) have been short-lived organizations. Actually, the "underdog" of modern times is the consumer.

In the second place, employers as a class are neither courageous nor devout believers in competition for themselves. Hence, they tend to grant concessions to union officials whenever threatened with a strike. This appeasatory attitude, however, causes union officials to overreach themselves and to make exorbitant demands which the employer cannot grant under the conditions he otherwise faces. He sees bankruptcy ahead either if he grants the demands on one hand, or if he suffers from a long-drawn-out strike on the other hand. This dilemma makes him belligerent. Usually labor troubles become most bitter just before and immediately after a financial crisis. Every outstanding panic in the United States has been preceded first by excessive union demands and then by marked belligerency usually in the form of a pronounced open-shop movement. The demands of the union officials had become greater than employers could profitably grant; their denial of concessions led to strikes or a threatened epidemic of strikes, which in turn caused the open-shop movements. Long before the revolt of the employers, however, there were clear forewarnings against the power-seeking union officials and their exorbitant demands, but as employers are very slow to act, seeming to prefer peace at any price than to face a showdown, the movement awaits what almost seems like a grass-roots uprising, like that of the "law and order leagues" discussed above. That one started in Sedalia, Missouri; the one of 1903 started in Dayton, Ohio, although there were flash-ups at Idaho Springs, Colorado as well as in Danbury, Connecticut. These flash-ups are clear warnings.

Employer reluctance to granting concessions may be simulated. Association officials have cautioned employers not to grant demands too readily, as such invited more and more demands. Automobile manufacturers, for instance, have proved to be such hard bargainers that it is possible that the automobile workers have obtained less through their union than they would have secured without it. Acting under that advice, employers even in boom times will haggle long over concessions that they had planned to grant; and the union officials will tell the union members how long and hard the fight was to get these concessions. In periods of deflation, however, union officials deceive themselves into thinking that employer reluctance is merely sham fighting, and the union members are told that if they will only stick together, the over-greedy, "bad" employers will be brought to their knees. The struggle thus becomes more and more bitter, with unionists resorting to violence and associationists to counter measures, notably the injunction and militia. Union officials by their militancy usually force the employers finally to fight and to take measures to prevent strikes. Yellow-dog contracts developed largely out of exorbitant demands by oath-bound union-ists in secret orders.

A coordination of factors has often operated to enable union officials to make demands which normally were excessive, yet obtain them. Before the strike, the employers could not profit-ably grant the concessions demanded. The strike cut down the supply of the product—and sometime stimulated a demand for it—so that the price rose and the concessions could be granted.

A practice prevalent among appeasatory associations often makes them seem nonexistent, namely, that of having members individually "negotiate" and sign the collective agreement. How-ever, their united opposition to the full union demands, their belligerency during the strike, and the uniformity of the con-cessions offered to the union, are conclusive evidence of the functioning of the association—a fact, however, which cannot be reconciled to the theory of strict parallelism. Opponents of industry-wide collective bargaining may easily be outmaneuvered by this informal method of collective bargaining, which is seem-ingly individual corporation bargaining with a union. The so-called "pattern" and "area-wide" collective bargaining can be as collusive as industry-wide bargaining.

In the third place, employers' associations are of different types; only the permanent belligerent associations regularly op-the twentieth century. Earlier the flare-ups of belligerency were by normally appeasatory associations resisting exorbitant demands pose unionism, and these organizations did not develop until by union officials. These demands were excessive because the eco-nomic system or the industries involved had not developed a high enough productivity to warrant the demands, or the phase of the business cycle was adverse to further concessions—even to con-tinuing current ones. It was a manifestation of poor union leader-ship when these flare-ups occurred. Propaganda by union officials against the "bloated profiteers" and "predatory class" did not change the economic conditions; in fact, the actions of the union officials often made the economic conditions worse—through a widespread wave of unemployment. However, a strike was occa-sionally welcomed, if not induced, by the association to curtail the supply of the product and even stimulate an artificial demand

for it. This has been notably true in coal mining where a strike
stimulated a demand for the unsold "coal dust," and other very
low grade coals. Under favorable economic conditions, appeasatory associations have freely granted union demands when the
union imposed terms or created conditions (polecat strikes, boycotts, violence, etc.) which put the "cutthroat" competitors out
of business. In the garment industry, for instance, the unions still
make war on the nonunion, nonassociation manufacturer (or contractor) and on certain chain clothing stores, and in this are
abetted by the associations. These unions set as their most important function "the policing" of the industry against the "cutthroat" competitor. For years, Northern textile manufacturers'
associations have combined with textile unions against Southern
textile mills which have generally opposed unionism singly and
have not combined effectively prior to 1953 to combat the
Northern collusion; then, however, 70 of the 71 mills combined
to fight the dollar-an-hour minimum wage. Ironically, Northern
associations, in order to get the aid of the unions against Southern
competition, have granted concessions which made the competitive situation even more adverse. The drastic restriction of immigration undoubtedly aided unionized textile mills and garment
manufacturers, as well as the respective unions, but the competition took on other forms, so that these groups resorted to the
Federal wage-hour legislation to stop the "cutthroat" competition
of the South. The vitality of competition has been thoroughly
tested by union-association collusion in industry after industry.
The "cutthroat" competitor is thus the "bad" employer—the
bête noire of union-association collusion.

Attempts by organized employers to suppress competition in
various ways often found that competition asserting itself in ways
and manners beyond their control. These employers have frequently been ready to support any movement to raise prices and
pass on all the increased costs to the consumers. Union officials,
notably of the molders' union, have urged employers to stand
together and raise the prices of stoves. However, the collusion
priced itself out of the market in at least two ways. One was by
the substitution of other methods of heating as supplied by the
sheet iron stove, the furnace, and the central heating plant; an-

other was by Southern competition. To maintain its higher wage rate in the North (since World War I) the molders' union has endeavored to unionize the Southern Negro molder, but did not attain any marked degree of success until after the passage of the Wagner Act.

Union literature abounds with the charges against capitalism and the employer that these resort regularly to the tactics of "divide and conquer." Whether the charge is true in whole or in part, the use of this tactic by union officials is almost universal. They normally tempt any employer who will listen to them by outlining to him the large profits he will make if he breaks with his association, signs up with the union, and has his strike called off. They promise him the patronage going with the union label as well as that arising from the union boycott. They tell him that he can gain permanently the customers of the struck association-ists—a chance otherwise he could not get. With the great demand for his product and the consequent expansion, they promise him his choice of union workmen for efficient production. Thus, "divide and conquer" has been essentially one of the outstanding tactics of union officials.

When no employer would "scab" on the association, the union sometimes formed a "cooperative" to give employment to the strikers and hurt the employers, but never primarily to give lower prices to the consumer. Such "cooperatives" were not planned to be permanent.

Union officials have not only been short-sighted; they have boasted of it, for example, Gompers. They have won strikes but lost the work, as the business of the appeasatory employers went elsewhere. As early as 1832, the ship carpenters won a victory in a New York strike, but the shipbuilding went to other ports. Union officials and appeasatory associations both have generally been blind to economic and industrial changes and quite generally stood in the way of progress. Union officials of the iron workers opposed wire nails in favor of cut nails, and leaders of the stove molders fought sheet steel and molding machines; and both found support among appeasatory employers.

Yet union officials regularly contend that improved standards of living are due to the activities of the unions and superficially this contention seems to be valid. However, the great gains in improved standards of living have come—not from unions and labor legislation—but almost solely from improved processes—machines and methods—in the factory, in transportation, in the field and on the farm. The anti-union Ford did more with his mass production for better standards of living than all that the union officials and their collusive association colleagues have done throughout our history. Relatively, workers of today have less skill and "know-how," work fewer hours, and exert less effort to do their assigned tasks, than workers of the past. In this sense, they earn less. Except for the mighty monopolistic groups, unions have not been able permanently to exact excess wages, or "wageteer," at the expense of the rest of the industrial order. These monopolistic unions have gained by combining with monopolistic associations to restrict production, raise wages and prices, and thus cause a lower standard of living for all the consumers. So long as the wage (and other) demands of the union conspirators did not exceed the amount that the association conspirators felt that they could exact from the users of the product made by members of the joint conspiracies, the necessary concessions were made and industrial peace prevailed in that industry. However, when the union demands became excessive, the association resisted, a strike resulted, and often a "labor war" broke out. Instead then, of collective bargaining conducing to industrial peace, it produced industrial warfare on an industry-wide scale. When union-association collective bargaining did conduce to industrial peace, the bargaining was actually collusive—a conspiracy against the consumer, nonunion workers, nonassociation employers, and the public. The unrestricted condemnation of competition and of the Sherman Anti-Trust Act by the conspirators in their collective bargaining conferences reveals clearly their motives in their joint activities.

Moreover, the greatest progress in industrial processes (machines and methods) was made in those industries where and when the joint union and association conspiracy did not fully succeed in monopolizing the field. For instance, the nonunion coal fields of West Virginia were important factors in keeping coal mining competitive in spite of the union-association con-

spiracy elsewhere. That competition produced the mechanization
of the mines and the resulting "surplus" of coal miners and of coal
mines. It also conduced to the great "labor wars" in West Virginia where the union officials were spurred on by the demands
of the unionized coal operators that the West Virginia operators
be made to meet the onerous conditions enforced by the union
on the members of the appeasatory association. Murder of nonunionists and dynamiting of West Virginia mines were often resorted to by the union officials in their campaigns to "unionize"
the West Virginia mines. Evidence abounds that such weapons
are still used against nonunion miners and coal operators.

With most of the coal mines unionized today, there is an
added purpose of the strike, "memorial holidays," and the like,
namely to stop the production of coal until great stocks of coal
(mostly unsalable normally) are sold usually at high prices.
Coal operators welcome such "stoppages" as a "stimulant to a
weak market" and as a procedure for permanently raising the
price of coal. Might it not be that John L. Lewis is sometimes a
"stooge" rather than the "master-mind" in some of the maneuver-
ings in the coal industry?

Unions and appeasatory associations, then, have been factors
in directly thwarting the improvement of conditions for everybody. Instead of allowing competition to lower the prices so that
everyone could buy the product cheaper, they have conspired with
each other to raise the price and get increased wages, as their
respective shares of the "hold-up." By obstructing changes in
methods and the introduction of machinery unless the union
reaped the major portion of the gain from the "increased productivity per man hour," (although the effort of the worker was
decreased) the union with the sanction of the appeasatory association prevented any gain for the public. The so-called "productivity wage" is on an entirely different basis from an "incentive
wage" whether applied to an individual or group. The latter is a
just reward for increased effort.

Thus, appeasatory-association and union officials, at best, have
given only lip service to free competitive enterprise. In their
conferences, monopolistic gain has been acknowledged as the
actual goal; both lip and actual service have been given to mo-

nopoly. Lacking government sponsorship for many years (but having it since NRA) they have tended to foster fascism, not free competitive enterprise.

Is Collective Bargaining a Solution?—Collective bargaining between association and union has been well established in the building industry as well as in coal mining. In the building industry, strikes and jurisdictional disputes have been probably more prevalent than in any other industry. The devastating effect of a series of jurisdictional disputes has been highly illustrated recently in the building of atomic energy installations throughout the country. The abuses have long been admitted, device after device has been tried to eliminate them, but the atomic energy experience adds only further proof that they are inherent in trade unionism. Closely akin to these abuses is that of graft and corruption in the building industry, recurrently exposed over the years, but regularly occurring. Graft seems also to be inherent in this type of trade unionism. Without passing judgment on whether the benefits of trade associations, trade union, and collective bargaining are greater than the evils, we can readily conclude that unqualified approval of collective bargaining is socially highly questionable.

In the coal industry, as noted before, collusion and violence are notorious. The collusion is obviously the natural result of the collective bargaining there. The violence has been so widespread and over so many years that it cannot be separated logically from the collective (and collusive) bargaining. Accordingly, the collusive association cannot escape the onus for its part in inciting union officials to violence against both nonunionist and nonassociationist. In the "collective" conference, these price-fixing associations have harped on the failure of the union to stop the "cutthroat" competition, and they knew what methods the union officials were using in the "mine wars" to stop that competition. Goon squads under the control of union officials and used to suppress competitors, were logically employed against the association when it was struck by the union. The sword cut both ways.

In collective bargaining outside of the collusive, practically all the advantages lie with the union as against most employers.

Rarely, if at all does the employer obtain any concession he would not have in the absence of collective bargaining. On the other hand, the union has all to gain and nothing to lose under the rules that the union has set up. Moreover, it is a truism in association circles that a union cannot be defeated in conference, that is, by argument or "talking it down." These union rules are so often "the laws of the Medes and Persians," and they are frequently exactions. On occasions these exactions have been set forth by associations, notably builders' associations who have enumerated the union practices, restrictions, and the like. Under these practices, the shorter workday was long fought by the builders' associations mainly because the machine process had not been allowed to advance enough to warrant the marked lessening of the working hours with no wage reductions and with adverse seasonal conditions—rain, cold, and such factors.

The Ethics of Collusion.—Since associationists justify their collusive actions as necessary measures to stop "cutthroat" competition and as a means to help the worker, it might be well to note the justification offered by unionists. For instance, the late President Gompers of the AFL boasted that he would appeal to the devil and his mother-in-law to help unionism. To him collusion was perfectly proper:

"In their struggle to obtain lasting improvements, the workers have occasionally been aided by employers whose interests for the time being were identified with theirs. For it sometimes occurs that the competitive interests of the employers may impel some of them to aid the working men in the establishment of what have become known as standardized conditions of the trade—the minima of standardization."

He also said in regard to the coal miners who engaged in the "Bloody Mine War of West Virginia" to stop the competition of the nonunion mines there: "In their first strike in 1897, not 3 percent of them was organized." The Anthracite Coal Strike Commission (of 1902) thus branded UMWA: "Its history is stained with a record of riot and bloodshed,"—murder, dynamiting of houses, assault and intimidation of nonstrikers, and they and their families terrorized and intimidated. Fifty years later, a similar situation was revealed:

The UMWA made in 1952 an out-of-court settlement of $171,000 with Charles Minton (a former UMWA official) and nine coal companies. Minton charged under oath that he had been deprived of a living by the union because he refused to kill two mine owners and blow up the mine property. He had previously carried out orders by the union to blow up the main substation of the Gladeville Coal Co., using three cases of dynamite in its destruction. Minton had sued in the Circuit Court of Wise, Wise County, Virginia.

This is the union in which John L. Lewis has long officiated, and in which the late President William Green of the AFL and the late President Phillip Murray of the CIO were indoctrinated. It remained, however, for Attorney Arthur Goldberg of the CIO to state: "The right to be nonunion does not exist."

Closed-shop unionism is largely the product of collusion. Collusion could not exist without the support of appeasatory associations. Accordingly, these are not blameless in the development of the ethical standards noted above. The closed shop is of far less benefit to the union member than to the member of a price-fixing association where the closed shop functions to maintain monopoly prices for the association.

Organization Begets Organization and fosters endless organization issues, thus enlarging and intensifying the conflict. The range of issues is growing, notably "fringe benefits" most of which would not have arisen were not the union officials seeking more power. Without the great strides in organization, there would have been no problems of industry-wide strikes and national strike emergencies adverse to the public interest and welfare. Moreover, the number of organization issues is growing rapidly. While nearly everyone knows about jurisdictional disputes and most know about dual unionism, few realize how organization has led to "professionalism" in industrial relations and all that it involves. Thus labor-management relations are becoming more and more complicated and industrial peace seems more and more difficult to attain. Governments by their partisan sponsorship of unionism have made the problem far greater, by making the organizations, directly and indirectly much larger than they would normally have been.

Final Conclusions; the Consumer Forgotten.—To the consumers and the public in general, the choice among the three types of associations is not an easy one to make. The appeasatory, negotiatory, or collective-bargaining type is characteristically a price-fixing organization directly, or indirectly through an affiliated group. It is, accordingly, in league with the union against the consumer and against a system of free competition. It partakes of a system of fascism, not of private enterprise. However, if it conduced to continued industrial peace, so that the consumer could regularly obtain the products he desired, he might feel that the higher price paid for the goods and services was not too high for the regularity of production.

But association-union collective bargaining has not conduced to permanent industrial peace and holds out no such promise so long as the strike is a part of the procedure of collective bargaining by the union. Either the union must voluntarily relinquish the "right" to strike, or the strike (including wildcats or outlaws) must be prevented by the power of governments. "No strike" clauses in agreements have proved to be inadequate in the past; moreover, agreements expire or have been violated by wildcat and even authorized strikes. In no industry has the practice of collective bargaining prevailed longer and more completely than in the building industry which has for years led all others in the number and frequency of strikes. Similarly, the coal mining industry is characteristically a collective-bargaining and strike-ridden one. The consumer has thus had both collusive price fixing and strike-interrupted production at the hands of appeasatory associations. Nation-wide appeasatory associations with their collusive agreements constitute a quadruple conspiracy against: (1) consumers of the product, (2) nonunion workers, (3) nonassociation employers, and (4) a menace to national welfare when the collective bargaining fails and a nation-wide strike occurs.

Mediatory associations have likewise failed to promote continuous industrial peace while at the same time condoning or even fostering collusion between association and union. Their usefulness has thus been limited to special cases where they functioned to bring public opinion to bear upon over-recalcitrant association and union. We need to remember that mediation which rests upon collusion, disregards the vital interests of the consumer.

Belligerent associations, however, are in bad favor with the public, partly because of the weapons they have used against aggressive unions, but largely as a result of union propaganda bitterly assailing such associations at every opportunity. As no belligerent association can be free from attacks upon one or more of its members by the militant union, it does not assure the public of continuous industrial peace. In fact, a militant union has as its basic principle that every nonunion shop or belligerent association is a menace to that union in all the other (unionized) shops. Unless checked by the opposition of permanently belligerent associations and of appeasatory associations (forced temporarily to be belligerent) the militant unions would inevitably obtain control over the industries of the United States and thus establish the "dictatorship of the proletariat" so devoutly and strongly advocated by the disciples of Karl Marx. Of course, should the consumer and the public desire such dictatorship, the belligerent associations are to be condemned as obstacles to that dictatorship. Without belligerency by associations, the militant unions would soon dominate the industrial life of the nation. The system of private enterprise has been preserved in the United State because of the belligerency of associations. The consumer and the public may think that the price of maintaining that system has been too high to pay in the industrial warfare which has often been fostered by government inaction at times and by government support at other times. The functioning of belligerent associations has been so greatly hindered by governments since 1932, that it seems possible that any effective checks upon the coming of that dictatorship have been removed. Only a great reaction in the form of a nation-wide open-shop movement can change the trend.

The heavy hand of government has already been laid on the belligerent associations, so that it seems ironical to advocate as a solution to the problem that a conference of the conspirators (officials of unions and appeasatory, price-fixing associations) be called to plan the future laws in this field. How can anyone who has read the record as set forth in the previous pages concur in a continuance of the anti-social "gains" carried over from the late fascistic NRA?

Legislation is long, long overdue in behalf of the consumer, that is, all of us outside the great conspiracies fostered by NRA and its successors—Wagner acts and the like. Laws directed solely against "labor monopolies" may have merit, but they are largely futile when governments bless the conspiracies of associations and unions as great "social gains" and resort to conferences of such conspirators to enact further legislation in the name of all of us. "Collective bargaining" practically ceases to benefit even the working man when it is distorted into an instrument for the price-fixing association. The consumer is entitled to more of the social and economic gains of improved machines and processes of our economic system. It is not the true function of government to foster the conspiracies against him.

REFERENCES

(to page and paragraph)

(Abbreviations are in Italics)

23; 1 *Ward's* History of ancient working people, vol. 1, 11, pp. 131-41; vol. 2, pp. 105, 444n

23; 2 Unearthed by W. H. Buckler; see comment in Oct. 1924 International m o l d e r s ' journal 601 (*IMJ*)

23; 3 See also *Stone's* A history of labour p. 70

25; 2 Stone 72

26; 1 *Bland,* Brown and Tawney's English economic history—select documents, p. 137; Stone 74

26; 2 *Salzman's* English industry of the middle ages, pp. 346-7; also 337; Ap. 6, 93 *IA* 781 (Iron age)

27; 1 *Unwin's* Industrial organization in the sixteenth and seventeenth centuries, pp. 48-9

27; 2 Bland 139-41; *Bretano's* On the history and development of gilds and the origin of trades unions, pp. 82-3 (also in *Toulman Smith's* English gilds cxlvii) ; Salzman 345-6

27; 3 Bretano 82-3; Toulman Smith cxlvi-vii; Bland 140-1; Stone 74

27; 4 Unwin 97-8, 101, 224; Salzman 345

28; 1 Bretano 14-5; Toulman Smith lxxvi-ix; Salzman 346; Unwin 54; see also Adam *Smith's* Wealth of Nations Bk. 1, Ch. 10, part 2

28; 2 Unwin 49

29; 1 *Unwin's Gilds* and companies of London, pp. 87-8; Salzman 331-2

29; 2 Unwin gilds 92

29; 3 Ashley's Economic history and theory, Bk. 1, p. 90; Unwin gilds 92; Salzman 333; Smith *idem.* Bretano 76; Toul-

man Smith cxi; Warner's Land-
marks in English history, pp.
127-8

30; 1 Unwin 118-20; Smith
idem. Bland 282-4, 296, 336

30; 2 Quoted from the ordinances by Bretano 96; Toulman Smith clx

31; 1 Bretano 13, 66, 73, 85-
7, 99-100; Toulman Smith lxvii,
cxxx, cxxxvi, cxlii, cxlix, ci,
cliii; Unwin 62; Salzman 331-
3, 338-9

31; 2 Bland 357-60

31; 3 Bland 617, 619-22; Unwin 220-3

31; 4 Bland 622-4, 626-31;
Bretano 104-5; Toulman Smith
clxviii-ix

32; 1, 2 Smith *idem.*

33; 1 Quoted in Bretano 129;
Toulman Smith cxciii-viii; Bretano 59-64; Toulman Smith
clxiii-viii; Bland 578-88

34; 1 Smith *idem.*

35; 1 New York Historical
Society: Collections, 1885, pp.
1-31 (*NYHS*)

35; 2 *Wright's* Industrial
Evolution of the United States,
pp. 105-9; *Weeden's* Economic
and social history of New England 162-1789, pp. 83, 99, 104,
167; June 1932 Machinists'
m o n t h l y journal, p. 243
(*MMJ*); *M c N e i l l'* s Labor
movement in the United States,
p. 70

35; 3 Weeden 184, 309; Massachusetts Archives I: x, 29, 33

36; 1 Weeden 274; NYHS 1-

31; Pennsylvania Historical Society, Pennsylvania magazine of
history, vol. 33; pp. 476-91, vol.
34, pp. 99-121; Pennsylvania
German Society, Proceedings
and addresses, vol. 16; also
Weeden 86, citing Boston town
record p. 13

36; 2 *Betts'* Carpenters' hall
and its historical memories
(Rev. Ed.) p. 4

37; 1 *Sampson's* Trial of the
journeymen cord-wainers in the
City of New York (1810) pp.
83, 103; 3 *Doc Hist* 309, 327
(Documentary history of American industrial society); Wright
294; Historical sketch and government of the general society
of mechanics and tradesmen of
the City of New York, pp. 3-9

37; 2 McNeill 70

37n Wright 294 (contra 1
Commons' History of labour
in the United States, pp. 53-4)

38; 1 Mr. 22, 1800 New York
Commercial Advertiser p. 3
(*NYCA*); I Commons 111
places the strike in New York
City

38; 2 *Swinton's* Striking for
life p. 175; Report of the Bureau of Statistics of New Jersey 1885, p. 272 (*NJLB*); Mc-
Masters' History of the people
of the United States, vol. 2, p.
618

39; 1 *Lloyd's* Trial of the
boot and shoe workers of Philadelphia, 1806, pp. 14, 29, 34,
37, 41, 47, 53, 61, 65, 104-5,

133-4; 3 Doc Hist 94, 119-20, 127, 217, 236 (Cf. Saposs in 1 Commons 132-3) ; Ap. 20, 1876 IA 24; Third annual report of the U. S. Commissioner of Labor pp. 1030-1

39; 2 3 Doc Hist 249, 371-2, 383-5; Swinton 175

39; 3 2 *Wheeler's* Criminal cases 268; see also Yates, Select cases; Sampson, *passim;* Wright 295-6

40; 1 *Gould's* Trial of the journeymen cord-wainers of Pittsburgh *passim; Swinton* 175

40; 2 Gould; 4 Doc Hist 28-9, 40, 47-8

41; 1 Jy. 24, 1819 *Niles* Register 356

42; 1 D. 2, 1815 Niles 230; O. 28, 1815 Niles 152; F. 2, 1817 Niles 429; O. 5, 1816 Niles 86-7; Mr. 29, 1817 Niles 75; Je. 28, 1817 Niles 273; Jy. 24, 1819 Niles 356; Jy. 5, 1817 Niles 290; My. 23, 1818 Niles 224; Au. 7, 1819 Niles 297, 385-90; Swinton 175; McNeill 333

42; 2 Brightly's Report of cases nisi prius, Pennsylvania pp. 36-43

42; 3 1 Wheeler 144-9

43; 1 4 Doc Hist 93-5; McNeill 74

43; 2 6 Doc Hist 76-81; McNeill 74

44; 1 5 Doc Hist 81-2; Gould 11-5; 37 Niles 298

44; 2 McNeill 74; *Simpson's* The workingman's manual p. 86

45; 2, 3, 4 *Luther's* An address to the workingman of New England p. 36—also 13, 17

46; 1 Luther 13, 17

46; 2 1880 *MSLB* 3-4 (Commonwealth of Massachusetts. . . . Annual report of the bureau of statistics of labor) ; McNeill 79-81, 84; Luther 7; Simpson 86; *Ely's* Labor movement in America 50

47; 1 1880 MSLB 3; McNeill 84-6; Luther 7, 33-4

47; 2 McNeill 84

47; 3 1880 MSLB 3-4; McNeill 84

48; 1 45 Niles 4, 66, 83, 399; McNeill 84

48; 2 45 Niles 66, 99, 133, 147, 150, 177; 47 Niles 52

48; 3 Connecticut Current Jy. 29, 1883 pp. 1-2, Au. 5, 1883 pp. 2-3

49; 1 45 Niles 373, 434; 5 Doc Hist 208-11; 6 Doc Hist 101-7

49; 2 14 Wendell 9; 1885 NJLB 272

50; 1 Wright 296-7; 46 Niles 5, 52, 147; 5 Doc Hist 303-8; 1880 MSLB 4

51; 1 48 Niles 450; 5 Doc Hist 251-4; 1880 MSLB 4, 273; 1885 NJLB 272-3; McNeill 85-7; 1881 *PALB* 263-4 (Commonwealth of Pennsylvania, Annual report of the bureau of labor statistics)

51; 2 1881 PALB 265; 5 Doc Hist 246, 248

51; 3 1881 PALB 264-5; 6 Doc Hist 27-35

52; 1 4 Doc Hist 314-22, 339; 5 Doc Hist 289, 314-22; 208 U S 274 (1908) Loewe v. Lawler—Danbury hatters; 1885 NJLB 273-5; Simpson 86; McNeill 84; 20 Am Fed 523 (American federationist)

52; 2 20 Am Fed 520; s. 19, 1835 Niles 34; S. 20, 1835 Niles 31

53; 1 McNeill 84-5, 878; 20 Am Fed 517, 522; 1880 MSLB 5; 50 Niles 74; S. 16, 1836 N Y Eve. Post; Bul 61 U.S. Bureau of Labor

54; 1 McNeill 84; 1885 NJLB 273; 50 Niles 74, 131; 5 Doc Hist 241, 245, 301-2, 309-13; 6 Doc. Hist 35, 50-7

54; 2 50 Niles 74; McNeill 87-8; F. 10, 1866 FTR (Finchers' trade review)

55; 1 McNeill 88; 52 Niles 291

55; 2 McNeill 348

56; 1 Thatcher's Criminal cases 616, 637; 4 Metcalf's Reports 112, 114, 136—Com. v. Hunt; 1870 MSLB 97-8; 5 Channing A history of the U. S. 103; Ja. 1951 Typographical journal 5

56; 2 1880 MSLB 5; 1881 PALB 277; Jy. 10, 1850 Baltimore Sun; My. 18, 1850 Philadelphia Ledger; S. 13, 1850 N. Y. Times

57; 1 1881 PALB 266-9; Persons' labor laws 46, 67

58; 1 1881 PALB 268-9; 1880 MSLB 5-6, 9; McNeill 96

58; 2 1881 PALB 270

58; 3 1881 PALB 271; McNeill 84, 108, 111-4

59; 2 1880 MSLB 6; 1881 MSLB 9; 1879 PALB 150; 1881 PALB 272-5; Persons 57; N. 30, 1939 Amalgamated Journal 3; Au. 12, 1880 IA 9

60; 1 Pamphlet itself

60; 2 McNeill 216; Persons 55; 1880 MSLB 9

61; 1 1880 MSLB 9; Ely 57; Persons 57, 68; McNeill 119-20

61; 2 1880 MSLB 9

62; 1 1880 MSLB 8-9; Ely 57; Persons 55, 68; McNeill 216; 1881 PALB 276; Mr. 19, 26, 28, Ap. 2, 5, 6, 14, My. 7, 12, 28 29, 1953 Sun

62; 2 Mr. 16, 17, 1853 Sun

62; 3, 4 Mr. 1853 Sun

63; 1 Mr. 17, 18, 21, 1853 Sun

63; 2 Mr. 22, 1853 Sun

63; 3 Mr. 16, 1853 Sun

63; 4 Mr. 28, 29, 1853 Sun

63; 5 Mr. 30, Ap. 6, 11, My. 12, 1853 Sun

63; 6 Ap. 12, 14, 1853 Sun

63; 7 Mr. 18, 26, Ap. 4-6, 1853 Sun

64; 1 Ap. 21, 23, My. 7, 14, 1853 Sun

64; 2 1880 MSLB 14; Ap. 6, 21, 22, 1853 Sun

65; 1 Mr. 18, 22, 24, 26, 29-31, Ap. 2, 4-6, 8, 11, 12, 22, 23, 25, 26, My. 12, 1853 Sun; McNeill 349

65; 2 Mr. 24, 28-30, Ap. 8-9, 11-2, 22, 28, 1853 Sun

66; 1 Ap. 13, 14, 25, 28, My. 3-5, 12, 1853 Sun

66; 2 Mr. 18, Ap. 22, 25, My. 11-2, 1853 Sun

66; 3 1881 PALB 276; 1880 MSLB 15

67; 1 My. 5-12, 1855 *Pic* (New Orleans Picayune) My. 5, 7, 9, 1885 Commercial bulletin; My. 6, 8, 1855 Daily True Delta

67; 2 McNeill 598; Ely 63

68; 1 O. 17, 1863 FTR; 1894 NHLB 459; 1880 MSLB 16; Mr. 25, 1855 N. Y. Daily Tribune p. 5; 1881 PALB 276; N. 26, 1894 Pic; *Powderly's* Thirty years of labor 36, 417

68; 2 McNeill 122

69; 1 My 26, 1892 IA 1026; O. 17, 1863 FTR; 5 *ILR* (International labor review) 540-1; 1866 *IMU* 5-6 (Proceedings iron molders' union) ; Jy. 1939 IMJ 425

69; 2 1887 NJLB 79-80; 1883 NJLB 155; McNeill 122, 197, 245, 247-8

70; 1 1880 MSLB 16-7; 1881 PALB 276-7; McNeill 216-7

71; 1 1881 PALB 277-8; 1880 MSLB 17-9; McNeill 607-9

71; 2 McNeill 245, 247, 248

73; 1 1883 NJLB 157; 1880 MOLB 129, 132, McNeill 258

73; 2 Je. 27, O. 3, 10, 17, 24, N. 7, 21, D. 5, 1864 FTR

74; 1 Au. 15, 1863, S. 10, O. 1, 29, 1864 FTR

74; 2 Jy. 1839 IMJ 338; Sylvis 57, 217; Je. 6, 13, 20, O. 3, 17, N. 7, 14, 1863, F. 20, Jy. 11, 1864 FTR

75; 1 Je. 13, N. 21, 28, 1863, Ja. 30, Mr. 26, Ap. 16, 30, My. 21, 28, Je. 11, Jy. 9, Au. 20, O. 29, 1864, Ja. 14, Mr. 11, 18, Ap. 22, 29, Je. 6, 1865 FTR; Sylvis 137-40

75; 2 Ap. 9, Je. 28, 1864 FTR; 9 Doc Hist 97-8

75; 3 My. 7, 28, Je. 4, 11, 18, D. 3, 1864 FTR

75; 4 Jy. 2, 9, S. 10, O. 8, 1864 FTR

76; 1 N. 21, 28, D. 5, 19, 26, 1863, Ja. 2, 9, F. 20, Ap. 16, Au. 6, 20, S. 10, O. 8, 29, 1864, Mr. 18, 25, Ap. 8, 15, Au. 26, 1886, Ja. 3, 17, 1866 FTR; 1881 MSLB 9; S. 5, 1878 IA 14

77; 1 Je. 6, 13, Jy. 11, 18, 1863, Mr. 26, Ap. 2, 16, 30, S. 24, 1864, Jy. 15, 29, N. 11, 1865 FTR; 9 Doc Hist 105-6 Mr. 26, 1864 Buffalo Sentinel

78; 1 N. 5, 12, 1864 FTR; 1887 NJLB 157

78; 2 My. 14, Je. 26, Au. 13, O. 15, 29, N. 5, D. 10, 1864 FTR; Jy. 25, 1864 Detroit Tribune; 9 Doc Hist 109-14

78; 3 Ja. 27, 1866 FTR

78; 4 O. 1, 29, N. 26, D. 10, 17, 1864, Ja. 14, Mr. 11, Jy. 7, S. 16, O. 14, D. 8, 1865 FTR

79; 1 Ap. 30, My. 14, 1864, S. 9, 30, O. 7, 1865 FTR

79; 2 F. 20, Jy. 16, Au. 10, D. 17, 1864, My. 6, 1865 FTR

79; 3 Ap. 8, 15, My. 6, 1865 FTR

79; 4 Mr. 16, Jy. 25, Au. 13, 1864, Je. 7, Jy. 22, 29, Au. 5, 12, 1865, Mr. 3, 24, 1866 FTR; 9 Doc Hist 107-14; McNeill 318-9, 321-4

80; 1 McNeill 126-7, 333; 85 *SLCH* 2 (Labor and capital . . . relations between . . . testimony on . . . 1885) ; *Andrews* 347 (in Je. 1905 Commons) My. 7, 21, Je. 4, O. 15, 1864 FTR; 1864 Printer 86-7, 102, 104-5, 119

81; 1 D. 5, 1863, Je. 4, Jy. 16, Au. 8, O. 1, D. 17, 31, 1864 FTR

81; 2, 1883 NJLB 155

81; 3 Je. 6, 13, 1863, Ja. 23, Je. 4, Jy. 16, D. 17, 1864, Ap. 15, 1865 FTR; *Fite* 188-92, 201, 204 (Social and industrial conditions in the North during the Civil War)

81; 4 Ja. 23, F. 20, O. 8, 1864; F. 22, Je. 7, Jy. 8, 15, 29, S. 2, 16, 30, O. 7, D. 23, 1865, Ja. 6, 1866 FTR

83; 1 1183 NJLB 156; 9 Doc Hist 102-4; O. 24, 31, N. 7, 14, 1863, F. 20, Mr. 19, 26, Au. 20, S. 30. 1, 29, N. 5, 1864, Ja. 28, Ap. 4, My. 6, 13, 20, 27, Je. 10, Jy. 8, 22, O. 7, 14, 21, D. 26, 1865, Ja. 20, F. 4, Mr. 25, 1866 FTR

83; 2 Je. 13, O. 24, 1863, Ap. 23, D. 24, 31, 1864, Jy. 11, D. 16, 1865 FTR

83; 3 Jy. 8, 1865 FTR; 9 Doc Hist 99-103

84; 1 Jy. 22, S. 2, 9, 16, 30, O. 15, 1864, Je. 3, 10, 17, Jy. 16, O. 4, 1865, Ja. 13, 1866 FTR; 1883 NJLB 155; 1887 NJLB 81

85; 1 Mr. 18, 25, Ap. 8, My. 20, Je. 3, 10, 17, 24, Jy. 1, 15, 22, 29, Au. 5, 12, S. 2, 16, 23, O. 21, 1865, Ja. 27, F. 3, Ap. 28, My. 19, 1866 FTR

85; 2 Jy. 29, S. 12, 1865 FTR

85; 3 F. 4, 11, My. 27, Je. 3, 10, Jy. 29, Au. 5, S. 9, 1865 FTR; 1880 MSLB 21

86; 1 Ja. 4, Mr. 18, Ap. 8, My. 13, Je. 3, 17, 24, Jy. 1, 1865 FTR

86; 2 Jy. 9, 1864, Mr. 11, My. 27, Jy. 8, 15, 22, 29, Au. 19, 26, S. 9, 16, O. 7, 28, D. 26, 1865, Ja. 22, 1866, FTR

87; 1 Au. 19, S. 9, 1865 FTR

87; 2 S. 5, 1878 IA 14; Ja. 21, F. 11, Ap. 9, Je. 3, Jy. 1, 1865 FTR; 1878 PALB 150-9; 1887 PALB 15-8; 1887-8 COLB 179; Je. 12, 1879 IA 14; Au. 12, 1880 IA 9, 11; Je. 30, 1881 14, Au. 9, 188 IA 206-7

88; 1 Je. 30, 1881 IA 14; Au. 12, 1880 IA 9; 1881 MSLB 9-13; Je. 30, 1881 IA 14; McNeill 306

89; 1 Jy. 15, 22, Au. 19, 26, S. 16, 30, O. 7, 14, 1865, Ja. 6, My. 19, 1866 FTR

90; 1 F. 13, My. 28, Jy. 2, 9, 23, 1864, F. 18, Je. 3, 10, S. 2, 30, 1865, Ja. 17, F. 3, Mr. 10, 31, Ap. 21, 28, My. 14, 1866

FTR; 1867 IMU 5-6; Jy. 1839
LMJ 388, 1881 PALB 281; 2
Commons 49-50, and cf. p. 55
that emplrs. assns. in stove and
foundry industry had disap-
peared from 1865-72; see also
1867 IMU; 1868 IMU; 1892
NASM (Proceedings Natl. assn.
of stove mfrs.)
90; 2 Ap. 7, 21, My. 5 1866
FTR
91; 1 1880 MSLB 21-2; 1883
NJLB 156; Mr. 1866 *BEV* (Boston evening voice) ; Mr. 31,
Ap. 7, 21, 28, My. 19, 1866
FTR
92; 1 Ja. 20, 27, F. 3, 10, 17,
24, Mr. 3, 10, 17, 24, 31, Ap.
14, 21, 1866 FTR
93; 1 1871 MSLB 48; 1880
MSLB 21, 23-4; McNeill 218;
1881 PALB 280; Persons 11;
Mr. 14, 1867 BEV; S. 9, 23, 30,
O. 7, 14, 1865 FTR
93; 2 Ap. 5, 12, 1866 FTR;
McNeill 352-3; Mr. 14, 1867
BEV 2
93; 3 O. 1, 15, 29, D. 10, 17,
1864 FTR; Mr. 4, 11, 18, My.
13, Je. 3, 10, Jy. 15, 22, Au. 5,
19, S. 9, 16, 23, O. 7, 14, 21, 28,
N. 11, 25, D. 2, 9, 16, 23, 1865
FTR; Ja. 13, F. 3, 24, Mr. 3,
10, 24, 31, Ap. 7, 21, 28, My.
5, 12, 19; Au. 18, 1866 FTR
94; 1 F. 13, 1867 Boston daily
advertiser; Mr. 8, 14, 23, 25,
27, 1867 BEV
95; 1 Mr. 14, 23, 25, 27, 1867
BEV
95; 2 McNeill 374; Mr. 14,

20, 1867 BEV; Sylvis 251, 253,
264, 432-3, 436
96; 1 1888 MOLB 129-30, 132
96; 2 1873 PALB 322-3; 1881
PALB 281, 285-6; Mr. 14, 1867
BEV
97; 1 1873 PALB 333-4; 1881
MSLB 23
97; 2 1873 PALB 336-7; 1881
PALB 287-91; Powderly 413
97; 3 1881 PALB 291
97; 4 1881 PALB 291-5;
PALB 347-52
98; 1 D. 3, 1874 IA 3;
1873 PALB 333-4, 346-64; 1881
MSLB 32-42; 1879 PALB 130-9
98; 2 1883 NJLB 155, 157
98; 3 McNeill 321
99; 1 107 Mass 555; 107 Mass
Briefs; 85 SLCH 2: 1105-9; Mc-
Neill 131-2, 137, 139, 353-4; 4
ILLB 470-1
100; 1 1887 OHLB 201; Mc-
Neill 601
100; 2 1883 NJLB 156
100; 3 1880 OHLB 1155-6;
1883 NJLB 155; 1880 MSLB 32
101; 1 1871 MSLB 47-93;
1880 MSLB 30
101; 2 1871 MSLB 136-49;
1880 MSLB 29-31
102; 1 1880 MSLB 29; 1877
MSLB 26-33; 1871 MSLB 93-8
103; 1 1880 MSLB 27-9
103; 2 1880 MSLB 31; 1872
MSLB 434-6
104; 1 1877 MSLB 31-40; Bul
8 U.S. B.L 5-7 This case is discussed as very illustrative of
collective bargaining in *Lowell*

JSS (Journal of social science no. 28, O. 1891)

105; 1 Birmingham v. Gallagher, 112 Mass 190; 1880 MSLB 33; Mr. 11, 75 IA 3

105; 2 72 MSLB 436-7

106; 1 Au. 14 73 IA 16

106; 2 F. 13, 73 IA 16; 73 MSLB 252; 90 NYLB 397; Andrews 347

107; 1 My. 15, 73 IA 17

107; 2 Pamphlet itself (in NYC Pub. Lib.)

107; 3 Questionaire itself (in NYC Pub. Lib.)

108; 1 109; 1 My. 15, 73 IA 17

109; 2 My. 15, 73 IA 17; McNeill 143; Andrews 347

110; 1 My. 15, 73 IA 17; 85 SLCH 2; 1121; cf. Hilbert in Hollander and Barnett's American trade unionism

110; 2 Andrews 347; McNeill 146, 376

111; 1 83 NJLB 154; 81 MSLB 13; Je. 30, 84 IA 14

112; 1 1873 I A: F. 13 p. 16, Mr. 6, p. 16, Ap. 17 p. 16, My. 13-17, Jy. 30-16, S. 4-16, S. 11-20, D. 25-16, 1874 IA: Ja. 8-16, Ja. 22-16; Mr. 19-14; Ja. 10, 74 St. Louis Journal of Commerce 7

112; 2 F. 13, 73 IA 16

113; 1 F. 13, 73 IA 16; 77 OHLB 199

114; 1 80 MSLB 33-4; McNeill 146; N. 27, 73 IA 17; 83 NJLB 157; 77 OHLB 276

114; 2 81 PALB 305

114; 3 McNeill 321-4; Ja. 8, 76 IA 16

115; 1 McNeill 147- 8, 154, 220-1, 240, 603; My. 7, 74 IA 19, quoting IMJ

115; 2 88 MOLB 130, 133

115; 3 D. 74 IA 3

116; 1 81 MSLB 42-6

116; 2 McNeill 259

117; 1 Ap. 17, 73 IA 7; My. 15, 73 IA 16; 81 PALB 302

117; 2 81 PALB 303-5

117; 3 81 PALB 310; My. 19, 74 IA 11

118; 1 Ja. 22, 74 IA 16; 81 PALB 308; 81 MSLB 42-6; Ap. 20, 76 IA 14

118; 2 73 PALB 479, 502; 81 PALB 306-8

118; 3 McNeill 243

119; 1 Wright 155-9; 80 OHLB 1159; 87 OHLB 276; 81 MSLB 57-63

119; 2 80 OHLB 1168

119; 3 N. 12, 74 IA 20; N. 19, 74 IA 11

120; 1 Ap. 30, 74 IA 14; S. 1, 81 IA 17; Mr. 5, 74 IA 14; Ap. 16, 74 IA 15

120; 2, 3 Au. 13, 74 IA 14

121; 1 Au. 13, 74 IA 14; Mr. 12, 74 IA 14; My. 28, 74 IA 14;

121; 2 See p. 123 for pol. act., p. 125 for yellow-dog contract and strike compensation.

121; 3 Ap. 16, 74 IA 19;

122; 1 My. 7, 74 IA 15, 19; D. 5, 78 Iron Age 15; 80 MSLB 35; D. 3, 74 IA 15; 87 NJLB 157; 74 PALB 421-2; 77 OHLB 276

122; 2 D. 3, 74 IA 24; D. 24, 74 IA 20; Ap. 1, 75 IA 14

123; 1 Mr. 4, 75 IA 9; Mr. 11, 75 IA 14; Mr. 25, 75 IA 11; Ap. 8, 75 IA 14; Au. 12, 75 IA 3; Ja. 20, 76 IA 14; My. 18, 76 IA 15; My. 25, 76 IA 3

124; 1 Ap. 29, 75 IA 15; My. 6, 75 IA 14; Je. 24, 75 IA 14; O. 23, 75 IA 14; Ja. 20, 76 IA 14; My. 25, 76 IA 3; Jy. 12, 76 IA 14

124; 2 81 PALB 314-5

124; 3 80 OHLB 1160

124; 5 N. 26, 74 IA 14; D. 3, 74 IA 14; D. 31, 74 IA 14

125; 1 83 NJLB 155; S. 30 75 IA 15; 80 MSLB 40-2

127; 1 1774 IA: D. 10, 14-5, 18; D. 17-15; 1775 IA: Mr. 4-15; Mr. 18-9; Mr. 23-17, 20; Ap. 22-14; Ap. 29-17; My. 6-14; D. 16-15; 1776 IA: F. 17-15; Mr. 9-14-5; My. 18-15; Je. 1-23; Je. 8-14; Je. 22-14-5; Jy. 20-14-5; Je. 12, 79 IA 14; Au. 12, 80 IA 11; 79 PALB 150-9; 81 PALB 311-3, 316; 87 PALB G15-8

127; 2 Ja. 14, 75 IA 14; Ap. 15, 75 IA 14-5; Ap. 22, 75 IA 14

128; 1 Ja. 14, 75 IA 11; O. 15, 74 IA 20; D. 31 IA 24; Ap. 1, 75 IA 7; My. 27, 75 IA 7

128; 2 Ap. 16, 74 IA 15

128; 3 Ap. 2, 74 IA 9

128; 4 Ap. 15, 75 IA 14-6; Ap. 29, 75 IA 23; Je. 30, 81 IA 14

128; 5 O. 26, 82 IA 4

129; 1 D. 2, 75 IA 14; Au. 24, 76 IA 15; Ap. 20, 76 IA 14; Ja. 11, 77 IA 15; Ap. 27, 76 IA 14; S. 14, 76 IA 17

129; 2 83 OHLB 248; Mc-Neill 223, 225, 609

130; 1 92 NASM; Ja. 16, 73 IA 17; Bul 62 USBL 124; Ja. 27, 76 IA 15, cf. Saposs in 1 Commons 53-4; Ap. 1, 75 IA 9; My. 4, 76 IA 14-5; Je. 20, 76 IA 14-5; Au. 3, 76 IA 15; Mr. 23, 76 IA 20

130; 2 D. 2, 76 IA 14

131; 1 Ja. 27, 75 IA 23; D. 7, 76 IA 3; 80 OHLB 1161; 77 OHLB 149

131; 2 88 PALB G5-7; Je. 22, 76 IA 15; O. 5, 76 IA 15

132; 1 87 MSLB 40-9; 80 MSLB 43, 47-8

132; 2 80 MSLB 447

134; 1 Jy. 19, 77 IA 14; N. 15, 77 IA 14; Au. 30, 77 IA 5

134; 2 O. 11, 77 IA 14; Powderly 417

135; 1 Mr. 15, 77 IA 24; 1877 Mich. Acts 11, p. 5

135; 2 My. 3, 77 IA 3, 5

135; 3 Logan's A city's danger and defense 13-4; Sylvis 430-2

135; 4 Au. 16, 77 IA 24; Au. 23, 77 IA 14

136; 1 81 PALB 317-65; Au. 2, 77 IA 14

136; 2 Swinton 179-209

137; 1 Jy. 26, 77 IA 14; Au. 2, 77 IA 14-5, 26; Au. 9, 77 IA 14; Au. 16, 77 IA 17, 24; Au. 23, 77 IA 14; S. 6, 77 IA 18; O. 25, 77 IA 14; N. 29, 77 IA 14;

153; 1 F. 6, 79 IA 17; F. 13, 79 IA 14; F. 27, 79 IA 3; Mr. 6, 79 IA 14; Je. 5, 79 IA 13-4; Jy. 13, 79 IA 26; Au. 28, 79 IA 14-5; S. 4, 79 IA 14; D. 2, 80 IA 3; Cf. 2 Commons 504— An injunction was granted against glassblowers interfering with Belgian strikebreakers at Zanesville, Ohio in Jan. 1880; 9 Abb NC 393 (NY 1880) Johnston Harvester v. Meinhardt

153; 2 N. 27, 79 IA 14

154; 1 F. 6, 79 IA 17; F. 13, 79 IA 15; O. 16, 79 IA 3, 57; O. 30, 79 IA 22; N. 6, 79 IA 14

154; 2 My. 22, 79 IA 13; O. 23, 79, IA 13; *Coffin's* Complaint of labor 15

154; 3 F. 20, 79 IA 1; Mr. 6, 79 IA 5, 29; Mr. 13, 79 IA 15

155; 1 Mr. 27, 79 IA 11; Je. 12, 79 IA 13; O. 16, 79 IA 13; D. 11, 79 IA 11, 13; Ja. 8, 80 IA 11

156; 1 O. 16, 79 IA 13; N. 20, 79 IA 20; D. 4, 79 IA 17; 80 OHLB 1153, 1164-9

157; 1 F. 13, 79 IA 16; Mr. 13, 79 IA 18, 24; Ap. 10, 79 IA 13; Jy. 17, 79 IA 13; Au. 7, 79 IA 24; N. 20, 79 IA 20; 81 PALB 382

157; 2 Ja. 79 IA 13; F. 20, 79 IA 11; Mr. 6, 79 IA 29; Mr. 20, 79 IA 15; Mr. 27, 79 IA 11, 22; Ap. 10, 79 IA 13, 20; My. 29, 79 IA 16; Je. 19, 79 IA 13

158; 1 Ap. 10, 79 IA 20; Ap.

17, 79 IA 20; My. 1, 79 IA 17; N. 13, 79 IA 9, 11, 13-4

159; 1 S. 18, 79 IA 13; O. 2, 79 IA 14; O. 30, 79 IA 22; N. 13, 79 IA 11; 81 MSLB 46-54

159; 2 N. 6, 79 IA 14; D. 11, 79 IA 13; 81 PALB 374, 376

160; 1 S. 4, 79 IA 13; D. 4, 79 IA 17; Ap. 19, 83 IA 15; Wright 145, 151, 153, 258; McNeill 252; 81 MSLB 54-6; 79 PALB 142-9; 81 PALB 373-6

161; 1 F. 6, 79 IA 19; F. 13, 79 IA 14; Mr. 13, 79 IA 14; Ap. 17, 79 IA 15; McNeill 307

162; 1 81 PALB 371; My. 22, 79 IA 14; My. 29, 79 IA 15; Je. 5, 79 IA 14; Je. 12, 79 IA 13-4; Au. 12, 80 IA 11; Au. 9, 88 IA 206-7

162; 2 81 MSLB 13-8; Au. 21, 79 IA 15; Au. 28, 79 IA 14-5

162; 3 Ap. 17, 79 IA 14, 20; My. 29, 79 IA 15-6; Jy. 3, 79 IA 14; D. 4, 79 IA 17; D. 11, 79 IA 13

163; 1 Wright 115

163; 2 F. 13, 79 IA 16; Mr. 6, 79 IA 29; Ap. 22, 79 IA 13; Au. 14, 79 IA 22; Au. 28, 79 IA 15; S. 4, 79 IA 13; O. 16, 79 IA 13

163; 3 S. 18, 79 IA 3; 81 PALB 370

164; 1 McNeill 232; 4 ILLB 370; Jy. 17, 79 IA 15; Au. 7, 79 IA 24; Je. 19, 79 IA 13; S. 11, 79 IA 20

165; 1 F. 20, 79 IA 11; My. 22, 79 IA 13; Jy. 3, 79 IA 26;

Jy. 17, 79 IA 13; Au. 21, 79 IA 11, 13; Au. 28, 79 IA 15; S. 28, 79 IA 13; Ja. 8, 80 IA 11; 83 NJLB 155

166; 1 Au. 7, 79 IA 24; S. 18, 79 IA 13; O. 9, 79 IA 7

168; 1 Ja. 29, 80 IA 14; Mr. 11, 80 IA 13; My. 6, 80 IA 15; My. 27, 80 IA 15; Je. 17, 80 IA 14; S. 23, 80 IA 15; O. 23, 80 IA 14; N. 4, 80 IA 14; D. 9, 80 IA 14; D. 23, 80 IA 14; Ja. 6, 81 IA 14; Mr. 3, 81 IA 13; Mr. 10, 81 IA 11, 13-4; Mr. 17, 81 IA 14; Ap. 28, 81 IA 13

168; 2 Ap. 26, 80 IA 3; S. 16, 80 IA 14; S. 23, 80 IA 3; D. 9, 80 IA 11; D. 16, 80 IA 14; F. 3, 81 IA 14; D. 15, 80 Times

168; 4 McNeill 310

168; 5 McNeill 461

169; 1 McNeill 462

169; 2 Quoted from the Duke of Argyle in *Weeks'* Labor differences 76; McNeill 309-10

169; 3 Abram S. Hewitt in 85 SCLH 1: 457

169; 4 Weeks 63

170; 1 Weeks 7-8

170; 2 McNeill 179; Weeks 30, 37, 57; 85 SCLH 1: 305

172; 1 F. 5, 80 IA 26; F. 12, 80 IA 15; Mr. 11, 80 IA 15; Ap. 15, 80 IA 13; Ap. 26, 80 IA 7; My. 20, 80 IA 26; My. 27, 80 IA 15; Je. 3, 80 IA 13, 22, 24; Je. 17, 80 IA 14, 23; Jy. 1, 80 IA 13; Jy. 22, 80 IA 14; Jy. 29, 80 IA 22; Au. 12, 80 IA 11; S. 16, 80 IA 15, 24;

Au. 9, 88 IA 206-7; Wright 117; 81 MSLB 15-8

172; 2 Ja. 29, 80 IA 22; F. 12, 80 IA 14; F. 26, 80 IA 13; My. 6, 80 IA 13

173; 1 F. 26, 80 IA 13; Mr. 11, 80 IA 13; Je. 24, 80 IA 20; 80 OHLB 1189

173; 2 O. 28, 80 IA 20

173; 3 My. 13, 80 IA 24; Jy. 8, 80 IA 20

174; 1 F. 26, 80 IA 13; Mr. 11, 80 IA 13; Mr. 18, 80 IA 22; Mr. 25, 80 IA 22; Ap. 1, 80 IA 13; Ap. 8, 80 IA 26; Ap. 15, 80 IA 14; Ap. 22, 80 IA 11; My. 20, 80 IA 26

174; 2 My. 20, 80 IA 15

174; 3 Jy. 22, 80 IA 14, 20; Je. 30, 81 IA 14; 81 PALB 383-4; McNeill 289

174; 4 F. 12, 80 IA 7

175; 1 F. 5, 80 IA 26; F. 12, 80 IA 22; F. 26, 80 IA 13; Mr. 18, 80 IA 22; Ap. 22, 80 IA 11; My. 16, 80 IA 13

175; 2 Au. 19, 80 IA 19; Au. 26, 80 IA 14; S. 2, 80 IA 11

175; 3 80 OHLB 1189

176; 1 Ja. 29, 80 IA 22; F. 5, 80 IA 26; F. 12, 80 IA 22; F. 19, 80 IA 14; F. 26, 80 IA 13; Mr. 11, 80 IA 14; Ap. 1, 80 IA 15, 22; 81 PALB 377

176; 2 81 PALB 378-9

176; 3 Jy. 29, 80 IA 22; Au. 5, 80 IA 24

176; 4 Au. 5, 80 IA 15; S. 6, 80 IA 24

176; 5 S. 30, 80 IA 13; O. 7, 80 IA 24; 81 PALB 379

176; 6 O. 21, 80 IA 22

177; 1 Jy. 22, 80 IA 20; Jy. 29, 80 IA 22; Au. 5, 80 IA 24; S. 2, 80 IA 11; S. 16, 80 IA 24; S. 23, 80 IA 13-4; S. 30, 80 IA 13; O. 28, 80 IA 20

177; 2 O. 28, 80 IA 20

178; 1 Ja. 29, 80 IA 9; O. 20, 80 IA 20; D. 30, 80 IA 14

178; 2 F. 5, 80 IA 11

178; 3 F. 5, 80 IA 26; F. 26, 80 IA 13; Mr. 11, 80 IA 13; Mr. 18, 80 IA 22; 95-6 COLB 66

179; 1 Mr. 11, 80 IA 13; My. 6, 80 IA 13; My. 13, 80 IA 24; My. 20, 80 IA 15, 26; Je. 10, 80 IA 21-2; Je. 17, 80 IA 22; S. 23, 80 IA 13; D. 30, 80 IA 13; Ja. 13, 81 IA 20

180; 1 87-8 COLB 136-8; 95-6 COLB 66; McNeill 612

180; 2 80 OHLB 1193-4; 83 NJLB 154; 156; 4 ILLB 369

181; 1 Ja. 29, 80 IA 22; Ap. 29, 80 IA 20; My. 13, 80 IA 15; Jy. 1, 80 IA 7, 9; Au. 26, 80 IA 22; S. 30, 80 IA 13; 83 NJLB 155; 87 NJLB 165-6

181; 2 F. 12, 80 IA 22; Au. 26, 80 IA 22; D. 2, 80 IA 13

182; 1 McNeill 166, 366-7; S. 9, 80 Times 5; O. 7, 80 Times 5; S. 19, 80 IA 19; F. 3, 81 IA 14

183; 1 McNeill 233, 240; 80 MSLB 53-63

183; 2 83 OHLB 248; 86 OHLB 1185-7; 4 ILLB 370

183; 3 Jy. 15, 80 IA 20; 80 OHLB 90-1; Au. 6, 29, S. 9, 80 Times

183; 5 S. 4, 81 IA 15; S. 28, 81 IA 17

184; 1 O. 27, 81 IA 15; D. 29, 81 IA 15

185; 1 D. 8, 81 IA 20; Jy. 28, 81 IA 24; 81 PALB 386; Au. 4, 81 IA 26; D. 1, 81 IA 26; D. 8, 81 IA 13; My. 5, 81 IA 14; Je. 2, 81 IA 17; Je. 9, 81 IA 13; Au. 18, 81 IA 13; S. 22, 81 IA 15; O. 13, 81 IA 20; Mr. 10, 81 IA 14; Mr. 31, 81 IA 24; Je. 16, 81 IA 13; Je. 30, 81 IA 17; Proceedings of the *Hocking* Valley investigating committee of the General Assembly of Ohio, 1885, pp. 180-1

185; 2 S. 15, 81 IA 26

185; 3 My. 5, 81 IA 28; Ap. 14, 81 IA 26; Au. 18, 81 IA 13;

186; 1 Jy. 21, 81 IA 19; S. 15, 81 IA 26; S. 22, 81 IA 15

186; 2 McNeill 290-1; 81 OHLB 212-7; Je. 30, 81 IA 14-5; Jy. 7, 81 IA 15; Jy. 21, 81 IA 19; Au. 4, 81 IA 6, 15, 26; S. 8, 81 IA 20; S. 15, 81 IA 26; O. 13, 81 IA 20; O. 27, 81 IA 17; N. 3, 81 IA 15, 28; N. 10, 81 IA 11, 15

187; 1 My. 5, 81 IA 28; My. 26, 81 IA 24; Je. 2, 81 IA 15, 17; Je. 16, 81 IA 22; Je. 23, 81 IA 22; Jy. 7, 81 IA 15; Jy. 21, 81 IA 19; Au. 4, 81 IA 14; S. 15, 81 IA 26

188; 1 81 MSLB 18; Mr. 3, 81 IA 24; Ap. 14, 81 IA 26; Je. 9, 81 IA 13; Je. 23, 81 IA 22,

26; Jy. 28, 81 IA 14; Au. 18, 81
IA 14; S. 15, 81 IA 26; O. 6,
81 IA 22; D. 22, 81 IA 14; D.
29, 81 IA 9
  188; 2 F. 24, 81 IA 14, 19;
Mr. 3, 81 IA 13; Mr. 17, 81 IA
13; Mr. 31, 81 IA 24; Ap. 14, 81
IA 26; Ap. 28, 81 IA 24; Au.
18, 81 IA 13; S. 1, 81 IA 26;
S. 8, 81 IA 20; O. 13, 81 IA 20;
83 NJLB 156
  189; 1 O. 6, 81 IA 22; O. 20,
81 IA 26; D. 27, 81 IA 17; 83
NJLB 154, 156-7; 81 PALB
385-6
  189; 2 F. 3, 81 IA 26; Je. 2,
81 IA 15, 17; Je. 9, 81 IA 11
  190; 1 Au. 18, 81 IA 13; S. 1,
81 IA 26; S. 15, 81 IA 26; S.
22, 81 IA 15; O. 27, 81 IA 17;
D. 22, 81 IA 9
  190; 2 McNeill 362
  191; 1 81 PALB 385; O. 27,
81 IA 17, 26; N. 17, 81 IA 17;
D. 26, 81 IA 26
  191; 2 Ap. 21, 81 IA 24; 81
PALB 385-6; 83-4 WILB 140-
4; 151-3
  191; 3 F. 3, 81 IA 14; S. 22,
81 IA 3; O. 13, 81 IA 20
  192; 1 81 PALB 386; 94
NHLB 459--60; 83 NJLB 155;
85 SCLH 1: 861-3
  192; 2 O. 20, 81 IA 26; 83
NJLB 154; 83 WILB 140-4
  193; 1 O. 27, 81 IA 17, 26; S.
8, 81 IA 20; S. 29, 81 IA 19;
83 NJLB 154
  194; 1 F. 16, 82 IA 14; Mr.
23, 82 IA 4; Je. 1, 82 IA 14;
Jy. 6, 82 IA 15, 17, 22; Jy. 20,

82 IA 19; Au. 10, 82 IA 14,
19; Au. 17, 82 IA 15
  194; 2 Je. 1, 82 IA 15; S. 28,
82 IA 14-5
  195; 1 Mr. 30, 82 IA 14; Ap.
6, 82 IA 13
  195; 2 My. 25, 82 IA 14; Je.
22, 82 IA 13
  196; 1 Ap. 20, 82 IA 15, 26;
Ap. 27, 82 IA 14; My. 4, 82 IA
15; My. 11, 82 IA 26; My. 18,
82 IA 19; My. 25, 82 IA 14
  196; 2 Ja. 4, 1940 Amal 3; Je.
22, 82 IA 14-5
  197; 1 Je. 8, 82 IA 14; Je. 15,
82 IA 14; Je. 29, 82 IA 14; Jy.
13, 82 IA 23; Au. 24, 82 IA 14;
Au. 31, 82 IA 24; 82 PALB
175-90
  197; 2 F. 23, 82 IA 19; Mr.
9, 82 IA 13; Ap. 6, 82 IA 30;
Jy. 6, 82 IA 14, 22; Au. 7, 82
IA 26; S. 7, 82 IA 21
  197; 3 Je. 1, 82 IA 14-5;
Jy. 20, 82 IA 14
  197; 4 S. 28, 82 IA 15; 82
PALB 175-90; 82 OHLB 113-7;
McNeill 293; F. 20, 1940 Amal
3; O. 12, 82 IA 15; O. 19, 82
IA 24; O. 26, 82 IA 4, 19; N.
16, 82 IA 15
  197; 5 N. 30, 82 IA 26; Mc-
Neill 294
  198; 1 N. 16, 82 IA 15; Je.
1, 82 IA 15; O. 12, 82 IA 15;
O. 19, 82 IA 24; O. 26, 82 IA
4, 19; N. 9, 82 IA 19; N. 16,
82 IA 15; D. 7, 82 IA 23; Jy.
20, 82 IA 22; Au. 10, 82 IA 24
  199; 1 Mr. 9, 82 IA 14, 22;
Mr. 23, 82 IA 11; My. 25, 82 IA

14; Je. 1, 82 IA 15, 30; Je. 22,
82 IA 14, 20; Je. 29, 82 IA 19,
24; Jy. 27, 82 IA 14, 24; Au.
3, 82 IA 30; Au. 17, 82 IA 15,
26; Au. 24, 82 IA 14; S. 28, 82
IA 26; O. 5, 82 IA 14; N. 9, 82
IA 15; N. 16, 82 IA 15; 82
OHLB 110-1, 149-50; N. 23,
82 IA 15; D. 21, 82 IA 14
    200; 1 F. 23, 82 IA 19; Mr.
9, 82 IA 13; My. 25, 82 IA 11;
N. 30, 82 IA 2, 26
    200; 2 F. 9, 82 IA 26; F. 23,
82 IA 19; Mr. 23, 82 IA 11; Mr.
30, 82 IA 24; Ap. 6, 82 IA 30;
My. 18, 82 IA 13; D. 7, 82 IA
23; D. 28, 82 IA 26; 82 PALB
190
    201; 1 Ja. 12, 82 IA 14-5; Mr.
28, 82 IA 14-5; Je. 29, 82 IA
15; Jy. 6, 82 IA 22
    202; 1 Ja. 5, 82 IA 13; Ja.
19, 82 IA 26; F. 16, 82 IA 19;
Mr. 23, 82 IA 11; Mr. 30, 82 IA
24; Ap. 13; 82 IA 24; Je. 1, 82
IA 30; Je. 15, 82 IA 11; Je.
22, 82 IA 20; Jy. 6, 82 IA 15,
22; Jy. 27, 82 IA 19; Au. 10,
82 IA 14, 24; Au. 17, 82 IA 26;
Au. 24, 82 IA 24; Au. 31, 82 IA
30; 82 PALB 147-63; McNeill
261
    203; 1 Mr. 30, 82 IA 24; Ap.
6, 82 IA 9, 28; Ap. 13, 82 IA
26; My. 18, 82 IA 13; Jy. 6, 82
IA 15; Au. 10, 82 IA 14, 24;
Au. 17, 82 IA 15, 30; Au. 24,
82 IA 14, 24; N. 2, 82 IA 17;
N. 23, 82 IA 14; N. 30, 82 IA
14; N. 9, 82 IA 19; O. 5, 82
IA 30; Ap. 27, 82 IA 11; My.

25, 82 IA 11; My. 4, 82 IA 21;
Ap. 27, 82 IA 11; Mr. 16, 82
IA 13; O. 5, 82 IA 30; 82
OHLB 81-3, 85-7; 82 PALB
163-70
    204; 1 Ap. 6, 82 IA 15; 82
PALB 144-5
    204; 2 F. 9, 82 IA 26; Au. 24,
82 IA 24; Au. 31, 82 IA 13; O.
26, 82 IA 19; 83 NJLB 150, 155
    205; 1 82 OHLB 31-41; Mr.
23, 82 IA 11; My. 18, 82 IA 13
    205; 2 82 OHLB 41-3; My.
18, 82 IA 13
    205; 3 82 OHLB 43-4
    206; 1 83 NJLB 154
    206; 2 82 OHLB 255-6; 85
OHLB 233-4
    207; 1 F. 6, 82 IA 7; McNeill
236; 85 SLCH 1: 80-1 Mr. 23,
82 IA 1; Ja. 19, 82 IA 26; Ap.
6, 82 IA 14
    207; 2 85 SCLH 1: 198, 200;
82 OHLB 60-5; Ely 85; Mc-
Neill 168-9
    208; 1 2 ILLB 265-78, 4 ILLB
390, 394; Je. 15, 82 IA 11;
    209; 1 F. 9, 82 IA 26; Jy. 27,
82 IA 19; Au. 17, 82 IA 26; 83
NJLB 151-2; 85-6 WILB 247-8;
SCLH 2: 303, 1115-6, 1118
    210; 2 Ap. 12, 83 IA 14, 17;
Ap. 19, 83 IA 14; Ap. 26, 83
IA 17; My. 17, 83 IA 14; My.
24, 83 IA 14; Je. 7, 83 IA 14;
Je. 14, 83 IA 14
    211; 1 My. 3, 83 IA 14; Ja.
11, 83 IA 26; Ja. 18, 83 IA 17,
19; Ja. 25, 83 IA 26; F. 7, 83 IA
17; F. 22, 83 IA 24; Mr. 15, 83
IA 11; Mr. 22, 83 IA 28; Ap.

84 IA 23; S. 4, 84 IA 22; S. 11, 84 IA 16; 84 PALB 73-8

224; 4 87 PALB F8-13; Mr. 20, 84 IA 16

225; 1 87-8 COLB 139-46

226; 1 My. 1, 84 IA 24; Jy. 10, 84 IA 16; Jy. 24, 84 IA 23; Au. 7, 84 IA 15; McNeill 375; 88 PALB F15-6

226; 2 5 ILLB 314-5; 4 ILLB 369; McNeill 169; 90 NYLB 410; 85-6 WILB 247-8; So the railroad kings itch for an empire, do they?

227; 1 McNeill 395

227; 2 *Lowell Ind.* 64-74 (Industrial Arbitration a n d Conciliation)

228; 1 McNeill 395; 85 COLB 31-4; 91 COLB 131-49, 175

229; 1 McNeill 237-8, 584

229; 2 D. 4, 84 IA 22, 31, 39; D. 11, 84 IA 27; D. 25, 84 IA 16, 32

229; 3 O. 15, 85 IA 20; McNeill 423

230; 1 McNeill 310-11; Ja. 29, 85 IA 15; Mr. 5, 85 IA 22; Mr. 19, 85 IA 18; My. 14, 85 IA 16; F. 22, 1940 Amal 3; Je. 4, 85 IA 22-3; Je. 11, 85 IA 17

231; 1 My. 21, 85 IA 11; My. 28, 85 IA 16; Je. 18, 85 IA 24; Je. 25, 85 IA 16-7; Au. 9, 98 IA 206-7

231; 2 Jy. 2, 85 IA 23;

232; 1 Jy. 30, 85 IA 16; Au. 6, 85 IA 22; Au. 13, 85 IA 14-5; S. 3, 85 IA 22; S. 10, 85 IA 17; O. 1, 85 IA 33; N. 19, 85 IA 24; N. 26, 85 IA 24; D. 17, 85 IA 22; F. 5, 85 IA 15; Ja. 6, 87 IA 31; McNeill 296-7

232; 2 O. 29, 85 IA 27; D. 31, 85 IA 22

232; 3 F. 19, 85 IA 16-7

232; 4 Mr. 19, 85 IA 19, 29; Ap. 9, 85 IA 17; Ap. 16, 85 IA 18; Ap. 30, 85 IA 16; S. 17, 85 IA 33; O. 29, 85 IA 27; N. 12, 85 IA 22; N. 19, 85 IA 31; N. 26, 85 IA 17, 31 D. 17, 85 IA 18, 22; D. 31, 85 IA 14, 20

233; 1 McNeill 256

233; 2 4 ILLB 395, 397, 399; 1 10LB 158; S. 17, 85 IA 33

233; 3 *Gould* and Wines's Report on the coal miners' strike in Northern Illinois, 1889, pp. 10, 22, 24

234; 1 N. 12, 85 IA 27; N. 26, 85 IA 17, 31; D. 17, 85 IA 18; D. 31, 85 IA 14; Hocking 4-5, 9, 14-6

234; 2 McNeill 210-1; Mr. 3, 87 IA 13; Ap. 2, 85 IA 11, 13; 0.29, 85 IA 18

235; 1 McNeill 137, 210-12

235; 2 Au. 27, 85 IA 33; 0.1, 85 IA 33; D. 10, 85 IA 31

236; 1 87 NJLB 157; McNeill 380-2;

236; 2 1 MDLB 206-8; 2 MDLB 70

237; 1 85-6 MGLB 92-126, 238-46; 6 KALB 120

237; 2 85-6 WILB 269-70; 85 MGLB 85; My. 21, 85 IA 17; N. 19, 85 IA 27; 87-8 CALB 81

252; 1, 253; 1, 2 Au. 5, 86 IA 20-1
254; 1 Ap. 29, 86 IA 18 quoting *Boston Commercial Advertiser*
254; 2 My. 20, 86 IA 22; Je. 10, 86 IA 13
254; 3 My. 13, 86 IA 24; My. 20, 86 IA 31; 90 NYLB 387
255; 1, 2 Ap. 29, 86 IA 18
255; 3 My. 13, 86 IA 24; 86 NYLB 492-3; 90 NYLB 387
257; 1 My. 6, 86 IA 22, 33; S. 9, 86 IA 35
258; 1 Ap. 1, 86 IA 17; Ap. 29, 86 IA 31; My. 6, 86 IA 33; My. 13, 86 IA 18, 22
258; 2 Je. 17, 86 IA 18; Jy. 29, 86 IA 14, 31; O. 7, 86 IA 17; D. 23, 86 IA 11, 14
259; 1 Jy. 29, 86 IA 31; Au. 12, 86 IA 33; S. 16, 86 IA 18; O. 21, 86 IA 15; N. 25, 86 IA 33
259; 2 Je. 3, 86 IA 26, 31; Je. 17, 86 IA 22, 25; Je. 24, 86 IA 15, 20; Jy. 29, 86 IA 15; 87 PALB G18-9; McNeill 305
261; 1 Ja. 7, 86 IA 22; Ja. 28, 86 IA 22; F. 18, 86 IA 17, 22; F. 25, 86 IA 16, 22; Mr. 18, 86 IA 16, 22; Ap. 22, 86 IA 13; Jy. 1, 86 IA 20; Au. 26, 86 IA 29; S. 21, 86 IA 33; S. 30 86 IA 20
261; 2 4 ILLB 392
262; 1 Je. 17, 86 IA 17-8; 87 NYLB 296-8, 306
262; 2 My. 13, 86 IA 18; Au. 19, 86 IA 29; S. 16, 86 IA 18;

N. 11, 86 IA 13; 86 NJLB 193-4; 87 NJLB 223-4
263; 1 Ja. 14, 86 IA 15; Mr. 18, 86 IA 15; D. 9, 86 IA 23; D. 23, 86 IA 30; 85 OHLB 252-3; 4 ILLB 396
263; 2 2 MDLB 72
264; 1 87 NJLB 232-42
264; 2 Ja. 28, 86 IA 22; F. 11, 86 IA 22; F. 18, 86 IA 22; F. 25, 86 IA 16, 22; Ap. 29, 86 IA 27; N. 25, 86 IA 17; D. 2, 86 IA 18-9; D. 30, 86 IA 30; 87 PALB F8-13
265; 1 4 ILLB 392; 86 NYLB 521; 90 NYLB 410; D. 23, 86 IA 13
265; 2 4 ILLB 377; My. 13, 86 IA 18; My. 20, 86 IA 31; 2 MDLB 68-9
266; 1 My. 20, 86 IA 31; 4 ILLB 381; 90 NYLB 418-20; My. 13, 86 IA 18; Je. 3, 86 IA 22
266; 2 4 ILLB 369, 393; 87 OHLB 36; 2 MDLB 78
267; 1 F. 4, 86 IA 39; 87 RILB 58-9; 87 NYLB 167-71; 90 NYLB 390
267; 2 My. 20, 86 IA 31; O. 14, 86 IA 33
269; 1 87 MGLB 430; 4 ILLB 369, 380, 384-6, 470; 86 NYLB 590; 90 NYLB 417; 91 NAB 82; 86 NJLB 206; My. 6, 86 IA 33; My. 20, 86 IA 31; My. 27, 86 IA 20, 31; Je. 3, 86 IA 22
269; 2 2 MDLB 68
269; 3 87 OHLB 36; 86 NJLB 216-17; My. 6, 86 IA 33

269; 4 89 NAB 13; Au. 19,
86 IA 13; S. 9, 86 IA 35
  270; 1 N. 4, 86 IA 17
  270; 2 S. 9, 86 IA 35; O. 7, 86
IA 17; O. 14, 86 IA 35
  271; 1 Ja. 21, 86 IA 31; F.
11, 86 IA 23; O. 28, 86 IA 29;
N. 18, 86 IA 35; N. 25, 86 IA
18, 35
  272; 1 Je. 3, 86 IA 31; Jy.
29, 86 IA 31; Au. 5, 86 IA
35; S. 9, 86 IA 35; 86 NJLB
195-8; 87 NJLB 83, 222-3; 90
NJLB 419-29; 2 MDLB 77; S.
16, 86 IA 18; S. 23, 86 IA 33;
S. 30, 86 IA 33; D. 2, 86 IA 15;
D. 30, 86 IA 31
  272; 2 Mr. 10, 87 IA 15; My.
13, 86 IA 18; Au. 26, 86 IA 15;
94 Chicago Strike 241
  272; 3 O. 21, 86 IA 15; N.
11, 86 IA 13
  272; 4 Au. 12, 86 IA 31; Au.
19, 86 IA 11
  273; 1 87-8 CALB 32, 54-5,
81; 91-2 CALB 171, 175-6, 179
  274; 1 Mr. 25, 86 IA 18; My.
27, 86 IA 29; O. 7, 86 IA 17;
N. 11, 86 IA 13; N. 18, 86 IA
33; 94 NHLB 462
  274; 2 Je. 26, 86 IA 15; Jy.
29, 86 IA 192; 87 NJLB 174-5
  275; 1 Ap. 1, 86 IA 17; Ap.
8, 86 IA 33; Je. 10, 86 IA 13;
O. 14, 86 IA 33; D. 2, 86 IA
13; D. 30, 86 IA 13, 18; 86
NYLB 576-83; 87 NYLB 317-9
  276; 1 86 NYLB 501, 539-43,
617-9
  276; 2 86 NYLB 220-1; 85-6

WILB 291; 4 ILLB 388, 391
  277; 1 86 NJLB 207-10
  278; 1 86 NYLB 544-5, 559-
60, 562; 90 NYLB 411-2; F. 4,
86 IA 39
  279; 1 Je. 17, 86 IA 18; S.
2, 86 IA 19; McNeill 206; 85-
6 WILB 292-3; 86 NJLB 219-20
  279; 2 86 NJLB 217-8; 87
NJLB 228-32; S. 30, 86 IA 30
  279; 3 86 NJLB 216; 86
NYLB 569
  280; 1 Jy. 29, 86 IA 31; Au.
12, 86 IA 33; O. 7, 86 IA 17;
O. 14, 86 IA 33; O. 21, 86 IA
21-2; O. 28, 86 IA 11, 20; N.
11, 86 IA 11; N. 18, 86 IA 17,
22, 33; 4 ILLB 369; 5 ILLB
314-5; 86 NYLB 500
  281; 1 91 MOLB 27-8
  281; 2 4 ILLB 368; 86 NYLB
497-8
  281; 3 Ja. 21, 86 IA 31; 86
NYLB 524-9; 2 MDLB 75-6;
92 MDLB 203; 85-6 WILB 319
  282; 1 Ap. 29, 86 IA 31; 86
NJLB 221-2; 86 NYLB 488-9
  282; 3 2 MDLB 73; 4 ILLB
369, 381, 395; 86 NYLB 556;
Jy. 29, 86 IA 31
  283; 2 Je. 30, 87 IA 25
  283; 3 Mr. 10, 87 IA 13; Je.
9, 87 IA 13, 33
  283; 4 Jy. 21, 87 IA 27; D.
23, 86 IA 14
  284; 2 Ap. 28, 87 IA 17
  284; 3 Je. 2, 87 IA 20, 26
  284; 4, 285; 1 F. 3, 87 IA 23
  285; 2 87 NYLB 148; Au. 11,
87 IA 20

285; 3 Ja. 20, 87 IA 33; F. 3, 87 IA 15, 18, 23, 37; Mr. 3, 87 IA 7; Mr. 10, 87 IA 19; Mr. 17, 87 IA 11-2, 23; Mr. 31, 87 IA 23; Ap. 7, 87 IA 27; My. 5, 97 IA 37; My. 12, 87 IA 13; Je. 2, 87 IA 16; Au. 11, 87 IA 13; O. 6, 87 IA 9

Mr. 17, 87 IA 11, 13; Mr. 24, 87 IA 19; Ap. 14, 87 IA 18-9; 286; 1 Mr. 3, 87 IA 7, 26; Mr. 17, 87 IA 11, 13; Mr. 24, 87 IA 19, Ap. 14, 87 IA 18, 9; Ja. 12, 88 IA 16

286; 2 Ap. 14, 87 IA 15; My. 26, 87 IA 13; Jy. 21, 87 IA 26

286; 3 Mr. 17, 87 IA 29; Je. 9, 87 IA 17, 31; Je. 16, 87 IA 17; Je. 30, 87 IA 19, 25; Je. 23, 87 IA 27; Jy. 21, 87 IA 17; D. 29, 87 IA 13; Ja. 12, 88 IA 55

287; 1 Je. 16, 87 IA 27; Ja. 19, 88 IA 113; Ja. 26, 88 IA 151

287; 2 Ap. 14, 87 IA 13; Ap. 21, 87 IA 16-7; 87 OHLB 35

288; 1 My. 5, 87 IA 25; My. 12, 87 IA 24

289; 1 Ap. 7, 87 IA 19; Ap. 14, 87 IA 13; Ap. 21, 87 IA 16; Ap. 28, 87 IA 17; My. 5, 87 IA 17; My. 12, 87 IA 17, 24; Je. 9, 87 IA 24; Jy. 21, 87 IA 26; Ja. 19, 88 IA 102; Ja. 26, 88 IA 154; Jy. 26, 88 IA 121; 87 MGLB 431; 88 KALB 296-7

290; 1 Ja. 6, 87 IA 37; F. 24, 87 IA 25; Ap. 7, 87 IA 39; My. 12, 87 IA 25; My. 26, 87 IA 16; Je. 9, 87 IA 33; Jy. 7, 87 IA 21; Au. 4, 87 IA 29; N. 24, 87 IA 30

290; 2 Labor troubles in Pennsylvania, 1887-88, Report of a Select Committee, House of Representatives of the United States; S. 15, 87 IA 22; O. 13, 87 IA 30; O. 27, 87 IA 27; N. 10, 87 IA 29; D. 1, 87 IA 29; D. 29, 87 IA 16; Ja. 12, 88 IA 78; F. 23, 88 IA 335, 339; Mr. 1, 88 IA 374; Mr. 22, 88 IA 490

291; 1 F. 10, 87 IA 18; Mr. 10, 87 IA 1; My. 12, 87 IA 16, 20-1, 35; My. 19, 87 IA 9, 15; Je. 9, 87 IA 13, 19; Je. 16, 87 IA 17; Je. 23, 87 IA 17; Je. 30, 87 IA 17; Jy. 28, 87 IA 15; Jy. 28, 87 IA 17; Au. 25, 87 IA 17; S. 8, 87 IA 23; S. 29, 87 IA 31; O. 6, 87 IA 9

292; 1 Je. 16, 87 IA 25; S. 29, 87 IA 11, 13; N. 10, 87 IA 20

292; 2 87 NYLB 220-4

293; 1 My. 5, 87 IA 39; O. 6, 87 IA 17; N. 10, 87 IA 20; 87 NYLB 134-6; 88 PALB F22

294; 1 F. 24, 87 IA 15; Mr. 17, 87 IA 29; Mr. 24, 87 IA 15; My. 19, 87 IA 15; O. 20, 87 IA 31; 91 NAB 166; Bul 124 USBLS 7

294; 2 Ap. 7, 87 IA 26-7

295; 1 Ap. 7, 87 IA 27; 91 NAB 221-2; 95 NAB 129-30; 93 *CBE* 86 (Cleveland builders' exchange handbook, 1893)

295; 3 93 CBE 86

295; 4 Jy. 21, 87 IA 26

89 NAB 14, 27; 91 NAB 73
(People v. Walsh)
313; 1 89 NAM 28; 89 NYLB
408, 418, 609-10, 618, 622-5,
627--30; 90 NYLB 418, 1001;
F. 2, 23, 87 IA 329
314; 2 Ap. 5, 88 IA 569
314; 3 Ap. 19, 88 IA 654
314; 4, 315; 1, 2 88 NYLB
115-26
315; 3 Je. 7, 88 IA 929-30
316; 1 My. 17, 88 IA 818; Je.
7, 88 IA 943; Je. 14, 88 IA 973-
4, 978; Je. 21, 88 IA 1012; Je.
28, 88 IA 1042, 1046; Jy. 5, 88
IA 21; Jy. 12, 88 IA 66; Jy. 19,
88 IA 90; Au. 9, 88 IA 206-7
316; 2 Jy. 26, 88 IA 138
317; 1 Jy. 26, 88 IA 127, 138;
Ap. 29, 89 IA 622
317; 2 Je. 6, 89 IA 842
317; 3 Mr. 22, 88 IA 488;
My. 5, 88 IA 571; F. 14, 89 IA
239, 262
318; 1 Ap. 19, 88 IA 654; My.
9, 89 IA 697; D. 12, 89 IA 922;
89 NYLB 134-6; 89 NYLB 671;
Swinton 182
318; 2 Jy. 26, 88 IA 124
319; 1 88 MOLB 120-2, 135-
8; O. 11, 88 IA 536; S. 12, 89
IA 1; Ja. 9, 90 IA 54; Gould
27, 54
319; 2 Ja. 10, 89 IA 48; F.
7, 89 IA 207; Au. 1, 89 IA 175;
Au. 15, 89 IA 248; S. 19, 89
IA 443
320; 1 89 NYLB 635-40
320; 2 Ap. 5, 88 IA 570; Jy.
5, 88 IA 13; Au. 2, 88 IA 163
320; 3 Ap. 4, 89 IA 512

320; 4 99 NYLB 661-2
320; 5 89 NYLB 692-6; Ap.
11, 89 IA 551
321; 1 Mr. 1, 88 IA 373; Mr.
22, 88 IA 496; Ap. 5, 88 IA
573; My. 10, 88, 772, 776; Mr.
14, 89 IA 396; Swinton 182
321; 2 Mr. 8, 88 IA 408
321; 3 88 NYLB 141; 89
NYLB 665-8, 687-9; Mr. 28, 89
IA 474
321; 4 Ap. 5, 88 IA 573; O.
18, 88 IA 605; Ja. 3, 89 IA 14;
Je. 20, 89 IA 927
322; 1 My. 22, 90 IA 864; Au.
21, 90 IA 317; S. 25, 90 IA 483,
491-2; 89 OHLB 33
323; 1 S. 10, 90 IA 443
323; 2 Au. 28, 90 IA 325
323; 3 F. 5, 91 IA 241; F.
12, 91 IA 289; Je. 10, 90 IA 47;
Jy. 10, 90 IA 57; Au. 7, 90 IA
239; 89 NJLB 179-95; 90 NJLB
417-36; S. 4, 90 IA 374; S. 25,
90 IA 483
323; 4 F. 6, 90 IA 217; Au.
14, 90 IA 255
324; 1 90 NYLB 421, 997,
1000-1, 1008, 1013-6; My. 8, 90
IA 775, 778; My. 15, 90 IA 810;
94 PALB B28; Lowell JSS 79
325; 1 90 NYLB 1001; Lowell
JSS 80; Lowell Ind 106-10; 90
OHLB 33
325; 2 Au. 14, 90 IA 255; N.
20, 90 IA 905
326; 1 91 MOLB 17-8; 90
NYLB 1009, 1013-4; Ap. 10, 90
IA 598, 602
326; 2 Lowell JSS 70-80; 91
NAB 46-9; 7 Ind Com 844

339; 2 91 NYLB 827-8; 91-2 WILB 119-20

339; 3 91 NYLB 794-5; Lowell JSS 79

340; 1 91 NYLB 788, 828-38

340; 2 91-2 COLB 174-5

341; 1 91 NYLB 844, 846; 91 MGLB 367; 91 MOLB 19; 91-2 WILB 119

341; 2 5 IOLB 287; 91 NYLB 847, 854-7; 91-2 WILB 119

341; 3 91 MOLB 12-3; 91-2 WILB 119

342; 1 Mr. 7, 91 IA 881; 91 NYLB 822-6, 952; 91 MOLB 20-1

342; 2 91 MOLB 24

342; 3 90 MOLB 49; 91 MOLB 16, 20; 91 NYLB 969

343; 1 My. 21, 91 IA 964; Je. 11, 91 IA 1130; Je. 18, 91 IA 1169, 1175-6; Je. 25, 91 IA 1235; Jy. 16, 91 IA 102; Jy. 30, 91 IA 190; S. 3, 91 IA 366; S. 10, 91 IA 412; O. 8, 91 IA 596; O. 15, 91 IA 647; O. 22, 91 IA 696; 91 MOLB 10-1; 91 PALB D1

343; 1 Ap. 23, 91 IA 774

344; 2 Jy. 16, 91 IA 104; Jy. 23, 91 IA 136

344; 3 Ap. 23, 91 IA 774

344; 4 N. 26, 91 IA 943

344; 5 My. 14, 91 IA 933; O. 29, 91 IA 733; N. 11, 91 IA 825

345; 1 Ja. 8, 91 IA 62; F. 5, 91 IA 246; F. 12, 91 IA 289; 292; F. 26, 91 IA 383; Mr. 5, 91 IA 441; Ap. 2 91 IA 609; Ap. 9, 91 IA 642-4, 691-2; My.

14, 91 IA 929; My. 28, 91 IA 1025; 91 PALB D2-13

346; 1 Ja. 1, 91 IA 13; Ap. 6, 91 IA 736-7; My. 7, 91 IA 876; Je. 25, 91 IA 1216; N. 12, 91 IA 825; D. 3, 91 IA 968; D. 24, 91 IA 1121; D. 31, 91 IA 1168; Ja. 14, 92 IA 62; 91 PALB D1-2

346; 2 Mr. 26, 91 IA 623; Ap. 2, 91 IA 641; My. 14, 91 IA 929-30; Jy. 2, 91 IA 14; O. 8, 91 IA 592; 91 NYLB 903, 936-42

347; 1 91 NYLB 885-96, 993-4

347; 2 Ja. 29, 91 IA 197; Mr. 19, 91 IA 540; Jy. 30, 91 IA 177; 91 NYLB 953, 993-4

348; 1 91 NYLB 880-1, 951-2; 91 MOLB 27-8; 91-2 CALB 13, 101-11

348; 2 S. 3, 91 IA 370; S. 10, 91 IA 425; S. 24, 91 IA 486

348; 3 91-2 CALB 90-4; 91-2 WILB 122; Ap. 16, 91 IA 736

349; 1 Ap. 23, 91 IA 782

349; 2 91 PALB D2; 91 NYLB 868-9, 871, 882-4; Mr. 19, 91 IA 535; Je. 12, 91 IA 62; S. 3, 91 IA 386

350; 1 My. 26, 92 IA 1040; Je. 9, 92 IA 1137; S. 8, 92 IA 435; S. 15, 92 IA 480-1; S. 29, 92 IA 580-2; O. 13, 92 IA 678; 92 NYLB 231-2

351; 1 F. 18, 92 IA 309; F. 25, 92 IA 353; Mr. 10, 92 IA 464; Mr. 31, 92 IA 619; My. 5, 92 IA 868; My. 26, 92 IA 1026-

7; Au. 4, 92 IA 195; Au. 18, 92 IA 290

351; 2 Mr. 10, 92 IA 464; Mr. 24, 92 IA 563-4; Mr. 31, 92 IA 619; Je. 23, 92 IA 1218, 1237

351; 3 My. 12, 92 IA 914

351; 4 Je. 2, 92 IA 1074-5; Jy. 21, 92 IA 110-1; Au. 11, 92 IA 238; Au. 25, 92 IA 335; 92 MGLB 1211

352; 1 Je. 2, 92 IA 1074-5

352; 2 Au. 11, 92 IA 244; S. 8, 92 IA 435; S. 29, 92 IA 580-2

352; 3 Ja. 28, 92 IA 159; Mr. 31, 92 IA 623; My. 12, 92 IA 927-8; Jy. 21, 92 IA 113; S. 23, 92 IA 520; S. 29, 92 IA 582; N. 17, 92 IA 936; 54 Fed 994

353; 1 Je. 9, 92 IA 1136

353; 2 S. 15, 92 IA 484

354; 1 F. 25, 92 IA 361-2

354; 2 Mr. 3, 92 IA 408

354; 3 Je. 23, 92 IA 1218, 1227, 1229-30; Je. 30, 92 IA 1277; Jy. 7, 92 IA 20; Jy. 14, 92 IA 71-2; Au. 4, 92 IA 185, 197, 204; Au. 11, 92 IA 244, 249; Au. 18, 92 IA 293, 299

355; 1 Je. 23, 92 IA 1207-8, 1217-8, 1240; Je. 30, 92 IA 1275-6, 1278; Jy. 7, 92 IA 21-2; Jy. 14, 92 IA 62

355; 2 Je. 9, 92 IA 1131-2; Je. 16, 92 IA 1184-5 Je. 30, 92 IA 1131-2; Au. 4, 92 IA 189, 200; Au. 11, 92 IA 237; Au. 18, 92 IA 293

356; 1 Mr. 31, 92 IA 607; My. 5, 92 IA 872, 874; My. 12, 92 IA 930; My. 26, 92 IA 1040;

Je. 30, 92 IA 1277; Au. 25, 92 IA 348

356; 2 Mr. 10, 92 IA 467; Mr. 31, 92 IA 624

356; 3 My. 26, 92 IA 1040; Je. 9, 92 IA 1137; S. 8, 92 IA 435; S. 29, 92 IA 580-2; O. 13, 92 IA 678

356; 4 S. 8, 92 IA 435; S. 29, 92 IA 580-2

356; 5 My. 26, 92 IA 1040; Je. 9, 92 IA 1137; O. 13, 92 IA 678

357; 1 50 IA 20-1, 33-4, 70-1, 114

357; 2 50 IA 116-8, 123, 159-60, 197, 199-200, 246, 294, 299, 338, 390, 483, 530, 572, 578, 584, 630-1, 679-80, 723, 736, 791, 840, 940, 996, 1000; Swinton 183-4

358; 1 My. 5, 92 IA 859; My. 26, 92 IA 1038-9; Jy. 14, 92 IA 60; O. 13, 92 IA 669-70; N. 10, 92 IA 880-1

358; 3 Mr. 17, 92 IA 503

359; 1 92 NYLB 200-1, 214

359; 2 92 NYLB 201; Lowell JSS 79; Andrews 348

359; 3 Au. 11, 92 IA 199, 242; 92 NYLB 179-80; Bul 124 USBLS

360; 1 92 NYLB 197, 200-3, 206, 208, 212, 217, 225-6, 230-3; Andrews 348

360; 2 92 NYLB 212, 232; N. 10, 92 IA 881

361; 1 92 NYLB 210-1

361; 2 92 NYLB 240-2

361; 3 92 MDLB 202-7

362; 1 Mr. 24, 92 IA 563-4;

O. 13, 92 IA 676; D. 15, 92 IA 1165; 92 NYLB 193-6; 92 MGLB 1216; My. 19, 92 IA 982

362; 2 Je. 23, 92 IA 1226; O. 20, 92 IA 734; N. 13, 92 IA 838

362; 3 Ap. 14, 92 IA 723; D. 22, 92 IA 1216

363; 1 92 NYLB 184-9, 212-4, 226-7, 248, 251, 274-5; 92 MOLB 31-5; 92 NYLB 213-4

363; 2 92 NYLB 208, 210

364; 1 92 MGLB 1221-2

364; 2 92 NYLB 203-5; N. 10, 92 IA 887

365; 1 92 NYLB 235-9, 242, 294-301; Swinton 183; 94 NHLB 463; 6 MELB 173-82, 207; My. 19, 92 IA 985; My. 26, 92 IA 1049; Au. 11, 92 IA 242; S. 22, 92 IA 529

365; 3 92 MOLB 25-7, 35-6

366; 1 92 NYLB 196-8, 233, 239; Lowell Ind 75-6, 99-110; 92 MGLB 1223-4; S. 22, 92 IA 523

367; 1 92 MGLB 1213-4; 5 10B 287; 92 NYLB 210-1, 227-9

367; 1 O. 13, 92 IA 678

367; 2 92 NYLB 223; 92 MGLB 1214-7

368; 1 92 NYLB 215, 217-8, 225-6, 292-3; 92 MOLB 28-9; 94 PALB B28

369; 1 My. 5, 92 IA 881; Au. 25, 92 IA 322; S. 1, 92 IA 377; O. 13, 92 IA 676

369; 2 S. 15, 92 IA 487

369; 3 5 10LB 286

370; 1 92 NYLB 267-9, 284, 293, 342-5; 92 MGLB 1221; 91-

2 COLB 181-9; 03 CNLB 422-3

370; 2 92 MDLB 207-9

371; 1 92 NYLB 278

371; 2 S. 15, 92 IA 481; O. 13, 92 IA 678; 92 NYLB 306-34

372; 1 N. 17, 92 IA 936; Mr. 30, 93 IA 731; 54 Fed 274; 208 US 274; 92 MGLB 1238-9; Swinton 183

372; 2 92 MOLB 22-5

374; 1 My. 12, 92 IA 933; Jy. 21, 92 IA 113; S. 8, 92 IA 434; S. 15, 92 IA 480-1; N. 10, 92 IA 887; N. 17, 92 IA 936

374; 1 92 NYLB 237, 253-4, 261, 272, 305, 347; 92 MGLB 1211, 1217

374; 2 F. 2, 93 IA 251; Ap. 6, 93 IA 781; My. 11, 93 IA 1069; Jy. 27, 93 IA 160; Au. 31, 93 IA 388; S. 21, 93 IA 519; D. 7, 93 IA 1038; D. 28, 93 IA 1184; F. 1, 94 IA 215

375; 1 F. 2, 93 IA 251; Ap. 13, 93 IA 851; My. 25, 93 IA 1206; N. 2, 93 IA 805

375; 2 93 MSLB 271-2, 279, 282, 284-5

376; 1 Ja. 5, 93 IA 22; Mr. 9, 93 IA 561; 93 MGLB 418-9

376; 2 Ap. 27, 93 IA 962; My. 11, 93 IA 11, 93 IA 1073; Au. 24, 93 IA 352; 93 MOLB 38-9, 41, 43-4; 94 PALB B28; 94 NAB 27

377; 1 94 NAB 29-30, 32ff, 86-7

377; 2 Ja. 4, 40 Amal 3; Mr. 23, 93 IA 675; Je. 8, 93 IA 1298; Je. 15, 93 IA 1342; Je. 22, 93 IA 1396; Jy. 6, 93 IA 17;

S. 21, 93 IA 519; O. 12, 93 IA
662; O. 19, 93 IA 713; O. 26,
93 IA 743, 769; N. 23, 93 IA
993-4; D. 28, 93 IA 937, 942-3;
N. 30, 93 IA 993-4; D. 28, 93 IA
1177; Mr. 8, 94 IA 464
    378; I Mr. 23, 93 IA 675; My.
25, 93 IA 1183, 1206; Je. 1, 93
IA 1244; Je. 8, 93 IA 1291,
1298; Je. 29, 93 IA 1443; Jy.
13, 93 IA 67; Jy. 20, 93 IA 113,
119; Jy. 27, 93 IA 159; Au. 3,
93 IA 222; S, 28, 93 IA 576; O.
5, 93 IA 616; O. 26, 93 IA 743
    378; 2 Au. 10, 93 IA 271; Au.
24, 93 IA 351; O. 5, 93 IA 616
    378; 3 N. 16, 93 IA 893
    379; 1 N. 9, 93 IA 862; N.
16, 93 IA 893; N. 23, 93 IA
935-7; D. 28, 93 IA 1177; Ja.
4, 94 IA 18; Ja. 11, 94 IA 64;
Mr. 8, 94 IA 464
    379; 2 Mr. 2, 93 IA 517; Je.
15, 93 IA 1342
    379; 3 Je. 8, 93 IA 1289-90
    380; 1 Ap. 13, 93 IA 865;
My. 11, 94 IA 1073; Je. 15, 93
IA 1340; Au. 3, 93 IA 209; Au.
24, 93 IA 348-9; O. 12, 93 IA
648
    380; 2 Au. 24, 93 IA 352
    380; 3 93 MOLB 37-8; 93
MSLB 274; Je. 1, 93 IA 1232;
Je. 22, 93 IA 1380; Jy. 27, 93
IA 159, 169; Au. 3, 93 IA 222;
Au. 10, 93 IA 272
    381; 1 93 MSLB 272-3, 277,
279
    382; 1 93 MOLB 25-7, 32-4;
94 PALB C1-2; My. 18, 93 IA
1119; N. 16, 93 IA 893

382; 2 95-6 COLB 68
    383; 1 Ja. 19, 93 IA 131; Ja.
26, 93 IA 192; Ap. 6, 93 IA
790; Ap. 13, 93 IA 851; Ap. 20,
93 IA 908; O. 13, 93 IA 678; 93
MSLB 279-81, 284-5; 99 NJLB
179; 93 MOLB 45, 440; Swinton 185-6
    384; 1 Ap. 5, 94 IA 659; My.
3, 94 IA 849; Je. 7, 94 IA 1103;
Je. 21, 94 IA 1182; Jy. 5, 94
IA 15; Jy. 12, 94 IA 63-4; Au.
9, 94 IA 226; 94 PALB C3-4
    385; 1 N. 22, 94 IA 904
    385; 3 Je. 14, 94 IA 1139
    385; 4 Swinton 163; Au. 30,
94 IA 352
    385; 5 N. 15, 94 IA 855, 866;
Ja. 31, 95 IA 219
    385; 6 O. 18, 94 IA 653
    386; 1 Je. 14, 94 IA 1139; Au.
9, 94 IA 223; Au. 16, 94 IA
263; Swinton 154
    387; 1 My. 17, 94 IA 949;
Jy. 5, 94 IA 15; 84 NYLB 358-
74; 94 Chicago strike; Swinton
85, 89-95, 102, 130, 133; 93-4
COLB 249
    387; 2 Ja. 18, 94 IA 114; F.
15, 94 IA 369; Mr. 8, 94 IA
464; Jy. 12, 94 IA 66; Au. 9,
94 IA 223, 226; Au. 16, 94 IA
263; Au. 30, 94 IA 353; N. 23,
93 IA 943
    387; 3 My. 17, 94 IA 930; Je.
14, 94 IA 1130; Je. 28, 94 IA
1235; Jy. 12, 94 IA 66
    388; 1 Ja. 4, 94 IA 18; Ja. 11,
94 IA 64; Mr. 8, 94 IA 469;
Mr. 15, 94 IA 496; Mr. 29, 94

IA 604; My. 5, 94 IA 661; S. 13, 94 IA 442

389; 1 Je. 28, 94 IA 1235; Jy. 12, 94 IA 66; S. 6, 94 IA 405; S. 13, 94 IA 451; S. 20, 94 IA 483; S. 27, 94 IA 494; O. 4, 94 IA 581; N. 8, 94 IA 794; N. 29, 94 IA 941, 958; D. 6, 94 IA 1022; Ja. 24, 95 IA 169; Ja. 31, 95 IA 222; F. 7, 95 IA 275; Mr. 28, 40 Amal 3

389; 2 Je. 14, 94 IA 1140

389; 3 F. 15, 94 IA 309-10; Je. 14, 94 IA 1128

389; 4 94 MGLB 511-2

390; 1 93-4 COLB 241-5

391; 1 F. 15, 94 IA 308; F. 22, 94 IA 367; Ap. 19, 94 IA 754; My. 10, 94 IA 895; My. 24, 94 IA 1001-2; My. 31, 94 IA 1043-9; 94 MDLB 172-93; 94 MOLB 523-4; Ap. 21, 94 *BD* 291-2, 295 (Black Diamond) Swinton 172, 188-91

391; 2 Je. 14, 94 IA 1139; Ap. 21, 94 BD 291

392; 1 Je. 21, 94 IA 1169; Jy. 5, 94 IA 17; Jy. 26, 94 IA 157; O. 4, 94 IA 571; D. 20, 94 IA 1121; D. 27, 94 IA 1158; Ja. 3, 95 IA 18; Ja. 17, 95 IA 113; 94 PALB C3-4

393; 1 Mr. 29, 94 IA 610; My. 10, 94 IA 902; S. 6, 94 IA 400; 94 PALB C2-3

393; 2 Ap. 12, 94 BD 263; 97-8 WVLB 63-8

394; 1 94 NHLB 469-71; 94 MSLB 308-9, 311; Ap. 12, 94 IA 713; Ap. 26, 94 IA 805; O. 18, 94 IA 665

394; 3 94 NAB 9, 212-3

394; 4 94 NAB 9

395; 1 S. 6, 94 IA 405; 94 MSLB 311-3; 94 NHLB 474; Swinton 187

395; 2 Ja. 18, 94 IA 114; F. 22, 94 IA 369

395; 3 Ap. 26, 94 IA 802; Jy. 12, 94 IA 66; Swinton 187

395; 4 94 NBLB 463-7

396; 1 Jy. 12, 94 IA 62; 94 MOLB 525

396; 3 Ja. 30, 95 IA 219; Ap. 11, 95 IA 771; N. 7, 95 IA 948; N. 14, 95 988-9

396; 4 My. 30, 95 IA 1134; N. 21, 95 IA 1057, 1072-3; D. 5, 95 IA 1180

397; 2 My. 30, 95 IA 1124; Je. 13. 95 IA 1232; Jy. 4, 95 IA 25-6; Au. 8, 95 IA 286

397; 3 O. 17, 95 IA 801; N. 7, 95 IA 941; N. 14, 95 IA 1035; D. 5, 95 IA 1175

398; 1 My. 9, 95 IA 979-80; My. 23, 95 IA 1085; My. 30, 95 IA 1131; Je. 6, 95 IA 1183, 1190; Jy. 4, 95 IA 25; S. 19, 94 IA 604; D. 12, 95 IA 1225; Ja. 2, 96 IA 14; Ja. 9, 96 IA 130

398; 2 Au. 1, 95 IA 236

399; 1 D. 12, 95 IA 1209, 1212

399; 2 O. 17, 95 IA 819; O. 31, 95 IA 902

399; 3 Jy. 25, 95 IA 177; Au. 1, 95 IA 236

399; 4 S. 5, 95 IA 494; S. 26, 95 IA 655; 95 MGLB 350-63; Jy. 25, 95 IA 177; Au. 1, 95 IA 230-1; Au. 15, 95 IA 335

410; 1 N. 26, 96 IA 1018
410; 3 My. 7, 96 IA 1080;
Je. 4, 96 IA 1313; Jy. 30, 96 IA
221; 8 Ind Com 355; 96 MSLB
314; 96 MGLB 377; 95-6 CALB
154-7
411; 1 Mr. 12, 96 IA 638;
My. 21, 96 IA 1186; Jy. 2, 96
IA 1-3; N. 26, 96 IA 1016
411; 2 96 MDLB 145-52; Je.
25, 96 IA 1475; 96 MSLB 312;
Jy. 30, 96 IA 221
412; 1 96 MSLB 315; 96
MGLB 376
412; 2 N. 21, 96 IA 1041
413; 2 My. 27, 97 IA 20; N. 4,
97 IA 70
414; 1 97-8 *INLB* 202 (Indiana)
414; 2 My. 20, 97 IA 19; Je.
3, 97 IA 23; S. 30, 97 IA 23-4; Au. 26, 97 IA 11; D. 9, 97
IA 23-4
415; 4 Ap. 15, 97 IA 22; My.
20, 97 IA 22; My. 27, 97 IA 20,
23; Je. 2, 97 IA 18; Je. 9, 97
IA 24; Je. 16, 97 IA 34; Jy. 1,
97 IA 18, 20, 24; Jy. 8, 97 IA
16; Jy. 15, 97 IA 22; Jy. 22,
97 IA 15; Jy. 29, 97 IA 16; Au.
18, 97 IA 8, 20
415; 2 Ap. 8, 97 IA 20; My.
27, 97 IA 20
415; 3 My. 20, 97 IA 22
416; 1 F. 2, 99 IA 5; My. 13,
97 IA 20
416; 3 Ap. 15, 97 IA 12; My.
20, 97 IA 22
417; 1 O. 14, 97 IA 10
417; 2 O. 28, 97 IA 16
418; 1 D. 16, 97 IA 9; D. 30,
97 IA 9; Ja. 27, 98 IA 27-9
418; 2 My. 13, 97 IA 19-20
418; 3 Mr. 25, 97 IA 2
419; 1 Ja. 7, 97 IA 16; Jy. 15,
97 IA 19; Jy. 22, 97 IA 31;
97-8 INLB 23, 28-9; 16 ILLB
sup 5
420; 1 97-8 WVLB 63-86; 97-8 INLB 28-9
420; 2 S. 16, 97 IA 15
420; 3 Au. 12, 97 IA 14; D.
23, 97 IA 23; 97-8 INLB 19,
23, 28-9; S. 30, 97 IA 19-20; N.
11, 97 IA 16; D. 2, 97 IA 16
420; 4 F. 25, 97 IA 2-3; D.
30, 97 IA 23
421; 1 97 MSLB 313-4, 317;
Mr. 4, 97 IA 16; My. 20, 97
IA 8; Jy. 1, 97 IA 14; Au. 19,
97 IA 14; 96 MDLB 156-7
422; 1 Mr. 4, 97 IA 16; My.
27, 97 IA 18; D. 30, 97 IA 23;
97 MOLB 440; 97 MSLB 316,
318; 320-1; 99 MSLB 84, 321;
4 ILLB 369; 98-00 CALB 118
422; 3 Ap. 28, 98 IA 10; Je.
30, 98 IA 21
423; 1 Ja. 27, 98 IA 22-3; F.
3, 98 IA 20-1; F. 24, 98 IA 17;
S. 8, 98 IA 16-8; S. 15, 98 IA 6;
S. 22, 98 IA 9, 15; O. 13, 98
IA 13; O. 20, 98 IA 22; O. 27,
98 IA 16
423; 2 F. 9, 98 IA 13; Mr.
31, 98 IA 30; Ap. 14, 98 IA 20;
Je. 16, 98 IA 34, 36; Je. 23, 98
IA 19-20; Je. 30, 98 IA 2-3, 25;
Jy. 14, 98 IA 29
424; 1 Ja. 27, 98 IA 27-9;
Mr. 10, 98 IA 12, 15; Mr. 17,
98 IA 29; Mr. 31, 98 IA 19;

434; 1 F. 2, 99 IA 5; N. 30,
99 IA 15; D. 14, 99 IA 29
434; 2 My. 18, 99 IA 38; Au.
10, 99 IA 16
434; 3 O. 5, 99 IA 37
434; 4 99 MDLB 1-4, 14-5;
99 NJLB 202
435; 1 Mr. 9, 99 IA 7; Au.
17, 99 IA 17; S. 14, 99 IA 12;
Ap. 6, 99 IA 30; Ap. 13, 99 IA
25-6, 32; O. 5, 99 IA 20; O. 19,
99 IA 29
436; 1 My. 4, 99 IA 29, 31;
14 KALB 327-54; 15 KALB
459-73
436; 2 Jy. 6, 99 IA 22; 00
MDLB 17-55; 99-00 COLB 187
437; 1 99 NJLB 198-201; S.
14, 99 IA 17
437; 2 99 MSLB 80-1; 00
CNLB 198; 99 MELB 158-9;
O. 12, 99 IA 28; D. 14, 99 IA
16
438; 1 99 MSLB 84, 99, 110
438; 3 Ap. 20, 99 IA 15; N.
16, 99 IA 17
439; 1 N. 23, 99 IA 4
439; 2 N. 23, 99 IA 4; N. 30,
99 IA 17; D. 14, 99 IA 16, 18;
Ja. 4, 00 IA 45; 12 ILLB 507
439; 3 Je. 15, 99 IA 24;99
MOLB 271, 273
440; 1 99-00 COLB 163, 165-
6, 168, 186
440; 2 99 MSLB 99-100, 106,
109-10; D. 14, 99 IA 16; D. 21,
99 IA 18
440; 3 99 MOLB 273
441; 1 99-00 MNLB 316-7; 99
MSLB 111

441; 2 99 NJLB 171-95, 198-9
442; 1 99 NJLB 198-9; 99
MOLB 272; 99-00 COLB 187;
99 MDLB 6-9
442; 2 99 MSLB 103; My. 4,
99 IA 17; My. 18, 99 IA 18
443; 1 N. 8, 00 IA 25-6
443; 2 00 MDLB 16
443; 3 Ja. 11, 40 Amal 31; Jy.
6, 99 IA 15; S. 21, 99 IA 11; O.
18, 00 IA 16-8; 7 Ind Com 396-
7 (for favorable union official
attitude); Jy. 19, 00 IA 13
444; 2 S. 23, 00 IA 17; Mr.
1, 00 IA 8
444; 3 F. 1, 00 IA 20; Je. 14,
00 IA 26h-7; Au. 9, 00 IA 20;
S. 20, 00 IA 17; O. 11, 00 IA 2;
O. 18, 00 IA 24-5; O. 25, 00 IA
17; D. 6, 00 IA 11; 00 MDLB
16
445; 1 Au. 9, 00 IA 20-1
445; 2 My. 4, 00 IA 23; Au.
9, 00 IA 20; S. 20, 00 IA 17; N.
22, 00 IA 28g-28h; D. 27, 00 IA
21
445; 3 N. 22, 00 IA 28c-28d;
D. 20, 00 IA 33; 00 NCF (Convention proceedings); 00 RILB
67
446; 1 S. 20, 00 IA 16
446; 2 Ja. 11, 00 IA 28; My.
24, 00 IA 23; Jy. 5, 00 IA 21;
Jy. 12, 00 IA 22; Jy. 26, 00 IA
16; Au. 9, 00 IA 9-10; Au. 23,
00 IA 34; S. 6, 00 IA 19; S. 13,
00 IA 33; S. 20, 00 IA 23; S.
27, 00 IA 33-4; O. 11, 00 IA 24;
O. 18, 00 IA 20; O. 25, 00 IA 5
447; 1 Gompers' American

GENERAL INDEX

(Cross references are in *italics*)

ACTIVITIES of assns. *passim*. In re specific ones, see *advertised, advocated, agitation, apprentices, armed guards, army, attack, battles, blacklist,* etc.

Advertised for nonunionists 49, 53, 64, 74-5, 98, 135

Advocated accident prevention 295

assns. *passim*
  industrial betterment (*welfare*) 19, 45, 108
  industrial education (*manual training, trade education*)
  old age pensions 295
  workmen's compensation 295
  (*conspiracy, eviction*)

Agitation and agitators 60, 69, 133, 142-4, 148, 152, 168, 180, 219-20, 239, 285, 333-4, 362, 435, 445, 469

Agreements, conference a n d collective, *passim*

Aims and objects of assns. (*principles*)

Anarchy (*battles, riots*) 356-7, 385, 408-9, Ch. 15

Apprentices 23, 25-6, 30, 32-3, 35-40, 49, 52, 69-70, 74, 78-81, 83, 93-4, 107, 130, 139, 142, 144, 152-3, 168, 191, 195, 218-21, 223, 239, 258-9, 261-2, 269-2, 274-5, 285, 289, 293-6, 299-300, 303, 306, 309, 311, 313, 317, 323, 325-8, 333-4, 338, 344, 346, 349, 361, 366, 394, 403, 406, 410, 418, 421, 424, 427, 437-8, 442, 449-50, 470-3

Arbitration *passim* (*compulsory*)

Armed guards 179, 202, 225, 345, 381-2, 393, 435 (*army, detectives, militia, p o l i c e , sheriffs*)

Army, regular 73, 84, 122, 136

Associations *passim* (See special index)

INDEX OF ASSOCIATIONS

(The word association is omitted when obvious)

INDEX OF UNIONS